Professional Apache Tomcat 5

Vivek Chopra
Amit Bakore
Jon Eaves
Ben Galbraith
Sing Li
Chanoch Wiggers

Professional Apache Tomcat 5

Published by
Wiley Publishing, Inc.
10475 Crosspoint Boulevard
Indianapolis, IN 46256
www.wiley.com

Published by Wiley Publishing, Inc., Indianapolis, Indiana

Published simultaneously in Canada

Library of Congress Card Number: 2004103742

ISBN: 0-7645-5902-8

Manufactured in the United States of America

10 9 8 7 6 5 4 3

1B/RR/QV/QU/IN

For general information on our other products and services or to obtain technical support, please contact our Customer Care Department within the U.S. at (800) 762-2974, outside the U.S. at (317) 572-3993 or fax (317) 572-4002.

Wiley also publishes its books in a variety of electronic formats. Some content that appears in print may not be available in electronic books.

About the Authors

Vivek Chopra

Vivek Chopra has over nine years of experience as a software developer, architect, and team lead, and is currently working on Web Services, J2EE, and middleware technologies. He has worked and consulted at a number of Silicon Valley companies (including Hewlett-Packard, Sun, and currently Sony) and startups. He actively writes about technology and has co-authored half a dozen books on topics such as Apache/open-source software, XML, and Web services. He is also a committer for UDDI4J, an open-source Java API for UDDI. His other areas of experience and interest include compilers, middleware, clustering, GNU/Linux, RFID systems, and mobile computing.

Sing Li

Sing Li, bitten by the microcomputer bug since 1978, has grown up with the Microprocessor Age. His first personal computer was a $99 do-it-yourself Netronics COSMIC ELF computer with 256 bytes of memory, mail-ordered from the back pages of *Popular Electronics* magazine. Currently, Sing is a consultant, system designer, open-source software contributor, and freelance writer specializing in Java technology, as well as embedded and distributed systems architecture. He writes for several popular technical journals and e-zines, and is the creator of the "Internet Global Phone," one of the very first Internet telephones available. He has authored and co-authored a number of books across diverse technical topics, including Tomcat, JSP, Servlets, XML, Jini, and JXTA.

Ben Galbraith

Ben Galbraith was introduced to Java in 1999, and has since become something of a Java enthusiast. He has written dozens of Java/J2EE applications for numerous clients, and has built his share of Web sites. He actively tinkers on several open-source projects and participates in the Java Community Process. He has also co-authored a gaggle of books on various Java/XML-related topics, including the one you're holding now. He is president of the Utah Java User's Group (`www.ujug.org`) and Director of Software Development for Amirsys (`www.amirsys.com`).

Jon Eaves

Jon Eaves is the Chief Technology Officer of ThoughtWorks Australia and has more than 15 years of software development experience in a wide variety of application domains and languages. He can be reached at `jon@eaves.org`.

Amit Bakore

Amit Bakore is a Sun-certified Web component developer and Java programmer. He works at Veritas Software R&D center, Pune (India). Earlier, he was a part of the Server Technologies group at Oracle, Bangalore (India), as a Senior Member Technical Staff. He has been working primarily on Java, J2EE, XML, and Linux. His areas of interest include open-source technologies and satellite-launching vehicles. He can be reached at `bakoreamit@yahoo.com`. Amit dedicates this work to his parents, Dr. Ramkrishna and Sau. Vaijayanti.

Chanoch Wiggers

Chanoch Wiggers is a senior developer with Kiwi DMD, U.K., programming with J2EE and VB. He previously worked as a technical architect with Wrox Press, editing, architecting, and contributing to Java books.

Credits

Acquisitions Editor
Robert Elliott

Development Editor
Kevin Shafer

Production Editor
William A. Barton

Copy Editor
Luann Rouff

Editorial Manager
Kathryn A. Malm

Vice President & Executive Group Publisher
Richard Swadley

Vice President and Executive Publisher
Bob Ipsen

Vice President and Publisher
Joseph B. Wikert

Executive Editorial Director
Mary Bednarek

Project Coordinator
Erin Smith

Graphics and Production Specialists
Beth Brooks, Sean Decker, Lauren Goddard, Shelley Norris, Lynsey Osborne

Quality Control Technician
Carl W. Pierce
Brian H. Walls

Media Development Specialist
Travis Silvers

Proofreading and Indexing
TECHBOOKS Production Services

Acknowledgments

The behind-the-scenes work undertaken to create this book was as critical as writing the book itself. For this, we would like to acknowledge the efforts of our editorial team: Bob Elliot (our executive editor), Kathryn Malm (our editorial manager), and Kevin Shafer (our development editor). In addition, we certainly couldn't have done this without the expert help of Rupert Jones, our technical reviewer.

We would also like to acknowledge our respective families for all the support they gave us in this project.

Contents

Introduction

Professional Apache Tomcat 5 is primarily targeted toward administrators. However, developers (especially those with additional responsibilities for Tomcat configuration, performance tuning, system security, or deployment architecture) will find this book extremely useful.

In this book, we have attempted to address the needs of two diverse groups of administrators. The first group has a job to do right away, and needs a line-by-line analysis of configuration options to assist in meeting the needs of a customer. The second group seeks to understand Tomcat's administrative features in their entirety for professional development, and to explore its capabilities. For example, this group might like to get some hands-on experience in building a cluster of Tomcat servers with inexpensive components.

This is the second edition in our Apache Tomcat series. Our first edition, *Professional Apache Tomcat*, covered Tomcat versions 3.x and the (then) new Tomcat 4.x. Since then, Tomcat has undergone a lot of changes, and hence the need for this book.

What's Changed Since the First Edition

Those of you who own a copy of our previous book will no doubt be wondering what's changed in this one.

Well, a lot has! There is a new specification (Servlet 2.4, JavaServer Pages 2.0) and a brand-new Tomcat version (Tomcat 5.x) implementing it. Other than updated content, you will find the following changes:

- Complete coverage of Tomcat 5.x. This book still retains the Tomcat 4.x-related sections, however, recognizing that it's going to be around for some time.
- A new chapter on the new and exciting JMX support in Tomcat.
- A new chapter on Tomcat clustering. Administrators (as well as system architects) should find this chapter interesting when planning for and deploying Tomcat installations for mission-critical production environments.
- A new chapter on embedded Tomcat.
- Coverage of the new JK2 Connector.
- Expanded coverage of security concepts in Tomcat.
- Coverage of support for Tomcat in popular IDEs such as IntelliJ IDEA, Eclipse, NetBeans/Sun Java Studio, and Jbuilder.
- Many other topics!

We value your feedback, and have improved on areas that needed some changes in our first edition. You will find several of our original chapters rewritten, with better organization and more content. As a small sample of the many improved areas, check out the streamlined coverage of Log4J and Apache Ant.

How to Use This Book

The best way to read a book is from cover to cover. We do recognize, however, that for a technical book of this nature, it is often not possible to do that. This is especially true if a busy administrator only wants to refer to this book for a particular urgent task at hand.

We have written this book to address both needs.

The chapters are structured so that they can be read one after another, with logically flowing content. The chapters are also independent to the degree possible, and include references to other sections in the book when it is necessary to have an understanding of some background material first.

This book is organized as follows:

- Chapter 1, "Apache and Jakarta Tomcat," provides an introduction to the Apache and Tomcat projects, their history, and information about the copyright licenses under which they can be used.
- Chapter 2, "JSP and Servlets," is a "10,000-foot overview" of Web technologies for administrators unfamiliar with them, including CGI, Servlets, JSPs, JSP tag libraries, MVC (Model-View-Controller) architecture, and Struts.
- Chapter 3, "Tomcat Installation," details the installation of JVM and Tomcat on Windows and Unix/Linux systems, and offers troubleshooting tips.
- Chapter 4, "Tomcat Architecture," provides a conceptual background on components of the Tomcat server architecture, including Connectors, Engines, Realms, Valves, Loggers, Hosts, and Contexts.
- Chapter 5, "Basic Tomcat Configuration," covers the configuration of the Tomcat server components introduced in Chapter 4, both by manually editing the XML configuration files and by using the Web-based GUI.
- Chapter 6, "Web Application Configuration," describes the structure of Web applications deployed in Tomcat, and their configurable elements.
- Chapter 7, "Web Application Administration," explains how these Web applications can be packaged, deployed, undeployed, and, in general, managed. There are three ways to do this in Tomcat: via HTTP commands, via a Web-based GUI, and through Ant scripts. This chapter describes all of them.
- Chapter 8, "Advanced Tomcat Features," details advanced Tomcat configuration topics, such as Access log administration, Single Sign-on across Web applications, request filtering, the Persistent Session Manager, and JavaMail session setup.
- Chapter 9, "Class Loaders," introduces Java class loaders and discusses their implications for Tomcat, including (but not limited to) security issues.

- Chapter 10, "HTTP Connectors," describes Tomcat's internal HTTP protocol stack that enables it to work as a Web server. It covers its configuration, as well as security and performance issues.
- Chapter 11, "Web Server Connectors," explains why using a Web server such as Apache or IIS is a better option than using Tomcat's internal HTTP implementation, and provides an overview of how this works.
- Chapter 12, "Tomcat and Apache Server," covers the use of Apache as a Web server front end for Tomcat. It also describes load-balancing configurations, as well as SSL setup.
- Chapter 13, "Tomcat and IIS," provides detailed coverage of the use of IIS as a Web server front end for Tomcat.
- Chapter 14, "JDBC Connectivity," discusses JDBC-related issues in Tomcat, such as connection pooling, JNDI emulation, configuring a data source, and alternative JDBC configurations.
- Chapter 15, "Tomcat Security," deals with a wide range of security issues, from securing Tomcat installations to configuring security policies for Web applications that run on it.
- Chapter 16, "Shared Tomcat Hosting," will prove very useful to ISPs and their administrators, as it covers Tomcat installations in virtual hosting situations.
- Chapter 17, "Server Load Testing," offers detailed coverage about how to load-test Web applications deployed in Tomcat using the open-source JMeter framework. It also notes alternatives to JMeter, such as commercially available products such as Silk Performer and Load Runner, and details strategies for optimizing performance.
- Chapter 18, "JMX Support," explores Tomcat 5's Java Management Extension (JMX) support in detail.
- Chapter 19, "Tomcat 5 Clustering," covers Tomcat configurations for providing scalability and high availability to Web applications. This is a "must read" chapter for production deployments of Tomcat.
- Chapter 20, "Embedded Tomcat," details the new mechanism for embedding Tomcat 5 within custom applications.
- Appendix A, "Log4J," provides a short (yet comprehensive) tutorial introduction to logging and the use of Log4j in Tomcat's Web applications. It provides configuration settings for various deployment scenarios, such as sending log alerts via e-mail.
- Appendix B, "Tomcat and IDEs," covers the support available for Tomcat in popular IDEs such as IntelliJ IDEA, Eclipse, NetBeans/Sun Java Studio, and JBuilder.
- Appendix C, "Apache Ant," provides a tutorial introduction to Ant. Apache Ant is used extensively in the book, both as a build/install tool, as well as a scripting engine. Ant is being used increasingly by administrators to automate repetitive tasks.

Conventions

To help you get the most from the text and keep track of what's happening, we've used a number of conventions throughout the book.

Boxes like this one hold important, not-to-be forgotten information that is directly relevant to the surrounding text.

Tips, hints, tricks, and cautions regarding the current discussion are offset and placed in italics like this.

As for styles in the text:

- New and defined terms are highlighted in **bold** when first introduced.
- Keyboard strokes appear as follows: Ctrl+A.
- Filenames, URLs, directories, utilities, parameters, and other code-related terms within the text are presented as follows: `persistence.properties`.
- Code is presented in two different ways:

```
In code examples, we highlight new and important code with a gray background.
```

```
The gray highlighting is not used for code that's less important in the given
context or for code that has been shown before.
```

Downloads for the Book

As you work through the examples in this book, you may choose either to type in all the code manually or to use the source code files that accompany the book. All of the source code used in this book is available for download at `http://www.wrox.com`. Once at the site, simply locate the book's title (either by using the Search box or by using one of the title lists) and click the Download Code link on the book's detail page to obtain all the source code for the book.

Because many books have similar titles, you may find it easiest to search by ISBN; this book's ISBN is 0-7645-5902-8.

Once you download the code, just decompress it with your favorite compression tool. Alternately, you can go to the main Wrox code download page at `www.wrox.com/dynamic/books/download.aspx` to see the code available for this book and all other Wrox books.

Errata

We made every effort to ensure that there are no errors in the text or in the code. However, no one is perfect, and mistakes do occur. If you find an error in one of our books, such as a spelling mistake or a faulty piece of code, we would be very grateful for your feedback. By sending us errata, you may save another reader hours of frustration, and you will be helping to provide even higher quality information.

To find the errata page for this book, go to `http://www.wrox.com` and locate the title using the Search box or one of the title lists. Then, on the book details page, click the Book Errata link. On this page, you can view all errata that has been submitted for this book and posted by Wrox editors. A complete book list, including links to each book's errata, is also available at `www.wrox.com/misc-pages/booklist.shtml`.

If you don't spot the error you found on the Book Errata page, go to `www.wrox.com/contact/techsupport.shtml` and complete the form that is provided to send us the error you have found. We'll check the information and, if appropriate, post a message to the book's errata page and fix the problem in a subsequent edition of the book.

p2p.wrox.com

For author and peer discussion, join the P2P forums at `p2p.wrox.com`. The forums are a Web-based system for you to post messages pertinent to Wrox books and related technologies and interact with other readers and technology users. The forums offer a subscription feature if you wish to be sent e-mail about topics of particular interest to you when new posts are made to the forums. Wrox authors, editors, other industry experts, and your fellow readers are present on these forums.

At `http://p2p.wrox.com`, you will find a number of different forums that will help you not only as you read this book, but also as you develop your own applications. To join the forums, just follow these steps:

1. Go to `p2p.wrox.com` and click the Register link.
2. Read the terms of use and click Agree.
3. Complete the required information to join as well as any optional information you wish to provide and click Submit.
4. You will receive an e-mail message with information describing how to verify your account and complete the joining process.

You can read messages in the forums without joining P2P, but in order to post your own messages, you must join.

Once you join, you can post new messages and respond to messages that other users post. You can read messages at any time on the Web. If you would like to have new messages from a particular forum e-mailed to you, click the Subscribe to this Forum icon by the forum name in the forum listing.

For more information about how to use the Wrox P2P, be sure to read the P2P FAQs for answers to questions about how the forum software works as well as many common questions specific to P2P and Wrox books. To read the FAQs, click the FAQ link on any P2P page.

Caveat

Finally, a caveat: Tomcat, like all active open-source projects, is a constantly evolving piece of software. This is usually good, because it keeps the software abreast of new technologies and improves existing ones. However, this can make the content in any related book outdated over time. This is especially true of new features that have been added in Tomcat 5 — JMX support, clustering, and support for the embedded mode of operation. While we have made every effort possible to ensure that the book remains current, we would like to point you to the following additional resources:

- *Book Errata* — Any changes in the book caused by new (or modified) Tomcat features will be posted in the book errata section of the Wrox Web site (`www.wrox.com`) under the Book List link.
- *Wrox P2P forum* — The place (`http://p2p.wrox.com`) where you can consult with the Wrox user community.
- *Tomcat User's mailing list* — Mailing list for Tomcat users. This is where questions relating to Tomcat's usage and configuration should be posted. The archives for the list are at `www.mail-archive.com/tomcat-user@jakarta.apache.org`, and directions for joining the list are at `http://jakarta.apache.org/site/mail2.html#Tomcat`.
- *Tomcat Developer's mailing list* — Mailing list for developers of the Tomcat Servlet container. This is the place to track new developments in Tomcat. *Do not post user questions on this list; use the Tomcat User's mailing list instead.* The archives for the list are at `www.mail-archive.com/tomcat-dev@jakarta.apache.org`, and directions for joining the list are at `http://jakarta.apache.org/site/mail2.html#Tomcat`.
- *The Apache bug database* — Apache currently uses a Bugzilla-based system to track bugs (`http://nagoya.apache.org/bugzilla`), but will eventually migrate to a Scarab-based system (`http://nagoya.apache.org/scarab/issues`). This is where (use the Query Existing Bug Reports option in Bugzilla) you can verify whether the issue you are facing is configuration-related or a known Tomcat bug.

1

Apache and Jakarta Tomcat

If you've written any Java Servlets or JavaServer Pages (JSPs), chances are good that you've downloaded Tomcat. That's because Tomcat is a free, feature-complete **Servlet container** that developers of Servlets and JSPs can use to test their code. Tomcat is also Sun Microsystems' reference implementation of a Servlet container, which means that Tomcat's first goal is to be 100 percent compliant with the versions of the Servlet and JSP API specifications that it supports. Sun Microsystems (Sun) is the creator of the Java programming language and functions as its steward.

However, Tomcat is more than just a test server. Many individuals and corporations are using Tomcat in production environments because it has proven to be quite stable. Indeed, Tomcat is considered by many to be a worthy addition to the excellent Apache suite of products of which it is a member.

Despite Tomcat's popularity, it suffers from a common shortcoming among open source projects: lack of complete documentation. Some documentation is distributed with Tomcat (mirrored at `http://jakarta.apache.org/tomcat/`), and there's even an open source effort to write a Tomcat book (`http://tomcatbook.sourceforge.net/`). Even with these resources, however, there is a great need for additional material.

This book has been created to fill in some of the documentation holes, and uses the combined experience of the authors to help Java developers and system administrators make the most of the Tomcat product. Whether you're trying to learn enough to just get started developing Servlets or trying to understand the more arcane aspects of Tomcat configuration, you should find what you're looking for within these pages.

The first two chapters are designed to provide newcomers with some basic background information that will become prerequisite learning for subsequent chapters. If you're a system administrator with no previous Java experience, you are advised to read these first two chapters, and likewise if you're a Java developer who is new to Tomcat. If you're well informed about Tomcat and Java, you'll probably want to jump straight ahead to Chapter 3, "Tomcat Installation," although skimming this chapter and its successor is likely to add to your present understanding.

The following points are discussed in this chapter:

- The origins of the Tomcat server
- The terms of Tomcat's license and how it compares to other open source licenses
- How Tomcat fits into the Java "big picture"
- An overview of integrating Tomcat with Apache and other Web servers

Humble Beginnings: The Apache Project

One of the earliest Web servers was developed by Rob McCool at the National Center for Supercomputer Applications (NCSA), University of Illinois, Urbana-Champaign, referred to colloquially as the NCSA project, or NCSA for short. In 1995, the NCSA server was quite popular, but its future was uncertain because McCool left NCSA in 1994. A group of developers got together and compiled all the NCSA bug fixes and enhancements they had found, and patched them into the NCSA code base. The developers released this new version in April 1995, and called it Apache, which was somewhat of an acronym for "A PAtCHy Web Server."

Apache was readily accepted by the Web-serving community from its earliest days, and less than a year after its release, it unseated NCSA to become the most used Web server in the world (measured by the total number of servers running Apache), a distinction that it has held ever since (according to Apache's Web site). Incidentally, during the same period that Apache's use was spreading, NCSA's popularity was plummeting, and by 1999, NCSA was officially discontinued by its maintainers.

For more information on the history of Apache and its developers, see **`http://httpd.apache.org/ABOUT_APACHE.html`**.

Today, the Apache Web server is available on just about any major operating system (as of this writing, binary downloads of Apache are available for 29 different operating systems, and Apache can be compiled on dozens more). Apache can be found running on some of the largest server farms in the world, as well as on some of the smallest devices (including several hand-held devices). In Unix data centers, Apache is as ubiquitous as air conditioning and UPS systems.

While Apache was originally a somewhat mangy collection of miscellaneous patches, today's versions are state-of-the-art, incorporating rock-solid stability with bleeding edge features. The only real competitor to Apache in terms of market share and feature set is Microsoft's Internet Information Server (IIS), which is bundled free with certain versions of the Windows operating system. As of this writing, Apache's market share is estimated at around 67 percent, with IIS at a distant 21 percent (statistics courtesy of `http://news.netcraft.com/archives/web_server_survey.html, January 2004`).

It is also worth noting that Apache has a reputation of being much more secure than Microsoft IIS. When new vulnerabilities are discovered in either server, the Apache developers fix Apache far faster than Microsoft fixes IIS.

The Apache Software Foundation

In 1999, the same folks who wrote the Apache server formed the Apache Software Foundation (ASF). The ASF is a nonprofit organization that was created to facilitate the development of open source software projects. Tomcat is developed under the auspices of the ASF. According to their Web site, the ASF accomplishes this goal by the following:

- Providing a **foundation** for open, collaborative software development projects by supplying hardware, communication, and business infrastructure
- Creating an independent legal entity to which companies and individuals can **donate resources** and be assured that those resources will be used for the public benefit
- Providing a means for individual volunteers to be sheltered from **legal suits** directed at ASF projects
- Protecting the Apache **brand** (as applied to its software products) from being abused by other organizations

In practice, the ASF does indeed sponsor a great many open source projects. While the best-known of these projects is likely the aforementioned Apache Web server, the ASF hosts many other well-respected and widely used projects, including such respected industry standards as the following:

- *PHP*—Perhaps the world's most popular Web scripting language
- *Xerces*—A Java/C++ XML parser with JAXP bindings
- *Ant*—A Java-based build system (and much more)
- *Axis*—A Java-based Web Services engine

The list of ASF-sponsored projects is growing fast. Visit `www.apache.org` to see the latest list.

The Jakarta Project

Of most relevance to this book is Apache's Jakarta project, of which the Tomcat server is a subproject. The Jakarta project is an umbrella under which the ASF sponsors the development of many Java subprojects. As of this writing, there is an impressive array of more than 20 such projects. They are divided into the following three categories:

- Libraries, tools, and APIs
- Frameworks and engines
- Server applications

Tomcat fits into the latter of these three.

Tomcat

The Jakarta Tomcat project has its origins in the earliest days of Java's Servlet technology. **Servlets** are a certain type of Java application that plugs into special Web servers, called **Servlet containers** (originally called Servlet engines). Sun created the first Servlet container, called the Java Web Server, which demonstrated the technology but wasn't terribly robust. Meanwhile, the ASF folks created the JServ product, which was a Servlet engine that integrated with the Apache Web server.

In 1999, Sun donated their Servlet container code to the ASF, and the two projects were merged to create the Tomcat server. Today, Tomcat serves as Sun's official reference implementation (RI), which means that Tomcat's first priority is to be fully compliant with the Servlet and **JavaServer Pages** (JSP) specifications published by Sun. JSP pages are simply an alternative, HTML-like way to write Servlets. This is discussed in more detail in Chapter 2, "JSP and Servlets."

An RI also has the side benefit of refining the specification. As an RI team seeks to implement a committee-created specification (for example, the Servlet specification) in the real world, unanticipated problems emerge that must be resolved before the rest of the world can successfully make use of the specifications. As a corollary, if an RI of a specification is successfully created, it demonstrates to the rest of the world that the specification is technically viable.

The RI is in principle completely specification-compliant and therefore can be very valuable, especially for people who are using very advanced parts of the specification. The RI is available at the same time as the public release of the specification, which means that Tomcat is usually the first server to provide the enhanced specification features when a new specification version is completed.

The first version of Tomcat was the 3.x series, and it served as the reference implementation of the Servlet 2.2 and JSP 1.1 specifications. The Tomcat 3.x series was descended from the original code that Sun provided to the ASF in 1999.

In 2001, Tomcat 4.0 (code-named Catalina) was released. Catalina was a complete redesign of the Tomcat architecture, and built on a new code base. The Tomcat 4.x series is the RI of the Servlet 2.3 and JSP 1.2 specifications.

Tomcat 5.0, the latest release of Tomcat, is an implementation of the new Servlet 2.4 and JSP 2.0 API specifications. In addition to supporting the new features of these specifications, Tomcat 5 also introduces many improvements over its predecessor, such as better JMX support and various performance optimizations.

Earlier in this chapter, it was mentioned that Tomcat is Sun's RI of the Servlet and JSP APIs. Yet, it is the ASF that develops Tomcat, not Sun. It turns out that Sun provides resources to the ASF in the form of Sun employees paid to work on Tomcat. Sun has a long history of donating resources to the open source community in this and other ways.

Other Jakarta Subprojects

Wise Java Web application developers who want to save valuable time will familiarize themselves with the other Jakarta projects. These peer projects of Tomcat include the following:

- *Commons*—A collection of commonly needed utilities, such as alternative implementations of the Collection Framework interfaces, an HTTP client for initiating HTTP requests from a Java application, and much more
- *JMeter*—An HTTP load simulator used for determining just how heavy a load Web servers and applications can withstand
- *Lucene*—A high-quality search engine written by at least one of the folks who brought us the Excite! search engine
- *Log4J*—A popular logging framework with more features than Java 1.4's logging API, and support for all versions of Java since 1.1
- *ORO* and *Regexp*—Two different implementations of Java-based regular expression engines
- *POI*—An effort to create a Java API for reading/writing the Microsoft Office file formats
- *Struts*—Perhaps the most popular Java framework for creating Web applications

This list is by no means comprehensive, and more projects are added frequently.

Distributing Tomcat

Tomcat is open source software, and, as such, is free and freely distributable. However, if you have much experience in dealing with open source software, you're probably aware that the terms of distribution can vary from project to project.

Most open source software is released with an accompanying license that states what may and may not be done to the software. At least 40 different open source licenses are in use, each of which has slightly different terms.

Providing a primer on all of the various open source licenses is beyond the scope of this chapter, but the license governing Tomcat is discussed here and compared with a few of the more popular open source licenses.

Tomcat is distributed under the Apache License, which can be read from the `$CATALINA_HOME/LICENSE` file. The key points of this license state the following:

- The Apache License must be included with any redistributions of Tomcat's source code or binaries.
- Any documentation included with a redistribution must give a nod to the ASF.
- Products derived from the Tomcat source code can't use the terms "Tomcat," "The Jakarta Project," "Apache," or "Apache Software Foundation" to endorse or promote their software without prior written permission from the ASF.
- Tomcat has no warranty of any kind.

However, through omission, the license contains the following additional implicit permissions:

- Tomcat can be used by any entity (commercial or noncommercial) for free without limitation.
- Those who make modifications to Tomcat and distribute their modified version do not have to include the source code of their modifications.
- Those who make modifications to Tomcat do not have to donate their modifications to the ASF.

Thus, you're free to deploy Tomcat in your company in any way you see fit. It can be your production Web server or your test Servlet container used by your developers. You can also redistribute Tomcat with any commercial application that you may be selling, provided that you include the license and give credit to the ASF. You can even use the Tomcat source code as the foundation for your own commercial product.

Comparison with Other Licenses

Among the previously mentioned and rather large group of other open source licenses, two licenses are particularly popular at the present time: the GNU General Public License (GPL) and the GNU Lesser General Public License (LGPL). Let's take a look at how each of these licenses compares to the Apache License.

GPL

The GNU Project created and actively evangelizes the GPL. The GNU Project is somewhat similar to the ASF, with the exception that the GNU Project would like all of the nonfree (that is, closed source or proprietary) software in the world to become free. The ASF has no such (stated) desire and simply wants to provide free software.

Free software can mean one of two entirely different things: software that doesn't cost anything, and software that can be freely copied, distributed, and modified by anyone (thus, the source code is included or is easily accessible). Such software can be distributed either free or for a fee. A simpler way to explain the difference between these two types of free is to compare "free as in free beer" and "free as in free speech." The GNU Project's goal is to create free software of the latter category. All uses of the phrase "free software" in the remainder of this section use this definition.

The differences between the Apache License and the GPL thus mirror the distinct philosophies of the two organizations. Specifically, the GPL has the following key differences from the Apache License:

- No nonfree software may contain GPL-licensed products or use GPL-licensed source code. If nonfree software is found to contain GPL-licensed binaries or code, it must remove such elements or become free software itself.
- All modifications made to GPL-licensed products must be released as free software if the modifications are also publicly released.

These two differences have huge implications for commercial enterprises. If Tomcat were licensed under the GPL, any product that contained Tomcat would also have to be free software.

Furthermore, while the Apache License permits an organization to make modifications to Tomcat and sell it under a different name as a closed source product, the GPL would not allow any such act to occur; the new derived product would also have to be released as free software.

LGPL

The LGPL is similar to the GPL, with one major difference: Nonfree software may contain LGPL-licensed products. The LGPL license is intended primarily for software libraries that are themselves free software, but whose authors want them to be available for use by companies who produce nonfree software.

If Tomcat were licensed under the LGPL, it could be embedded in nonfree software, but Tomcat could not itself be modified and released as a nonfree software product.

For more information on the GPL and LGPL licenses, see `www.gnu.org`.

Other Licenses

Understanding and comparing open source licenses can be a rather complex task. The preceding explanations are an attempt to simplify the issues. For more detailed information on these and other licenses, the following two specific resources can help you:

- The Open Source Initiative (OSI) maintains a database of open source licenses. Visit them at `www.opensource.org`.
- The GNU Project has an extensive comparison of open source licenses with the GPL license. See it at `www.gnu.org/licenses/license-list.html`.

The Big Picture: J2EE

As a Servlet container, Tomcat is a key component of a larger set of standards collectively referred to as the Java 2 Enterprise Edition (**J2EE**) platform. The J2EE standard defines a group of Java-based **APIs** that are suited to creating Web applications for **enterprises** (that is, large companies). To be sure, companies of any size can take advantage of the J2EE technologies, but J2EE is especially designed to solve the problems associated with the creation of large software systems.

J2EE is built on the Java 2 Standard Edition (J2SE), which includes the Java binaries (such as the JVM and bytecode compiler), as well as the core Java code libraries. J2EE depends on J2SE to function. Both the J2SE and J2EE can be obtained from `http://java.sun.com`. Both J2SE and J2EE are referred to as **platforms**, as they provide core functionality that acts as a sort of platform or foundation upon which applications can be built.

Java APIs

As mentioned, J2EE is a standardized collection of Java APIs. The term **API** (or **application programming interface**) is used by software developers in general to describe services made available to applications by an underlying service provider (such as an operating system). In the Java world, this term is used to describe many of the services that the Java Virtual Machine (JVM) and its code libraries make available to Java programs.

An important characteristic of APIs is that they are separated from the services that provide them. In other words, an API is a kind of technical contract defining the functionality that two parties must provide: a service provider (often called an **implementation**), and an application. If both parties adhere to the contract, an API is **pluggable** (that is, a new service provider can be plugged into the relationship). Of course, if a service provider fails to conform to the contract, the applications that use the API will fail to function properly.

The Java Community Process (JCP)

APIs in the Java world are created and modified by a standards body known as the Java Community Process (JCP). The JCP is composed of hundreds of **Java Specification Requests (JSRs)**. Each JSR is a request to either change an existing aspect of Java (including its APIs) or introduce a new API or feature to Java. New JSRs can be submitted by a **member** of the JCP. Anyone can become a member of the JCP and, notably, individuals may do so at no cost (organizations pay a nominal fee). Once submitted, the JCP **Executive Committee** must approve the JSR. The Executive Committee consists of JCP members who have been elected to three-year terms in an annual election.

When a JSR is approved, the submitter becomes the **Spec Lead**. The Spec Lead forms an **Expert Group** composed of JCP members who assist the Spec Lead in creating a specification detailing the change or addition to the Java language. The Expert Group shepherds the specification along through various review processes (to other JCP members and to the public) until, finally, the JSR is judged completed and is approved by the Executive Committee. If a JSR results in an API, the Expert Group must also provide a reference implementation of the API (discussed earlier in this chapter in the context of Tomcat) and a **technology compatibility kit** (TCK) that other implementers can use to verify compatibility with the API.

Thus, via the JCP, any Java developer can influence the Java platforms, either by submitting a JSR, by becoming a member of an existing JSR's Expert Group, or by simply giving feedback to JSR Expert Groups. While not the first attempt to create a technology standards body, the JCP is probably the world's best combination of accessibility and influence. As a contrast, the influential World Wide Web Consortium (W3C) standards body charges almost $6,000 for individuals to join. Visit the JCP at `www.jcp.org`.

The J2EE APIs

As mentioned, the J2EE 1.4 platform consists of many individual APIs. The Servlet and JSP APIs are two of these. The following table describes some of the other J2EE APIs.

J2EE API	Description
Enterprise JavaBeans (EJB)	Provides a mechanism that is intended to make it easy for Java developers to use advanced features in their components, such as remote method invocation (RMI), object/relational mapping (that is, saving Java objects to a relational database), distributed transactions across multiple data sources, statefulness, and so on.
Java Message Service (JMS)	Provides high-performance asynchronous messaging. Among other things, enables J2EE applications to communicate with non-Java systems on top of various transports.

J2EE API	Description
JAX-RPC	Binds Java objects to Web services. This is the key API around which J2EE Web services support revolves.
Java Management Extensions (JMX)	Standardizes a mechanism for interactively monitoring and managing applications at run-time.
Java Transaction API (JTA)	JTA enables applications to gracefully handle failures in one or more of its components by establishing transactions. During a transaction, multiple events can occur, and if any one of them fails, the state of the application can be rolled back to how it was before the transaction began. JTA provides the functionality of database-transactions technology across an entire distributed application.
Connector	Provides an abstraction layer for connecting with enterprise information systems, especially those that have no knowledge of Java and expose no Java-compatible interfaces (such as JDBC drivers).
JavaMail	Provides the capability to send and receive e-mail via the industry-standard POP/SMTP/IMAP protocols.

In addition to the J2EE-specific APIs, J2EE applications also rely heavily on J2SE APIs. In fact, over the years, several of the J2EE APIs have been migrated to the J2SE platform. Two such APIs are the Java Naming and Directory Interface (JNDI), used for interfacing with LDAP-compliant directories (and much more), and the Java API for XML Processing (JAXP), which is used for parsing and transforming XML (using XSLT). The vast collection of J2EE and J2SE APIs form a platform for enterprise software development unparalleled in the industry. In the coming years, Microsoft's .NET platform may present itself as a viable alternative to J2EE, but that day is still far off.

J2EE Application Servers

As mentioned, an API simply defines services that a service provider (i.e., the implementation) makes available to applications. Thus, an API without an implementation is useless. While the JCP does provide RIs of all the APIs, most of the J2EE API reference implementations are inefficient and difficult to use (with the exception of Tomcat, of course). Furthermore, the various J2EE RIs are not well integrated, making it all the more difficult to write applications that make use of several different APIs. Enter the **J2EE application server**.

Various third parties provide commercial-grade implementations of the J2EE APIs. These implementations are typically packaged as a **J2EE application server**. Whereas Tomcat provides an implementation of the Servlet and JSP APIs (and is thus called a **Servlet container**), application servers provide a superset of Tomcat's functionality: the Servlet and JSP APIs plus all the other J2EE APIs, and some J2SE APIs (such as JNDI).

Dozens of vendors have created **J2EE-compatible** application servers. Being "J2EE-compliant" means that a vendor of an application server has paid Sun a considerable sum and passed various compatibility tests. Such vendors are said to be **J2EE licensees.**

For a list of the J2EE licensees, visit **`http://java.sun.com/j2ee/licensees.html`**.

It is worth mentioning that several open source J2EE application servers are emerging. Currently, none of these products have paid Sun the requisite fees to become officially J2EE-compatible, but the products make informal claims stating that they are as good as such. One example is the popular JBoss project. The ASF has itself recently begun a project to develop a J2EE-compatible application server named Geronimo.

"Agree on Standards, Compete on Implementation"

Developers who use the J2EE APIs can use a J2EE-compatible application server from any vendor, and it is guaranteed to work with their applications. This flexibility is intended to help customers avoid vendor lock-in problems, enabling users to enjoy the benefits of a competitive marketplace. The Java slogan along these lines is "Agree on standards, compete on implementation," meaning that the vendors all cooperate in establishing universal J2EE standards (through participation in the JCP) and then work hard to create the best application server implementation of those standards.

That's the theory, at least. In reality, this happy vision of vendor neutrality and open standards is slightly marred by at least two factors. First, each application server is likely to have its own eccentricities and bugs. This leads to a popular variation on the famous "Write Once, Run Anywhere" Java slogan: "Write Once, Test Everywhere." Second, vendors are rarely altruistic. Each application server typically includes a series of powerful features that are outside the scope of the J2EE APIs. Once developers take advantage of these features, their application is no longer portable, resulting in vendor lock-in. Developers must, therefore, be vigilant to maintain their application's portability, if such a capability is desirable.

Tomcat and Application Servers

Up to this point, Tomcat has been referred to as an implementation of the Servlet/JSP APIs (i.e., a Servlet container). However, Tomcat is more than this. It also provides an implementation of the JNDI and JMX APIs. However, Tomcat is not an application server; it doesn't provide support for even a majority of the J2EE APIs.

Interestingly, many application servers actually use Tomcat as their implementation of the Servlet and JSP APIs. Because Tomcat permits developers to embed Tomcat in their applications with only a one-line acknowledgment, many commercial application servers quietly rely on Tomcat without emphasizing that fact. The JBoss application server mentioned previously makes explicit use of Tomcat (although it can also use other Servlet/JSP implementations).

Developers seeking to create Java Web applications that utilize the Servlet, JSP, JNDI, and JMX APIs will find Tomcat an excellent solution. However, those seeking support for additional APIs will probably be better served to either find an application server, or use Tomcat in addition to an application server. A third option is to find an implementation of the individual J2EE APIs required and use them in conjunction with Tomcat. This piecemeal approach is perfectly valid, although integration problems are likely to manifest themselves.

Tomcat and Web Servers

Tomcat's purpose is to provide standards-compliant support for Servlets and JSPs. The purpose of Servlets and JSPs is to generate Web content such as HTML files or GIF files on demand, using changing data. Web content that is generated on demand is said to be **dynamic**. Conversely, Web content that never changes and is served up as is is called **static**. Web applications commonly include a great deal of static content, such as images or Cascading Style Sheets (CSS).

While Tomcat is capable of serving both dynamic and static content, it is not as fast or feature-rich as Web servers written specifically to serve up static content. While it would be possible for Tomcat to be extended to support many additional features for serving up static content, it would take a great deal of time. The popular Apache Web server (and others like it) has been under development for many years. In addition, because most Web servers are written in low-level languages such as C and take advantage of platform-specific features, it is unlikely that Tomcat (a 100-percent Java application) could ever perform as well as such products.

Recognizing that Tomcat could enjoy a synergistic relationship with conventional Web servers, the earliest versions of Tomcat included a connector that enabled Tomcat and Apache to work together. In such a relationship, Apache receives all of the HTTP requests made to the Web application. Apache then recognizes which requests are intended for Servlets/JSPs, and passes these requests to Tomcat. Tomcat fulfills the request and passes the response back to Apache, which then returns the response to the requestor.

The Apache connector was initially crucial to the Tomcat 3.x series, because its support for both static content and its implementation of the HTTP protocol were somewhat limited.

Starting with the 4.x series, Tomcat features a much more complete implementation of HTTP and better support for serving up static content, and should by itself be sufficient for people who aren't looking for maximum performance, but do need compliance with HTTP. However, as mentioned above, Apache and other Web servers will most likely always have superior performance and options when it comes to serving up static content and communicating with clients via HTTP. For this reason, anyone who is using Tomcat for high-traffic Web applications may want to consider using Tomcat together with another Web server.

This book describes how to integrate Tomcat with the Apache and Internet Information Server (IIS) Web servers in Chapters 11–13.

If you're not using either Apache or IIS, then don't give up hope entirely. It is still very possible to integrate Tomcat with other Web servers, even one that resides on the same machine. All you have to do is set up Tomcat to run on a port other than 80 (the default HTTP port). Note that, by default, Tomcat runs on port 8080. Thus, any normal Web requests to a server are sent to an HTTP server sitting on port 80, and any requests to port 8080 are sent to Tomcat. You can then design your Web application's HTML to request its static resources from the Web server on port 80.

Summary

To conclude this chapter overview of Tomcat, let's review some of the key points that have been discussed:

- The Apache Software Foundation (ASF) is a nonprofit organization created to provide the world with quality open source software.
- The ASF maintains an extensive collection of open source projects. Many of the ASF's Java projects are collected under the umbrella of a parent project called Jakarta.
- Tomcat is one of the most popular subprojects in the Jakarta project.
- Tomcat can be freely used in any organization. It can be freely redistributed in any commercial project so long as its license is also included with the redistribution and proper recognition is given.
- J2EE is a series of Java APIs designed to facilitate the creation of complex enterprise applications. J2EE-compatible application servers provide implementations of the J2EE APIs.
- Tomcat is a J2EE-compliant Servlet container and is the official reference implementation for the Java Servlet and JavaServer Pages APIs. Tomcat also includes implementations of the JNDI and JMX APIs, but not the rest of the J2EE APIs, and is not, thus, an application server.
- While Tomcat can also function as a Web server, it can also be integrated with other Web servers.
- Tomcat has special support for integrating with the Apache, IIS, and Netscape Enterprise Server (NES) servers.

This chapter has provided a basic introduction to Tomcat. Chapter 2 describes what Tomcat-served Web applications look like and what files comprise them.

2

JSP and Servlets

From its humble beginnings as a document-exchange medium, the Internet has now become a much more complex beast that is the backbone of much industry and social discourse. It quickly outgrew its beginnings as a document publishing forum when it was obvious that these documents were changing very quickly. To prevent it from being filled with great amounts of stale information, a system was needed to keep the information up-to-date.

It was also realized that the Internet represented an excellent medium for communication. Customers and companies, service providers and clients, and all peer groups could communicate over it. To facilitate this exchange of information and the provision of dynamic content, additional technologies were designed.

This chapter examines why there was a need for another type of server when Apache was already doing such a good job as a Web server. We look at the types of services that Tomcat provides for the programmer and the applications that run on it. This chapter also provides an introduction to the following technologies for building dynamic Web sites:

- CGI scripts
- Servlets and JSP pages
- JSP tag libraries
- Web application architecture
- MVC architecture

First Came CGI

Well, perhaps HTML (static content) came first. However, as far as dynamic content was concerned, the first mechanism was the **Common Gateway Interface** (**CGI**). Executable applications (usually written in Perl or C) were provided with an interface that enabled clients to access them in a standard way across HTTP.

The World Wide Web Consortium (W3C) has more details on CGI at **`www.w3.org/CGI/`**.

A URL for a CGI program looks something like this:

```
http://www.myserver.com/cgi-bin/MyExecutable?name1=value1&name2=value2
```

The first part of the URL is the **protocol name** (Hypertext Transfer Protocol, or HTTP, in this case), followed by the name of the server. Everything after this and before the question mark is the **context path.**

The `/cgi-bin/` part of the URL alerts the server that it should execute the CGI program specified in the next part of the URL. The section after the question mark is known as the **query string,** and it enables the client to send information to the CGI program specific to the client. In this way, the program can run with client-specific information affecting the results.

CGI suffers from several drawbacks. The languages used to write applications must be procedural. Instability in a CGI program can bring the entire machine down. In terms of performance, CGI applications require that a new instance of the application be created for every request, creating a new thread, and thus making scalability difficult. This can cause a significant drain on the server. Each user requires the same amount of resources, and any setup of those resources must be performed once per user request. However, improvements in CGI (such as the FastCGI extension) have meant that CGI suffers less from performance problems than it did previously.

Note that CGI describes only the contract between the Web server and the program. No services are provided to help implement user-centric systems. These include maintaining the identity of the client, providing access to ways of maintaining a user's information, restricting access to the application to authorized users, and storing run-time information in the application.

Thus, it became necessary to provide a framework in which applications that were created for the Web could reside. This framework would provide the services mentioned previously, in addition to providing a more mature life-cycle management service so that performance becomes less of an issue.

Then Servlets Were Born

Servlets are portions of logic written in Java that have a defined form and which are invoked to dynamically generate content and provide a means for deploying an application on the Internet. All Servlets implement an interface called `Servlet`, which defines a standard life cycle (a list of methods that are called in a predictable way). Servlets were created by Sun Microsystems to address the problems with CGI discussed in the preceding section.

Initialization is facilitated through a method called `init()`. Any resources needed by the Servlet, along with any initialization that the Servlet must do before it can service client requests, is done in this method, which is called just once for each instance of the Servlet.

Each Servlet may handle many requests from many clients. The `Servlet` interface defines a method called `service()` that is called for each client request. This method controls the computation of the response that is returned to the client. When a request has been serviced and the response returned to the client, the Servlet waits for the next request. In HTTP applications, the `service()` method checks which type of HTTP request was made (whether `GET` or `POST`, and so on), and forwards the request to methods defined for handling these requests.

Finally, a method called `destroy()` is called once before the `Servlet` class is disposed of (see Figure 2-1). This method can be used to free any resources acquired in the `init()` method.

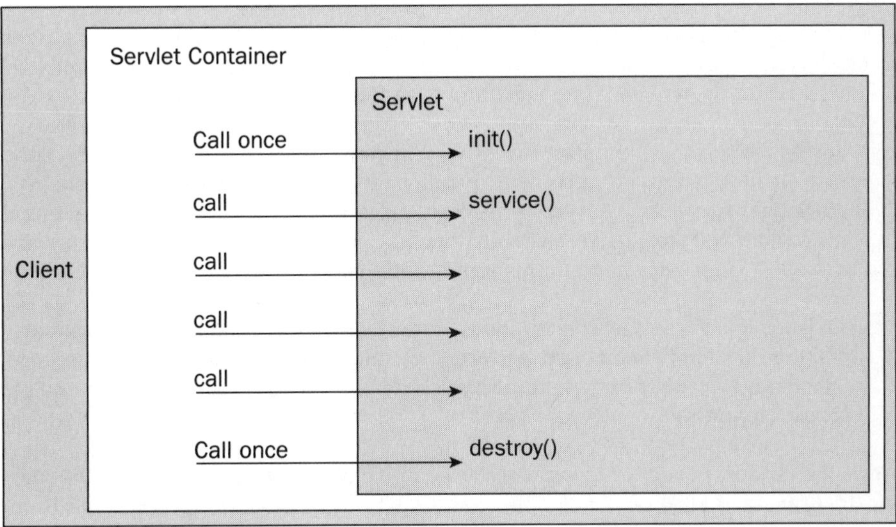

Figure 2-1: Servlet methods.

Servlet Containers

The fact that the life cycle of the Servlet is predetermined means that many vendors may implement an execution environment for Servlets (known as a **Servlet container**). All they must do is ensure that they follow the contract defined for Servlets in the Servlet specifications. Therefore, a Servlet written according to the specifications should run without modification in any compliant Servlet container.

Furthermore, Web containers provide services to the Servlet in addition to life-cycle management (such as making initialization parameters available, enabling database connections, and enabling the Servlet to find and execute other resources in the application). Containers can also maintain a session for the Servlet. HTTP by design is stateless — once the response is returned to the client, there is nothing in HTTP that enables the server to recognize the client when it makes another request.

To circumvent this issue, the container maintains the client's identity through temporary **cookies** that store a special token referencing the user. This token is known as the **user's session.** By doing this, the container can identify a client to the Servlet across multiple requests. This enables more complex interactions with the client. If cookies are unavailable, the container can also rewrite links in the HTML that is returned to the client, which offers an alternative way to maintain session information.

This means that instead of the application setting cookies in the client browser (and then failing if cookies are disabled), the container automatically determines whether cookies are enabled. If so, it uses them, or alternatively uses URL rewriting to maintain the session. The application developer can then create objects that are stored in the user's session and which are available to other Servlets in subsequent client requests.

Security (that is, authentication and authorization) is provided through a declarative security framework. This means that restricted resources and authorized users are not hard-coded into the application. Instead, a configuration document specifies the types of users to whom the resources are available. Thus, security policies can be changed easily according to requirements.

Tomcat is one such Servlet container. It provides an execution environment for Servlets, provides them with access to system resources (such as the file system), and maintains the client's identity. As mentioned in Chapter 1, it is also the reference implementation for the Servlet specifications.

Although the Servlet specifications allow for other transports besides HTTP, in practice, Servlets are almost exclusively used to provide application functionality across the Internet, servicing HTTP requests. Like CGI, the Servlet specifications were designed to provide a standard way for extending Web servers beyond static content and creating Web-enabled applications. Unlike CGI, the Servlet specifications are confined to the Java language, although this carries with it the benefits of platform-independence.

Like the Java language, the Servlet specifications were created with the purpose of enabling third parties to offer containers that compete on price, performance, and ease of use. In principle, because these containers are standard, customers of these third parties are free to choose between them and can enjoy a relatively painless migration.

In practice, the vendors of Servlet containers also compete with services that exceed the specifications. In addition, there are several areas in which the exact way to implement the specifications is open to interpretation. One example of this is the way in which class loaders (responsible for making classes available within the container so that they can be used by the application) work within the container.

However, migration is usually more a container configuration issue than a matter of reprogramming and recompiling the application. This assumes, however, that the programmers were not tempted into using nonstandard services of the Servlet container, and programmed the application with cross-container compatibility in mind.

Tomcat, as a result of its reference implementation status, does not provide extra-specification features that create application dependencies on it.

Accessing Servlets

If you consider Servlets as program resources, how are these resources accessed? Well, like CGI, the server maps URLs to programmatic resources.

In the case of Servlets, this can be done in two ways. As part of the application configuration, each Servlet is mapped to a Servlet name. The name is arbitrary, but is often descriptive of the service the Servlet provides. The Servlet can then be accessed by entering a URL such as the following:

```
www.server.com/servlet/ServletName
```

where `ServletName` is the name given to the Servlet in the configuration files. Alternatively, a Servlet may be accessed by its fully qualified name as follows:

```
www.server.com/servlet/com.wrox.db.ServletName
```

where `com.wrox.db.ServletName` is the fully qualified name of the Servlet.

Servlets can also be accessed through a **logical mapping,** which maps context paths to Servlets. This is often more obvious in its intention than the straight Servlet name, because it is possible to add information into the path that provides users with a clue as to the intention of the Servlet's action. For example, a Servlet that loads all available documents to enable administrative procedures may be called `AdminLoaderServlet`, and may be mapped to a context path such as the following:

```
/admin/LoadDocumentsForAdministration
```

thus giving the user a better idea of what is occurring at this point in the application.

The container intercepts all requests and looks for patterns in the URL that correspond to a specified Servlet, invoking the Servlet that matches that pattern. For example, all URLs that end with the `.db` extension may be mapped to `com.wrox.db.ServletName`.

Another possibility is matching a character sequence to a Servlet. For example, a system could match all requests that include the character sequence `upload` to an upload manager Servlet that manages the uploading process. Thus, in principle, all of the following URLs would invoke this Servlet:

```
http://localhost:8080/upload?file=Hello&locationResolver=World

http://localhost:8080/admin/uploadUserDocument/Hello/World/auth

http://localhost:8080/core/Hello.World.upload
```

Although Servlets are an improvement over CGI (especially with respect to performance and server load), they too have a drawback. Their primary use is processing logic. For the creation of content (i.e., HTML) they are less usable. Firstly, hard-coding textual output (including HTML tags) in code makes the application less maintainable, because when text in the HTML must be changed, the Servlet must be recompiled. Take a look at an excerpt of Servlet code:

```
out.println("<html>");
out.println("  <head>");
out.println("    <title>Hello World example</title>");
out.println("  </head>");
out.println("  <body bgcolor=\"white\">");
out.println("    <h1>Hello World</h1>");
out.println("  </body>");
out.println("</html>");
```

The intended effect of this section of code is to output the following HTML:

```
<html>
  <head>
    <title>Hello World example
```

```
    </head>
    <body bgcolor="white">
      <h1>Hello World</h1>
    </body>
  </html>
```

This is a rather cumbersome way of doing Web programming.

Secondly, it requires the HTML designer to understand enough about Java to avoid breaking the Servlet. More likely, however, the programmer of the application must take the HTML from the designer and then embed it into the application, which is an error-prone task.

To solve this problem, the **JavaServer Pages (JSP)** technology was created by Sun Microsystems.

And on to JSPs . . .

The first edition of the JavaServer Pages (JSPs) specifications resembled **Active Server Pages (ASPs)**, a Microsoft technology. Both have since evolved from those early days so much that the resemblance is now purely superficial. JSP has made a huge leap forward with the introduction of **tag libraries.** These tag libraries are collections of custom tags, and each tag corresponds to a reusable Java module. In addition, ASP.NET introduces a more object-oriented way of creating Web applications and includes a system similar to JSP tags for moving code away from the HTML in which it is embedded. JSP tags are discussed later in this chapter.

ASP is a technology for creating dynamic content. In its initial (and still the most popular) incarnation, the programmer inserts sections of code into the page. These snippets of code are executed by the server, and the returned content appears to the browser to be just HTML. The insertion of dynamic content is done in a way that is transparent to the user. Following is an ASP page, `HelloWorld.asp`:

```
<% @Language = "VBScript" %>
<% Response.buffer = true %>
<html>
  <head>
    <title>Hello World</title>
  </head>
  <body>
    <%
    Dim HelloMessage
    HelloMessage="Hello World"
    If request.QueryString("message") <> "" Then
      HelloMessage=request.QueryString("message")
    End If

    response.write HelloMessage
    %>
  </body>
</html>
```

This page carries out one of two actions. The default is to show the message "Hello World" should the URL `http://localhost/HelloWorld.asp` be called. However, if the URL provided is, for example, `http://localhost/HelloWorld.asp?message=HelloHello`, then the message "HelloHello" will be shown instead.

JSP initially resembled this style very closely. The same page coded in JSP could look like the following:

```
<%@ page language="java" %>
<html>
  <head>
    <title>Hello World</title>
  </head>
  <body>
    <%
    String message = request.getAttribute("message");
    if(message == null || message.equals("")) {
      message = "Hello World";
    }
    %><%=message%>
  </body>
</html>
```

Behind the scenes, the JSP pages are compiled into Servlet classes the first time the JSP is invoked. The Servlet is called for each request, thus making the process far more efficient than ASP because it avoids parsing and compiling the document every time a user accesses the site. This means that a developer can write software whose output is easy to verify visually (because the intended result is a visual one), and the result works like a CGI program (a piece of software). In fact, JSP took off largely as a result of its suitability for creating dynamic visual content at a time when the Internet was growing massively in popularity.

One major practical difference between Servlets and JSP pages is that Servlets are provided in compiled form, whereas JSP pages are often not (although pre-compilation is possible). What this means for a system administrator is that Servlet files are held in the private resources section of the server, whereas JSP files are mixed in with static HTML pages, images, and other resources in the public section. You will see later how this can affect maintenance.

In the early days of JSP, the logic of the site, including what content should be shown, was always present in the JSP pages themselves, and user interaction was entirely managed by the JSP pages. This is known as **Model 1 architecture.** This architecture is suitable only for small sites with limited functionality, or Web pages with minimal requirements for expansion. It is quite easy to create sites in this way and, therefore, productivity is improved when complexity is low. This model is not recommended for larger sites. The cost of this initial productivity is the time lost in debugging complex pages as the complexity and the size of the site increase. The architecture for Model 1 is illustrated in Figure 2-2.

Each JSP page must know where the user should be sent next, and from where the user has originated. This is embedded in information about how the site should be presented, the color of the fonts, and so on. As such, this approach is quite inflexible.

There are, however, quite severe limitations to implementing large projects using only JSP pages. Mixing code and HTML on the same page means that the designer must be sufficiently proficient with code to avoid breaking the functionality of the page, as well as be able to work with the logic on the page to produce the desired output. At the same time, the developer must do some of the designer's work of laying out the page when the logic is sufficiently convoluted.

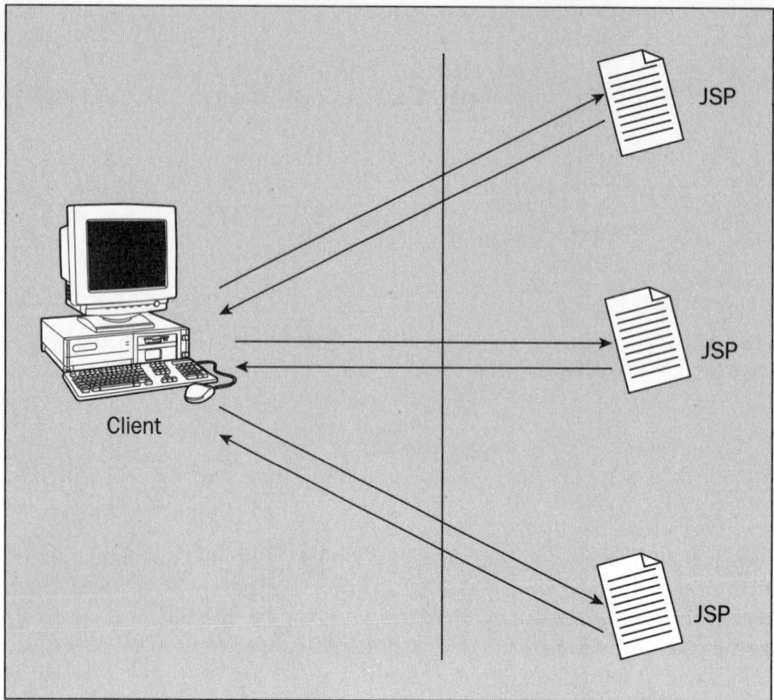

Figure 2-2: Model 1 Architecture.

In addition, because pieces of logic may be strewn around the page embedded in sections of HTML, it is by no means straightforward to figure out the intended result without a fair amount of inspection. This can cause significant problems with maintenance, as the code is mixed with markup. As such, code reusability is very limited, so that sections of code are often repeated across the site and, unlike in traditional code, it is not easy to identify where a piece of code is.

The obvious alternative to this is to keep the pages as free from Java as possible, and have the processing logic localized to Java classes.

JSP pages are often used like templates. For example, the header that includes the company logo may be in one page, the main menu for the site may be in another, and a current news table may be defined in a third. When the client makes a request, these separate elements of the page are assembled together and presented to the user as though they were all created as one, as shown in Figure 2-3.

This enables the designer to effect changes globally by updating a single page. The HTML has been centralized. However, code may be spread out according to functionality across the various parts of the site.

Like Servlets, JSP pages operate within a container. The JSP container provides the same services as a Servlet container, but requires the additional steps of conversion to Servlet code and compilation before the JSP pages are executed. Tomcat includes both the Servlet container that executes Servlets and compiled JSP pages (named Catalina), and the compiler service for JSP pages (the `Jasper` compiler). The combination of a JSP container and a Servlet container is known as a **Web container** (a container capable of hosting Java Web applications).

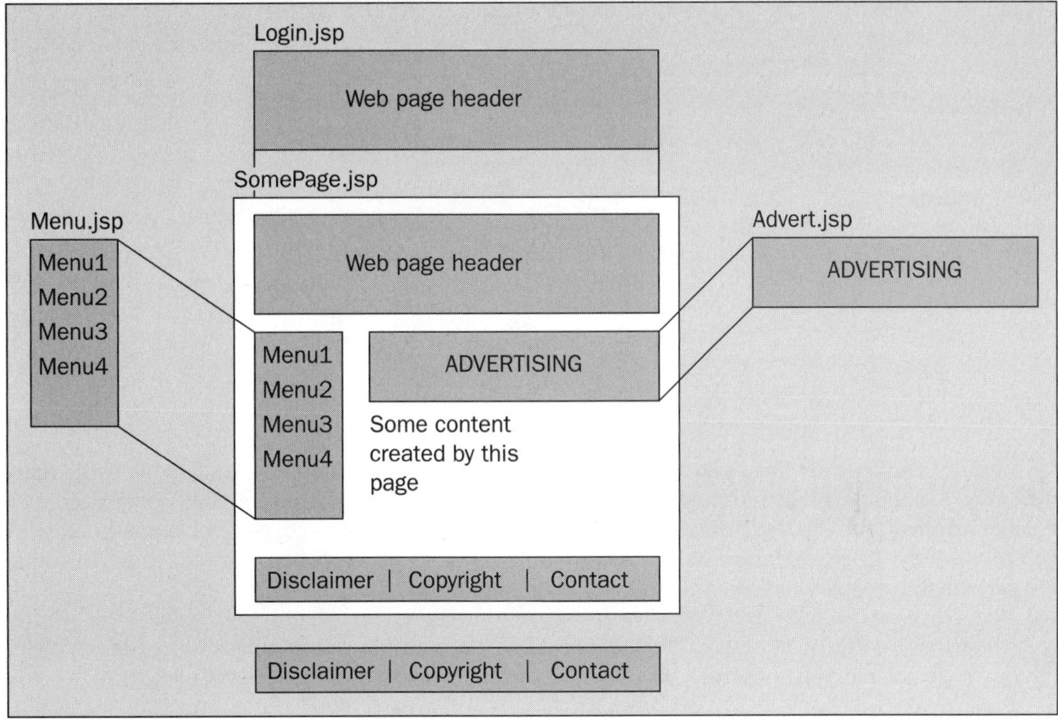

Figure 2-3: JSP pages.

A Web container provides the JSP developer with the services required to create complex, interactive, and personalized applications on the Internet.

JSP Tag Libraries

Since the introduction of JSP tag libraries (also known as **JSP tag extensions**), JSP files look more like the following (only the changed portions of the previous JSP are illustrated here):

```
<%@ page language="java" %>
<html>
  <head>
    <title>Hello World</title>

  </head>
  <body>
    <app:HelloWorld/>
  </body>
</html>
```

Compare this with the previous incarnation of the page:

```
<%@ page language="java" %>
<html>
  <head>
    <title>Hello World</title>
  </head>
  <body>
    <%
    String message = request.getAttribute("message");
    if(message == null || message.equals("")) {
      message = "Hello World";
    }
    %><%=message%>
  </body>
</html>
```

You can already see that this is an improvement. An HTML-like tag has encapsulated the entire functionality behind our code. In fact, the more complex the application is, the more this replacement of Java code scriptlets with JSP tags improves the readability of the site. The page designer is presented with sections of dynamic content that are far more familiar, and, more important, the page designer could insert the `HelloWorld` tag without understanding how it works.

Each tag has a corresponding Java class that contains the code that would otherwise appear on the page. Tags are structured in pairs, with a start tag followed by an end tag, with optional content:

```
<aTag>Something here</aTag>
```

The tag life cycle includes a method that is called when the start tag is encountered, called `doStartTag();` a method that is called when the end tag is encountered, called `doEndTag();` and a method that is called to reset any state (request specific data) in readiness for the next request.

The tag also has power over which parts of the page are parsed by the application. Depending on the behavior of the tag, it can stop the execution of the page, conditionally include its contents, and have its contents evaluated multiple times. You can use this tag as shown here:

```
<app:if cookie="user" value="">
  Please enter your name...
</app:if>
```

The `app:` prefix denotes a group of tags to which this tag belongs. In the preceding example, the contents of the `<app:if>` tag are evaluated if the cookie named `user` has an empty string as its value. In this case, the user is prompted for a name.

Here is an example of a JSP page that uses the Struts Framework tags:

```
<%@ page language="java" %>
<%@ taglib uri="struts-bean.tld" prefix="bean" %>
<%@ taglib uri="struts-html.tld" prefix="html" %>

<html:html locale="true">
  <head>
```

```
    <title>Intranet Title</title>
    <html:base/>
  </head>
  <body bgcolor="white">

    <html:errors/>

    <html:form action="/ChangePassword" focus="email">
      <table border="0" width="20%">

        <tr>
          <th><bean:message key="prompt.username"/></th>
          <td align="left">
            <html:text property="email" size="20" maxlength="50"/>
            <html:errors property="email"/>
          </td>
        </tr>

        <tr>
          <th><bean:message key="prompt.oldpassword"/></th>
          <td>
            <html:password property="oldPassword"
                           size="16" maxlength="16" redisplay="false"/>
            <html:errors property="oldPassword"/>
          </td>
        </tr>

        <tr>
          <th><bean:message key="prompt.password"/></th>
          <td>
            <html:password property="password"
                           size="16" maxlength="16" redisplay="false"/>
            <html:errors property="password"/>
          </td>
        </tr>

        <tr>
          <th><bean:message key="prompt.confirmpassword"/></th>
          <td>
            <html:password property="password2"
size="16" maxlength="16" redisplay="false"/>

            <html:errors property="password2"/>
          </td>
        </tr>

        <tr>
          <th><html:submit property="submit" value="Submit"/></th>
          <td><html:reset/></td>
        </tr>

      </table>
    </html:form>
  </body>
</html:html>
```

The scripted version of this page runs to several pages, and, hence, is not included here. The point is that tags present an elegant way to write pages that create dynamic content.

The encapsulation of code within tags means that, in principle, page designers could use them to construct sites. This depends, however, on the tags being quite generic so that they can be reused in many situations. Moreover, there must be sufficient information in the form of documentation and training in order for the designer to understand the significance of what they are doing and to correctly define the tags.

> **Tags represent the future of JSP and Java-based dynamic content.**

The next section briefly looks at the structure of a typical Web application. Chapter 6, "Web Application Configuration," discusses this structure in far more detail.

Web Application Architecture

The set of all the Servlets, JSP pages, and other files that are logically related constitute a **Web application.** The Servlet specification defines a standard directory hierarchy in which all of these files must be placed. It is described in the following table.

Relative Path	Description
`/`	Web application root: all files that are publicly accessible are placed in this directory. Examples include HTML, JSP, and GIF files.
`/WEB-INF`	All files in this directory and its subdirectories are not publicly accessible. A single file, `web.xml`, called the **deployment descriptor,** contains configuration options for the Web application. The various options for the deployment descriptor are defined by the Servlet API.
`/WEB-INF/classes`	All of the Web application's class files are placed here.
`/WEB-INF/lib`	Class files can be archived into JAR files and placed in this directory.

All Servlet containers are required to use this directory hierarchy. What's more, because the location and features of the deployment descriptor (the `web.xml` file mentioned previously) are set by the specification, Web applications only need to be configured once and they are compatible with any Servlet container. The deployment descriptor defines options such as the order in which Servlets are loaded by a Servlet container, parameters that can be passed to the Servlets on startup, which URL patterns map to which Servlets, security restrictions, and so on. Chapter 6 provides a full description of the deployment descriptor.

To make distribution easier, all the files in the directory hierarchy described in the preceding table can be archived in a WAR (Web ARchive) file. Server administrators can then place this WAR file into the directory specified by the Servlet container, and the Servlet container takes care of the rest.

This means that developers need only expend effort creating a Web application once. They can then take their WAR file and simply install it into the proper location in their Servlet container, and the Web application will be deployed and ready to run. Thus, distributing and deploying Web applications is remarkably simple, even if you switch Servlet containers.

Chapter 7, "Web Application Administration," provides more detail on deploying Web applications and WAR files.

Java Site Architecture

The ideal balance for the majority of sites is, as seen previously, a mix of Servlets and JSP pages. Servlets are ideal for encapsulating the logic of the application, while being somewhat poor at visual representation, whereas JSP pages are designed for displaying visual material. This suggests that the combination of the two can provide a balance and cover the needs of the majority of sites.

The architecture that aids this separation between logic and presentation is known as **Model 2 architecture** or **Model View Controller** (**MVC**) architecture. The **Model** is the logic of the site—the rules that determine what is shown and to whom it is shown. The **View** component of this architecture is naturally the JSP pages that display the content that is created. Finally, the **Controller** designates which part of the Model is invoked, and which JSP page is used to render the data. Another way to put this is that the Controller defines the structure of the site. Figure 2-4 shows a diagram of the MVC architecture.

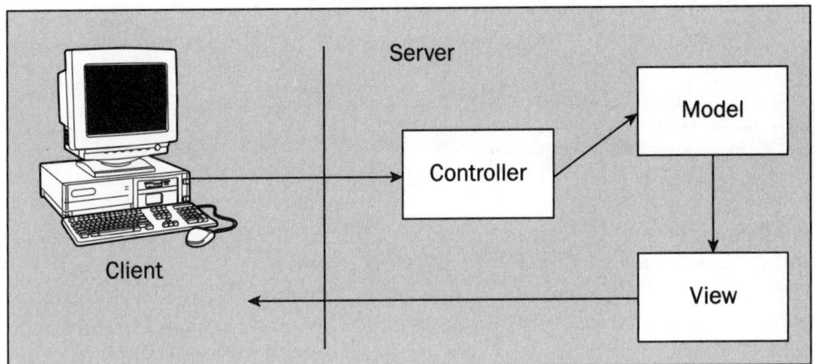

Figure 2-4: MVC architecture.

There are two typical types of Model 2 architectures: strict and loose. The strict version designates the role of the Controller to a single Servlet, which extracts the information needed to route the query to a piece of logic, executes the logic component, and then forwards the result of the execution to a JSP page.

An example of a strict MVC architecture is the Struts Framework, which was introduced in Chapter 1. This framework implements a standard Servlet for routing execution. Each piece of functionality is implemented as a special type of Struts component known as an Action. Each Action defines a single method and can place a variety of objects where the JSP that is invoked can use them to render the page. In this type of architecture, the sequence of execution is often very reliable. Figure 2-5 illustrates this sequence.

Figure 2-5: Sequence of execution in the Struts Framework.

An expanded example of the MVC strict architecture is shown in Figure 2-6. In this diagram, you can see that the single Controller selects the correct logic to execute, and then forwards the result to the View, which renders the results for the client.

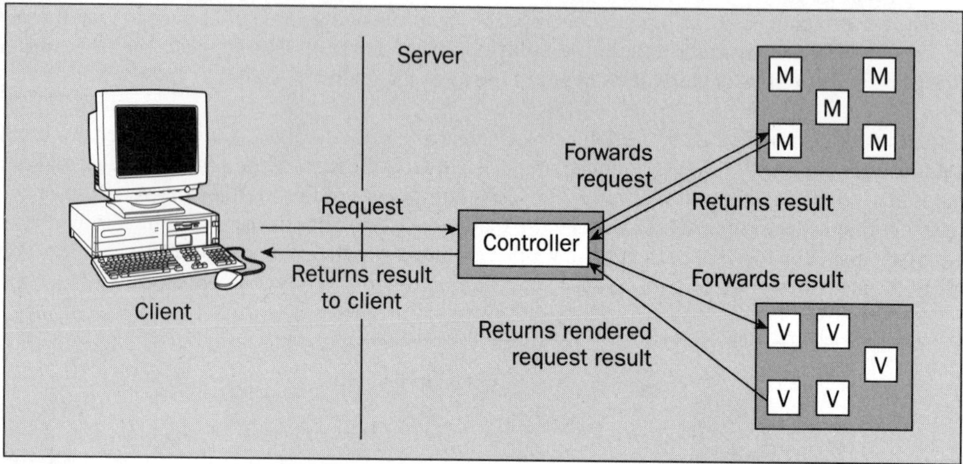

Figure 2-6: Expanded MVC architecture.

Small-scale, homegrown sites that are not based on a framework are often a looser version of this architecture. Several Servlets each take the role of a Controller and part of the Model. In this version of the Model 2 architecture, the JSP pages are still designed so that they contain very little or no logic, and the Servlets handle all of the function of the application. This second model is quite popular because it promotes high productivity in the short term, and can be easier to understand than the strict MVC architecture.

In sites that have a pure MVC architecture, the structure of the site is (at least in principle) quite flexible. The site is divided into units of functionality that can be reused in multiple situations, as well as pages that can be reused. This structure, therefore, represents the most work for the administrator in frequently changing sites. For example, a page that displays contact details in a Web site may be used for creating a new contact, updating an old contact, viewing an existing contact, and updating a user's contact details.

A site that allows content management may use the same JSP page and Servlet code for uploading a variety of documents, each with different needs (such as a report, a tender request, and a procedures manual). As the site expands, these components will need to be integrated with new functionality. The flow control must be configured before the various components will work together correctly.

This does, however, represent a very reusable and updateable site. The site can be reconfigured according to business needs and customer requests without rewriting code, and can be extended without affecting existing code to any great extent.

Summary

To conclude this chapter, let's review some of the key points that have been discussed:

- Tomcat came about as a result of a need for complex sites that provide dynamic content and features such as personalization through maintaining client identity, authentication and authorization, and an environment for providing system services to simplify the creation of Web applications.
- Servlets are portions of logic written in Java that have a defined form and which are invoked to dynamically generate content and provide a means for deploying an application on the Internet.
- As part of the application configuration, each Servlet is mapped to a Servlet name. The name is arbitrary, but is often descriptive of the service the Servlet provides. The Servlet can then be accessed by entering a URL. Alternatively, Servlets can be accessed through a logical mapping, which maps context paths to Servlets.
- Although Servlets are an improvement over CGI (especially with respect to performance and server load), they are primarily suitable for processing logic. For the creation of content (that is, HTML), they are less usable.
- JSP has made a huge leap forward with the introduction of tag libraries. In addition, ASP.NET introduces a more object-oriented way of creating Web applications and includes a system similar to JSP tags for moving code away from the HTML in which it is embedded.
- JSP pages are compiled into Servlets, which are then kept in memory or on the file system indefinitely, until either the memory is required back or the server is restarted. One major practical difference between Servlets and JSP pages is that Servlets are provided in compiled form and JSP pages are often not (although pre-compilation is possible).
- The more complex the application is, the more the replacement of Java code scriptlets with JSP tags improves the readability of the site. Each tag has a corresponding Java class that contains the code that would otherwise appear on the page.
- The set of all the Servlets, JSP pages, and other files that are logically related constitute a **Web application.** The Servlet specifications define a standard directory hierarchy in which all of these files must be placed.
- Servlets are ideal for encapsulating the logic of the application, while being somewhat poor at visual representation; conversely, JSP is designed for displaying visual material. Therefore, the combination of the two can provide a balance and cover the needs of most sites. The architecture that aids this separation between logic and presentation is known as Model 2 architecture or **Model View Controller** (**MVC**) architecture.

In Chapter 3, you will learn how to install Tomcat.

3

Tomcat Installation

Having read a couple of chapters on the history of and reason for Tomcat's existence, you are now probably raring to start with Tomcat. This chapter covers the following aspects of installation:

- How to install Tomcat on both Windows and Linux
- How to install Java
- The Tomcat installation directory structure
- How to troubleshoot typical problems encountered while installing Tomcat

Installing the Java Virtual Machine

Tomcat, like any Java-based application, requires a Java Virtual Machine (JVM) to function. Sun Microsystems distributes a free JVM for Windows, Linux, and Solaris. Other third-party vendors and open-source groups make JVMs for other platforms — some for free, others commercially.

Installing the Sun JVM on Windows

In the Windows environment, the installer is an executable with easy-to-follow steps. First, download the latest JVM from Sun's Java Web site:

```
http://java.sun.com
```

Once downloaded, double-click the downloaded file and you will shortly have the JDK installed. The folder in which you have chosen to install the JDK is known as your Java Home folder. It contains several subfolders, but the only one of interest here is the `bin` directory in which the various executables are stored (including the JVM, the compiler, the debugger, and a packaging utility).

The next step of the installation is to add the Java Home folder as an environment variable named `JAVA_HOME` so that Windows can find it when it is invoked. The `bin` subdirectory of the Java Home folder should also be added to the `PATH` environment variable.

To do this, select Start ➪ Settings ➪ Control Panel and choose the System option. Now choose the Advanced tab and select the Environment Variables button. If desired, you can add the variable settings to the specific user that you are operating as, so that it will only exist when you are logged in as that user. Alternatively, you could add the settings for the entire system.

To add the `JAVA_HOME` environment variable for the entire system, select the New button in the lower half of the window, as shown in Figure 3-1.

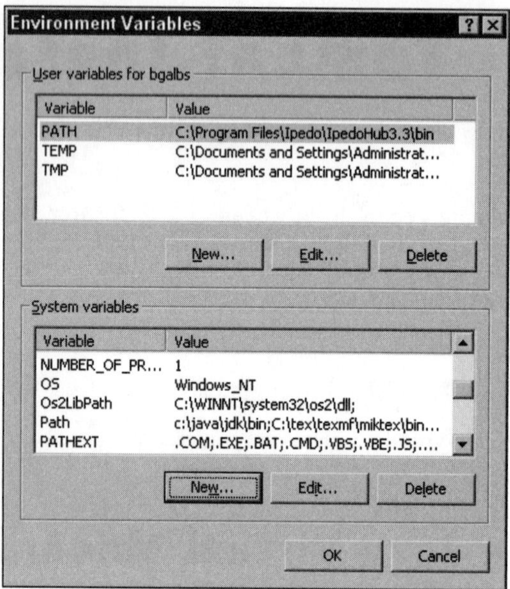

Figure 3-1: Selecting the New button.

Now enter the information shown in Figure 3-2.

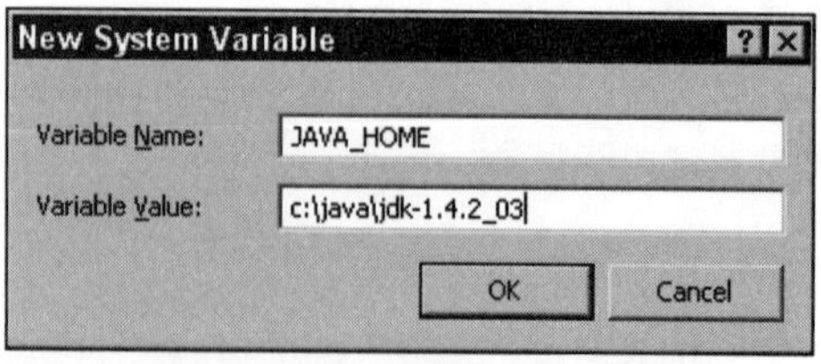

New System Variable
Variable Name: JAVA_HOME
Variable Value: c:\java\jdk-1.4.2_03
OK
Cancel

Figure 3-2: The JAVA_HOME information.

This information may vary depending on the specific version of the JVM you have installed and the location of your installation. Next, modify the `PATH` variable to include `%JAVA_HOME%\bin`, making sure that it is the first entry in `PATH`, as shown in Figure 3-3.

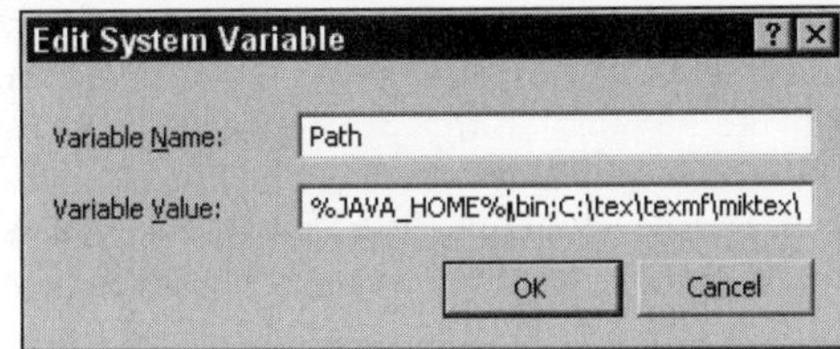

Figure 3-3: Modifying the Windows PATH.

This will make the Java executables available to the command prompt. To test the installation, open an instance of the command prompt (Start ➪ Programs ➪ Accessories ➪ Command Prompt) and enter the following instruction in the command window:

```
> javac
```

This should bring up a standard usage message such as the following (cropped short here):

```
Usage: javac <options> <source files>
where possible options include:
  -g                          Generate all debugging info
  -g:none                     Generate no debugging info
  -g:{lines,vars,source}      Generate only some debugging info
```

Linux Installation

For a Linux installation, first download a suitable distribution from the following URL:

```
http://java.sun.com
```

The official supported platform is Red Hat Linux, but Sun's JDK can be adapted to work with other distributions without too much trouble.

The following sections describe the two types of download: a tar/gzip version and an RPM package for systems supporting RPMs.

Tar/gzip installation

For the tar/gzip version, the installation process is as follows: Once the archive has been downloaded, extract its contents, which is a single self-extracting binary file. In these instructions, installing the JDK for all users is demonstrated. You should sign in as `root` using the `su` command. Begin by moving the file into the directory in which you would like to install the JDK.

If you are installing the JDK for a specific user, then you must install it into the user's home directory. Alternatively, if you wish to install the JDK for all users (which the Sun installation documentation assumes), then an accepted location is `/usr/java/jdk-[`*`version number`*`]` where *version number* is the version number of the JDK being installed.

Now add execute permissions for the file as follows:

```
# chmod o+x j2sdk-1_4_2_03-linux-i586.bin
```

Run the file using the following line:

```
# ./j2sdk-1_4_2_03-linux-i586.bin
```

You will be presented with a license agreement before installation commences. Once installation has finished, you should add the environment variable `$JAVA_HOME` to your system, with the location of the JDK. For example, if you installed it in `/usr/java/j2sdk-1_4_2_03-linux-i586`, you should give it this value. This value can be added to the `~/.bashrc` file for personal use or to `/etc/profile` for all users. Alternatively, `/etc/profile` runs any shell scripts in `/etc/profile.d`, so the following lines can be added to a script (here named `tomcat.sh`) in that directory (changing the details of the Java directory as appropriate):

```
JAVA_HOME=/usr/java/jdk-1.4.2_03/
export JAVA_HOME
PATH=$JAVA_HOME/bin:$PATH
export PATH
```

Note that you may have to log out and log in again for `/etc/profile` or `tomcat.sh` to be read by your system. You should also allow execute permissions for the `$JAVA_HOME/bin` folder for all users or for yourself as owner as appropriate.

To test the installation, type the following:

```
# javac
```

This should provide the following output (cropped for the sake of brevity):

```
Usage: javac <options> <source files>
where possible options include:
  -g                        Generate all debugging info
  -g:none                       Generate no debugging info
  -g:{lines,vars,source}        Generate only some debugging info
```

RPM installation

To install the JDK using the RPM, you must first download the file. The format is as follows:

```
j2sdk-[version number]-linux-i586-rpm.bin
```

On executing this file, you will be presented with the license terms for Apache. After execution, an RPM with the same name, but with the trailing `.bin` removed, is automatically uncompressed. If you wish to install the JDK for all users, you must now sign in as `root`. Set execute permissions for the file as follows:

```
# chmod o+x j2sdk-1_4_2_03-linux-i586-rpm.bin
# ./j2sdk-1_4_2_03-linux-i586-rpm.bin
```

The script will display a binary license agreement, which you will be asked to agree to before installation can proceed. Once you have agreed to the license, the install script will create the RPM file in the current directory. To install the RPM, type the following:

```
# rpm -iv j2sdk-1_4_2_03-linux-i586-rpm
```

This will install the Java 2 SDK at `/usr/java/j2sdk1.4.2_03`. You should now follow the previous instructions to modify various environment settings. You should also test the installation as described earlier.

Installing Tomcat

For each of the following steps (for Windows, Linux, and Unix systems), you can download the distributions from the same folder on the Jakarta Web site. Navigate to the following URL:

```
http://jakarta.apache.org/tomcat
```

Click the download binaries link (which at the time of this writing is on the left-hand side). The link will take you to a page of various Jakarta projects; choose the most recent Tomcat 5.x link.

Tomcat Windows Installer

The Jakarta download page contains many different links for Tomcat 5.x. The one you want has an extension of .EXE. Save this file at a convenient location on your machine, and double-click it to begin installation.

Once you've agreed to the Apache license, the installer will present you with a screen labeled "Choose Components," as shown in Figure 3-4. You should probably select the Full option, which will install all of the Tomcat components. Some of the components deserve some discussion, however.

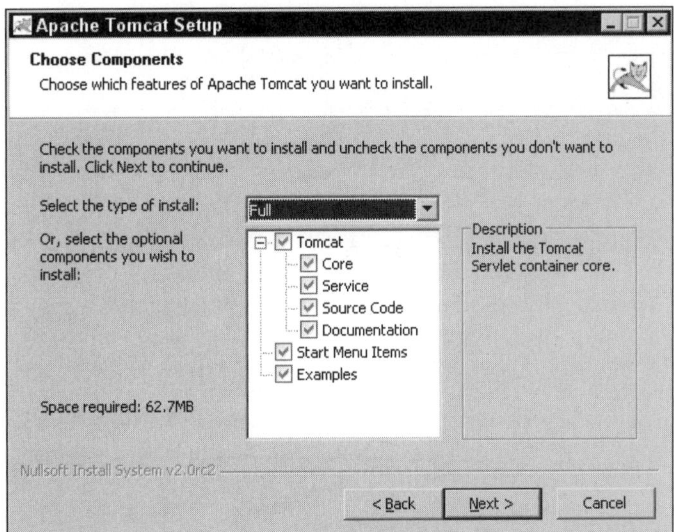

Figure 3-4: The Tomcat setup's Choose Components screen.

NT Service

One component you may not wish to install is the Service component (a subcomponent of Tomcat; if you can't see it, click the plus symbol next to Tomcat). The Service component enables you to start, stop, and restart Tomcat in the same way as any other Windows NT service, and this option is recommended if you are accustomed to managing your system services in this way. The chief advantage of a service is that it will automatically start Tomcat for you when your system starts, and it will do so without displaying any command prompts or other open windows.

An NT service is clearly the better option for production servers, but may not be what you want for development; starting and stopping an NT service repeatedly can be a pain.

Example Web Applications

The example Web applications may be useful as a reference. However, if they are installed and operational, they represent a certain security risk because they provide a documented and known path into your server. Choose to install them for now, as you will use them to confirm that the installation is working correctly. Chapter 15, "Tomcat Security," describes the possible security implications.

Finishing the Installation

Once you've chosen the components you wish to install, click the Next button. You will be prompted to choose a directory into which Tomcat should be installed. While the default directory is `C:\Program Files\Apache Software Foundation\Tomcat 5.0`, you should consider installing Tomcat into a path that does not contain spaces in the name, such as `c:\java\tomcat-5.0`. Once you've reviewed the destination folder, click Next.

The next screen requests the Tomcat port and an administrator login. Leave the port value as 8080, but choose a unique user name for the administrator login, and select a hard-to-guess password. Once done, click Next.

The final screen will ask for the location of the JDK you installed earlier. Enter it if it was not automatically found. Then, click Install.

Setting Environment Variables

While not strictly required when Tomcat's Windows installer is used, it is a good idea to add an environment variable that points to the directory in which you installed Tomcat. The environment variable is named `CATALINA_HOME`. To add the environment variable, navigate to Start ➪ Settings ➪ Control Panel and choose System. Now choose the Advanced tab and select the Environment Variables button. Now select the New button in the system variables (lower half) section and enter `CATALINA_HOME` as the variable name and the path to your Tomcat installation (for example, `c:\java\tomcat-5.0`).

Testing the Installation

To test the installation, you must first start the server. You can start Tomcat manually or, if you installed Tomcat as a service, you can start the service.

Starting the Server Manually

You can start the server manually by selecting Start ➪ Programs ➪ Apache Tomcat 5.0 and choosing Start Tomcat. A new command-prompt window will appear, demonstrating that the server is running.

Alternatively, you can start Tomcat by opening a command-prompt window, navigating to `%CATALINA_HOME%\bin`, and typing `startup`, as shown in Figure 3-5.

Figure 3-5: Starting Tomcat from the command line.

If Tomcat does not start up, you can find some troubleshooting tips at the end of this chapter. You may also get error messages if your `%JAVA_HOME%` variable is not defined, and if the `%JAVA_HOME%\bin` directory within the JDK is not in the `PATH`. If this is the case, you will get an error message such as the following:

```
'java' is not recognized as an internal or external command, operable program or
batch file.
```

Refer to the instructions in the section "Installing the Java Virtual Machine," earlier in this chapter, if this is the case.

To shut down Tomcat, use the Shutdown shortcut, Start ➪ Programs ➪ Apache Tomcat 5.0 ➪ Stop Tomcat, or type **`shutdown`** into the command prompt from Tomcat's `bin` directory.

Starting the Server as a Service

If you wish to start the server as a service (and assuming you chose this option when installing Tomcat), you will need to start up the service. This is done by double-clicking Administrative Tools in the Control Panel. In Administrative Tools, you should select Services. In the window that opens, you should find an entry for Tomcat, as shown in Figure 3-6.

To start the server, right-click the Tomcat entry and choose Start. No window will appear because the server is running as a service in the background. Once the server is started, the options for restarting and stopping the server will also be enabled.

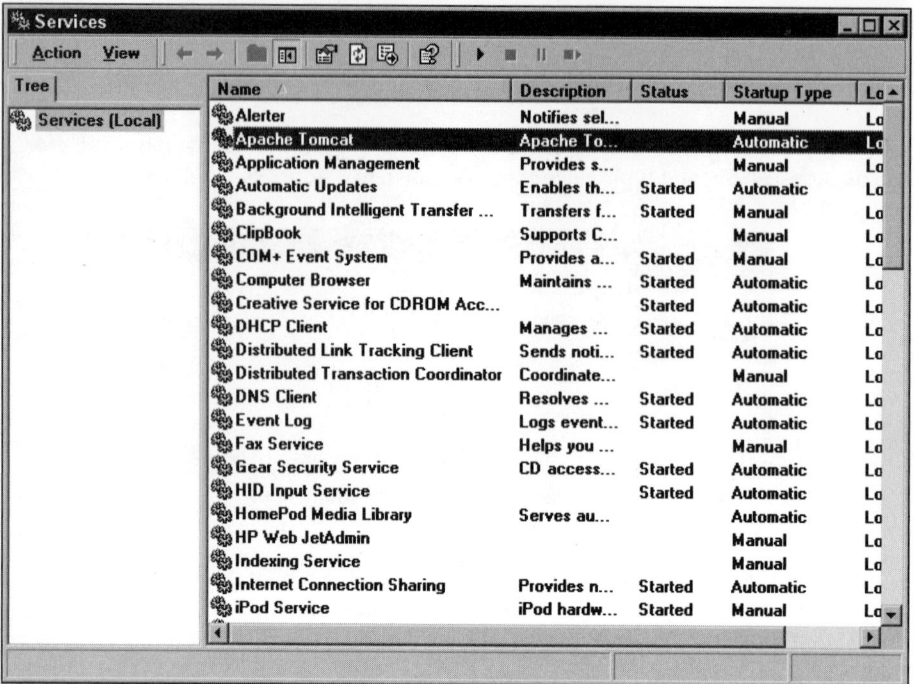

Figure 3-6: The Apache Tomcat service.

Changing NT Service Options

Looking at Figure 3-6, you can see that the Startup Type is set to Automatic, which means that restarting the computer also starts an instance of Tomcat automatically. From now on, every time Windows is started, Tomcat will automatically start up at boot time and will be available from then on.

You can further customize the service by choosing the Properties option from the context menu. This enables the startup type to be changed to Manual, or for the service to be disabled entirely. It also enables you to choose to automatically restart the service should it crash. This last option is especially useful because it enables you to run a script should the server fail, as well as reboot the computer.

You can also perform different actions depending on how many times the service has failed (by choosing the Recovery tab), so you can initially request a reboot of the service, then a reboot of the machine, after which any subsequent failures will cause a script to run that perhaps alerts you of the failure.

If you wish to set the recovery options, right-click the Tomcat service entry in the list and choose Properties. In the window that opens, choose Recovery, and you should be presented with the options shown in Figure 3-7.

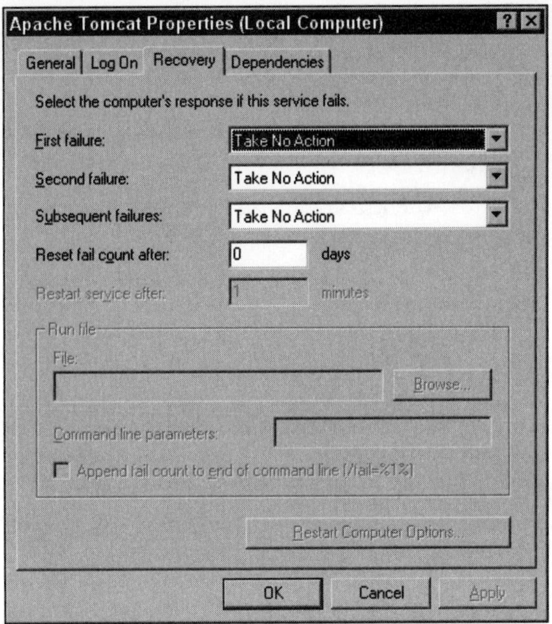

Figure 3-7: The Recovery options.

As you can see, the default is for no action to be taken. As you desire, you can configure the service to be restarted on failure, and/or run programs when a failure occurs.

Tomcat 5 as a Daemon Thread

If you chose not to run Tomcat as an NT service, you can still run Tomcat without a command prompt/DOS prompt window being open all the time that Tomcat is running.

To do this, you need to amend the `catalina.bat` file in `%CATALINA_HOME%\bin`. Search and replace the text

```
%_RUNJAVA%
```

with

```
%_RUNJAVAW%
```

Note the added `w` character. This new command calls the windowless version of the Java executable using `startup.bat`, which is also in the `%CATALINA_HOME%\bin` directory. Tomcat will now start without an attached Tomcat window, although one will appear and disappear.

You should create a shortcut to `startup.bat` because the provided shortcuts in the Start menu will not start a daemon process.

Because the appearing and disappearing window resembles a port contention problem, you should verify that the server is running by attempting to connect to it with a Telnet session or using a browser. If it is not running, run the `startup.bat` file from the `%CATALINA_HOME%\bin` folder and look at the error message, which should explain the problem.

Viewing the Default Installation

Tomcat, like most servers, comes with a default home page that can be used to confirm that the installation is working. Enter the following address in a browser:

```
http://localhost:8080/
```

The page shown in Figure 3-8 should appear.

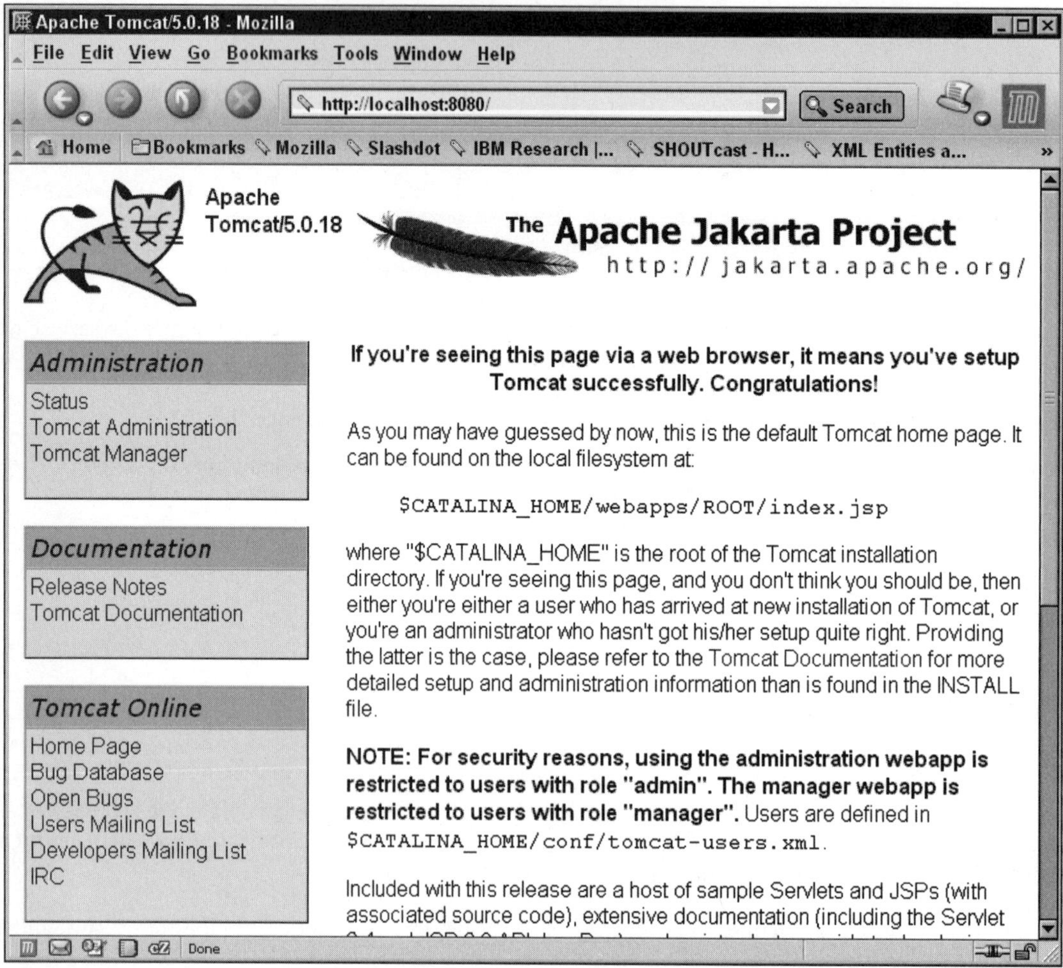

Figure 3-8: The default Tomcat home page.

Assigning Port Numbers

Note that if you are not accustomed to the port number assignation (the **:8080** section of the address), including it in the address of the server is required in the default installation. Ports are logical addresses in a computer that enable multiple communications with the server and the channeling of different protocols. For example, POP3 traffic is commonly addressed to port 25, SMTP is addressed to port 110, SSL is addressed to port 21, Telnet to 23, and so on. Browsers automatically point at port 80 if no port is specified (443 for HTTPS); hence, the use of ports is not immediately visible to the average user.

Because the majority of server hardware already includes a standard Web server installation (usually Apache for Linux, and IIS for Windows), Tomcat does not attempt to connect to the standard HTTP traffic port (which is 80 by default), but rather to port 8080.

The configuration file that specifies the port number is called `server.xml` and can be found in the installation folder of Tomcat in the `%CATLINA_HOME%\conf` directory. It's just a text file, and somewhere within it you should find an entry similar to the following:

```
<!-- Define a non-SSL Coyote HTTP/1.1 Connector on port 8080 -->
<Connector acceptCount="100" connectionTimeout="20000" debug="0"
    disableUploadTimeout="true" enableLookups="false" maxSpareThreads="75"
    maxThreads="150" minSpareThreads="25" port="8080" redirectPort="8443"/>
```

You can find this entry by searching for the string `port="8080"`. Changing this to another number will change the Tomcat port number. Changing it to 80 will enable you to connect to Tomcat using the following URL without the trailing colon and port number:

```
http://localhost/
```

If you have any problems, refer to the "Troubleshooting and Tips" section at the end of this chapter.

Conversely, if all has gone well, you are now the proud owner of your own Tomcat instance. Before you are finished, you should check Tomcat's capability to serve JSP pages and Servlets.

To do this, choose the JSP Examples link from the left-hand menu and select some of the examples to run. Confirm that they all run as they are supposed to without error messages. Do the same for the Servlet Examples link to test this functionality.

Installing Tomcat on Windows Using the ZIP File

Installing Tomcat using the ZIP file is not much different from the process described earlier. The ZIP file is provided for those who prefer manually installing Tomcat.

To install Tomcat using the ZIP file, simply unpack the contents of the file to your directory of choice, such as `c:\java\tomcat-5.0`.

Now add the `%CATALINA_HOME%` environment variable as shown in the preceding directions. To check your installation, you need to follow slightly different instructions than before. Because the shortcuts for the server are not created automatically, you need to call a couple of batch files provided in the `%CATALINA_HOME%\bin` directory for this purpose.

To start the server, type the following at the command prompt:

```
> cd %CATALINA_HOME%\bin
> startup.bat
```

As with the preceding installation method, a new window will open, indicating that the server has started. To shut down Tomcat, type **shutdown.**

Installing Tomcat on Linux

Installing Tomcat on Linux or Unix is easy. Download the tar/gzip file of the latest Tomcat 5.x binary release from the following URL:

`http://jakarta.apache.org/tomcat`

Extract the downloaded file onto your hard drive to a path such as `/usr/java/jakarta-tomcat-5`. Note that you should use the GNU version of the `tar` utility to ensure that long filenames are handled properly.

You should now export the `$CATALINA_HOME` variable, using the following command (in `bash`):

```
# CATALINA_HOME=/usr/java/jakarta-tomcat-5
# export CATALINA_HOME
```

Alternatively, add these commands to `~/.bashrc` or `/etc/profile` as you did for the JDK installation or create a shell file, `tomcat.sh`, and place it in `/etc/profile.d`. It will be run automatically by `/etc/profile` at boot time to make the variable available to all users.

You can now start Tomcat by running the following shell command:

```
# $CATALINA_HOME/bin/startup.sh
```

Viewing the Default Installation

To confirm that Tomcat is running, point your browser to the following URL:

`http://localhost:8080/`

Choose the JSP Examples link from the menu on the left-hand side and select some of the examples to run. Confirm that they run without error messages. Do the same for the Servlet Examples to test their functionality.

Modifying Port Numbers

Tomcat uses port 8080 by default. Because the majority of server hardware already includes a standard Web server installation, usually Apache, Tomcat does not attempt to connect to the standard HTTP traffic port, 80, by default.

If you wish to have Tomcat use port 80 (and thus eliminate the need for a port number to be provided in the URL), you first need root privileges.

The configuration file that specifies the port number is called `server.xml` and can be found in the `$CATALINA_HOME/conf` directory. Somewhere within it you should find the following entry:

```
<!-- Define a non-SSL Coyote HTTP/1.1 Connector on port 8080 -->
<Connector acceptCount="100" connectionTimeout="20000" debug="0"
    disableUploadTimeout="true" enableLookups="false" maxSpareThreads="75"
    maxThreads="150" minSpareThreads="25" port="8080" redirectPort="8443"/>
```

You can find this entry by searching for the string `port="8080"`. Changing this to another number (higher than 1024 in Linux) will change the Tomcat port number. Changing it to 80 will enable you to connect to Tomcat using the following URL, providing that the server is started with root permissions:

```
http://localhost/
```

If you have any problems, refer to the "Troubleshooting and Tips" section at the end of this chapter.

The Tomcat Installation Directory

The Tomcat installation directory contents are as follows:

```
(Tomcat Directory)/
                bin/
                common/
                        classes/
                        endorsed/
                        lib/
                conf/
                logs/
                server/
                        classes/
                        lib/
                        webapps/
                shared/
                        classes/
                        lib/
                temp/
                webapps/
                work/
```

The bin Directory

The `bin` directory contains the shell scripts and batch files for starting Tomcat in various modes. It also includes a pre-compiler for JSP pages that can improve startup time and first-time response (the time it takes for the server to respond to a request for a JSP page that has not been previously compiled). Compilation occurs only once, but it can frustrate the first visitor to a site after the server is restarted because of the long response time.

The shared Directory

The `shared` directory contains Java classes to which any Web application can have access, such as JDBC drivers or shared utility libraries. Class files are placed in `shared/classes`, and JAR files are placed in `shared/lib`. See Chapter 9, "Class Loaders," for more details.

The common Directory

The `common` directory's subdirectories are for class files and JAR files that are available to all Web applications and to Catalina's internal class files as well. Users should not place their own libraries in these directories.

The conf Directory

The `conf` directory contains the configuration files for Tomcat. These include general server configuration files, a default user list for file-based authentication and security for Web applications, and a global configuration file. Later chapters discuss these files in greater detail.

The logs Directory

The `$CATALINA_HOME/logs` directory contains the server logs.

The server Directory

Classes that are to be made available to Catalina only are placed within the `server` directory's subdirectories. You should not place files here.

The webapps Directory

The Web applications provided with Tomcat are contained in `webapps`. The Web applications provided with Tomcat are as follows:

- `servlet-examples` and `jsp-examples` — These are numerous example Servlets and JSP pages. These are the examples used earlier to test the Tomcat installation.
- `manager` — This Web application enables remote management of the server, including installing and uninstalling Web applications. Chapter 7, "Web Application Administration," covers this application in detail.
- `ROOT` — This is the default Web application for Tomcat. The contents of this folder are shown when no subcontext is provided in the URL to the server. For example, `http://localhost:8080/` will load `index.html`, or `index.jsp`, whichever is present, with the latter taking precedence if both exist.
- `tomcat-docs` — The documentation for Tomcat is available with a default installation.

Your own Web applications will also be installed in this directory. The structure of the `webapps` directory is discussed in greater detail in Chapter 6, "Web Application Configuration."

The work Directory

The `work` directory contains temporary files, precompiled JSP pages, and other intermediate files.

Troubleshooting and Tips

This final section deals with some common problems you may encounter after installing Tomcat. If you have further problems, more material can be found on the Tomcat Web site at the following URLs (as well as on various forums):

```
http://jakarta.apache.org/tomcat/
http://java.sun.com/
```

You should also read the release notes available with each download.

Sometimes, when you attempt to launch Tomcat, the Tomcat window will appear briefly and then disappear. This usually occurs because of an error that causes Tomcat to crash and, thus, its window to disappear. The error message is also displayed, but because the window disappears so rapidly, the error cannot be seen.

If Tomcat does not start, it can be run in the current shell or as a command prompt (as opposed to a new pop-up window) so that the problem can be seen. To do this in Linux, type the following:

```
# $CATALINA_HOME/bin/catalina.sh run
```

Or, in Windows, type the following:

```
> %CATALINA_HOME%/bin/catalina run
```

This will produce the normal startup messages, and any errors will be displayed. These errors also appear in the `stdout.log` file in the $CATALINA_HOME/logs subdirectory.

Some common problems are discussed next.

The Port Number Is in Use

One possible error is that the chosen port is already in use. The error message will look similar to the following:

```
LifecycleException:  Protocol handler initialization failed:
java.net.BindException: Address already in use: JVM_Bind:8080
```

Tomcat uses port 8080 by default, as mentioned previously. You can determine whether another program is using this port by using the `netstat` utility on both Windows and Linux. Typing **netstat -ao** on Windows and **netstat -lp** on Linux into your shell/command prompt will list open ports on your system, which should indicate any process that is interfering with Tomcat. You have two options: shut the process down or change Tomcat's port as described earlier.

Running Multiple Instances

A common problem is trying to start a new Tomcat instance when one is already running. This is especially true if it's running as a daemon thread. Check to ensure that you aren't already running another instance of Tomcat.

A Proxy Is Blocking Access

If you have a proxy set up for all HTTP services, it may be blocking access to the server. You should bypass the proxy for all local addresses. Instructions are provided below.

Choose Edit ➪ Preferences. Choose the Advanced option and choose Proxies. Select Manual proxy configuration and enter **localhost** and **127.0.0.1** in the No proxies for box. This may vary between different versions of Netscape and Mozilla, but the principles remain the same.

Choose Tools ➪ Internet Options and choose the Connections tab. Select the Lan Settings button and enter your proxy configuration by selecting the Advanced button in the window that opens. Enter **localhost** and **127.0.0.1** in the Exceptions box. This should work in all versions of Internet Explorer.

Summary

This chapter has provided a great deal of information about selecting and installing a JDK and Tomcat in a variety of ways. Key points of this chapter include the following:

- In the majority of cases, installing the server is a very straightforward process, as binary versions are available for the common platforms.
- The Tomcat installation directory structure includes eight important directories.
- Common installation problems include the port number being in use, multiple instances running, and a proxy blocking access.

If you have any problems, you can contact the support network at the following URL:

```
http://p2p.wrox.com/
```

The following URL also offers several lists that can be helpful to the beginner:

```
http://jakarta.apache.org/
```

The user list is also archived and you will find that most questions have been asked, and answered, before.

Chapter 4 examines Tomcat's architecture.

Tomcat Architecture

An understanding of Tomcat's architecture is important both for its effective use and for getting the most out of the remainder of this book. Tomcat's internal architecture closely mirrors the way that it should be administered. Each section of the Tomcat architecture is closely associated with a function of the Server. It is possible to group administration tasks around these functional components, making administration more intuitive.

In this chapter, you will gain an understanding of the Tomcat architecture, including the following roles:

- Connectors
- Engines
- Realms
- Valves
- Loggers
- Hosts
- Contexts

An Overview of Tomcat Architecture

Tomcat's architecture was completely revised for version 4. It was rebuilt from the ground up because some users felt that the refactoring done in the previous Tomcat release, while improving its performance and flexibility, was always going to result in a somewhat limited server. A rather heated debate ensued regarding whether this was actually the case. The result of this controversy was the 3.2 architecture branching from the main development tree in a continued refactoring effort, leaving the 4.0 version to become the main focus of the project.

Tomcat 5 is the latest iteration of the Tomcat 4 architecture. Tomcat 5 supports the latest Servlet and JSP specifications, versions 2.4 and 2.0, respectively.

Tomcat 5 consists of a nested hierarchy of components. Some of these components are called **top-level components** because they exist at the top of the component hierarchy in a rigid relationship with one another. **Containers** are components that can contain a collection of other components. Components that can reside in containers, but cannot themselves contain other components, are called **nested components**. Figure 4-1 illustrates the structure of a typical Tomcat 5 configuration.

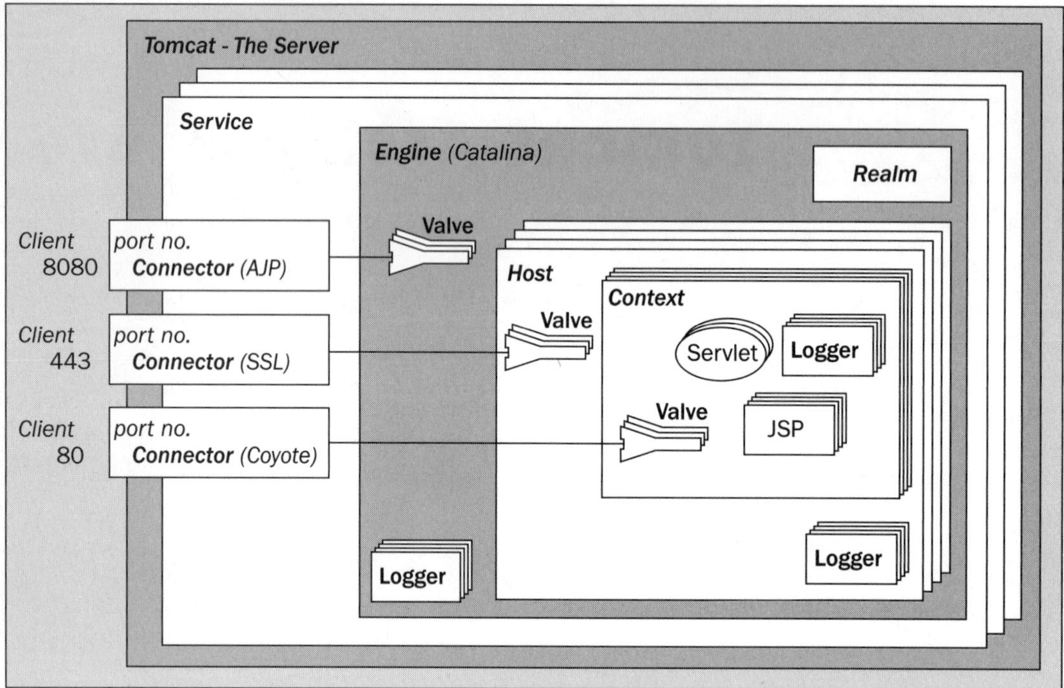

Figure 4-1: Tomcat's architecture.

This diagram represents the most complete topology of a Server. However, you should be aware that some of these objects may be removed without affecting the Server's performance. Notably, the Engine and Host may be unnecessary if an external Web server (such as Apache) is carrying out the tasks of resolving requests to Web applications.

Here, components that can be contained multiple times are denoted by a symbol that has multiple profiles, including Logger, Valve, Host, and Context. Connectors are drawn separately to illustrate a point that is covered in just a moment.

The following sections examine each component in turn. Chapter 5 discusses each component's configuration.

The Server

The **Server** is Tomcat itself — an instance of the Web application server — and is a top-level component. It owns a port that is used to shut down the server. In addition, the Server can be set in debug mode, which instantiates a version of the Java Virtual Machine (JVM) that enables debugging.

Only one instance of the Server can be created inside a given Java Virtual Machine (JVM).

Separate Servers configured to different ports can be set up on a single machine to separate applications so that they can be restarted independently. That is, if one Server running in a JVM were to crash, the other applications would be safe in another Server instance. This is sometimes done in hosting environments in which each customer has a separate instance of a JVM, so a badly configured/written application will not cause others to crash.

The Service

A **Service** groups a container (usually of type Engine) with that container's Connectors and is a top-level component.

An Engine is a request-processing component that represents the Catalina Servlet engine. It examines the HTTP headers to determine the virtual host or context to which requests should be passed.

Each Service represents a grouping of Connectors (components that manage the connection between the client and server) and a single container, which accepts requests from the Connectors and processes the requests to present them to the appropriate Host. Each Service is named so that administrators can easily identify log messages sent from each Service.

In other words, the container contains the Web applications. It is responsible for accepting requests, routing them to the specified Web application and specific resource, and returning the result of the processing of the request. Connectors stand between the client making the request and the container. They provide additional services such as SSL support.

The Connectors

Connectors connect the applications to clients. They represent the point at which requests are received from clients and are assigned a port on the server. The default port for nonsecure HTTP applications is kept as 8080 to avoid interference with any Web server running on the standard HTTP port, but there is no reason why this cannot be changed as long as the port is free. Multiple Connectors may be set up for a single Engine or Engine-level component, but they must have unique port numbers.

The default port to which browsers make requests if a port number is not specified is port 80. If Tomcat is run in standalone mode, the port for the primary Connector of the Web application can be changed to 80 by reconfiguring this component.

The default Connector is Coyote, which implements HTTP 1.1. Alternative Connectors are Apache JServ Protocol (AJP), an SSL Connector for secure connections, and an HTTP 1.0 Connector. These are discussed as part of Chapters 10–13, which deal with Tomcat's Connectors and integrating Tomcat with Web servers such as Apache and IIS.

The Engine

The next component in the architecture is the top-level container—a container object that cannot be contained by another container. This means that it is guaranteed not to have a parent container. It is at this level that the objects begin to aggregate child components.

Strictly speaking, the container does not need to be an Engine, it just has to implement the container interface. This interface mandates the following: that the object implementing it is aware of its position in the hierarchy (it knows its parent and its children), that it provides access to logging, that it provides a Realm for user authentication and role-based authorization, and that it has access to a number of resources, including its session manager (and some internally important aspects that you do not need to worry about).

In practice, the container at this level is usually an **Engine** and so it makes sense to discuss it in that role. As mentioned previously, an Engine is a request-processing component that represents the Catalina Servlet engine. It examines the HTTP headers to determine the virtual host or context to which requests should be passed.

When the standalone configuration is used, the Engine that is used is the default one. This Engine does the checking mentioned earlier. When Tomcat is configured to provide Java Servlet support for a Web server, the default class used to serve requests is overridden because the Web server has normally determined the correct destination of the request.

The host name of the server to which the Engine belongs is set here in multi-homed machines. An Engine may contain hosts representing a group of Web applications and contexts representing a single Web application.

The Realm

The Realm for an Engine manages user authentication and authorization. During the configuration of an application, the administrator sets the roles that are allowed for each resource or group of resources, and the Realm is used to enforce this policy.

Realms can authenticate against text files, database tables, LDAP servers, and the Windows network identity of the user. You will learn more about this in Chapter 15.

A Realm applies across the entire Engine or top-level container, so applications within a container share user resources for authentication. This means that, for example, a manager for the intranet will have the same rights as the manager of the e-commerce site should both these applications be in the same Engine.

By default, a user must still authenticate separately to each Web application on the server. You will see how this can be changed in Chapter 8 using Single Sign-on, but, in brief, this is implemented as a Valve in Tomcat.

The Valves

Valves are components that enable Tomcat to intercept a request and pre-process it. They are similar to the filter mechanism of the Servlet specifications, but are specific to Tomcat. Hosts, contexts, and Engines may contain Valves.

Valves are commonly used to enable Single Sign-on for all Hosts on a Server, as well as log request patterns, client IP addresses, and server usage patterns (peak traffic, bandwidth use, mean average requests per time unit, the resources that most requests ask for, and so on). This is known as **request dumping,** and a **request dumper Valve** records the header information (the request URI, accept languages, source IP, host name requested, and so on) and any cookies sent with the request. Response dumping logs the response headers and cookies (if set) to a file.

Valves are typically reusable components, and can therefore be added and removed from the request path according to need. Their inclusion is transparent to Web applications, although the response time will increase if a Valve is added). An application that wishes to intercept requests for pre-processing and responses for post-processing should use the **filters** that are a part of the Servlet specifications.

A Valve may intercept a request between an Engine and a Host/context, between a Host and a context, and between a context and a resource within the Web application.

The Loggers

Loggers report on the internal state of a component. They can be set for components from top-level containers downward. Logging behavior is inherited, so a Logger set at the Engine level is assigned to every child object unless overridden by the child. The configuration of Loggers at this level can be a convenient way to decide the default logging behavior for the server.

This establishes a convenient destination for all logging events for those components that are not specially configured to generate their own logs.

The Host

A **Host** mimics the popular Apache virtual host functionality. In Apache, this enables multiple servers to be used on the same machine, and to be differentiated by their IP address or by their host name. In Tomcat, the virtual hosts are differentiated by a fully qualified host name. Thus, the two Web sites `www.websitea.com` and `www.websiteb.com` can both reside in the same server, with requests for each routed to different groups of Web applications.

Configuring a Host includes setting the name of the host. The majority of clients can be depended on to send both the IP address of the server and the host name they used to resolve the IP address. The host name is provided as an HTTP header that an Engine inspects to determine the Host to which a request should be passed.

If the Host is not within an Engine, it is possible that it is the top-level container.

The Context

Finally, there is the Web application, also known as a **context**. Configuration of a Web application includes informing the Engine/Hosts of the location of the root folder of the application. Dynamic reloading can also be enabled so that any classes that have been changed are reloaded into memory. However, this is resource-intensive, and is not recommended for deployment scenarios.

The context may also include specific error pages, which enable a system administrator to configure error messages that are consistent with the look and feel of the application, and usability features (such as a search Engine, useful links, or a report-creating component that notifies the administrator of errors in the application).

Finally, a context can also be configured with initialization parameters for the application it represents and for access control (authentication and authorization restrictions). Chapter 15 provides more information on these two aspects of Web application deployment.

The Remaining Classes in the Tomcat Architecture

Tomcat also defines classes for representing a request, a response, a session that represents a virtual connection between a server and a client, and listeners. These classes are described in detail in the remainder of the book.

Listeners listen for significant events in the component they are configured in. Examples of significant events include the instantiation of the component and its subsequent destruction.

Summary

To conclude this chapter on Tomcat's architecture, let's review some of the key points that have been discussed:

- A Web application is represented by the context component. It may include Loggers that log messages and Valves that intercept and process requests and responses. Valves intercept just before and just after a request is processed and a response is generated.
- A context sits within a Host that represents a virtual host (an alias assigned to the currently assigned IP address) and many contexts may share a Host. The context component may define Valves and Loggers.
- The Host sits in an Engine that resolves requests to virtual hosts. It can define Valves and Loggers, too.
- Finally, an Engine sits inside a Service that groups together the Engine with the Connectors that connect the Engine with clients. The entire object tree lives within the Server component that is Tomcat.

Now you should be comfortable with Tomcat's architecture. In Chapter 5, you will examine the steps for configuring Tomcat.

5

Basic Tomcat Configuration

The focus of this chapter is on the basic configuration of Tomcat 5. The Tomcat 5 server is configured by setting parameter values for the components of Tomcat 5 before starting the server. All architectural components (such as Service, Servers, Engine, Connectors, Realm, and Valves) can be configured. This chapter describes how to configure these components, the range of allowed parameter values, and how they affect Tomcat's operation. Major differences between Tomcat 5 and Tomcat 4.1.x configuration files will be noted wherever applicable.

Tomcat 5 can be completely configured using a Web-based GUI configurator called the `admin` application. The `admin` application is itself a Tomcat-hosted Web application. This chapter includes step-by-step coverage of how to use the `admin` application.

As with the Tomcat 4.1.x series of servers, the persistent data of a Tomcat 5 configuration (even if configuration changes are made through the `admin` application) is stored within XML file(s). There are numerous XML elements in these files, and each element has attributes that correspond to a configurable aspect of a Tomcat 5 architectural component (see Chapter 4 for more information about Tomcat 5 architecture). This chapter examines each of these configurable attributes, and describes how they affect the behavior of the corresponding Tomcat 5 components.

Some hard-core administrators may insist on hand-editing the underlying configuration XML files instead of using the Web-based GUI to gain maximum control. Others may not enable the `admin` utility for security reasons during deployment. If you belong in either of these categories, this chapter provides a detailed, line-by-line explanation of the most important Tomcat 5 configuration files, including the `server.xml` file (the primary configuration file for Tomcat servers).

Special attention is paid to the default Tomcat 5 configuration in this chapter's coverage. This default configuration exists in the form of a set of default configuration files that are included with the Tomcat 5 distribution. If you start Tomcat 5 without first editing any of the XML configuration files, this is the configuration that is used. Incidentally, it is also the **bootstrap** configuration used if you start up Tomcat 5 to gain access to the `admin` application to make configuration changes.

Therefore, it is important to understand what this special bootstrap configuration will do, and how you may be able to modify it for specific production environments.

This chapter also touches on some advanced configuration topics, (such as Realm configuration and the configuration of fine-grained security policy control over Tomcat 5 server instances), but detailed descriptions of these concepts are provided in later chapters.

By the end of this chapter, you will be fluent with basic Tomcat 5 configuration, and be able to configure Tomcat 5 using either one of the following two methods:

- The `admin` application
- Editing the XML configuration file by hand

You will also be completely familiar with the basic (default) configuration of the Tomcat 5 server, and will be able to modify this configuration for your own production needs.

Tomcat 5 Configuration Essentials

A Tomcat 5 server instance reads a set of configuration XML files upon startup. To configure a Tomcat 5 server instance, it is necessary to modify these XML files. The following table shows the files that affect the behavior of the Tomcat 5 instance.

File Name	Description
`server.xml`	Primary configuration file for the Tomcat server components. This includes the configuration of Service, Connector, Engine, Realm, Valves, Hosts, and so on.
`web.xml`	Default deployment descriptor for Web applications. This is used by Tomcat 5 for all automatically deployed Web applications, or applications without their own specific deployment descriptor. If a Web application has its own deployment descriptor, its content will always override the configuration settings specified in this default descriptor.

Tomcat 5 looks for these configuration files in a specified configuration directory. This configuration directory is specified via an environment variable. Tomcat 5 first checks the `$CATALINA_BASE` (`%CATALINA_BASE%` on Windows) environment variable. If this environment variable is defined, Tomcat 5 looks in the specified directory for a `conf` subdirectory. The configuration files are expected to reside in this `conf` subdirectory. It is quite straightforward to configure multiple, concurrently running Tomcat 5 instances on the same physical machine. This can be done by specifying different `$CATALINA_BASE` directories for each Tomcat instance. Typically, this is performed using a different shell script or batch file to set the `$CATALINA_BASE` variable and start each instance.

If `$CATALINA_BASE` is not specified, the `$CATALINA_HOME` (`%CATALINA_HOME%` on Windows) environment variable is used instead. The `$CATALINA_HOME` environment variable is a required variable that specifies where Tomcat 5 is installed on your system. In fact, the `$CATALINA_HOME` variable is used to locate the executables (i.e., Catalina, Jasper, and Coyote) to run Tomcat. In this case, Tomcat 5 will look into the `conf` directory under `$CATALINA_HOME` for the server configuration files. This behavior is compatible with Tomcat 4.x servers. However, if you need to run multiple instances on the same machine (using `$CATALINA_HOME`), you must duplicate the entire Tomcat 5 distribution (including the large `bin`, `common/lib`, `server/lib` directories, and so on). In the rest of this chapter, references to the `$CATALINA_HOME` variable can be taken to mean `$CATALINA_BASE` if you are using Tomcat 5's multi-instances support.

Tomcat 5 Web-Based Configurator

Tomcat 5 configuration can be performed via a Web browser using the included Web-based configurator application (called the `admin` application). Figure 5-1 shows a typical screen from this Web-based configurator. In this case, a JDBC data source is being configured.

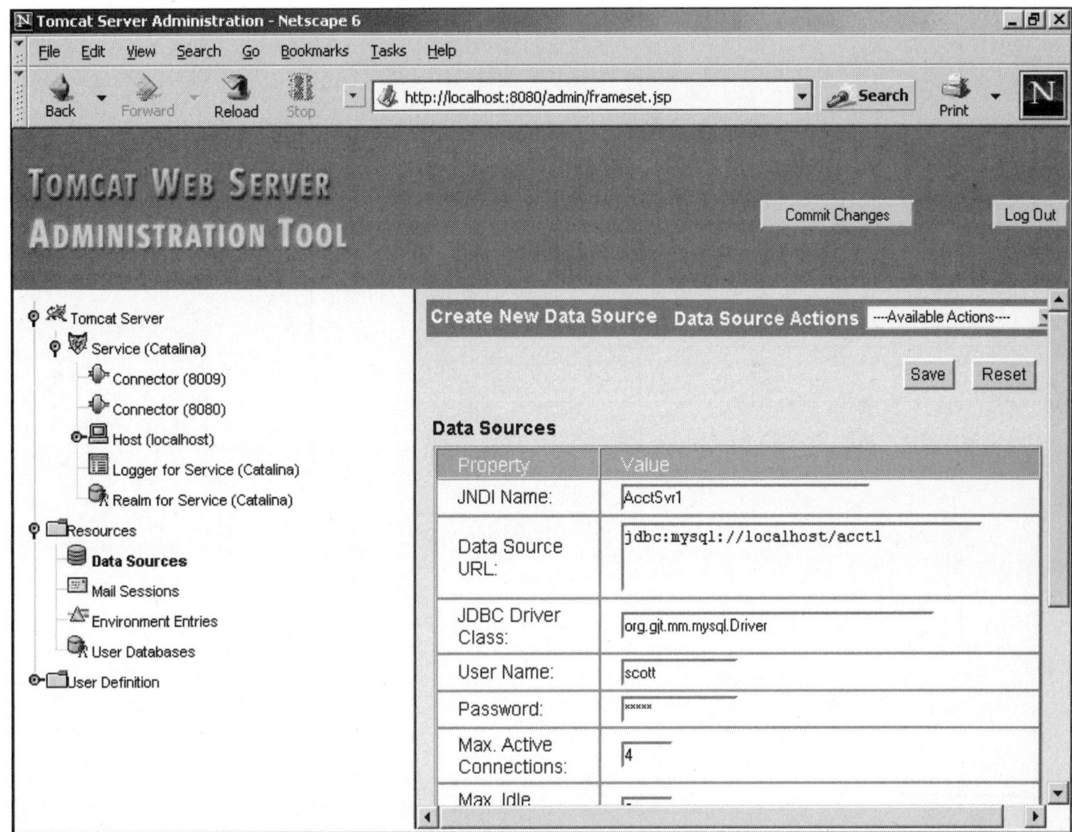

Figure 5-1: Tomcat 5 Web-based configurator (admin).

Some earlier versions of Tomcat supported only file-based configuration, mandating hand editing of the configuration files via a text editor. While manual editing of configuration file is still supported, this error-prone approach can be completely avoided by using the Web-based GUI provided by the `admin` application. Another major advantage of a Web-based GUI configuration is the capability to perform remote, off-site administration. With Tomcat 5, administrators can now reconfigure and maintain server instances wherever a Web browser connected to the Internet is available.

Even though the configuration is performed graphically, the XML configuration files are still being modified. These files are kept in the `$CATALINA_HOME/conf` directory of the Tomcat 5 distribution (or, if you have configured multiple Tomcat 5 instances, the corresponding `$CATALINA_BASE/conf` directory).

Figure 5-2 illustrates how Web-based Tomcat 5 configuration can be performed, and the behind-the-scenes work that takes place.

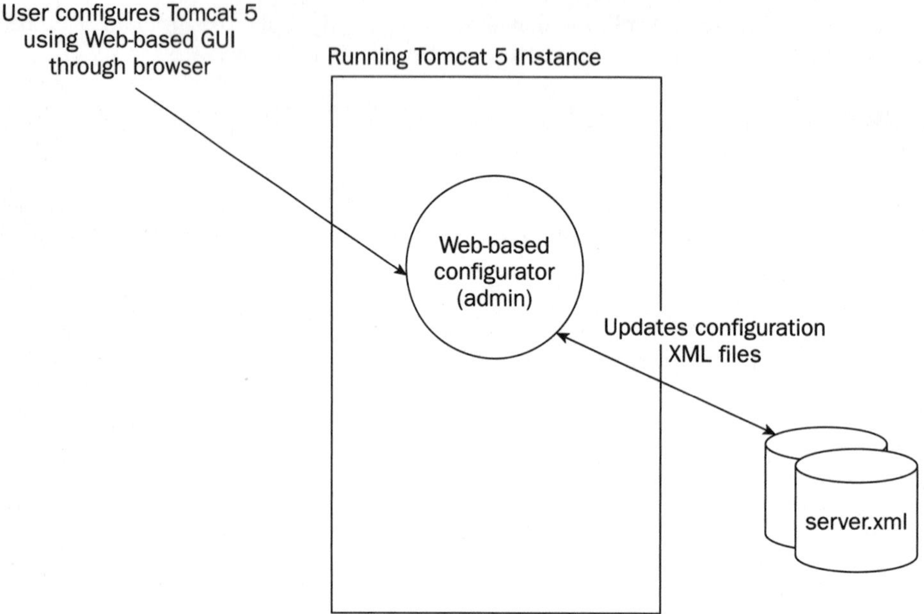

Figure 5-2: How Tomcat 5 Web-based configuration works.

In Figure 5-2, the user changes the value of a certain attribute of a Tomcat 5 component via the Web-based GUI. The `admin` Web application then makes the corresponding change in the configuration XML file. The user can control when the change to the XML file occurs by clicking the Commit Changes button on the top panel of the user interface. The `admin` Web application can be conceptually viewed as a user-friendly editor for the XML-based configuration files, whereby the Commit Changes button enables the user to save any changes to the files.

Enabling Access to Configurator

Before you can use the configurator, you must enable access to it. For security reasons, only users with an `admin` role are allowed to access the Web-based configurator, and the role of `admin` is not defined for any user in the list of users that comes with the default installation. This means that no one can access the `admin` application by default. Instead, a user must be explicitly configured for the admin role before access is granted. Therefore, to use the Web-based configurator, you should follow these steps:

1. Define the role of **admin.**
2. Assign this role to one of the Tomcat users.

To perform these two tasks, it is necessary to edit one of the XML files in the `$CATALINA_HOME/conf` directory. The `tomcat-users.xml` file contains user and password information used by the `admin` application. Following is the modification required for this file:

```
<?xml version='1.0' encoding='utf-8'?>
<tomcat-users>
<role rolename="admin"/>
<user username="tomcat" password="tomcat" roles="tomcat,admin "/>
  <user username="both" password="tomcat" roles="tomcat,role1"/>
  <user username="role1" password="tomcat" roles="role1"/>
</tomcat-users>
```

The modification here first adds the role "admin." This role is then assigned to the user named "tomcat," with a password of "tomcat."

If you had installed Tomcat on Windows using the installer executable, the admin user name and password would have been specified during the install. In this case, your **`tomcat-users.xml`** *file will have these values already set.*

Of course, in a production scenario, you need to ensure that access to the `admin` application is secured. Some of the mechanisms for securing the `admin` application are as follows:

- Use a more rigorous mechanism of authentication than BASIC, such as one that is client-certificate-based (CLIENT-CERT).
- Use JDBC or JNDI-based Realm implementations to store the manager and admin user name/password.
- Configure the Realm implementation to use encrypted passwords.
- Use `RemoteAddrValve` or `RemoteHostValve` in the admin's Context to restrict the machines from which the `admin` application can be accessed.

See Chapter 15, "Tomcat Security," for details about performing some of these steps. You may even want to completely disable access to `admin` and require that all configuration be hand-edited.

The **`admin`** *utility accesses this* **`tomcat-users.xml`** *file through a UserDatabase Realm. See Chapter 15 for a detailed discussion of Realms configuration and system security in general. Instead of XML files, it is possible to use specialized Realms that access an external directory service, or an external table in a relational database containing user and password information for added security and ease of maintenance during production deployment.*

Once the admin role has been assigned, you can start Tomcat 5 and use the following URL to access the `admin` utility (assuming you are using the default configuration and have not manually modified the configuration files):

```
http://localhost:8080/admin/
```

The custom login screen is then displayed, as shown in Figure 5-3.

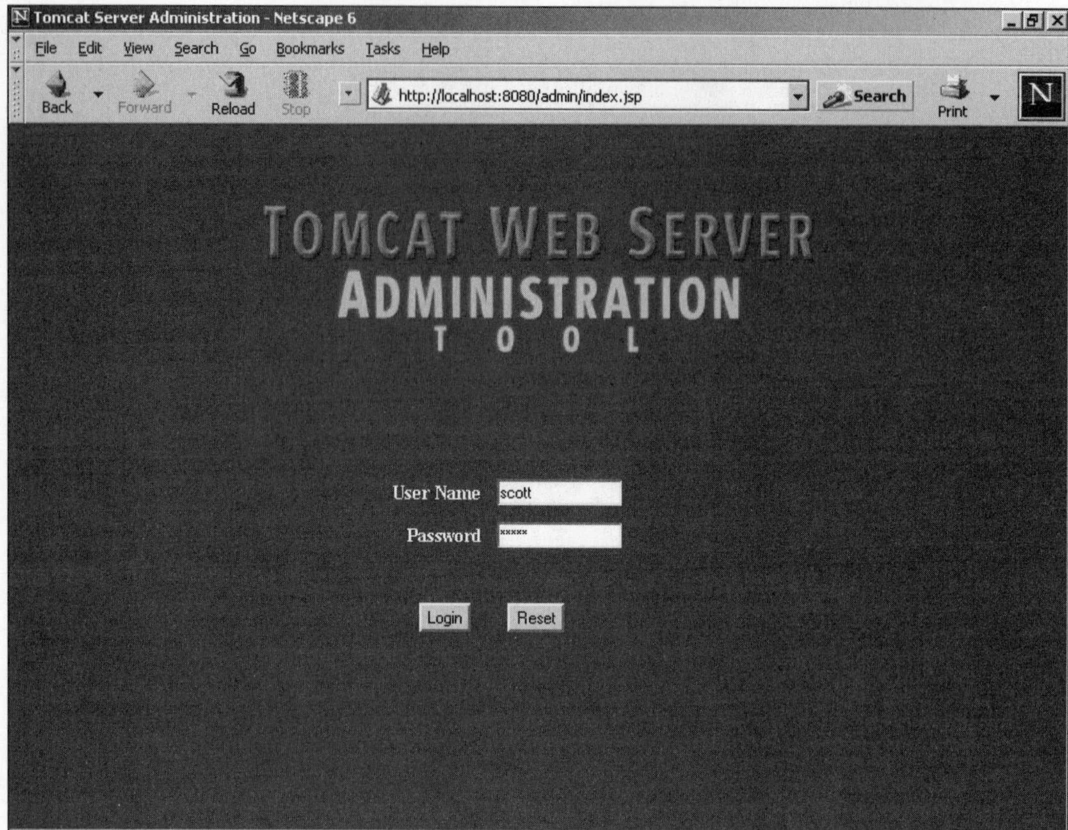

Figure 5-3: Web-based configurator custom login screen.

You can now use the user name "tomcat" and the password "tomcat" to log in to the `admin` application. However, once the `admin` application is up and running, a new user can easily be added via the GUI. Simply click the User Definition link on the left pane of the admin GUI, and then click the Users selection. You will see the list of users in the right pane, as shown in Figure 5-4.

In the User Actions drop-down list in the right pane, select the Create New User option. You can then enter the user name and password of the new user, and assign it the admin role. Figure 5-5 shows this in action.

Click the Save button to add the user. This will update the underlying `tomcat-users.xml` file immediately with the new user and password information. There is no need to click the Commit Changes button when working with user definitions in this case.

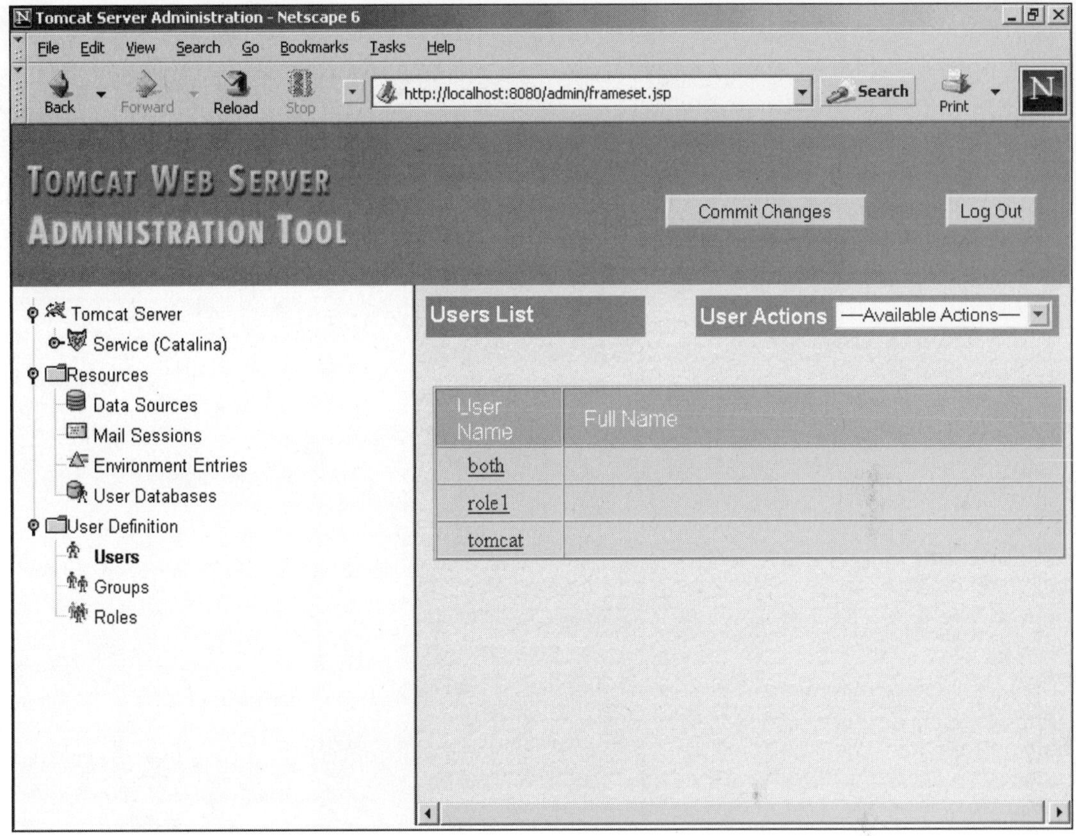

Figure 5-4: Users and role management via Tomcat 5's Web-based configurator.

Once the administrative user gains access to the `admin` application, it is possible to use the GUI to perform detailed Tomcat 5 component configuration. The following discussion assumes that you are already familiar with the hierarchical, components-based internal architectural model of Tomcat 5 (presented in Chapter 4). This is the same model that the `admin` application presents to the administrator for configuration.

All the components in the component-based model are represented by elements in XML files. This makes it very easy to change component nesting relationships and configuration (indirectly via the `admin` application, or directly via a text editor). All the configuration files for a specific Tomcat configuration are located in its `$CATALINA_HOME/conf` directory. The next section describes the tabulation of files.

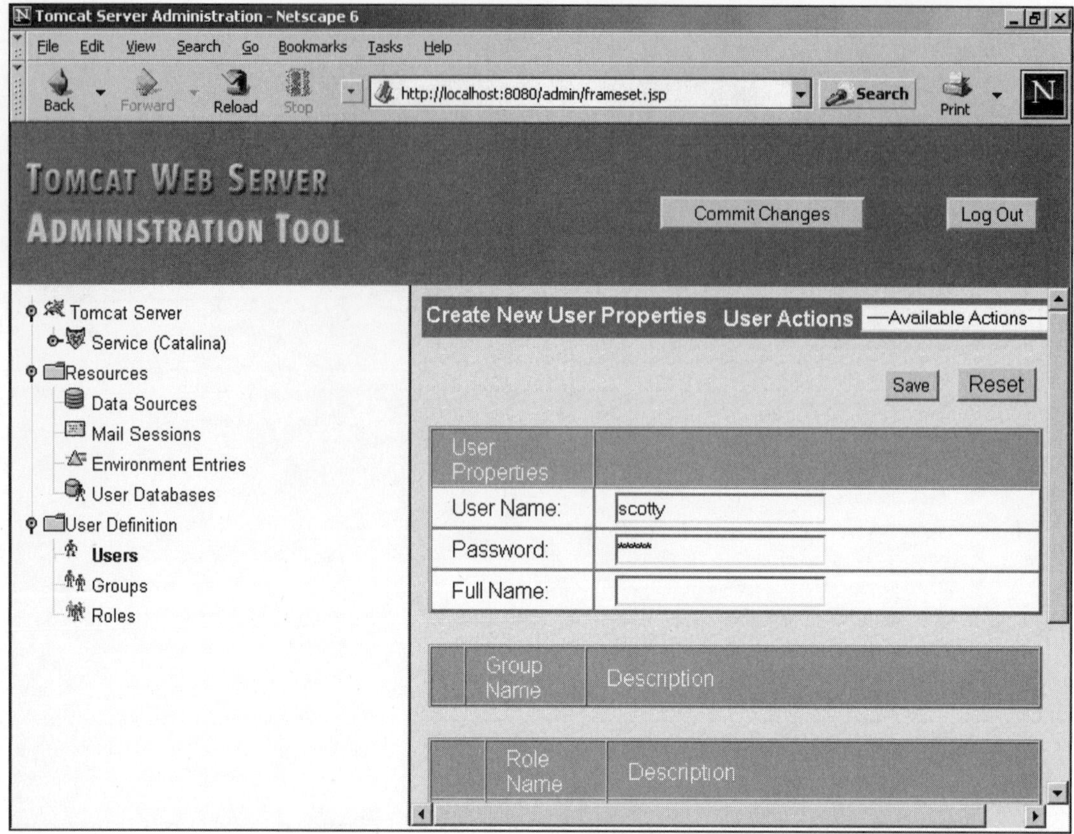

Figure 5-5: Adding a user with Tomcat 5's Web-based configurator.

Files in $CATALINA_HOME/conf

In the `$CATALINA_HOME/conf` directory of the Tomcat 5 server distribution, you will see several configuration files (this list of files varies between the Tomcat 5 and Tomcat 4.1.x series of servers). Following is a brief synopsis of each of these files:

- `server.xml` — This is the main configuration file for the Tomcat server and is the one that Tomcat actually reads at startup. By default, it contains a configuration that is ready to run on your machine immediately.

  Note that any changes made using the Web-based configurator are saved to the `server.xml` file. Comments in the XML file are *not* preserved during the save operations. However, Tomcat 5 will make a backup copy of the `server.xml` file in the same directory. The name of this commented `server.xml` file is suffixed by the date and time that the backup is created, enabling multiple versions of the `server.xml` file to be maintained in the same directory.

In Tomcat 4.1.x, the `server.xml` file contains declarations for the Context of many example Web applications that come with the Tomcat 4 distribution. Because the example applications take up memory space and consume processing time to load, it is usual practice to remove them in production systems, as they are not needed. This is the main reason for a `server-noexamples.xml.config` file in Tomcat 4.1.x server distributions. Tomcat 5 servers no longer maintain any Web-application-specific information in the `server.xml` file.

- `server-minimal.xml` — This is a minimal `server.xml file`, similar to the default `server.xml` above, but without the extensive comments and optional features support (clustering, persistence manager, and so on).
- `server-noexamples.xml.config` (Tomcat 4.1.x only) — This file contains a template of `server.xml`. This enables you, as the administrator, to easily create your own version of `server.xml` without having to remove standard Tomcat `examples` definitions from it. In practice, if you need to custom configure your server, it may be easier to start with this file and then rename the resulting file to `server.xml`. Also contained in this file are detailed comments to assist in understanding the options available when configuring the server.
- `server.xml.2004-08-21.23-45-49` (date suffix varies) — The existence of these files indicates that you have executed the Tomcat 5's `admin` application to modify the configuration. These are backup versions of the `server.xml` file before a new one is saved. The suffix indicates the time when the backup is performed. Because the `admin` application does not preserve comments when it writes a new `server.xml file`, this is the one way to retain comments/annotations in your `server.xml` configuration file.

  Only the file named `server.xml` will be used by the Tomcat 5 server upon startup. You can store multiple configuration files here, and rename the one you want to use to `server.xml` before starting Tomcat 5. Other configuration files in the `$CATALINA_HOME/conf` directory include the following:

  - `tomcat-users.xml` — This file contains user authentication and role-mapping information for setting up a UserDatabase Realm. Both Tomcat's `admin` and `manager` applications use this file by default. UserDatabase Realm is a component in Tomcat 5 used to implement a database of users/passwords/roles for authentication and Container-managed security. In Tomcat versions prior to 4.1.x, a more limited memory Realm may be used instead (see Chapter 15 for the difference between memory Realms and UserDatabase Realms), requiring a slightly different `tomcat-users.xml` file.
  - `web.xml` — This is a default deployment descriptor file for any Web applications that are deployed on this Tomcat server instance. It provides basic Servlet definition and MIME mappings common to all Web applications, and also acts as the deployment descriptor for any Web application that does not have its own deployment descriptor.
  - `catalina.policy` — Java 2 has a fine-grained security model that enables the administrator to control in detail the accessibility of system resources. This is the default policy file for running Tomcat 5 in secured mode. This is covered in detail later in this chapter.
  - `catalina.properties` — Tomcat 5 reads and uses the properties value in this file upon startup. It provides for internal package access and definition control, as well as control over contents of Tomcat class loaders (see Chapter 9).

You may also find other properties files (e.g., `jk2.properties`) in this configuration directory. See Chapter 12 for JK2 Connector configuration information.

Basic Server Configuration

This section provides a line-by-line analysis of the default server.xml file. This file is created as an XML 1.0 document; it is assumed that you are familiar with XML.

Server Configuration via the Default server.xml

The default server configuration is stored in the server.xml file included with the distribution. Figure 5-6 illustrates this default configuration, as viewed from the admin application. If you have started admin from the default distribution, this is also the configuration used to run the admin application.

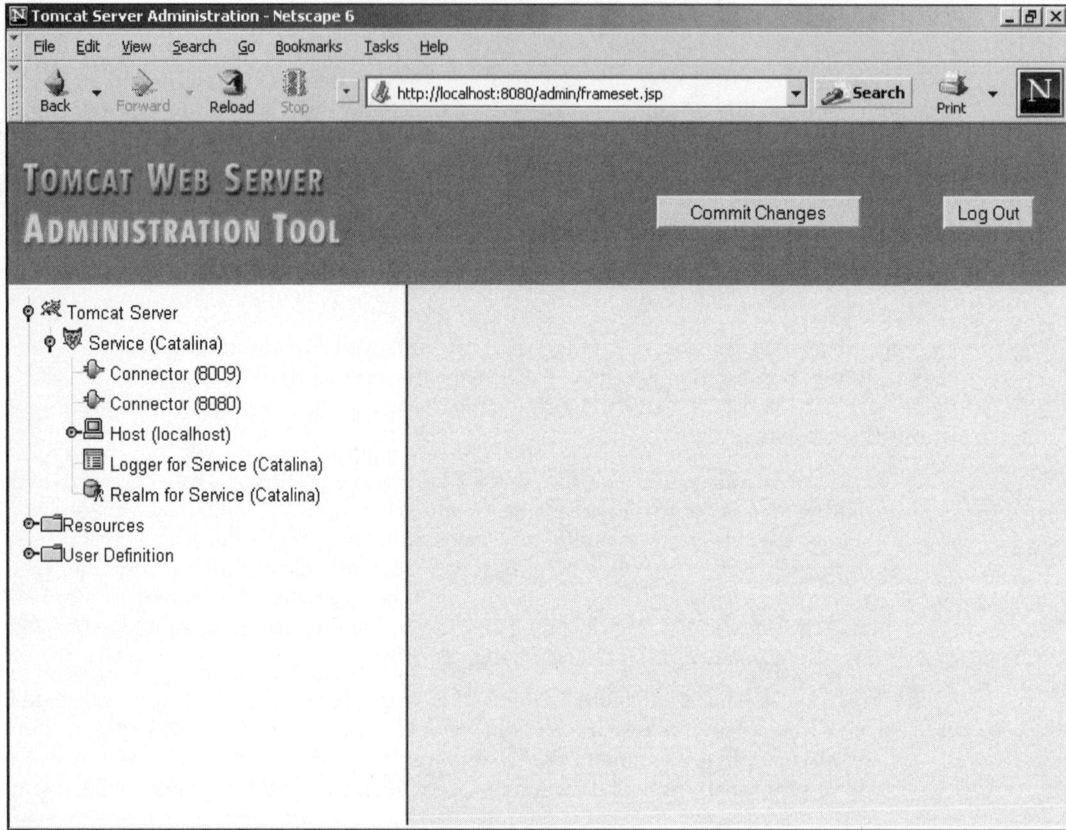

Figure 5-6: The Tomcat 5 default server.xml configuration.

The Tomcat 5 primary configuration file, server.xml, is not backwardly compatible. Tomcat 5 has additional features such as new configurable component attributes, decoupled application Context, and so on. The server.xml file from previous versions of Tomcat servers may require significant changes to work with Tomcat 5.

The `server.xml` file associated with the default configuration is listed here. In the listing, advanced configuration components have been deleted (indicated by the ellipses, "..."), and comments have also been removed. The focus in this chapter is on the configuration of the remaining basic components. Chapter 8 discusses configuration of the advanced components.

```
<Server port="8005" shutdown="SHUTDOWN" debug="0">
...

<Service name="Catalina">

    <Connector port="8080"
               maxThreads="150" minSpareThreads="25" maxSpareThreads="75"
               enableLookups="false" redirectPort="8443" acceptCount="100"
               debug="0" connectionTimeout="20000"
               disableUploadTimeout="true" />

    <Connector port="8009"
               enableLookups="false" redirectPort="8443" debug="0"
               protocol="AJP/1.3" />

<Engine name="Catalina" defaultHost="localhost" debug="0">

   <Logger className="org.apache.catalina.logger.FileLogger"
              prefix="catalina_log." suffix=".txt"
              timestamp="true"/>

   <Realm className="org.apache.catalina.realm.UserDatabaseRealm"
                 debug="0" resourceName="UserDatabase"/>

      <Host name="localhost" debug="0" appBase="webapps"
       unpackWARs="true" autoDeploy="true">

        <Logger className="org.apache.catalina.logger.FileLogger"
            debug="0" directory="logs" prefix="localhost_log."
            suffix=".txt" timestamp="true" verbosity="1"/>
      </Host>

    </Engine>
  </Service>
</Server>
```

The default configuration has the following nesting of components:

```
Server
    Service
        Connector
        Connector
        Engine
    Logger
    Realm
        Host
            Logger
```

The next few sections examine each of these configurable components.

The Server Component

Our initial examination of the default `server.xml` file reveals that it configures a single service inside a single instance of the server component. When viewed from the Web-based configurator, the top-level server element appears, as shown in Figure 5-7.

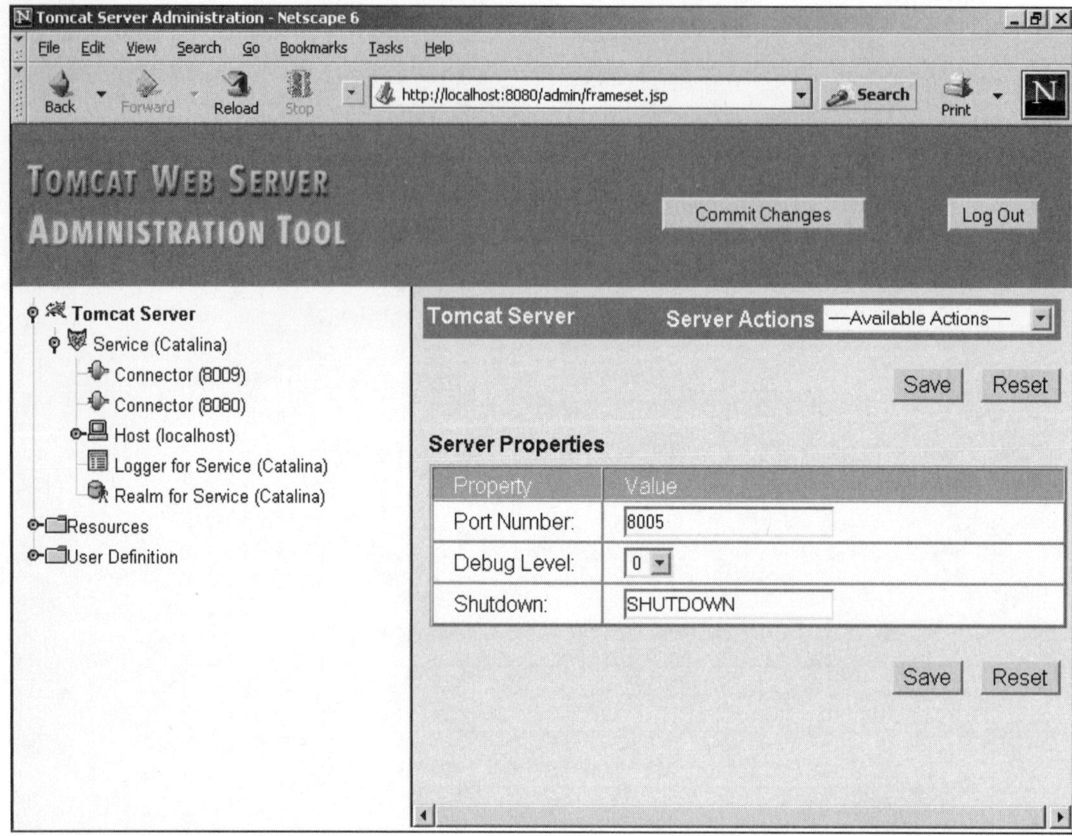

Figure 5-7: Configuring the Server component.

In the `server.xml` file, the very first active line of the file defines the server component, which corresponds to the XML `<Server>` element. Here is the line from the configuration file:

```
<Server port="8005" shutdown="SHUTDOWN" debug="0">
```

This tells Tomcat 5 to start a server instance (a JVM) listening to port 8005 for a shutdown command. Be careful if you need to change this port number. Tomcat or other servers may not start properly if identical ports are configured—causing a conflict. The shutdown command will contain the text "SHUTDOWN." This provides a graceful way for an administrator (or management console software) to shut down this Tomcat server instance. The server instance will not print debugging messages to the log because debug is set to "0." Any unspecified attributes will take on default values. The following table describes the allowed attributes of the `<Server>` element and their default values, followed by a list of the sub-elements that the XML `<server>` may contain.

Attribute	Description	Required
className	The Java class of the server to use. This class is required to implement the org.apache.catalina.Server interface. By default, the Tomcat 5 supplied code is used.	No
Port	The TCP port to listen to for the command specified by the shutdown attribute before shutting down gracefully. Tomcat will confirm that the connection is made from the same physical server machine. Together with a custom shutdown command string that you can specify (discussed next), this provides a measure of security against hacker attacks.	Yes
Shutdown	The command text string that the server should monitor for, at the TCP port specified by the port attribute, before shutting down gracefully.	Yes
Debug	Controls the amount of debug information logged by the server instance. Setting this to a higher number provides more debugging details. For Tomcat 5, the levels can range from 0 to 4. A value of 0 will log only fatal failure messages. A value of 4 will log all debug messages. The default is 0. See configuration for the Logger component, later in this chapter, for more information on the range of allowed values.	No

Within the <Server> element, the XML sub-elements shown in the following table are allowed.

Sub-element	Description	How Many?
<Service>	A grouping of Connectors associated with an Engine. The Connectors handle different client protocols (HTTP, HTTPS, JK2, and so on) and manage request concurrency, while the Engine processes the requests.	1 or more
<Listener>	Life-cycle listener for interception of the server's life-cycle events (start, stop, before start, before stop, after start, after stop). The installed listener is called at a prescribed point of the server's life cycle. Life-cycle events can be used by developers to add custom components, additional logging, management, resource allocation, or other added functionality to the server instance. See Chapter 8 for more details on the configuration this advanced component.	0 or more
<GlobalNamingResources>	JNDI resources that are defined to be globally available throughout this server component instance. See Chapter 8 for more details on the configuration of this advanced component.	0 or more

The Service Component

The next line in the file defines a service component. The main purpose of a Service component is to group a request processing Engine with its configured set of protocol/concurrency handling Connectors. The service component is a top-level element, and it appears in the `admin` application, as shown in Figure 5-8.

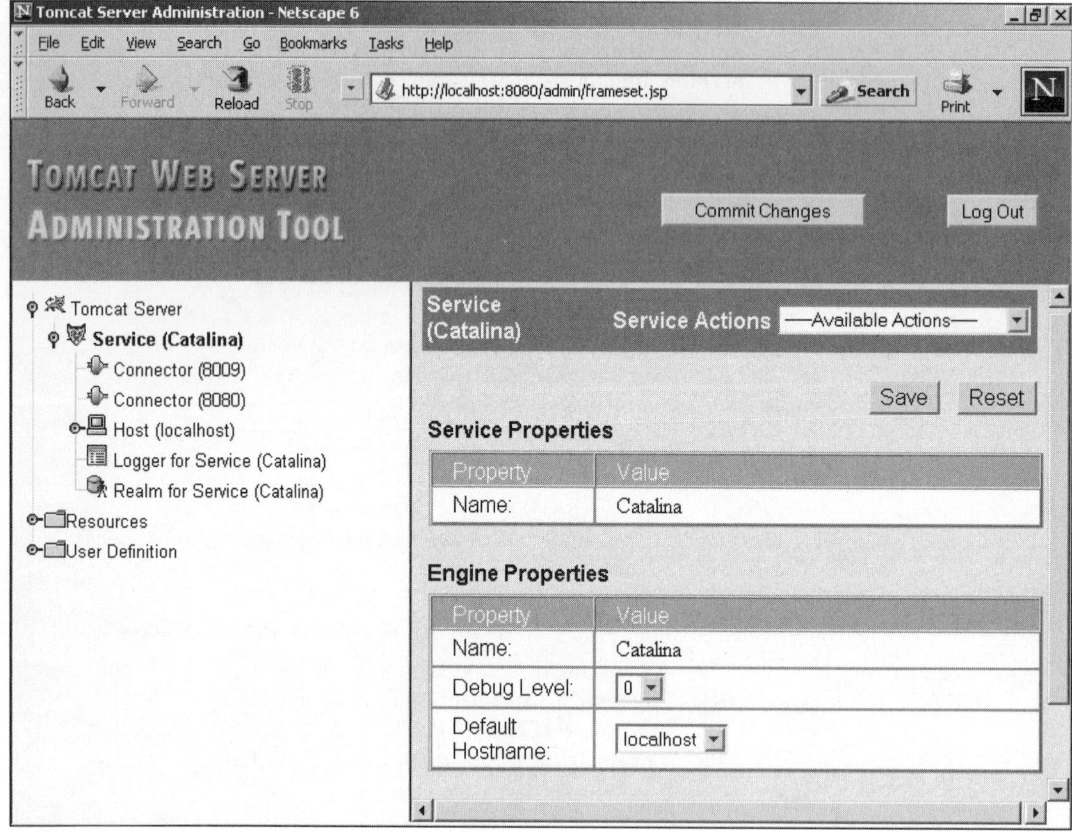

Figure 5-8: Configuring a service component.

The figure shows how a service component is used to group together all the Connectors that may be used with the Catalina request processing Engine. This is defined by the `<Service>` element shown here:

```
<Service name="Catalina">
```

Here, a service instance was defined with the name "Catalina." This name will be visible in logged messages, clearly identifying the component. It is also used as the name to identify the service instance when using the `admin` application.

A `<Service>` element can have the attributes shown in the following table.

Attribute	Description	Required
`className`	The Java class name for the service class to use. By default, the Tomcat 5–supplied Catalina container code `org.apache.catalina.core.StandardService` is used. The default is adequate unless you're modifying Tomcat's source code.	No
`name`	A name for the service, used in logging, administration, and management. If you have more than one `<Service>` element inside the `<Server>` element, you must make sure their name attributes are different.	Yes
`debug`	Controls the amount of debug information logged by the service instance. Setting this to a higher number provides more debugging details. The default is 0.	No

The sub-elements that a `<Service>` element can have are shown in the following table.

Sub-element	Description	How Many?
`Connector`	This is a nested component that handles external client connections and feeds them to the Engine for processing. A Connector also manages the number of threads and their allocation for request handling. The configuration of Connectors is explained in detail in the next section.	1 or more
`Engine`	This is the request-processing component in Tomcat: Catalina.	Exactly 1

The Connector Component

It is necessary to understand the two modes of Tomcat operations before you can appreciate the role of the Connector component. Following are two very different ways of operating Tomcat 5:

- *Tomcat as an application server* — In this configuration, a front-end Web server (Apache, iPlanet, IIS, and so on) serves static content to end-users, while all JSP and Servlet requests are routed to the Tomcat server(s) for processing. In turn, Tomcat-hosted Web applications interface to back-end J2EE-compliant services. (See Chapters 11–13 for an in-depth examination of this mode of Tomcat operation.)
- *Tomcat in standalone mode* — In this case, any static pages and graphic files from your Web application are served directly from the Tomcat 5 server. In this mode, an additional front-end Web server is not necessary because Tomcat is acting as both the Web server and the JSP/Servlet container. Tomcat 5 uses its built-in HTTP Connector to process the incoming HTTP request, bypassing the need for an external Web server altogether. Tomcat-hosted Web applications can interface to back-end J2EE services.

This mode of operation is seldom used in production because of the huge gap in performance, support, and industry experience between production Web servers (such as Apache, iPlanet, and IIS) and Tomcat's built-in Web server. The only exception may be the case in which the production site's operation is almost completely Web-application-driven, requiring relatively few static pages and elements. (See Chapter 10 for an in-depth exploration of this mode of Tomcat operation.)

Operating Tomcat in Application Server Configuration

In the application server configuration, some intelligent piece of software must run inside the Web server and decide on the requests that will be routed to the Tomcat server for processing. This usually exists in the form of a loadable module (that is, `mod_jk2` in Apache 2.0) containing a redirector plug-in.

In this case, multiple independent Tomcat servers may be running simultaneously (that is, across a networked bank of machines for scalability and load balancing), and the loadable module or redirector plug-in may also decide to which Tomcat server instance requests are sent. This sort of hardware configuration is technically known as a **Tomcat cluster.** (See Chapter 19 for a detailed description of clustering with Tomcat 5.)

For operational efficiency, the protocol between the Web server and the Tomcat instance(s) is not HTTP. It is typically one of two specially designed protocols: AJP or WARP. For Tomcat 5, the official support for the Web server to Tomcat link is the AJP protocol. As of this writing, the WARP protocol, managed by the `mod_webapp` project, has not been modified for Tomcat 5 compatibility. Chapters 11–13 provide more information about these protocols. For now, you only need to appreciate that there must be a native code extension to the Web server that routes incoming requests to Tomcat, and a corresponding piece of request receiving software (a Connector component) at the Tomcat server-side that understands this protocol and connection convention.

Figure 5-9 shows the Connector component as it appears in the `admin` application.

In the default `server.xml` file, an HTTP 1.1 Connector is also defined for the Catalina service:

```
<Connector port="8080"
        maxThreads="150" minSpareThreads="25" maxSpareThreads="75"
        enableLookups="false" redirectPort="8443" acceptCount="100"
        debug="0" connectionTimeout="20000"
        disableUploadTimeout="true" />
```

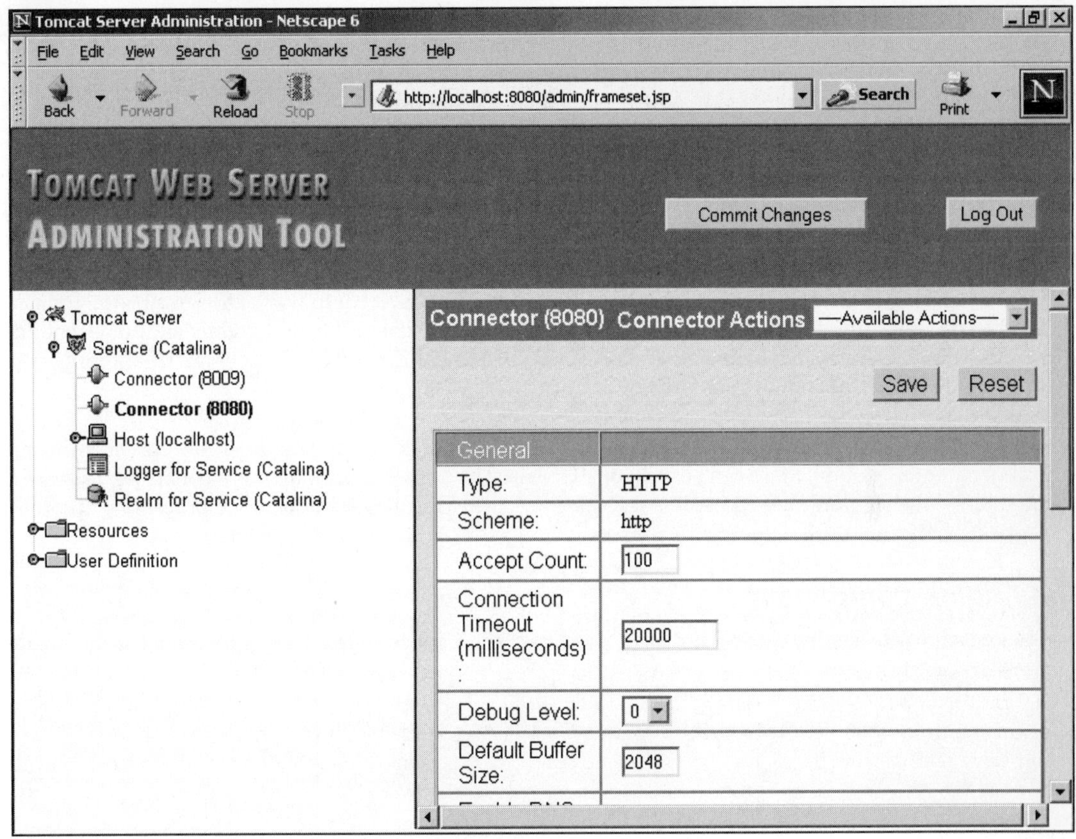

Figure 5-9: Configuring the Connector component.

The following table describes two standard Connectors supplied with Tomcat 5.

Connector Name	Description
HTTP/1.1	Connects browser or Web services to the Catalina Engine using HTTP 1.1 if supported by the client, and adaptively falls back to using HTTP 1.0 if necessary. This Connector can also be configured to support secured HTTPS/SSL connections.
JK2	Used for connecting between external Web servers (Apache included) and Tomcat 5 using the AJP 1.3 protocol. It uses the external Web server for static Web content, while Tomcat 5 will handle Servlet and JSP processing. It can also use the Web server's SSL support. See Chapter 12 for more details.

In the default `server.xml` file, you can see an additional configuration for the JK2 Connector, supporting the AJP 1.3 protocol:

```
<Connector port="8009"
           enableLookups="false" redirectPort="8443" debug="0"
           protocol="AJP/1.3" />
```

Note that the 4.x.x versions of Tomcat may include up to four standard Connectors, although several are deprecated by 4.1.2x releases. The new Connector technology, code-named **Coyote** in Tomcat 5, unified the support of HTTP 1.0, HTTP 1.1, and HTTPS/SSL into a single Connector. Coyote also provides a JK2 Connector for AJP protocol support. Coyote was created from scratch to work efficiently with Tomcat 5's (and a later revision of Tomcat 4.1.x) optimized architecture. This unification greatly simplifies configuration, administration, management, and operation of Tomcat Connectors in general. Chapters 11–13 provide the details of configuring Connectors.

While you can have as many Connectors as you need in a service (to handle the different incoming client protocol requirements), there can be only one Engine. The Engine component is a container; think of it as Catalina — the Servlet/JSP processor. An Engine executes Web applications while processing incoming requests and generating outgoing responses.

The Engine Component

The one and only Engine component associated with the **Catalina** service is defined next in the default `server.xml` file:

```
<Engine name="Catalina" defaultHost="localhost" debug="0">
...
</Engine>
```

An Engine is a container (see Chapter 4 for an architectural discussion of containers and nested elements), essentially representing a running instance of the Servlet processor. The name "Catalina" is given to this configured Engine instance. An Engine can process a request destined for multiple configured virtual hosts. The `defaultHost` attribute indicates the virtual host to which Tomcat will direct a request if the request is not specifically destined for one of the virtual hosts configured in the `server.xml` file. The `debug="0'` indicates that no Engine-specific debug messages will be written to the log — only fatal failure messages will be logged.

The attributes that an `<Engine>` element can have are shown in the following table.

Attribute	Description	Required
`className`	The Java class name for the Engine code. If not specified, the default Tomcat code, `org.apache.catalina.core.StandardEngine`, is used, and is seldom overridden unless you're modifying Tomcat code.	No

Attribute	Description	Required
backgroundProcessDelay	The delay in seconds before the background processing is enabled for this Engine and other nested Host and Context components. Any nested component with its own backgroundProcessDelay set to a negative value will be ignored, indicating that it will manage its own background processing (if any). Background processing is typically used by components to perform low-priority tasks such as lazy reclamation of unused resources. One example of background processing is the occasional checking for Web application changes by a <Host> component for hot application re-deployment. See Chapter 4 for more details on background processing resources. The default delay is 10 seconds.	No
defaultHost	Selects one of the virtual hosts within this Engine to field all the incoming requests by default. This is only used if the Engine cannot find the host named on the request within this server.xml file.	Yes
jvmRoute	This is an identifier used in load-balancing Tomcat 5. See Chapter 19 for more information on using this attribute and configuring Tomcat 5 for clustering and load balancing.	No
name	A name given to this Engine, which will be used in error logging and by management applications such as the admin application.	Yes
debug	Controls the level of debugging information written by this Engine to the log files.	No

As a container, the <Engine> element can have the sub-elements shown in the following table.

Sub-Element	Description	How Many?
Host	Each <Host> element specifies a virtual host handled by the Engine. Tomcat 5 can handle multiple virtual hosts per Engine/Service instance. This mirrors one of the most popular features of the Apache Web server.	1 or more
DefaultContext	Creates a Context (collection of settings for configurable properties/elements) for the Web applications that are automatically deployed when Tomcat 5 starts. The properties specified in this default Context are also available to all Web applications running within the Engine.	0 or 1

Table continued on following page

Sub-Element	Description	How Many?
`Logger`	Specifies the logging component instance used by this Engine for logging messages. Unless overridden by inner containers, this is the default Logger instance for any nested components inside the Engine.	0 or 1
`Realm`	This Realm is used by default in the declarative security support (see Chapter 15 for more details) to map users into roles; it is used for authentication purposes. Each individual virtual host's `<Host>` and `<Context>` elements may have their own Realm for this purpose. If they do not define their own, the Realm configured at the Engine level is used.	0 or 1
`Valve`	Valves add processing logic into the request- and response-handling pipeline at the Engine level. Standard Valves are used to perform access logging, request filtering, implement Single Sign-on, and so on. Chapter 8 discusses the configuration of these standard Valves, as well as advanced configuration.	0 or more
`Listener`	This is used to configure lifecycle listeners that monitor the starting and stopping of the Engine. See Chapter 4 for information about how lifecycle listeners fit into Tomcat 5's architecture.	0 or more

The Logger Component

The first nested component inside the Engine component is a Logger component. This component is configured as an XML `<Logger>` element:

```
<Logger className="org.apache.catalina.logger.FileLogger"
      prefix="catalina_log." suffix=".txt"
      timestamp="true"/>
```

A Logger is a nested component that collects log information (information, debug, or error messages) from the Tomcat system, as well as application programming code, and stores or displays it in an efficient manner. Web application programmers can access the configured Logger through the Servlet Context that is passed into their code. These log files are placed in the `$CATALINA_HOME/logs` directory by default. This location can be changed by configuring the directory attribute, described later in this section.

You can define an optional default Logger at the Engine level. In the default configuration, the standard Catalina `FileLogger` class is configured as the default Logger for the Engine.

For the Engine component, the default Logger configuration will create files in the `$CATALINA_HOME/logs` directory. The sample log files that follow were created with the default values of the `prefix` (`catalina_log`) and `timestamp` (`true`) attributes:

```
catalina_log.2003_11_02.txt
catalina_log.2003_11_03.txt
```

All <Logger> elements can have the attributes shown in the following table.

Attribute	Description	Required
`className`	The Java class to use for this instance of the Logger	Yes
`verbosity`	Controls what level of logging is performed. The range is from 0 to 4, with a default of 1: 0 — Log fatal messages only 1 — Log error messages 2 — Log warning messages 3 — Log information messages 4 — Log debug information The numbers are cumulative (that is, 4 logs all messages, 3 logs everything but debug information, and so on).	No

Unlike other components, the `<Logger>` element *must* specify a `className` attribute. This attribute specifies which standard Logger implementation (all included with Tomcat 5) you want to be used. The following table shows the available standard Logger implementations included with Tomcat 5.

Java Class Name	Description
`org.apache.catalina.logger.FileLogger`	Log to a file. This option is most frequently used.
`org.apache.catalina.logger.SystemErrLogger`	Log to the standard error stream (configurable in most operating systems). Seldom used; may be suitable for console-based debugging.
`org.apache.catalina.logger.SystemOutLogger`	Log to the standard output stream (configurable in most operating systems).

If `org.apache.catalina.logger.FileLogger` is selected, then the optional attributes shown in the following table can also be configured.

Attribute	Description
`directory`	Specifies where to place the log files; relative or absolute paths may be used. `$CATALINA_HOME/logs` is the default.
`prefix`	A prefix for all generated log filenames; `catalina_log` is the default.
`suffix`	A suffix for all the generated log filenames; `.txt` is the default.
`timestamp`	Specifies whether the messages in the log files will have a date and time stamp. The default is to have no time stamps. It is recommended that this setting be set to `true` for production systems.

The Realm Component

In the default `server.xml` file, after the configuration of the Logger component, the only other configured nested component inside the Engine is a Realm component:

```
<Realm className="org.apache.catalina.realm.UserDatabaseRealm"
       debug="0" resourceName="UserDatabase"/>
```

This configures a `UserDatabase` Realm to load the `tomcat-users.xml` file into memory for use in authentication by default applications such as the `admin` application and the `manager` application. Chapter 15 discusses the attributes for the `<Realm>` element, including how to specify your own XML file or data source for user authentication information.

A Realm is a security mechanism used to perform authentication and implement container-managed security. Essentially, Realms are data sources that provide mappings between user names and passwords (for authentication), and between user names and roles that users assume (for container-managed security). For example, user `johnf` may have password `xyzzy` (authentication) and a role of `supervisor`.

A Realm can access data sources external to Tomcat 5 where the user/password/role relationships are stored. There are many different implementations of Realms, differing only in the source from which they retrieve the information. Following are several types of Realms that are standard with Tomcat 5:

- *Memory*—Uses a memory based table that is populated with the user/password/role mappings. Typically, this is read into memory from an XML file during server startup and stays static throughout the lifetime of the server. For the default implementation that comes with Tomcat, the size of the mappings is seriously constrained by the memory available. This is typically used only in testing and development, and seldom in production.
- *UserDatabase*—UserDatabase implements a completely updateable and persistent memory Realm. It is backwardly compatible with the standard Memory Realm. This Realm implementation is also available on Tomcat 4.1.x servers. Chapter 15 provides extensive coverage of UserDatabase.
- *JDBC*—Uses a relational database sources for obtaining authentication information. Any other data sources with a JDBC-compatible access interface may also be used (for example, ODBC-compliant sources via the JDBC-to-ODBC bridge).
- *JNDI*—This uses JNDI (Java Naming and Directory Interface) to access the Realm data. This data is typically stored in an LDAP-based directory, although any authentication system compatible with the LDAP protocol can be used. (For instance, OpenLDAP, Microsoft, or Novell all have LDAP-compatible access drivers.)
- *JAAS*—Works in conjunction with the Java Authentication and Authorization Service (JAAS) to obtaining the authentication and authorization information for the Realm.

Chapter 15 provides details about how to configure different Realms.

The Host Component

After the default Logger and global UserDatabase Realm component configuration, the next configured component is a Host component. A Host component is a container; it can contain other nested components. The Host component represents a virtual host handled by a Tomcat 5 server instance. It is configured as a <Host> element within the server.xml file. Each <Host> element defined within the enclosing <Engine> element represents another virtual host that is handled by this Engine. In our case, the Host definition is as follows:

```
<Host name="localhost" debug="0" appBase="webapps"
        unpackWARs="true" autoDeploy="true">
```

This defines a virtual host named localhost matching the defaultHost specified in the <Engine> outer container. The applications to be deployed for this virtual host are located under the $CATALINA_HOME/webapps directory (all the examples from the Tomcat 5 distribution are installed there). In addition, the unpackWARs attribute specifies that if Tomcat 5 finds any WAR files in the appBase directory, they will be expanded before the Web application is executed. If you set unpackWARs to false, Tomcat will execute the Web applications in place, without unarchiving them — saving space but sacrificing performance. The autoDeploy attribute is set to true, meaning that Tomcat will actively scan for the addition of new Web applications or changes in existing ones, and then automatically deploy, or re-deploy, them. See the description of the autoDeploy attribute in the next section for more details.

Chapter 16, "Shared Tomcat Hosting," discusses the techniques used to support virtual hosting. For now, however, Figure 5-10 illustrates the basic concept of virtual hosting.

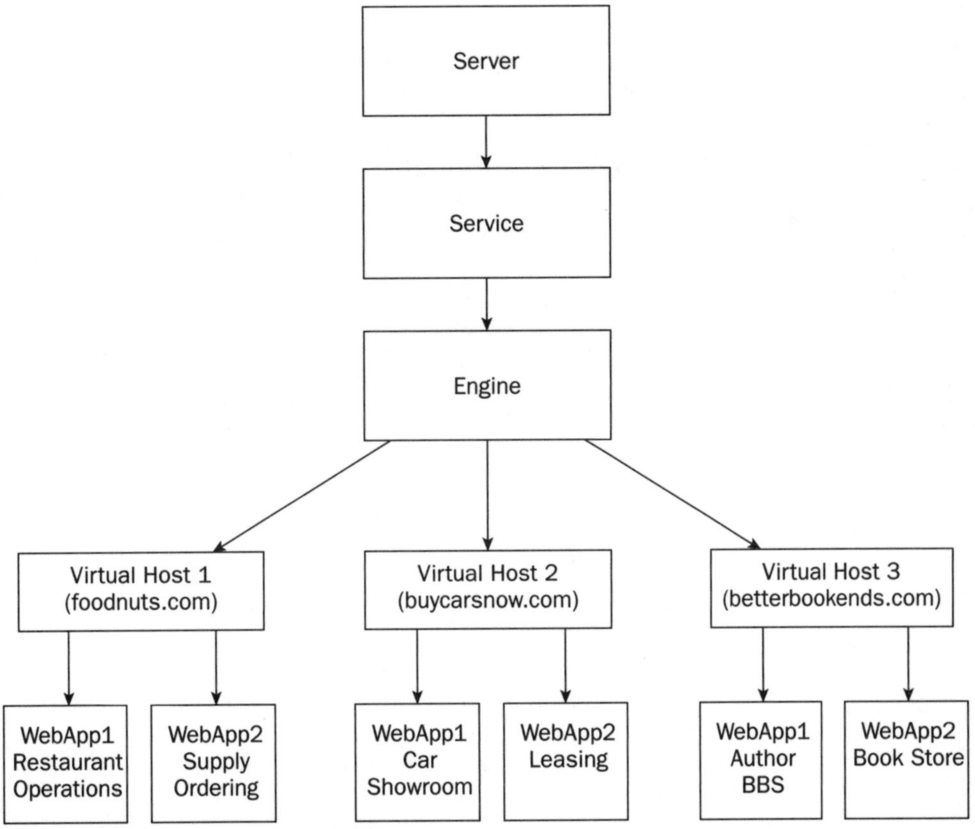

Figure 5-10: Virtual hosting in Tomcat 5.

In this figure, a single Engine supports three different Web sites via virtual hosts. The first one is `foodnuts.com`, the second one is `buycarsnow.com`, and the third one is `betterbookends.com`. Each virtual host is running a completely different Web application. The Engine is responsible for forwarding any incoming request to the corresponding host. If the system were to be configured as depicted in the figure, there would be three `<Host>` nested elements nested within the single `<Engine>` definition.

A `<Host>` element is a container. It can have any one of the attributes shown in the following table.

Attribute	Description	Required
`className`	The Java class that is used to handle requests for the host. The default is the Tomcat-supplied class `org.apache.catalina.core.StandardHost`, and this almost never needs to be changed.	No
`appBase`	Used to set the default application-deployment source directory. Tomcat 5 will look in this directory for applications to be deployed. The path should be specified relative to the installation or per-instance base directory for the Tomcat 5 server.	Yes
`autoDeploy`	Setting this attribute to `true` means that Web applications will be automatically deployed or re-deployed while Tomcat 5 is running. This includes any new applications placed into the directory specified by `appBase` (in WAR form or unarchived), any application whose `web.xml` deployment descriptor has bee modified, and any application whose Context descriptor has been modified. The default value is `true`. Background processing must be enabled for this to work properly. See `deployOnStartup` for auto application deployment during Tomcat startup.	No
`name`	The resolvable name of this virtual host.	Yes
`debug`	Sets the level of debugging information that will be emitted for the log from the virtual host.	No
`backgroundProcessDelay`	The delay in seconds before the background processing is enabled for this host and other nested components. Any nested component with its own `backgroundProcessDelay` set to a negative value will be ignored, indicating that it will manage its own background processing (if any). The default delay is 10 seconds.	No
`configClass`	Specifies the Java class name of the Context configuration class for Web applications on this virtual host. The default is `org.apache.catalina.startup.ContextConfig`.	No

Attribute	Description	Required
contextClass	Specifies the Java class name of the Context implementation class for Web applications on this virtual host. The default is org.apache.catalina.core.StandardContext.	No
deployOnStartup	When set to true, will automatically deploy Web applications from this host during component startup. The default is true.	No
deployXML	Used primarily in shared Tomcat hosting to restrict access. Set this to false if you'd like to restrict the capability to deploy an application based on a Context XML Descriptor file. When set to false, Web applications must be placed in the appBase directory (see appBase attribute) under $CATALINA_HOME/conf/<engine>/<host> to be deployed successfully. The default value is true.	No
errorReportValveClass	Specifies the Java class that implements the error reporting Valve used by this host. The default implementation is org.apache.catalina.valves.ErrorReportValve.	No
unpackWARs	Set this to false if you want Tomcat 5 to run Web applications without unarchiving the WAR files found at the directory specified by the appBase attribute. The default is true and Tomcat 5 will unpack these applications. The trade-off here is typically performance (lower performance when WAR files are not unarchived) versus storage (no need to write to the appBase directory).	No
xmlNamespaceAware	Indicates if the XML parser used by Tomcat is namespace aware. The default is false.	No
xmlValidation	Pass through to control the XML parser used by Tomcat 5 (Apache Xerces by default), indicates if XML document validation is enabled. The default is false.	No

Note that there must be at least one <Host> entry associated with the <Engine> element. This makes sense because you must be able to reach the Engine by at least one virtual host name. Due to this reason, the defaultHost attribute of the <Engine> element must be assigned with one of the <Host> entries.

The XML subelements that can be placed inside a <Host> element are described in the following table.

Sub-Element	Description	How Many?
Context	A <Context> can contain a set of property values for a Web application deployed within this host. There can be as many <Context> elements as there are Web applications. The default server.xml included with the Tomcat 5 distribution does not include any application Context. This enables a clean separation between server configuration and Web application configuration. Instead, all Web application contexts are maintained under the $CATALINA_HOME/conf/<engine>/<host> directory.	0 or more
DefaultContext	The <DefaultContext> specifies the set of property values for a Web application that is deployed within this host, but that does not have its own <Context> specified. Typically, this <DefaultContext> is used for Web applications that are part of the standard behavior of the Tomcat server, and Web applications that are automatically deployed.	0 or 1
Logger	A default Logger that is configured for this host, and any application Context within. It overrides any previously specified Logger.	0 or 1
Realm	A Realm that can be accessed across all the Web applications running within this host, unless a lower-level component specifies its own Realm.	0 or 1

A Nested Logger Inside the Virtual Host

Inside the Host component is another configured Logger component. This one overrides the default specified earlier in the parent Engine component. For this Host component, the newly configured Logger will create log files in the $CATALINA_HOME/logs directory. Sample log files are as follows:

```
localhost_log.2005_11_02.txt
localhost_log.2005_11_03.txt
```

Overriding the default Logger enables you to log component-specific debug or error messages. This is vital in configurations that involve many virtual hosts. By overriding the default, the debug or error messages from each virtual host will be placed in their own file instead of being mixed within the Engine-level log file.

Web Application Context Definitions

Administrators familiar with earlier versions of Tomcat may wonder where the <Context> elements for Web applications are defined. In Tomcat 5, application Context Descriptor XML files are placed in the $CATALINA_HOME/conf/*<engine name>*/*<host name>* directory. This is done to maximize the decoupling between server and application configuration, and to improve deployment security.

Each deployed Web application will have a Context Descriptor XML file in the directory. If the original Web application does not have one, Tomcat 5 can generate one.

This concludes the examination of the default `server.xml` file. The remainder of the chapter examines the other configuration files found in the `$CATALINA_HOME/conf` directory.

Authentication and the tomcat-users.xml File

Another configuration file found in the `$CATALINA_HOME/conf` directory is `tomcat-users.xml`. Earlier examples showed that the `tomcat-users.xml` file is used by Tomcat 5 to authenticate `admin` application users. Tomcat 5 makes use of a UserDatabase Realm component to accomplish this. The UserDatabase Realm enables modification of the loaded data and will properly persist (write back to the XML file) any changes made to the data (that is, by the `admin` application). The Tomcat 5 `manager` application also uses this UserDatabase Realm for authentication. Only users assigned to role "admin" will be able to access the Web-based configurator; only users assigned to role "manager" will be able to access the `manager` application.

The Default Deployment Descriptor – web.xml

According to the Servlet 2.4 specification, every Web application should include a deployment descriptor (`web.xml` file). This file must be placed in the `WEB-INF/` directory of the Web application.

There is also a `web.xml` file under the `$CATALINA_HOME/conf` directory. This file is similar to a Web application's `web.xml` file. However, this particular `web.xml` file is used to specify the default properties for all Web applications that are running within this server instance. Be very careful when making modifications to this file (such as any additions or changes) because they will affect all Web applications running on the same server instance. Note also that other application servers may or may not support a global default `web.xml`, as this is not a requirement for Servlet 2.4 standard compliance.

It is time to see what default server-wide properties are configured in this `web.xml` file. First, there is the standard XML header and a reference to the Servlet 2.4 schema. Unlike `server.xml`, `web.xml` can be formally validated against a schema:

```
<?xml version="1.0" encoding="ISO-8859-1"?>

<web-app xmlns="http://java.sun.com/xml/ns/j2ee"
    xmlns:xsi="http://www.w3.org/2001/XMLSchema-instance"
    xsi:schemaLocation="http://java.sun.com/xml/ns/j2ee web-app_2_4.xsd"
    version="2.4">
```

Servlet 2.3 (and Tomcat 4.x) uses a DTD instead of a schema. The Servlet 2.4 schema provides a significantly more rigorous mechanism for document validation. Chapter 6 provides detailed coverage of the Servlet 2.3 Document Type Definition (DTD) and the Servlet 2.4 schema.

Default Servlet Definitions

In the following `<servlet>` definition, a default Servlet is specified. This default Servlet is used to serve any static resources (static HTML files, GIF files, and so on) within all Web applications:

```
<servlet>
  <servlet-name>default</servlet-name>
  <servlet-class>
     org.apache.catalina.servlets.DefaultServlet
  </servlet-class>
  <init-param>
    <param-name>debug</param-name>
    <param-value>0</param-value>
  </init-param>
  <init-param>
    <param-name>listings</param-name>
    <param-value>true</param-value>
  </init-param>
  <load-on-startup>1</load-on-startup>
</servlet>
```

The `invoker` Servlet can be used to load and execute any Servlet directly using a URL similar to the following:

```
http://<host name>/<web app name>/servlet/<servlet name>
```

Because of its capability to invoke any Servlet directly (with or without prior configuration within a Web application) the `invoker` Servlet is considered a major security risk in production systems. Therefore, this Servlet should only be used in test configurations. Tomcat 5's default `web.xml` file has the `invoker` Servlet configuration commented out for this security-related reason. You can uncomment it and enable the Servlet on test configurations.

The `invoker` Servlet is configured as follows:

```
<!--
  <servlet>
    <servlet-name>invoker</servlet-name>
    <servlet-class>
      org.apache.catalina.servlets.InvokerServlet
    </servlet-class>
    <init-param>
      <param-name>debug</param-name>
      <param-value>0</param-value>
    </init-param>
    <load-on-startup>2</load-on-startup>
  </servlet>
-->
```

The JspServlet converts JSP pages to Servlets and executes them. It is used to process JSP pages:

```
<servlet>
        <servlet-name>jsp</servlet-name>
        <servlet-class>org.apache.jasper.servlet.JspServlet</servlet-class>
        <init-param>
            <param-name>fork</param-name>
            <param-value>false</param-value>
        </init-param>
```

```
        <init-param>
            <param-name>xpoweredBy</param-name>
            <param-value>false</param-value>
        </init-param>
        <load-on-startup>3</load-on-startup>
    </servlet>
```

The next set of Servlets is commented out. You should uncomment them if you plan to add Apache-style server-side include (SSI) processing features to the standalone Tomcat 5 server.

```
<!--
  <servlet>
    <servlet-name>ssi</servlet-name>
    <servlet-class>org.apache.catalina.ssi.SSIServletServlet</servlet-class>
    <init-param>
      <param-name>buffered</param-name>
      <param-value>1</param-value>
    </init-param>
    <init-param>
      <param-name>debug</param-name>
      <param-value>0</param-value>
    </init-param>
    <init-param>
      <param-name>expires</param-name>
      <param-value>666</param-value>
    </init-param>
    <init-param>
      <param-name>isVirtualWebappRelative</param-name>
      <param-value>0</param-value>
    </init-param>
    <load-on-startup>4</load-on-startup>
  </servlet>
-->
```

The next Servlet definition is also used exclusively for configuring the Tomcat 5 server to mimic an Apache Web server. If you would like the standalone Tomcat 5 server to process CGI, you need to uncomment the following section:

```
<!--
  <servlet>
    <servlet-name>cgi</servlet-name>
    <servlet-class>org.apache.catalina.servlets.CGIServlet</servlet-class>
    <init-param>
      <param-name>clientInputTimeout</param-name>
      <param-value>100</param-value>
    </init-param>
    <init-param>
      <param-name>debug</param-name>
      <param-value>6</param-value>
    </init-param>
    <init-param>
      <param-name>cgiPathPrefix</param-name>
```

```
        <param-value>WEB-INF/cgi</param-value>
      </init-param>
       <load-on-startup>5</load-on-startup>
    </servlet>
-->
```

Matching URLs: Servlet Mappings

A <servlet-mapping> element specifies how incoming requests containing a specific URL pattern are to be handled:

```
    <servlet-mapping>
      <servlet-name>default</servlet-name>
      <url-pattern>/</url-pattern>
    </servlet-mapping>
```

The rule set up here specifies the following:

- When you see a URL request fitting the pattern /, route it to the default Servlet.

For example, if the host is www.wrox.com, and a standalone version of the Tomcat 5 server is running, then the following URL will map to the Servlet named default:

```
http://www.wrox.com/
```

Looking back at the <servlet> definition earlier in this file, it was specified that the `org.apache.catalina.servlets.DefaultServlet` will be handling this request.

The second <servlet-mapping> is commented out because it is for the security-sensitive `invoker` Servlet. You may uncomment this to enable the `invoker` Servlet in test configurations:

```
<!--
    <servlet-mapping>
      <servlet-name>invoker</servlet-name>
      <url-pattern>/servlet/*</url-pattern>
    </servlet-mapping>
-->
```

The rule here specifies the following: When you see a URL request fitting the pattern `/servlet/*`, route it to the `invoker` Servlet.

Therefore, the following URL request is sent to a Servlet called `invoker`:

```
http://www.wrox.com/servlet/<name of servlet>
```

Referring back in the file, the `org.apache.catalina.servlets.InvokerServlet` is specified to process the request. This `invoker` Servlet will in turn invoke the Servlet that is named by examining the incoming URL.

The next two <servlet-mapping> elements specify that all URLs containing *.jsp and *.jspx should be passed to the Servlet named jsp for processing. In the earlier <server-mapping>, the jsp Servlet is declared to be the org.apache.jasper.servlet.JspServlet class:

```
<servlet-mapping>
  <servlet-name>jsp</servlet-name>
  <url-pattern>*.jsp</url-pattern>
</servlet-mapping>

<servlet-mapping>
      <servlet-name>jsp</servlet-name>
      <url-pattern>*.jspx</url-pattern>
  </servlet-mapping>
```

How server.xml, Context Descriptors, and web.xml Work Together

Figure 5-11 illustrates how an incoming URL is parsed by the various components of a Tomcat 5 server, and how a <servlet-mapping> with a <url-pattern> controls the final mapping of the request to a specific Servlet in a Web application.

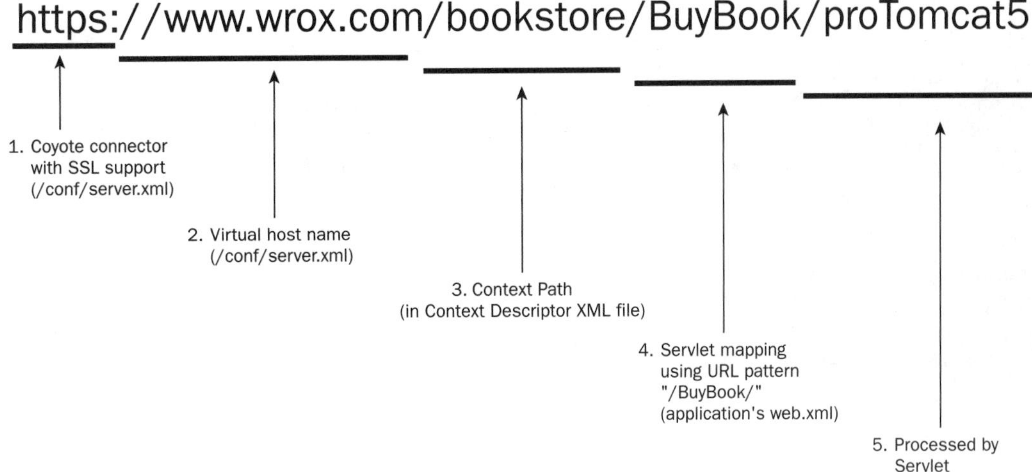

Figure 5-11: How server.xml and web.xml collaborate in Tomcat 5 URL parsing.

In the figure, the URL `https://www.wrox.com/bookstore/BuyBook/proTomcat5` is parsed through the nested components that make up a Tomcat server. First, the protocol portion (`https://`) is parsed by the **Service** and the Coyote Connector with SSL support is selected, and the request is passed to the **Engine.** Next, the host name (`www.wrox.com`) is parsed by the Engine and one of its **Host** components is selected (the one that matches the www.wrox.com host name).

The Host then attempts to match the URL against the contexts of its deployed Web applications — the match in this case is /bookstore and the bookstore Web application is selected to handle the request (the Context information itself is stored in a Context descriptor file). Last, but not least, the **Context** hosting the Web application performs a match against the <servlet-mapping> defined in the deployment descriptor (the web.xml file of the Web application), and the URL pattern /BuyBook/* matches the BookPurchase Servlet. This Servlet is finally handed the URL request to process. It is easy to see how the component hierarchy helps in forwarding the request to a single Servlet in a Web application for processing.

SSI and CGI Mappings

Now it's time to take a look at the next section of the default web.xml file.

The next two default Servlet mappings are commented out. They support SSI and CGI when Tomcat 5 is configured to work in standalone mode:

```
<!--
  <servlet-mapping>
    <servlet-name>ssi</servlet-name>
    <url-pattern>*.shtml</url-pattern>
  </servlet-mapping>
-->

  <!-- The mapping for the CGI Gateway servlet -->
<!--
  <servlet-mapping>
    <servlet-name>cgi</servlet-name>
    <url-pattern>/cgi-bin/*</url-pattern>
  </servlet-mapping>
-->
```

Session Timeout Configuration

The <session-config> element configures the amount of time during which Tomcat 5 will maintain a session on the server side on behalf of a client. For example, the client may be in the middle of an online shopping transaction and still has products in the shopping cart. In this case, if the client does not return to the cart for 30 minutes, and no session persistence is used (see Chapter 8 for a description of the session persistence manager), all their cart information will be lost. As administrators, it is important to carefully balance the <session-timeout> value with the potential of overloading the server with too many stale sessions:

```
  <session-config>
    <session-timeout>30</session-timeout>
  </session-config>
```

Handling Client-Side Helper Activation — Mime Mappings

The next set of elements contains the default <mime-mapping> elements. Tomcat 5 uses these mappings to serve static files with specific extensions to the client. It will generate an HTTP Content-Type header when transmitting the file to the client (typically a browser). Most browsers use a helper application to process the file being transmitted if they recognize the content type specified. For example, Microsoft Internet Explorer may start Microsoft MediaPlayer when it detects the video/x-mpeg content type.

Note that these are only the default mappings; a Web application's own deployment descriptor (`web.xml` file) can override or add to this list:

```
<mime-mapping>
  <extension>abs</extension>
  <mime-type>audio/x-mpeg</mime-type>
</mime-mapping>
<mime-mapping>
  <extension>ai</extension>
  <mime-type>application/postscript</mime-type>
</mime-mapping>
<mime-mapping>
  <extension>aif</extension>
  <mime-type>audio/x-aiff</mime-type>
</mime-mapping>
<mime-mapping>
  <extension>aifc</extension>
  <mime-type>audio/x-aiff</mime-type>
</mime-mapping>

  ... more mime mappings...

<mime-mapping>
  <extension>Z</extension>
  <mime-type>application/x-compress</mime-type>
</mime-mapping>
<mime-mapping>
  <extension>z</extension>
  <mime-type>application/x-compress</mime-type>
</mime-mapping>
<mime-mapping>
  <extension>zip</extension>
  <mime-type>application/zip</mime-type>
</mime-mapping>
```

Simulating Apache Web Server: Welcome File Handling

The last section in the `web.xml` file pertains only to Tomcat's standalone mode of operation. To be compatible with the default behavior of the Apache Web server, the default Servlet will display a welcome file if the incoming URI is terminated in `/`, as shown in the following example:

```
http://www.wrox.com/
```

The default Servlet will examine the root directory of the named virtual host (`www.wrox.com`) and look for `index.html`, `index.htm`, or `index.jsp` in turn to be displayed. Each Web application may override this list in its own deployment descriptor (`web.xml`) file:

```
  <welcome-file-list>
    <welcome-file>index.html</welcome-file>
    <welcome-file>index.htm</welcome-file>
    <welcome-file>index.jsp</welcome-file>
  </welcome-file-list>
</web-app>
```

In the following section, the last file in the $CATALINA_HOME/conf directory—catlina.policy—is examined.

Fine-Grained Access Control: catalina.policy

Chapter 15, "Tomcat Security," provides complete coverage of the role of the Tomcat security manager and its use of this policy file. For now, it is adequate to take a quick browse through the file to understand how it provides access control for a Tomcat 5 server administrator.

Tomcat 5 leverages the built-in fine-grained security model of Java 2. When enabled, the basis of the security system is as follows:

> *Any access to system resources that is not explicitly allowed is prohibited.*

This means that we must anticipate all the resources that the Tomcat 5 server will access, and explicitly grant permission for it to do so.

By default, Catalina starts up without security. You need to start Tomcat 5 with the following option for it to run with a security manager:

```
> startup -security
```

It is only in this secured mode that the catalina.policy file will be read, processed, and enforced. Some of the more important sections of the catalina.policy file are discussed below, but details of the file are not covered at this time. The general policy entry is in the following form, where the <security principal> is typically a body of trusted code:

```
grant <security principal> { permission list... };
```

Looking at the catalina.policy file, the first set of permissions grant code from the Java compiler directories all access to all resources (this is essentially the Java compiler and run-time system code):

```
// These permissions apply to javac
grant codeBase "file:${java.home}/lib/-" {
        permission java.security.AllPermission;
};

// These permissions apply to all shared system extensions
grant codeBase "file:${java.home}/jre/lib/ext/-" {
        permission java.security.AllPermission;
};

// These permissions apply to javac when ${java.home] points at $JAVA_HOME/jre
grant codeBase "file:${java.home}/../lib/-" {
        permission java.security.AllPermission;
};

// These permissions apply to all shared system extensions when
// ${java.home} points at $JAVA_HOME/jre
grant codeBase "file:${java.home}/lib/ext/-" {
        permission java.security.AllPermission;
};
```

One clear message here is that you must protect these directories using your operating system file-protection features (that is, via file ownership and permission settings).

The next section grants Catalina server code and API libraries access to all resources:

```
// These permissions apply to the launcher code
grant codeBase "file:${catalina.home}/bin/commons-launcher.jar" {
        permission java.security.AllPermission;
};

// These permissions apply to the server startup code
grant codeBase "file:${catalina.home}/bin/bootstrap.jar" {
        permission java.security.AllPermission;
};

// These permissions apply to the Servlet API classes
// and those that are shared across all class loaders
// located in the "common" directory
grant codeBase "file:${catalina.home}/common/-" {
        permission java.security.AllPermission;
};

// These permissions apply to the container's core code, plus any additional
// libraries installed in the "server" directory
grant codeBase "file:${catalina.home}/server/-" {
        permission java.security.AllPermission;
};

// These permissions apply to shared web application libraries
// including the Jasper page compiler in the "lib" directory
grant codeBase "file:${catalina.home}/lib/-" {
        permission java.security.AllPermission;
};

// These permissions apply to shared web application classes
// located in the "classes" directory
grant codeBase "file:${catalina.home}/classes/-" {
        permission java.security.AllPermission;
};
```

Again, in a secure configuration, you must be careful to lock down the preceding directories, thus preventing an attacker from adding malicious code to them. Any class files introduced into these directories will automatically be granted access to all system resources.

The final set contains the permissions given to Web applications by default. They are significantly more restrictive (that is, they are never granted the all-powerful permission "`java.security.AllPermission`").

The first section enables access to system properties that enable JNDI and JDBC access:

```
grant {
        // Required for JNDI lookup of named JDBC DataSource's and
        // javamail named MimePart DataSource used to send mail
        permission java.util.PropertyPermission "java.home", "read";
        permission java.util.PropertyPermission "java.naming.*", "read";
        permission java.util.PropertyPermission "javax.sql.*", "read";
```

The next section enables read-only access to some operating system description properties (the type of operating system that is running and what it uses to separate file extensions in a filename):

```
        // OS Specific properties to allow read access
        permission java.util.PropertyPermission "os.name", "read";
        permission java.util.PropertyPermission "os.version", "read";
        permission java.util.PropertyPermission "os.arch", "read";
        permission java.util.PropertyPermission "file.separator", "read";
        permission java.util.PropertyPermission "path.separator", "read";
        permission java.util.PropertyPermission "line.separator", "read";
```

The third section enables read-only access to some JVM-specific properties that are often used in application programming:

```
        // JVM properties to allow read access
        permission java.util.PropertyPermission "java.version", "read";
        permission java.util.PropertyPermission "java.vendor", "read";
        permission java.util.PropertyPermission "java.vendor.url", "read";
        permission java.util.PropertyPermission "java.class.version", "read";
        permission java.util.PropertyPermission "java.specification.version",
                                            "read";
        permission java.util.PropertyPermission "java.specification.vendor",
                                            "read";
        permission java.util.PropertyPermission "java.specification.name",
                                            "read";
        permission java.util.PropertyPermission "java.vm.specification.version",
                                             "read";
        permission java.util.PropertyPermission "java.vm.specification.vendor",
                                            "read";
        permission java.util.PropertyPermission "java.vm.specification.name",
                                            "read";
        permission java.util.PropertyPermission "java.vm.version", "read";
        permission java.util.PropertyPermission "java.vm.vendor", "read";
        permission java.util.PropertyPermission "java.vm.name", "read";
```

The next section is required for the use of MX4J (formerly called OpenJMX), providing JMX support for Tomcat 5 (see Chapter 18 for more information on JMX):

```
        // Required for OpenJMX
        permission java.lang.RuntimePermission "getAttribute";
```

The last two sections provide access to XML parser debug and precompiled JSPs, required frequently during code development (see JavaBean and JAXP specifications for more details on these properties):

```
        // Allow read of JAXP compliant XML parser debug
        permission java.util.PropertyPermission "jaxp.debug", "read";

       // Precompiled JSPs need access to this package.
       permission java.lang.RuntimePermission
           "accessClassInPackage.org.apache.jasper.runtime";
       permission java.lang.RuntimePermission
   "accessClassInPackage.org.apache.jasper.runtime.*";};
```

These are minimal permissions that are granted by default to Web applications. Typical secured production configuration will require opening up additional access to the Web applications, such as socket access to a JDBC server or network access to an external authentication system.

catalina.properties: Finer-Grained Control over Access Checks

The `catalina.properties` file is read during a secured Tomcat 5 server startup, and allows administrators to configure access control at a Java package level. This level of restriction will cause a SecurityException to be reported should an errant or malicious Web application attempt to access these Tomcat 5 internal classes directly, or if new class definition is attempted under these highly privileged packages.

The following lines in the `catalina.properties` file specify the name of the internal packages that should be restricted. Where partial package names are specified, any subpackages are protected as well.

```
package.access=sun.,org.apache.catalina.,org.apache.coyote.,org.apache.tomcat.,org.
apache.jasper.,sun.beans.
package.definition=sun.,java.,org.apache.catalina.,org.apache.coyote.,org.apache.to
mcat.,org.apache.jasper.
```

Configurator Bootstrapping and the Future of Tomcat Configuration

Before concluding this chapter, it is important to reiterate that the `admin` application is itself a Tomcat 5 hosted Web application. This means that Tomcat 5 must be running and operating for you to be able to access it. Tomcat 5 includes a default bootstrap configuration to ensure that the `admin` application can start under most circumstances. However, in the unlikely event that you have made manual modifications and the Tomcat 5 instance will not start up, your only remaining recourse is to edit the XML configuration files via a text editor. This is the primary reason why this chapter has devoted considerable coverage to Tomcat administration from the perspective of manually editing the XML configuration files.

It is rather ironic that beyond the initial release of Tomcat 5, the art of hand-editing XML files for configuration may quickly become obsolete. The introduction of support for the Java Management Extensions (JMX) enables Tomcat configuration to be automated and integrated as part of a larger configuration process. See Chapter 18 for more information on Tomcat 5's brand-new support for JMX. While JMX support is still in its nascent stage within Tomcat 5, it is envisioned that today's `server.xml` file will eventually become a collection of persisted JMX MBean descriptors meant for machine-based read/write, and not intended for manual editing. Until this happens, however (likely to be in the Tomcat 5.1.x or Tomcat 6 time frame), the capability to understand and edit XML configuration files will still be a valuable Tomcat administrator asset.

A Final Word on Differentiating Between Configuration and Management

Inexperienced Tomcat administrators often confuse the Web-based configurator (`admin`) application with the Web-based manager (the `manager` Web application, covered in more detail in Chapter 7) application. At first glance, they appear to offer similar capabilities. In reality, however, they are completely separate Web applications that offer a mutually exclusive set of administrative capabilities. One easy way of distinguishing between the two is to realize that the Web-based configurator is used primarily to modify static configuration files that will be read and used by Tomcat **before server startup,** and that the `manager` application is used to manage Tomcat operations **after server startup.** In other words, `admin` is used for configuration, and `manager` is used during operations.

Summary

This chapter has described the setup and operation of the Web-based configurator (`admin` application) for Tomcat 5 in detail. Because every configurable component maps to elements in XML files in the configuration directory, all the Tomcat server configuration files in the `$CATALINA_HOME/conf` directory of the Tomcat 5 distribution have also been covered. These files include the following:

- `server.xml`
- `server-noexamples.xml.config`
- `tomcat-users.xml`
- `web.xml`
- `catalina.policy`
- `catalina.properties`

It is obvious from the discussion that `server.xml` is the essential server configuration file for Tomcat 5. To understand the model of configuration, it is necessary to understand the concept of a top-level component, a container hierarchy, and nested components. In addition, the function and configuration of the following Tomcat components were covered:

- Server
- Service
- Connector
- Engine

- Host
- Logger
- Realm

An understanding of how these components relate to each other and work together during normal Tomcat 5 operation was developed. To conclude this chapter, let's review some of its key points:

- The `tomcat-users.xml` file is the authentication and authorization data supply for a Memory Realm that is used by the Tomcat `manager` application, as well as a sample Realm implementation that programmers may use. In a production system, a more robust implementation of a Realm (such as a JDBC Realm or a JNDI Realm) should be used.
- The default `web.xml` file in `$CATALINA_HOME/conf` specifies properties that are used in every single Web application running on the server. Many of the default Servlets configured here provide Web server-like features (serving static content, SSI, CGI, and so on) for running Web applications.
- While Tomcat 5 starts up by default in an unsecured mode, the `catalina.policy` file is very important in secured Tomcat 5 installations. It specifies in excruciating detail what can be accessed by whom — and anything else that is not specified cannot be accessed. Tomcat 5 takes advantage of the sophisticated, built-in security infrastructure of Java 2. To protect against tampering with Tomcat internal classes, the `catalina.properties` file can be used to restrict internal package access and definition.
- The in-depth analysis of these configuration files should provide an understanding of the basic configuration features of the Tomcat 5 server.

Chapters 6 and 7 discuss the configuration and administration of Web applications that execute within a Tomcat 5 server instance.

6

Web Application Configuration

Web applications consist of static content (such as HTML pages and images files) as well as dynamic content (such as Servlets, JSPs, and Java classes). Chapter 2 briefly discussed Servlets and JSPs.

Though these Web applications usually are created by developers, they often require a system administrator to configure and deploy them. There are a number of things that a systems administrator needs to know about in order to administer Web applications, such as the structure of a Web application and its configuration files.

This chapter describes the configuration-related issues for Web applications:

- The structure and content of a Web application
- The deployment descriptor for a Web application (that is, the `web.xml` configuration file). Significant changes to this file resulted from the Servlet 2.4 specification, and there is a new XML schema definition for the deployment descriptor.

Chapter 7 discusses other administrative activities for Web applications (for example, deploying, undeploying, and listing Web applications).

The Contents of a Web Application

Web applications are usually installed under the `CATALINA_HOME/webapps` directory. The Servlet 2.4 specification requires that a certain basic directory structure be followed. Figure 6-1 shows a sample Web application structure.

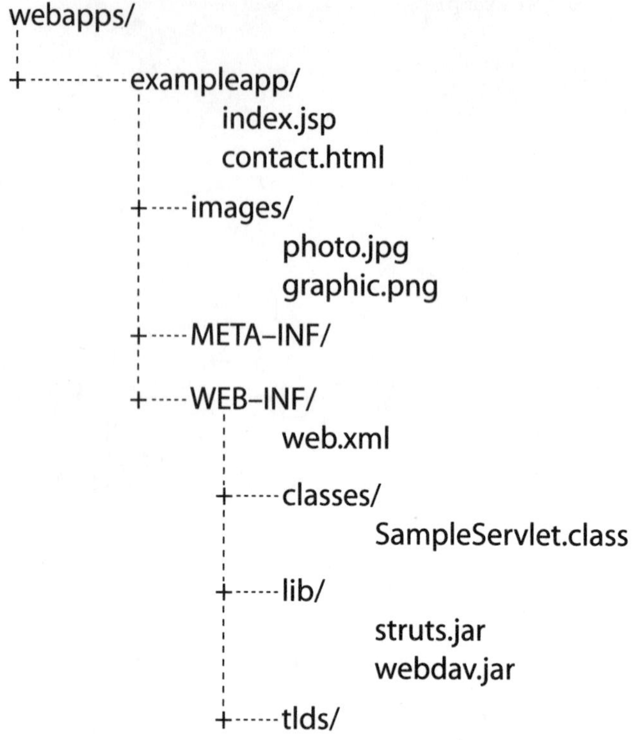

Figure 6-1: Directory structure for a sample Web application.

The Web application is deployed in a directory typically named after the Web application. This name is also used in the Web application URL. For example, the sample Web application in Figure 6-1 is located in a directory called `exampleapp`, and can be accessed by the URL `http://localhost:8080/exampleapp/`. Here, `/exampleapp/` is called the **context path** for the Web application. The context path refers to everything in the URL after the server and port number, and is the part of the URL that is used to resolve the location of the resource.

An exception to this is the `ROOT` application. The `ROOT` application is the application that is available when no context path is specified, as shown in the following URL:

```
http://servername:8080/
```

Regarding the structure of the Web application, the minimum that is required is a `WEB-INF` directory with a `web.xml` file in it. As discussed previously in Chapter 2, HTML and JSP pages belong to the public resources that a client may request directly. All the contents of the `WEB-INF` and `META-INF` directories fall into the category of an application's private resources, and cannot be accessed directly by client applications.

Public Resources

Everything outside the `WEB-INF` and `META-INF` directories are **public resources**, and can be accessed via an appropriate URL. For example, the `contact.html` file can be accessed as follows:

```
http://localhost:8080/exampleapp/contact.html
```

The placement of publicly accessible files (such as JSP and HTML pages, CSS, and images) is arbitrary as far as the specifications for Web applications are concerned, and they can be accessed directly by a client.

By arbitrary we do not mean that they can be placed anywhere and the server will find them. Rather, as long as the files are put within the Web application directory, and outside of the **`WEB-INF`** *directory, then the application itself (and its designer) decides where files are placed.*

In the example Web application shown in Figure 6-1, `index.jsp` is the default welcome page for the Web application. The **welcome page** is the Web page served up when you access the Web application URL — in this case, at the following URL:

```
http://localhost:8080/exampleapp/
```

If this Web page were not present, then, by default, `index.html` and `index.htm` will be looked for and served. These welcome pages are subject to configuration and can be modified, as you will see later in the chapter. Besides `index.jsp` and `contact.html`, the other public resources in the example application are the image files in the `images` directory.

URL Mappings

In most cases, when you request a Web resource from your browser (such as an HTML page), it is served to you without modification by the Web server. JSP pages are an exception to this. A JSP page is first passed through a JSP compiler that compiles the file to a Java file, and then compiles the Java file to a Servlet class. This Servlet class then executes, and the output is displayed on your browser.

The code that makes this happen is a URL mapping defined using a `<servlet-mapping>` element, as shown next. This URL mapping is defined in `CATALINA_HOME/conf/web.xml`. This file is the deployment descriptor for all the Web applications — individual Web applications can define their own deployment descriptors.

```
<servlet-mapping>
  <servlet-name>jsp</servlet-name>
  <url-pattern>*.jsp</url-pattern>
</servlet-mapping>
```

The preceding code specifies that any URL that ends in `.jsp` should be passed to a Servlet named `jsp` that is defined elsewhere in the same `$CATALINA_HOME/conf/web.xml` configuration file. The definition for this Servlet is as follows:

```
<servlet>
  <servlet-name>jsp</servlet-name>
  <servlet-class>org.apache.jasper.servlet.JspServlet</servlet-class>
  <init-param>
    <param-name>logVerbosityLevel</param-name>
    <param-value>WARNING</param-value>
  </init-param>
  <load-on-startup>3</load-on-startup>
</servlet>
```

As you can see, the fully qualified name of the Servlet is `org.apache.jasper.servlet.JspServlet`. The Servlet is handed the request, uses the context path to load the JSP page, and passes it to Tomcat's JSP compiler, known as Jasper. The remaining options set the logging level for the JSP compilation and execution process, and ensure that the Servlet class is loaded into memory on startup with a priority of 3 (where 1 is most important) to ensure that it is loaded before any JSP pages are requested.

The WEB-INF Directory

The contents of the `WEB-INF` directory are also shown Figure 6-1. As shown, it has a deployment descriptor (`web.xml`) and three subdirectories. These subdirectories include the following:

- The `classes` directory
- The `lib` directory
- The `tlds` directory

The classes Directory

The `classes` directory contains Servlet and utility classes, including JavaBeans. It may also contain a number of resource files such as key/value message lists, which contain error messages and user prompts for the application, and application-specific configuration information.

Each class is stored within a directory hierarchy that matches its Fully Qualified Name (FQN). Therefore, a class with package structure `com.wrox.db.DatabaseServlet` will be stored in the `classes/com/wrox/db` directory structure. Because Servlets are merely Java classes that implement a specified interface, they are stored in the `classes` directory, too. Previously, it was common to place Servlets in an additional directory within the `WEB-INF` directory named `servlets`. Classes placed into this directory are no longer on the classpath by default, and they need to be moved into the `classes` directory.

Ideally, an administrator need not be concerned with the contents of the `classes` directory. However, it is worth noting that there may be configuration files present in it. The resource files mentioned earlier may be within this directory and are typically text files that contain configuration information or are used to externalize error messages. This is merely a programming practice and you may have any kind of file here.

For example, there may be an `ApplicationResources.properties` file (the name is determined by the application developer) that looks like the following:

```
prompt.username=User Name (your email address)
prompt.password=Please enter you password
error.password.mismatch=The password is incorrect. Please try again.
```

This type of list enables an application developer to refer to the text by its name (for example, `prompt.username`), thereby enabling an administrator to change the values, minimizing the need to touch the sensitive JSP code.

The tlds Directory

An optional `tlds` directory within the `WEB-INF` directory contains configuration files for tag libraries.

A **tag library** is a group of Java classes that define the functionality of dynamic markup tags. For example, you could use a tag that you define as follows:

```
<date:today/>
```

This would output the current date whenever it is placed in a JSP file. To enable the container to recognize which Java class to invoke when it comes across the tag, you must provide a configuration file that lists the number of arguments the tag can have, its name (in this case, the tag's name is `today` and the library it belongs to is `date`). The tag library configuration files have a `.tld` extension. The configuration of a tag library is the territory of developers and designers, and thus beyond the scope of this book.

The lib Directory

This directory contains packaged Java libraries that the application requires and that are bundled with the application. JAR files that are placed here are available only to the Web application.

The following section describes what aspects of the `web.xml` configuration file you can administer.

The META-INF Directory

As mentioned, the `WEB-INF` directory represents the private resources of an application. However, this is not the only directory for private resources. A Web application may have an optional `META-INF` directory that contains deployment information for tools that create `war` files and resources that applications may rely on. Therefore, a Servlet container will refuse to show the contents of the `META-INF` directory to a client.

The `META-INF` directory often contains only one file, named `MANIFEST.MF`. This file may contain a list of `jar` files on which an application relies. The container can then check all the required libraries that are to be made available for the Web application.

An entry in this text file should be provided as follows, on a single line:

```
Extension-List: extension1 extension2 extension3
```

Each extension name is separated by a space and is placed as a separate entry in the `MANIFEST.MF` file. The entries are named with a prefix, followed by the string `-Extension-Name`, which is an attribute name, as shown here:

```
extension1-Extension-Name: com.wrox.extension1
extension1-Specification-Version: 1.0
extension1-Implementation-Version: 0.8
extension1-Implementation-Vendor: WROX Press Ltd
extension1-Implementation-Vendor-Id: com.wrox
extension1-Implementation-URL: http://www.wrox.com/extension1/
```

As you can see, the name of the extension is referenced in each entry. This is suffixed by a specific attribute name describing the extension. The name of the extension in this file is an alias for the extension's name as defined in the `jar` file. Thus, the declaration of the extension's alias is accomplished by simply prefixing it to the attribute names; it does not need to be explicitly defined.

The extension's proper name is referred to in the first entry. The server will investigate the contents of each jar file installed on it and check packages to determine whether the names match. The specifications and implementation version numbers are self-explanatory, as should be the vendor name that is specified in the Implementation-Vendor attribute. The vendor should be a globally unique ID. The custom of including the reversed host name is common. In the preceding example, this is com.wrox.

Finally, the Implementation-URL should be provided, providing the location of additional information and often download instructions. For our purpose, this is the most useful line. If the extension is not installed, the URL should provide enough information to ensure that it is made available to the Web application by other means.

The jar files may be placed in the application's lib directory, the Web application shared $CATALINA_HOME/shared/lib directory, the system-wide $CATALINA_HOME/server/lib directory, or alternatively placed on the classpath in some way.

The MANIFEST file is typically generated automatically when a Web application is packaged as a Web archive (.war) file. Packaging Web applications for distribution as .war files is described in Chapter 7.

The Deployment Descriptor (web.xml)

A **deployment descriptor** is an XML file that contains configuration information used by the Web application for execution on the Servlet engine. The deployment descriptor for a Web application is the CATALINA_HOME\webapps\<webapp name>\WEB-INF\web.xml file. There is another web.xml file that is applicable for all Web applications deployed in the Servlet engine, and this is located under CATALINA_HOME\conf. This section examines application-specific deployment only. However, the configuration-related information is valid for all deployment descriptors.

The Servlet 2.4 specifications introduce a new schema for the deployment descriptor — the previous specifications provided a Document Type Definition (DTD). However, the older Servlet 2.3-style web.xml is still supported for backward compatibility with existing Web applications. Because you might need to support existing Web applications, this chapter covers both the Servlet 2.3-style web.xml and the new schema-based version. The first few lines of the deployment descriptor will indicate whether it is the Servlet 2.4 schema-based web.xml or the older DTD-based version.

Following is a Servlet 2.3 DTD-based web.xml:

```
<?xml version="1.0" encoding="ISO-8859-1"?>

<!DOCTYPE web-app
    PUBLIC "-//Sun Microsystems, Inc.//DTD Web Application 2.3//EN"
    "http://java.sun.com/dtd/web-app_2_3.dtd">
<web-app>
   ...
</web-app>
```

Following is a Servlet 2.4 schema-based web.xml:

```
<?xml version="1.0" encoding="ISO-8859-1"?>

<web-app xmlns="http://java.sun.com/xml/ns/j2ee"
    xmlns:xsi="http://www.w3.org/2001/XMLSchema-instance"
    xsi:schemaLocation="http://java.sun.com/xml/ns/j2ee web-app_2_4.xsd"
    version="2.4">
  ...
</web-app>
```

Servlet 2.3-Style Deployment Descriptor

The web.xml file takes the following generalized form:

```
<?xml version="1.0"?>
<!DOCTYPE web-app
    PUBLIC "-//Sun Microsystems, Inc.//DTD Web Application 2.3//EN"
    "http://java.sun.com/j2ee/dtds/web-app_2_3.dtd">
<web-app>
  <icon>
  <display-name>
  <description>
  <distributable>
  <context-param>
  <filter>
  <filter-mapping>
  <listener>
  <servlet>
  <servlet-mapping>
  <session-config>
  <mime-mapping>
  <welcome-file-list>
  <error-page>
  <taglib>
  <resource-env-ref>
  <resource-ref>
  <security-constraint>
  <login-config>
  <security-role>
  <env-entry>
  <ejb-ref>
  <ejb-local-ref>
</web-app>
```

The order of elements inside the <web-app> element must be as shown previously, but some elements are optional, and others may appear multiple times. The following table may be used as a quick reference to the functionality of each element. A more detailed explanation is provided later in the chapter.

Element	Description	How Many?
<icon>	Image for an application	0 or 1
<display-name>	Display name for a Web application	0 or 1
<description>	Description used for display	0 or 1
<distributable>	A Boolean value indicating whether an application is distributable across servers	0 or 1
<context-param>	Initialization parameters for the entire application	0 or more
<filter>	Defines a filter Valve	0 or more
<filter-mapping>	Defines a URL pattern to which the given filter needs to be applied	0 or more
<listener>	Defines a lifecycle event listener	0 or more
<servlet>	Defines a Servlet	0 or more
<servlet-mapping>	Defines a URL pattern to invoke a named Servlet	0 or more
<session-config>	Defines session configuration	0 or 1
<mime-mapping>	Defines the MIME type for a given file type	0 or more
<welcome-file-list>	A list of files to be served if no resource is specified explicitly in the URL	0 or 1
<error-page>	Defines a Java exception or an HTTP code-based error page	0 or more
<taglib>	Declares a tag library	0 or more
<resource-env-ref>	Declares a resource-administered object	0 or more
<resource-ref>	Declares an external resource	0 or more
<security-constraint>	Restricts access to a resource to a required transport guarantee and by user role	0 or more
<login-config>	Defines authentication parameters	0 or 1
<security-role>	Declares a security role by name	0 or more
<env-entry>	Defines a Web application's environment entry	0 or more
<ejb-ref>	Declares a reference to an EJB's home	0 or more
<ejb-local-ref>	Declares a reference to an EJB's local home	0 or more

In the following sections, you will examine a minimal `web.xml` file to understand what must be present.

The XML Header

Every web.xml file complies with the XML specifications that require an XML header in the beginning of the file, as shown here:

```
<?xml version="1.0"?>
```

Optionally, the declaration may also include an encoding type that identifies the character encoding of the document, as is standard for XML. For example, if the document is encoded in UTF-8, the declaration may be provided as follows:

```
<?xml version="1.0" encoding="UTF-8"?>
```

The DTD Declaration

The next tag is a Document Type Definition (DTD) tag. A DTD is a document that outlines the structure of the web.xml elements, what elements are allowed and in which order, and their content. The inclusion of a standard DTD declaration in our web.xml file looks as follows:

```
<?xml version="1.0"?>
<!DOCTYPE web-app
    PUBLIC "-//Sun Microsystems, Inc.//DTD Web Application 2.3//EN"
    "http://java.sun.com/dtd/web-app_2_3.dtd">
```

Applications that comply with the Servlet specifications prior to 2.3, such as Tomcat 3 web.xml files, for example, will have the following DTD reference:

```
<!DOCTYPE web-app
    PUBLIC "-//Sun Microsystems, Inc.//DTD Web Application 2.2//EN"
    "http://java.sun.com/j2ee/dtds/web-app_2_2.dtd">
```

Backward compatibility is required as per the Servlet 2.3 specifications, so applications that were written for the Servlet 2.2 specifications will work unaltered on Tomcat 5, except for any dependencies on the exact configuration of the server (such as the location of databases, network authentication, and the name of the server and the host). Because the Servlet 2.3 specifications have introduced a number of new tags since 2.2, we will also highlight these tags where appropriate.

<web-app>

The root element of the web.xml file is <web-app>, and all other XML elements reside inside it:

```
<?xml version="1.0"?>
<!DOCTYPE web-app
    PUBLIC "-//Sun Microsystems, Inc.//DTD Web Application 2.3//EN"
    "http://java.sun.com/dtd/web-app_2_3.dtd">
<web-app>
</web-app>
```

This is all that is required for the web.xml file to be complete. However, in many practical cases, there will be more. Let's begin by covering elements that describe the application. A number of elements are provided so that deployment tools can identify Web applications visually and textually.

<icon>

This tag holds the location of the image files within the Web application that may be used by a tool to represent the Web application visually. The `<icon>` tag may contain two child elements (`<small-icon>` and `<large-icon>`) that carry the location of a 16 × 16 pixel image file and a 32 × 32 pixel image file, respectively.

```
<icon>
  <small-icon>/images/icons/exampleapp_small.gif</small-icon>
  <large-icon>/images/icons/exampleapp_large.gif</large-icon>
</icon>
```

<display-name>

This tag provides a name that can be used for display in a GUI. The name need not be unique. For example, the following display name is typical:

```
<display-name>Example Application</display-name>
```

<description>

This tag contains the description of a Web application, as shown in the following example:

```
<?xml version="1.0"?>
<!DOCTYPE web-app
    PUBLIC "-//Sun Microsystems, Inc.//DTD Web Application 2.3//EN"
    "http://java.sun.com/dtd/web-app_2_3.dtd">
<web-app>
  <icon>
    <small-icon>/images/icons/exampleapp_small.gif</small-icon>
    <large-icon>/images/icons/exampleapp_large.gif</large-icon>
  </icon>

  <display-name>Wrox Example Application</display-name>

  <description>
    The Wrox example application contains a number of simple resources
    for illustrating configuration points.
  </description>
</web-app>
```

These element tags must be listed in the same order as shown earlier in the section (refer to `http://java.sun.com/dtd/web-app_2_3.dtd` for more information). The actual number of tools for deploying Web archives (especially in a drag-and-drop manner as suggested by the use of icon files) is somewhat low, so it is common for these values not to be provided. The `web.xml` may be heavily commented. XML comments take the same form as HTML ones:

```
<!--
This is a comment
-->
```

<distributable>

This tag describes a Web application that is designed to be distributable for load balancing and fail-over. By default, the value of this is `false`.

<context-param>

Context parameters are mechanisms used for setting application-initialization parameters. For example, you could set the URL to a database here. The following example enables the administrator to change the title and greeting of the example application:

```
<context-param>
  <param-name>title</param-name>
  <param-value>Wrox example application - Chapter 6</param-value>
</context-param>
<context-param>
  <param-name>greeting</param-name>
  <param-value>Welcome to the example application</param-value>
</context-param>
```

There may be any number of context parameters in the application, known as **initial parameters.** Each dynamic resource (such as a Servlet, a JSP page, or a class) with access to the application context is able to look up the value associated with a given parameter name. Typical items provided as a context parameter are the debug status of the application, the verbosity of logging (these two are often inter-linked), and as much other externalized configuration as the application developer has allowed.

<filter>

Filters are new to the Servlet 2.3 specifications. Filters are reusable components that intercept the client request and response and apply some type of processing to them. For example, a filter may apply compression to the contents of the response, thus reducing bandwidth usage and improving the performance of the application by minimizing the size of the response packet. This is just an example, of course, and to make it work in a real-world situation would require additional support in the browser.

Filters are intended to be the ultimate reusable Web components. They should be virtually independent of the content being created. Examples include the compression filter, a transformation filter that may convert XML to HTML or WML, a filter to provide logging of resource usage, and a filter to restrict access to resources.

A filter, like all Web application resources, can be mapped to a URL pattern, including the extension of the resource, a section of the site (such as everything within the `images` directory), or even a URL alias such as the `servlet` alias that exists on most default installations of Java Web servers.

In addition, filters can have an icon associated with them, and configuration parameters (initialization parameters). An example configuration is shown here:

```
<filter>
  <icon>/images/icons/filter.jpg</icon>
  <filter-name>Compressor</filter-name>
  <display-name>Compression Filter</display-name>
  <description>This filter applies compression</description>
  <filter-class>com.wrox.utils.CompressionFilter</filter-class>
  <init-param>
    <param-name>compression_type</param-name>
    <param-value>gzip</param-value>
  </init-param>
</filter>
```

Once a filter is defined, it can be mapped against any number of URL patterns. In addition, when many filters are defined for a given URL pattern, they are all applied in the order in which they are defined in the web.xml file. In the following example, the compression filter is applied to every URL:

```
<filter-mapping>
  <filter-name>Compressor</filter-name>
  <url-pattern>*</url-pattern>
</filter-mapping>
```

Chapter 8 provides further information on filters, listeners, and Servlet configuration.

<listener>

Listeners are designed to respond to events in an application. For example, a JavaBean could send an e-mail when an event requiring administration is recorded:

```
<listener>
  <listener-class>com.wrox.listeners.ExampleListener</listener-class>
</listener>
```

<servlet>

A Servlet is declared in the web.xml file by assigning it a unique name, which references its fully qualified name against a shorter, more intuitive name:

```
<servlet>
  <icon>/images/icons/DownloadServlet.jpg</icon>
  <servlet-name>Download</servlet-name>
  <display-name>File Download Servlet</display-name>
  <description>
    This Servlet manages file downloads in the application
  </description>
  <servlet-class>com.wrox.servlets.DownloadServlet</servlet-class>
  <!-- require terms and conditions agreement? -->
  <init-param>
    <param-name>require_tc</param-name>
    <param-value>true</param-value>
  </init-param>
  <load-on-startup>5</load-on-startup>
  <!-- uncomment this if Servlets must run in user role
  <run-as>
    <description>
      This Servlet does not require authorization to resources
    </description>
    <role-name>admin</role-name>
  </run-as>
  -->
</servlet>
```

In the preceding example, the Servlet manages the download process, enabling you to decide at run-time if a user is required to sign a terms and conditions acceptance form before download commences. The optional <icon>, <display-name>, and <description> elements work in the same way as described previously. The fully qualified name of the Servlet is specified in the <servlet-class> element.

Because JSP pages are ultimately compiled into Servlets, an alternative to the Servlet class name (`<servlet-class>` element) is to specify the JSP filename (`<jsp-file>` element) to which these configuration parameters should be applied, thus making JSP files fully configurable. The reference is a full path, from the root of the application to the JSP file, as shown in the following example:

```
<servlet>
  <servlet-name>ExampleJSP</servlet-name>
  <jsp-file>/admin/users/ListAllUsers.jsp</jsp-file>

  <!-- list disabled user accounts -->
  <init-param>
    <param-name>list_disabled_accs</param-name>
    <param-value>false</param-value>
  </init-param>
</servlet>
```

The initialization parameters work in the same way as the application context parameters. However, they are specific to the Servlet.

The `<load-on-startup>` element specifies an integer value indicating whether the Servlet must be loaded when the Tomcat server boots, rather than on a client's request. If this value is not specified or it is negative, the container loads the Servlet into memory when the first request comes in.

If the value is zero or a positive integer, the container must load the Servlet into memory at startup of the Web application. Servlets assigned lower integers are loaded before those with higher integers. Servlets with the same `<load-on-startup>` values are loaded in an arbitrary sequence by the container.

In the `Download Servlet` example, the `<run-as>` attribute is not specified because it is commented out. However, if the Servlet requires a privileged role, it can be specified here, so that any resource requiring a privileged user will discover it while calling the `isUserInRole()` method.

<session-config>

Session configuration enables sessions to be configured for every application. The `<session-timeout>` element can be used to set a session timeout value. This value can be calculated by considering typical client usage patterns, along with security requirements. For example, if a user is asked to enter a great deal of information, the session timeout value may be set to a larger number to avoid information being lost.

Alternatively, in low security environments with serializable sessions, it is possible to set sessions to never expire so that the user is always recognized.

The session configuration is defined as follows:

```
<session-config>
  <session-timeout>40</session-timeout>
</session-config>
```

If the value is zero or less, the session is never expired and the application must explicitly remove it as required. If the element is not provided, the default value of 30 is used as specified in the global `web.xml` file within Tomcat's `$CATALINA_HOME/config` directory.

<mime-mapping>

MIME types enable browsers to recognize the file type of the content being returned by the server so that the browser can handle it correctly, to determine whether to display it (as HTML, plain text, images); pass the content to a plug-in (such as Flash); or prompt the user to save the file locally.

Tomcat comes preconfigured with the majority of MIMI mappings set, which can be seen in the `$CATALINA_HOME/conf/web.xml` file. MIME mappings set in this file apply to all applications. Additional MIME mappings may be configured on each Web application with the `<mime-mapping>` element. This can be especially useful when the developer defines new extensions to suit the application. In addition, this can be useful if you wish to have a certain MIME type treated differently from how it is normally. For example, for a content management application, you may want to prevent Internet Explorer from recognizing the MIME type and thus opening the file in the appropriate application, and instead prompt the user with the File Save dialog box.

Another example might be the automatic generation of Excel files. Excel will accept comma-separated values and convert them to an Excel spreadsheet if the MIME type sent to Internet Explorer is set to the Excel MIME type of `application/x-excel` or `application/ms-excel`. This will open Excel, although the file is a CSV file. This technique is used in Web applications for non-integrated applications in which a company administrator wants to be able to dynamically generate Excel files from a site into their reports, as creating Excel sheets on-the-fly is quite complex.

*For those interested in creating Excel sheets or manipulating documents on-the-fly, a number of programs can be used for this, such as JExcel (**`http://jexcelapi.sourceforge.net/`**) or Jakarta POI (**`http://jakarta.apache.org/poi/index.html`**).*

This is a common technique when it is desirable to use an external application to view content from a Web application/script. The following example shows how the Excel-CVS MIME mapping is done:

```
<mime-mapping>
  <extension>csv</extension>
  <mime-type>application/x-msexcel</mime-type>
</mime-mapping>
...
```

<welcome-file-list>

Sometimes a request is made from a client to an application without a definite resource specified in the URL. For example, the root of the application is requested as follows:

```
http://localhost:8080/exampleapp/
```

whereas a definite resource is requested as shown in the following URL:

```
http://localhost:8080/exampleapp/whatsnew.jsp
```

In such cases, the Web application looks for a file called `index.jsp` in the Web application's directory and executes this file if it exists. If this file cannot be found, it looks for `index.htm` and `index.html` in turn. This is because the welcome file list defined in `$CATALINA_HOME/conf/web.xml` lists these files by default. If the `web.xml` file in the `WEB-INF` directory of your Web application does not mention a welcome file list, the default will be used.

The format for the welcome file list is as follows (this will apply to each request that does not specify a resource). This means that each of the subdirectories within the application root will also have this rule applied to it. In the following example, `default.jsp` will be loaded instead of `index.jsp`:

```
<welcome-file-list>
  <welcome-file>default.jsp</welcome-file>
  <welcome-file>default.htm</welcome-file>
  <welcome-file>UserWelcome.jsp</welcome-file>
</welcome-file-list>
```

Note that if none of the files in the example list are found, then, depending on the configuration, an HTTP 404–Not Found error message is displayed.

<error-page>

The default behavior for Web applications written in JSP is to return a **stack trace**, which is a complex view into the internals of the virtual machine that greatly reduces the user-friendliness of the application.

You can configure error pages to provide a user-friendly mechanism for informing users about a problem, enabling them to continue using the application. The errors are mapped to the HTTP specification error mappings (such as a code for a resource that cannot be found, server malfunctioning, authentication issues, resource issues, and so on).

In addition, because there are no one-to-one correspondences between HTTP errors and Java exceptions, the exception class type may be specified. This enables the creation of error pages that are generic, and follows good programming practice. Someone without an understanding of the application's internals can configure them. Following is an example for the common 404 message for a `NullPointerException`:

```
<error-page>
  <error-code>404</error-code>
  <location>/errors/oops.jsp</location>
</error-page>
<error-page>
  <exception-type>java.lang.NullPointerException</exception-type>
  <location>/errors/badlycodedpage.jsp</location>
</error-page>
```

Like the JSP page example, `<location>` must be a reference from the root of the application.

These pages often have a message that notifies the user of the problem, and provisionally provides both a search box so that users can locate the resources they need and a list of likely links in the site from which they might receive help.

Often the problem is a configuration issue, and users are best served by being informed that the problem will be fixed and they should return later. The developer may be informed through automated parsing of error logs or through a notification system that sends e-mails to a watched e-mail address or directly to the administrator or the development team.

Should any problem occur in a page (such as missing resources, a bug in the software, or parts of the system being down), a page configured here would be returned. Error pages can also be written so that they display contextual information (that relates to the specific problem at hand), but this requires an understanding of the inner workings of the system and can only be provided by a developer.

HTTP return codes can be found at the following URL:

```
www.w3c.org/Protocols/HTTP/HTRESP.html
```

Error pages are configured by associating them with the HTTP return code that covers the error group. Two examples are provided in the following example, one for the `HTTP 404` code and one for a `NullPointerException` (an internal error is often hard to debug in an application and may require a developer's intervention to correct it):

```
<error-page>
  <error-code>404</error-code>
  <location>/errors/ResourceNotFound.htm</location>
</error-page>
<error-page>
  <exception-type>java.lang.NullPointerException</exception-type>
  <location>/errors/ApplicationProblem.jsp</location>
</error-page>
```

<taglib>

Tag libraries, as previously discussed in Chapter 2, are reusable Java components that may be invoked using markup tags in the page. The tag library definition is specified by the application developer and the HTML designers. However, the main configuration of these reusable components is done in a separate file (one with a `.tld` extension), as this entry simply enables aliasing of the location of this configuration document against a URI. The exact location of the configuration file, which is given as a reference to the file from the Web application's root directory, can then be referred to by its alias.

This aliasing enables location-independence (that is, the tag library configuration files can be moved around without editing the JSP pages that refer to the tag library configuration file, so long as the tag entry points to it). An example entry is shown here:

```
<taglib>
  <taglib-uri>applicationtags.tld</taglib-uri>
  <tablib-location>/WEB-INF/tlds/web-app.tld</taglib-location>
</taglib>
```

In this example, the tag library configuration file that the Web application container needs for resolving references, looking up initialization parameters, and enforcing proper use of the tags is referred to by its alias, `applicationtags.tld`. The location of the configuration file is customarily within the `WEB-INF` directory in a directory called `tlds`. If this location is changed, you must adjust the `<taglib-location>` entry, but any code referencing it can stay the same.

<resource-ref>

Two elements, `<resource-ref>` and `<resource-env-ref>`, are provided for configuring resources for a Web application environment. These elements enable two things:

- *The management of connections to resources, such as a reference to the object pooling resource connection (much like database-connection pooling), to make the process more efficient*

Object pooling enables efficient use of resources by defining a component that manages connections to those resources. In the case of databases, the pool will make a number of connections and when a client requests one, it is handed over to the client to be used. When the client requests the connection to be closed, the pool retrieves the connection, but rather than closing it and establishing a new connection, it reuses the connection by handing it over to the next client (as long as the authority constraints and the type of connection matches).

Because establishing a connection to a database is a resource-intensive process, this can affect application performance. A pool can also be configured to refresh the connections periodically and to restore dropped connections so that the application can efficiently recover from database failures.

- *A reference to administered objects, which provides the application with access to run-time administration of the resource*

Administered objects enable the application configuration to be changed without restarting the server. They can also be used to monitor the state of the application by interrogating administered objects for their current state.

<security-constraint>

Web resources may be associated with some security constraints for authentication purposes. The constraints limit access to the resource according to user roles (such as manager, administrator, user, and guest) and by transport guarantee (which can include SSL secure data transmission), guaranteeing delivery and non-interference.

The `<security-constraint>` element enables a Web resource to be defined against an authentication constraint and a user data constraint.

An entry takes the following form:

```
<security-constraint>
  <display-name>Name String</display-name>
  <web-resource-collection>
    <web-resource-name>GETServlet</web-resource-name>
    <description>
      Group together all Servlet GET requests on the server using
      /servlet/servletname. We are grouping these requests as (we have
      decided) they require additional security being inherently less secure
      than the POST method and aliased Servlet calls.
    </description
    <url-pattern>/servlet/*</url-pattern>
    <http-method>GET</http-method>
  </web-resource-collection>
  <auth-constraint>
    <description>
       All roles are constrained to secure connection to Servlet resource
       via GET calls
    </description>
    <role-name>*</role-name>
  </auth-constraint>
  <user-data-constraint>
    <description>
```

```
        Constrain the user data transport for GET Servlet requests to secure
        sockets
      </description>
      <transport-guarantee>INTEGRAL</transport-guarantee>
    </user-data-constraint>
  </security-constraint>
```

<web-resource-collection>

The `<web-resource-collection>` element identifies a group of resources and the methods by which these resources can be requested. In the previous example, all Servlets identified by the pattern `/servlet` can be accessed via the HTTP `GET` method. Any number of URL patterns and valid HTTP methods may be provided to exactly define the resource collection.

<auth-constraint>

The `<auth-constraint>` element uses role-based authentication to constrain access to Web resources. You can limit groups of users to whom this security constraint is applied to using role-based authentication. Therefore, placing `administrator` in the `<role-name>` tag above would allow only users belonging to that role to be able to access the Servlets. Role-based authentication is discussed in more detail in Chapter 15.

Valid values are specified by the developer of the application. In the preceding example, `*` indicates that all roles should be allowed access. An empty element indicates that no roles should be allowed access to the resource.

There is no constraint on the number of `<role-name>` elements required to define security constraints. If none are provided, then the resource is unavailable as no authentication is possible. You might make resources unavailable for security reasons by removing all references to `<role-name>` elements in the `web.xml` file and then restarting Tomcat.

<user-data-constraint>

The `<user-data-constraint>` element indicates what guarantees are given about the communication of data from and to the client. A value of `NONE` indicates that no guarantees are provided that the data has not been tampered with or intercepted by anyone other than the client and the system (the server). Conversely, a value of `INTEGRAL` requires the authenticity of the data to be guaranteed, or that the data has not been interfered with, while `CONFIDENTIAL` requires guarantees that the data has not been intercepted by a third party. Specifying `INTEGRAL` or `CONFIDENTIAL` means that SSL will be used by redirecting the client to the SSL port of the server.

This type of configuration is likely to be defined at design time. However, in a well-designed application, it is up to the deployment engineer/system administrator to follow the design architecture to enforce the security constraints defined within it. This enables authentication requirements to be absent from the application code itself, thus allowing the application to be very flexible so that it can be configured as business needs dictate.

<login-config>

This element relates to the configuration of login authentication in the application. The `<login-config>` element contains the authentication method, the Realm name and login page, and the authentication error page that should be used if form-based authentication is specified:

```
<login-config>
  <auth-method>FORM</auth-method>
  <realm-name>MemoryRealm</realm-name>
  <form-login-config>
    <form-login-page>login.jsp</form-login-page>
    <form-error-page>notAuthenticated.jsp</form-error-page>
  </form-login-config>
</login-config>
```

The authentication method consists of the HTTP methods available—namely, `BASIC`, `DIGEST`, `FORM`, and `CLIENT-CERT`. These correspond to basic authentication (plain text), digest (base64-encoded responses), `FORM`-based authentication (which enables an HTML page with a form that prompts the user to log in and returns the user name and password), and client-certificate-based authentication, respectively.

The `<realm-name>` identifies the Realm that the server should use to authenticate the user against—in our example, the Realm name alludes to the file-based list of users and passwords provided by the memory Realm with Tomcat. In a production environment, using the memory Realm is not recommended. Instead, a JDBC or JDNI Realm is far more robust and maintainable.

Having chosen form-based authentication, we must specify the login page and the error page, in case a login fails. In this case, we have specified that `login.jsp` contains the login request form. Bad authentication requests are redirected to `notAuthenticated.jsp`.

<security-role>

Security roles have been discussed in brief earlier in the chapter. The `<security-role>` element enables roles to be defined along with the optional description:

```
<security-role>
  <description>
    Administrator of the application is allowed read/write rights to the
    content
  </description>
  <role-name>administrator</role-name>
</security-role>
```

Further detail is provided in Chapter 15.

<env-entry>

The `<env-entry>` element is used to declare environment entries. These are JNDI value parameters that can be used to configure the application. Unlike context initialization parameters, these values are dynamic. They can be referred to and updated at run-time so that the application can be reconfigured dynamically, and resources outside the Web application can access them. In particular, they can be administered by non-Java application components, and can be managed as part of the entire enterprise administration system.

This works like all JNDI resources; the parameter is referenced from the JNDI initial context and can be accessed using the `java:comp/env` environment naming context. The `env-entry` is defined as relative to this context.

The environment entry must be typed to a Java data type (such as `String` or `Integer`) so that it can be used within the application and can be used to define environment limits (such as minimum and maximum values). The general structure of an environment entry is as follows:

```
<env-entry>
  <description>Lower limit - minimum allowable value</description>
  <env-entry-name>MinimumValue</env-entry-name>
  <env-entry-value>5</env-entry-value>
  <env-entry-type>java.lang.Integer</env-entry-type>
</env-entry>
```

Environment entries are usually specific to the environment in which they are operating (that is, they are application-specific). However, accepted norms for resource naming may be adopted in an attempt to harmonize resource configuration.

The value can then be accessed using code such as the following:

```
// obtain the initial context.
Context initCtx = new InitialContext();
Context envCtx = (Context) initCtx.lookup("java:comp/env");

// Look up environment entry
Integer minValue = (Integer)envCtx.lookup("MinimumValue");
```

Servlet 2.4-Style Deployment Descriptor

In the new `web.xml` schema, the `web-app` element is the root element for the deployment descriptor. A sample `web-app` element is shown here:

```
<web-app xmlns="http://java.sun.com/xml/ns/j2ee"
    xmlns:xsi="http://www.w3.org/2001/XMLSchema-instance"
    xsi:schemaLocation="http://java.sun.com/xml/ns/j2ee web-app_2_4.xsd"
    version="2.4">
    ...
</web-app
```

The `web-app` element contains all other elements. Unlike the DTD-style 2.3 Deployment Descriptor, the enclosed elements can be in any order.

These elements are listed in the following table. Except for `session-config`, `jsp-config`, and `login-config`, all other elements can occur multiple times in the `web.xml` file.

Element Name	Description
`context-param`	Contains the Web application's Servlet context initialization parameters
`description`	Provides a description for the Web application
`display-name`	Specifies a short name for the Web application

Element Name	Description
distributable	Indicates that this Web application is programmed to be deployed in a distributed Servlet container
ejb-local-ref	Declares a reference to the Enterprise bean's (EJB) local home
ejb-ref	Declares the references to the EJB's home
env-entry	Declares the Web application's environment entries
error-page	Defines a mapping between an error code or exception and an error page
filter	Declares and configures a filter for the Web application
filter-mapping	Specifies the filters to be applied to the Web application, and the order in which they are applied
icon	Specifies filenames for icons used to represent the parent elements
jsp-config	Specifies global configuration properties for the JSP pages in the Web application
listener	Configures the properties of an application listener bean
locale-encoding-mapping-list	Specifies the mapping between locales and their encoding
login-config	Specifies the authentication methods to be used for accessing the Web application
message-destination	Specifies a message destination
message-destination-ref	Contains the deployment component's reference to a message destination
mime-mapping	Defines the mapping between an extension and a MIME type
resource-env-ref	Contains a reference to an administered object associated with a resource
resource-ref	Contains a reference to an external resource
security-constraint	Specifies security constraints for one or more groups of Web resources
security-role	Defines the security roles used in the security-constraint element
service-ref	Contains the reference to a Web service
servlet	Configuration for a Servlet
servlet-mapping	Specifies the mapping between a Servlet and URL pattern
session-config	Defines the session parameters for the Web application
welcome-file-list	Specifies a list of welcome files for a Web application

The following sections describe these elements in more detail.

Some of the deployment descriptor elements deal with configuration for J2EE components, such as Enterprise JavaBeans (EJBs) and Web services. The following sections cover their configuration, but do not explain these components in any detail.

context-param

The `context-param` element contains name-value pairs containing a Web application's Servlet context initialization parameters. The `context-param` has the following sub-elements:

- `description` — A text description of the name-value pair
- `param-name` — Name of the initialization parameter
- `param-value` — Value of the initialization parameter

A sample usage is shown here:

```
<context-param>
  <param-name>webmaster</param-name>
  <param-value>webmaster@foobar.com</param-value>
  <description>Email address of webmaster</description>
</context-param>
```

description

The `description` element provides a textual description for its parent element. When included under the `web-app` element (as shown in the "JSP examples" section of the Web application included in the Tomcat distribution), it describes the Web application. This element is used elsewhere, too (for example, the `context-param` element and the `filter` element), where it provides a description for that element:

```
<description>
  JSP 2.0 Examples
</description>
```

The `description` element has an optional attribute, `xml-lang`, which indicates the language of the description text. This defaults to `en` for English. There can also be multiple description elements, usually with different `xml-lang` attributes, to support localization.

display-name

The `display-name` element gives a short, descriptive name for the parent element. For example, when used directly under the `web-app` element, it provides a name for the Web application. This name is displayed by software tools that work with deployment descriptors. Like the description element, it too has an `xml-lang` attribute (which defaults to `en`) to indicate the language; and multiple `display-name` elements with different `xml-lang` values can be used to handle multiple-language support. A sample `display-name` element is shown here:

```
<display-name xml-lang="en">JSP 2.0 Examples</display-name>
```

distributable

The presence of a `distributable` element indicates that the Web application has been programmed to be deployed (if required) in a distributed Servlet container. Such a Servlet container may distribute the Web application to multiple JVMs for scalability or performance considerations.

```
<distributable/>
```

Chapter 19 discusses a deployment scenario in which this is used.

ejb-local-ref

The `ejb-local-ref` element declares a reference to the enterprise bean's (EJB) local home. This element has the following child elements:

- *ejb-ref-name*—The EJB reference name
- *ejb-ref-type*—The EJB reference type
- *ejb-link*—Specifies that the EJB reference is linked to an enterprise bean
- *local*—The fully qualified name of the EJB's local interface
- *local-home*—The fully qualified name of the EJB's local home interface

ejb-ref

This element contains a reference to an EJB's home. It has the following child elements:

- *ejb-refname*—The name used in the deployment component to refer to the EJB
- *ejb-ref-type*—Type of the EJB (Entity/Session)
- *home*—Fully qualified name of the EJB's home interface
- *remote*—Fully qualified name of the EJB's remote interface
- *ejb-link*—Specifies that the EJB reference is linked to an enterprise bean
- *description*—A text description of the EJB reference

A sample `ejb-ref` element is shown here:

```
<ejb-ref>
  <description>Employee bean/description>
  <ejb-ref-name>EmployeeBean</ejb-ref-name>
  <ejb-ref-type>Session</ejb-ref-type>
  <home>com.foobar.employee.EmployeeHome</home>
  <remote>com.foobar.employee.Employee</remote>
</ejb-ref>
```

env-entry

The env-entry element declares environment parameters for a Web application. Each env-entry has the following child elements:

- *env-entry-name*—The JNDI name of the deployment component's environment entry. This name is relative to the java:comp/env context, and must be unique within a context.
- *env-entry-type*—The type for the environmental entry (for example, java.lang.Integer, java.lang.String)
- *env-entry-value*—The value of the deployment component's environment entry

The following example shows a sample env-entry:

```
<!-- Environment entry examples -->
   <env-entry>
       <env-entry-name>maxExemptions</env-entry-name>
       <env-entry-type>java.lang.Integer</env-entry-type>
       <env-entry-value>15</env-entry-value>
   </env-entry>
   <env-entry>
       <env-entry-name>minExemptions</env-entry-name>
       <env-entry-type>java.lang.Integer</env-entry-type>
       <env-entry-value>1</env-entry-value>
   </env-entry>
```

error-page

The error-page element specifies the mapping between an error code or Java exception type and a Web resource. It contains the following child elements:

- *error-code*—The HTTP error code
- *exception-type*—The fully qualified class name of the Java exception type

Either the error-code or the exception-type should be specified in an error-page element, but not both.

- *location*—The location of the resource (that is, the error Web page) that handles the error. The location is relative to the root of the Web application, and must have a leading slash (/).

A sample error-page is shown in the following code:

```
<error-page>
    <error-code>404</error-code>
    <location>/myApp/jsp/notFound.jsp</location>
</error-page>
<error-page>
    <error-code>500</error-code>
    <location>/myApp/jsp/SystemErr.jsp</location>
</error-page>
```

filter

The `filter` element declares a filter in the Web application. The filter is mapped to either a Servlet or a URL pattern in the `filter-mapping` element, using the `filter-name` value as a reference key.

The filter element consists of the following sub-elements:

- *`filter-name`*—The name of the filter. This must be unique in the Web application, and should not be empty. This name must match the `filter-name` specified in the `filter-mapping` element described in the next section.
- *`filter-class`*—The fully qualified Java class name of the filter
- *`init-param`*—Initialization parameters for the filter specified as name-value pairs. These have the same structure as the `context-param` element described earlier, and consist of the `param-name`, `param-value`, and `description` sub-elements.
- *`description`*—A text description of the filter
- *`display-name`*—A short, descriptive name that can be used by tools while displaying the filter configuration
- *`icon`*—The `icon` element specifies icons that can be used by tools to symbolically represent the filter in GUI tools. It has two sub-elements: a `small-icon` and `large-icon` (see the `icon` element, described later in this chapter).

A sample `filter` configuration is shown in the following example:

```
<filter>
    <filter-name>Compression Filter</filter-name>
    <filter-class>compressionFilters.CompressionFilter</filter-class>

    <init-param>
      <param-name>compressionThreshold</param-name>
      <param-value>10</param-value>
    </init-param>
    <init-param>
      <param-name>debug</param-name>
      <param-value>0</param-value>
    </init-param>
</filter>

<filter>
    ...
    </filter>
```

filter-mapping

As specified earlier, the filter is mapped to either a Servlet or a URL pattern in the `filter-mapping` element, using the `filter-name` value for reference. The `Compression Filter` was declared in the `filter` element above, and the following example shows it being mapped to URL patterns that begin with `/CompressionTest`:

```
<filter-mapping>
    <filter-name>Compression Filter</filter-name>
    <url-pattern>/CompressionTest</url-pattern>
</filter-mapping>
```

The `filter-mapping` element can contain the following sub-elements:

- *`filter-name`*—The filter name. This must match the `filter-name` specified in the `filter` element.
- *`url-pattern`*—The URL pattern to which the filter applies
- *`servlet-name`*—The Servlet to which the filter applies. You should specify either the `url-pattern` or `servlet-name`, but not both.

icon

The `icon` element specifies icons that can be used by GUI tools to symbolically represent the parent element. It can occur under the `web-app` element (specifying icons to represent the Web application) or other elements (for example, the `filter` element described earlier). It has two sub-elements:

- *`small-icon`*
- *`large-icon`*

These set the small and large icon images, respectively. The images are relative path names to `gif` or `jpeg` files. The following is an example `icon` element:

```
<icon>
   <small-icon>an-icon16x16.jpg</small-icon>
   <large-icon>an-icon32x32.jpg</large-icon>
</icon>
```

jsp-config

The `jsp-config` element is used to configure JSP files in the Web application. It has the following child elements:

- *`taglib`*—Configure tag libraries used within the JSP pages. This is done via its two child elements: `taglib-uri` and the `taglib-location` (the location of the tag configuration `.tld` file).
- *`jsp-property-group`*—Configure JSP pages. This in turn has a number of child elements of its own:
    - *`url-pattern`*—The URL pattern for the JSPs

If a URL pattern is also specified in the **`servlet-mapping`** *(described later in this section), then the more specific pattern applies. If both match, then the* **`jsp-property-group`** *takes precedence.*

- *`el-ignored`*—Sets the `isELIgnored` property for JSP pages. EL evaluation is enabled by default. JSP EL is a new expression language for accessing data from JSP pages.
- *`page-encoding`*—The encoding to be used for the page (for example, ISO-8859-1)

- *scripting-invalid*—Used to disable scripting in JSP pages (enabled by default)
- *is-xml*—If `true`, implies that the documents matching the pattern are JSP pages, and can be interpreted as XML.
- *include-prelude*—Specifies the path to a Web resource to be included in the beginning of the JSP page
- *include-coda*—Specifies the path to a Web resource to be included at the end of the JSP page
- *description*—A text description of the filter
- *display-name*—A short, descriptive name that can be used by tools while displaying the filter configuration

- *icon*—The icon element specifies icons that can be used by GUI tools to symbolically represent the filter. It has two sub-elements: a small-icon and large-icon (see the icon element, described in more detail earlier in the chapter).

The `jsp-config` element for the example JSPs bundled along with Tomcat is shown here:

```
    <jsp-config>
            <taglib>
               <taglib-uri>
               http://jakarta.apache.org/tomcat/examples-taglib
           </taglib-uri>
               <taglib-location>/WEB-INF/jsp/example-taglib.tld</taglib-location>
            </taglib>

            <taglib>
         <taglib-uri>
               http://jakarta.apache.org/tomcat/jsp2-example-taglib
               </taglib-uri>
               <taglib-location>
                   /WEB-INF/jsp2/jsp2-example-taglib.tld
               </taglib-location>
            </taglib>

           <jsp-property-group>
               <description>
                 Special property group for JSP Configuration JSP example
               </description>
               <display-name>JSPConfiguration</display-name>
               <url-pattern>/jsp2/misc/config.jsp</url-pattern>
               <el-ignored>true</el-ignored>
               <page-encoding>ISO-8859-1</page-encoding>
               <scripting-invalid>true</scripting-invalid>
               <include-prelude>/jsp2/misc/prelude.jspf</include-prelude>
               <include-coda>/jsp2/misc/coda.jspf</include-coda>
           </jsp-property-group>
</jsp-config>
```

listener

The `listener` element specifies the deployment properties for an application listener bean. It has the following sub-elements:

- *`listener-class`*—The fully qualified class name of the Java class corresponding to the listener
- *`description`*—A text description of the listener
- *`display-name`*—A short, descriptive name that can be used by tools while displaying the listener configuration
- *`icon`*—The icon element specifies icons that can be used by GUI tools to symbolically represent the listener. It has two sub-elements: a small-icon and large-icon (see the icon element, described in more detail earlier in the chapter).

A sample listener element is shown here:

```
<listener>
    <listener-class>listeners.ContextListener</listener-class>
</listener>
<listener>
    <listener-class>listeners.SessionListener</listener-class>
</listener>
```

locale-encoding-mapping-list

This element contains the `locale-encoding-mapping` element that specifies the mapping between the locale and the encoding. The `locale-encoding-mapping` element has two child elements:

- *`locale`*—The locale to be encoded
- *`encoding`*—The encoding to be used

A sample is shown here:

```
<locale-encoding-mapping-list>
    <locale-encoding-mapping>
        <locale>en</locale>
        <encoding>en_US</encoding>
    </locale-encoding-mapping>
</locale-encoding-mapping-list>
```

login-config

This element is used to configure the authentication method, the Realm name, and the attributes needed for `FORM`-based login. It has the following child elements:

- *`auth-method`*—The authentication method to be used. It must be one of the following: `BASIC`, `DIGEST`, `FORM`, or `CLIENT-CERT`.

- *realm-name*—The name of the Realm
- *form-login-config*—If FORM-based authentication is used, this element is used to configure it. It specifies the form's login page (form-login-page element) and the error page (form-error-page element).

The login-config element is described in more detail in Chapter 15. A sample login-config is shown here:

```
<!-- Default login configuration uses form-based authentication -->
<login-config>
    <auth-method>FORM</auth-method>
    <realm-name>Example Form-Based Authentication Area</realm-name>
    <form-login-config>
        <form-login-page>/security/protected/login.jsp</form-login-page>
        <form-error-page>/security/protected/error.jsp</form-error-page>
    </form-login-config>
</login-config>
```

message-destination

The message-destination element specifies a message destination. The destination specified here is mapped to a physical destination by the deployer. It consists of the following child elements

- *message-destination-name*—The name of the message destination. This name must be unique across all message destinations described in the deployment descriptor.
- *description*—A text description of the destination
- *display-name*—A short, descriptive name that can be used by tools while displaying the destination
- *icon*—The icon element specifies icons that can be used by GUI tools to symbolically represent the message-destination. It has two sub-elements: a small-icon and large-icon (see the icon element, described in more detail earlier in the chapter).

message-destination-ref

The message-destination-ref element declares a reference to a message destination associated with a resource in the deployment component's environment. It consists of the following child elements:

- *message-destination-ref-name*—Name of the message destination reference. This name is a JNDI name, relative to the java:comp/env context, and must be unique within the deployment descriptor.
- *message-destination-type*—Type of the destination. The type is specified as a fully qualified Java interface that is implemented by the destination.
- *message-destination-usage*—Specifies the use of the message destination. The destination is used for consuming messages (Consumes), producing messages (Produces), or both (Both).

- `message-destination-link`—Links the message destination reference to a message destination (see the `message-destination` element described earlier) or a message-driven bean. This value should match the `message-destination-name` defined in the `message-destination` element.
- `description`—Used for documentation

mime-mapping

The `mime-mapping` element specifies the mapping between the extension for a resource and its MIME type. It has two child elements for this: `extension` and `mime-type`. A sample `mime-mapping` is shown in the following example:

```
<mime-mapping>
    <extension>pdf</extension>
    <mime-type>application/pdf</mime-type>
</mime-mapping>
```

resource-env-ref

This element contains a reference to the administered object associated with a resource. It has the following child elements:

- `resource-env-ref-name`—Name of the resource environment reference. This name is a JNDI name, relative to the `java:comp/env` context, and must be unique within the deployment descriptor.
- `resource-env-ref-type`—The type of the resource environment reference. This must be the fully qualified name of a Java class or interface.
- `description`—Used for documentation

resource-ref

The `resource-ref` element specifies a reference to an external resource. It consists of the following child elements:

- `res-ref-name`—Name of the resource manager connection factory reference. This name is a JNDI name, relative to the `java:comp/env` context, and must be unique within the deployment descriptor.
- `res-type`—Type of the data source. The type is specified as a fully qualified Java class or interface that is implemented by the data source.
- `res-auth`—Specifies whether the deployment component code signs on programmatically to the resource manager (Application), or whether the container signs on to the resource manager on its behalf (Container). If the container handles this, the deployer needs to supply information for the sign on.
- `res-sharing-scope`—Specifies if the connections obtained through the resource manager are sharable (Sharable) or not (Unsharable)
- `description`—Used for documentation

The example `resource-ref` element shown here is reference to a JDBC DataSource:

```
<!-- JDBC DataSources (java:comp/env/jdbc) -->
  <resource-ref>
      <description>The default JDBC datasource</description>
      <res-ref-name>jdbc/DefaultDS</res-ref-name>
      <res-type>javax.sql.DataSource</res-type>
      <res-auth>Container</res-auth>
  </resource-ref>
```

security-constraint

This element specifies the security constraints on one or more Web resource collections, as follows:

- *`display-name`*—The display name for the security constraint
- *`web-resource-collection`*—Specifies the resources (`url-pattern` element) and the HTTP methods (`http-method` element) that are allowed on these resources
- *`auth-constraint`*—Indicates the user roles (`role-name` element) that are permitted to access the Web resources protected by this security constraint. These role names must match those defined in the `security-role` element described later in the chapter. The pattern `*` matches all roles defined in the Web application.
- *`user-data-constraint`*—Specifies how the data transmitted between the client and the Servlet container is protected. This is done via its `transport-guarantee` child element, and it can be set to `NONE`, `INTEGRAL`, or `CONFIDENTIAL`.

A sample `security-constraint` is shown in the following example:

```
<security-constraint>
      <display-name>Example Security Constraint</display-name>
      <web-resource-collection>
           <web-resource-name>Protected Area</web-resource-name>
               <!-- Define the context-relative URL(s) to be protected -->
           <url-pattern>/security/protected/*</url-pattern>
               <!-- If you list http methods, only those methods are protected -->
               <http-method>DELETE</http-method>
           <http-method>GET</http-method>
           <http-method>POST</http-method>
               <http-method>PUT</http-method>
      </web-resource-collection>
      <auth-constraint>
           <!-- Anyone with one of the listed roles may access this area -->
           <role-name>tomcat</role-name>
               <role-name>role1</role-name>
      </auth-constraint>
  </security-constraint>
```

security-role

The `security-role` element lists all the security roles used in the Web application. These role names are specified via the `role-name` child element, and are used in the `security-constraint` (see the previous element) to specify the security constraints for a Web application. A sample `security-role` element is shown in the following example that corresponds to the role used in the `security-constraint` in the previous example:

```
<security-role>
    <role-name>role1</role-name>
</security-role>
<security-role>
    <role-name>tomcat</role-name>
</security-role>
```

service-ref

A `service-ref` element declares a reference to a Web service. It consists of the following child elements:

- *`service-ref-name`*—The logical name that components in the module use to look up the service. It is recommended that this name start with `/service/`.
- *`service-interface`*—The fully qualified class name of the JAX-RPC Service interface on which the client depends
- *`wsdl-file`*—The URI location for the WSDL file. The location is relative to the Web application root.
- *`jaxrpc-mapping-file`*—File that specifies the JAX-RPC mapping between the Java interfaces used by the application and the descriptions in the WSDL file
- *`service-qname`*—The name of the WSDL service element
- *`port-component-reference`*—This element declares the service endpoint interface or provides the link to a port component that specifies this. It has two child elements:
    - *`service-endpoint-interface`*—A fully qualified Java class that represents the service endpoint interface of a WSDL port
    - *`port-component-link`*—Links the port component reference to a specific port component
- *`handler`*—Declares the handler for the port component. This in turn has a number of child elements:
    - *`handler-name`*—Name of the handler. The name must be unique within the module.
    - *`handler-class`*—Fully qualified Java class name for the handler
    - *`init-param`*—This contains parameter name (`param-name`) and value (`param-value`) pairs for initialization parameters.
    - *`soap-header`*—Qualified name (QName) of the SOAP header that will be processed by this handler

    - *soap-role*—SOAP actor definitions that the handler will play as a role
    - *port-name*—WSDL port name that the handler is associated with
- *description*—A text description of the service reference
- *display-name*—A short, descriptive name that can be used by tools while displaying the service reference
- *icon*—The `icon` element specifies icons that can be used by GUI tools to symbolically represent the element. It has two sub-elements: a `small-icon` and `large-icon` (see the `icon` element, described in more detail earlier in the chapter).

servlet

The `servlet` element is used to configure a Servlet or JSP file. It consists of the following child elements:

- *servlet-name*—The name of the Servlet. This must be unique across the Web application.
- *servlet-class*—The fully qualified Java class name of the Servlet
- *jsp-file*—The full path of the JSP file within the Web application (that is, beginning from /). If the `load-on-startup` element is enabled (described later), then the JSP should be pre-compiled.

  Only one of the ***servlet-class*** or ***jsp-file*** elements should be specified.
- *init-param*—The `init-param` element is used to pass initialization time parameters to the Servlet. This is done via its `param-name` and `param-value` elements. It also has a `description` element that is used to document the parameters.
- *load-on-startup*—The `load-on-startup` element indicates to the Servlet container that this Servlet should be loaded at startup time. This element can also contain an optional positive integer value that specifies the startup sequence (lower-integer-valued Servlets are loaded before the higher-integer-valued ones). A negative or missing value indicates that the order doesn't matter.
- *run-as*—The security role to be used for the execution of the Servlet or JSP page. This has two child elements: an optional `description` and a `role-name` that specifies the role.
- *security-role-ref*—This element declares the security role reference in a component's code. It consists of the security role name (`role-name` element) and a link to the security role (`role-link` element). It also has an optional `description` element, again used for documentation purposes.
- *description*—A text description of the listener
- *display-name*—A short, descriptive name that can be used by tools while displaying the listener configuration
- *icon*—The `icon` element specifies icons that can be used by GUI tools to symbolically represent the listener. It has two sub-elements: a `small-icon` and `large-icon` (see the `icon` element, described in more detail earlier in the chapter).

A sample servlet element is shown here:

```
<servlet>
    <servlet-name>org.apache.jsp.num.numguess_jsp</servlet-name>
    <servlet-class>org.apache.jsp.num.numguess_jsp</servlet-class>
</servlet>
```

servlet-mapping

The `servlet-mapping` element defines the mapping between a Servlet (`servlet-name` element) and a URL pattern (`url-pattern` element). The `servlet-name` must match the name defined in the `servlet` element, as shown in the following example:

```
<servlet-mapping>
    <servlet-name>org.apache.jsp.num.numguess_jsp</servlet-name>
    <url-pattern>/num/numguess.jsp</url-pattern>
</servlet-mapping>
```

session-config

This element defines the session parameters for the Web application. It has a `session-timeout` element, which specifies the default session timeout interval, in minutes, for all sessions for this application. The following example specifies a session timeout of 30 minutes:

```
<session-config>
     <session-timeout>30</session-timeout>
</session-config>
```

If set to 0 (zero) or less, the session is set to never timeout.

welcome-file-list

This element contains an ordered list of welcome files (for example, `index.html`), and is specified via the `welcome-file` child element. This file is displayed when someone browses to the Web application URL:

```
http://hostname:port/<web application name>/
```

Following is a sample `welcome-file-list` element:

```
<welcome-file-list>
    <welcome-file>index.jsp<welcome-file>
    <welcome-file>index.html<welcome-file>
    <welcome-file>home.html<welcome-file>
  </welcome-file-list>
```

If more than one of these files are present in the Web application, then the order in which they are specified determines which one is shown — the file listed earlier has higher precedence. If none of the files in the example list are found, then, depending on the configuration, an HTTP 404–Not Found error message is displayed.

Summary

Configuring Web applications on production and test systems is an important part of an administrator's job. This involves tasks such as adding or removing filters for given URL patterns, session configuration, error page configuration, the addition of tag libraries, and the configuration of initialization parameters for the Web application. Understanding the Web application structure, and the deployment descriptor is, therefore, important for administrators. This chapter focused on these issues, and described the various elements that make up a Web application. It highlighted the following aspects:

- The directory structure for a typical Web application
- A detailed examination of both the Servlet 2.3-style (DTD-based) deployment descriptor and the Servlet 2.4-style (schema-based) deployment descriptor.

Chapter 7 covers how Web applications are managed within Tomcat.

7

Web Application Administration

This chapter discusses the management of Web applications using tools available with Tomcat versions 4.x and 5.x. Tomcat's management tools include the `manager` application and the `admin` application. The `manager` application helps manage Web application deployment. It enables administrators to deploy Web applications, view deployed applications, and finally undeploy them. While these tasks can also be performed manually by editing Tomcat's configuration files, this method requires Tomcat to be restarted. The `manager` application automates these tasks and enables them to be performed on a running instance of Tomcat. This way, applications that are already running are left undisturbed.

The `admin` application enables management of the Tomcat server itself: You can add, delete, or modify Connectors, Hosts, and Context; manage Resources such as DataSources and Environment parameters, and manage users and roles. In short, it provides a Web-based GUI for tasks that otherwise would require editing Tomcat's configuration files (`server.xml`, `tomcat-users.xml`, and so on) and restarting the Tomcat server.

Chapter 5 discussed the `admin` application, along with basic Tomcat configuration. This chapter covers the `manager` application. The chapter first looks at a sample Web application that is used as an example throughout the chapter. Then it discusses in detail the `manager` application, including the following areas:

- Enabling access to the `manager` application
- The three ways of interacting with the `manager` application (via HTTP commands, Ant scripts, and the new Web-based user interface)
- Security considerations while using the `manager` application

Sample Web Application

This chapter uses a simple Web application for testing the `manager` commands. This application consists of nothing more than one HTML file and one JSP file.

The HTML file (`index.html`) contains a form that asks for the user's name and uses HTTP POST to send the result to a JSP page:

```
<html>
  <head>
    <title>Hello Web Application</title>
  </head>

  <body>
    <h1>Hello Web Application</h1>
    <form action="/hello/hello.jsp" method="POST" >
      <table width="75%">
        <tr>
          <td width="48%">What is your name?</td>
          <td width="52%">
            <input type="text" name="name" />
          </td>
        </tr>
      </table>
      <p>
        <input type="submit" name="Submit" value="Submit name" />
        <input type="reset" name="Reset" value="Reset form" />
      </p>
    </form>
  </body>
</html>
```

The JSP page (`hello.jsp`) then prints a `Hello` `<name>` message. The `<name>` portion is the name that the user entered in the `index.html` form:

```
<html>
  <head>
    <title>Hello Web Application</title>
  </head>
  <body>
    <h1>Hello Web Application</h1>
    <br/><br/>

    <%
    String name   = request.getParameter("name");
    if (name.trim().length() == 0) {
    %>
      You didn't tell me your name!<br><br><br>
    <%
    } else {
    %>
      Hello <%=name%><br><br><br>
```

```
    <%
    }
    %>
    <a href="/hello/index.html">Try again?</a>
  </body>
</html>
```

This Web application will be deployed with the `/hello` context path; therefore, `http://localhost:8080/hello/index.html` would be the URL to access it.

The commands for building the WAR file are as follows:

```
$ cd /path/to/hello
$ jar cvf hello.war.
```

The `/path/to/hello` is the directory in which the `index.html` and `hello.jsp` files reside.

Tomcat Manager Application

The Tomcat `manager` application is a Web application that enables you to carry out various system administration tasks related to deploying, undeploying, and managing a Web application.

Following are the three ways of interacting with the `manager` application:

- *Using HTTP requests*—This can be done either via the browser or by writing scripts to automate the process. The section "Tomcat Manager: Using HTTP Requests," later in this chapter covers this in more detail.
- *Using the Ant based interface*—This is discussed in the section "Tomcat Manager: Managing Applications with Ant," later in this chapter.
- *Using the Web interface to the Admin application*—This is discussed in the section "Tomcat Manager: Web Interface," later in this chapter.

Future versions of Tomcat might add a Web Service interface, thus enabling easier integration of the Tomcat management tasks from third-party applications.

Access to the `manager` application is restricted to authorized users. This prevents unauthorized users from undeploying (or deploying) applications, or performing any other operation that they shouldn't. The next section discusses how this access control is configured, and then examines the other configuration parameters for the `manager` application. Finally, it describes all the `manager` application commands in more detail.

Following is a summary of some of the tasks that the `manager` application can perform:

- Deploy a new Web application
- List the currently deployed Web applications, as well as the sessions that are currently active for those Web applications
- Reload an existing Web application

- List the available global JNDI resources
- List the available security roles
- Start a stopped application
- Stop an existing application, but not undeploy it
- Undeploy a Web application
- Display session statistics

An application can be deployed manually, too. Following are the ways to do this:

- Add a `<Context>` entry in Tomcat's `server.xml` configuration file. This enables you to place the Web application in a location other than the default `$CATALINA_HOME/webapps` directory.
- Copy the entire application directory into the `$CATALINA_HOME/webapps` directory. The `server.xml` file does not have to be edited in this case.
- Copy the WAR file for the application into the `$CATALINA_HOME/webapps` directory. In this option, too, the `server.xml` file does not have to be edited.

However, there are advantages to using a `manager` application. First, all these ways of deploying just described require you to restart Tomcat. When deploying is done via the `manager` application, Tomcat is not restarted and, hence, the other running Web applications are not affected.

Alternatively, the `autoDeploy` attribute in the `Host` (see `server.xml`) could be set to `true`, which is actually the default in Tomcat 5.x. This would cause any Web application dropped into Tomcat's application base to be deployed automatically. Doing this compromises performance, however, because Tomcat must continually monitor the application base directory; hence, `autoDeploy` is often set to `false`.

Another advantage of using the `manager` application is that it supports remote installs. That is, the Web application directory (or WAR file) doesn't need to be transferred via FTP or some other means to the host machine running Tomcat. The `deploy` command takes care of transferring the Web application WAR file from the local development machine to the remote machine running the Tomcat server.

Enabling Access to the Manager Application

Before using the `manager` application, the server needs to be configured to enable access. Access to this application is controlled via a Security Realm. Any Realm implementation can be used (Memory, User Database, JDBC, JNDI, or JAAS). This example uses a User Database Realm for simplicity.

In a User Database Realm, the user names and their supporting information are stored in memory and are initialized at startup from an XML configuration file (`$CATALINA_HOME/conf/tomcat-users.xml`) kept on the file system. This file needs to be edited to add a user with a role of `manager`. In the following entry, the user name and password for this role are `"admin"` and `"secret"` respectively:

```
<tomcat-users>
  ...
  <user username="admin" password="secret" roles="manager" />
  ...
</tomcat-users>
```

Tomcat now needs to be restarted to make it re-read the `tomcat-users.xml` file. To determine whether the `manager` application setup was successful, browse to the default Tomcat URL (`http://localhost:8080`), and click the Tomcat Manager link. The user is then prompted for a user name and password. After entering the values set in the `tomcat-users.xml` file, the Web page of the `manager` application shown in Figure 7-1 should be displayed.

Figure 7-1: The Tomcat Web Application Manager.

As you can see in the figure, the response for a successful command execution (the `Message` parameter) is an `OK` string. A missing `OK` is an indication of failure, and the rest of the message provides the cause. The possible causes of failure for each command are listed later in this chapter in the section "Possible Errors."

During installation of Tomcat 4.1 and 5.x on Windows using the installer executable (and not the zip file), the installer asks the user for the admin user name and password. The user name and password entered at install time are used to generate entries for the **`tomcat-users.xml`** *file for both the* **`manager`** *and* **`admin`** *Web applications. Hence, no configuration is needed in this case, unless another user with manager privileges is to be added or the manager password is to be changed.*

Manager Application Configuration

The previous section looked at tomcat-users.xml, which defines the user name and password for the manager role. The other manager application related configuration parameters are the **manager context entry** and the **deployment descriptor.**

No changes have to be made for the manager application to work—the settings are configured by default. They can, however, be modified for deployment requirements—for example, to change the security constraints for the manager application, to change the authentication mechanism for users in the manager role, or even to change the name of the role from "manager" to some other name if required. This section covers these configurable parameters for the manager application.

Manager Application Context Entry

In Tomcat 4.0, the manager context is configured in the same way as the other application contexts. Following is the default configuration for the manager application from the $CATALINA_HOME/conf/server.xml file:

```
<!-- Tomcat Manager Context -->
<Context path="/manager" docBase="manager" debug="0" privileged="true"/>
```

In Tomcat 4.1 and 5.x, the configuration information for the manager application is picked up from the manager.xml file. The default manager context from the configuration file is listed here:

```
<Context path="/manager" docBase="../server/webapps/manager"
        debug="0" privileged="true">

  <!-- Link to the user database we will get roles from -->
  <ResourceLink name="users" global="UserDatabase"
               type="org.apache.catalina.UserDatabase"/>
</Context>
```

The manager.xml file is located under $CATALINA_HOME/webapps/ for Tomcat 4.1 and under the application base for your host in Tomcat 5.x (for example, $CATALINA_HOME/conf/Catalina/localhost). If you have multiple virtual hosts, you need to configure a manager for each virtual host via a manager.xml file.

The Context entry specifies the context path for the manager application via the path and the document base directory for the Web application via the docBase attribute ("../server/webapps/manager"). The privileged attribute is set to true. This enables the application to access the container's Servlets. This attribute is false for a normal Web application deployed in Tomcat. The <ResourceLink> element creates a link to a global JNDI resource database from which the user names and roles are retrieved.

Manager Application Deployment Descriptor

The tomcat-users.xml file shown earlier defined the user name and password for the manager role. This section discusses how the security constraints for this role are specified. The deployment descriptor for the Tomcat 4.0 manager application is $CATALINA_HOME/webapps/manager/WEB-INF/web.xml. In Tomcat 4.1 and 5.x, the web.xml file is in $CATALINA_HOME/server/webapps/manager/WEB-INF.

The `web.xml` defines, among other things, the security constraints on the `manager` application. The following snippet describes the default security constraint definition for the `manager` Web application. The `<role-name>` defined here (shown in bold) specifies that only users in that role can access the `manager` Web application:

```
<!-- Define a Security Constraint on this Application -->
<security-constraint>
    <web-resource-collection>
      <web-resource-name>HTMLManger and Manager command</web-resource-name>
      <url-pattern>/jmxproxy/*</url-pattern>
      <url-pattern>/html/*</url-pattern>
      <url-pattern>/list</url-pattern>
      <url-pattern>/sessions</url-pattern>
      <url-pattern>/start</url-pattern>
      <url-pattern>/stop</url-pattern>
      <url-pattern>/install</url-pattern>
      <url-pattern>/remove</url-pattern>
      <url-pattern>/deploy</url-pattern>
      <url-pattern>/undeploy</url-pattern>
      <url-pattern>/reload</url-pattern>
      <url-pattern>/save</url-pattern>
      <url-pattern>/serverinfo</url-pattern>
      <url-pattern>/status/*</url-pattern>
      <url-pattern>/roles</url-pattern>
      <url-pattern>/resources</url-pattern>
    </web-resource-collection>
    <auth-constraint>
       <!-- NOTE:  This role is not present in the default users file -->
       <role-name>manager</role-name>
    </auth-constraint>
  </security-constraint>
```

The authentication mechanism for the `manager` application is also defined here. The default setting is `BASIC` authentication. Administrators could set up a more rigorous mechanism for `manager` application authentication—for example a client-certificate-based mechanism (`<auth-method>` set to `CLIENT-CERT`):

```
<login-config>
    <auth-method>BASIC</auth-method>
    <realm-name>Tomcat Manager Application</realm-name>
  </login-config>
```

The `<security-role>` lists all the roles that can log in to the `manager` application. In this case, it is restricted to only one user role (that is, the `manager` role):

```
<!-- Security roles referenced by this web application -->
<security-role>
  <description>
    The role that is required to log in to the Manager Application
  </description>
  <role-name>manager</role-name>
</security-role>
```

Tomcat Manager: Using HTTP Requests

The manager application commands that are issued via the Web browser have the following format:

```
http://{hostname}:{portnumber}/manager/{command}?{parameters}
```

In this command, the various parts are as follows:

- hostname — The host on which the Tomcat instance is running
- portnumber — The port on which the Tomcat instance is running
- command — The manager command to be run. The allowed values for command are list, sessions, start, stop, install, remove, deploy, undeploy, reload, serverinfo, roles, resources, status, and jmxproxy. These commands are covered in more detail later in this chapter.
- parameters — The parameters passed to the commands listed above. These are command-specific, and are explained in detail along with the specific command below. Many of these parameters contain the context path to the Web application (the path parameter) and the URL to the Web application file (the war parameter). The context path for the ROOT application is an empty string. For all other Web applications, the context path must be preceded by a slash (/). The URL to the Web application can be in one of the following formats:
    - file:/absolute/path/to/a/directory — This specifies the absolute path to a directory in which a Web application is present in an unpackaged form. This entire path is then added as the context path of the Web application in Tomcat's configuration.
    - file:/absolute/path/to/a/webapp.war — This specifies the absolute path to a WAR file. The Tomcat documentation states that this format is not allowed for the install command. However, our tests with Tomcat 4.1.3 indicate that it works fine for install, too.
    - jar:file:/absolute/path/to/a/warfile.war!/ — The jar protocol enables the specifying of the URL for a WAR file. This is handled by the java.net.JarURLConnection that provides a URL connection to a JAR/WAR file. Here, the URL specified is for a file on the local file system.
    - file:/absolute/path/to/a/context.xml — This specifies the absolute path to the context configuration file. This is an XML file that contains the <Context> configuration for the Web application.
    - directory — This is the directory name for the Web application within the Tomcat application base directory. The application base directory is typically $CATALINA_HOME/webapps.
    - webapp.war — This is the directory name for the Web application archive (that is, WAR file). This WAR file is looked for in the Tomcat application base directory (typically, $CATALINA_HOME/webapps).

The !/ characters at the end of these URLs enable them to be used in a Web browser and not cause the default MIME type action for the .war extension to take effect. For example, if the following URL is used to install a Web application and the !/ is omitted at the end, the user may be prompted to (depending on how the browser's MIME settings are configured) save to disk, open the file in the browser, or open the file in an application (for example, Winzip):

```
http://localhost:8080/manager/install?path=/hello&war=jar:file:/path/to/hello.war!/
```

Numerous problems can occur while working with the `manager` application. The possible causes of failure are listed later in this chapter in the section "Possible Errors."

List Deployed Applications

The format for the `list` command URL that lists all deployed and installed applications is as follows:

```
http://{hostname}:{portnumber}/manager/list
```

Figure 7-2 shows the `list` command being run.

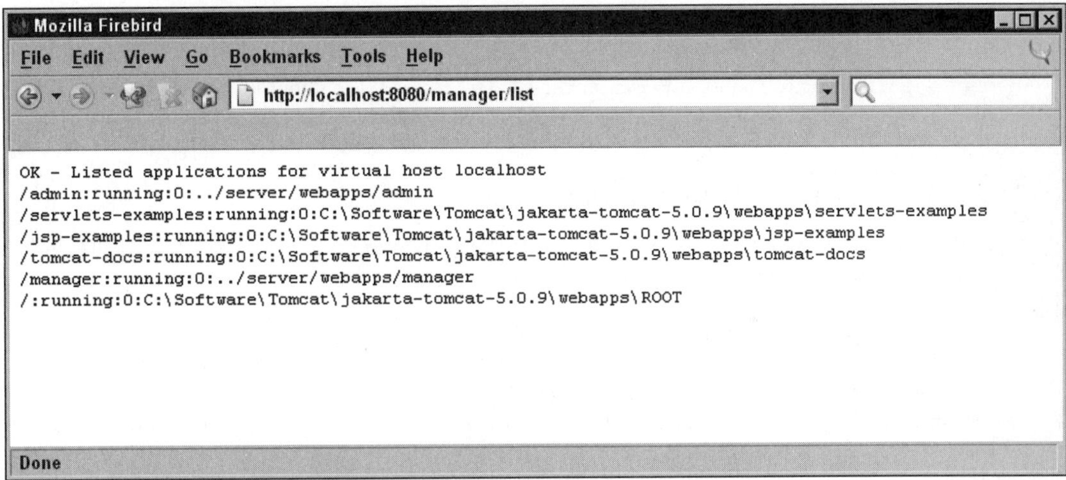

Figure 7-2: Listing deployed applications.

As shown in the figure, the response for a successful command execution begins with an `OK` string (`OK – Listed applications of virtual host {hostname}`). A missing `OK` is an indication of failure, and the rest of the response page provides the cause(s). The possible causes of failure for each command are covered later in the chapter. The response page is in the `text/plain` format (that is, it contains no HTML markup).

The data fields returned in a manager command response are always delimited by the colon (:) character. In Figure 7-2, each line indicates the (unique) context path of the Web application, the status (running or stopped), the number of active sessions for the application, and the document base for the Web application.

These conventions enable scripts to be written that retrieve the output of the `manager` command and perform appropriate actions.

Installing/Deploying Applications in Tomcat 4.x

Tomcat 4.x has both an install command and a deploy command. At first glance, these look the same. However, there are differences as far as the Tomcat manager application is concerned.

When a Web application is deployed, it makes permanent changes to Tomcat's configuration, so the Web application is available across Tomcat restarts. The install option, however, does not make permanent changes to Tomcat's configuration. Thus, the install command is useful for test purposes. Developers can build a Web application, install it, and then try it out. Once it is sufficiently robust, it can then be deployed via the deploy command to permanently place it into a Tomcat installation.

Furthermore, the deploy command enables administrators to deploy a Web application remotely. With install, the Web application JAR file (or the extracted Web application path) must be on the same machine as that of the Tomcat instance.

The undeploy and uninstall commands undo the effects of deploy and install. These are discussed later in this chapter.

However, note that Tomcat 4.0 has a command called install that actually has an effect similar (though not identical) to the deploy command in Tomcat 4.1. The Tomcat documentation, to help matters, calls it the command to deploy applications (even though the name of the command is install).

Deploying a New Application

The deploy command is used to deploy a Web application to a running instance of Tomcat. The effect of this command is as follows:

- The WAR file for the Web application is uploaded from the client machine to the machine on which Tomcat is running, and copied into the application base directory of the given virtual host. For example, if the virtual host name configured in server.xml were localhost itself, the WAR file would be copied under $CATALINA_HOME/work/Standalone/localhost/manager.
- The client machine may very well be the same machine on which Tomcat is running.
- An entry for the Web application's context is added into Tomcat's run-time data structures.
- The Web application is loaded.
- The WAR file can contain a <Context> element definition (META-INF/context.xml), and this would take precedence over the default Context that the manager application generates for it.

The general format for the deploy command is as follows:

```
http://{hostname}:{portnumber}/manager/deploy?path={context_path}
```

Here, hostname and portnumber are the host and port for the Tomcat instance, and context_path is the context path for the application. The WAR file to be deployed is passed inside the request data of the HTTP PUT request. Therefore, to deploy the hello application shown at the beginning of the chapter at the context path /hello, an HTTP PUT request would need to be directed to the URL http://{*hostname*}:{*portnumber*}/manager/deploy?path=/hello.

Because the WAR file is passed as the request data, this command cannot be invoked directly via a Web browser. Instead, it should be invoked from a tool — for example, within an Ant script (see the section "Tomcat Manager: Managing Applications with Ant," later in this chapter) or via the manager Web interface (see the section "Tomcat Manager: Web Interface," later in this chapter).

Essentially, the tool that sends the `deploy` command will have to build an HTTP request that looks something like the one shown in Figure 7-3, and execute an HTTP `PUT` command to send it over to the `manager` Servlet.

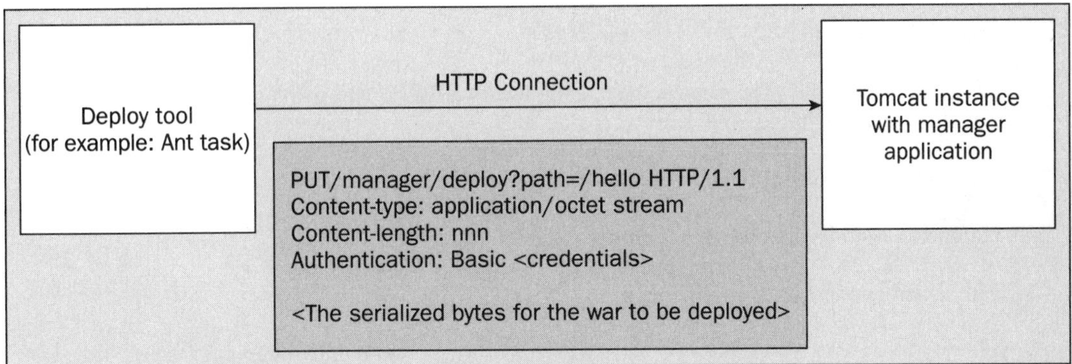

Figure 7-3: Deploy command sent over an HTTP connection.

A successful `deploy` command returns the success message "OK — Deployed application at context path {*context_path*}." If the operation failed, the error message would start with a `FAIL` string, and contain the cause for failure.

Recall that Tomcat 4.0 has an `install` command that it calls a `deploy` command! The behavior of the `install` command varies between versions 4.0 and 4.1. This difference is discussed in the next section.

Installing a New Application

The Tomcat 4.0 documentation says that the command called `install` **deploys** an application. This is true because this command has a permanent effect in Tomcat's configuration. The effect that the Tomcat 4.0 `install` command has is as follows:

1. The Web application WAR file (or extracted directory) is copied into the application base directory.
2. The Web application is started.
3. Tomcat's internal run-time data structures are updated to reflect the new application context.

The last two steps ensure that the new Web application is available for use immediately. The first step (the copying) makes the installation permanent (that is, across Tomcat restarts).

In Tomcat 4.1, the `install` option performs only the last two steps: It updates Tomcat's internal runtime data structures and starts the application. Thus, if Tomcat is restarted, the Web application is not reloaded. This is the correct behavior, because the `install` command is meant for developers to test new Web applications. Once they are happy with them, the `deploy` command (shown earlier) should be used to update Tomcat's installation.

The general format for the `install` command URL (in both Tomcat 4.0 and 4.1) is as follows:

```
http://{hostname}:{portnumber}/manager/install?path={context_path}&war={war_url}
```

To install from a WAR file, the following command is used. Here, `file:/path/to/hello.war` is the URL for the local file system location of `hello.war`:

```
http://localhost:8080/manager/install?path=/hello&war=jar:file:/path/to/hello.war!/
```

The extracted Web application can also be installed from a file system path (`/path/to/hello`). The following command entered via the browser does this:

```
http://localhost:8080/manager/install?path=/hello&war=file:/path/to/hello
```

The command assumes that the `hello` application is extracted into `/path/to/hello`.

The Windows version uses the following:

```
http://localhost:8080/manager/install?path=/hello&war=file:/C:\path\to\hello.war
```

If this succeeds, the message `OK—Installed application at context path /hello` is displayed in the browser window. If the operation fails, an appropriate error message is displayed.

Figure 7-4 shows the `hello` application WAR file (`hello.war`) being installed with the context path `/hello`:

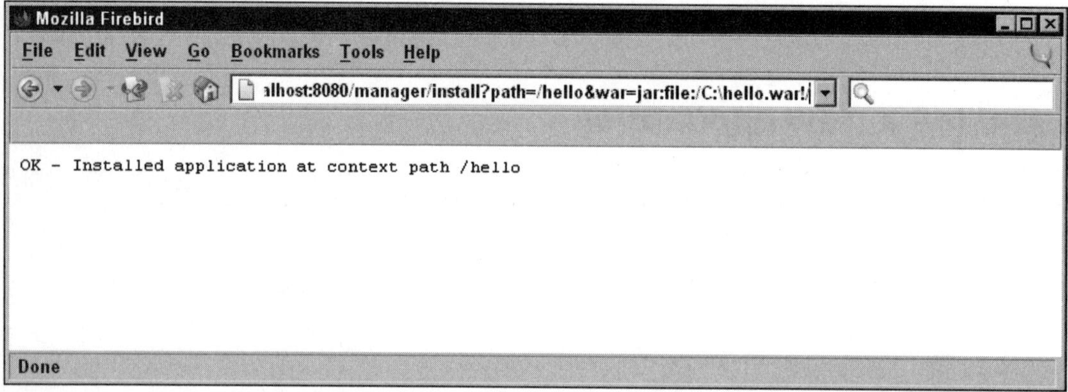

Figure 7-4: Installing a Web application from a WAR file in Tomcat 4.x.

If this command is rerun, it fails with an `Application already exists` error message, as shown in Figure 7-5. The context path for a Web application is unique. If an already installed application is to be updated, it needs to be either reloaded or removed and installed again. These options are covered later in this chapter:

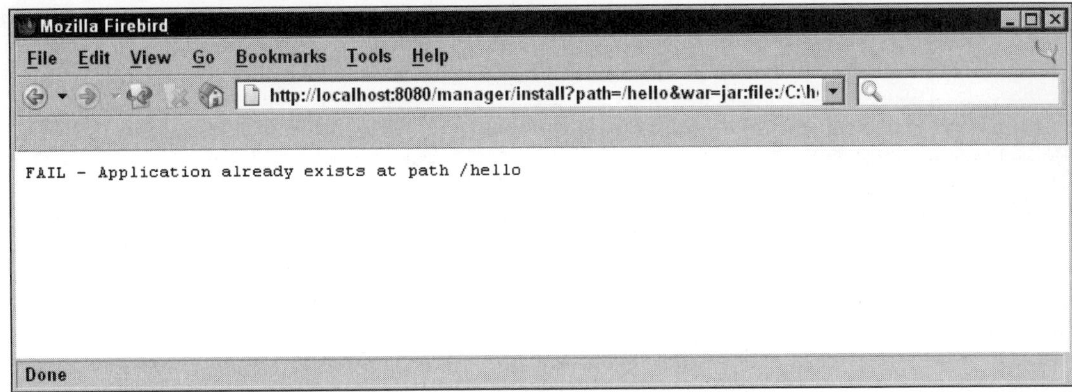

Figure 7-5: Error message returned after trying to install over an existing Web application in Tomcat 4.x.

Tomcat 4.1 introduces two new options in the `install` command (unfortunately, these are not listed in the current Tomcat documentation):

```
http://{hostname}:{portnumber}/manager/install?config={config_url}
http://{hostname}:{portnumber}/manager/install?config={config_url}&war={war_url}
```

The `config_url` is the URL for a context configuration file. This file contains the `<Context>` element entry for the Web application. The document base in the context is used to point to the location of the WAR file or to the directory in which the Web application is extracted. The second version of the command enables administrators to pass the URL to the WAR file (`war_url`). This overrides the document base specified in the context configuration file.

Installing/Deploying Applications in Tomcat 5.x

Tomcat 5.x simplifies the confusion around the 4.x `install`/`deploy` commands by having just one command: `deploy`. Correspondingly, there is no `uninstall` command in 5.x, just an `undeploy` command.

The `deploy` command enables Web applications to be deployed either from the local file system (local to the machine on which Tomcat is running) or remotely. The deployment changes are permanent (that is, it survives Tomcat restarts) until the application is undeployed.

Deploying a New Application Remotely

The minimum format for the remote `deploy` command is as follows:

```
http://{hostname}:{portnumber}/manager/deploy?path={context_path}
```

In addition to this, the (remote) `deploy` command can take three additional and optional parameters:

- `update`—When set to `true`, the previously deployed instance of the Web application will first be undeployed, and then the new one deployed. This defaults to `false`.
- `tag`—This assigns a version tag to the deployed Web application. This enables versioning of Web applications, and a subsequent redeployment of the Web application using only this version tag.

- `pause`—This property causes the Web application to be paused during the deployment so that incoming requests are not lost. The `pause` property defaults to `false`, and is used in conjunction with the `update` property.

Thus, deploying the `hello` Web application with default parameters and a tag of *hello_ver1* could look like the following:

```
http://localhost:8080/manager/deploy?path=/hello&update=false&tag=hello_ver1&pause=false
```

Because the WAR file is passed as the request data (via an HTTP `PUT`), this command cannot be invoked directly via a Web browser. Instead, it should be invoked from a tool—for example, within an Ant script (see the section "Tomcat Manager: Managing Applications with Ant," later in this chapter) or via the manager Web interface (see the section "Tomcat Manager: Web Interface," later in this chapter). This is similar to the `deploy` command in Tomcat 4.x (see the previous section).

Deploying a New Application from a Local Path

The `deploy` command also enables the installation of a Web application from a local path. That is, the Web application is present either as a WAR file or a directory on the same machine on which Tomcat is installed. The directory from which the Web application is installed must, as always, have a directory structure corresponding to the conventions of a Web application.

A lot of combinations are possible while deploying from a local path. These enable you to do the following:

- Install from a local directory or WAR file (anywhere on the file system)
- Install from a local directory or WAR file within the Tomcat application base
- Install using a Context configuration file
- Redeploy a previously deployed version of a Web application

If installation is being done from a file system location outside the Tomcat application base (`$CATALINA_HOME/webapps`), the fully qualified path to the WAR file or directory needs to be specified.

For example, the following is used to install from a directory:

```
http://localhost:8080/manager/deploy?path=/hello&war=file:/path/to/hello
```

Alternatively, the following is used from a WAR file:

```
http://localhost:8080/manager/deploy?war=jar:file:/path/to/hello.war!/
```

Figure 7-6 shows a deployment of a WAR file (`C:\hello.war`) with tag `hello_ver1`.

In the current version of Tomcat 5.x (5.0.9), a **`local path`** *deployment as shown above does not copy the WAR files into the Tomcat application base, and, hence, the deployment does not persist across Tomcat restarts. In this case, it behaves similarly to the Tomcat 4.1* **`install`** *command. Deployment on the local machine can also be done by copying the WAR file (or directory) to the application base. In this case, the deployment would naturally persist across Tomcat restarts.*

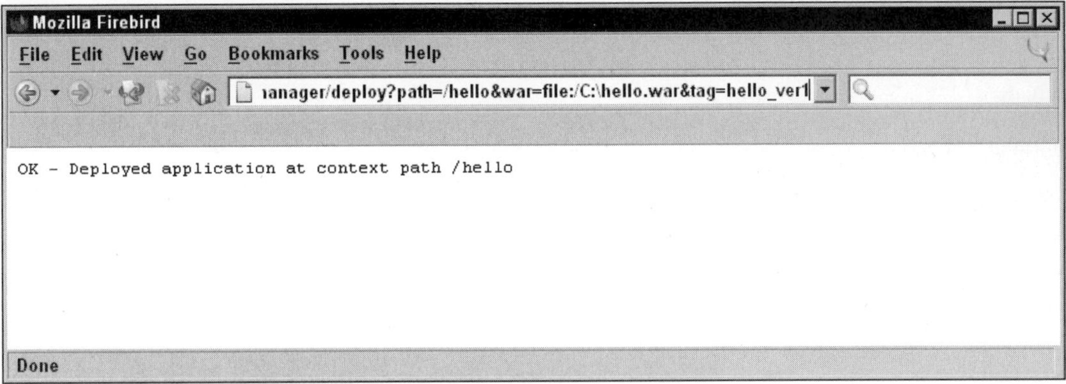

Figure 7-6: Deploying a Web application from a local path in Tomcat 5.x.

Another way to deploy is to first copy the directory or WAR file over to the Tomcat application base directory. If the `autoDeploy` attribute in the Host (see `server.xml`) had been set to `true` (that is, the default), the Web application would be automatically deployed once it was copied over. Because this is turned off for performance reasons (at least it should be), the administrator would need to deploy the Web application explicitly. As the directory or WAR file is copied to the application base directory (`$CATALINA_HOME/webapps`), the full pathname does not need to be specified (see Figure 7-7):

```
http://localhost:8080/manager/deploy?war=hello.war
```

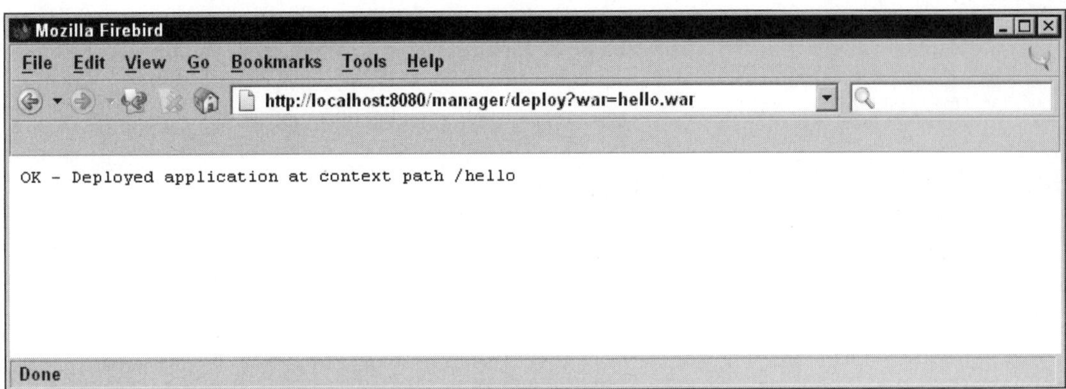

Figure 7-7: Deploying a Web application from a WAR file in Tomcat 5.x.

In this command, the Web application would be accessible under the context named `/hello`. If it is to be deployed under another context name (such as `/bye`), it could be specified as follows:

```
http://localhost:8080/manager/deploy?path=/bye&war=hello.war
```

In each of these cases, the WAR file or the expanded directory can contain a `context.xml` file with a `Context` entry for the Web application. The context file can, however, be overridden by specifying it in the following command:

```
http://localhost:8080/manager/deploy?config=file:/path/context.xml&war=jar:file:/path/hello.war!/
```

Finally, installation can be done via a `context.xml` file:

```
http://localhost:8080/manager/deploy?config=file:/path/context.xml
```

The `context.xml` in this case would contain the details for the Web application — the context name (`/hello`) and the `docBase`:

```
<Context path="/hello" docBase="/path/to/hello"
         debug="0">

  <!-- Link to the user database we will get roles from -->
  <ResourceLink name="users" global="UserDatabase"
                type="org.apache.catalina.UserDatabase"/>

</Context>
```

However, using a **`context.xml`** *file is subject to the* **`deployXML`** *flag in the Host element (***`server.xml`***). If this is set to* **`false`** *(the default is* **`true`***), applications cannot be installed via a context definition. Nor can they be installed outside the Host's config base directory (***`$CATALINA_HOME/conf/[engine_name]/[host_name]`***).*

If a Web application has already been deployed with a version tag (either remotely or locally), it can be redeployed using the tag name. This is very useful during development because it enables rolling back to an older version:

```
http://localhost:8080/manager/deploy?path=/hello&tag=hello_ver1
```

Another Host attribute to note for deploying Web applications is **`unpackWARs`***. This controls whether the WAR is unpacked into a directory (***`unpackWARs=true`***), or the Web application is run from a WAR file itself (***`unpackWARs=false`***).*

Reloading an Existing Application

An existing application can be reloaded by accessing the `manager` application via the following URL:

```
http://{hostname}:{portnumber}/manager/reload?path={context_path}
```

This causes the existing application to shut down and then restart. The application's deployment descriptor (`web.xml`) is not reread (at least not in the current version of Tomcat), even though the Tomcat documentation states that it is. This is a known bug, and it is expected that a future version of Tomcat will fix it. The workaround is to stop and then start the application again. The `server.xml` configuration file is not reread either, but this is by design.

The `reload` command is useful when a Web application has not been configured to be reloadable. A Web application's `<Context>` entry in the `server.xml` file has a `reloadable` attribute. When this attribute is set to `true`, Tomcat monitors all its classes in `/WEB-INF/classes` and `/WEB-INF/lib` and reloads the Web application if a change is detected. This causes a performance hit in production environments, as the class loader keeps comparing the date and time stamps for Servlets in memory with those on disk. To avoid this, the `reload` command can be used to make Tomcat reload the Web application when developers change any classes.

The standard Java class loader is designed to load a Java class just once. So how does the `reloadable` attribute work? Tomcat implements its own custom class loader that is used to reload the classes in `/WEB-INF/classes` and `/WEB-INF/lib` if required. Chapter 9 discusses this topic in more detail.

The current version of Tomcat supports reloading only if a Web application has been installed from an unpacked directory. It does not support reloading if the Web application has been installed from a WAR file. The workaround with a WAR file is to either restart Tomcat or remove and then deploy the application again.

Figure 7-8 shows the `hello` Web application being reloaded.

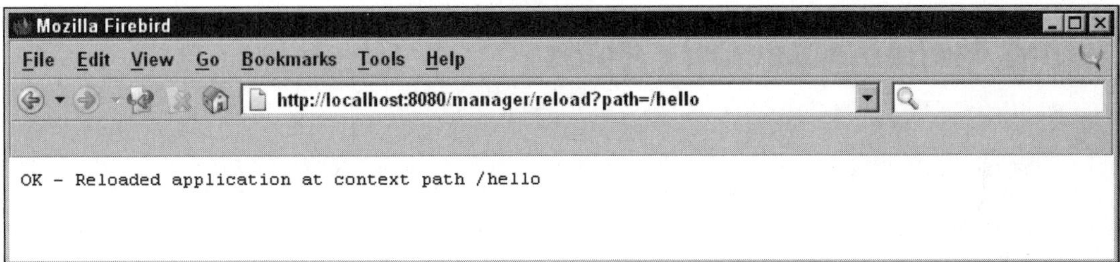

Figure 7-8: Reloading a Web application.

A successful execution of the `reload` command returns an `OK–Reloaded application at context path` *`{context_path}`* message, where *`{context_path}`* is the context path for the application.

Listing Available JNDI Resources

The general format of the URL for listing available JNDI resources is as follows:

```
http://{hostname}:{portnumber}/manager/resources[?type={jndi_type}]
```

In this URL, the `type` argument is optional. When it is not specified, all the available JNDI resources are listed. Otherwise, JNDI resources corresponding to the specified type alone are listed. The `type` field needs to be a fully qualified Java class name. For example, for JDBC data sources, the type needs to be specified as `javax.sql.DataSource`:

```
http://localhost:8080/manager/resources?type=javax.sql.DataSource
```

The response to this contains a success string (`OK–Listed global resources of all types` or `OK–Listed global resources of type {jndi_type}`), followed by information about the resources (one per line). Each line contains the global resource name and the global resource type. The global resource name is the name of the JNDI resource as specified in the `global` attribute of the `<ResourceLink>` element in Tomcat's configuration. The global resource type is the fully qualified Java class name of this JNDI resource (see Figure 7-9).

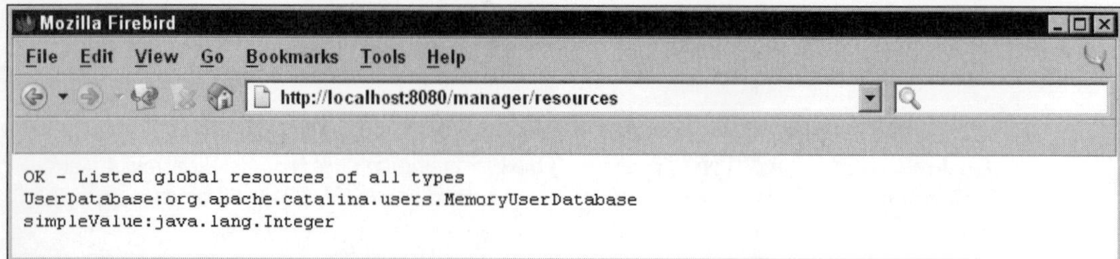

Figure 7-9: Listing JNDI resources.

Listing Available Security Roles

The URL for listing all security role names is as follows:

```
http://{hostname}:{portnumber}/manager/roles
```

On successful execution, the output of this command is an `OK – Listed security roles` message, followed by the security role name and a (optional) description. There is one security role listed per line, and the fields are separated by colons (`:`) as before, as shown in Figure 7-10.

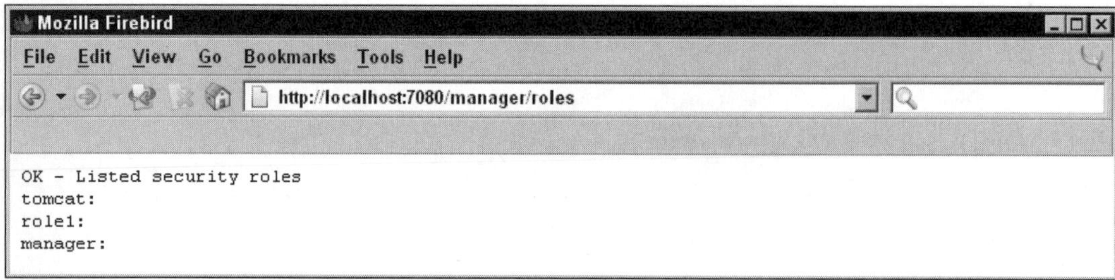

Figure 7-10: Listing available security roles.

The security roles listed by this command are those that are defined in the user database. The `manager` application's configuration defines the user database resource that should be searched for the roles in its `<ResourceLink>` section.

Listing OS and JVM Properties

The URL for listing these properties is as follows:

```
http://{hostname}:{portnumber}/manager/serverinfo
```

Figure 7-11 shows the `serverinfo` command being run. It displays the OS name, the OS version, and information about the Java Virtual Machine (JVM) being used.

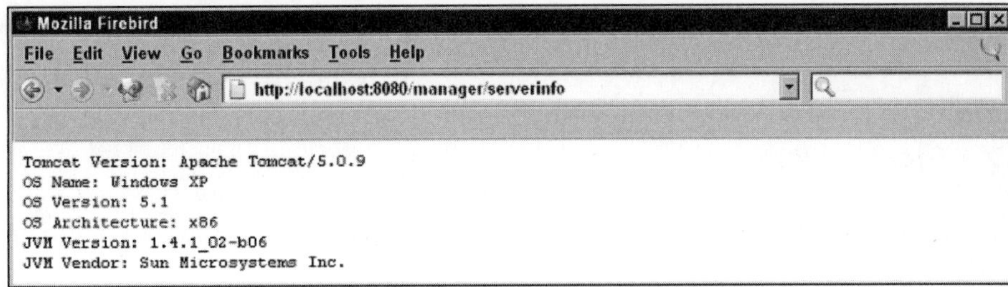

Figure 7-11: Listing OS and JVM properties.

Stopping an Existing Application

The `manager` application can be used to stop a running application. The following URL shows how this can be done:

```
http://{hostname}:{portnumber}/manager/stop?path={context_path}
```

This command sends a signal to the Web application to stop. This application is no longer available to users, though it still remains deployed. If the `list` command is run again, the state of the application is shown as "stopped" (see Figure 7-12).

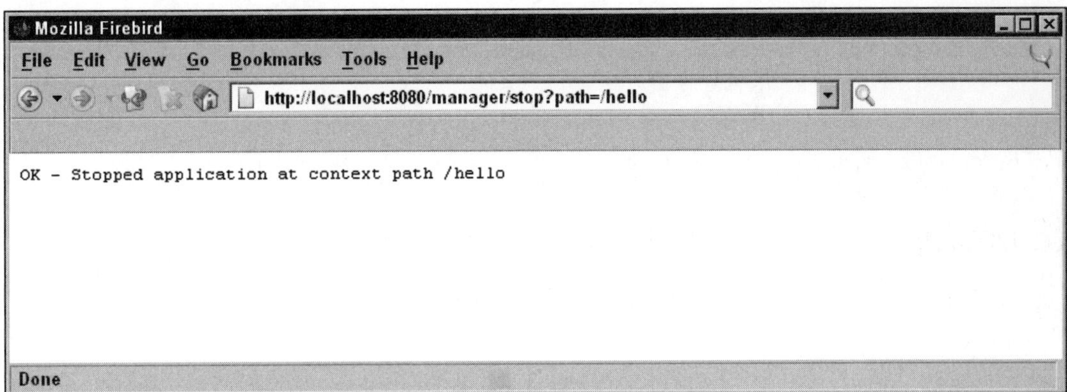

Figure 7-12: Stopping a Web application.

If the application stops successfully, the message `OK—Stopped application at context path {context_path}` is displayed. If the operation fails, a `FAIL` message with appropriate error information is shown. Stopping a Web application does not affect any Tomcat configuration information kept on the file system, so if Tomcat is restarted, the application is started, too.

The application can be restarted using the `start` command.

Starting a Stopped Application

The `manager` application can be used to start a stopped application. The following URL shows how this can be done:

```
http://{hostname}:{portnumber}/manager/start?path={context_path}
```

Here, *{context_path}* is the context path for the Web application (an empty string for the `ROOT` application).

If the application starts successfully, the message `OK—Started application at context path {context_path}` is displayed (see Figure 7-13).

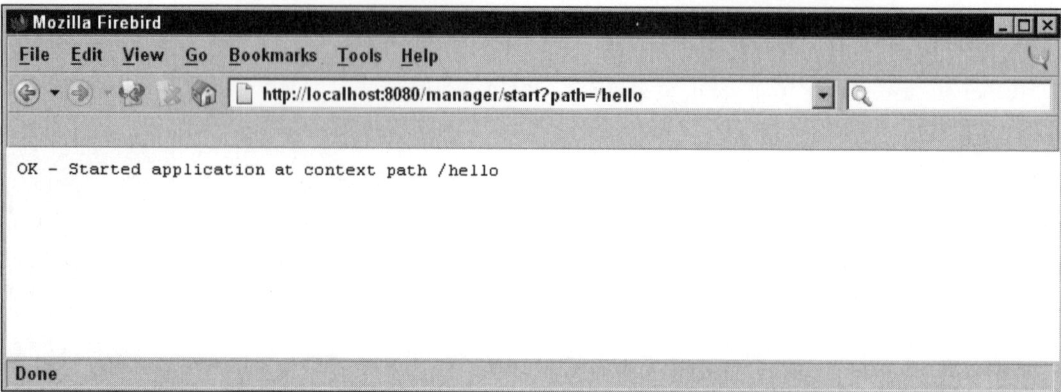

Figure 7-13: Starting a stopped Web application.

If the operation fails, a `FAIL` message with appropriate error information is displayed.

Removing an Installed Application (Tomcat 4.x Only)

The **`remove`** *command is obsolete in Tomcat 5.x. It is replaced by the* **`undeploy`** *command.*

The format of the `remove` command URL is as follows:

```
http://{hostname}:{portnumber}/manager/remove?path={context_path}
```

This command is the opposite of the `install` command. It signals the Web application to shut down gracefully, and then makes the application context available for reuse. This is done by removing the context entry from Tomcat's run-time data structures.

As described previously, the Tomcat 4.0 `install` command behaves like a `deploy` command, because it copies the Web application to `$CATALINA_HOME/webapps`. The `remove` command should undo this and remove the Web application directory and/or the WAR file, but because of a bug in Tomcat, it does not. The extracted Web application directory needs to be removed manually.

Figure 7-14 shows the Web application running at context path `/hello` being removed. Its context entry is deleted from Tomcat's internal run-time data structures, so any attempt to access `http://localhost:8080/hello` will now fail.

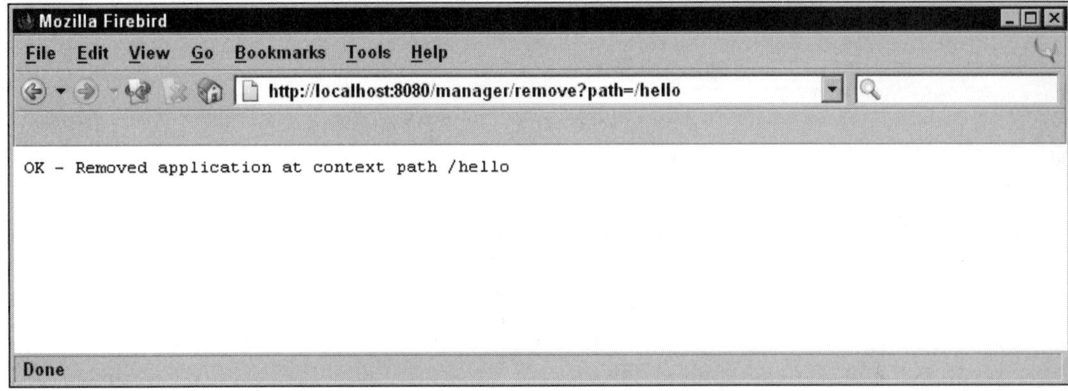

Figure 7-14: Removing a Web application in Tomcat 4.x.

If the application is removed successfully, the message `OK – Removed application at context path {`*`context_path`*`}` is displayed.

Undeploying a Web Application

> *This command should be used with care. It deletes the Web application directory that was created when the application was deployed. In Tomcat 4.x, there is an option to use the* **`remove`** *command instead, which does not remove the Web application permanently, but only for the current Tomcat lifetime.*

This command first signals the application to shut down (if it is still running) and then deletes the Web application directory and the application WAR file. It then removes the `<Context>` entry for the Web application from `$CATALINA_HOME/conf/server.xml`.

In short, the `undeploy` command does the opposite of the `deploy` command described earlier in the chapter. However, the `undeploy` command works only on applications installed in the application base directory of the virtual host (the location where the `deploy` command put the Web application WAR files or the extracted directories).

The URL for the `undeploy` command is as follows:

```
http://localhost:8080/manager/undeploy?path={context_path}
```

If the application undeploys successfully, the message `OK – Undeployed application at context path {`*`context_path`*`}` is displayed, as shown in Figure 7-15. If the operation fails, a `FAIL` message with appropriate error information is displayed.

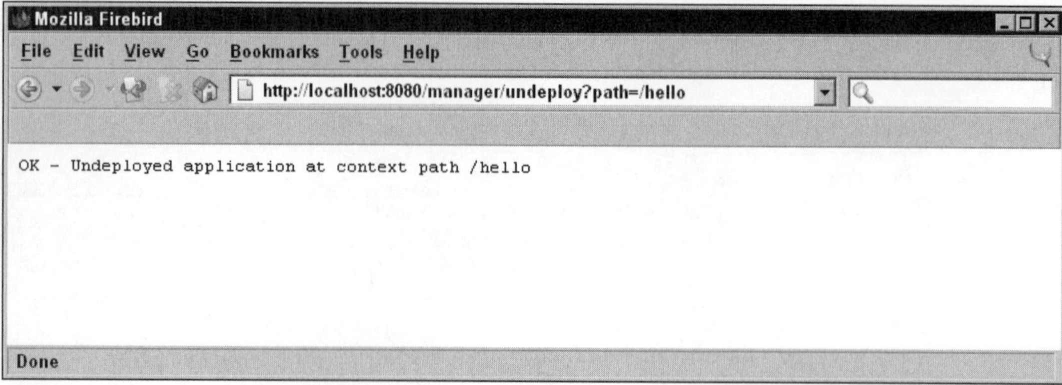

Figure 7-15: Undeploying a Web application.

Displaying Session Statistics

The `manager` application can be used to retrieve statistics about a particular Web application. The statistics shown are the default session timeout and the number of current active sessions.

The URL for accessing this information is as follows:

```
http://localhost:8080/manager/sessions?path={context_path}
```

For example, the statistics for the `hello` application can be checked using the following command (see Figure 7-16):

```
http://localhost:8080/manager/sessions?path=/hello
```

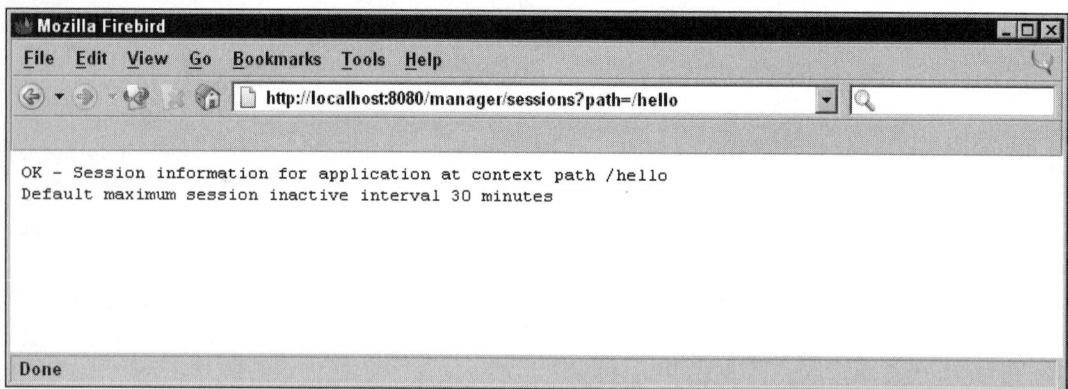

Figure 7-16: Displaying session statistics.

Querying Tomcat Internals Using the JMX Proxy Servlet

The JMX `proxy` Servlet enables the querying of Tomcat internals classes (or any other class exposed via MBeans). The general format of this command is as follows:

```
http://{hostname}:{portnumber}/manager/jmxproxy/?qry=QUERY_STRING
```

A missing query string (that is, only `http://{hostname}:{portnumber}/manager/jmxproxy/`) will show all the MBeans (a long listing!). The query parameters are not well documented and some experimentation is required to see what works. For example, a query string "`qry=*:j2eeType=Servlet,*`" shows all loaded Servlets. As a browser URL, this would be written as follows (see Figure 7-17):

```
http://localhost:8080/manager/jmxproxy/?qry=*%3Aj2eeType=Servlet%2c*
```

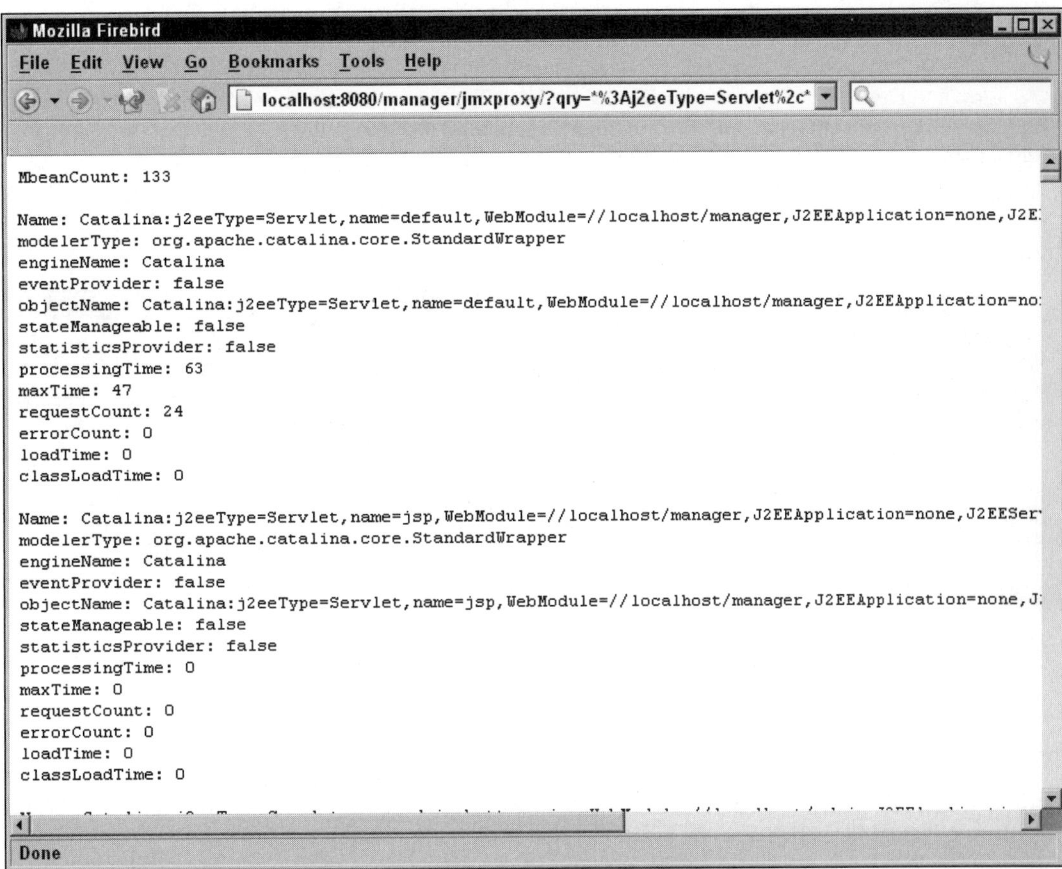

Figure 7-17: Querying Tomcat internals using the JMX proxy Servlet.

The % values in the command are hexadecimal escape sequences for reserved characters used in URLs (as defined in RFC 2396): %3A for the colon (:), %2C for the comma (,), and %3D for the equals sign (=). When this command is run via the Ant task interface (see the section "Tomcat Manager: Managing Applications with Ant," later in this chapter), the escape sequences don't have to be used.

The JMX proxy Servlet also allows for changes to these values.

Setting Tomcat Internals Using the JMX Proxy Servlet

The general format for the JMX `set` command is as follows:

```
http://{hostname}:{portnumber}/manager/jmxproxy/?set=BEANNAME&att=MYATTRIBUTE&val=NEWVALUE
```

Here `BEANNAME` is the bean name, `MYATTRIBUTE` is the name of the bean attribute that needs to be modified, and `NEWVALUE` is the new value for the bean attribute.

As shown in Figure 7-18, the following command sets the debug level for the `ErrorReportValve` to `10` in a running Tomcat instance (set the `debug` attribute in the bean `Catalina:type=Valve,name=ErrorReportValue,host=localhost` to `10`):

```
http://localhost:8080/manager/jmxproxy/?set=Catalina%3Atype%3DValve%2Cname%3DErrorR
eportValve%2Chost%3Dlocalhost&att=debug&val=10
```

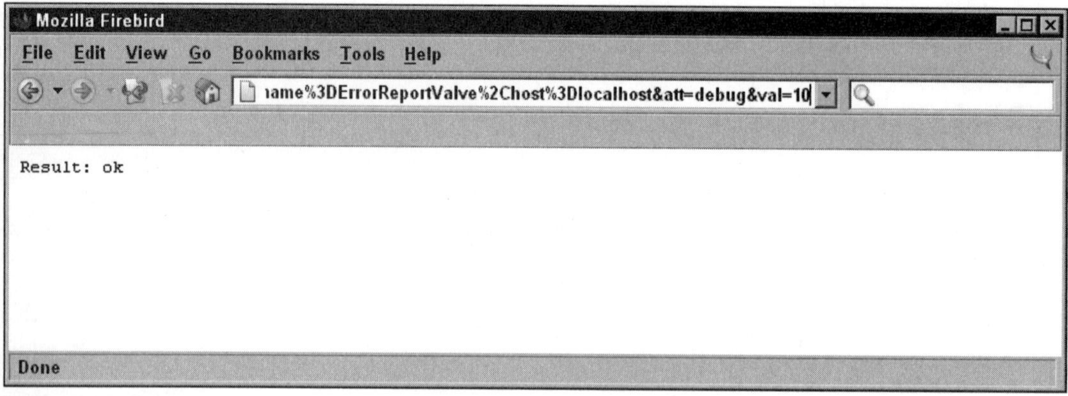

Figure 7-18: Setting Tomcat internals using the JMX proxy Servlet.

As before, the % values in the command are hexadecimal escape sequences for reserved characters. When this command is run via the Ant task interface (see the section "Tomcat Manager: Managing Applications with Ant," later in this chapter), the escape sequences don't have to be used.

Chapter 18 discusses JMX support in Tomcat in more detail.

Tomcat Manager: Web Interface

Tomcat also has a Web interface for the `manager` application. This interface enables you to start, stop, remove, reload, and install Web applications without having to type the command URL.

To access the Tomcat manager Web application, access `http://localhost:8080/` and click the Tomcat Manager link on the left-hand side of the Tomcat home page, as shown in Figure 7-19.

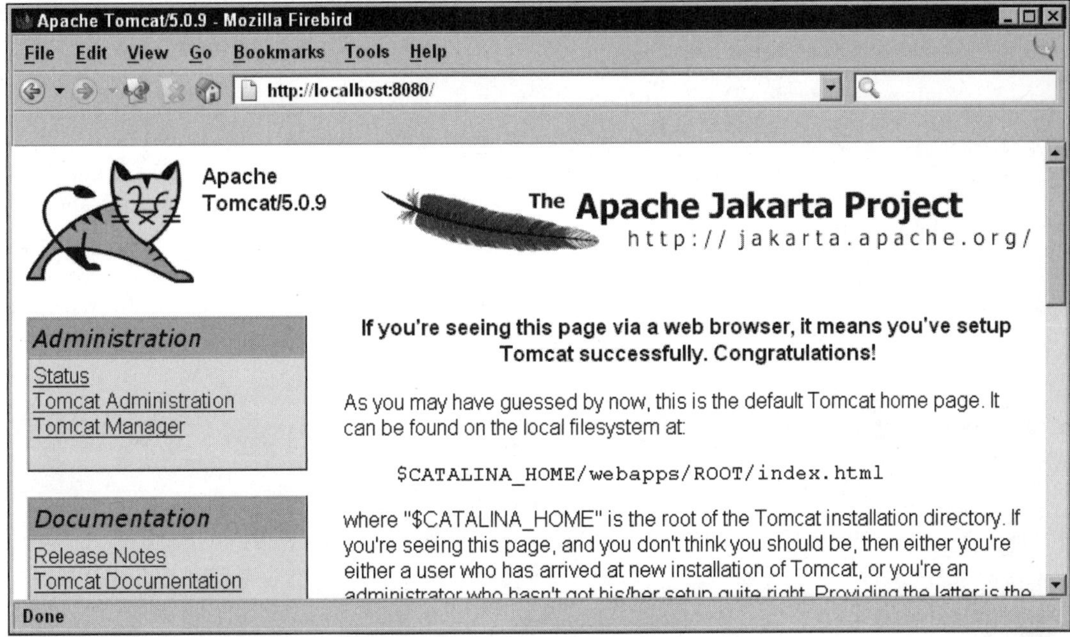

Figure 7-19: Tomcat Manager's Web interface.

You will then be prompted for a user name and password. This will take you to the `manager` application home page.

Displaying Tomcat Server Status

The `status` command retrieves miscellaneous information about a running instance of Tomcat (such as the free and total memory used by the JVM, number of threads, and so on). This is accessible via the `Server Status` command.

Information such as the class load time, processing time, and so on, on every Servlet class/JSP for all the deployed Web applications can be obtained using the Complete Server Status option (visible while viewing the server status).

Managing Web Applications

Administrators can start, stop, reload, and remove Web applications by clicking on the relevant links provided at the end of each application.

In Tomcat 4.0 and 4.1.3, the Manager tasks were handled by a Servlet called `ManagerServlet` (`org.apache.catalina.servlets.ManagerServlet`). From Tomcat 4.1.7 onward, the new interface is `HTMLManagerServlet`. This class extends the `ManagerServlet` and internally invokes the same commands that were discussed earlier in the chapter.

The Applications table has five columns (see Figure 7-20):

- *Path* — This lists the Web application path. The pathname links to the URL for the Web application.
- *Display Name* — This is picked up from the `<display-name>` element in the application's deployment descriptor (`web.xml`).
- *Running* — This indicates the running status for the application (`true` if the application is running, and `false` otherwise).
- *Sessions* — This indicates the number of active sessions for the Web application. Clicking the link for the number of sessions returns the session statistics for that particular Web application. This internally invokes the `sessions` command discussed earlier.
- *Commands* — These are the links to the`start`, `stop`, `reload`, and `remove` commands for the Web application. The manual commands for this were shown earlier, but using the Web application manager saves the effort (and possible errors) of typing a command URL for performing these tasks.

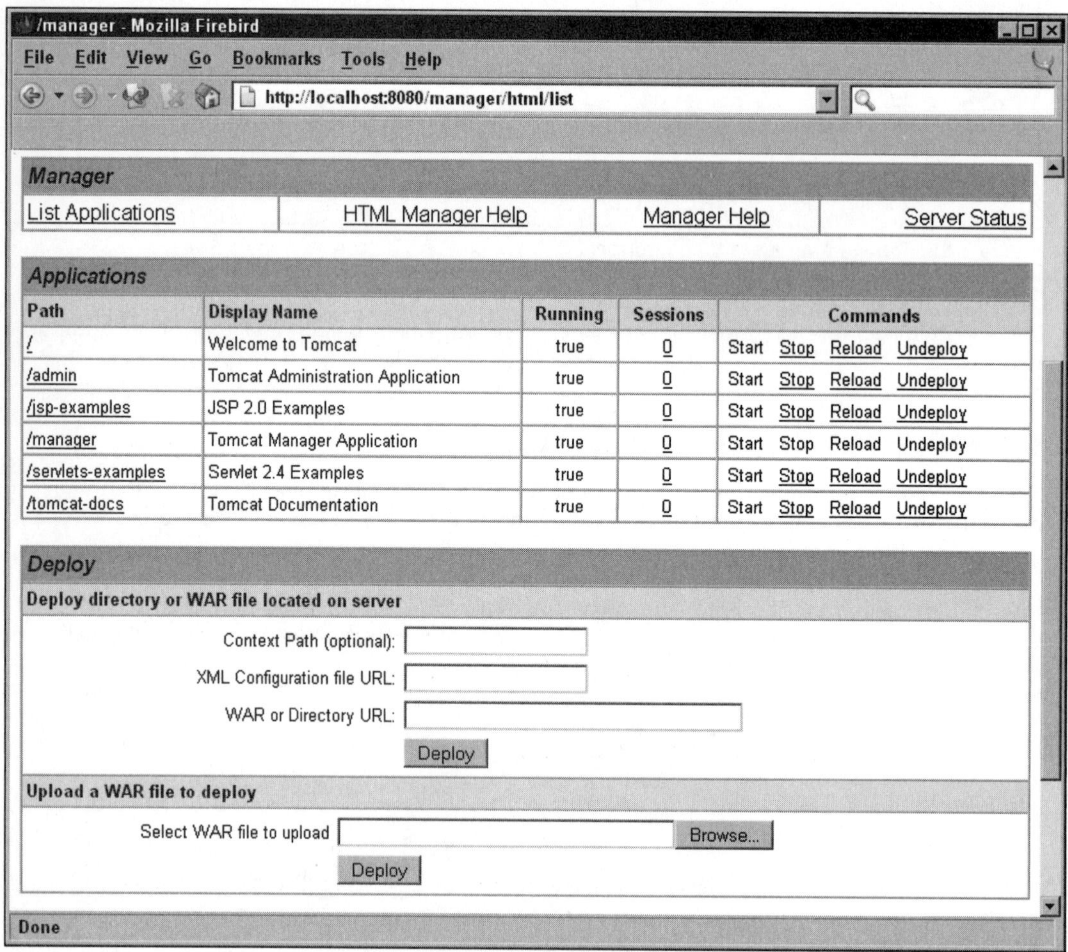

Figure 7-20: Commands for Tomcat Manager's Web interface.

Deploying a Web Application

A new Web application can be deployed using the manager application both locally ("Deploy directory or WAR file located on server") as well as remotely ("Upload a WAR file to deploy").

Some of the options available via the HTTP command interface (such as the **`tag`**, **`update`**, *and* **`pause`** *parameters) are not currently usable from the Web interface.*

Figure 7-21 shows the manager Web interface after successfully executing the `deploy` command to deploy the `hello` application. As you can see, Tomcat adds another row for the application in the list of deployed applications.

Figure 7-21: Successful deployment of a Web application.

Tomcat Manager: Managing Applications with Ant

Tomcat 4.1 and 5.x enable administration commands to be run from an Ant script. Ant is a Java-based build tool from the Apache Software Foundation. Appendix C provides a brief introduction for those unfamiliar with it.

Using the Tomcat Manager commands from Ant is convenient for development purposes because the Ant build file can be used to compile, deploy, and even start a Web application. The steps for doing this once Ant is installed are as follows:

- Copy the `$CATALINA_HOME/server/lib/catalina-ant.jar` file into Ant's library directory (`$ANT_HOME/lib`). This JAR file contains the Tomcat management task definitions for Ant.
- Add `$ANT_HOME/bin` to your `PATH`.
- Add a user with the `manager` role to Tomcat's user database if such a user does not exist.
- Add to your custom `build.xml` script the `<taskdef>` elements that call the Tomcat `manager` commands.

The following sample `build.xml` file builds and deploys the `hello` Web application discussed at the beginning of the chapter:

```
<project name="HelloApplication" default="compile" basedir=".">

  <!-- Configure the directory into which the web application is built -->
  <property name="src" value="."/>
  <property name="build"    value="${basedir}/build"/>

  <!-- Configure the context path for this application -->
  <property name="path"     value="/hello"/>
```

The `<project>` tag has attributes for the name of the project and the default target. The default target in this case is called `compile`. Running Ant with no options will invoke the tasks associated with this default target. The `basedir` attribute is the base directory for all path calculations in the Ant build script. This is set to . (the current directory), so all the paths for the build process are assumed to be relative to the directory from which Ant is run. The properties for the build are defined next, such as the location of the source directory and the target directory to which the compiled `.class` files will be sent.

The following properties specify the access URL and user name/password for the `manager` application. This password can be passed via the command line, too:

```
  <!-- Configure properties to access the Manager application -->
  <property name="url"      value="http://localhost:8080/manager"/>
  <property name="username" value="myusername"/>
  <property name="password" value="mypassword"/>
```

The task definitions for the `manager` application are now specified. Ant allows for custom tasks that extend its functionality. Tomcat implements the custom tasks shown in the following example for executing the `manager` application commands. For example, `org.apache.catalina.ant.DeployTask` executes the `deploy` command against the `manager` application:

```
<!-- Configure the custom Ant tasks for the Manager application -->
<taskdef name="deploy"
         classname="org.apache.catalina.ant.DeployTask"/>
```

The following `install` and `remove` commands are deprecated in Tomcat 5.x. The `deploy/undeploy` commands should be used instead.

```
<!-- Valid for Tomcat 4.x only, deprecated in 5.x -->
<taskdef name="install"
         classname="org.apache.catalina.ant.InstallTask"/>

 <!-- Valid for Tomcat 4.x only, deprecated in 5.x -->
<taskdef name="remove"
         classname="org.apache.catalina.ant.RemoveTask"/>
```

The rest of the commands (`list`, `resources`, `roles`, `start`, `stop`, and `undeploy`) are the same in Tomcat 4.x and 5.x:

```
<taskdef name="list"
         classname="org.apache.catalina.ant.ListTask"/>
<taskdef name="reload"
         classname="org.apache.catalina.ant.ReloadTask"/>
<taskdef name="resources"
         classname="org.apache.catalina.ant.ResourcesTask"/>
<taskdef name="roles"
         classname="org.apache.catalina.ant.RolesTask"/>

<taskdef name="start"
         classname="org.apache.catalina.ant.StartTask"/>
<taskdef name="stop"
         classname="org.apache.catalina.ant.StopTask"/>
<taskdef name="undeploy"
classname="org.apache.catalina.ant.UndeployTask"/>
```

The following Ant tasks (`serverinfo`, `sessions`, `jmxquery`, and `jmxset`) are missing from Tomcat 4.x, and are found only in Tomcat 5.x, from version 5.0.10 onward:

```
<taskdef name="serverinfo"
         classname="org.apache.catalina.ant.ServerinfoTask"/>
<taskdef name="sessions"
         classname="org.apache.catalina.ant.SessionsTask"/>
<taskdef name="jmxquery"
         classname="org.apache.catalina.ant.JMXQueryTask"/>
<taskdef name="jmxset"
         classname="org.apache.catalina.ant.JMXSetTask"/>
```

Next is the Ant target that performs initializations (in this case, creates the build directory):

```
<target name="init">
  <!-- Create the build directory structure used by compile -->
  <mkdir dir="${build}"/>
  <mkdir dir="${build}/hello"/>
  <mkdir dir="${build}/hello/WEB-INF"/>
  <mkdir dir="${build}/hello/WEB-INF/classes"/>
</target>
```

The default `compile` target is shown here. This has Ant instructions to compile all the Java files into class files. The `hello` application doesn't have any class files, so nothing will be done, but any serious Web application will contain Java files. Notice how the `compile` task depends on the `init` task. This ensures that the initializations steps are performed before Ant compiles the Java files:

```
<!-- Executable Targets -->
<target name="compile" description="Compile web application"
        depends="init">
  <javac srcdir="${src}" destdir="${build}"/>
</target>
```

The `build` target builds the application WAR file. It has instructions to move the files to the correct directory format for a Web application and build the WAR file:

```
<target name="build" description="Build web application"
        depends="compile">
  <copy file="index.html" toDir="${build}/hello"/>
  <copy file="hello.jsp" toDir="${build}/hello"/>
  <jar destfile="${build}/hello.war" basedir="${build}/hello"/>
</target>
```

Finally, the manager tasks for listing all Web applications, and installing/uninstalling and deploying/undeploying Web applications:

```
<target name="list" description="List all web applications">
  <list url="${url}" username="${username}" password="${password}"/>
</target>

<target name="reload" description="Reload web application"
        depends="build">
  <reload  url="${url}" username="${username}" password="${password}"
          path="${path}"/>
</target>


<target name="deploy" description="Deploy web application"
        depends="build">
  <deploy url="${url}" username="${username}" password="${password}"
          path="${path}" war="file:${build}/hello.war"/>
</target>

<target name="undeploy" description="Undeploy web application">
  <undeploy url="${url}" username="${username}" password="${password}"
          path="${path}"/>
</target>
</project>
```

Before using the Ant script, `$CATALINA_HOME/server/lib/catalina-ant.jar` must be added to the `CLASSPATH`, and the Ant install directory must be added to the system path (Ant version 1.5 was used for this example):

```
$ CLASSPATH=$CLASSPATH:$CATALINA_HOME/server/lib/catalina-ant.jar
$ PATH=$PATH:/path/to/ant1.5/bin
$ export CLASSPATH PATH
```

The `password` property in the Ant script contains the password for the user with manager privileges. This is useful for development environments in which developers don't want to specify the password each time. The password value can be overridden from the command line, or even omitted from the build file altogether and passed only from the command line. This avoids the security risk of putting the password in a clear text file:

```
$ ant --Dpassword=secret list
```

The capability to run the manager commands from within Ant files allows for a very integrated develop-deploy-test cycle for Web application development. For example, after developing the HTML pages, Servlets, JSP pages, and other Java classes for the Web application, the developer would need to compile all the Java code:

```
$ ant build
```

The `build` target in the `build.xml` file compiles all the Java code and puts the class files into the appropriate location (the `/WEB-INF/classes` directory). It then builds the deployable JAR file. Developers may need to fix compilation errors, if any, and then rerun the `Ant` command.

The `deploy` target can then be used to deploy the Web application in the Tomcat instance specified in the Ant build file:

```
$ ant deploy
```

This installed application can then be tested, and errors ironed out. During each iteration, developers would (re)build, undeploy the previous installation, and then (re)deploy the new Web application.

Possible Errors

Numerous things can go wrong while working with the `manager` application. The following list describes some of the typical error messages and the possible causes of failure. These errors are applicable for the HTTP command interface, the Web application interface, and the Ant task interface to the manager application commands.

- *Application already exists at path {context_path}* — A Web application already exists at the path specified. The context path for each Web application must be unique. Tomcat returns an error if there is another application with the same context path. This can be the same application (that is, `deploy` was executed twice for the same application) or a different one with the same context path. To fix this, the previous application must be undeployed/removed, or a different context path chosen.
- *Encountered exception* — An exception occurred while trying to start the Web application. The Tomcat log files will contain error messages relating to the specific error. Typical causes of this error are missing classes/JAR files while loading the application, and invalid commands in the application's `web.xml` file.
- *Invalid context path specified* — The context path must start with a slash (`/`). The exception to this is when the `ROOT` Web application (that is, at context path `/` itself

) is being deployed, in which case the context path must be a zero-length string.

- *No context path specified* — The context path is mandatory.
- *Document base does not exist or is not a readable directory* — The value specified for the WAR file path/URL in the `war` parameter is incorrect. This parameter must point to an expanded Web application or an actual WAR file.
- *No context exists for path {context_path}* — The context path is invalid; there is no Web application deployed that corresponds to it.
- *Reload not supported on WAR deployed at path {context_path}* — The Web application was installed from a WAR file, instead of from an unpacked directory. The current version of Tomcat does not support this.
- *No global JNDI resources* — No JNDI global resources were configured for this Tomcat instance.
- *Cannot resolve user database reference* — There was an error looking up the appropriate user database. For example, in the case of the roles stored in a JNDI Realm, a JNDI error would result in such a message. Tomcat's log files would have more error information.
- *No user database is available* — The `<ResourceLink>` element has not been configured properly in the `manager.xml` configuration file. See the section "Manager Application Configuration," earlier in this chapter for more information.

The error messages shown here are in English, but Tomcat supports numerous languages. The locale-specific versions of these messages (error as well as the success messages) are picked up from resource bundles.

Security Considerations

Securing the `manager` application is critical. An insecurely configured manager could be used to cause denial of service by stopping existing applications, or worse, to install malicious Web applications over existing ones. Some of the ways in which the `manager` application can be secured are as follows:

- Use a more rigorous mechanism of authentication for the `manager` application than `BASIC`. Administrators can, for example, set the authentication method to be client-certificate-based (`CLIENT-CERT`) in the deployment descriptor. `BASIC` authentication is very insecure, because the password is sent across as a standard base64-encoded string. `CLIENT-CERT` uses SSL for securing the transport layer. The manager deployment descriptor configured for `CLIENT-CERT` is shown as follows:

```
<login-config>
  <auth-method>CLIENT-CERT</auth-method>
  <realm-name>Tomcat Manager Application</realm-name>
</login-config>
```

- Use JDBC or JNDI-based Realm implementations to store the manager user name/password. These are more secure than Memory/UserDatabase Realms because they don't save the password in a text file on the file system. This can be a security risk if the file permissions aren't set correctly, though similar problems can occur with JDBC/JNDI realms, too, if the access rights to the database, LDAP server, and so on, were too permissive.

- Configure the Realm implementation to use encrypted passwords. This is especially useful if Memory or UserDatabase Realm implementations are used. Two sample configurations of this are as follows.

  The `server.xml` file:

```
<Realm className="org.apache.Catalina.realm.UserDatabaseRealm"
          debug="5"
          digest="sha"
          pathname="conf/tomcat_users.xml" />
```

  The `tomcat-users.xml` file:

```
    <user name="manager"
          password="c23e4c2003a93af2dad4dae78f5e1c4a4735732"
          roles="manager" />
```

  The character sequence in the `password` attribute is the SHA digest version of the password.

- Use a `RemoteAddrValve` or `RemoteHostValve` Valve in the manager's Context to restrict the machines from which the manager application can be accessed. In the following example, access is restricted to the host on which Tomcat runs by using the loopback IP address (127.0.0.1):

```
<Context path="/manager"
         debug-"0"
         privileged="true"
         docBase="/usr/local/tomcat/server/webapps/manager">

          <Valve className="org.apache.Catalina.valves.RemoteAddrValve"
                 allow="127.0.0.1"/>
 </Context>
```

- The `deployXML` parameter in the configuration for a `Host` (see `server.xml`) controls whether Web applications can be deployed using a context configuration file, and whether they can be installed outside the Host's config base directory (`$CATALINA_HOME/conf/[`*`engine_name`*`]/[`*`host_name`*`]`). This is set to `true` by default (that is, allowing an install outside the config base). Setting it to `false` can prevent users from deploying Web applications anywhere else on the file system, where the admin may not be able to control file permissions as can be seen in the following example:

```
<Host name="localhost"
 deployXML="false"
 debug="0"
 appBase="webapps"
 unpackWARs="true"
 autoDeploy="false">
        ...
 </Host>
```

Tomcat Deployer

Tomcat comes with a "deployer" distribution that can be downloaded from the Apache Web site. These distributions are named as `jakarta-tomcat-5.x.y-deployer.tar.gz` or `jakarta-tomcat-5.x.y-deployer.zip`, where `x.y` is the Tomcat version.

The deployer distribution is a stripped-down version of Tomcat that includes the following:

- Tomcat's Ant tasks for managing the Web application. These tasks are discussed in detail earlier in the chapter.
- A sample build file (`build.xml`) for deploying a Web application. This build file uses a property file (`deployer.property`) that can be modified as per requirements.
- A JSP compiler (Jasper) for precompiling JSP pages

The deployer distribution can be used to validate, compile, deploy, and manage Web applications, and includes only those parts of Tomcat that are required for this.

Summary

The `manager` application provides an easy-to-use interface (via the Web-based interface), and enables the automation of tasks (for example, via the `manager` application's Ant tasks). This chapter covered issues related to the `manager` Web application, including the following:

- Configuration for the `manager` application
- Administration capabilities of the Tomcat 4.x and 5.x `manager` application
- Security-related issues

Securing the `manager` application is important. As discussed earlier, someone who gains unauthorized access to applications can do a lot of harm, such as deploy malicious applications or cause a Denial of Service (DoS) by shutting down running ones. Administrators concerned about security should perform the appropriate configuration as specified in the section "Security Considerations," or, if they are paranoid, disable the `manager` Web application altogether from production deployments.

Chapter 8 discusses advanced features of Tomcat.

8

Advanced Tomcat Features

Earlier chapters discussed Tomcat 5 administration basics, system architecture, and Web applications deployment. Basic administrative functions were performed using the Web-based `admin` or `manager` application, or by editing XML configuration files. This chapter explores a collection of administrative tasks that involve advanced features built into standard Tomcat 5. As a Tomcat 5 administrator, you are likely to encounter requests for many of these features from the development team.

More specifically, the following advanced administration tasks are explored:

- ❑ Access log administration
- ❑ Single Sign-on across Web applications
- ❑ Request filtering
- ❑ Installation of a Persistent Session Manager
- ❑ Setting up Tomcat JNDI emulation resources to enable developers access to external JDBC and JNDI resources
- ❑ Setting up Tomcat for access to a JavaMail session
- ❑ Configuration of lifecycle listeners

Note that configuration of Realms, a very important advanced Tomcat 5 administration topic, is discussed in Chapter 15. A basic understanding of Tomcat 5's security infrastructure is a prerequisite for appreciating the configuration options in Realms configuration.

This chapter serves as a "cookbook" for these specific tasks. For each task, the reasons why a user or a developer may need the feature are provided, followed by the configuration and administrative details. Finally, a practical sample configuration is presented, which you can experiment with. Useful hints, tips, or problems that may apply are pointed out along the way.

Valves — Interception Tomcat-Style

Valves are intrinsic architectural elements, similar to filters and specific to Tomcat, that have been available since early versions of Tomcat 4. As a Filterlike element, a Valve can intercept any incoming request and outgoing response. In Tomcat 5, a set of standard Valves is delivered with the distribution. Architecturally, they are managed by the Engine and are given access to the incoming request from the Connectors before (and after) they are handled by the Servlet and JSP processing logic. Logically, they can also be applied on a per-virtual-host or per-Web-application level (although application developers will typically use Tomcat 5 application filters instead of Valves if they need per-application filtering). Valves offer value-added functionality that includes the following:

- Access logging
- Single Sign-on for all Web applications running under Tomcat
- Requests filtering/blocking by IP address and/or host name
- Dumping of incoming and outgoing request headers for debugging purposes

The following sections examine the set of standard Valves available with Tomcat 5.

Standard Valves

Valves are **nested components** in the Tomcat 5 configuration component model (configured using the `<Valve>` XML element in the `server.xml` file) that can be placed inside `<Engine>`, `<Host>`, or `<Context>` containers (refer to Chapter 4 for architectural details on containers). The Engine passes an incoming request and outgoing response through any Valve that is incorporated within these containers. This process is illustrated in Figure 8-1.

Before the addition of a Valve

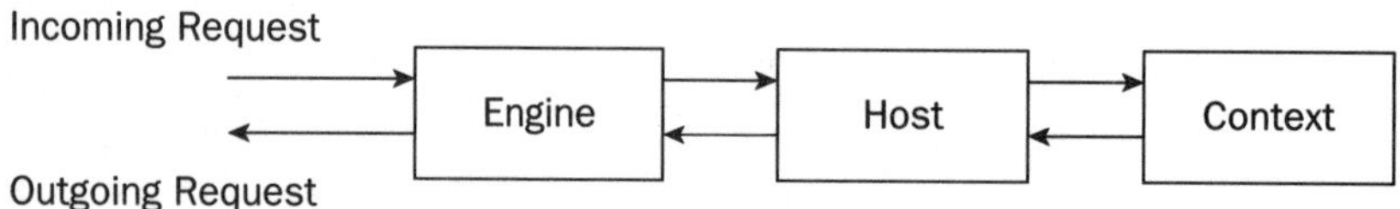

After the addition of a Valve

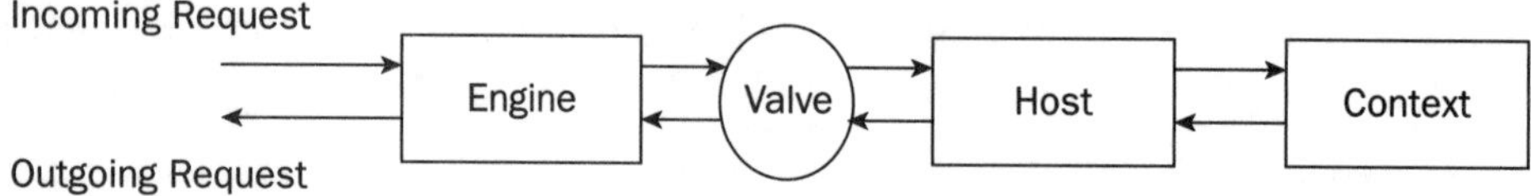

Every request to every virtual host in this engine goes through the added Valve

Figure 8-1: Position of Valves in Tomcat 5's architecture.

In Figure 8-1, every single incoming request is passed through the added Valve. Because of this, Valves can be configured to perform work on each request. The Java language programming interface, `org.apache.catalina.Valve`, is well-documented. Java application programmers may create their own Valves using this programming interface. For the most common application of Valves, however, Tomcat 5 already has basic implementations built in. The following table describes these standard Valves.

Valve Name	Description
Access Logging	Enables logging of the request (the URL of the resource requested, date and time of request)
Single Sign-on	Enhances the user experience by requesting a password only once, even when the user accesses different Web applications on the same host or server
Request Filtering	Enables selective filtering (blocking) of incoming requests based on a list of IP addresses or host names
Request Dump	Prints the headers and cookies of incoming requests and outgoing responses to a log

The configuration of each of these Valves is illustrated in the following sections.

Access Log Implementation

Logging access to resources is a very common activity for Web server administrators. This can include either static resources (such as Web pages and graphic files) or dynamic resources (such as CGI, JSP, and Servlets). In Tomcat 5, access logs can be generated by inserting an **Access Log Valve.**

Note that this standard Valve is completely separate and different from the `<Logger>` nestable component. The `<Logger>` component provides Tomcat—as well as applications running within it—with a method to capture information, warning, and error messages. The standard Access Log Valve uses its own logic to examine each incoming request for Web resources (that is, the URL requested), and captures only the access request information to its own log file.

In the case of the `<Logger>` component, the format of the log file content is variable (it depends on the system or application), whereas the typical format for the standard Access Log Valve is a well-known `common` log file format (for more information, see W3C link `http://www.w3.org/Daemon/User/Config/Logging.html#common-logfile-format`). This format is supported by almost all popular Web servers, including Apache. Analysis tools are widely available for the analysis of log files in the `common` log file format.

Scope of Log Files

The scope of logging depends on where the Access Log Valve is inserted. For example, to log all the access within a specific Web application, the Valve (the `<Valve>` element) should be placed in the `<Context>` container in the `$CATALINA_HOME/conf/server.xml` file. To log all the resource access within a virtual host across all Web applications, the Valve should be placed in the `<Host>` container.

Finally, if you want to track all access to all resources on a particular instance of the Catalina engine (across all the virtual hosts in that Engine and across all the Web applications), the Valve should be placed in the `<Engine>` scope.

If you are using the default Access Log Valve (that is, if the `className` attribute is set to `org.apache.catalina.valves.AccessLogValve`), then you can specify the attributes shown in the following table.

Attribute	Description	Required?
`className`	The Java programming language executable class representing the Valve, `org.apache.catalina.valves.AccessLogValve`	Yes
`directory`	The directory in which the log files will be placed. Usually relative to the `$CATALINA_HOME`, but can also specify an absolute path instead. The default value is `logs`.	No
`pattern`	This attribute specifies the format used in the log. You can customize the format, or you can use the `common` format or the combined format (common log file entry plus referrer and user-agent logged). The default format is `common`. To customize the format, you can use any of the following pattern identifiers interspersed with a literal string in this pattern attribute: `%a`—Insert remote IP address. `%A`—Insert local IP address (of URL resource). `%b`—Insert bytes sent count, excluding HTTP headers; will show - if zero. `%B`—Insert bytes sent count, excluding HTTP headers. `%h`—Insert remote host name (or IP address if the `resolveHosts` attribute is set to `false`). `%H`—Insert the request protocol (HTTP). `%l`—Insert remote logical user name (always -). `%m`—Insert request method such as `GET` or `POST`. `%p`—Insert the local TCP port on which the request is received. `%q`—Insert the query string of the request. `%r`—Insert the first line of the request. `%s`—Insert the HTTP status code of the response. `%S`—Insert the user session ID. `%t`—Insert the date and time in `common` log file format. `%u`—Insert the remote user that has been authenticated (otherwise, it is -). `%U`—Insert the URL path of the request. `%v`—Insert the name of the local virtual host from the request.	No

Attribute	Description	Required?
resolveHosts	Determines if the log will contain host names via a reverse DNS lookup. This can take significant time if enabled. The default is disabled (false).	No
prefix	The prefix added to the name of the log file.	No
suffix	The suffix (extension) added to the name of the log file.	No

The Access Log Valve supports rolling logs automatically. A new log file will be created for each day at midnight.

Testing the Access Log Valve

Here is a practical example for the configuration of access logs. If you examine the default $CATALINA_HOME/conf/server.xml file, you will see a commented <Valve> entry that specifies the access log. It is placed immediately within the <Host name='localhost' ...> entry:

```
<!--
    <Valve className='org.apache.catalina.valves.AccessLogValve'
           directory='logs'
           prefix='localhost_access_log.'
           suffix='.txt'
           pattern='common'
           resolveHosts='false'
     />
-->
```

> **If you do not see the commented section detailed here, type in the <Valve> entry manually as shown below. It is possible that you may have modified some Tomcat settings using the admin application. Some versions of this administration tool will strip comments when changes are saved.**

Uncomment this entry and modify the directory and prefix attributes as shown here:

```
    <Valve className='org.apache.catalina.valves.AccessLogValve'
           directory='wroxlogs'
           prefix='wroxtest_localhost_access_log.'
           suffix='.txt'
           pattern='common'
           resolveHosts='false'
    />
```

Now, create a wroxlogs/ directory under the $CATALINA_HOME directory (the standard Valve will actually create it for you if you forget). Start/restart Tomcat 5, and then open a browser and point it to the following URL:

```
http://localhost:8080/
```

The default Tomcat 5 welcome page should be displayed. Shut down the Tomcat server and examine the `$CATALINA_HOME/wroxlogs/` directory. You will find the access logs created by the Valve.

Note that the log file's prefix is the same as the one configured in the `<Valve>` element. If you look inside this log file, you will see the access log entries to the home page and the associated GIF files, all in the `common` log file format:

```
127.0.0.1 - - [07/Jul/2004:17:33:14 -0500] 'GET / HTTP/1.1' 302 -
127.0.0.1 - - [07/Jul/2004:17:33:21 -0500] 'GET /index.jsp HTTP/1.1' 200 -
127.0.0.1 - - [07/Jul/2004:17:33:21 -0500] 'GET /tomcat.gif HTTP/1.1' 200 1934
127.0.0.1 - - [07/Jul/2004:17:33:21 -0500] 'GET /jakarta-banner.gif HTTP/1.1' 200 8006
127.0.0.1 - - [07/Jul/2004:17:33:21 -0500] 'GET /tomcat-power.gif HTTP/1.1' 200
2324
```

You may want to experiment further with other attributes of the standard Access Log Valve. This can be done by modifying the `<Valve>` entry. If you are running multiple virtual hosts, you may want to try configuring the `<Valve>` at the `<Host>` level as well as the `<Context>` level to experiment with the scope difference. Logging involves disk writes, and will inherently introduce additional overhead into the server hosting Web applications. This is especially true for global Engine-wide or virtual host-wide request logging. For a production site, it is important to discuss and formulate an optimal logging strategy between developers and administrators, based on the application and demand of a server.

Single Sign-On Implementation

Another standard Valve that is frequently used is the **Single Sign-on Valve**. During conventional Web access, whenever a user of a Web application reaches a protected page, the user will be required to sign on. This is required for each Web application that may be accessed. Using Single Sign-on, it is possible to eliminate this annoying repetition (provided the user name and password are identical for each sign-on, and usually authenticating against the same Tomcat Realm).

The Single Sign-on Valve caches credentials (passwords) on the server side, and will invisibly authenticate users as they traverse between Web applications on a given virtual host. Without activating this Valve, the user will be prompted to authenticate for each and every protected Web application, even in cases where all applications use the same user name and password. The credential is cached against a host-wide client session on the server side. This means that a Single Sign-on will be effective throughout the session.

Multiple Sign-On Without the Single Sign-On Valve

Before configuring the Single Sign-on Valve, you should understand what the user must go through without Single Sign-on. To do this, we must protect (enable authentication on) two Web applications within the same virtual host. We will do this for two of the default applications included with the Tomcat 5 distribution. These sample Web applications are as follows:

- The `jsp-examples` Web application
- The Tomcat documentation Web application

To begin, secure the documentation application, and edit the `web.xml` file in the `$CATALINA_HOME/webapps/tomcat-docs/WEB-INF` directory by adding the lines shown here:

```
<?xml version='1.0' encoding='ISO-8859-1'?>
<!DOCTYPE web-app
    PUBLIC "-//Sun Microsystems, Inc.//DTD Web Application 2.3//EN"
    "http://java.sun.com/dtd/web-app_2_3.dtd">


<web-app>
<display-name>Tomcat Documentation</display-name>
  <description>
     Tomcat Documentation.
  </description>
    <security-constraint>
      <display-name>Example Security Constraint</display-name>
      <web-resource-collection>
         <web-resource-name>Protected Area</web-resource-name>
         <url-pattern>/*</url-pattern>
      </web-resource-collection>
      <auth-constraint>
         <role-name>tomcat</role-name>
      </auth-constraint>
    </security-constraint>
 <login-config>
      <auth-method>BASIC</auth-method>
      <realm-name>Single Sign-on Example</realm-name>
 </login-config>
</web-app>
```

This modification will protect all the pages of the documentation, via the `<url-pattern>/*</url-pattern>` element, by requiring an authentication for access. Only users belonging to the `tomcat` role can access these pages, as specified by the `<auth-constraint>` element. The `<security-constraint>` and `<login-config>` elements are part of the Servlet 2.4 (since 2.2) specification. Note that the `<login-config>` in this case specifies a `BASIC` authentication. This means the browser's Security dialog box will be used to obtain authentication information from the user.

Next, the `jsp-examples` Web application is protected. In the `$CATALINA_HOME/webapps/jsp-examples/WEB-INF/web.xml` file, make the following modifications:

```
<security-constraint>
      <display-name>Example Security Constraint</display-name>
      <web-resource-collection>
         <web-resource-name>Protected Area</web-resource-name>
         <!-- Define the context-relative URL(s) to be protected -->
         <url-pattern>/*</url-pattern>
         <!-- If you list http methods, only those methods are protected -->
         <http-method>DELETE</http-method>
         <http-method>GET</http-method>
         <http-method>POST</http-method>
         <http-method>PUT</http-method>
      </web-resource-collection>
      <auth-constraint>
```

```
            <!-- Anyone with one of the listed roles may access this area -->
            <role-name>tomcat</role-name>
            <role-name>role1</role-name>
         </auth-constraint>
   </security-constraint>

   <!-- Default login configuration uses form-based authentication -->
   <login-config>
      <auth-method>FORM</auth-method>
      <realm-name>Example Form-Based Authentication Area</realm-name>
      <form-login-config>
         <form-login-page>/jsp/security/protected/login.jsp</form-login-page>
         <form-error-page>/jsp/security/protected/error.jsp</form-error-page>
      </form-login-config>
   </login-config>
```

Here, the `<url-pattern>` element is modified to protect all the resources within the `jsp-examples` Web application. Note that the `<login-config>` in this case specifies `FORM`-based authentication. This means a custom-created form will be used to obtain authentication information from the user, instead of the browser's Security dialog box.

Start Tomcat 5, and try to access the `tomcat-docs` Web application via the following URL:

```
http://localhost:8080/tomcat-docs/
```

Because `BASIC` authentication has been configured for `tomcat-docs`, the browser prompts you to enter a user name and password, as shown in Figure 8-2.

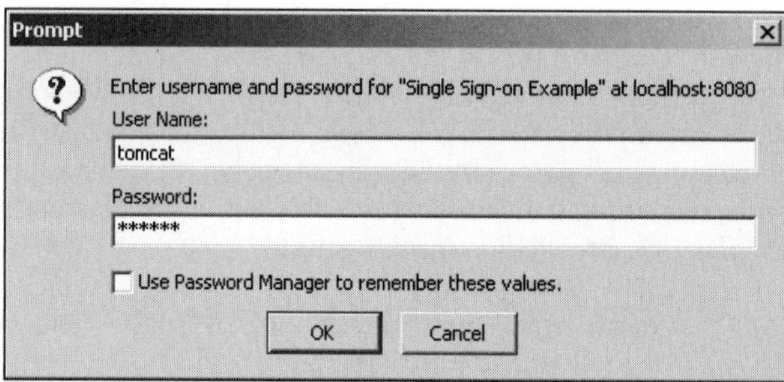

Figure 8-2: BASIC authentication for tomcat.docs application access.

You can use `tomcat` for User name, and `tomcat` for Password (the password is case-sensitive). This corresponds to one of the password entries added earlier in `$CATALINA_HOME/conf/tomcat-users.xml`, which is the default location of the XML file for loading the Memory Realm or UserDatabase Realm (see Chapter 15 for detailed coverage of security Realms). Once you authenticate successfully, you will be able to reach the Tomcat documentation home page. Now, let's switch to another Web application on the same virtual host. Try the following URL:

```
http://localhost:8080/jsp-examples/
```

Note that you are requested to authenticate again, this time using a custom form that has been created as part of the Web application, as shown in Figure 8-3.

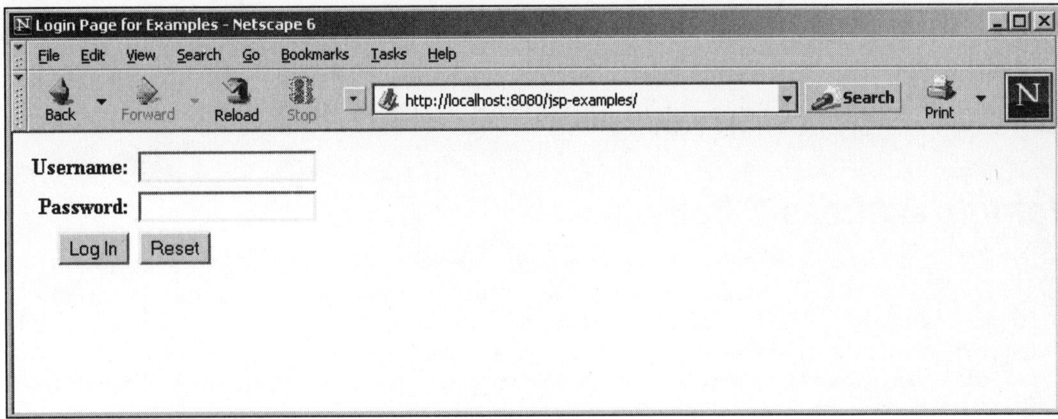

Figure 8-3: Authentication for accessing other applications on the same virtual host.

If you enter `tomcat` for Username, and `tomcat` for Password again, you can gain access to the `examples` pages. In fact, if you have more Web applications that require authentication, the user will be prompted again when first accessing them unless you enable the Single Sign-on Valve.

Configuring a Single Sign-On Valve

To enable the Single Sign-on Valve, place a `<Valve>` element inside the `<Host>` element in the `$CATALINA_HOME/conf/server.xml` file. To specify the Single Sign-On Valve, set the `className` attribute to the value `org.apache.catalina.authenticator.SingleSignOn`. The only additional attribute allowed with this Valve is `debug`, and this attribute sets the debug level:

```
<Valve className='org.apache.catalina.authenticator.SingleSignOn'
       debug='0'/>
```

Restart Tomcat as well as your browser. (This is necessary because most browsers cache credentials for `BASIC` authentication.) Try accessing the two URLs again, in any order. This time, because the Single Sign-on Valve caches the access credentials across multiple Web applications on the same virtual host, you will only be asked to enter the user name and password once. You can test this again by trying the URLs in a different order after restarting the browser (to clear the browser's password cache and create a new session).

> **Note that `BASIC` authentication was purposely not used for both applications because the client browser will typically cache login user names and passwords. This Valve is not as useful whenever all the applications use `BASIC` authentication (because the browser may already cache credentials for `BASIC` authentication, providing single sign-on capability in this special case). Therefore, depending on the authentication method used by Web applications, your mileage on the Single Sign-on Valve may vary. The Single Sign-on Valve is most effective when multiple authentication schemes are involved (common in most production scenarios).**

Restricting Access via a Request Filter

A **Request Filter** is a very useful Valve that enables you to block or Filter specific client requests. This Valve is useful for implementing policies that are based on the characteristics of requests passing through it. These Filters are discussed next.

Remote Address Filter

If the `className` attribute of the `<Valve>` component has the value `org.apache.catalina.valves.RemoteAddrValve`, then a **Remote Address Filter** is created. A Remote Address Filter enables the administrator to specify a list of IP addresses (or regular expressions representing IP addresses) from which to accept or deny requests. Any denied request is not passed through the Valve, effectively blocking it completely from further processing. The following table describes the attributes allowed with the Remote Address Filter.

Attribute	Description	Required?
`className`	The Java programming language executable class representing the Valve — typically, `org.apache.catalina.valves.RemoteAddrValve`	Yes
`allow`	An IP address specified using a regular expression that matches the address of incoming requests	No
`deny`	An IP address specified using a regular expression that matches the address	No

This Valve examines the IP address of the client's request against its `allow/deny` list, and attempts to match the specified regular expression representing IP addresses. Any address that does match the `allow` attribute will be passed through to downstream components. If `allow` is not specified, all IP addresses other than the ones specified in `deny` are allowed.

Remote Host Filter

If the `className` attribute of the `<Valve>` component has the value `org.apache.catalina.valves.RemoteHostValve`, a **Remote Host Filter** is created. A Remote Host Filter functions like the Remote Address Filter, except the filtering performed is based on host names, rather than IP addresses. The allowed attributes are `allow` and `deny`, but the regular expression specified is used to match a host name, rather than an IP address.

Use of the Remote Host Filter requires a reverse DNS lookup. Therefore, the DNS service must be accessible from the server side. In addition, you must be careful to specify all variants (or use a regular expression) of host names that a particular remote host can assume. For example, if a host has only two names, `printserver.wrox.com` and `charlie.wrox.com`, you should be careful to use `printserver.wrox.com,charlie.wrox.com` to match it; `*.wrox.com` will also work, but will potentially match many other hosts.

Configuring Request Filter Valves

Let's look at the details of configuring both Request Filter Valves discussed in the preceding section. Before starting Tomcat, add the following line to the `$CATALINA_HOME/conf/server.xml` file inside the `'localhost'` `<Host>` container, and then start Tomcat:

```
<Valve className='org.apache.catalina.valves.RemoteAddrValve'
allow='121.121.121.*,111.111.111.*'/>
```

This will set up a Request Filter Valve to allow only requests from the two subnets: `121.121.121.*` and `111.111.111.*`.

Now, try accessing the following URL:

```
http://localhost:8080/examples/jsp/index.html
```

The list of allowed IP addresses does not have an entry that matches the IP (`127.0.0.1`); therefore, the request is filtered out. The server returns an HTTP "Forbidden" 403 error and you get a blank page.

If you need to have a custom page returned when access is denied, you must use Servlet 2.4 filters within a Web application instead. Custom error pages are configurable inside the deployment descriptor.

Now, edit the previous line again to include your IP address:

```
<Valve className='org.apache.catalina.valves.RemoteAddrValve'
allow='121.121.121.*,127.*.*.*'/>
```

Restart Tomcat, and now the URL can be accessed again, as the IP is explicitly enabled by the `allow` list.

You can also explicitly deny access by changing the line as shown here:

```
<Valve className='org.apache.catalina.valves.RemoteAddrValve'
       deny='127.0.0.1'/>
```

When you try to access the URL again, a blank page is returned, as the request is filtered out again.

The Remote Host Filter works identically, but with host names instead. You can try it out by simply editing the previous configuration line as follows:

```
<Valve className='org.apache.catalina.valves.RemoteHostValve'
       allow='*.wrox.com'/>
```

Notice the change in `className` from `org.apache.catalina.valves.RemoteAddrValve` to `org.apache.Catalina.valves.RemoteHostValve`, and that the `deny` list now contains a host name instead of an IP address. Restart Tomcat and try accessing the URL again.

The access fails and you get a blank page, as only hosts from `wrox.com` with names that are DNS-resolvable are explicitly allowed.

The Request Filter Valve can be quite effective in implementing a security policy, although if filtering on a physical server level is desired, router-based hardware filtering may be more suitable. Regardless, the Request Filter Valve is handy for temporarily removing access to specific remote client(s).

Request Dumper Valve

A lesser-known standard Valve (useful for debugging Web applications that most administrators/users typically overlook) is called the **Request Dumper Valve.** This Valve dumps the headers and cookies of requests and responses to a log. The Request Dumper Valve assumes that a `<Logger>` element is properly configured (see Chapter 5 for configuration of the `<Logger>` nested element).

For administrators, it serves the following two purposes:

- It visually illustrates how the scope of a Valve affects the requests that are processed.
- It is used to debug the actions of other Valves (that is, when a Request Filter Valve does not appear to work) or to request processing components.

To configure a Request Dumper Valve, simply add the following to the `<Context>`, `<Host>`, or `<Engine>` elements:

```
<Valve className='org.apache.catalina.valves.RequestDumperValve'/>
```

Make sure you remove any definitions of `RemoteAddrValve` or `RemoteHostValve` before using this Valve. Otherwise, you may not gain access to the application at all.

Persistent Sessions

Tomcat 5 features a **Persistent Session Manager** to manage the backup of user sessions onto disk. This manager is not configured by default. This section covers the need for the Persistent Session Manager, as well as its configuration details.

The Need for Persistent Sessions

When Tomcat 5 is shut down, typically all session information is lost. Furthermore, sessions that are idle consume valuable working memory until session timeout, which can be a long period, as some users may leave their computers in the middle of a session.

With Persistent Session Manager, the following features can be enabled:

- Sessions that are inactive can be configured to be **swapped onto disk,** thereby releasing the memory consumed by them, and making memory available for other active sessions.
- When Tomcat is shut down, all the current sessions are **saved to disk.** Upon restart, the saved sessions are restored.
- Sessions lasting beyond a specified threshold period are **automatically backed up** on disk, enabling the system to survive an unexpected crash.

The last feature listed here enables continuous reliable execution of the Web application despite minor server failure (crash), and goes a long way toward enhancing the availability and robustness of the system. However, the Persistent Session Manager is still considered to be of experimental quality, rather than production quality, as of this writing.

Configuring a Persistent Session Manager

The Persistent Session Manager is configured through the `<Manager>` element in the context descriptor of a Web application: `$CATALINA_HOME/conf/<engine name>/<host name>/<app name>.xml`. The Session Manager is a nested component that must be configured at the context level. Therefore, the `<Manager>` element must be configured as a sub-element of the `<Context>` element within the application's context descriptor XML file.

The <Manager> Element

The following table describes the most common attributes of the `<Manager>` element that are available for configuration.

Attribute	Description	Required?
`className`	The Java programming language class that implements the Persistent Session Manager	Yes
`debug`	Controls the level of debug messages	No
`saveOnRestart`	If this is set to `true`, Tomcat will save all the active sessions to the Store upon shutdown, and will reload the session (except the expired ones) from the Store on startup. The default is `true`.	No
`maxActiveSessions`	The ceiling on the number of active sessions before swapping out of the session via the Persistent Session Manager begins. The default value of `-1` allows an unlimited number of active sessions.	No
`minIdleSwap`	The minimum number of seconds before a session will be considered for swapping. The default value of `-1` disables swapping.	No
`maxIdleSwap`	The maximum number of seconds before a session is swapped out to the Store. Used with `minIdleSwap` also to tune the session persistence mechanism. The default value of `-1` disables swapping.	No
`maxIdleBackup`	The number of seconds a session is active before it is backed up on the Store. This can be used to avert a sudden crash, as the backed up sessions will be restored from the Store upon the next startup. The default value of `-1` will disable the backup action altogether.	No
`checkInterval`	Expiry check interval for cleanup, specified in seconds. The default is 60 seconds.	No

The <Manager> element can have only one sub-element, as described in the following table.

Sub-Element	Description	How Many?
Store	Used by the Persistent Session Manager to determine how and where to save the session. Currently, the only options available for a Store implementation are org.apache.catalina.session.FileStore or org.apache.catalina.session.JDBCStore.	1

Store uses object serialization to store the session. The following hands-on example uses the FileStore Store implementation. By default, the FileStore's serialized session information is placed under the $CATALINA_HOME/work/<service name>/<host name>/<web-app name>/ directory.

Hands-On Configuration with the Persistent Session Manager

To configure the Persistent Session Manager, it is necessary to add a <Manager> element definition into the context descriptor of the Web application. In this example, the servlets-examples Web application will be used.

If you have already tried the servlet-examples Web application on your local Tomcat installation, a default context descriptor will be created for you. Look for the $CATALINA_HOME/conf/Catalina/localhost/servlets-examples.xml file (look for your host name if you're not using localhost). If you find this file, make the following modifications to it:

```
<Context displayName='Servlet 2.4 Examples'
docBase='C:\jdk1.4\tc5\webapps\servlets-examples' path='/servlets-examples'>
  <Environment name='foo/name4' type='java.lang.Integer' value='10'/>
  <Environment name='minExemptions' type='java.lang.Integer' value='1'/>
  <Environment name='foo/bar/name2' type='java.lang.Boolean' value='true'/>
  <Environment name='name3' type='java.lang.Integer' value='1'/>
  <Environment name='foo/name1' type='java.lang.String' value='value1'/>
   <Manager className='org.apache.catalina.session.PersistentManager'
         debug='0'
         saveOnRestart='true'
         maxActiveSessions='3'
         minIdleSwap='0'
         maxIdleSwap='60'
         maxIdleBackup='0'>
   <Store className='org.apache.catalina.session.FileStore'/>
   </Manager>
</Context>
```

If you do not find the context descriptor, add the file manually by creating a $CATALINA_HOME/conf/Catalina/localhost/servlets-examples.xml file containing the following:

```
<Context docBase=' C:\jdk1.4\tc5\webapps\servlets-examples' path='/servlets-
examples'>
   <Manager className='org.apache.catalina.session.PersistentManager'
         debug='0'
         saveOnRestart='true'
         maxActiveSessions='3'
         minIdleSwap='0'
         maxIdleSwap='60'
         maxIdleBackup='0'>
   <Store className='org.apache.catalina.session.FileStore'/>
   </Manager>
</Context>
```

Make sure you have adjusted the `docBase` attribute in this file to point to your Web application directory.

This configures a Persistent Session Manager that will allow up to three active sessions before activating session swapping. Any session is available for swapping at any time. All idle sessions will be swapped within 60 seconds. An active session is backed up regularly; a value of `0` indicates that sessions should be backed up immediately after being used.

Start Tomcat 5, start a session, and view the session information by going to the following URL:

```
http://localhost:8080/servlets-examples/servlet/SessionExample
```

Note on a piece of paper the session ID and the start date of your session.

Now, wait for about two minutes for the Persistent Session Manager to go to work. At this point, simulate a crash via an ungraceful shutdown. This can be done by a Ctrl+C in the Tomcat window. Make sure you do not close the browser.

Next, start Tomcat again. When Tomcat starts, it will restore all the sessions that were backed up. Try the following URL again:

```
http://localhost:8080/servlets-examples/servlet/SessionExample
```

Note that the session ID and backed-up session information is identical to what appeared before the (simulated) crash. In effect, our Tomcat server has survived an unexpected sudden crash. The Persistent Session Manager already backed up the session by the time you crashed Tomcat. Therefore, when you restart Tomcat, it restores the session from the backed-up Store, and you resume the previous session.

To see where the persisted sessions are stored, go to the `$CATALINA_HOME/work/Catalina/localhost/servlets-examples/` directory and look for filenames with the `.session` extension.

JNDI Resource Configuration

Within the `server.xml` configuration file, **Java Naming and Directory Interface (JNDI)** resources can be defined; and they may be accessed in a standard J2EE-compliant manner by any Web applications. This section provides a brief introduction to JNDI. Examples illustrate how it is used and the type of administrative requests that developers typically make. A basic understanding of these requests is important to any administrator, because they have an impact on how the JNDI resources must be configured.

What Is JNDI?

JNDI is an API used to look up information pertaining to the network (via naming and directory services). JNDI is designed to work with any compatible naming and directory service, regardless of its native interface API. Some common information that can be obtained through JNDI includes (but is not restricted to) the following:

- User name and password (authentication)
- Access control policy (who can access what)
- Organizational directories
- Servers (e-mail, database, and so on)
- Printers
- Other objects or resources

Before the advent of JNDI, developers had to program specifically to a particular network's directory service. On Microsoft-based networks, they programmed to NT Domains or the Active Directory Service Interface (ADSI). On Solaris/Unix networks, they programmed to the Network Information Service (NIS). On Novell networks, they programmed to the Netware Directory Service (NDS). This made the programming even more complex because each of the network directory services assumes a different naming convention for the resources/information that it stores, and has completely different programming interfaces (APIs) to search for and locate this information.

Figure 8-4 shows how JNDI unifies directory service access across different networks:

As shown in Figure 8-4, JNDI is the top layer that provides a uniform programming interface to applications, while translating the API commands to the network-specific operations that are sent out through its plug-in drivers. In fact, many of the modern directory services support the Lightweight Directory Access Protocol (LDAP). JNDI often gains compatibility with new or legacy directory services through its LDAP driver.

Beyond providing interfaces to existing directory services, JNDI has become a standard way for Java applications (especially in the context of J2EE) to locate network resources. That is, even if there is no physical directory service involved over the network, many of the standard Java APIs have adopted JNDI as the de facto way of obtaining network resources. Developers expect to use JNDI to obtain these Tomcat managed resources. The next section discusses two such examples.

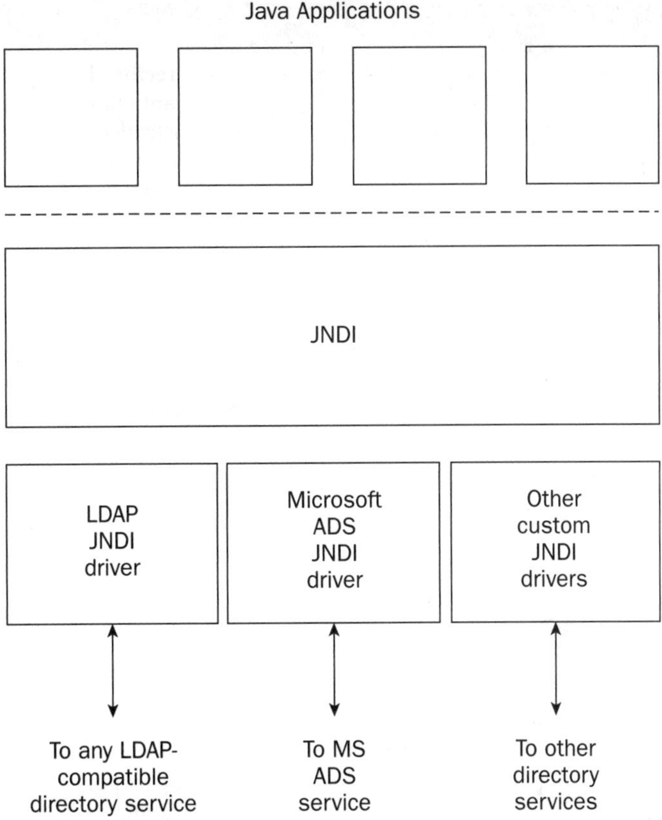

Figure 8-4: JNDI unifies access of different directory services.

Tomcat and JNDI

The role of the Tomcat server, with respect to supporting JNDI, is quite interesting. In fact, the role of Tomcat in this case is only to provide the JNDI lookup facilities (acting as a sort of go-between to provide a standard interface) for any Web application. Tomcat is a J2EE-compliant and Servlet 2.4-compliant server that will facilitate the use of JNDI by hosted Web applications, as shown in Figure 8-5.

In Figure 8-5, the Web application running inside Tomcat is retrieving certain JNDI resources through standard programming convention and APIs (specified by JNDI and Servlet 2.4 specifications). This enables the requests to be placed in a manner independent of the application server—enabling the Web applications to be portable across different vendors' application servers.

The Tomcat container intercepts the standard JNDI requests from the application. To fulfil these JNDI API requests, Tomcat must check its set of preconfigured resources (in the `server.xml` file) to determine what needs to be passed back to the application. Tomcat essentially provides JNDI emulation service for accessing these resources. Tomcat's administrator must configure these resources in the `sever.xml` file.

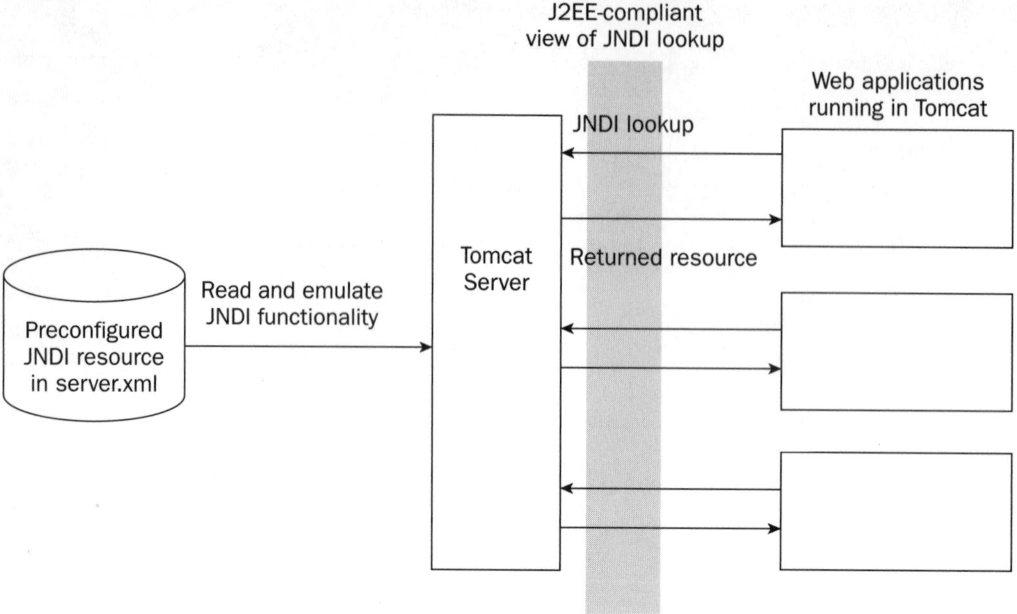

Figure 8-5: Tomcat facilitates resource acquisition by emulating JNDI.

Typical Tomcat JNDI Resources

Two interesting resources that are accessed via JNDI requests from Web applications include the following:

- A JDBC DataSource
- A JavaMail session

JDBC is a well-known standard API that enables application programmers to access relational databases (such as MySQL, Oracle, and SQL Server) in a uniform and standard way. To access data from these relational databases, the application must first obtain a DataSource object. (See Chapter 14 for extensive JDBC coverage. For now, it is sufficient to view a DataSource as a class from which it is possible to obtain connections for a remote database.)

JavaMail is another well-known standard API that provides an interface to access e-mail client capabilities (that is, to create and send mail) across different methods of handling e-mail, in a uniform and standard manner. For a Web application to access mail servers and send mail, the application must first obtain a JavaMail `Session` object.

The JDBC 3 and JavaMail 1.3 specifications are synchronized with the latest J2EE specification. In both cases, it is the responsibility of the container (application server) to provide Web applications with JNDI access to these resources. The administrator needs to configure these resources for Tomcat 5 to find them, passing them through to the requesting Web application by emulating JNDI action.

Configuring Resources via JNDI

For JNDI, you have the following three options for configuring the resource within the hierarchy of Tomcat configuration components:

- At the server's global `<GlobalNamingResources>` level
- At the virtual host's `<DefaultContext>` level
- At the `<Context>` level associated with a single Web application, typically residing in the application's context descriptor XML file

Any JNDI resource configured at the `<DefaultContext>` level will be available to all Web applications running on the same virtual host, whereas any JNDI resource configured at the `<Context>` level will be available only within the specific Web application associated with that context.

Resources configured at the `<GlobalNamingResources>` level are available server-wide (across all services and engines). These resources can then be referred to in subsequent resource configurations via `<ResourceLink>` elements.

You can add the sub-elements described in the following table inside the `<Context>` or `<DefaultContext>` element to support and configure JNDI Resources.

Sub-Element Name	Description	How Many?
`Environment`	Creates environment entries available from the JNDI `InitialContext` that Tomcat will supply to an application	0 or more
`Resource`	Provides the name of a datatype of a JNDI resource to the application	0 or more
`ResourceParams`	Specifies the Java programming language class that is used to create the resources, and specifies a configuration JavaBean	0 or more
`ResourceLink`	Adds a link to a resource defined in the `<GlobalNamingResource>` element, which is server-wide	0 or more

It is also possible for developers to directly embed environment or resource parameters into their Web applications. This is done by defining `<env-entry>`, `<resource-env-entry>`, and `<ResourceParams>` elements inside the `web.xml` descriptor. This will make a resource specific to a Web application. However, the `web.xml` deployment descriptor must be changed each time a change occurs in the resource information.

The following sections examine each of the JNDI supporting sub-elements.

The <Environment> Element

The `<Environment>` element is used to pass named data values (like environment variables in a command shell) to the Web applications. Web applications can access these values through the JNDI context. The following table describes the available attributes for an `<Environment>` element.

Attribute	Description	Required?
`name`	The JNDI name for this element	Yes
`description`	Text description for this element	No
`override`	Application programmers can use the `<env-entry>` element to override the one defined here. You can disable the override by setting it to `false`.	No
`type`	Java class name of the datatype represented by this element	Yes
`value`	The actual value of the environment entry	Yes

For example, the following will add a JNDI entry named `maxUsers` with a value of `100`:

```
<Environment name='maxUsers' type='java.lang.Integer' value='100' />
```

The <Resource> Element

The `<Resource>` element is used to pass a reference via resource managers (classes that manage and assign resources — such as JDBC connections) to Web applications using a name in simple text. A Web application can access the reference to the resource manager through a lookup based on the textual name using the JNDI context. The following table describes the attributes a `<Resource>` element can have.

Attribute	Description	Required?
`auth`	Indicates who does the authentication. If the value is `application`, then the application itself must sign-on with the resource manager. If the value is `container`, then the container does a sign-on with the resource manager.	No
`description`	Text description for this element	No
`name`	Name of the resource	Yes
`scope`	Value can be either `Shareable` or `Unsharable`; determines if the resource can be shared	No
`type`	Java class name of the datatype represented by this resource	Yes

For example, the following will add a UserDatabase implementation (for storing authentication and role information on Tomcat 5):

```
<Resource name='myDatabase'
          type='org.apache.catalina.UserDatabase'>
</Resource>
```

The <ResourceParams> Element

The <ResourceParams> element associates parameters with the resource manager already configured in a <Resource> element. This element is often used to configure the resource manager. For example, if the <Resource> is a JDBC DataSource, the <ResourceParams> may contain the Relational Database Management Server (RDBMS) server location, login name, and password to use. The <ResourceParams> element can contain the attribute shown in the following table.

Attribute	Description	Required?
`name`	Name of corresponding resource	Yes

Each <ResourceParams> element can contain one or more <nam>/<value> sub-elements, expressed as follows:

```
<ResourceParams name='jdbc/wroxDatabase'>
   <parameter>
      <name>password</name>
      <value>wrox123</value>
   </parameter>
</ResourceParams>
```

The <ResourceLink> Element

The <ResourceLink> element refers to a previously configured JNDI resource (typically in the <GlobalNamingResource> sub-element associated with a server), making these resources available to all <Service>, <Host>, and <Context> components. This enables resources to be defined and shared across servers or globally. A <ResourceLink> element can have the attributes described in the following table.

Attribute	Description	Required?
`global`	The name of the resource being linked to	Yes
`name`	The name of the resource, accessible by Web application via JNDI lookup	Yes
`type`	The Java programming language class name indicating the type of resource returned	Yes

For example, if the UserDatabase `<Resource>` element is already defined in the server's `<GlobalNamingResource>` sub-element (see the `<Resource>` element example earlier), then it can be referred to within a `<Context>` element of a Web application using the following:

```
<ResourceLink name='localDatabase' global='myDatabase'
              type='org.apache.catalina.UserDatabase'/>
```

This entry will link the previously defined UserDatabase instance (named `myDatabase` in `<GlobalNamingResource>`) to the JNDI addressable resource called `localDatabase`. The Web application can perform a JNDI lookup for `localDatabase` and obtain access to the UserDatabase instance.

The next section shows how to apply these elements to configure a JDBC DataSource and JavaMail session.

Configuring a JDBC DataSource

JDBC 2.1 features, including DBCP connections pooling (a Jakarta Commons library for efficient management of JDBC connections), are directly supported by Tomcat 5. JDBC is discussed at length in Chapter 14. For now, it is only necessary to know how JDBC connections (as a JNDI resource) can be passed to Web applications.

Your JDBC driver can be placed in the `$CATALINA_HOME/common/lib/` directory. This enables the Tomcat server and your applications to find and access this driver.

Finally, you must configure the JNDI resource factory using `<Resource>` and `<ResourceParams>` elements. In this case, you are configuring the database factory to use the MySQL database, with a host-wide scope. This instance of the database will be shared between all the Web applications running within the same virtual host:

```
<Host>
  ...
  <Resource name='jdbc/wroxTC5' auth='Container'
            type='javax.sql.DataSource'/>
```

This segment configures Tomcat's built-in JDBC DataSource factory. The built-in DataSource factory implementation in Tomcat is `org.apache.naming.factory.DbcpDataSourceFactory`. A DataSource factory is a class from which new instances of DataSource objects can be obtained. Using this factory, the configuration parameters described in the following table are possible.

Parameter	Description
`driverClassName`	Java programming language class name of the JDBC driver. This driver should be placed in the `$CATALINA_HOME/common/lib` directory for easy location by the DataSource factory code.
`maxActive`	The maximum number of active connections in this pool
`maxIdle`	The maximum number of idle connections in this pool

Parameter	Description
maxWait	In milliseconds, indicates the maximum wait for a connection by the DataSource factory before throwing an exception
user	The user ID used to log on to the database
password	The password used to log on to the database
url	The JDBC-compatible URL specifies the database instance to be used
validationQuery	An optional SQL query used to validate a connection. Essentially, the factory will perform this query to ensure that rows are returned before considering the connection valid.

For example, you can parameterize the defined JDBC resource by using the following `<ResourceParams>` elements:

```
<ResourceParams name='jdbc/WroxTC5'>
    <parameter>
        <name>driverClassName</name>
        <value> com.mysql.jdbc.Driver </value>
    </parameter>
    <parameter>
        <name>url</name>
        <value>jdbc:mysql://localhost/wroxtomcat</value>
    </parameter>
    <parameter>
        <name>username</name>
        <value>empro</value>
    </parameter>
    <parameter>
        <name>password</name>
        <value>empass</value>
    </parameter>

    <parameter>
        <name>maxActive</name>
        <value>20</value>
    </parameter>
    <parameter>
        <name>maxIdle</name>
        <value>30000</value>
    </parameter>
    <parameter>
        <name>maxWait</name>
        <value>100</value>
    </parameter>
</ResourceParams>
```

In addition to this configuration, the developer must declare the use of the resource in a deployment descriptor (`web.xml`) using a `<resource-ref>` element, as shown in the following example:

```
<resource-ref>
  <res-ref-name> jdbc/WroxTC5 </res-ref-name>
  <res-type> javax.sql.DataSource </res-type>
  <res-auth> Container </res-auth>
</resource-ref>
```

Within the Web applications, the DataSource can be looked up relative to the `java:comp/env` naming context. The code used will be similar to the following:

```
Context myInitialContext = new InitialContext();
Context localContext = (Context) myInitialContext('java:comp/env');
DataSource myDataSource = (DataSource)
  localContext.lookup('jdbc/wroxTC5');

Connection myConn = myDataSource.getConnection();
...
```

At this point, `myConn` contains an instance of a database connection, which can be used to access the MySQL database immediately.

Configuring Mail Sessions

JavaMail is a standard programming API used by Java developers to create and send e-mail. Tomcat 5 supports JavaMail by providing the JNDI configuration of a JavaMail session as a resource, using its own "factory code" to create a JavaMail session for the Web application. This enables any Web applications running under Tomcat to use JNDI to look up and use the session. The example in the following section shows how to send e-mail from within a JSP using a JavaMail session configured as a JNDI resource. The JSP will post a form to a collaborating Servlet. The Servlet will use the configured JavaMail session to send the actual e-mail. It takes advantage of the `jsp-examples` sample Web application that is distributed with Tomcat 5.

Adding a Resource Definition to the Application Context Descriptor

The first step is to configure a mail session as a JNDI resource. In the context descriptor of the `jsp-examples` Web application (the `$CATALINA_HOME/conf/Catalina/localhost/jsp-examples.xml` file), add the following resource definition inside the `<Context>` element. If this file does not exist, add it explicitly:

```
<Context path='/jsp-examples' docBase='jsp-examples' debug='0' privileged='true'>
 <Resource name='mail/Session' auth='Container' type='javax.mail.Session'/>
 <ResourceParams name='mail/Session'>
           <parameter>
             <name>mail.smtp.host</name>
             <value>localhost</value>
           </parameter>
 </ResourceParams>
</Context>
```

This will configure the JNDI `mail/Session` context, referring to an SMTP server running on `localhost`. If you are connecting to a remote SMTP server, change the value of `localhost` to the name or IP address of your server. You can also modify the port used (if it is not at the standard port 25) by setting the `mail.smtp.port` parameter.

Adding a Reference to a Mail Session Resource in the Deployment Descriptor

In the deployment descriptor (the `$CATALINA_HOME/webapps/jsp-examples/WEB-INF/web.xml` file), you must declare a reference to JNDI resource. Add the following lines after the `<security-role>` declarations, but before the `<env-entry>` descriptions in the `web.xml` file:

```
...
</security-role>
<resource-ref>
        <res-ref-name>mail/Session</res-ref-name>
        <res-type>javax.mail.Session</res-type>
        <res-auth>Container</res-auth>
</resource-ref>
<env-entry>
...
```

Downloading and Installing JavaMail 1.3.1 and the JavaBeans Activation Framework 1.0.2 Libraries

Check the `%CATALINA_HOME%/common/lib` directory to determine whether you have `mail.jar` and `activation.jar` libraries there. These are the JavaMail and JavaMail-dependent JAF libraries. If they are not there, they will need to be downloaded.

JavaMail support is a part of the J2EE download, or it can be obtained as an optional download. You can find the required `mail.jar` library as part of the JavaMail distribution, downloadable from the following URL:

```
http://java.sun.com/products/javamail/downloads/index.html
```

The latest version available at the time of writing is JavaMail 1.3.1. Because JavaMail 1.3.1 depends on JAF, you will also need to download the JavaBeans Activation Framework from the following URL:

```
http://java.sun.com/products/javabeans/glasgow/jaf.html
```

The library that you will need from this download is `activation.jar`.

Compiling and Configuring the SendMailServlet

The code distribution includes the source code of `SendMailServlet.java` and a `compile.bat` file for its compilation. This sample Servlet may already be part of your Tomcat 5 distribution. If not, place the `SendMailServlet.java` and `compile.bat` files into the `webapps/jsp-examples/WEB-INF/classes` directory.

Be sure to edit the `compile.bat` file to set the path to your own `servlet-api.jar` and `mail.jar`. Otherwise, compilation will fail. Compile the Servlet.

To configure the Servlet, add the following Servlet definition and mapping to the `web.xml` deployment descriptor of the `jsp-examples` Web application:

```
<servlet>
    <servlet-name>SendMailServlet</servlet-name>
    <servlet-class>SendMailServlet</servlet-class>
</servlet>
<servlet-mapping>
    <servlet-name>SendMailServlet</servlet-name>
    <url-pattern>/mail/SendMailServlet</url-pattern>
</servlet-mapping>
```

Creating the sendmail.jsp JSP

If `sendmail.jsp` is not included with your Tomcat 5 distribution, copy it from the code distribution to the `%CATALINA_HOM%/webapps/jsp-examples/mail` subdirectory (create this directory if necessary). This is the JSP that will accept user input and submit the e-mail details to the SendMailServlet for sending.

Sending E-mail via JavaMail Sessions

Start Tomcat 5, and you can test the example that uses JavaMail to send e-mail. Use the following URL:

```
http://localhost:8080/jsp-examples/jsp/mail/sendmail.jsp
```

Figure 8-6 shows the JSP-generated form that you can fill out to send e-mail.

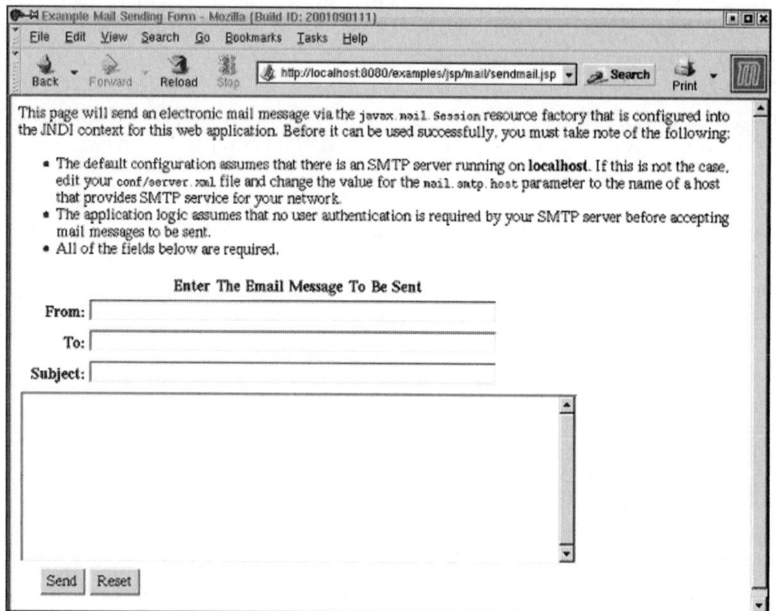

Figure 8-6: Accessing JavaMail via JNDI.

You can fill out the form shown in Figure 8-6 to actually send an e-mail message (assuming that you have the SMTP server configured properly).

This JSP collects information for an e-mail message from the user, and then submits it to the SendMailServlet for processing and sending. The following code shows how SendMailServlet (or other Web application code) can look up and utilize the JNDI mail session:

```
// Acquire our JavaMail session object
   Context initCtx = new InitialContext();
   Context envCtx = (Context) initCtx.lookup('java:comp/env');
   Session session = (Session) envCtx.lookup('mail/Session');
   ...
```

Configuring Lifecycle Listeners

Many top-level and nested components in the Tomcat 5 architecture (including Server, Service, Logger, Realm, and so on) support the configuration of **lifecycle listeners.** Lifecycle listeners are Java code modules that can be hooked into the server logic and executed during specific moments during the lifecycle of a component. This capability enables new custom functionality to be introduced to the Tomcat 5 server without having to change the core server code base.

With Tomcat 5, the only explicit use of a lifecycle Listener is to insert code that enables the server to be managed remotely (through JMX support). Using a simple example, the following section shows how this support code is configured.

Lifecycle Events Sent by Tomcat Components

Lifecycle listeners are customized code that listens to specific lifecycle events. Lifecycle events are sent by a component, to any configured Listener, at well-defined points in a component's lifecycle. These points include the following:

- Just before component startup
- During component startup
- Just after component startup
- Just before component stop
- During component stop
- Just after component stop

Developers may use lifecycle listeners to add new processing logic to the Tomcat server. As an administrator, you can add these custom listeners by creating a `<Listener>` XML element within the associated component.

The <Listener> Element

You can add a lifecycle Listener to a Tomcat component (if the component supports lifecycle listeners) by configuring a `<Listener>` XML element within the XML definition of the component. Most Tomcat 5 architectural components support lifecycle listeners.

In Tomcat 5, listeners for the <Server> component are used to create JMX MBeans that represent run-time server structures and global resources. **JMX MBeans** are objects that enable Tomcat components, structures, and resources to be monitored or accessed via an external management system. Chapter 18 provides more extensive coverage of JMX.

More specifically, Tomcat 5 uses the following default `server.xml` fragment to add JMX MBean support:

```
<Server port='8005' shutdown='SHUTDOWN' debug='0'>
  <Listener className='org.apache.catalina.mbeans.ServerLifecycleListener'
            debug='0'/>
  <Listener className='org.apache.catalina.mbeans.GlobalResourcesLifecycleListener'
            debug='0'/>
```

Although the XML configuration syntax of a lifecycle Listener configuration is similar to the configuration of a nested component inside a container, technically, a Listener is *not* an architectural component (and definitely not a nested component). A lifecycle Listener should be thought of as an extended attribute of the containing XML element. The main reasons why lifecycle listeners are configured as XML sub-elements instead of XML element attributes are as follows:

- Multiple lifecycle listeners can be associated with a single component.
- Each Listener can be configured with its own set of attributes.

The `<Listener>` element, representing a lifecycle Listener, can be configured with the attributes described in the following table.

Attribute	Description	Required?
`className`	The Java programming language class that implements the Listener logic. This class must implement the `org.apache.catalina.LifecycleListener` Java interface.	Yes
`debug`	Controls the level of debug messages	No
`descriptors`	A semicolon-separated list of MBean descriptor XML files. This attribute is used to provide JMX compatibility (see Chapter 18 on Tomcat's JMX support) for custom components (that is, custom Valves and custom Realms).	No

Tomcat 5 Lifecycle Listeners Configuration

Tomcat 5 has two custom Listener classes that will intercept lifecycle events and create (or destroy) management objects (called MBeans) to support external management of Tomcat. These two custom Listener classes are as follows:

- *`org.apache.catalina.mbeans.ServerLifecycle`*—A Listener to create/destroy MBeans for management of Tomcat architectural components
- *`org.apache.catalina.mbeans.GlobalResourcesLifecycle`*—A Listener to create/destroy MBeans for management of any global resources that may be externally manageable

Displaying MBeans Created by Lifecycle Listeners Using the Manager JMX Proxy

In the default `server.xml` file, the two lifecycle listeners are configured. You can see the result of the created MBeans by using the `manager` application's JMX proxy Servlet. Try the following URL:

```
http://localhost:8080/manager/jmxproxy/?qry=*%3Atype%3DRole%2C*
```

This proxy Servlet enables you to query specific MBeans that are created within the Tomcat 5 server. MBeans representing roles are created only by the lifecycle listeners described earlier. When these lifecycle listeners are not hooked in, the **roles** MBeans are not created.

The preceding query will enumerate all the roles MBeans. The query should return a list of the four manageable objects (MBeans) for the roles that are defined in `tomcat-users.xml`, as shown in Figure 8-7.

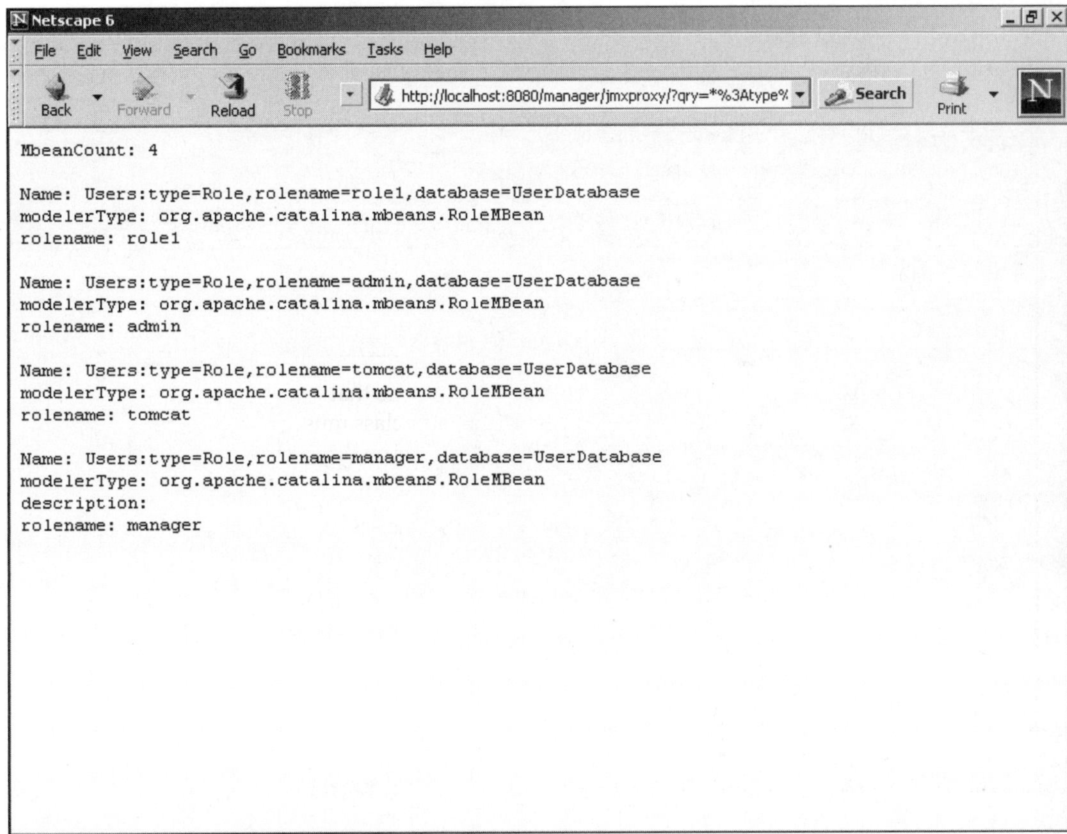

Figure 8-7: Lifecycle Listener–created role-type MBeans.

Note that you will have to authenticate to use the **`manager`** *application. This means that the manager role must be added to the* **`tomcat-users.xml`** *file (either manually or via the* **`admin`** *application) for the* **`manager`** *application user. In this test case, the manager role was added to the default Tomcat user. (Chapter 7 discusses the* **`manager`** *application.)*

Removing Default Lifecycle Listeners

Next, the lifecycle listeners will be removed. As a result, it is expected that the dynamically created MBeans will no longer be available. To try this out, first stop Tomcat 5. Edit the `server.xml` file by hand and comment out the two `<Listener>` elements. The following code shows the elements commented out:

```
<Server port='8005' shutdown='SHUTDOWN' debug='0'>
<!--
 <Listener className='org.apache.catalina.mbeans.ServerLifecycleListener'
           debug='0'/>
  <Listener className='org.apache.catalina.mbeans.GlobalResourcesLifecycleListener'
           debug='0'/>
-->
```

This means that no lifecycle Listener will be configured for the server component, and no role-typed MBeans will be created.

Start Tomcat 5 and try the previous proxy URL again. This time, no role-typed MBean will be found, as shown in Figure 8-8.

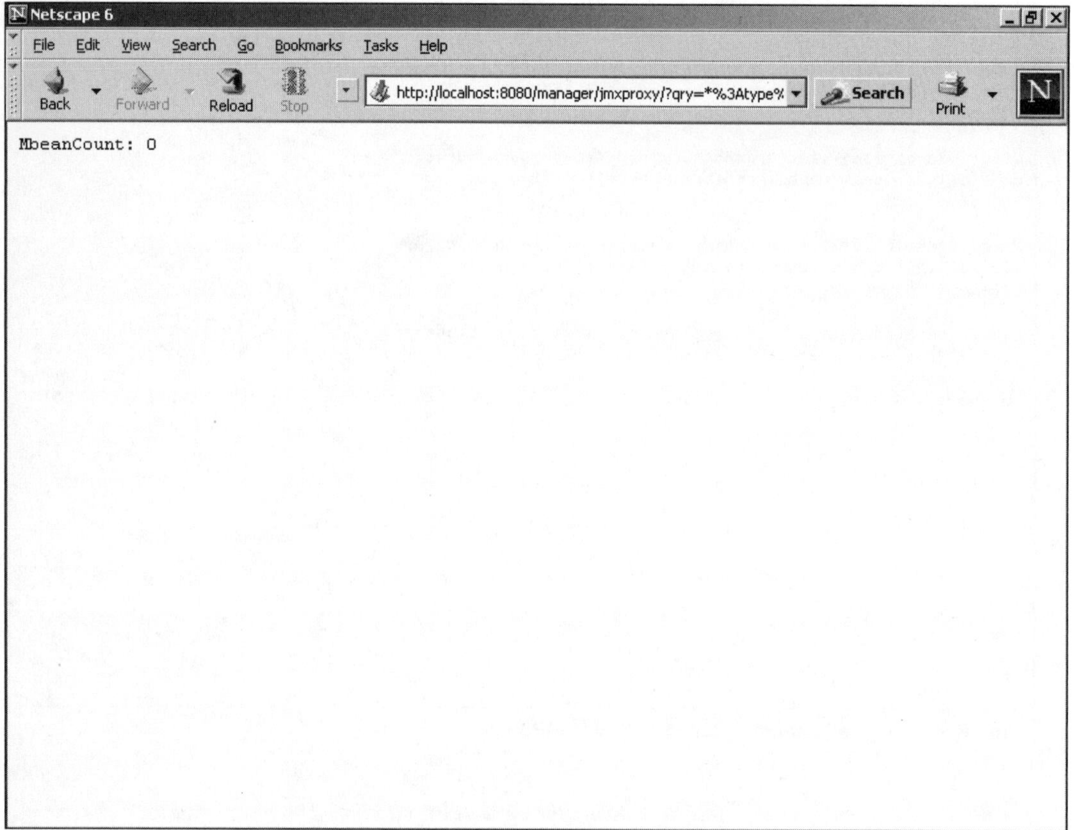

Figure 8-8: No role-typed MBean is available when lifecycle listeners are disabled.

Because the lifecycle listeners responsible for creating the role-typed MBeans are not configured, the query reveals that no role-typed MBeans are available.

Summary

This chapter discussed Tomcat configuration topics that are beyond the basic "up-and-running" requirements. The following important areas were covered:

- The Access Log Valve can enable logging of resource access at different levels: the Web application, the virtual host, or globally across all the virtual hosts. This Valve is highly configurable and you can customize the name as well as the actual format of the log entries, although the `common` format is the best known.
- The standard Single Sign-on Valve enhances the user experience because users no longer must type in a user name and password every time they switch between Web applications running on the same host. This Valve caches the credentials on the server and passes them between the applications as required.
- The Request Filter Valves are easily configured to control all incoming requests that are to be processed or blocked entirely. These Valves can block a list of IP addresses or host names.
- The lesser-known Request Dumper Valve can be used to debug other Valves and/or components, and to visualize the effects of scoping.
- The configurable Persistent Session Manager component can be used to provide a measure of reliability to Tomcat. It can periodically back up sessions on disk, and also swap out dormant sessions to make room for active sections. Most important, it will restore sessions from disk when it starts up. This enables sessions to persist between restarts of the Tomcat server.
- JNDI provides a uniform interface to different directory services. This makes it possible to write only one set of lookup code across different directory services. Examples presented included the configuration of JNDI resources (such as JDBC connections and JavaMail sessions).
- Lifecycle listeners are Java code modules and are configured as XML sub-elements of a Tomcat component. Configured listeners are invoked by the component during well-defined points in the lifecycle of a component. In Tomcat 5, lifecycle listeners are used to create manageable objects (MBeans) for supporting Tomcat manageability (via JMX).

Chapter 9 discusses Tomcat's class loaders.

Class Loaders

Every Java developer makes extensive use of class loaders, often without realizing it. Each time a class is instantiated as an object or referenced statically, that class must be loaded by the Java Virtual Machine (JVM) into memory. Thus, even statements as simple as `String greeting = "hello"` or `int maxValue = Integer.MAX_VALUE` make use of a class loader. They require the `String` class and the `Integer` class to be loaded, respectively.

While class loaders are designed to operate fairly transparently from the developer's point of view, there are subtleties to their use that are important to understand. Why a chapter on class loading in a Tomcat book? It turns out that class loaders and their behavior are a big part of Tomcat. Following the Servlet specification, Tomcat is required to allocate a unique class loader to each Web application. This chapter explains what this means and why it is important.

Following an explanation of class loaders in general and Tomcat's class loaders in particular, common problems related to class loaders are discussed. By the end of this chapter, not only will you be familiar with class loaders in general, but you'll also understand how they relate specifically to Tomcat.

The following topics are covered in this chapter:

- An overview of class loaders
- Security issues with class loaders
- Tomcat and class loaders
- Dynamic class reloading
- Common class loader issues

Class Loader Overview

Java was designed to be platform-independent and to support distributed network architectures. To fulfill both of these goals, Java had to innovate in many key areas. One of these areas is the basic issue of how to load code libraries. If Java is to be truly platform-independent, it cannot rely on a specific type of file system (or even a set of dozens of file systems) for loading its libraries. Many small embedded computer systems don't even have a file system!

Furthermore, because Java was designed to load classes from various sources spread across a network, simply loading classes from a file system won't work.

To deal with these issues, the Java architects introduced the notion of a **class loader.** The role of the class loader is to abstract the process of loading classes, making it completely independent of any type of underlying data store, be it a network or a hard drive.

For example, consider the following simple program:

```
import com.wrox.MyObject;

public class Simple {
    public static void main(String[] args) {
        MyObject myObject = new MyObject();
    }
}
```

When the line `MyObject myObject = new MyObject()` is executed, the Java Virtual Machine (JVM) asks a class loader to find a class named `com.wrox.MyObject` and return it as a `Class` object. The class loader is then free to do whatever it is designed to do to locate the class. Possible actions include searching a file system, checking a ROM chip, or loading a class from a network. Once returned, the `Class` object that represents the `MyObject` class is then used to instantiate the `myObject` instance. Figure 9-1 depicts this process.

Standard J2SE Class Loaders

Ever since the J2SE 1.2 specification, the JVM has made use of three distinct class loaders, which are discussed next, along with their roles:

- **Bootstrap** class loader (also called the **primordial** class loader)
- **Extension** class loader
- **System** class loader

These class loaders occupy a hierarchy, with the system class loader at the bottom and the bootstrap class loader at the top. The relationships are parent-child, so the parent of the system class loader is the extension class loader. The importance of this relationship shall soon become clear.

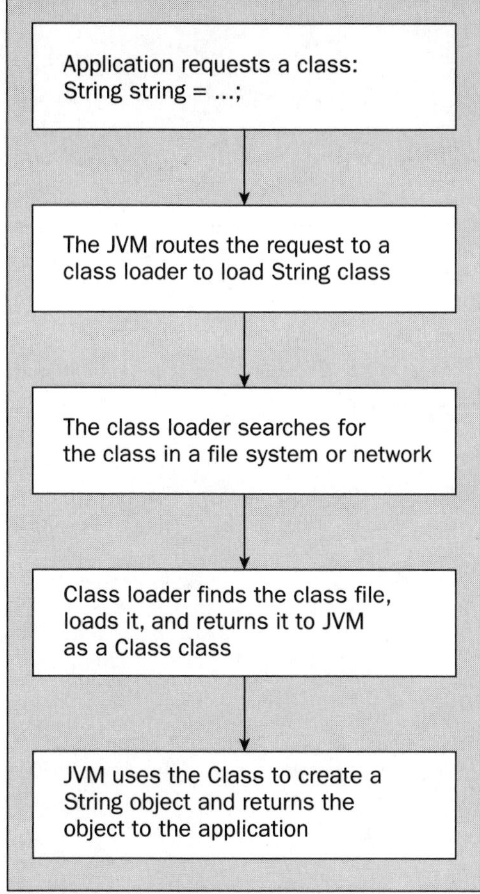

Figure 9-1: JVM and class loaders.

Bootstrap Class Loader

As its name implies, the bootstrap class loader is used by the JVM to load those Java classes that are necessary for the JVM to function. Actually, the bootstrap class loader is responsible for loading *all* the core Java classes (such as `java.lang.*` and `java.io.*`).

Because class loaders are written in Java, the bootstrap class loader solves a high-tech "chicken-and-egg" problem: How can the JVM load a Java-based class loader when the class loader itself must be loaded in? Including the bootstrap class loader in the JVM itself solves this problem, and various JVM vendors (including Sun) implement the bootstrap class loader using native code.

Although it has been explained that the bootstrap class loader loads the core Java classes, you may be wondering where exactly the bootstrap class loader finds these classes.

It turns out that the answer to this question varies from vendor to vendor. Sun's JVM 1.3.1 looks in the following locations:

```
jdk/jre/lib/rt.jar
jdk/jre/lib/i18n.jar
jdk/jre/lib/sunrsasign.jar
jdk/jre/classes
```

The paths for Sun's JVM 1.4 include a few additional items (highlighted):

```
jdk/jre/lib/rt.jar
jdk/jre/lib/i18n.jar
jdk/jre/lib/sunrsasign.jar
jdk/jre/lib/jsse.jar
jdk/jre/lib/jce.jar
jdk/jre/lib/charsets.jar
jdk/jre/classes
```

Apple's JVM 1.3.1 uses the following locations instead:

```
/System/Library/Frameworks/JavaVM.framework/Versions/1.3.1/Classes/ui.jar
/System/Library/Frameworks/JavaVM.framework/Versions/1.3.1/Classes/classes.jar
/System/Library/Frameworks/JavaVM.framework/Versions/1.3.1/Classes/i18n.jar
/System/Library/Frameworks/JavaVM.framework/Versions/1.3.1/Classes/sunrsasign.jar
```

Extension Class Loader

Java 1.2 introduced the standard extension mechanism. Normally, when developers want the JVM to look in certain locations for class files, they make use of the CLASSPATH environment variable. Sun introduced the standard extension mechanism as an alternative method. You can drop JAR files into a standard extension directory and the JVM will automatically find them.

The extension class loader is responsible for loading all the classes in one or more extension directories. Just as the bootstrap class loader's paths can vary on different JVMs, so can the standard extension paths. On Sun's JVM, the standard extension directory is as follows:

```
/jdk/jre/lib/ext
```

One advantage of the standard extension mechanism is that developers don't have to struggle with a huge CLASSPATH environment variable as they add more and more libraries to their system. Another advantage is considered a little later in this chapter.

System Class Loader

The system class loader locates its classes in those directories and JAR files specified in the CLASSPATH environment variable. The system class loader is also used to load an application's entry point class (that is, the class with the main() method), and is the default class loader for loading in any other classes not covered by the other two class loaders.

The Delegation Model

As discussed, J2SE has three different class loaders. If a `java.lang.String` is instantiated, the bootstrap class loader is responsible for loading its class, and if a user class is instantiated, the system class loader is usually the responsible class loader. How does the JVM know which class loader to use?

The JVM knows which class loader to use by utilizing the **delegation model.** In every version of Java since JDK 1.2, whenever a class loader receives a request to load a class, it first asks its parent to fulfil the request (in other words, it *delegates* the request to its parent class loader). Before the class loader's parent loads the requested class, it delegates the request to *its* parent, and so on, until the bootstrap class loader is reached. If the parent is successful in loading the class, then the resulting class object is returned so that it may be instantiated (or statically referenced). Only if a class loader's parent (and its parent, and so on) fails to load the class does the original class loader attempt to load the class.

Thus, when a class is referenced in a Java program, the JVM will automatically route a request to the system class loader to load the necessary class. The system class loader will then request that the extension class loader load the specified class, which in turn will request that the bootstrap class loader load the class. The process stops with the bootstrap class loader, which will then check the core Java libraries (and whatever else it's configured to search) for the requested class.

If the class doesn't exist in the bootstrap class loader's domain, then the extension class loader will check the standard extensions location for the class. If it's still not found, then the system class loader will check the locations specified by the `CLASSPATH` variable for the class. If the class still cannot be located, then a `ClassNotFoundException` will be thrown. Figure 9-2 summarizes this process.

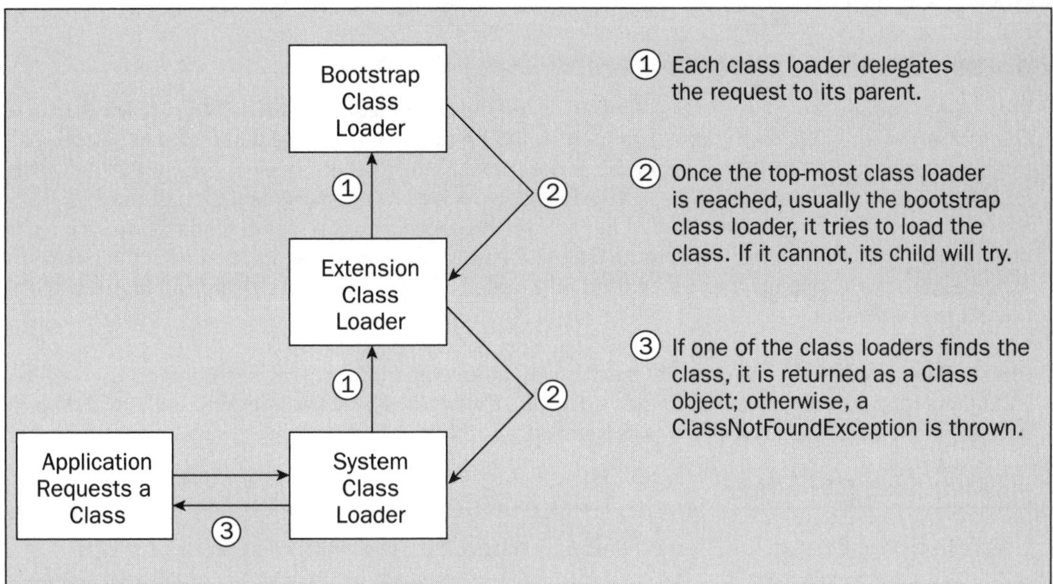

Figure 9-2: Delegation model.

Consider the following example:

```
import com.wrox.MyObject;

public class Simple {
  public static void main(String[] args) {
    String myString = "test";
    MyObject myObject = new MyObject();
  }
}
```

In this example, when the JVM sees the reference to `java.lang.String`, it will request that the system class loader try to load the class. However, before attempting to load the class itself, the system class loader will request that the extension class loader load it, and the extension class loader will pass the request to the bootstrap class loader. Because the bootstrap class loader has no parent, it will check its paths for `java.lang.String`, and it will find it in the `rt.jar` file (at least, on Sun JVMs). The bootstrap class loader will then return the class back down the chain until it is returned to the JVM.

The reference to `com.wrox.MyObject` will also trigger the JVM to make the same request to the system class loader and, as with the `String` class, the system class loader will delegate this to the extension class loader, which will delegate to the bootstrap class loader. However, the bootstrap class loader will not find the `com.wrox.MyObject` class, and will return nothing to the extension class loader. The extension class loader will check its paths, and it will also not find the class (unless, of course, the class has been explicitly placed in the extensions directory), and it, too, will return nothing to the system class loader. The system class loader will search in the `CLASSPATH` locations, where it will find the `com.wrox.MyObject`. The system class loader will then return the class to the JVM.

Endorsed Standard Override Mechanism

Java 1.4 has introduced an interesting concept called the **Endorsed Standards Override Mechanism.** Over time, the core J2SE distribution has been including more and more of what used to be optional extensions to Java. The best example of this is the Java API for XML Processing (JAXP) that is distributed with J2SE 1.4. Sun included both the JAXP API classes as well as an implementation of the API. Because the implementation classes are included in `rt.jar`, the bootstrap class loader loads them. As a result, if developers try to place newer versions of the JAXP implementations that shipped with the JDK in their `CLASSPATH`, their version will never be used. The system class loader will delegate all requests to the bootstrap class loader.

The problem is solved by the override mechanism. If developers place JAR files containing an alternate JAXP implementation in this class loader's domain, the bootstrap class loader will load their class files instead. In the J2SE 1.4, this location is as follows:

```
$JAVA_HOME/lib/endorsed
```

Users can change the path for this mechanism by setting the `java.endorsed.dirs` property.

Before developers start thinking about replacing all of the core libraries, an important limitation must be addressed: only certain packages can be overridden. The complete list of packages can be found in the J2SE 1.4 documentation (`http://java.sun.com/j2se/1.4.1/docs/guide/standards/`). In short, only the CORBA classes and the JAXP classes can be overridden with this mechanism.

More on Class Loader Behavior

Now that the standard J2SE class loaders have been discussed, as well as the delegation model that governs how these class loaders interact, the following sections address additional aspects of class loader behavior.

Lazy Loading (Loading Classes on Demand)

None of the three class loaders preloads all classes in the paths that they search for classes. Instead, they load the classes on demand. Such behavior is said to be *lazy* because the object waits to load the data until it is requested. While laziness in human beings is generally regarded as a negative trait, it is actually quite a positive one for class loaders, for the following reasons:

- *Faster performance* — At the time of initialization, if each class loader had to load every class, it would take much longer to initialize the JVM.
- *Efficiency* — Loading on demand results in more efficient memory usage because loading all the classes immediately would consume more memory than necessary.
- *Flexibility* — JAR files and classes can be added to the search paths of all the class loaders even after the class loaders have been initialized.

Note that when a class is loaded, all of its parent classes must also be loaded. Thus, if ClassB extends ClassA, and ClassB is loaded, then ClassA is also loaded.

Class Caching

The standard J2SE class loaders look up classes on demand, but once a class is loaded into a class loader, it will stay loaded (cached) for a period of time. However, the JVM's garbage collector can reclaim these `Class` objects. This is generally desirable, unless one such garbage-collected `Class` object is actually a stateful singleton class (that is, a class that maintains a static reference to itself, is either noninstantiable or not instantiated in practice, and that maintains some aspects of an application's state). For this reason, Sun JVM's allow class garbage collection to be turned off with the `-Xnoclassgc` option.

Separate Namespaces

Each class loader is assigned a unique namespace. In other words, if the bootstrap class loader loads a class named `sun.misc.ClassA`, and the system class loader loads a class named `sun.misc.ClassB`, the two classes will be considered to be in distinct packages. They will not have access to each other's package-private members.

Creating a Custom Class Loader

Java allows for the creation of custom class loaders, which may seem like one of those pointless tasks that only hard-core professional Java academics would ever want to do. However, not only is creating custom class loaders fairly easy, it can provide enormous flexibility in controlling aspects of an application's behavior.

The key to creating a custom class loader is the `java.lang.ClassLoader` class. This abstract class contains all the logic necessary for transforming the bytes of a compiled class file into a `Class` object that can then be used in an application. It does not, however, provide any mechanism for locating and loading such files.

The J2SE comes with two concrete implementations of `ClassLoader`: `SecureClassLoader` and `URLClassLoader`. The `SecureClassLoader` is a relatively thin wrapper around `ClassLoader` that ties class loading into Java's security model (security issues are discussed in the section "Security and Class Loaders," later in this chapter). Like `ClassLoader`, it does not provide a mechanism for loading class files.

`URLClassLoader` (a subclass of `SecureClassLoader`) provides the default Java mechanism for locating class files in directories or JAR files on a file system, or across a network. The extension and system class loaders are both descended from `URLClassLoader`, though they do not directly extend this class. Tomcat uses its own class loaders extensively. This is discussed in more detail later in this chapter.

Following are some neat tricks that you can perform with a custom class loader:

- Search a database instead of a file system for classes.
- Load different classes with the same fully qualified name.
- Swap your classes with new versions at run-time.
- Load classes before you need them.

Additional Class Loader Information

Covering all the details associated with writing custom class loaders is an advanced development topic and beyond the scope of this chapter. More information about this topic can be gleaned from the following resources:

- `http://java.sun.com/j2se/1.4/docs/api/java/lang/ClassLoader.html` — The `ClassLoader` API JavaDoc file, which is fairly transparent and easy to understand
- `http://www.javageeks.com/Papers/` — A few white papers related to class loaders, notably "Understanding Class.forName()" and "Using the BootClasspath"

Security and Class Loaders

Class loading is at the very center of the Java security model. After all, it would clearly be undesirable for a rogue third party to be able to inject into an application a custom version of `java.lang.String` that had the nasty side effect of deleting the hard drive whenever it is instantiated. Understanding the security features of the class loader architecture will help you understand how Tomcat's class loader system works.

The Java class loader architecture tackles the security problem with the following strategies:

- Class loader delegation
- Core class restriction

- Separate class loader namespaces
- A Security Manager

The following sections describe each of these strategies.

Class Loader Delegation

Recall the class loader delegation model discussed previously. Each class loader first determines whether its parent has the requested class before it attempts to load it.

The delegation model is described by many as a security feature. After all, it seems like it should be. Anyone trying to load false versions of the core Java classes will fail because the bootstrap class loader has first shot at any class, and it will always find the real copies of the core Java classes.

However, the delegation model on its own is flawed as a security mechanism because class loaders are *not required* to implement it. In other words, developers are free to create a class loader that doesn't follow the delegation model.

This security flaw doesn't impeach the class loader delegation model. Indeed, optional enforcement of the delegation model is actually an important feature, and other aspects of the class loader architecture resolve the security issues discussed here, as you will see shortly.

Core Class Restriction

If a custom class loader doesn't have to delegate requests to the system class loader, what would prevent it from loading in its own copy of `java.lang.String`?

Fortunately, it's not possible for any class loader written in Java to instantiate a core Java class. The `ClassLoader` abstract class (from which all class loaders must descend) blocks the creation of any class whose fully qualified name begins with `java`. Thus, no false `java.*` classes can be caught hanging around. Because the bootstrap class loader is not written in Java and does not descend from `ClassLoader`, it is not itself subject to this restriction.

By implication, this restriction indicates that all class loaders must at least delegate to the bootstrap class loader. Otherwise, when the class is loaded, there is no way for its class loader to load `java.lang.Object`, from which all objects must descend.

Thus, the delegation model by itself does not provide security. Instead, the core class restriction mechanism prevents rogue class loaders from tampering with the core Java libraries (at run-time).

Separate Class Loader Namespaces

As discussed previously, each class loader has its own namespace (thus, two different classes with the same fully qualified name). Because every single class loader has its own completely distinct namespace, class loader A can load a class named `com.wrox.Book`, and class loader B can also load a completely different class also named `com.wrox.Book`.

Having separate namespaces is an important security feature because it prevents custom class loaders from stepping over each other, or the system class loader. No matter how hard a renegade class loader may try, it cannot replace a class loaded by a different class loader. Furthermore, classes loaded by different class loaders but otherwise in the same package cannot access each other's package-private members.

Security Manager

If you really want to ensure that no damage can be done to a program with custom class loaders, you can disallow their use completely in an application. This can be done through the `SecurityManager` class, which is Java's general mechanism for applying security restrictions in applications.

With a Security Manager and its associated policy files, you can disallow (or allow) a large number of tasks. For example, a program can be prevented from opening a socket to some network host, or be prevented from opening files on the local file system. In addition, of course, an application can be prevented from loading a class loader. Developers have the following options for preventing class loader-related operations:

- ❑ Prevent the loading of any class loader.
- ❑ Prevent a reference to any class loader being obtained (including the system class loader).
- ❑ Prevent the context class loader of any thread being changed.

Only two steps are required:

1. Configure a policy file with the permissions you want for a given application.
2. Turn on the application's Security Manager.

For more detailed information on Security Managers, see Chapter 15.

Tomcat and Class Loaders

Recall the default Java class loader hierarchy, as summarized in Figure 9-3. Tomcat builds on these class loaders by adding its own after the system class loader, as shown in Figure 9-4.

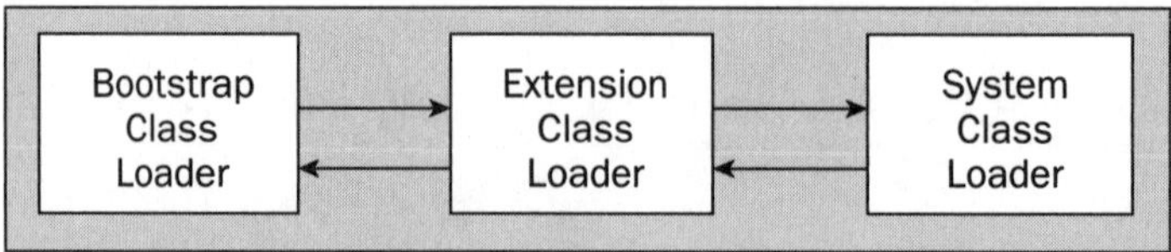

Figure 9-3: The Java class hierarchy.

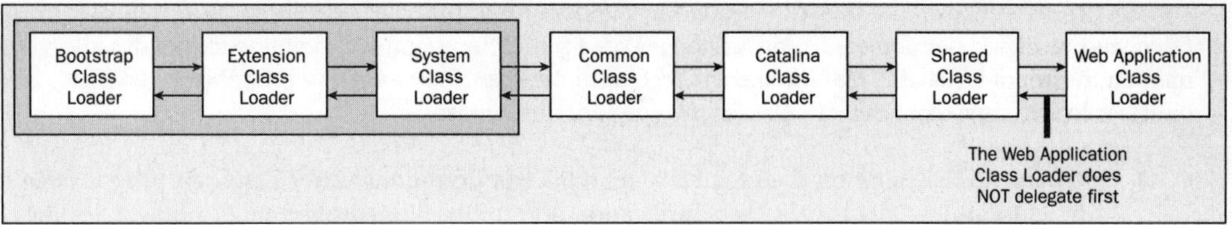

Figure 9-4: Tomcat's class loaders.

Each of these additional Tomcat-specific class loaders is discussed in the following sections.

System Class Loader

Tomcat uses the default system class loader, but it does something a little different from the default behavior of the JVM. In the Tomcat startup file (`startup.bat` on Win32, `startup.sh` on Unix, which in turn call `catalina.bat/sh`), the `CLASSPATH` environment variable is cleared. In its place, Tomcat points `CLASSPATH` to two Tomcat files: `bootstrap.jar` and `tools.jar`.

Recall that the system class loader searches the `CLASSPATH`. Because Tomcat sets the `CLASSPATH` variable to these two files, the normal effect of this class loader is nullified. Whatever the `CLASSPATH` is set to prior to launching Tomcat is simply disregarded as far as Tomcat is concerned.

The `bootstrap.jar` file contains Tomcat start-up classes; `tools.jar` contains the `javac` compiler, which is used to compile JSP pages into class files at run-time.

Endorsed Standards Override Mechanism

On startup, Tomcat changes the Endorsed Standards Override Mechanism to point to the following directory, rather than the default ones mentioned previously:

```
$CATALINA_HOME/common/endorsed
```

Tomcat ships with a version of the popular Apache Xerces XML parser in this directory and a version of the JAXP API. The net result is that this parser (a JAXP implementation) is preferred to any that may have shipped with the JRE that was used to launch Tomcat (such as the Crimson parser that ships with Java 1.4).

Common Class Loader

Next in the hierarchy is the **common class loader,** which is responsible for classes that are used by Tomcat and publicly available to all Web applications. It searches for such class files from two different locations:

```
$CATALINA_HOME/common/lib
$CATALINA_HOME/common/classes
```

Tomcat includes a number of JAR files in `$CATALINA_HOME/common/lib`, such as a version of Apache Ant, many of the Jakarta Commons projects, Jasper (a JSP compiler), as well as the API classes for those APIs that Tomcat supports (Servlet, JSP, JNDI, and JMX).

Tomcat can reference all the classes included in the domain of this class loader in their own Web applications, and exclude such classes from their own Web applications (indeed, developers are not allowed to include the Servlet/JSP API classes in their Web applications). However, it's probably a good idea not to reference anything except the API classes, for the following reasons:

- Relying on the common class loader to load Jakarta Commons, Ant classes, and so on, from this directory potentially breaks Web application portability. No requirement is made of Servlet containers to provide such classes, and other Servlet containers probably don't provide them. Thus, when a Web application is moved from Tomcat to another such Servlet container, problems will occur.
- The versions of such libraries that Tomcat includes may be different than the versions a Web application expects. Such bugs can be maddeningly difficult to track down.

Developers should not place their own classes or JARs in this class loader's domain. Another class loader, the **shared class loader,** is provided for just this purpose and is discussed in the section "Shared Class Loader," later in this chapter. Putting your own custom classes in the common class loader paths would be bad for at least two reasons, one trivial and one nontrivial:

- The trivial reason is that it's easy to forget which classes/JAR files are custom and which belong to Tomcat. Maintenance would, therefore, be tricky, especially for others who would not expect user classes to be in those locations.
- The nontrivial reason is that placing custom classes in the common class loader domain could cause compatibility problems with Tomcat. For example, if an earlier version of the Xerces XML parser were placed in the domain, and it wasn't tested with Tomcat, it could cause mysterious bugs. The same would be true if an older version of the Servlet API were placed into these paths.

Catalina Class Loader

The **Catalina class loader** is used to load all the Tomcat classes that are Tomcat-specific. These classes are not visible to other applications. They are stored in the following locations:

```
$CATALINA_HOME/server/lib
$CATALINA_HOME/server/classes
```

It is a good idea to ignore the contents of this class loader.

Shared Class Loader

The **shared class loader** is a bit like the common class loader, except that developers can place their own classes and JAR files into the shared class loader domain. The shared class loader looks in the following directories:

```
$CATALINA_HOME/shared/lib
$CATALINA_HOME/shared/classes
```

Anytime developers want to share general classes among two or more Web applications, these are the locations in which they should be placed.

Web Application Class Loader

Each Web application also has its own class loader, which looks in the following locations:

```
$CATALINA_HOME/webapps/<webapp>/WEB-INF/classes
$CATALINA_HOME/webapps/<webapp>/WEB-INF/lib
```

Two properties of the **web application class loader** make it unique. First, the Web application class loader does *not* use the delegation model that class loaders are encouraged to use. Instead, it tries to load classes first, before delegating the request to the other class loaders (except in certain conditions detailed below). This behavior makes it easy for Web applications to override classes in the shared and common class loaders on a per-Web-application basis.

Second, each Web application has its own instance of this class loader, which means that no two Web applications can see each other's class files.

Web Application Class Loader Details

Actually, the Web application class loader does delegate to other class loaders; however, it does so in a way that is not consistent with the traditional delegation model.

When a class is requested, this class loader first checks its cache of classes to determine whether the class has already been loaded. If the class is not found among those cached, the Web application class loader will then delegate the request to the system class loader. This is done to prevent Web applications from attempting to instantiate classes shipped with the JRE.

If the system class loader fails to find the class, the Web application class loader will next try to determine whether the class belongs to any of the following packages:

```
javax.*
org.xml.sax.*
org.w3c.dom.*
org.apache.commons.logging.*
org.apache.xerces.*
org.apache.xalan.*
```

If the class does belong to one of these packages, the Web application class loader will delegate the request to its parent, the shared class loader.

If the class has still not been found, the Web application class loader will check its domain for the class. If it fails to find it, and it has not already delegated the request to its parent (that is, if the class belongs to one of the packages listed previously), it will do so now.

Class Loader Order Revisited

To review how these various Tomcat class loaders work together, let's examine what happens when an individual application requests a class. Following is a list of class loaders, and the order in which they will look for classes:

- The Web application class loader looks in `$CATALINA_HOME/webapp/<webapp>/WEB-INF/lib` and `$CATALINA_HOME/webapp/<webapp>/WEB-INF/classes` (except for those situations mentioned in the section "Web Application Class Loader Details," earlier in this chapter).

- The bootstrap class loader looks in the core Java classes.
- Under Java 1.4, the bootstrap class loader will also look in `$CATALINA_HOME/common/endorsed` for alternative CORBA and JAXP classes.
- The system class loader looks in `$CATALINA_HOME/bin/bootstrap.jar` and `$JAVA_HOME/lib/tools.jar`.
- The common class loader looks in `$CATALINA_HOME/common/lib` and `$CATALINA_HOME/common/classes`.
- The shared class loader looks in `$CATALINA_HOME/shared/lib` and `$CATALINA_HOME/shared/classes`.

Dynamic Class Reloading

As discussed earlier, once a class loader has loaded a class, it caches the class. This means that future requests for the class always get the cached copy returned to them. Thus, if the class in the file system is changed while the JVM is running, the changed copy will be ignored.

However, because Tomcat uses its own class loader to load each Web application, it can accomplish dynamic class reloading simply by halting the Web application and then reloading it using a new class loader.

The Web application's original class loader is then orphaned and thus garbage-collected at the JVM's convenience. This eliminates the need to restart the JVM when new versions of classes are deployed.

Following are two mechanisms for instructing Tomcat to reload a Web application:

- Configure Tomcat to scan the Web application's `WEB-INF/lib` and `WEB-INF/classes` directories for changed files.
- Explicitly reload the Web application with the Tomcat `manager` application.

Note that in both cases, Tomcat does not simply direct its class loaders to dump their caches and reload from disk. Rather, when it detects a change or receives an explicit reload instruction, it reloads and restarts the entire Web application.

Because Tomcat cannot modify the JRE's built-in class loaders, classes loaded from their domains cannot be part of Tomcat's reload mechanism (that is, the contents of `$CATALINA_HOME/common/endorsed` won't be reloaded with this mechanism).

Performing either of these tasks is fairly simple and is described in Chapter 5 and Chapter 7.

Common Class Loader Pitfalls

A couple of common problems may occur when dealing with Tomcat's class loaders. The solutions to these problems, outlined in the following sections, are derived from information covered in the preceding sections.

Packages Split Among Different Class Loaders

If an application has multiple classes in the same package (for example, `com.wrox.servlets`), they must be loaded by the same class loader. For example, consider the following two classes:

```
com.wrox.servlets.MyServlet
com.wrox.servlets.Constants
```

These classes must be placed in the same class loader domain (such as `/WEB-INF/classes` or `$CATALINA_HOME/classes`). If they are split up, they will no longer have access to each other's private, protected, or package-private (default) members.

Singletons

A **singleton** is a class designed so that it can only be instantiated one time in any given JVM. Consider the example of a singleton class that is an entry point to an object pool of some sort. The designers of this class want to share this singleton among multiple Web applications, and want to maintain the contract that only one instance be created in a single JVM.

The singleton class could look something like the following:

```
public class ObjectPool {
    private static ObjectPool objectPool = null;

    private ObjectPool {
        // initialize object
    }

    public synchronized static ObjectPool getInstance() {
        if (objectPool == null) {
            objectPool = new ObjectPool();
        }
        return objectPool;
    }
}
```

Placing this class in the Web application class loader domain guarantees that each Web application will create a new instance of this class. This is because each Web application has its own class loader, and class loaders maintain distinct namespaces.

The solution is to place this class in the shared class loader domain, where the singleton will be shared among all Web applications because they all share the same class loader.

Recall, however, that the JVM can garbage-collect loaded class objects if memory is low. If the singleton is not currently referenced by any classes in the JVM, it could be garbage-collected, even when its contents are still important to the application. This scenario is a regrettable side effect of the singleton design pattern. Because they can be accessed statically at any time, applications need not maintain a reference to them. Without a reference, the JVM garbage collector cannot determine that the class is currently in use by the application.

Sun's JVMs provide a solution to this problem. Use the `-Xnoclassgc` start-up parameter. This parameter can be utilized when launching Tomcat by setting the `JAVA_OPTS` environment variable to this value. An example of doing this on Windows is as follows:

```
set JAVA_OPTS=-Xnoclassgc
```

Another solution is to ensure that the singleton class is always referenced in some way by the application. This can be as simple as adding the following member to a class that is always loaded in an application:

```
private ObjectPool objectPool = ObjectPool.getInstance();
```

XML Parsers

Unfortunately, the whole issue of XML parsers in Java has become somewhat confusing. Java defines an API for XML parsers based on the W3C organization's DOM standard, called the Java API for XML Processing, or JAXP.

Starting with Java 1.4, the JAXP API was included in the J2SE platform, along with an implementation of JAXP: the Apache Crimson parser. However, Crimson was soon discontinued by the Apache group, in favor of the Xerces XML parser. Xerces was also soon discontinued, in favor of Xerces2.

As a result of this high level of churn, the Java community must now deal with having multiple JAXP implementations in the marketplace and *many* versions of those parsers. Because these disparate versions often have classes with the exact same fully qualified names, using JAXP can often lead to weird results and buggy behavior. The situation is further complicated by the presence of multiple versions of JAXP.

As mentioned previously, the Endorsed Standards Override Mechanism exists to prevent the JRE's class loaders from loading the JAXP classes in situations where an alternate JAXP API version or alternate implementation is desired. Tomcat uses this mechanism to sidestep the XML parser issues by including its own JAXP API and implementation (Xerces).

Unfortunately, under Java 1.4, Tomcat must share the same version of the Xerces XML parser as its Web applications (as well as the same version of Xalan, an XSLT engine). Tomcat relies on the Endorsed Standards Override Mechanism for the version of Xerces it requires, and as discussed previously, the Web application class loader delegates to this mechanism under all conditions (see the section "Web Application Class Loader Details," earlier in this chapter).

This is likely not a problem unless a Web application relies on an old version of Xerces/Xalan for a particular behavior. Or, it is possible that a version of Xerces/Xalan that is newer than the one that shipped with Tomcat is required for a Web application (the version of Xerces/Xalan shipped with Tomcat can be determined by checking the `MANIFEST.MF` file in the Xerces JAR). In such circumstances, the only alternative is to change the parser in the `$CATALINA_HOME/common/endorsed` directory and hope that such a change doesn't break Tomcat.

Of course, these parser version issues really only apply if the Apache family of XML parsers is used. If you use another JAXP implementation whose classes are in entirely different package names, all of the issues just described are eliminated. However, Xerces is by far the world's most popular JAXP implementation.

Summary

To conclude this chapter on class loaders, let's review some of the key points that have been discussed:

- Class loaders abstract the process of loading class files before the first instantiation and make them available for use. Java's default class loaders support loading classes from the local file system and from a network. Java also provides developers with a facility to create their own custom class loaders. The three basic class loaders discussed are the bootstrap, extension, and system class loaders.
- Class loaders use the delegation model. Every class loader passes a request to load a class to its parent until the bootstrap class loader is reached. Each class loader looks for the class, and if it can't be found, the request goes back down the chain. Implementing the delegation model is optional, but class loaders are basically useless if they don't delegate to the bootstrap class loader at some point. Every class loader has a unique namespace.
- The Java security model prevents the misuse of custom class loaders by allowing only the bootstrap class loader to load classes that start with `java.*`. By using the security manager, an application can forbid the use of custom class loaders.
- Tomcat introduces four different class loaders: common, Catalina, shared, and Web application. To share classes among all Web applications, developers should place their classes and JARs in the domain of the shared class loader.

Chapter 10 examines the first of the Tomcat Connectors: HTTP Connectors.

10

HTTP Connectors

When used out of the box to run Web applications, Tomcat can serve HTML pages without any additional configuration. The reason this works is because Tomcat has been preconfigured with an HTTP Connector that can handle requests from a user's Web browser. Because of this Connector, Tomcat can function as a standalone Web server. It can serve static HTML pages, as well as handle Servlets and JSP pages.

Tomcat Connectors provide the external interface (over HTTP or HTTPS) to Tomcat clients. There are two kinds of Connectors — those that implement an HTTP stack of their own (called **HTTP Connectors**) and those that tie Tomcat to an external Web server such as Apache or IIS (called **Web server Connectors**). This chapter examines in detail the configuration of the new Coyote HTTP/1.1 Connector in Tomcat 4.1.x and 5.x. Chapters 11–13 discuss Web server Connectors.

The new Coyote HTTP/1.1 Connector is the default Connector configured for Tomcat 4.1x and 5.x. It supercedes the older HTTP/1.0 and HTTP/1.1 Connectors in Tomcat 3.x and 4.0. The Coyote Connector is backwardly compatible, and it can be installed in both Tomcat 3.x and 4.0.

Although no additional configuration is required to get the HTTP Connector working, you may want to fine-tune some of its features. This chapter describes what to do when your Connector configuration needs to be modified, such as for specific deployments (for example, running Tomcat behind a proxy), SSL setup, or performance tuning.

The following areas are covered in this chapter:

- Tomcat 4.0 HTTP/1.1 Connector
- Tomcat 4.1 HTTP/1.1 Connector
- Tomcat 5.x HTTP/1.1 Connector
- Running Tomcat behind a proxy server
- Performance tuning

HTTP Connectors

The HTTP Connectors are Java classes that implement the HTTP protocol. Tomcat's Connector class (for example, the `org.apache.coyote.tomcat5.CoyoteConnector` class in Tomcat 5.x) is invoked when there is an HTTP request on the Connector port. The port that the Connector listens on is specified in the `$CATALINA_HOME/conf/server.xml` configuration file, and is usually set to 8080. The Connector class has code to parse the HTTP request and take the required action of either serving up static content or passing the request through the Tomcat Servlet engine. This Connector class implements the HTTP/1.1 protocol.

Tomcat 4.0: HTTP/1.1 Connector

Tomcat 4.0 introduced a new HTTP/1.1 Connector. However, the very next release (4.1) comes with an improved HTTP Connector called the Coyote HTTP/1.1 Connector that makes the old container obsolete.

The configuration attributes for the HTTP/1.1 Connector are the same as those for the Coyote HTTP/1.1 Connector. Hence, for further details, refer to the section "Tomcat 4.1: Coyote HTTP/1.1 Configuration," later in this chapter. The only difference between the two is the value of the `className` attribute.

- *`className`*—The className attribute specifies the Java class name for the Connector implementation. This class must implement the `org.apache.catalina.Connector` interface. For the Tomcat 4.0 HTTP/1.1 Connector, this value must be `org.apache.catalina.connector.http.HttpConnector`.

  The default configuration for this Connector (from `$CATALINA_HOME/conf/server.xml`) is as follows. As you can be see from the configuration, the port attribute is set to 8080. Because of this, Tomcat listens on port 8080 for HTTP requests.

```
<Connector
          className="org.apache.catalina.connector.http.HttpConnector"
          port="8080"
          minProcessors="5"
          maxProcessors="75"
          enableLookups="true"
          redirectPort="8443"
          acceptCount="10"
          debug="0"
          connectionTimeout="60000"/>
```

The other attributes of this Connector (`minProcessors`, `maxProcessors`, `enableLookups`, and so on) are discussed in the next section.

Tomcat 4.1: Coyote HTTP/1.1 Connector

As a new Connector architecture introduced in Tomcat 4.1, Coyote is a higher-performance HTTP/1.1 Connector that has been completely rewritten. Coyote also comes with adaptors for Tomcat 4.0 and Tomcat 3.x.

Coyote HTTP/1.1 Configuration

The default Coyote HTTP/1.1 Connector configuration is as follows (from `$CATALINA_HOME/conf/server.xml`):

```
<Connector
        className="org.apache.coyote.tomcat4.CoyoteConnector"
        port="8080"
        minProcessors="5"
        maxProcessors="75"
        enableLookups="true"
        redirectPort="8443"
        acceptCount="10"
        debug="0"
        connectionTimeout="20000"
        useURIValidationHack="false" />
```

When Tomcat is serving HTML pages, a URL of `http://localhost:8080/foo.html` refers to the `foo.html` file in the `ROOT` Web application (`$CATALINA_HOME/webapps/ROOT`). Similarly, `http://localhost:8080/examples/bar.html` refers to the `bar.html` HTML file present in the `examples` Web application (`$CATALINA_HOME/webapps/examples`).

Following are the other configurable attributes for this Connector:

- *`acceptCount`*—This is the maximum queue length for incoming connection requests when all possible request processing threads are in use. Any requests received when the queue is full will be refused. This value is passed as the backlog parameter while creating a Tomcat server socket. The default queue length is 10, and the maximum is dependent on the operating system.
- *`address`*—This attribute specifies the IP address to which the Tomcat server binds. If the `address` attribute is not specified, Tomcat would bind to all addresses (if the host has multiple IP addresses).
- *`buffersSize`*—The `bufferSize` attribute specifies the size (in bytes) of the input stream buffer created by this Connector. The default value is 2,048 bytes.
- *`className`*—The `classname` attribute is set to the Java class implementing the Connector. This class must implement the `org.apache.catalina.Connector` interface. For the Coyote HTTP Connector, this attribute should be set to the `org.apache.coyote.tomcat4.CoyoteConnector` class.
- *`connectionTimeout`*—This is the number of milliseconds this Connector will wait (after accepting a connection) for the request URI line to be presented. The default value is 60,000 milliseconds (60 seconds).
- *`debug`*—This attribute sets the detail level of the log messages. Higher values will return higher levels of detail. (The maximum value for this attribute is not documented. However, turning it to 4 or 5 will print most log messages.) The default value for this attribute is zero, which turns off debugging. All logging and exception information is automatically redirected to the Logger component. Logger components can be associated with the related Engine, a virtual host, or even specified for a particular application Context. A sample Logger is shown next. This is the

default Logger that redirects all debug/error messages for this virtual host (in this case, localhost) into the `$CATALINA_HOME/logs/localhost_log.txt` file. (Chapter 5 discusses Logger components.)

```
<Host name="localhost" debug="0" appBase="webapps"
      unpackWARs="true" autoDeploy="true">

  <Logger className="org.apache.catalina.logger.FileLogger"
          directory="logs"
          prefix="localhost_log."
          suffix=".txt"
          timestamp="true"/>
```

- *`enableLookups`*—When this is set to `true`, all calls to `request.getRemoteHost()` (a J2EE Servlet API call) perform a DNS lookup to return the host name for the remote client. When this attribute is `false`, the DNS lookup is skipped and only the IP address is returned. The default value for `enableLookups` is `false`. The `enableLookup` can remain turned off for performance considerations, to avoid the overhead of the DNS lookup. These and other performance considerations are discussed in the section "Performance Tuning," later in this chapter.
- *`maxProcessors`*—This specifies the maximum number of request-processing threads to be created by this Connector, which determines the maximum number of simultaneous requests that can be handled. If there are more than `maxProcessors` concurrent requests, the remaining incoming requests are queued. See the `acceptCount` attribute for information about specifying the queue length. If not specified, this attribute is set to `20`.
- *`minProcessors`*—This specifies the number of request processing threads that will be created when this Connector is first started. This attribute should be set to a value smaller than the one set for `maxProcessors`. The default value is `5`.
- *`port`*—The `port` attribute specifies the TCP port number on which this Connector will create a server socket and await incoming connections. Only one server application can bind to a particular port number-IP address combination.
- *`proxyName`*—The `proxyName` attribute (along with the `proxyPort` attribute) is used when Tomcat is run behind a proxy server. It specifies the server name to be returned for `request.getServerName()` calls. See the section "Running Tomcat Behind a Proxy Server," later in this chapter for more information.
- *`proxyPort`*—As mentioned, the `proxyPort` attribute is used in proxy configurations. It specifies the port number to be returned for `request.getServerPort()` calls. See the section "Running Tomcat Behind a Proxy Server," later in this chapter for more information.
- *`redirectPort`*—If the Connector supports only non-SSL requests and a user request is directed to this Connector for an SSL resource, Catalina will redirect the request to the `redirectPort` port number.
- *`scheme`*—The `scheme` attribute is set to the name of the protocol. The value specified in scheme is returned by the `request.getScheme()` method call. The default value is "`http`." For an SSL Connector, this should be set to "`https`."
- *`secure`*—This attribute is set to `true` for an SSL Connector. This value is returned by the `request.getScheme()` method calls. The default value is `true`.

- *tcpNoDelay*—When this attribute is set to true, it enables the TCP_NO_DELAY network socket option. This improves performance, as explained in the section "Performance Tuning," later in this chapter. The default value is true.
- *useURIValidationHack*—The useURIValidationHack attribute was added for a Tomcat 4.0-related fix. This attribute performs additional validations and normalization on the URI for security reasons. Some of these normalizations are changing /%7E at the beginning of the URI to /~ and resolving relative path encoding in the URI (for example, /. / and /./). This attribute is only required for Tomcat 4.0, and, hence, can be turned off in Tomcat 4.1.

Configuring Tomcat 4.x for SSL

The Connector for the Catalina instance that supports HTTPS connections must have its secure attribute set to true and its scheme attribute set to https. In addition, it must contain a <Factory> element with the SSL-related configuration. The <Factory> attributes for SSL are as follows:

- *algorithm*—The algorithm attribute specifies the certificate encoding algorithm to use. It defaults to SunX509 if not specified.
- *className*—The className attribute specifies the Java class that implements the SSL server socket factory. This must be set to org.apache.coyote.tomcat4.CoyoteServerSocketFactory.
- *clientAuth*—If the clientAuth attribute is set to true (the default is false), the client must have a valid certificate for authenticating itself.
- *keystoreFile*—This specifies the pathname of the keystore file. The default value is a file called keystore in the home directory of the user running Tomcat. The home directory is operating system-specific.
- *keystorePass*—The keystorePass attribute specifies the password for the keystore file. The default password is changeit. This password is selected while creating the certificate keystore (see Chapter 15 for more details).

  In cases where the default password is changed, the keystorePass attribute must be set to the same value. The following is an error message that appears during Tomcat startup when this is not done:

```
LifecycleException:  Protocol handler initialization failed: java.io.IOException:
Keystore was tampered with, or password was incorrect.
```

- *keystoreType*—This specifies the type of keystore file to be used for the server certificate. It defaults to JKS (Java Keystore). Currently, JKS is the only keystore type supported.
- *protocol*—The protocol attribute specifies the version of the SSL protocol to use. It defaults to TLS if not specified.

Following is an example Connector with SSL configuration. This configuration is already present in the $CATALINA_HOME/conf/server.xml file, but is commented out. Note that if the SSL port (8443) is changed to something else, the redirectPort attribute for all the non-SSL Connectors must be changed to that port number, too. As mentioned, the non-SSL Connectors redirect users to this port if they try to access pages with a security constraint that specifies that SSL is required.

```
<Connector className="org.apache.catalina.connector.http.HttpConnector"
           port="8443"
           minProcessors="5"
           maxProcessors="75"
           enableLookups="true"
           acceptCount="10"
           debug="0"
           scheme="https"
           secure="true">

  <Factory className="org.apache.catalina.net.SSLServerSocketFactory"
           clientAuth="false"
           protocol="TLS"/>
</Connector>
```

Tomcat 5.x: Coyote HTTP/1.1 Connector

Even though Tomcat 5.x has a Coyote HTTP/1.1 Connector that is mostly similar to the 4.1 Connector, there are differences in some of the configuration attributes, such as those used for thread pool and SSL configuration.

Coyote HTTP/1.1 Configuration

The default Coyote HTTP/1.1 Connector configuration is as follows (from `$CATALINA_HOME/conf/server.xml`):

```
<!-- Define a non-SSL Coyote HTTP/1.1 Connector on port 8080 -->
<Connector port="8080"
           maxThreads="150"
           minSpareThreads="25"
           maxSpareThreads="75"
           enableLookups="false"
           redirectPort="8443"
           acceptCount="100"
           debug="0"
           connectionTimeout="20000"
           disableUploadTimeout="true" />
```

Although the only mandatory attribute for the Connector configuration is the `port` attribute, numerous other important attributes can be configured, as described in the following list:

- *`acceptCount`*—This is the maximum queue length for incoming connection requests when all possible request processing threads are in use. Any requests received when the queue is full will be refused. This value is passed as the backlog parameter while creating a Tomcat server socket. The default queue length is 10, and the maximum is operating system-dependent.
- *`address`*—This attribute specifies the IP address to which the Tomcat server binds. If the `address` attribute is not specified, Tomcat would bind to all addresses (if the host has multiple IP addresses).
- *`allowTrace`*—This enables the `TRACE HTTP` method if set to `true`. The default is `false`.
- *`buffersSize`*—The `bufferSize` attribute specifies the size (in bytes) of the input stream buffer created by this Connector. The default value is 2,048 bytes.

- *compressibleMimeTypes*—This is a comma-separated list of MIME types for which HTTP compressions (see the next attribute) can be used. The default value is `text/html,text/xml,text/plain`.
- *compression*—The Connector can use HTTP/1.1 GZIP compression to get better bandwidth from the server. This can be enabled via the `compression` attribute. The valid values are `off` (disables compression), `on` (enables compression), `force` (forces compression in all cases) or a numerical value that specifies the minimum amount of data required before the output is compressed. The default value of the compression attribute is `off`.
- *connectionLinger*—This sets the number of milliseconds for which socket connections will persist after the connection is closed. A value less than `0` means don't linger (this is the default).
- *connectionTimeout*—This is the number of milliseconds that this Connector will wait, after accepting a connection, for the request URI line to be presented. The default value is 60,000 milliseconds (60 seconds).
- *debug*—This attribute sets the detail level of the log messages. Higher values will provide higher levels of detail. (The maximum value for this attribute is not documented. However, turning it to 4 or 5 will print most log messages. The default value for this attribute is zero, which turns off debugging. All logging and exception information is automatically redirected to the Logger component. Logger components can be associated with the related Engine, a virtual host, or even specified for a particular application Context. The following code illustrates a sample Logger configuration. This is the default Logger that redirects all debug/error messages for this virtual host (in this case, localhost) into the `$CATALINA_HOME/logs/localhost_log.txt` file. (Chapter 5 discusses Logger components.)

```
<Host name="localhost" debug="0" appBase="webapps"
     unpackWARs="true" autoDeploy="true">

  <Logger className="org.apache.catalina.logger.FileLogger"
          directory="logs"
          prefix="localhost_log."
          suffix=".txt"
          timestamp="true"/>
```

- *disableUploadTimeout*—The `disableUploadTimeout` attribute enables a separate timeout to be set (or not set) for data uploads during a Servlet execution. The attribute's value defaults to `false`.
- *enableLookups*—When this is set to `true`, all calls to `request.getRemoteHost()` perform a DNS lookup to return the host name for the remote client. When this attribute is `false`, the DNS lookup is skipped and only the IP address is returned. The default value for `enableLookups` is `false`. Keeping this attribute turned off increases performance, avoiding the overhead required for the DNS lookup. These and other performance considerations are discussed in the section "Performance Tuning," later in this chapter.
- *maxKeepAliveRequest*—This attribute controls the "keep-alive" behavior of HTTP requests that enables persistent connections (that is, multiple requests to be sent over the same HTTP connection). It specifies the maximum number of requests that can be pipelined until the connection is closed by the server. The default value of `maxKeepAliveRequest` is 100, and setting it to 1 disables HTTP keep-alive behavior and pipelining.

- *maxPostSize*—This specifies the maximum size, in bytes, of the `POST` that can be handled by the container. It defaults to 2,097,152 (2 MB). If set to 0 or negative, this feature is disabled.
- *maxSpareThreads*—The `maxSpareThreads` attribute controls the maximum number of unused threads that are allowed to exist before Tomcat starts stopping the unused ones. `maxSpareThreads` defaults to 50.
- *minSpareThreads*—The `minSpareThreads` attribute specifies the minimum number of threads that are started when the Connector is initialized. `minSpareThreads` defaults to 4.
- *maxThreads*—This attribute specifies the maximum number of threads that are created for this Connector to process requests. This, in turn, specifies the maximum number of concurrent requests that the Connector can handle. `maxThreads` defaults to 200 threads.
- *noCompressionUserAgents*—This is a comma-separated list that matches the HTTP UserAgent value of Web browsers that have a broken support for HTTP/1.1 compression. Regular expressions can be used here.
- *port*—The `port` attribute specifies the TCP port number on which this Connector will create a server socket and await incoming connections. Only one server application can bind to a particular port number-IP address combination.
- *protocol*—This specifies the HTTP protocol to use, and must be set to `HTTP/1.1` (the default). Setting it to anything else (such as `HTTP/1.0`) causes the Connector initialization to fail, returning a "Protocol handler start failed" error.
- *proxyName*—The `proxyName` attribute (along with the `proxyPort` attribute) is used when Tomcat is run behind a proxy server. It specifies the server name to be returned for `request.getServerName()` calls. See the section "Running Tomcat Behind a Proxy Server," later in this chapter for more information.
- *proxyPort*—As mentioned, the `proxyPort` attribute is used in proxy configurations. It specifies the port number to be returned for `request.getServerPort()` calls. See the section "Running Tomcat Behind a Proxy Server," later in this chapter for more information.
- *redirectPort*—If the Connector supports only non-SSL requests and a user request is sent to this Connector for an SSL resource, Catalina will redirect that request to the `redirectPort` port number. The default Tomcat configuration specifies `8443` as the redirect port, as shown in the sample configuration presented earlier. If this is omitted, it defaults to `443`.
- *restrictedUserAgents*—This is a comma-separated list that matches the HTTP UserAgent value of Web browsers that have a broken support for HTTP/1.1 keep-alive behavior. Regular expressions can be used here.
- *scheme*—The `scheme` attribute is set to the name of the protocol. The value specified in scheme is returned by the `request.getScheme()` method call. The default value is `http`. For an SSL Connector, this would be set to `https`.
- *secure*—This attribute is set to `true` for an SSL Connector. This value is returned by the `request.getScheme()` method calls. The default value is `false`.
- *socketBuffer*—This specifies the size, in bytes, of the buffer to be used for socket output buffering. Use of a socket buffer helps to improve performance. By default, a buffer of size 9,000 bytes is used, and setting `socketBuffer` to `-1` turns buffering off.

- *tcpNoDelay*—When this attribute is set to `true`, it enables the `TCP_NO_DELAY` network socket option. This improves performance, as explained in the section "Performance Tuning," later in this chapter. The default value is `true`.
- *URIEncoding*—This specifies the character encoding used to decode URI bytes. It defaults to `ISO-8859-1`.
- *useBodyEncodingForURI*—If set to `true`, this attribute causes the URI encoding specified in the `contentType` to be used for encoding, rather than the `URIEncoding` attribute. This defaults to `false`.
- *xpoweredBy*—If set to `true` (the default value is `false`), an `X-Powered-By` header is output in Servlet-generated responses returned by the Connector. The value of the header is `Servlet/2.4`, as shown in the following sample HTTP response header:

```
HTTP/1.1 200 OK
X-Powered-By: Servlet/2.4
Content-Type: text/html
Content-Length: 1437
Date: Thu, 09 Oct 2003 17:25:52 GMT
Server: Apache-Coyote/1.1
```

In addition to these attributes, there are others that are specific to SSL Connectors. These are valid only if the `secure` attribute is set to `true`, and are discussed next.

Configuring Tomcat 5.x for SSL

The Connector for the Catalina instance that supports HTTPS connections must have its `secure` attribute set to `true` and its `scheme` attribute set to `https`. Unlike Tomcat 4.x, no Factory element is required for SSL-related configuration, although it is still supported for backward compatibility.

The new SSL-related Connector attributes are as follows:

- *algorithm*—This attribute specifies the certificate encode algorithm to use. This defaults to `SunX509`.
- *ciphers*—This is a comma-separated list of encryption ciphers.
- *clientAuth*—This attribute can be set to either `true` or `false` (the default is `false`). When set to `true`, the client connection would need to present a valid certificate. However, if `clientAuth` is set to `false`, and the Web resource being requested is protected by `CLIENT-CERT` authentication, the latter would take precedence (that is, the client would still need to present a certificate).
- *keystoreFile*—This specifies the pathname to the keystore file. The keystore file contains the server's public and private keys in the form of certificates. `keystoreFile` defaults to `keystore` in the user's home directory. The home directory varies by operating system (for example, `/home/<tomcat_user_name>` in Linux).
- *keystorePass*—The `keystorePass` attribute should be set to the password required to access the `keystoreFile`. The default password is `changeit`.
- *keystoreType*—This specifies the keystore file type. It defaults to `JKS` (Java Keystore).
- *sslProtocol*—This indicates which version of the SSL protocol to use (the default value is `TLS`).

Following is an example Connector with SSL configuration. This configuration is already present in the `$CATALINA_HOME/conf/server.xml` file, but is commented out. Note that if the SSL port (8443) is changed, the `redirectPort` attribute for all the non-SSL Connectors must be changed to that port number, too. As mentioned, the non-SSL Connectors redirect users to this port if they try to access pages with a security constraint that specifies that SSL is required.

```
<!-- Define a SSL Coyote HTTP/1.1 Connector on port 8443 -->
 <Connector port="8443"
            maxThreads="150"
            minSpareThreads="25"
            maxSpareThreads="75"
            enableLookups="false"
            disableUploadTimeout="true"
            acceptCount="100"
            debug="0"
            scheme="https"
            secure="true"
            clientAuth="false"
            sslProtocol="TLS" />
```

Configuring Tomcat for CGI Support

Support for CGI scripts is new for Tomcat 4.x and 5.0. This support is accomplished by a Servlet (the `org.apache.catalina.servlets.CGIServlet`) that simulates the way a Web server would handle a CGI script—processing the CGI environment variables and then executing the CGI executable.

However, CGI is disabled in the default Tomcat configuration for security reasons. For instance, a CGI script would bypass the security policies defined for programs in the `catalina.policy` file. More on these security policies is covered in Chapter 15.

Enabling CGI support in Tomcat requires the following steps:

1. Rename `CATALINA_HOME/server/lib/servlets-cgirenametojar` to `CATALINA_HOME/server/lib/servlets-cgi.jar`.
2. Uncomment the `servlet` and `servlet-mapping` settings for CGI in `CATALINA_HOME/conf/web.xml`—these settings are commented by default. The `servlet-mapping` causes all requests for Web pages with a `/cgi-bin/` prefix to be passed to the CGI Servlet, and the `servlet` element specifies the fully qualified Java class name of the Servlet and its configurable parameters. The sample settings are shown below and the configurable parameters are as follows:
    - *`cgiPathPrefix`*—The directory containing CGI scripts
    - *`clientInputTimeout`*—The timeout value in milliseconds
    - *`debug`*—The debug level to be enabled for the CGI Servlet

```
<!-- Common Gateway Includes (CGI) processing servlet, which supports     -->
<!-- execution of external applications that conform to the CGI spec      -->
<!-- requirements.  Typically, this servlet is mapped to the URL pattern  -->
<!-- "/cgi-bin/*", which means that any CGI applications that are         -->
<!-- executed must be present within the web application.  This servlet   -->
<!-- supports the following initialization parameters (default values     -->
<!-- are in square brackets):                                             -->
<!--                                                                      -->
<!--   cgiPathPrefix        The CGI search path will start at             -->
<!--                        webAppRootDir + File.separator + this prefix. -->
<!--                        [WEB-INF/cgi]                                 -->
<!--                                                                      -->
<!--   clientInputTimeout   The time (in milliseconds) to wait for input  -->
<!--                        from the browser before assuming that there   -->
<!--                        is none.  [100]                               -->
<!--                                                                      -->
<!--   debug                Debugging detail level for messages logged    -->
<!--                        by this servlet.  [0]                         -->
<!--                                                                      -->
<!--   executable           Name of the executable used to run the script. -->
<!--                        [perl]                                        -->
<!--                                                                      -->
<!-- IMPORTANT: To use the CGI servlet, you also need to rename the       -->
<!--            $CATALINA_HOME/server/lib/servlets-cgi.renametojar file   -->
<!--            to $CATALINA_HOME/server/lib/servlets-cgi.jar             -->
  <servlet>
      <servlet-name>cgi</servlet-name>
      <servlet-class>org.apache.catalina.servlets.CGIServlet</servlet-class>
      <init-param>
        <param-name>clientInputTimeout</param-name>
        <param-value>100</param-value>
      </init-param>
      <init-param>
        <param-name>debug</param-name>
        <param-value>6</param-value>
      </init-param>
      <init-param>
        <param-name>cgiPathPrefix</param-name>
        <param-value>WEB-INF/cgi</param-value>
      </init-param>
       <load-on-startup>5</load-on-startup>
  </servlet>

    ...

  <!-- The mapping for the CGI Gateway servlet -->
  <servlet-mapping>
      <servlet-name>cgi</servlet-name>
      <url-pattern>/cgi-bin/*</url-pattern>
  </servlet-mapping>
```

3. Restart Tomcat to cause the changes to be reread. Now Tomcat should serve up CGI scripts from the directory (typically, `/WEB-INF/cgi`) defined in the `cgiPathPrefix` element in `web.xml`.

Configuring Tomcat for SSI Support

Tomcat 4.x and 5.0 support SSIs (server-side includes). SSI enables the adding of directives to HTML pages that are evaluated when the pages are served to the browser, and they are a popular mechanism for adding dynamic content. SSI support in Tomcat is achieved via a Servlet (`org.apache.catalina.ssi.SSIServlet`) that simulates the way in which a Web server would handle an SSI in Web pages.

However, SSI is disabled in the default Tomcat configuration for security reasons. For instance, SSI could be used to execute external programs, and thus bypass the security policies defined in the `catalina.policy` file. More on these security policies is covered in Chapter 15.

Enabling SSI support in Tomcat requires the following steps:

1. Rename `CATALINA_HOME/server/lib/servlets-ssirenametojar` to `CATALINA_HOME/server/lib/servlets-ssi.jar`.
2. Uncomment the `servlet` and `servlet-mapping` settings for SSI in `CATALINA_HOME/conf/web.xml`. These setting are commented by default. The sample settings are shown after the following descriptions of some configurable parameters:
   - *`buffered`*—Enables (1) or disables (0) buffered output from the SSIServlet
   - *`debug`*—The debug level to be enabled
   - *`expires`*—The expiry time, in seconds, for a Web page with SSIs
   - *`isVirtualWebappRelative`*—Virtual paths to be relative to context root (1) or server root (0)

```
<!-- Server Side Includes processing servlet, which processes SSI          -->
<!-- directives in HTML pages consistent with similar support in web       -->
<!-- servers like Apache.  Traditionally, this servlet is mapped to        -->
<!-- URL pattern "*.shtml".  This servlet supports the following           -->
<!-- initialization parameters (default values are in square brackets):   -->
<!--                                                                       -->
<!--   buffered             Should output from this servlet be buffered?   -->
<!--                        (0=false, 1=true)  [0]                         -->
<!--                                                                       -->
<!--   debug                Debugging detail level for messages logged     -->
<!--                        by this servlet.  [0]                          -->
<!--                                                                       -->
<!--   expires              The number of seconds before a page with SSI   -->
<!--                        directives will expire.  [No default]          -->
<!--                                                                       -->
<!--   isVirtualWebappRelative                                             -->
<!--                        Should "virtual" paths be interpreted as       -->
<!--                        relative to the context root, instead of       -->
<!--                        the server root?  (0=false, 1=true) [0]        -->
<!--                                                                       -->
<!--                                                                       -->
<!-- IMPORTANT: To use the SSI servlet, you also need to rename the        -->
```

```
<!--           $CATALINA_HOME/server/lib/servlets-ssi.renametojar file    -->
<!--           to $CATALINA_HOME/server/lib/servlets-ssi.jar              -->

    <servlet>
        <servlet-name>ssi</servlet-name>
        <servlet-class>
          org.apache.catalina.ssi.SSIServlet
        </servlet-class>
        <init-param>
          <param-name>buffered</param-name>
          <param-value>1</param-value>
        </init-param>
        <init-param>
          <param-name>debug</param-name>
          <param-value>0</param-value>
        </init-param>
        <init-param>
          <param-name>expires</param-name>
          <param-value>666</param-value>
        </init-param>
        <init-param>
          <param-name>isVirtualWebappRelative</param-name>
          <param-value>0</param-value>
        </init-param>
        <load-on-startup>4</load-on-startup>
    </servlet>
      ...

    <!-- The mapping for the SSI servlet -->
    <servlet-mapping>
        <servlet-name>ssi</servlet-name>
        <url-pattern>*.shtml</url-pattern>
    </servlet-mapping>
```

3. Restart Tomcat to cause the changes to be reread. Now Tomcat should handle SSIs in all Web pages that end with `*.stml`.

Running Tomcat Behind a Proxy Server

A common deployment scenario involves running Tomcat behind a proxy server. In this kind of environment, the host name and port number that should be returned to the client in the HTTP response should be those specified in the request, and not the actual host name and port on which Tomcat is running. These are controlled via the `proxyName` and `proxyPort` attributes discussed earlier. These attributes affect the values returned for the `request.getServerName()` and `request.getServerPort()` Servlet API calls.

Apache's HTTP server can be used as the proxy server. If so, Apache's proxy module (mod_proxy) is configured to pass on the servlet requests to the Tomcat server:

```
# Load mod_proxy
LoadModule proxy_module libexec/mod_proxy.so

# AddModule only required for Apache 1.x, not 2.x
AddModule mod_proxy.c

# Pass all requests for the context path '/servlets' to Tomcat running
# at port 8080 on host 'hostname'
ProxyPass /servlets http://hostname:8080/servlets
ProxyPassReverse /servlets http://hostname:8080/servlets
```

On the Tomcat side, following is the configuration in server.xml for the Coyote HTTP Connector:

```
<Connector
                port="8080"
                proxyName="www.mydomain.com"
                proxyPort="80"
                ...
/>
```

If the proxyName and proxyPort attributes were not specified, the response message would have indicated that it came from *hostname* (i.e., the host on which Tomcat is installed), and 8080 instead of www.mydomain.com and port 80.

Typically, Apache logs incoming requests, so logging shouldn't be enabled on Tomcat — to avoid duplicate access logging.

Performance Tuning

The configuration sections previously covered in this chapter discussed some of the attributes that impact performance characteristics of the HTTP Connector.

Following are some of the actions you can perform to fine-tune Tomcat 4.x performance:

- **Turn debug off.** The debug attribute in the HTTP/1.1 and Coyote Connectors controls the detail level for the log messages. This should be set to zero (the default value) to have minimal logging.
- **Set tcpNoDelay to true.** When this attribute is set to true, it enables the TCP_NO_DELAY network socket option. This improves performance because it disables the **Nagle algorithm,** which is used to concatenate small buffer messages, which decreases the number of packets sent over the network. While this may result in better response time in a non-interactive network application because it enables greater throughput, it results in slower response times in interactive client-server environments (such as a Web browser interacting with the Web server).

- **Set `enableLookups` to `false`.** Setting `enableLookup` to `false` disables DNS lookups for the `request.getRemoteHost()` API calls. This improves performance by decreasing the time required for the lookup.
- **Use a thread pool.** Tomcat is a multi-threaded Servlet container, and each incoming request requires a Tomcat thread to handle it. Using a thread pool is hence very important for performance. If the thread pool were disabled, a new thread would be started for every request. If a very large number of requests arrived concurrently, they would cause Tomcat to allocate an equivalent number of threads. This would degrade performance, and could even cause Tomcat to crash. To prevent this, you should use a thread pool. In Tomcat 4.x, the attributes that control the thread pool behavior are as follows:
    - *`maxProcessors`*—This is the maximum number of request processing threads to be created by this Connector, which therefore determines the maximum number of simultaneous requests that can be handled. If there are more than `maxProcessors` concurrent requests, the remaining incoming requests are queued. The `acceptCount` attribute then controls the number of requests that are queued.
    - *`minProcessors`*—This is the number of request processing threads that will be created when this Connector is first started. This attribute should be set to a value smaller than the one set for `maxProcessors`.

  Setting these to appropriate values depends on the Web site load and the server machine's characteristics.
- **Java Virtual Machine (JVM) memory settings.** Another limiting factor here is the JVM memory settings. To add a larger number of threads, Tomcat startup scripts (`tomcat.bat/tomcat.sh`) must be modified to pass JVM-specific parameters (such as `-Xms` and `-Xmx` to set the initial and maximum heap size). Refer to your JVM documentation for additional information.

Now let's revisit some of the attributes for tuning Tomcat 5.x:

- **Turn `debug` off.** The `debug` attribute in the HTTP/1.1 and Coyote Connectors controls the detail level for the log messages. This should be set to zero (the default value) to have minimal logging.
- **Set `tcpNoDelay` to `true`.** When this attribute is set to `true`, it enables the `TCP_NO_DELAY` network socket option. This improves performance as it disables the Nagle algorithm, which is used to concatenate small buffer messages, which decreases the number of packets sent over the network. While this may result in better response time in a non-interactive network application because it enables greater throughput, it results in slower response times in interactive client-server environments (such as a Web browser interacting with the Web server).
- **`maxKeepAliveRequest`**—This attribute controls the "keep-alive" behavior of HTTP requests, enabling persistent connections (that is, multiple requests to be sent over the same HTTP connection). It specifies the maximum number of requests that can be pipelined until the connection is closed by the server. The default value of `maxKeepAliveRequest` is `100`, and setting it to 1 disables HTTP keep-alive behavior and pipelining.
- **Tune the `socketBuffer` parameter.** As mentioned, this specifies the size, in bytes, of the buffer to be used for socket output buffering.

- **Set `enableLookups` to `false`.** Setting `enableLookup` to false disables DNS lookups for the `request.getRemoteHost()` API calls. This improves performance by decreasing the time required for the lookup.
- **Use a thread pool.** Tomcat is a multi-threaded Servlet container, and each incoming request requires a Tomcat thread to handle it. Using a thread pool is hence very important for performance. In Tomcat 5.x, three thread-pool-related attributes can be tuned. Setting these to appropriate values varies according to the Web site load and the server machine's characteristics:
    - *`maxThreads`*—This is the maximum number of threads allowed. This defines the upper bound to the concurrency, as Tomcat will not create any more threads than this. If there are more than `maxThreads` requests, they will be queued until the number of threads decreases. Increasing `maxThreads` increases the capability of Tomcat to handle more connections concurrently. However, threads use up system resources. Thus, setting a very high value might degrade performance, and could even cause Tomcat to crash.
    - *`maxSpareThreads`*—This is the maximum number of idle threads allowed. Any excess idle threads are shut down by Tomcat. Setting this to a large value is not good for performance; the default (`50`) usually works for most Web sites with an average load. The value of `maxSpareThreads` should be greater than `minSpareThreads`, but less than `maxThreads`.
    - *`minSpareThreads`*—This is the minimum number of idle threads allowed. On Tomcat startup, this is also the number of threads created when the Connector is initailized. If the number of idle threads falls below `minSpareThreads`, Tomcat creates new threads. Setting this to a large value is not good for performance, as each thread uses up resources. The default (`4`) usually works for most Web sites with an average load. Typically, sites with "bursty" traffic would need higher values for `minSpareThreads`.
- **JVM memory settings.** Another limiting factor here is the JVM memory settings. To add a larger number of threads, Tomcat startup scripts (`tomcat.bat/tomcat.sh`) must be modified to pass JVM-specific parameters (such as `-Xms` and `-Xmx` to set the initial and maximum heap size). Refer to your JVM documentation for additional information.

Summary

To conclude this chapter on Connectors, let's review some of the key points that have been discussed:

- HTTP connectors are Java classes that implement the HTTP protocol. For Tomcat, this class is invoked when there is an HTTP request on the Connector port.
- A new HTTP/1.1 Connector was introduced with Tomcat 4.0. Configuration attributes for the HTTP/1.1 Connector are the same as those for the Coyote HTTP/1.1 Connector, with the exception of the `className` attribute.

- Coyote HTTP/1.1 was introduced with Tomcat 4.1 and is a higher-performance Connector that has been completely rewritten.
- Configuration for the Coyote HTTP/1.1 Connector in Tomcat 4.1 and 5.x, including support for SSL and performance tuning has been covered in detail in the chapter.
- The HTTP Connector is often not used in a production environment where performance is a major concern. This Connector is useful for test deployments, or in situations for which not a lot of static content is being used. For production Web deployments, it is common to use another Web server to serve up static content, and to have Tomcat handle only the dynamic JSP/Servlet content. This improves performance, and enables the integration of existing Web applications and scripts, some of which may have been written in another language, such as Perl or Python.

Chapters 11–13 discuss the Web server Connectors that enable Tomcat to work with Web servers such as Apache and IIS.

11

Web Server Connectors

Chapter 10 examined the HTTP Connectors that enable Tomcat to work as a standalone Web server. A Web server (such as Apache or IIS) can also be used along with Tomcat to serve up HTTP content. In this configuration, the Web server and Tomcat communicate with each other using Tomcat's Web server Connectors.

This chapter looks at the reasons for using such a configuration, and introduces the various Tomcat Connectors (`jk`, `jk2`, `jserv`, and `webapp`), including the protocols that they implement, which include Apache JServ Protocol (AJP) and WARP.

This chapter includes sections on the following topics:

- Reasons for using a Web server
- The architecture of Web server Connectors
- What to look for when choosing a Connector

Reasons for Using a Web Server

You may be wondering why a separate Web server is needed when Tomcat already has an HTTP Connector. Following are some reasons:

- *Performance* — Tomcat is inherently slower than a Web server. Therefore, it is better for the Web server to serve up static content, while Tomcat handles the dynamic content (JSPs and Servlets). Passing requests for static HTML pages, images, and style sheets through a Servlet container written in Java is not as efficient compared to a Web server.
- *Security* — A Web server such as Apache has been around for much longer than Tomcat, and has far fewer security holes.

- *Stability*—Apache is much more stable than Tomcat. In the event of a Tomcat crash, the entire Web site will not come down. Only the dynamic content served by Tomcat would be unavailable.
- *Configurability*—Apache is also far more configurable than Tomcat. Using Apache as a front end enables you to take advantage of its rich functionality.
- *Legacy support*—Web sites often have legacy code in the form of CGI programs. They might also use scripting languages (such as Perl or Python) to implement specific functionality. Web servers such as Apache have modules for Perl and Python, whereas Tomcat does not. Tomcat does have limited support for CGI, however, using a special `CGIServlet` that mimics the CGI functionality.

Connector Architecture

All the Connectors work on the same principle. They have an Apache module end (`mod_jk`, `mod_jk2`, or `mod_webapp`) written in C that Apache (or other supported Web servers) loads just like the other Apache modules.

On the Tomcat end, each Servlet container instance has a Connector module component written in Java. In Tomcat 4.x and 5.x, this is a class that implements the `org.apache.catalina.Connector` interface. For example, the Connector class for the WARP Connector is `org.apache.catalina.connector.warp.WarpConnector`; for AJP version 13 it is `org.apache.ajp.tomcat4.Ajp13Connector`.

Communication Paths

The Web server handles all requests for static content, as well as all non-Servlet/JSP dynamic content (CGI scripts, for example). When it comes across content targeted for the Servlet container, the Web server passes the request to the module in question (that is, `mod_jk`, `mod_webapp`, and so on). The Web server knows what content to pass to the Connector module because the directives in the Web server's configuration specify this.

To illustrate, if the JK Connector is being used, Apache's configuration would have entries similar to the following:

```
# Configuration directives in Apache's httpd.conf for mod_jk
# Send all request for JSP (extension *.jsp) or
# servlets (web application path /servlet) to the
# AJP Connector
JkMount /*.jsp ajp13
JkMount /servlet/* ajp13
```

Alternatively, if the `webapp` Connector is being used, the entries would be similar to the following:

```
# Configuration directives in Apache's httpd.conf for mod_webapp
# Send all request in the URL path /servlet to the webapp Connector
WebAppDeploy servlet warpConnection /servlet
```

The Connector module then sends the request encoded in a manner specific to a protocol (AJP or WARP) over a network connection to a Connector. (There can be more than one instance of the Servlet container in the back end.) The Connector gets the request serviced by the Servlet container, and sends the response back to the Apache module. Figure 11-1 illustrates this.

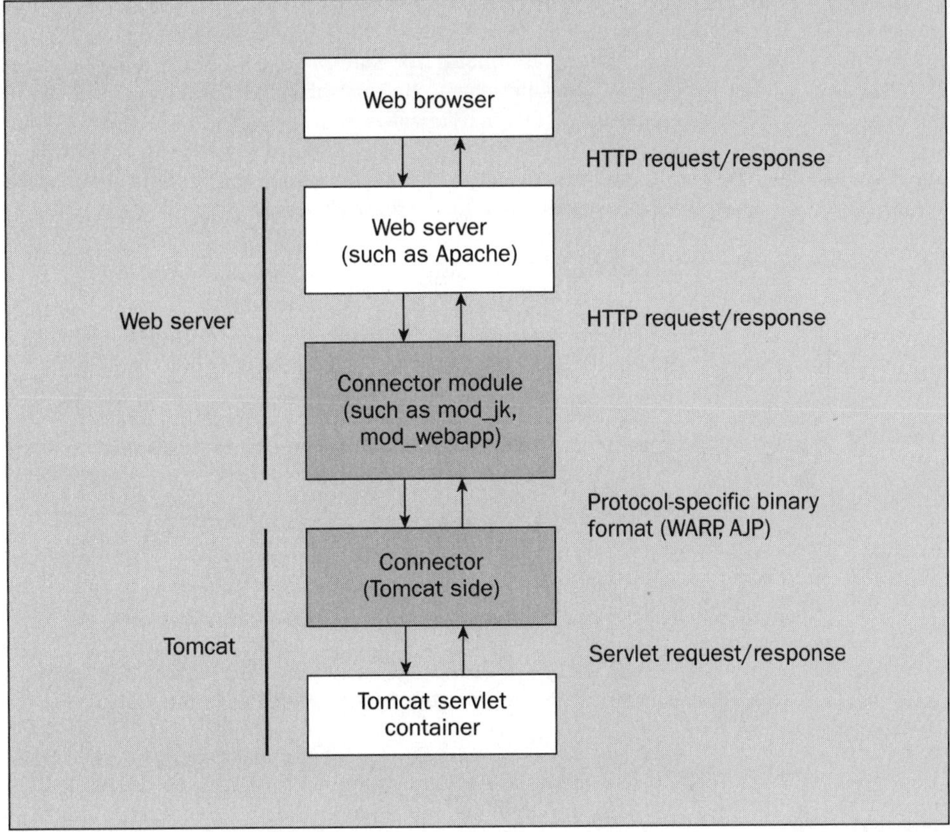

Figure 11-1: Communication between Connector and Apache modules.

Connector Protocols

Tomcat has two protocols for its Web server Connectors: AJP and WARP. These protocols essentially define the (binary) format for the data transmitted between the Web server and Tomcat and the control commands.

AJP Protocol

The **Apache JServ Protocol** (**AJP**) is a historical name, as AJP10 and AJP11 were the protocols that the now-obsolete JServ Connector implemented. The current version of AJP is AJP13, and is implemented by the JK and JK2 Connectors.

AJP13 uses a binary format for transmitting data between the Web server and Tomcat. The earlier versions of AJP (AJP10 and AJP11) used a text-based data format. The communication between the Web server and the Servlet container is over a network socket, and the same connection is reused for multiple requests and responses. The connection is made persistent for better performance. However, once a connection has been assigned to a particular request, it is not assigned to any other request until the request-handling cycle is complete.

The AJP packet format consists of a packet header and the actual payload. The packet header indicates the payload size. The type of message is in the first byte of the payload. The message could be an HTTP request/response packet, or even a control command (for example, the Web server asks the Servlet container to shut down). The protocol defines binary encoding for the HTTP commands and headers (for example, the `GET` command is represented by the byte value `2`).

Figure 11-2 shows the AJP packet structure from the Web server side to the Servlet container. Figure 11-3 shows the packet structure from the Servlet container to the Web server.

Byte #	0	1	2	3	4 (length+3)
Contents	0x12	0x34	Data length		Actual data payload

Figure 11-2: AJP packet structure from the Web server side to the Servlet container.

Byte #	0	1	2	3	4 (length+3)
Contents	A	B	Data length		Actual data payload

Figure 11-3: AJP packet structure from the Servlet container to the Web server.

As you can see, the binary data packet from the Web server side starts with the sequence 0x1234. This is followed by the packet size (two bytes) and then the actual payload data. On the return path, the packets are prefixed by AB (the ASCII codes for A and B). The protocol then defines the structure for the payload data (the type of message is in the first byte of the payload, and so on).

Administrators or Web developers do not need to know the AJP protocol and its packet structure. The specifics of the AJP protocol and packet structure are relevant only to people who are working on (or curious about) Tomcat internals, or who are interested in implementing a Connector for AJP. Users of Tomcat should have no reason to implement a Connector.

For further information on the details of AJP, see the documentation that comes with the JK Connector source code or visit the Web site at `http://jakarta.apache.org/tomcat/tomcat-4.1-doc/jk2/common/AJPv13.html`.

WARP Protocol

WARP derives its name from the Star Trek television series. Warp is a measure of speed. Traveling at "warp speed" means moving faster than the speed of light. Playing on this concept, the intent of the WARP protocol was to provide a very fast mechanism for communication between the Web server and the Servlet container.

WARP defines a packet structure for transferring data between the Web server and the Servlet container. This consists of an 8-bit, packet-type field; a 16-bit, payload-length field (to be dropped in new WARP versions); and then the actual content. All data is transmitted over a network socket (Apache and Tomcat could be on different machines) and encoded in the network byte order (that is, big-endian style).

The packet could contain request data from the user, such as the HTTP method (GET, POST), a request URI, a query argument, or a protocol (HTTP/1.0, HTTP/1). It also could be an administrative command that, for example, could deploy an application. On the response side, the WARP packet could contain the response to be sent back to the user's browser, or error information. The packet type distinguishes between these various types of packets.

The Web server parses the HTTP request that it receives. WARP takes this pre-parsed request and transmits it in a format that is encoded such that the Connector at the receiving end does not have to parse the data again.

Figure 11-4 shows the WARP packet structure. As you can see, the first byte contains the packet type, which is followed by the payload data length, and then the actual payload.

Byte #	0	1	2	3 (length+3)
Contents	Packet type	Data length		Actual data payload

Figure 11-4: WARP packet structure.

As in the case of the AJP protocol, the specifics of the WARP protocol and packet structure are relevant only to people implementing Connectors for WARP, and hence are not discussed here. Tomcat users have no reason to implement a Connector for these protocols. For more information on the protocol, see the WARP documentation that comes with the webapp Connector source code.

Choosing a Connector

Choosing a Connector was very confusing in earlier versions of Tomcat. In Tomcat 5.x, sticking to JK2 implifies the task. The use of the other major Connector (webapp) is deprecated. For historical interest (or for those examining such deployments), the following sections introduce all Tomcat Connectors.

JServ

Apache JServ (http://java.apache.org/jserv/) was a Servlet engine that implemented the JavaSoft Servlet API, version 2.0 (the current version of the API is 2.4). JServ is now in maintenance mode, and has been superseded by Tomcat. JServ did not have an HTTP stack, and so it came with a Connector (mod_jserv) that used Apache (versions 1.2 and 1.3) for this. The mod_jserv module also works as a Connector for Tomcat 3.x and earlier versions, though the JK Connector should be used for all new installations.

Following are some sample mod_jserv directives from Apache's httpd.conf configuration file:

```
LoadModule jserv_module libexec/mod_jserv.so
AddModule mod_jserv.c
...
ApJServMount  /examples   ajpv12://tomcat_host_name:8007/examples
```

mod_jserv defined the AJP protocol that specified the packet format for communication between the Apache and Tomcat ends of the Connector. mod_jserv implemented versions AJP11 and AJP12 of this protocol. This protocol lives on in the JK and JK2 Connectors.

JK

The JK Connector is a cleaned-up version of the JServ Connector, and has a refactored code base. It implements the same protocol (AJP) that JServ did. The versions that it supports include AJP11, AJP12, and AJP13.

JK adds support for many more Web servers than JServ supported, including Apache 1.3 and 2.x, Netscape, Domino, AOLServer, and IIS. On the Servlet side, it supports Tomcat 3.x, 4.x, and JServ. It also supports redirection of incoming requests, and thus can be used to achieve load-balanced request sessions.

The JK Connector renders mod_jserv obsolete. It offers a less complex configuration and better support for SSL. (For example, mod_jserv couldn't reliably differentiate between HTTP and HTTPS requests.) If you are looking for a stable Connector that supports a large(r) number of Web servers and Tomcat versions, mod_jk is the Connector for you.

webapp

The webapp Connector implements the WARP protocol for connecting Tomcat and Apache. This protocol has built-in support for auto-deployment and Web-application configuration.

webapp uses the Apache Portable Runtime (APR) library for operating-system portability, so it can only be used with Apache 1.3 and 2.0. It is limited also by the versions of Tomcat it supports (currently only Tomcat 4.x).

Furthermore, it is limited in the features it supports. The current version of webapp does not support load balancing and fault-tolerance, and has known problems in its Windows support.

webapp implements the WARP protocol, which was designed with performance as a major consideration. However, it is an experimental Connector, and has a number of known bugs. Its use has been deprecated, so this Connector is not discussed in this book.

JK2

JK2 is the next generation for the JK Connector and implements the AJP13 protocol. It supports all the Web servers that mod_jk does (Apache 1.3/2.0, Domino, Netscape, AOLServer, and IIS). It also supports the Tomcat 3.x, 4.x, and 5.x Servlet containers.

The JK2 Connector improves on the JK Connector in many ways, including the following:

- Developed with Apache 2.0 in mind, it works with Apache 1.3 as well
- It is better suited than JK for multi-threaded Web servers such as IIS and iPlanet
- It is more modular than JK
- It supports fast UNIX sockets
- It can be extended to support other communication channels
- It is better suited for JNI
- It offers support for monitoring

Tomcat 4.1 and 5.x ship with a JK2 Connector called `Coyote jk2`. Coyote is a new architecture/API for the Java code that talks to the Connectors. Tomcat 4.1 and 5.x have a Coyote HTTP/1.1 Connector (discussed in Chapter 10) in addition to the `Coyote jk2` Connector.

JK2 supersedes the JK Connector in Tomcat versions 4.x and 5.x.

Summary

This chapter on Web server connectors contained the following main points:

- Performance, security, stability, configurability, and legacy support are some of the reasons for configuring a Web server as the front end for Tomcat.
- The two protocols for these Connectors are AJP and WARP. WARP is currently not supported for Tomcat 5.
- Tomcat's Connectors have a variety of implementations and associated feature sets.

Chapter 12 discusses the JK2 Connector in the context of Tomcat and the Apache server.

12

Tomcat and Apache Server

A typical scenario in production environments is to use Tomcat along with a Web server. In this scenario, the Web server is used as a front end to Tomcat. The Web server serves all static content and Tomcat serves all dynamic content. Tomcat does have its own built-in HTTP server, but there are some practical advantages (as discussed in Chapter 11) to using Tomcat with a Web server front end. A number of Web servers can be used as the front end for Tomcat (including Apache, IIS, and Netscape). This chapter describes the process of connecting the Apache Web server as a front end to Tomcat.

Tomcat can be integrated with Apache using the JK2 Connector. This chapter explains how to install and configure this Connector. The JK2 Connector, like its predecessor, the JK Connector, uses the Apache JServ Protocol (AJP) for communication between Tomcat and the Apache Web server.

The following topics are covered in this chapter:

- The AJP (Apache JServ Protocol) and the JK2 Connector (`mod_jk2` module)
- The configuration of Tomcat with Apache
- Configuring SSL
- Load balancing multiple Tomcat instances with Apache

The configuration described in this chapter has been tested using **Tomcat 5.0.19, Apache 2.0.43,** and **mod-jk2-2.0.43** with **Sun J2SDK-1.4.2.** It is assumed that Apache is installed, configured, and running on the system. The JK2 Connector can also work with Apache 1.3.x and Apache 2.x. It is recommended to use Apache 2 because JK2 performs better with it.

Apache binaries are available for download at the following URL:

```
http://www.apache.org/dist/httpd/binaries/
```

The complete Apache documentation is available at the following URL:

```
http://httpd.apache.org/docs-2.0/
```

Introducing the JK2 Connector

The integration between the Apache Web server and Tomcat is made possible by an Apache module (`mod_jk2`) on the Apache end, a Java-based Connector implementation on the Tomcat end, and a protocol for passing the data passed between the two (AJP). The `mod_jk2` is the JK2 Connector implementation for integrating Tomcat with the Apache Web server.

The mod_jk2 Apache module

Figure 12-1 shows how `mod_jk2` works with Tomcat and Apache. All requests first come to Apache, which (with the help of `mod_jk2`) redirects all requests for any JSP or Servlet component to Tomcat. There may be one or more running instances of Tomcat for serving these client requests. The redirector usually comes as a DLL or shared object module (`.dll` for Windows and `.so` file for Unix or Linux) that plugs into the Web server. Tomcat processes the requests and generates the appropriate response. Finally, Tomcat sends this response back to the client via the `mod_jk2` module.

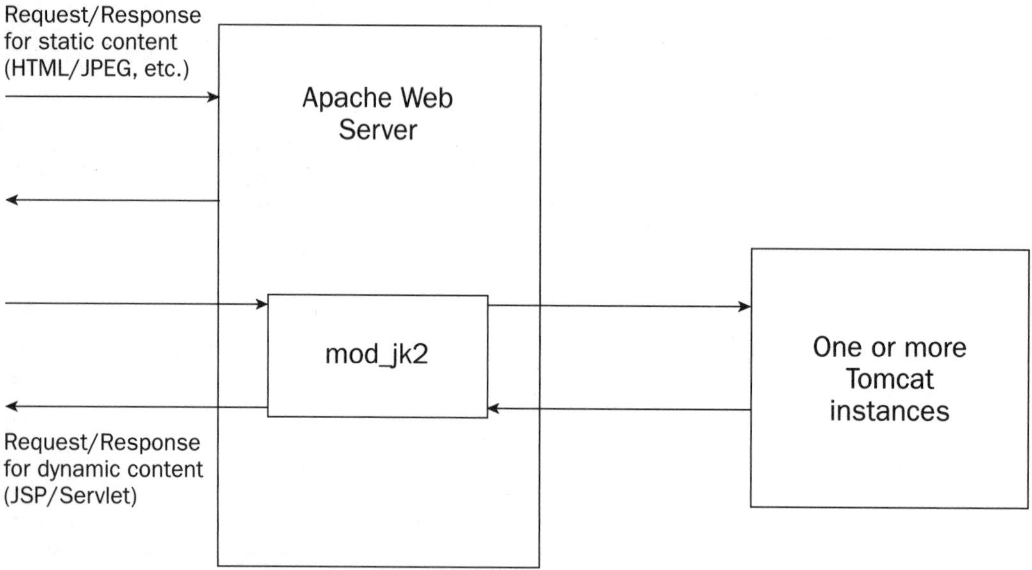

Figure 12-1: The mod_jk2 Apache module.

The Apache JServ Protocol (AJP)

AJP is a packet-oriented, TCP/IP-based protocol. It provides a communication channel between Apache and the running instances of Tomcat. There are various versions of the AJP protocol (AJP1.0, AJP1.1,

AJP1.2, and AJP1.3), as described briefly in Chapter 11. Tomcat 5 supports AJP1.3, which is the well-tested version. Some of its major features include the following:

- Improved performance
- Better support for SSL, encryption, and client certificates

One of the ways in which AJP enhances performance is by making the Web server reuse already open TCP-level connections with Tomcat. This saves the overhead of opening new socket connections for each request. This concept is similar to that of a connection pool. In the request-response cycle, when a connection is assigned to a particular request, it will not be reused until that request-response cycle is completed.

Coyote JK2 Connector

Tomcat provides a Connector implementation for the AJP 1.3 protocol as a Java class in the Tomcat distribution. Tomcat's `server.xml` configuration file contains the following entry for the Connector:

```
<!-- Define a Coyote/JK2 AJP 1.3 Connector on port 8009 --><Connector port="8009"
enableLookups="false" redirectPort="8443" debug="0" Protocol="AJP/1.3"/>
```

This JK2 Connector implementation provides several additional features not included with the older JK Connector it replaces, including the following:

- Support for the JNI mode of running Tomcat
- Better separation between the protocol and physical layers
- Better monitoring support using JMX

Understanding Tomcat Workers

Before going ahead with the configuration of the JK2 Connector, you must understand the concept of the **worker.** A worker represents a running instance of Tomcat. This worker serves the requests for all the dynamic components. The requests may come from the Apache Web server or directly from a client. In most cases, there is only a single Tomcat process or instance. However, sometimes multiple workers must be running to implement load balancing or site partitioning (mainly required for sites with heavy traffic). This topic is discussed in the section "Tomcat Load Balancing with Apache," later in this chapter.

Each worker is identified by a unique host name or a unique combination of IP address and port number. The host refers to the machine name on which the given Tomcat instance is running, and the port refers to the port on which that Tomcat instance is listening for any incoming requests.

Plug-In versus In-Process

Worker implementation in Tomcat with Apache can be achieved in two ways:

- *Using Tomcat as a plug-in for the Apache Web Server* — The most common implementation of Tomcat with Apache is using the Tomcat process as a plug-in to the running Web server process. In this case, `mod_jk2` is required as a redirector component. When Apache is configured with this plug-in, it can look up different Tomcat workers and forward requests accordingly.

- *Using Tomcat as an in-process worker*—This is a special type of worker implementation. Here, the Web server starts Java in its own process and executes Tomcat. Tomcat shares the same memory address space as that of the server process. This is a special type of deployment that provides an advantage in terms of request processing speed and better use of resources.

Multiple Tomcat Workers

There are a number of situations in which you may need to use multiple workers, including the following:

- When you want different Web application contexts to be served by different Tomcat workers. This setup will provide a development environment in which all the developers share the same Web server but have a dedicated Tomcat worker.
- When you want different virtual hosts served by different Tomcat processes to provide a clear separation between sites belonging to different entities.
- When you want to facilitate load balancing. You can run multiple Tomcat workers, each on a machine of its own (or maybe on the same machine), and distribute the requests between them.

Types of Workers

With many different types of workers, each defined Tomcat worker must be assigned a type. Tomcat 5 with the `mod_jk2` Connector supports the following types of workers:

- *`ajp13`*—This type of worker represents a running Tomcat instance. There are various possible attributes for this worker. The main attributes include `tomcatId` (which represents the identity of the Tomcat instance), `channel` (which indicates the communication channel associated with this worker), and `max_connections` (which is used to specify the maximum number of connections). By default, the maximum number of connections is unlimited. The default port for AJP 1.3 is 8009.
- *`lb`*—This type of worker is used for **load balancing.** In a load-balancing scenario, the worker doesn't actually process any requests. Rather, it handles the communication between a Web server and other defined Tomcat workers of type `ajp13`. The worker supports round-robin load balancing with a certain level of fault tolerance. One of the main properties for this worker is `worker`, which indicates the name of the worker to be used as a load balancer. A number of attributes are provided by the `lb` worker. Some of the attributes are `noWorkerMsg`, `noWorkerCode`, `timeout`, and so on, which are explained later in this chapter.
- *`status`*—This is a special type of worker that is used to show useful information about how the load among the various Tomcat workers is distributed. To use it, add a URI component assigned to this worker. Its use is explained in the section "Tomcat Load Balancing with Apache," later in this chapter. The `jkstatus` Web page (again, described later) normally displays some very vital information, including the available number and names of workers, the associated `lb_factor`, and JVM routes. It also indicates the number of requests served by a specific worker and any context mappings served. If any worker goes into an error state, this can be easily detected from this page.
- *`jni`*—Used in-process, this worker handles the forwarding of requests to in-process Tomcat workers using JNI. In the in-process mode, the Tomcat Web container and the Web server share the same memory address space. They communicate via interprocess communication. This

worker holds the details of the Tomcat class to start up, and which parameters to pass. There are two predefined `jni` workers: `onStartup` and `onShutdown`. These are executed during the startup and shutdown phase of the Connector, respectively. Both must exist in the configuration in order to be able to start and shut down Tomcat.

Worker configuration is covered later in this chapter in the section "Configuring Tomcat Workers ."

Connecting Tomcat with Apache

Connecting Tomcat with Apache involves the following steps:

1. Install the Apache `mod_jk2` module.
2. Configure the AJP 1.3 Connector in `server.xml`.
3. Configure Tomcat workers (using the `workers2.properties` file).
4. Add directives to load the `mod_jk2` module (`httpd.conf`).
5. Configure the `jk2.properties` file.

During this process, both Tomcat and Apache's configuration files are modified. The modified files are as follows:

- *`server.xml`*—This is Tomcat's main configuration file, located in `<CATALINA_HOME>/conf`. This is the file in which the AJP Connector is configured.
- *`workers2.properties`*—This file provides information about all available Tomcat instances (that is, the workers) for Apache. This file is kept under `<APACHE2_HOME>/conf`.
- *`httpd.conf`*—This is Apache's main configuration file and is located under `<APACHE2_HOME>/conf`. You add directives to load the `mod_jk2` module to this file.
- *`jk2.properties`*—This file specifies the communication channel details needed for connecting Tomcat with Apache. This file is located under `<CATALINA_HOME>/conf`.

Installing the Apache mod_jk2 Module

The Jakarta Project manages a separate subproject for Tomcat Connectors. A rich repository of various combinations exists for JK2 Connectors on many platforms. Both the source and binaries are available for download. You can get the latest binary version of the `mod_jk2` Connector module from the following URL:

```
http://jakarta.apache.org/site/binindex.cgi
```

Although the binaries of `mod_jk2` for Apache versions 1.3.x and 2.x are available, you should use Apache 2.0, because JK2 performs better, taking advantage of the new features of Apache 2.

For Windows, download `mod_jk2-2.0.43.dll` and copy it to the `modules` directory of the Apache Web server. For Unix and variant platforms, download `mod_jk2-2.0.43.so` and copy the module file to the `<APACHE2_HOME>/libexec` directory.

For each version of the Apache Web server, a separate version of the mod_jk2 module is available. Therefore, if you are using a version other than 2.0.43, select the corresponding version of mod_jk2 for download.

Building mod_jk2 on Windows

Use the following steps to build `mod_jk2` on the Windows platform:

1. Download the source of the latest Apache 2 Web server from the following URL:

   `http://httpd.apache.org/download.cgi`

   Unpack the distribution into any convenient directory, such as `D:\Apps\Apache2`.
2. Download the latest Connector source from the following URL:

   http://jakarta.apache.org/site/sourceindex.cgi

   Unpack it to a convenient directory, such as `D:\Apps\Tomcat5-connectors-src`.
3. Set `%APACHE2_HOME%` for the Apache source distribution (for example, `D:\Apps\Apache2`).
4. Set `%JAVA_HOME%` for the J2SE installation (for example, `D:\Apps\J2SDK-1.4.2`).
5. With Microsoft Visual C++, open the DSP file in `D:\Apps\Tomcat-connectors-src\jk\native\server\apache2\mod_jk2.dsp`.
6. Using the build option, build the `mod_jk2.dll`.
7. Copy `mod_jk2.dll` to the `modules` directory of the binary Apache installation.

Building mod_jk2 on Linux/Unix

Get the source code for Tomcat 5 and the JK2 Connectors from the following URL:

```
http://jakarta.apache.org/site/sourceindex.cgi
```

It is a good idea to download the source for a stable version of `mod_jk2`, such as 2.0.2.

Now get Apache Ant (preferably version 1.5.4) from the following URL:

```
http://ant.apache.org
```

Follow these steps to build the module:

1. Make a copy of the sample `build.properties` file from the Jakarta Tomcat Connector source (for your customized requirements). Edit the file and provide appropriate paths for Tomcat and Apache (that is, `tomcat5.home` and `apache2.home`).
2. Run Ant from the top-level Tomcat Connectors directory. To build `mod_jk2` for Linux, you may need to put Linux headers into the `include` directory of the J2SDK distribution.
3. Copy the `mod_jk2.so` module into the Apache modules directory.

Refer to the Jakarta Tomcat Connectors source documentation for any minor variations in the aforementioned steps.

Configuring the AJP 1.3 Connector in server.xml

The default `server.xml` file already has a configuration entry for the AJP 1.3 Connector, but it may be commented out. Uncomment this tag if commented. This is what you should see:

```
<!-- Define a Coyote/JK2 AJP 1.3 Connector on port 8009 -->
<Connector port="8009"
           enableLookups="false" redirectPort="8443" debug="0"
           protocol="AJP/1.3" />
```

These lines represent an AJP Connector that will use AJP version 1.3 and listen on AJP's default port (8009). The `port` attribute is configurable, and is the port on which Tomcat will listen for AJP requests. The other configurable attributes for this Connector are as follows:

- *`enableLookups`*—If set to `true`, calls to `request.getRemoteHost()` will perform DNS lookup to return the actual host name of the remote client. Setting this to `false` will skip the DNS lookup and return the IP address as a string (thereby improving performance). By default, DNS lookups are disabled.
- *`redirectPort`*—If a request is received for which a matching `<security-constraint>` requires SSL transport, Tomcat will automatically redirect the request to the port number specified here.
- *`scheme`*—Set this attribute to the name of the protocol you want to have returned by calls to `request.getScheme()`. For example, you would set this attribute to `https` for an SSL Connector. The default value is `http`.
- *`secure`*—If set to `true`, calls to `request.isSecure()` will return `true` where the Connector is SSL-enabled. The default value is `false`.

For Tomcat 5, the class `org.apache.coyote.tomcat5.CoyoteConnector` is the standard implementation of the AJP Connector, which supports AJP protocol version 1.3. This implementation supports the following additional attributes:

- *`debug`*—This attribute specifies the debugging level for the log messages generated by the Connector component, with higher numbers generating more detailed output. If not specified, this attribute is set to zero (`0`).
- *`protocol`*—This attribute value must be `AJP/1.3` in order to use the JK2 handler.

Configuring Tomcat Workers

Each running Tomcat instance is represented as a single worker. In order for Apache to communicate with Tomcat, it must know the host name and port of the available Tomcat instances. Using this information, Apache can route the dynamic requests to one of the available Tomcat workers. The information about the Tomcat workers is provided to Apache through the `<APACHE2_HOME>/conf /workers2.properties` configuration file.

Format of the workers2.properties File

The `workers2.properties` file uses a simple format to provide information about Tomcat workers. In this file, each component is represented by a name, its type, and associated attributes. For each attribute of the component, some default values are supported. Typically, each component in the `workers2.properties` file has a type and a local name, separated by a semicolon. Below this information, the associated attributes of that component are listed. The attribute name is a simple string, with no dots or special characters. The value is a string without quotation marks.

Normally, the entries in the file follow this format:

```
[TYPE:NAME]
ATTRIBUTE=VALUE
```

For backward compatibility, the following format is also supported:

```
TYPE:NAME.ATTRIBUTE=VALUE
```

Note that the square brackets in the first example are a part of the syntax. For example, `[channel.socket:localhost:8009]` will create a socket communication channel with host as localhost and port 8009.

Steps for Configuring the workers2.properties File

As already mentioned, the `workers2.properties` file provides information about the Tomcat workers available to Apache. For connecting Tomcat with Apache, the `ajp13` worker should be configured. In addition to the `ajp13` worker, some other components must be specified. These include the Logger, configuration settings, the communication channel, and the URI mappings. The URI mappings are used by Apache to dispatch requests to various Tomcat workers. All of these components and their associated configuration options are discussed individually in the next section.

Setting up a Logger

The JK2-based Connectors provide a default Logger. For Apache2, a `logger.apache2` file is available, which logs messages in the `error.log` file of the Apache Web server. For Windows, the default Logger is `logger.win32`. This is used by IIS, and logs messages to the Windows Application Event Log. In addition to the default Logger supported by the JK2 Connectors, an explicit log file location can also be provided using the `logger.file` attribute. Set the logging level for this default Logger to `INFO`. Other supported logging levels are `EMERG`, `ERROR`, and `DEBUG`. The followingconfiguration shows the log filename and debug level being set:

```
# Set a Logger
[logger.apache2]
file=<APACHE2_HOME>\logs\error.log
level=INFO
debug=1
```

Configuration Settings

In addition to the Logger, another important component of the `workers2.properties` file are the `config` settings specified by the `config` directive. These settings provide detailed information about the configuration setup to Apache, including the location of the `workers2.properties` file and the debugging level of the `config` component. In the actual configuration, use the exact location of `<APACHE2_HOME>`:

```
# config settings
[config]
file=<APACHE2_HOME>\conf\workers2.properties
level=INFO
debug=1
```

Setting up a TCP Socket Communication Channel

Tomcat 5 and JK2-based Connectors support four different types of communication channels for Tomcat to talk to Apache. The most commonly used standard is the TCP socket-based communication channel. The other possible options include a Unix channel (on a Unix system, of course), APR, and JNI communication channels.

A TCP socket channel is declared by providing details about the host name and port on which the Tomcat instance is running. The typical format for declaring a communication channel is `channel.socket:`*`HOST`*`:`*`PORT`*. Here, *`HOST`* and *`PORT`* specify where a Tomcat worker listens for AJP requests.

The `TomcatId` attribute indicates the identity of the Tomcat worker that will use this communication channel. The default value is `localhost:port`.

The following configuration shows a sample channel setup. Additional attributes not shown here include `lb_factor`, `group`, and `route`. These attributes are used in load balancing configurations and are discussed later in this chapter.

```
# communication channel settings for our "myTomcat"
[channel.socket:localhost:8009]
host=localhost
port=8009
tomcatId=myTomcat
```

On Unix systems, the other type of communication channel supported is `channel.un`. This uses Unix sockets. Typically, Unix sockets are faster than TCP/IP sockets. A sample entry for this type of communication channel will look something like the following:

```
# Example UNIX domain socket/named pipe
[channel.un:/usr/local/tomcat/work/jk2.socket]
```

The Shared Memory (SHM) File

When Tomcat is connected with a Web server such as Apache, the processes of Tomcat and Apache must share some information. A Shared Memory (SHM) file needs to be specified to share the information. Typically, this file is located in the `conf` directory of the Apache Web server. The maximum size for this file can be configured, as can be seen in the following configuration:

```
# Shared Memory file settings
[shm]
file=<APACHE2_HOME>/conf/jk2.shm
size=100000
```

Setting Up an AJP Worker

An important step in setting up an AJP worker is to provide an `ajp13` type worker using TCP socket-based communication. A sample worker will look something like the following:

```
# Declare a Tomcat worker
[ajp13:localhost:8009]
channel=channel.socket:myTomcat
```

The Tomcat ID used here (`myTomcat`) must match that defined earlier while setting up the communication channel.

URI Mappings

Using the AJP Connector, Apache dispatches the incoming requests for JSP or a Servlet to one of the available Tomcat workers. For a proper request-dispatching mechanism, Apache needs some rules. These rules are provided in the form of URI mappings in the `workers2.properties` file. The URI mappings specify a pattern that is used to match requests to workers. This pattern includes a host name and an associated port. The combination can be an exact host name and a nondefault port number, or any host name and a specific port number. A wildcard can be part of the URL to be matched. An additional attribute called `info` can be used to provide information about this pattern-matching. Typically, a Tomcat context is mapped along with some specific file types, such as JSP or Servlet:

```
# URI mappings for the tomcat worker
# All the incoming requests for any JSPs will be served.
# Map the "jsp-examples" web application context to the Web server uri space
[uri:/jsp-examples/*.jsp]
info= Mapping for jsp-examples context of tomcat
```

The Sample workers2.properties File

Now that you have examined all the configuration details to be put in the `workers2.properties` file, it's time to look at a sample one:

```
# settings for Logger of type Apache2
[logger.apache2]
file="D:\Apps\Apache2\logs\error.log"
level=INFO
debug=1

# Provide the basic config needed
[config]
file=D:/Apps/Apache2/conf/workers2.properties
debug=0

# Define a socket communication channel
[channel.socket:localhost:8009]
host=localhost
port=8009
tomcatId=myTomcat

# Shared Memory file settings
[shm]
file=D:/Apps/Apache2/conf/jk2.shm
```

```
size=1000000

# define a tomcat worker which will use the communication channel defined
# in the previous step
[ajp13:localhost:8009]
channel=channel.socket:myTomcat

# Map the Tomcat jsp-examples webapp to the Web server uri space
[uri:/jsp-examples/*]
info=mapping the jsp-examples context of Tomcat
```

Adding Directives to Load the jk2 Module (httpd.conf)

The `mod_jk2` module must be loaded as an Apache module. Edit the `httpd.conf` file by adding an entry as shown here in the `LoadModules` section.

For Windows, use the following:

```
# For Windows include the actual mod_jk2 DLL path in double quotes
# if the path contains any white spaces.
LoadModule jk2_module modules\mod_jk2-2.0.43.dll
```

For Unix/Linux, use the following:

```
LoadModule jk2_module modules/mod_jk2-2.0.43.so
```

Configuring the jk2.properties File

The JK2 Connector needs a communication channel and shared memory file for connecting Tomcat with the Apache Web server. This information is specified in the `jk2.properties` file. A sample `jk2.properties` file is provided under the `<CATALINA_HOME>\conf` directory in the standard Tomcat distribution. In most cases, the default settings provided in the `jk2.properties` work, and no additional tuning needs to be done.

The commonly used channel is `channelSocket`. Its configurable attributes are as follows:

- *`address`*—The machine on which Tomcat is running
- *`port`*—The port on which Tomcat listens. This defaults to 8009.
- *`maxThreads`*—The maximum number of threads the setup should allow at a given time
- *`serverTimeout`*—Specifies the timeout interval

The following example illustrates these attributes:

```
# Set the default port for the channelSocket
channelSocket.address=localhost
channelSocket.port=8009
channelSocket.serverTimeout=600
channelSocket.maxThreads=50
```

A sample `jk2.properties` file is shown here:

```
# Sample jk2.properties file
channelSocket.address=localhost
channelSocket.port=8009
shm.file=D:/Apps/Apache2/conf/jk2.shm
```

On Unix platforms, in addition to the `channelSocket`, an additional available channel option is `channelUnix`.

Testing the Final Setup

Now that the configuration is complete, it must be tested. Before testing this setup, restart Tomcat and then restart Apache. This ensures that the configuration changes made for Tomcat and Apache have been read.

To test the setup, point your browser to the following URL and browse to sample JSPs bundled with Tomcat:

```
http://localhost/jsp-examples/
```

Note that you are browsing to `http://localhost/` (the host/port on which Apache is listening) and not `http://localhost:8080/` (Tomcat's host/port). If everything was configured properly, the Web page shown in Figure 12-2 should be displayed.

Now try executing one of the JSPs. Point your browser to the following URL:

```
http://localhost/jsp-examples/jsp/dates/date.jsp
```

This should display the Web page shown in Figure 12-3.

This test confirms that requests for JSPs are being redirected by Apache to Tomcat correctly. After testing the deployment from a local machine, test the installation from any other machine across the network.

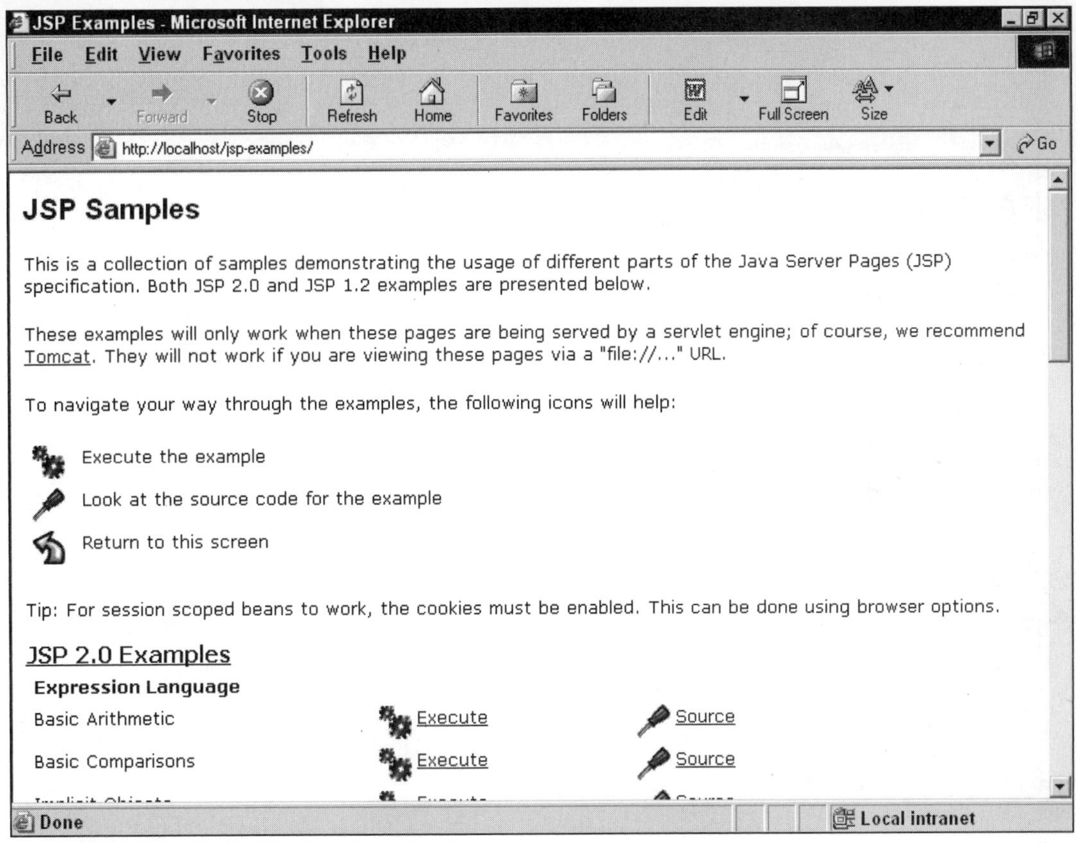

Figure 12-2: Proper configuration should result in this JSP Samples page.

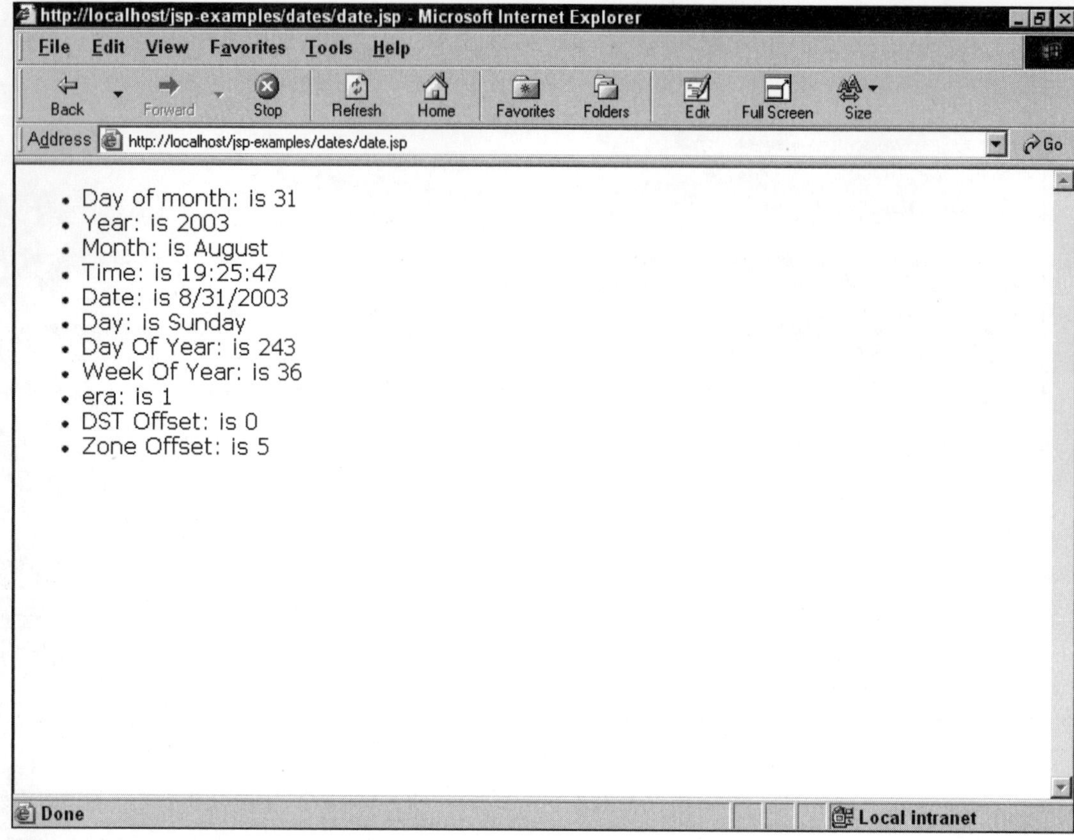

Figure 12-3: Another test of executing a JSP.

Configuring SSL

SSL provides a secure communication channel between the browser and the Web server. Chapter 10 explored how SSL is set up for the HTTP Connector. When Apache is used with Tomcat, you can use SSL at either the Apache end or the Tomcat end.

The preferred option is to enable SSL at the Apache end because of the better SSL support in Apache. In addition the SSL support, the Apache level can also be used by other deployed applications on the same server.

This section discusses both options.

Configuring SSL in Tomcat

Chapter 15 discusses this configuration in detail. In brief, it involves the following steps:

1. Download and install an SSL implementation.
2. Create a certificate **keystore** and add a self-signed certificate to it.
3. Purchase a certificate from a certificate authority such as VeriSign, Thawte, or Trustcenter. The self-signed certificate created here is used to generate a certificate-signing request.
4. Configure Tomcat for SSL.

Configuring SSL in Apache

Apache can be enabled with SSL using the `mod_ssl` Apache module. This section provides an overview of the major steps involved in configuring Apache 2 with SSL on Windows. A similar setup will work on Unix/Linux by changing the appropriate system-specific paths.

On Windows, ensure that no other Web servers (for example, IIS) are running on the server using port 80.

As mentioned in the introduction of this chapter, it is assumed that Apache is configured and running on the server. The versions and installation locations should be as follows:

- Apache version 2.0.43
- `APACHE2_HOME` is `D:\Apps\Apache2`
- `WINDOWS_HOME` is `C:\winnt`

Configuring the httpd.conf File

The first step is to get Apache to listen for SSL requests. This is done by adding another `Listen` directive in the Apache main configuration file (`httpd.conf`). You will find a line containing `Listen` directives in the `httpd.conf` file. This line indicates that the Apache Web server will listen to requests on port 80 (the default HTTP port):

```
Listen 80
```

Add another line below this line, to make Apache listen on the SSL port as well. The default SSL port is 443. A sample entry is shown here:

```
Listen 80
Listen 443
```

Ensure that the `serverName` directive is properly configured in `httpd.conf`. A valid server name is required because this is used while generating the server certificate:

```
serverName myserver.com
```

Now it's time to test whether Apache can listen on the SSL port 443. Restart the Apache server and browse to the following URL:

```
http://myserver.com:443
```

If the configuration is correct, Apache's home page should be displayed.

Building Apache with SSL Support

An SSL-enabled Apache server can be either built from source or downloaded in a binary version. Several Web sites (such as the one shown here) maintain binary versions of Apache. For the Apache version referred to in this chapter, i.e., 2.0.43, download the SSL-enabled binary (`Apache_2.0.43-OpenSSL_0.9.6g-Win32.zip`) from the following location:

```
http://tor.ath.cx/~hunter/apache/
```

Unzip the downloaded binary file at an appropriate location. This location will be referred to in the rest of this discussion as `APACHE2_SSL_HOME`. In our example, we will use `APACHE2_SSL_HOME` at `D:\Apps\Apache_2.0.43-OpenSSL_0.9.6g-Win32`.

> *Note that we have two separate locations:* **`APACHE2_HOME`** *and* **`APACHE2_SSL_HOME`**. *Though the server certificate will be generated using* **`APACHE2_SSL_HOME`**, *the final setup and SSL configuration will be done in* **`APACHE2_HOME`** *only. There will not be any changes in the Tomcat configuration because Tomcat will be communicating with* **`APACHE2_HOME`** *as before.*

Copying Files to a Windows Installation

Copy the files `ssleay32.dll` and `libeay32.dll` from `APACHE2_SSL_HOME\bin` directory to `C:\winnt\system32` directory.

Configuration File for Generating a Certificate

A configuration file is required for generating the server certificate. A sample configuration file is presented here. Save the following contents in a file named `myconfig.file` at `APACHE2_SSL_HOME\bin\myconfig.file`:

```
RANDFILE                 = $ENV::HOME/.rnd

[ req ]
 default_bits            = 1024
 default_keyfile         = keyfile.pem
 attributes              = req_attributes
 distinguished_name      = Wiley
 prompt                  = no
 output_password         = mypassword

 [ Wiley ]
 C                       = US
 ST                      = NJ
 L                       = Hoboken
 O                       = Wiley
 OU                      = Wrox Press
 CN                      = myserver.com
 emailAddress            = mail@myserver.com

 [ req_attributes ]
 challengePassword       = mypassword
```

Generating a Test Certificate

This section describes the steps required to generate a test certificate. Typically, in a production environment, a commercial-grade certificate from a Certificate Authority (CA) is used. Following are the main steps involved:

1. Create a certificate signing request
2. Remove the passphrase from the private key
3. Purchase a certificate from a CA or create a self signed certificate
4. Install the certificate

Create a certificate signing request

The command for creating a certificate signing request is shown as follows:

```
cd D:\Apps\Apache_2.0.43-OpenSSL_0.9.6g-Win32\bin
openssl req -new -out server.csr -config myconfig.file
```

Using the configuration from the `myconfig.file`, this step creates a certificate signing request (`server.csr`) and a private key (`keyfile.pem`). When asked for "Common Name" (for example, your Web site's domain name), give the exact domain name of your Web server (for example, `www.myserver.com`).

Remove the passphrase from the private key

This is an optional step that should be performed for security reasons (explained in the following text):

```
openssl rsa -in keyfile.pem -out server.key
```

It removes the passphrase from the private key. Provide the same password as mentioned in the `myconfig.file`. The `server.key` should be readable only by the Apache server and the administrator. It is highly recommended to delete the `.rnd` file, because it contains the entropy information for creating the key and could be used for cryptographic attacks against your private key.

Create a self signed certificate

In a production environment, the certificate signing request file generated (server.csr) is sent to a Certificate Authority and a certificate purchased. For test deployments, you can generate a self signed certificate. The following command shows this being done:

```
openssl x509 -in server.csr -out server.crt -req -signkey server.key -days 365
```

The `-days` option specifies the number of days after which the certificate will expire.

Install the certificate

On Windows, create a directory named `ssl` under the `APACHE2_HOME\conf` directory, and move the `server.key` and `server.crt` files into this directory.

Linux users must create two directories under APACHE2_HOME/conf — ssl.key and ssl.crt. Move server.crt into ssl.crt and move server.key into ssl.key.

Setting Up mod_ssl in Apache

Copy all the executable files from APACHE2_SSL_HOME\bin to the APACHE2_HOME\bin directory. This action will prompt for a confirmation of the overwriting of a few files. Choose to overwrite all files.

Similarly copy all the shared modules (*.so) from APACHE2_SSL_HOME\modules to the APACHE2_ HOME\modules directory. This action also will prompt for overwriting of a few files. Opt for overwriting all the files.

While performing the preceding step, don't delete the mod_jk2 module!

Now, copy the SSL configuration file APACHE2_SSL_HOME\conf\ssl.conf to the APACHE2_ HOME\conf\ directory. This file is included in the httpd.conf.

Finally, add the following lines in the httpd.conf file located at APACHE2_ HOME\conf, so that Apache can use the mod_ssl extension:

```
LoadModule ssl_module modules/mod_ssl.so

# Refer www.modssl.org for more details
SSLMutex sem
SSLRandomSeed startup builtin
SSLSessionCache none
ErrorLog logs/ssl.log
# You can change the log level later
LogLevel info

<VirtualHost www.myserver.com:443>
SSLEngine On
SSLCertificateFile conf/ssl/server.crt
SSLCertificateKeyFile conf/ssl/server.key
</VirtualHost>
```

Testing the SSL-Enabled Apache-Tomcat Setup

To test the SSL setup, the virtual host declared in the ssl.conf file plays a key role. A DocumentRoot different from the main configuration can be used for this SSL virtual host. This host will take care of all the requests coming for port 443. For simplicity, in the configuration used in this chapter, the virtual host uses the same DocumentRoot as that of the main configuration.

First, restart Tomcat and then restart Apache. To test the SSL-enabled Apache-Tomcat setup, try the following URL:

```
https://myserver/jsp-examples/dates/date.jsp
```

This should execute the date example bundled with the Tomcat distribution. In case of any errors, kindly refer to the ssl.log. In addition to this, an appropriate log level can be set in the configuration files httpd.conf and ssl.conf.

If you use SSL at the Apache end only, the connection between Apache and Tomcat may still be unsecured. This may be of concern in deployments where Apache runs on a server in the DMZ (demilitarized zone), and Tomcat is behind an internal firewall. One way of addressing this is by using an SSH (Secure Shell) tunnel to encrypt the AJP data passing between Apache and Tomcat. The details of setting up an SSH tunnel are not covered here, but if you do set up such a tunnel, you should remember to change the host/port values in Apache's **`workers2.properties`** *file to point to the tunnel, instead of directly to the Tomcat server.*

Tomcat Load Balancing with Apache

In this chapter, only a basic implementation of load balancing is discussed. Chapter 19 describes a more sophisticated environment, with support for persistent sessions with in-memory session replication.

Enterprise Web application must be fast, scalable, and reliable, and offer fail-safe behavior. For high-traffic Web sites, it is a good idea to route the requests coming from Apache to multiple Tomcat instances, instead of just one. The `mod_jk2` module supports load balancing with `seamless sessions`. It uses a simple round-robin scheduling algorithm. For each Tomcat worker, a weight can be assigned in the `workers2.properties` file, which specifies how the request load is distributed between the workers.

The concept of a **seamless session** is also known as **session affinity** or a **sticky session.** When a client requests any dynamic resource for the first time, the load balancer will route this request to any of the available Tomcat instances. Any subsequent requests from the same browser session should be routed to the **same** Tomcat Web container to keep the same user session. If the maximum number of connections for a Tomcat worker is reached, then `mod_jk2` waits for it until it is free. This behavior is known as a seamless session. The client experiences no break in application functionality, because the associated client session is kept intact.

The `mod_jk2` module inherently supports load balancing. The Apache Web server needs some configuration and multiple Tomcat instances to enable load balancing. The next section describes in detail how to set up a load balancer. The example setup consists of one Apache server and three Tomcat instances (workers) running on a single machine, though they could very well be distributed across different machines.

The steps involved in setting up Tomcat load balancing are as follows:

1. Change `CATALINA_HOME` in the Tomcat startup files to point to different locations for each of the Tomcat instances.
2. Set different AJP Connector ports for the instances.
3. Set different server ports.
4. Disable the Coyote HTTP/1.1 Connector.
5. Set the `jvmRoute` in the Standalone Engine.
6. Comment out the Catalina Engine.

7. Configure the Tomcat worker in `jk2.properties`.
8. Configure the Tomcat worker in `workers2.properties`.

These steps are covered in detail in the following sections. The three Tomcat workers used for load balancing are referred to as `Tomcat5A`, `Tomcat5B`, and `Tomcat5C`. All of them are on the same machine as Apache. Because multiple Tomcat workers are running on the same machine, they will use different ports for listening to AJP requests. Had these instances been running on different physical machines, they could have used the same port.

Before configuring Tomcat workers for Apache, make sure you stop all running instances of Apache and Tomcat. Once the configuration is complete, first start all Tomcat instances one by one and then start the Apache Web server.

Changing CATALINA_HOME in the Tomcat Startup Files

The basic requirement for all the Tomcat instances participating in this load-balanced framework is that all of them should be available simultaneously. Each instance needs a separate `CATALINA_HOME` variable at run-time. A different `CATALINA_HOME` variable can be provided for each of the Tomcat workers by editing the `startup.bat` (`startup.sh` on Unix/Linux) script file. Modify the `startup.bat` file for Tomcat5A as shown here:

```
set CATALINA_HOME=D:\Apps\Tomcat5A
```

For Tomcat5B, use this:

```
set CATALINA_HOME=D:\Apps\Tomcat5B
```

For Tomcat5C, use this:

```
set CATALINA_HOME=D:\Apps\Tomcat5C
```

The CATALINA_HOME environment variable should not be set in a load-balancing environment when you have more than one Tomcat instance running on the same machine. This is because each Tomcat worker needs its own **`CATALINA_HOME`***, as shown in the previous configuration.*

This step is not required if you run each Tomcat worker on a different machine.

Setting Different AJP Connector Ports

Because all the Tomcat workers (Tomcat5A, Tomcat5B, and Tomcat5C) are running on the same machine, it is required that each of them listen on a different port to avoid port conflicts. By default, the AJP 1.3 Connector listens on port 8009, which is preconfigured in Tomcat. Use port 8010 for Tomcat5B, and port 8011 for Tomcat5C.

To configure the AJP Connector for a Tomcat instance, edit the `server.xml` file and set the AJP port for each of them as mentioned earlier. Edit the information for the `<Connector>` tag in this file with appropriate values for the current Tomcat instance:

```
<!-- Define a Coyote/JK2 AJP 1.3 Connector on port 8009 -->
<Connector port="8009" enableLookups="false" redirectPort="8443" debug="0"
           protocol="AJP/1.3" />
```

Modify the AJP Connector port for each Tomcat worker as shown here:

- For Tomcat5A: 8009
- For Tomcat5B: 8010
- For Tomcat5C: 8011

This step is not required if you run each Tomcat worker on a different machine.

Setting Different Server Ports

Edit `server.xml` and set each Tomcat worker's server port. Locate and modify the following entry for each Tomcat worker:

```
<Server port="8005" shutdown="SHUTDOWN" debug="0">
```

For each Tomcat worker, set the port as follows:

- For Tomcat5A: 8005
- For Tomcat5B: 8006
- For Tomcat5C: 8007

This step is not required if you run each Tomcat worker on a different machine.

Disabling the Coyote HTTP/1.1 Connector

Because all the Tomcat instances will be running in conjunction with the load-balancer worker, it's possible that someone could directly access any of the available workers via the Coyote/HTTP Connector, bypassing the load-balancer path. To avoid this, comment out the HTTP Connector configuration of all the Tomcat instances in the `server.xml` file as shown here:

```
<!-- Define a non-SSL Coyote HTTP/1.1 Connector on port 8080
<Connector port="8080"
           maxThreads="150" minSpareThreads="25" maxSpareThreads="75"
           enableLookups="false" redirectPort="8443" acceptCount="100"
           debug="0" connectionTimeout="20000"
           disableUploadTimeout="true" />
           -->
```

Setting the jvmRoute in the Standalone Engine

An important step for load balancing is specifying the `jvmRoute`. Each Tomcat worker has an Engine directive in the `server.xml` file. The Engine is a top-level container in the Catalina hierarchy and represents the entire Catalina Servlet engine. This `Engine` directive has an attribute called `jvmRoute` that acts as an identifier for that particular Tomcat worker. Typically, a unique string is provided as the value for this attribute. This string must be unique across all the available Tomcat instances participating in the load-balancing environment.

Add a unique `jvmRoute` attribute to each Tomcat worker's `server.xml` file as described here. This unique `jvmRoute` ID will be used in the `workers2.properties` file for identifying each Tomcat worker. Ensure that the strings used are unique for each Tomcat worker. For the configuration discussed here, use the following entries:

For `Tomcat5A` on the `localhost` machine, the entry will be as follows:

```
<!-- You should set jvmRoute to support load-balancing via JK/JK2 ie : -->
<Engine name="Standalone" defaultHost="localhost" debug="0"
jvmRoute="Tomcat5A">
```

For Tomcat5B on the `localhost` machine, the entry would look as follows:

```
<!-- You should set jvmRoute to support load-balancing via JK/JK2 ie : -->
<Engine name="Standalone" defaultHost="localhost" debug="0"
jvmRoute="Tomcat5B">
```

For Tomcat5C on the `localhost` machine, the entry would look like this:

```
<!-- You should set jvmRoute to support load-balancing via JK/JK2 ie : -->
<Engine name="Standalone" defaultHost="localhost" debug="0"
jvmRoute="Tomcat5C">
```

Commenting Out the Catalina Engine

After adding the Engine directive as shown earlier, you are left with two entries for the Engine directive in your `server.xml` file(s). The first is the `Standalone` Engine and the second is the `Catalina` Engine. You need to comment out the `Catalina` Engine directive for each of the Tomcat workers, as shown here:

```
<!-- Define the top level container in our container hierarchy
    <Engine name="Catalina" defaultHost="localhost" debug="0">
-->
```

Tomcat Worker Configuration in jk2.properties

This section explains how to specify the properties of the Tomcat workers in the `jk2.properties` file. A separate AJP listener must be specified for each Tomcat worker. The following listings show how this is done.

For Tomcat5A, the `jk2.properties` file settings will be as follows:

```
# Sample jk2.properties file for Tomcat5A
channelSocket.address=localhost
channelSocket.port=8009
shm.file=D:/Apps/Apache2/conf/jk2.shm
```

For Tomcat5B, the `jk2.properties` file settings will be as follows:

```
# Sample jk2.properties file for Tomcat5B
channelSocket.address=localhost
channelSocket.port=8010
shm.file=D:/Apps/Apache2/conf/jk2.shm
```

For Tomcat5C, the `jk2.properties` file settings will be as follows:

```
# Sample jk2.properties file for Tomcat5C
channelSocket.address=localhost
channelSocket.port=8011
shm.file=D:/Apps/Apache2/conf/jk2.shm
```

Tomcat Worker Configuration in workers2.properties

This section discusses how to set up the `workers2.properties` file for load balancing.

Settings for Tomcat Workers

For setting up the load-balanced environment, the `<APACHE2_HOME>/conf /workers2.properties` configuration file must be suitably configured.

Some of the settings (shown here) are the same as those discussed earlier in the chapter:

```
# Usually commented out on production environments
[logger.apache2]
file="D:\Apps\Apache2\logs\error.log"
level=ERROR

# Provide the basic config needed
[config]
file=D:/Apps/Apache2/conf/workers2.properties
debug=1

# Provide the location of shm file on the Apache web server
[shm]
file=D:/Apps/Apache2/conf/jk2.shm
size=1000000
```

Now, define a socket communication channel for the first Tomcat instance (Tomcat5A). Some additional load-balancing-related attributes must be configured here.

These include an attribute called `group`, which informs the `mod_jk2` Connector that a particular Tomcat instance is a part of a certain group. For the setup discussed here, the load-balanced group name is `balanced`. Next, set the `tomcatId` attribute. This is used to identify which Tomcat instance is using a particular communication channel. In addition to this, an attribute called `lb_factor` indicates the load-balanced factor of the corresponding Tomcat instance.

The `lb_factor` indicates the relative weight of the associated Tomcat worker with respect to others for dispatching requests. The greater the `lb_factor` value, the less priority is given to that Tomcat worker.

Typically, the `lb_factor` is set by taking into account how powerful the hardware is on which the corresponding Tomcat instance is running. The last attribute used is `route`. The value for this attribute has to be exactly the same as the value of the `jvmRoute` attribute of the Engine directive. For more information, refer the section "Setting the jvmRoute in the Standalone Engine," earlier in this chapter. The settings for the `lb_factor` are shown as follows:

```
# Socket communication channel for Tomcat5A
[channel.socket:localhost:8009]
host=localhost
port=8009
tomcatId=Tomcat5A
group=balanced
lb_factor=1
route=Tomcat5A
```

Now, set up an `ajp13` type Tomcat worker using the communication channel declared previously:

```
# Tomcat5A worker
[ajp13:localhost:8009]
channel=channel.socket:Tomcat5A
```

Here are the settings for Tomcat5B:

```
# Tomcat5B
[channel.socket:localhost:8010]
host=localhost
port=8010
tomcatId=Tomcat5B
group=balanced
lb_factor=1
route=Tomcat5B

# Tomcat5B worker
[ajp13:localhost:8010]
channel=channel.socket:Tomcat5B
```

Here are the settings for Tomcat5C:

```
# Tomcat5C
[channel.socket:localhost:8011]
host=localhost
port=8011
tomcatId=Tomcat5C
group=balanced
lb_factor=1
route=Tomcat5C

# Tomcat5B worker
[ajp13:localhost:8011]
channel=channel.socket:Tomcat5C
```

Settings for the Load-Balancing Worker

After all the Tomcat instances have been configured for load balancing, it is time to configure the load-balancing worker (`lb`) in the `workers2.properties` file. The load-balancing worker is responsible for the management of several request-processing workers. By itself, the load-balancing worker does not process any requests; it just hands over the requests to the available Tomcat workers. Apache uses the load-balancing worker to dispatch all the requests for dynamic content. In turn, the load-balancing worker will route these requests to available Tomcat workers.

A load-balanced worker handles the following tasks:

- Instantiating the workers in the Web server
- Using the workers' **load-balancing factor** (`lb_factor`) to perform weighted round-robin load balancing. A lower `lb_factor` indicates a more powerful machine that can handle more requests than other Tomcat instances in the same load-balancing group.
- Keeping requests belonging to the same session executing on the same Tomcat worker (that is, providing **seamless sessions)**
- Identifying failed Tomcat workers, suspending requests to them, and falling back to other workers managed by the load-balanced worker. It also periodically looks up the availability of the failed Tomcat workers, as specified by the `recovery` attribute.

The overall result is that workers managed by the same load-balanced worker are load-balanced (based on their `lb_factor` and current user session) and covered by a fallback mechanism so that the death of a single Tomcat process does not bring down the entire deployment.

Declare the load-balanced worker and specify the worker group to which it belongs:

```
# Declare a Load balanced worker group named 'balanced'
[lb:balanced]
```

Various attributes can be used with this load-balancing worker. The following sections discuss each of them in detail.

worker

This attribute states the different workers participating in the load-balancing setup. For each worker participating in the load-balancing environment, a separate entry is needed. For the configuration discussed here, the entries will be as follows:

```
# Add three tomcat workers in this Load balanced worker group named 'balanced'
worker=ajp13:localhost:8009
worker=ajp13:localhost:8010
worker=ajp13:localhost:8011
```

timeout

A timeout can happen when one or more of the Tomcat workers to which the load-balanced worker is communicating are down or cannot serve the request for some reason. The default value is `0`, which is disabled. This attribute is very useful for sites with a large number of hits. The timeout value should be set to the maximum application call time, but not less than 1 second. An example is shown here:

```
timeout=90
```

attempts

This is the number of attempts that the load-balanced worker will try on each worker before giving up. The default value is 3:

```
attempts=2
```

recovery

This attribute indicates the amount of time a load-balanced worker will wait before checking to see whether a worker came out of the error state. By default, the value is 60 seconds, but you can modify it as desired:

```
recovery=30
```

stickySession

This attribute decides if seamless sessions are being used. By default, it is `true` (that is, 1). If needed, it can be set to 0, which will disable the feature:

```
stickySession=1
```

noWorkerMsg

This indicates what message is to be displayed if there are no workers available to process the current request:

```
noWorkersMsg=Server Busy please retry after some time.
```

noWorkerCode

The `noWorkerCode` attribute indicates the HTTP status code to be returned if no workers are available to process the current request. The default is Service Unavailable (that is, 503):

```
noWorkerCodeMsg=503
```

Finally the load-balanced worker will have settings like the following:

```
# Load balanced worker
[lb:balanced]
worker=ajp13:localhost:8009
worker=ajp13:localhost:8010
worker=ajp13:localhost:8011
timeout=30
attempts=2
recovery=90
stickySession=1
noWorkersMsg=Server Busy please retry after some time.
noWorkerCodeMsg=503
```

URI mappings

Now configure the load-balanced worker to handle the requests for the context `jsp-examples`. This is simply done by putting the URI mappings in the `workers2.properties` file as shown here. This will make `mod_jk2` forward any requests that match these patterns to the load-balanced worker:

```
# URI mapping
[uri:/jsp-examples/index.jsp]
info=Mappings for the Tomcat context jsp-examples
context=/jsp-examples
group=balanced
```

Adding the jkstatus worker

As discussed earlier, the `jkstatus` worker provides valuable information about the status of each Tomcat worker in the setup, and provides the associated performance statistics. Here is the configuration for the `jkstatus` worker:

```
# Define a status worker to test the run-time request behavior of all workers
[status:]

# Status URI mapping
[uri:/jkstatus/*]
group=status
```

Sample workers2.properties File

Now you will define a `workers2.properties` file for the load balancing. Here, a single load-balanced worker is defined. This load-balanced worker will in turn use the three separate Tomcat workers (Tomcat5A, Tomcat5B, and Tomcat5C). The load-balanced worker will be the single entry point for any requests delegated by Apache, and will handle the other workers:

```
# Usually commented out on production environments
[logger.apache2]
file="D:\Apps\Apache2\logs\error.log"
level=ERROR

# Provide the basic config needed
[config]
file=D:/Apps/Apache2/conf/workers2.properties
debug=1

# Provide the location of shm file on the Apache web server
[shm]
file=D:/Apps/Apache2/conf/jk2.shm
size=1000000

# Tomcat5A
[channel.socket:localhost:8009]
host=localhost
port=8009
tomcatId=Tomcat5A
group=balanced
lb_factor=1
```

```
route=Tomcat5A

# Tomcat5A worker
[ajp13:localhost:8009]
channel=channel.socket:Tomcat5A

# Tomcat5B
[channel.socket:localhost:8010]
host=localhost
port=8010
tomcatId=Tomcat5B
group=balanced
lb_factor=1
route=Tomcat5B

# Tomcat5B worker
[ajp13:localhost:8010]
channel=channel.socket:Tomcat5B

# Tomcat5C
[channel.socket:localhost:8011]
host=localhost
port=8011
tomcatId=Tomcat5C
group=balanced
lb_factor=1
route=Tomcat5C

# Tomcat5C worker
[ajp13:localhost:8011]
channel=channel.socket:Tomcat5C

# Load balanced worker
[lb:balanced]
worker=ajp13:localhost:8009
worker=ajp13:localhost:8010
worker=ajp13:localhost:8011
timeout=30
attempts=2
recovery=90
stickySession=1
noWorkersMsg=Server Busy please retry after some time.
noWorkerCodeMsg=503

# URI mapping
[uri:/jsp-examples/index.jsp]
info=Mappings for the Tomcat context jsp-examples
context=/jsp-examples
group=balanced

# Define a status worker to test the run-time request behavior to the all workers
[status:]

# Status URI mapping
[uri:/jkstatus/*]
group=status
```

The balanced worker is of type `lb`. It will use a weighted, round-robin algorithm for load balancing and will support seamless sessions as discussed earlier. If a worker dies, the balanced worker will check its state over the configured time intervals of recovery. Until it is back online, all work is redirected to the other available workers.

Testing the Load Balancer

This section explains how to test the load-balancing setup that was configured in the previous sections. To do this, create three similar JSPs for each of the Tomcat workers (using the same filename) and place them into the `jsp-examples` directory of each Tomcat worker. Create a file `index.jsp` with the following contents:

```
<%@ page language="java" %>
<html>
  <body>
    <h1><font color="red">Index Page Served By Tomcat5A</font></h1>
    <table align="centre" border="1">
      <tr>
        <td>Session ID</td>
        <td><%= session.getId() %></td>
      </tr>
      <tr>
        <td>Created on</td>
          <td><%= session.getCreationTime() %></td>
      </tr>
    </table>
  </body>
</html>
```

Make the following change to the `index.jsp` file of these copied versions (to identify that the corresponding Tomcat instance has processed the request).

For Tomcat5A, change the following line in the `index.jsp` file as follows:

```
    <h1><font color="red">Index Page Served By Tomcat5A</font></h1>
```

For Tomcat5B, change this line as follows:

```
    <h1><font color="blue">Index Page Served By Tomcat5B</font></h1>
```

For Tomcat5C, change the line as follows:

```
<h1><font color="green">Index Page Served By Tomcat5C</font></h1>
```

Make sure that all the Tomcat instances (Tomcat5A, Tomcat5B, and Tomcat5C) are up and running properly.

You are now ready to test load balancing. Make sure Apache is serving the static pages. This can be tested by visiting the following URL:

```
http://localhost/
```

Apache will return the `index.htm` page. Now, visit the following URL to confirm that Apache is serving dynamic requests:

```
http://localhost/jsp-examples/index.jsp
```

The request can be served by any of the three Tomcat instances. If Tomcat5A has served the index JSP, then the response would be something like the one shown in Figure 12-4. Depending on which Tomcat worker gets the request, the `index.jsp` page will be served.

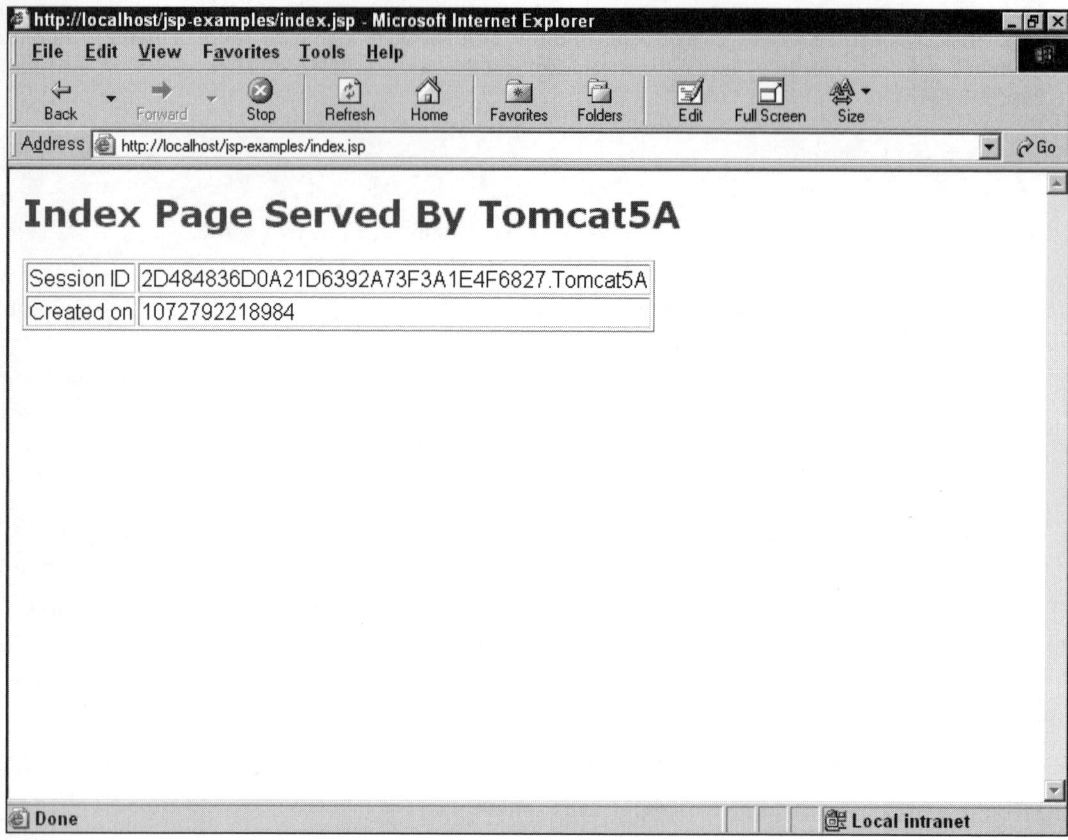

Figure 12-4: Testing the load-balancing behavior.

Testing Sticky Sessions

To test whether the same Tomcat worker maintains the session, make a note of the session ID for each request. In this case, the corresponding Tomcat worker name is appended to the session ID. In Figure 12-4, `Tomcat5A` is the unique string appended to the session ID. This confirms that `Tomcat5A` has served the request. The Tomcat worker name is determined by the `jvmRoute` attribute, which is set in the `server.xml` file. Whether the same Tomcat worker (which has served the first request) maintains a session can be confirmed by refreshing the browser window repeatedly. You can confirm that the session ID always remains the same for a given Tomcat instance. Hence, the session information remains intact.

If more browser instances are opened, then, for each of them, the request will be served by one of the Tomcat instances based on the `lb_factor`. Refreshing each browser window will confirm that the sticky sessions are supported by other Tomcat instances as well.

If you notice that load balancing with sticky session support is not working properly, then check whether you have properly (1) configured the **`jvmRoute`** *attribute of the Standalone Engine directive in* **`server.xml`** *and (2) commented out the Catalina Engine directive in all the* **`server.xml`** *files of the Tomcat workers.*

Testing Round-Robin Behavior

The `mod_jk2` module implements a round-robin algorithm. To test this, open a few browser windows and visit the following page:

```
http://localhost/jsp-examples/index.jsp
```

You will notice that with different requests from different browsers, different Tomcat workers will serve the request.

The run-time behavior of the Tomcat workers can be tested using the `jkstatus` Web page. The `jkstatus` page keeps track of the status of each worker and maintains a record of the traffic to each Tomcat worker. Apart from this, a lot of other useful information about the performance of each worker can be gathered. To view the status, visit the following URL (see Figure 12-5):

```
http://localhost/jkstatus/
```

Now, taking this to the next level, check whether Tomcat workers will serve the incoming requests in a round-robin fashion. Keep the browser windows open and you will notice that all three Tomcat workers do serve the incoming requests in a round-robin fashion. This means that if the first request is served by Tomcat5A, Tomcat5B will serve the second, and Tomcat5C will serve the third. Tomcat5A will again serve the fourth request. This is shown in the following table.

Tomcat5A	Tomcat5B	Tomcat5C
1	2	3
4	5	6
7	8	9
-	-	-

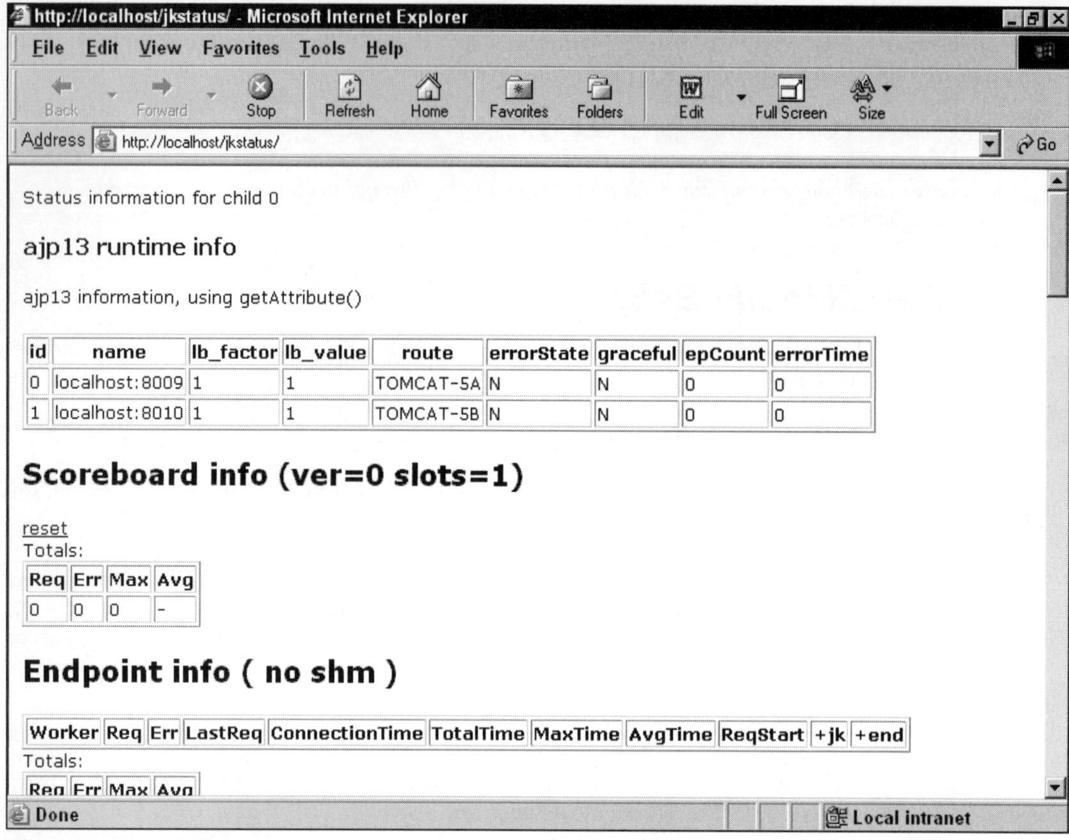

Figure 12-5: The jkstatus Web page.

Now, stop the Tomcat5B worker and try the same thing. This time, Apache uses the round-robin rule for the remaining two Tomcat workers. The following table reflects the modified request processing.

Tomcat5A	Tomcat5B	Tomcat5C
1	X	2
3	X	4
5	X	6
-	-	-

What happens if Tomcat5B is started again? Does the load balancer realize that Tomcat5B is again available? Moreover, when will the load balancer start using it? The answer is that the load balancer will start using Tomcat5B as soon as it finds that the server is up. It periodically checks the status of the worker, and will start using it as soon as it is made available. This lookup period is equal to the value set for the recovery attribute of the load-balanced worker. The default value is 60 seconds. This can be cross-checked by starting Tomcat5B again and continuing the testing cycle. The response will be something like the following:

Tomcat5A	Tomcat5B	Tomcat5C
1	X	2
3	X	4
5	6	7
8	9	10
-	-	-

Testing with Different Load Factors

In some deployment scenarios, the hardware configurations of all the machines may not be the same. In addition, there is a good chance that even though the hardware configurations are the same, the machines may be serving different online content. Therefore, every machine may not be in a position to contribute exactly the same resources as the others in the final load-balancing setup. This can be handled by setting an appropriate load factor (lb_factor) for each of them. The run-time load balancer will distribute the request load appropriately.

To carry out the test, change the lb_factor settings in the worker2.properties file. Modify the lb factor entries shown in the workers2.properties file.

For Tomcat5B, use this:

```
# Tomcat5B
[channel.socket:localhost:8009]
host=localhost
port=8010
tomcatId=Tomcat5B
group=balanced
lb_factor=2
route=Tomcat5B
```

For Tomcat5C, use this:

```
# Tomcat5C
[channel.socket:localhost:8011]
host=localhost
port=8011
tomcatId=Tomcat5C
group=balanced
lb_factor=2
route=Tomcat5C
```

Now, restart all three Tomcat workers and then restart Apache. Perform the same test you used to check the load balancing. Browse to the following URL a few times and notice the behavior:

```
http://localhost/jsp-examples/index.jsp
```

You will notice in this case that the behavior has changed. This is because the `lb_factor` is causing `mod_jk2` to distribute the request load proportionally, as shown in the following table.

Tomcat5A	Tomcat5B	Tomcat5C
1	X	X
2	X	X
X	3	X
X	X	4
5	X	X
6	X	X
X	7	X
X	X	8
-	-	-

Summary

This chapter presented details about the JK2 Connector and configuration for connecting Tomcat with Apache. The topics covered included the following:

- An overview of the JK2 Connector
- Getting and building `mod_jk2`
- Configuration of `mod_jk2` and the Connector for connecting Tomcat with Apache
- The different types of Tomcat workers
- Tomcat Load balancing, and testing load-balancing configurations

Chapter 13 discusses connecting Tomcat with an IIS front end.

13

Tomcat and IIS

Chapter 12 discussed how Apache could be used as a front end to Tomcat. This chapter details the use of Internet Information Services (IIS) with Tomcat. IIS is a popular Web server for Web sites hosted on Microsoft platforms, and is used for deploying server-side solutions developed in ASP, C#, and other Microsoft technologies. The advantage of using IIS is that it allows service providers to support heterogeneous server-side solutions (for example, both ASPs and JSPs) on the same platform.

The Jakarta project provides an Internet Services Application Programming Interface (ISAPI) filter for connecting IIS and Tomcat. ISAPI filters are components or plug-ins for third-party products to communicate with IIS. This chapter covers installation, configuration, and tuning of the ISAPI filter to connect Tomcat with IIS, including the following topics:

- Role of the ISAPI filter
- Configuration of Tomcat
- Settings, installation, and configuration of the ISAPI filter for IIS
- Testing and setup
- Troubleshooting tips

The configuration described in this chapter has been tested using Tomcat 5.0.19, Microsoft IIS 5.0, ISAPI filter (`isapi_redirector2.dll`) version 2.0.1, and Sun J2SDK 1.4.0 on Microsoft Windows 2000 Professional and Server editions. For the configuration discussed in this chapter, it is assumed that Tomcat and IIS are already installed, configured, and running on the system. The following locations are used in this chapter for configuration-related discussions:

- `JAVA_HOME`—`D:\Apps\j2sdk1.4.0`
- `CATALINA_HOME`—`D:\Apps\Tomcat5`
- `IIS Document Root`—`c:\Inetpub\wwwroot`

Role of the ISAPI Filter

The integration of Tomcat with a Web server is done with the help of two components: a Web server-specific component (the ISAPI filter) and a Java-based Connector implementation. These two components communicate with each other using the Apache JServ Protocol (AJP).

The ISAPI (`isapi_redirector2.dll`) filter is implemented as a Dynamic Link Library (DLL) and extends the functionality of IIS. In this case, it is used by IIS to serve requests for JSP and Servlets. IIS redirects all requests for JSP or Servlets to Tomcat using this filter. Tomcat then handles these requests and sends the response back to the client via IIS. Figure 13-1 shows how IIS communicates with Tomcat using the ISAPI filter. There can be one or more instances of Tomcat to serve the client requests.

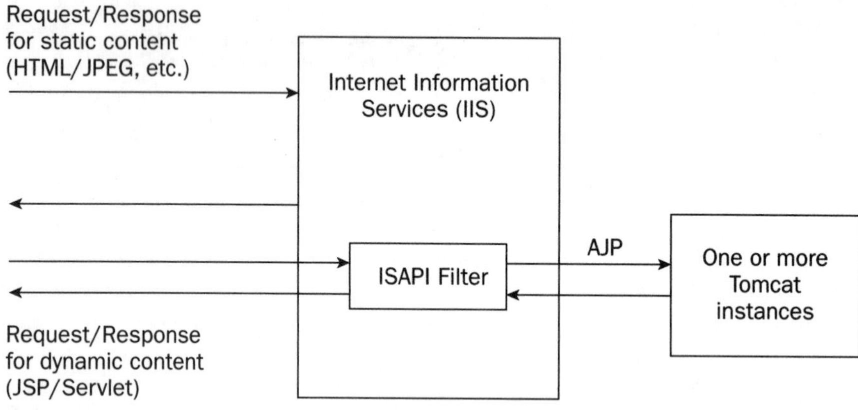

Figure 13-1: The ISAPI filter.

Connecting Tomcat with IIS

Following are the steps involved in configuring Tomcat to work with IIS:

1. Testing Tomcat and IIS installations
2. Configuring the Connector in Tomcat's `server.xml` file
3. Installing the ISAPI filter
4. Updating the Windows registry for the ISAPI filter
5. Configuring Tomcat workers (`workers2.properties` file)
6. Configuring the `jk2.properties` file
7. Creating a virtual directory under IIS
8. Adding the ISAPI filter to IIS

Testing Tomcat and IIS Installations

Before starting the actual configuration, you should test the installations of Tomcat and IIS. By default, Tomcat listens on port 8080 and IIS on port 80. This can be confirmed by accessing the corresponding home pages.

Start IIS by selecting the following in the Windows menus: Start ➪ Settings ➪ Control Panel ➪ Administrative Tools ➪ Internet Services Manager. Double-clicking the Internet Services Manager will open the IIS administration console. In the left pane of the console, expand the top-level server node. Right-click the default Web site and start the server. Once the server has been started, browse over to the IIS default home page at the following URL (see Figure 13-2):

```
http://localhost
```

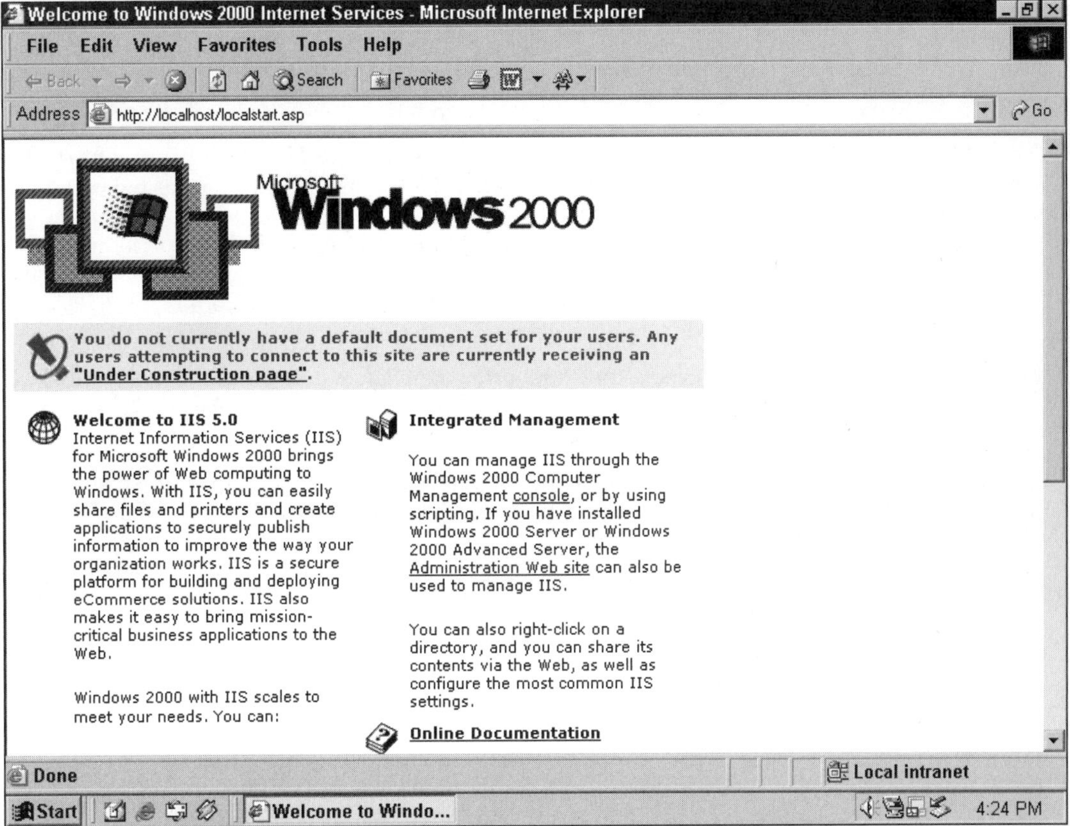

Figure 13-2: The default IIS Web page.

Next, confirm that Tomcat is properly configured. If it is not already running, start Tomcat and browse to the Tomcat home page at the following URL:

```
http://localhost:8080/
```

This should display the default Tomcat home page.

Configuring the Connector in Tomcat's server.xml file

Tomcat's `server.xml` file contains the configuration entry for the AJP Connector, as shown here. Uncomment the following lines if they have been commented out:

```
<!-- Define a Coyote/JK2 AJP 1.3 Connector on port 8009 -->
     <Connector protocol="AJP/1.3"
                port="8009"
                enableLookups="false"
                redirectPort="8443"
                debug="0" />
```

These lines represent an AJP Connector that will use AJP version 1.3 and will listen on port 8009. This listening port is configurable. The other configurable parameters of this Connector are as follows:

- *`enableLookups`*—If set to `true`, calls to `request.getRemoteHost()` will perform DNS lookup to return the actual host name of the remote client. Setting this to `false` will skip the DNS lookup and return the IP address as a string (thereby improving performance). By default, DNS lookups are disabled.
- *`redirectPort`*—If this Connector is supporting non-SSL requests, and a request is received for which a matching `<security-constraint>` requires SSL transport, Tomcat will automatically redirect the request to the port number specified here.
- *`scheme`*—Set this attribute to the name of the protocol you wish to have returned by calls to `request.getScheme()`. For example, you would set this attribute to `https` for an SSL Connector. The default value is `http`.
- *`secure`*—If set to `true`, calls to `request.isSecure()` will return `true` where the Connector is SSL enabled. The default value is `false`.
- *`debug`*—This specifies the debugging detail level of log messages generated by this component, with higher numbers creating more detailed output. If not specified, this attribute is set to zero (`0`).
- *`protocol`*—This attribute value must be AJP/1.3 to use the JK2 handler.

Installing the ISAPI Filter

The binaries of the ISAPI filter can be downloaded from the Jakarta Project Web site. The sources are also available. A separate version of the ISAPI filter DLL is available for each version of the Windows operating system. For Windows 2000, the `isapi_redirector2.dll` version is 2.0.1. For Windows XP, use `isapi_redirector2.dll` version 2.0.2.

For the configuration discussed in this chapter (Windows 2000), the `isapi_redirector2.dll` version 2.0.1 can be downloaded from the following URL:

```
http://archive.apache.org/dist/jakarta/tomcat-connectors/jk2/v2.0.1/bin/win32/
```

The 2.0.2 version for Windows XP can be downloaded from the same location by selecting the version 2.0.2 in the `jk2` directory.

After downloading, copy the ISAPI filter (`isapi_redirector2.dll`) into a directory under the Tomcat installation directory (for example `<CATALINA_HOME>\bin\win32\i386`). You must create this directory structure, because it is not a part of the standard distribution of Tomcat.

Write down the path where you copied the ISAPI filter. This same path must be specified while creating the virtual directory under IIS. The virtual directory path helps IIS locate the ISAPI filter. The step of creating a virtual directory is discussed later in this chapter.

Updating the Windows Registry for the ISAPI Filter

Windows uses the registry system to store configuration information about any system component. IIS also uses the Windows registry as a reference for getting information about its extensions. The ISAPI filter settings also need to be stored in the Windows registry. This can be done either manually or by running a registry script. It is always a good practice to create the registry manually. Creating a registry by running the script is also discussed later in this chapter.

It is highly recommended that you make a backup of the current registry before proceeding further. This will enable you to restore the original configuration if anything goes wrong.

Editing the Registry Manually

To update the Windows registry manually, select Start ➪ Run from the Windows menu. Type the command **regedit** in the command box and click OK, as shown in Figure 13-3.

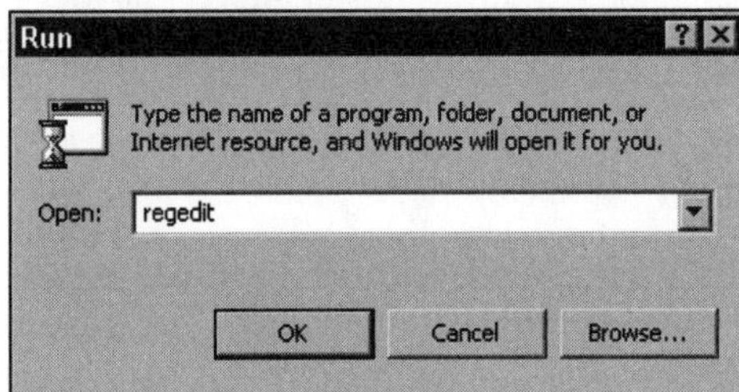

Figure 13-3: Invoking regedit.

The execution of the `regedit` command opens the Windows registry. The registry is a hierarchical collection of keys. The left pane shows the registry entries as a tree. The right pane shows associated subkeys for a selected key in the left panel. A typical Windows registry is shown in Figure 13-4.

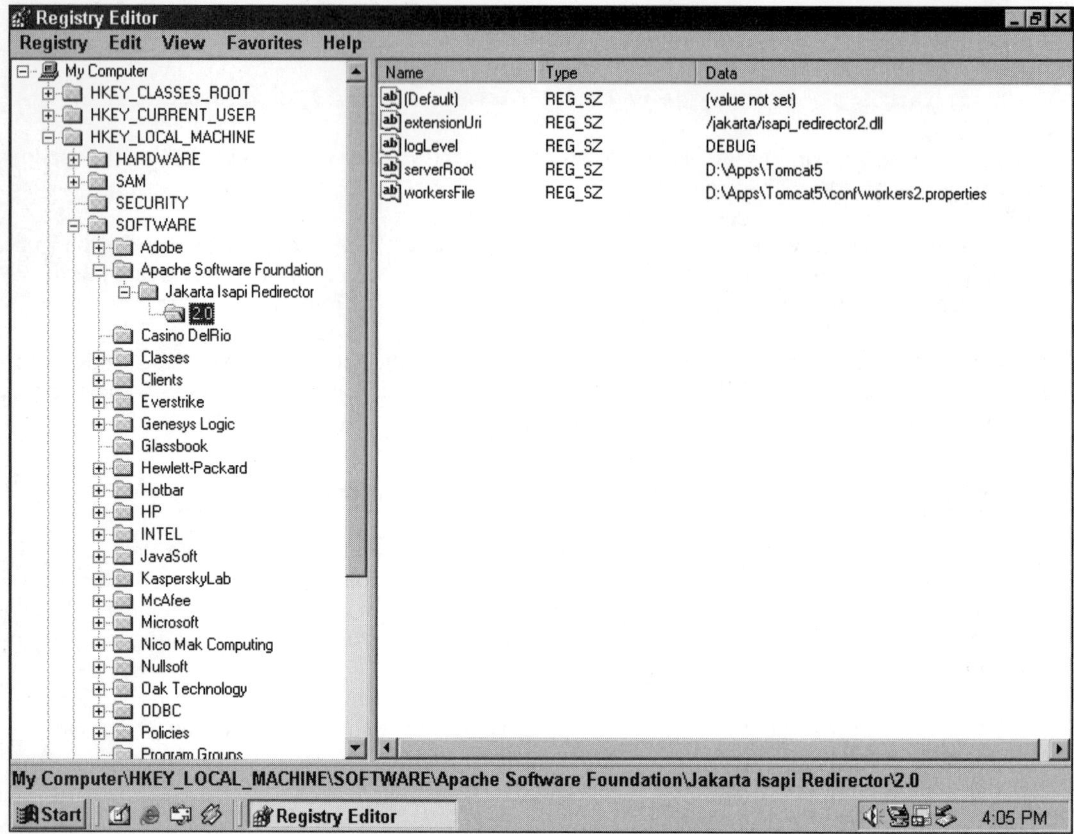

Figure 13-4: The Windows Registry Editor window.

To add the required new keys in the Windows registry, first locate the `HKEY_LOCAL_MACHINE > Software` branch in the left pane.

> *If any of the keys mentioned in this discussion already exists in your system's registry, then you can use the same. Note that the keys Apache Group and Apache Software Foundation are not the same.*

Now, create a new key called Apache Software Foundation under Software by right-clicking and selecting New ➪ Key. Under this, create another key named `Jakarta ISAPI Redirector`. Finally, create another key named `2.0` under `Jakarta ISAPI Redirector`.

Once this is done, you are ready to add the configuration parameters for the ISAPI filter. All parameters are of the type `string`. Right-click on branch `2.0` and add the first `string` parameter named `serverRoot` with the value of the Tomcat installation directory (`CATALINA_HOME`). For the configuration presented in this chapter, this would be `D:\Apps\Tomcat5`.

Add the second string parameter named `extensionUri`. This should point to the location of the ISAPI filter with respect to the IIS Web server context root. In later steps, a virtual directory named `jakarta` will be created under which the ISAPI filter is placed. For the present, specify the string as `/jakarta/isapi_redirector2.dll`.

Add a third string parameter named `workersFile`. This entry should point to the location of the `workers2.proprties` file (such as `D:\Apps\Tomcat5\conf\workers2.properties`). The `workers2.properties` file is used by the ISAPI filter to retrieve information about available Tomcat workers, and is discussed in detail later in this chapter.

Finally, add a fourth string value named `logLevel`. This parameter configures the logging level of the ISAPI filter. Any option of `DEBUG`, `INFO`, or `ERROR` can be specified here. Start with `INFO` as the log level; you can change it later if a different log level is required.

Editing the Registry via a Script

The Windows registry can also be updated at one pass by running a script. To update the registry using a script, create a script file as shown here and save it as `iis_redirect2.reg`. You may need to change some parameters in the script (such as the Tomcat install directory).

```
REGEDIT4

[HKEY_LOCAL_MACHINE\SOFTWARE\Apache Software Foundation\Jakarta Isapi
Redirector\2.0]
"serverRoot"="D:\\Apps\\Tomcat5"
"extensionUri"="/jakarta/isapi_redirector2.dll"
"logLevel"="INFO"
"workersFile"="D:\\Apps\\Tomcat5\\conf\\workers2.properties"
```

The script file should be edited in a plaintext editor such as Notepad. Note that the double quotation marks used in the script file should be the double quotation marks used in a plain ASCII text file. Double quotation marks used in a special word editor (such as Microsoft Word) will introduce problems in the execution of the script.

Modify the contents of the script as per your local settings and save it on the disk. Run the script for updating the windows registry by double-clicking the script file. This will pop up a message box. Select Yes and proceed. On execution, the script will create the entries in the Windows registry. Cross-check whether the registry is correctly updated or not. Look at the generated entries under `HKEY_LOCAL_MACHINE\SOFTWARE\Apache Software Foundation\Jakarta Isapi Redirector\2.0`.

Configuring Tomcat Workers (workers2.properties)

A **worker** represents a Tomcat instance that serves up JSP or Servlet requests to IIS. The ISAPI filter needs a properties file providing information about all Tomcat workers available. This file is the `workers2.properties` file. This configuration file also provides URI mappings to the ISAPI filter. These URI mappings are used for request dispatching by IIS. The other information contained in the `workers2.properties` file includes host name, port number, and load-balancing information for all the available Tomcat workers.

The standard Tomcat distribution doesn't have a sample `workers2.properties` file. It must be added explicitly in the setup. Typically, this file is placed under `<CATALINA_HOME>\conf`. For the syntax and other details of `workers2.properties` file, refer to Chapter 12.

Following are the step-by-step details for setting up a `workers2.properties` file to be connected to Tomcat with IIS. You will first create an empty `workers2.properties` file and then start adding all the needed components one by one as explained in the following sections.

Setting Up the Logger

A Logger will be the first component in the `workers2.properties` file. The ISAPI filter provides a default Logger for IIS called `logger.win32`. It logs messages to the Windows native application log. It can be viewed by selecting Start ➪ Settings ➪ Control Panel ➪ Administrative Tools ➪ Event Viewer. The available logging levels are `INFO`, `EMERG`, `ERROR`, and `DEBUG`.

The following lines show the Logger declaration in the `workers2.properties` file:

```
# Setup the windows application logging for the ISAPI filter
[logger.win32]
level=INFO
```

*If the logging level configured in the **`workers2.properties`** file is **`DEBUG`** and the level set in the Windows registry is **`INFO`**, then messages with both the **`DEBUG`** and **`INFO`** logging levels will bet logged in the Windows application log.*

Setting Up a Communication Channel

For the AJP communication between Tomcat and IIS, a TCP/IP-based socket communication channel must be set up in the `workers2.properties` file. The typical format for declaring a TCP/IP-based channel is `channel.socket:`*`HOST`*`:`*`PORT`*, where *`HOST`* represents the server on which a Tomcat instance is running, and *`PORT`* indicates the listening port of Tomcat for AJP communication. Typically, just the addition of the line `[channel.socket:localhost:8009]` serves the purpose; other parameters with default values may also work. A commonly used entry for declaring a communication channel looks like the following:

```
# communication channel settings
[channel.socket:localhost:8009]
host=localhost
port=8009
```

Setting Up a Shared Memory File

A **Shared Memory** (**SHM**) file must be set up in the `workers2.properties` file. This file is required for reconfiguration and status with multiprocess servers. Typically, the SHM file is located under `<CATALINA_HOME>\work`. The information about the location and maximum size of the SHM file is configured in the `workers2.properties` file, as shown here:

```
# SHared Memory file settings
[shm]
file=D:/Apps/Tomcat5/conf/jk2.shm
size=100000
```

Setting Up an AJP Worker

Each Tomcat worker must be represented in the `workers2.properties` file. Each of these workers uses a communication channel. The next step shows how a TCP/IP-based communication channel is configured. The Tomcat worker declared in the following code is of type `ajp13` and will use the TCP-based communication channel, `localhost:8009`:

```
# Declare a Tomcat worker and assign it the above declared communication channel.
[ajp13:localhost:8009]
channel=channel.socket: localhost:8009
```

Setting Up URI Mappings

The ISAPI filter refers to URI mappings in the `workers2.properties` file for dispatching requests to Tomcat. URI mappings consist of some combination of Web application names and file types. Typically, the entry includes a host name and its associated port. Wildcards can also be used in various forms. For example, the pattern for the default server name will be `[uri:*]`. Similarly, `[uri:*:port]` can be used when matching any host to a specific port:

```
# URI mappings for jsp-examples web application context
# Requests for any web component(indicated by the wild card *) are dispatched to
# Tomcat.
[uri:/jsp-examples/*]
info= Mapping for jsp-examples context of tomcat
```

Sample workers2.properties File

After following all the previously mentioned steps, a sample `workers2.properties` file is presented, as shown here. You may need to modify it to reflect your local settings. Once the file is ready, copy it to `<CATALINA_HOME>\conf`.

```
# Sample workers2.properties file

# Setup the windows application logging for the ISAPI filter
[logger.win32]
level=INFO

# Provide the location of shm file
[shm]
file=D:/Apps/Tomcat5/conf/jk2.shm
size=1000000

# Define a socket communication channel
[channel.socket:localhost:8009]
host=localhost
port=8009

# Define a tomcat worker by providing the communication channel
[ajp13:localhost:8009]
channel=channel.socket:localhost:8009
```

```
# URI Mapping for jsp-examples context of Tomcat
# This setting will forward all incoming requests for any JSP pages to Tomcat
[uri:/jsp-examples/*.jsp]
info= Mapping for jsp-examples context of tomcat
```

Configuring the jk2.properties File

The Connector needs a properties file that provides details about the communication channel and SHM file used for the communication between Tomcat and IIS. This information is provided in the `jk2.properties` file. The standard Tomcat distribution provides a sample `jk2.properties` file under `<CATALINA_HOME>\conf`. In most cases, the default settings provided in the `jk2.properties` file serve the purpose. However, in a production environment, you may need to customize these settings.

The SHM file entry specifies the location of the shared memory file, which is used for reconfiguration and status information with multiprocess servers. It also lists a TCP-based communication channel. Following is a sample `entry`:

```
# Sample jk2.properties file
channelSocket.address=localhost
channelSocket.port=8009
shm.file=D:/Apps/Tomcat5/conf/jk2.shm
```

In case the setup doesn't work with localhost, specify the actual server name.

Save the edited `jk2.properties` file under `<CATALINA_HOME>\conf`.

Creating a Virtual Directory Under IIS

IIS needs to locate the ISAPI filter as a server extension. Adding a virtual directory under IIS and loading the ISAPI filter addresses this requirement.

The first part of this process is to add a virtual directory. The IIS manager provides a wizard for this task. In Windows, select Start ➪ Settings ➪Control Panel ➪ Administrative Tools ➪ Internet Services Manager. Open the Internet Services Manager by double-clicking it. The left panel displays the components of the server. Upon expanding the main server node, the subnodes Default Web Site, Administration Web Site, and Default SMTP Virtual Server are displayed.

Add a virtual directory by right-clicking the Default Web Site node and select New ➪ Virtual Directory, as shown in Figure 13-5.

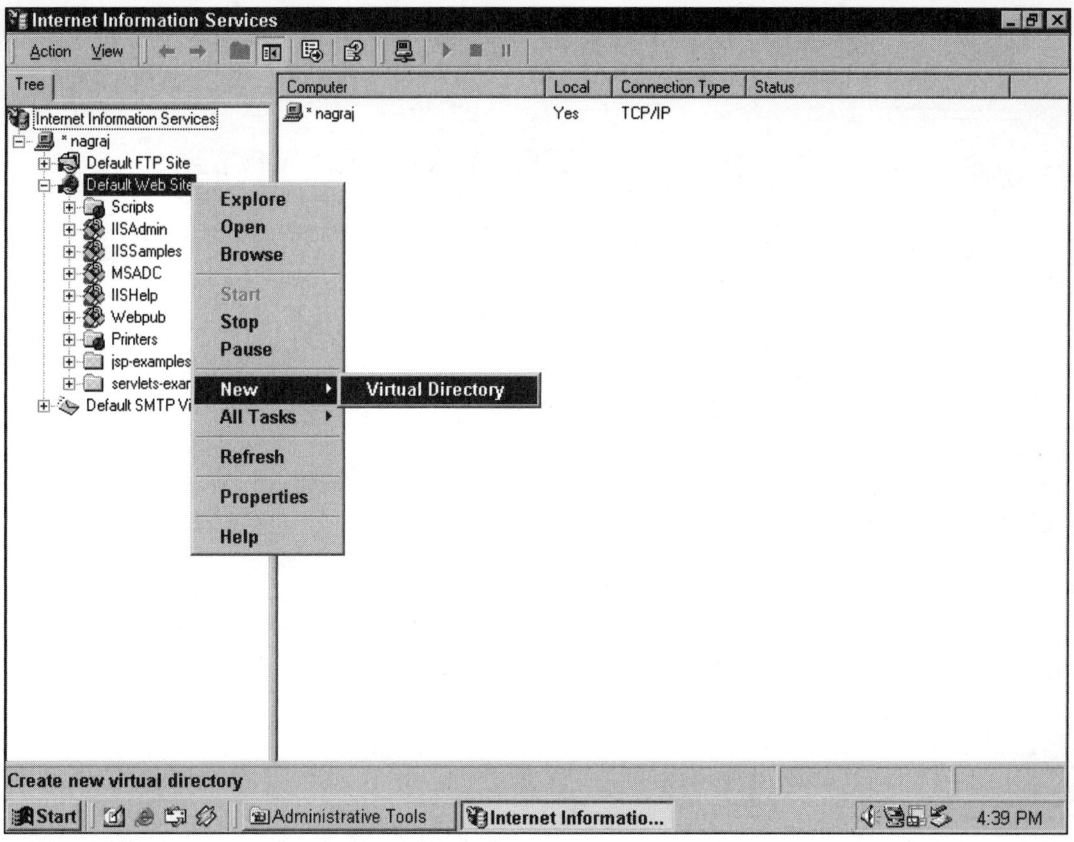

Figure 13-5: Starting the Virtual Directory Creation wizard.

This will start the wizard, as shown in Figure 13-6.

After clicking the Next button, the next screen will request an alias name for the virtual directory. Enter **jakarta** as the alias name. This is the same name that was specified earlier in the Windows registry in the `extensionUri` parameter. Take care to ensure that both the Windows registry and virtual directory alias are the same.

After you click Next, the wizard will ask for the actual location for the virtual directory. Click the `Browse` button to specify the directory in which the ISAPI filter is located. For the configuration discussed in this chapter, it is `D:\Apps\Tomcat5\bin\win32\i386`. Again, confirm that this was the location to which the ISAPI filter was copied (see the section, "Installing the ISAPI Filter," earlier in this chapter).

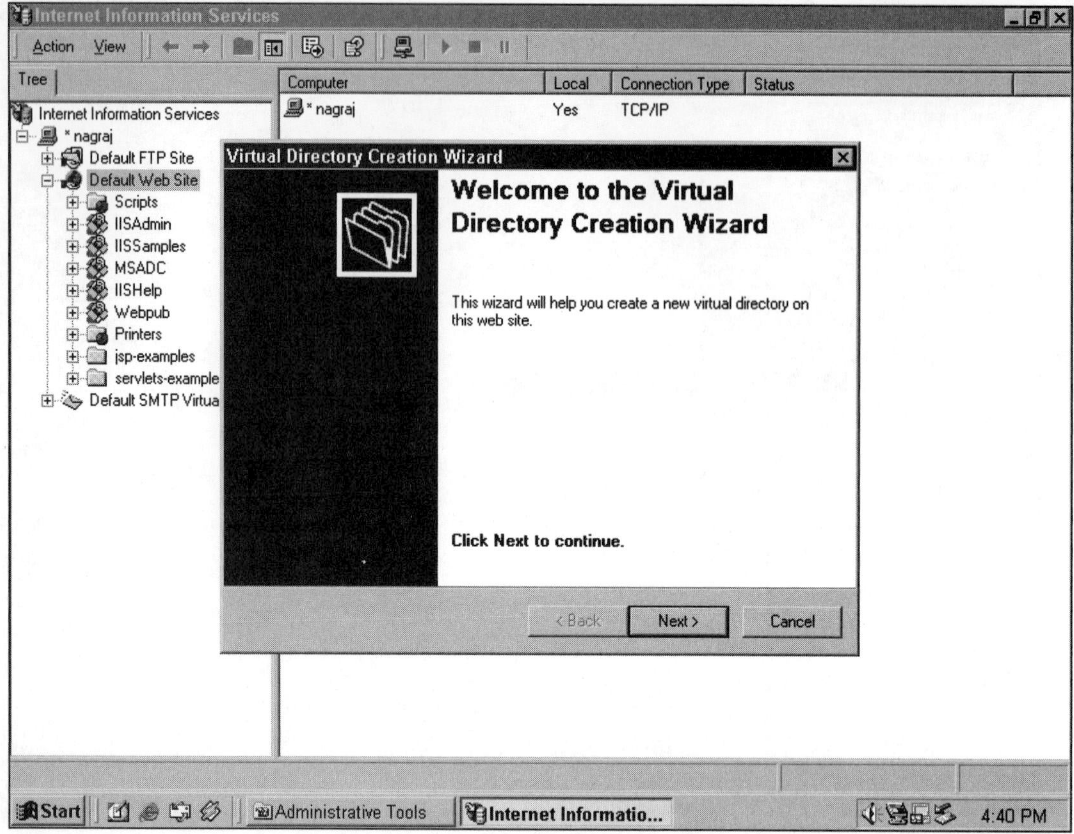

Figure 13-6: The first window of the Virtual Directory Creation wizard.

In the next screen, select the permissions that you want to provide for accessing the directory. Select options `Read`, `Run Scripts`, `Execute(such as ISAPI applications or CGI)`, and `Browse`.

> *The **`Browse`** option enables directory browsing for the virtual directory. The **`Browse`** option can be disabled later, after the setup is tested.*

Complete the final step of the wizard. On completion, the default Web site (named `jakarta`) will be displayed as a sub-branch.

After creating the virtual directory, recheck all the values specified. To do this, right-click the virtual directory and select `Properties`. A screen with all the details will be displayed, as shown in Figure 13-7.

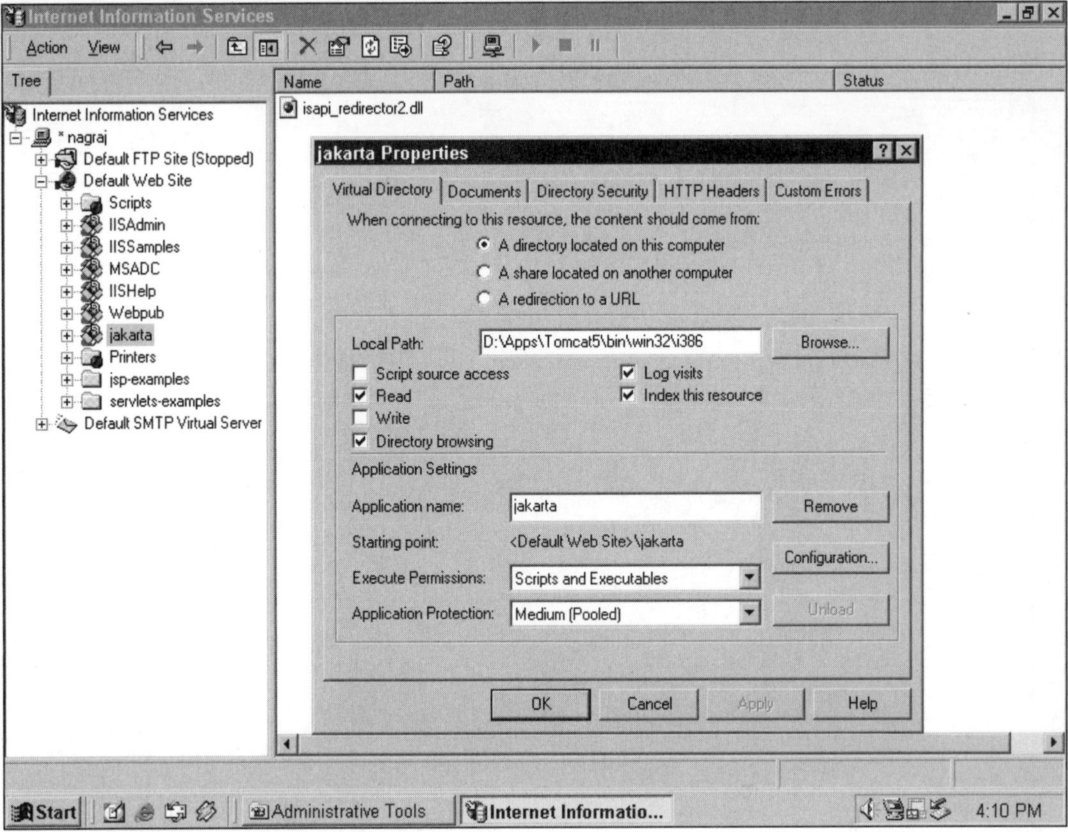

Figure 13-7: Checking the virtual directory settings.

Adding the ISAPI Filter to IIS

The next part of the configuration is to load the ISAPI filter as an extension to the IIS main Web service. In Windows, select Start ➪ Settings ➪ Control Panel ➪ Administrative Tools ➪ Internet Services Manager. Open the Internet Services Manager by double-clicking it. The left panel displays the server's component tree.

Now, right-click the Default Web Site node and select `Properties`. This will open the Default Web Site properties dialog box. Click the ISAPI Filters tab and click the Add button to add a new ISAPI filter.

Another dialog box will appear, requesting the filename and the location of the executable of the ISAPI filter to be added, as shown in Figure 13-8. Provide the ISAPI filter filename of `jakarta`, and provide the executable location of `D:\Apps\Tomcat5\bin\win32\i386\isapi_redirector2.dll`. These were the same values that you configured earlier.

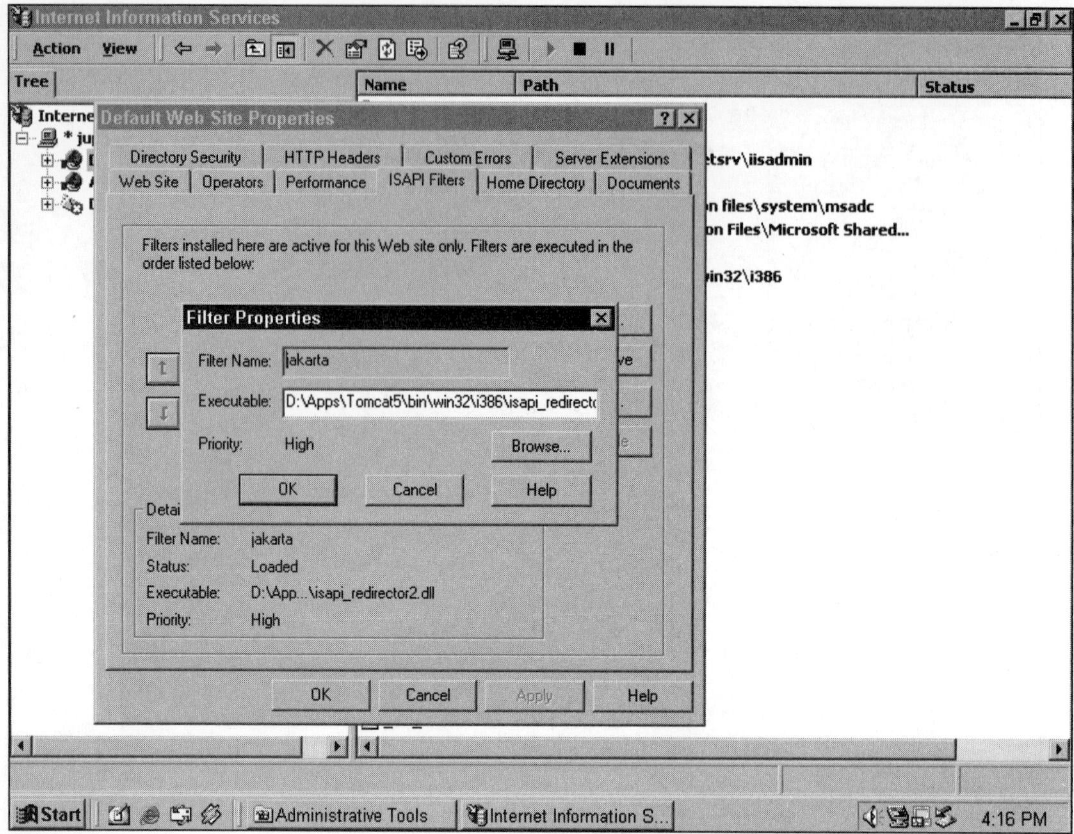

Figure 13-8: Adding the ISAPI filter to IIS.

Click OK to add the ISAPI filter named `jakarta`. This will add an entry in the ISAPI filter list. At this stage, the filter is not yet usable by IIS. This unavailability is indicated by the missing upward-pointing green status arrow for this filter in the ISAPI filter list.

IIS is stopped and started by right-clicking the Default Web Site node located in the left pane of the Internet Services Manager. After restarting the Default Web Site of IIS, again check the list of ISAPI filters. This time the `jakarta` filter will be displayed with an upward-pointing green status arrow, as shown in Figure 13-9.

> *The ISAPI filter can also be configured at the Main Server instead of the Default Web Site. If the setup is not working after setting up the ISAPI filter for the Default Web Site, try setting up the ISAPI filter at the Main Server.*

The newly added `jakarta` ISAPI filter is now loaded. The IIS Web server can use this filter as a server extension and apply it to all the incoming requests. This completes the configuration needed to connect Tomcat with IIS.

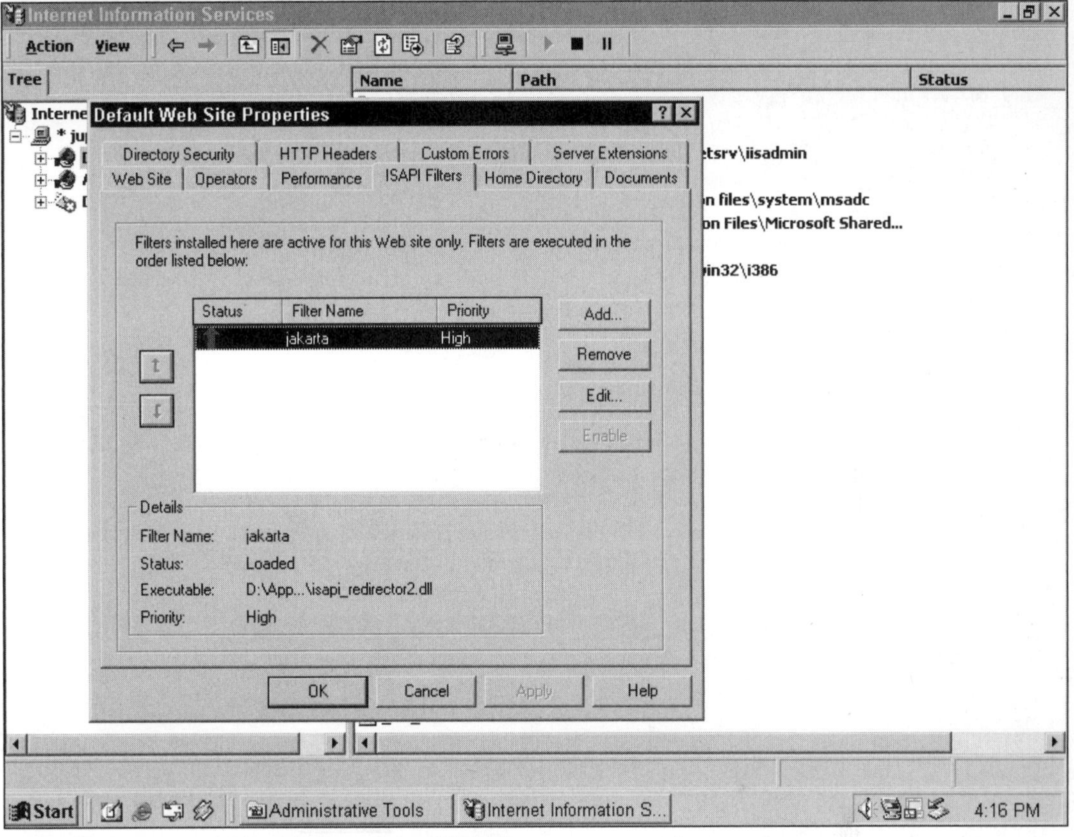

Figure 13-9: Successful installation of the ISAPI filter.

In case of failure, check the Windows registry entries and verify the `isapi_redirector2.dll` path that was specified while adding the ISAPI filter.

Testing the Final Setup

After successfully completing the previous steps, you are now ready to test connectivity between Tomcat and IIS.

One way to do this is to execute the example JSPs bundled with the Tomcat distribution. You had earlier mapped the `jsp-examples` context in the `workers2.properties` file. Now copy the complete `jsp-examples` directory from Tomcat's `webapps` folder to the IIS document root:

- Source: JSP samples directory (for example, `D:\Apps\Tomcat5\webapps\jsp-examples`)
- Destination: IIS document root (for example, `C:\inetpub\wwwroot`)

Once all the files are copied to the IIS document root, delete only the JSP files from the destination `C:\inetpub\wwwroot\jsp-examples`. This ensures that Tomcat serves the dynamic content, and IIS serves the static content (such as HTML and images used by the example JSPs). Now, restart Tomcat and then restart the IIS Web server.

Note that only the JSP files are to be deleted from the IIS document root. This can be done by searching for ***.jsp** *files and deleting them.*

Executing any of the sample examples under the `jsp-examples` context will test the final setup. Point your browser to the following location:

```
http://localhost/jsp-examples/dates/date.jsp
```

This should execute the `date.jsp` page, as shown in Figure 13-10.

*If you get a 404 Error while accessing the test URL (**http://localhost/jsp-examples/dates/date.jsp**), then try using the actual server name instead of localhost.*

This confirms successful connectivity between Tomcat and IIS. In this configuration, Tomcat serves up only the dynamic content, and IIS serves up all the static content (images, HTML pages, CSS files, and so on).

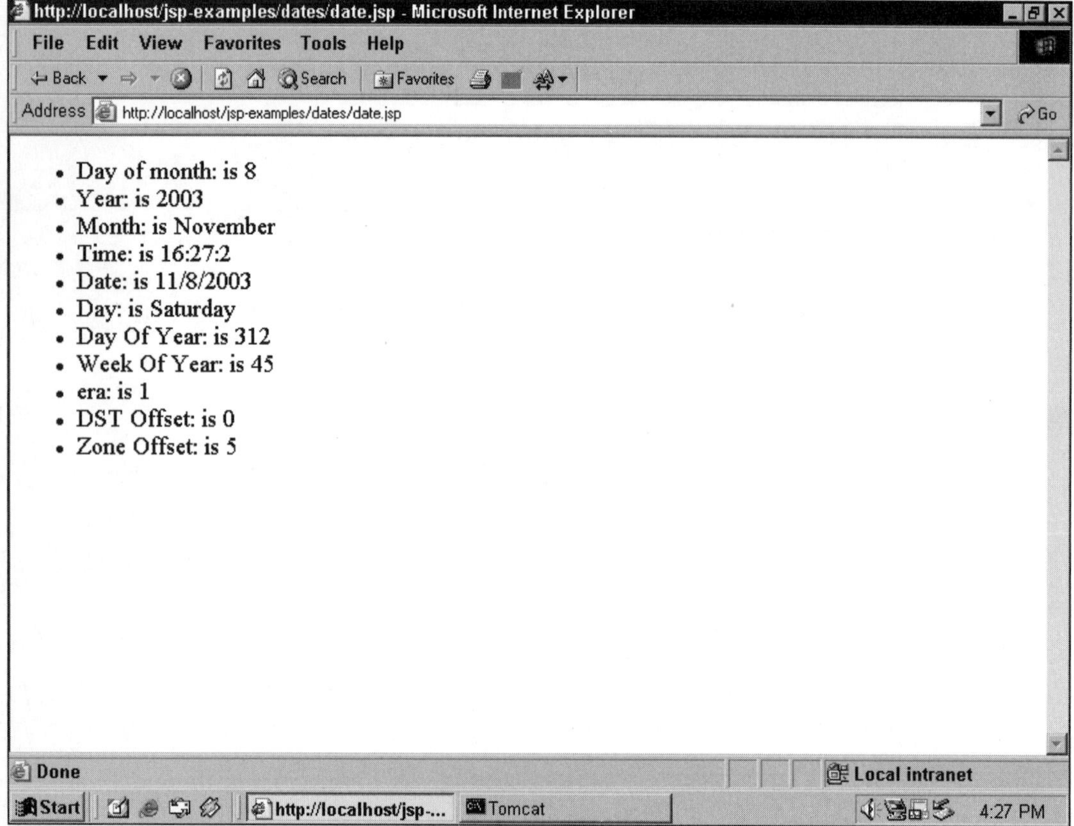

Figure 13-10: Testing the setup reveals a successful JSP execution.

Troubleshooting Tips

The procedure described in this chapter for configuring Tomcat with IIS is a bit tricky. Sometimes even when you think you followed the steps properly, the setup does not work. This section discusses some common pitfalls and provides debugging tips to help resolve any configuration-related issues.

If all the configuration steps were followed, but you still experience problems with IIS rendering JSPs, use the following guidelines to troubleshoot the most common problems:

- Check whether the IIS Web server is running. This can be tested by visiting the IIS home page. You should get the default IIS home page at `http://localhost`, which is shown in Figure 13-2. If the use of `localhost` as server name doesn't work, then try using the actual server name or IP address.
- Confirm that the ISAPI filter is properly installed. In the left pane of the Internet Services Manager, right-click the Default Web Site node and select the Properties option. Click the ISAPI Filters tab. In the list of ISAPI filters, check if the status column for the `jakarta` filter has a green upward-pointing arrow. If you do not see the green arrow, then there may be a problem with the installation of the ISAPI filter. Check the Windows registry entries and verify the `isapi_redirector2.dll` path that was specified while adding the ISAPI filter.
- Verify that the virtual directory (`jakarta`) is defined properly in IIS. If something is wrong with it, IIS will indicate this by flagging it with a red symbol. In addition, verify that the name of this virtual directory matches the name specified in the registry (in the example setup, the name `jakarta` was used).
- Visit the Windows system application log used by the ISAPI filter. You can configure the logging level of this log to `DEBUG` in the `workers2.properties` file under the component `logger.win32`, as shown here:

```
# Provide the logging level
[logger.win32]
level=DEBUG
```

  If there are any configuration errors, then `isapi_redirector2.dll` will log them in the Windows system application log.

- Check the IIS log file. By default, the IIS server log is located at `C:\Winnt\system32\LogFiles\W3SVC1\`. This path can also be checked in the IIS Default Web Site Properties dialog box. A different log file is generated every day. The following code shows some typical entries in the log file that indicate successful access of the ISAPI filter:

```
#Software: Microsoft Internet Information Services 5.0
#Version: 1.0
#Date: 2003-11-20 15:29:18
#Fields: time c-ip cs-method cs-uri-stem sc-status
15:29:18 127.0.0.1 GET /jakarta/isapi_redirector2.dll 200
15:29:20 127.0.0.1 GET /jakarta/isapi_redirector2.dll 200
15:29:20 127.0.0.1 GET /jakarta/isapi_redirector2.dll 200
```

  The log entries show the time, client IP address, HTTP method, URL requested, and HTTP status code for the request. If similar entries do not exist in the IIS log file, then the ISAPI redirector is not being called by IIS. The value `200` is an HTTP status code that indicates that the resource was found.

A status code of `400`, `404`, or `500` indicates an error in the ISAPI filter installation or configuration (as shown here):

```
15:29:18 127.0.0.1 GET /jsp-examples/dates/date.jsp _400
```

- Make sure Tomcat is running and that the AJP13 Connector is listening on the correct port. By default, the listening port is 8009 and is defined in the `server.xml` file of Tomcat. It's a good idea to open a DOS prompt and run the command `netstat`. This will list all the active ports on the system.
- Verify the ISAPI Windows registry settings. Cross-check whether they are correct as per your local installation paths.
- Verify the contents of the `workers2.properties` file. Refer to the sample `workers2.properties` file. The most common mistake is not properly declaring the `ajp` worker and communication channel.

  At least one Tomcat worker should be available to IIS for dispatching the requests. If no Tomcat workers are available to IIS, then an error message (shown in Figure 13-11) is displayed. Typically, such an error is reported when the configured Tomcat workers are not running. To resolve this problem, ensure that the Tomcat workers are properly configured and running.

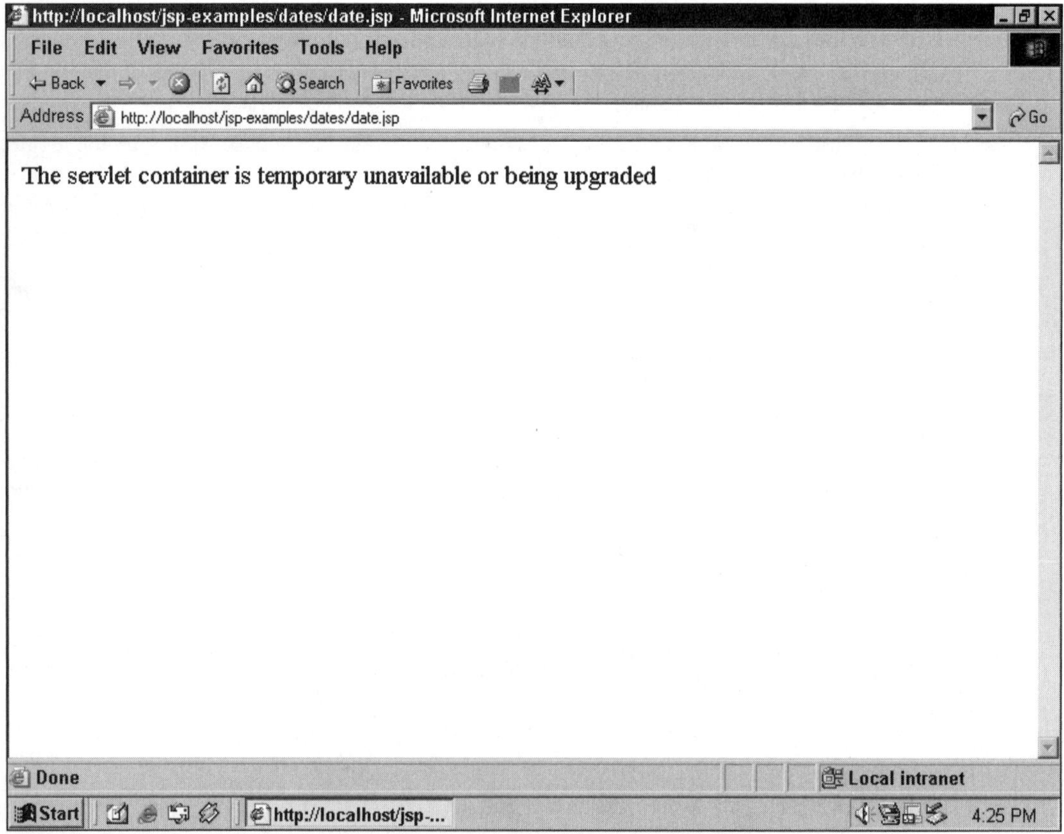

Figure 13-11: Error message indicating that no Tomcat worker is available.

Performance Tuning

The configuration discussed in this chapter is for out-of-the-box settings for Tomcat and IIS. Web sites serving a lot of traffic need optimum utilization of resources. IIS provides some additional options to tune the ISAPI filter configurations. The following sections describe some of these optimization options.

Web Site Hits per Day

IIS can be configured for the expected number of hits on the Web site. This option is available in the Performance tab on the Default Web Site Properties dialog box. Figure 13-12 shows the details of this option. It is a good idea to set the expected number of hits per day to be slightly higher than what is expected. However, if this value is set too high, excess server memory will be allocated, which will degrade performance.

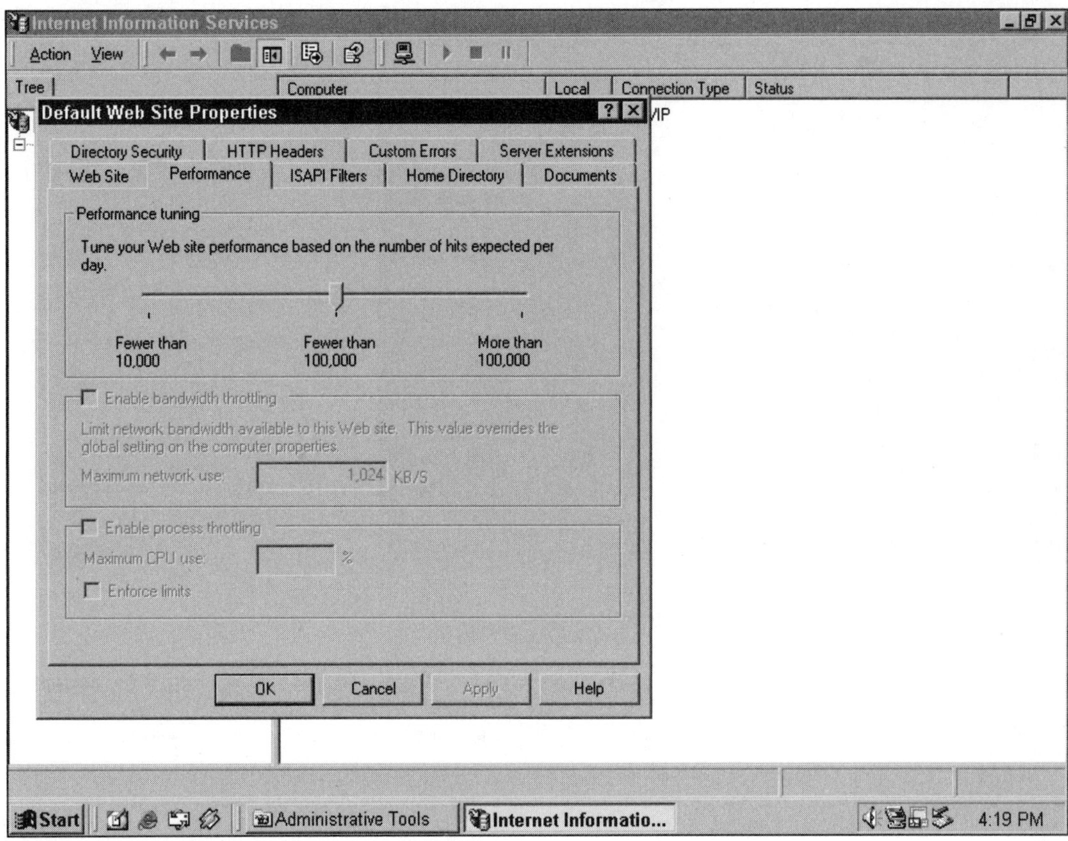

Figure 13-12: Tuning IIS for expected Web traffic.

Keep Alive and TCP Connection Timeout

The default IIS configuration has HTTP `keep-alive` enabled. HTTP is a stateless protocol, and each HTTP request from a client to the Web server causes a connection to be established, serviced, and then closed. If the Web server were to set up and close TCP connections for each HTTP request, this would cause serious performance issues. When the HTTP `keep-alive` attribute is enabled, the Web server keeps the TCP connection open for a specified period of time to optimize performance for back-to-back HTTP requests between a client and the Web server.

In addition to this parameter, a TCP connection timeout parameter can be set. This is the amount of time that idle TCP connections will be left open. Figure 13-13 shows these parameters being configured.

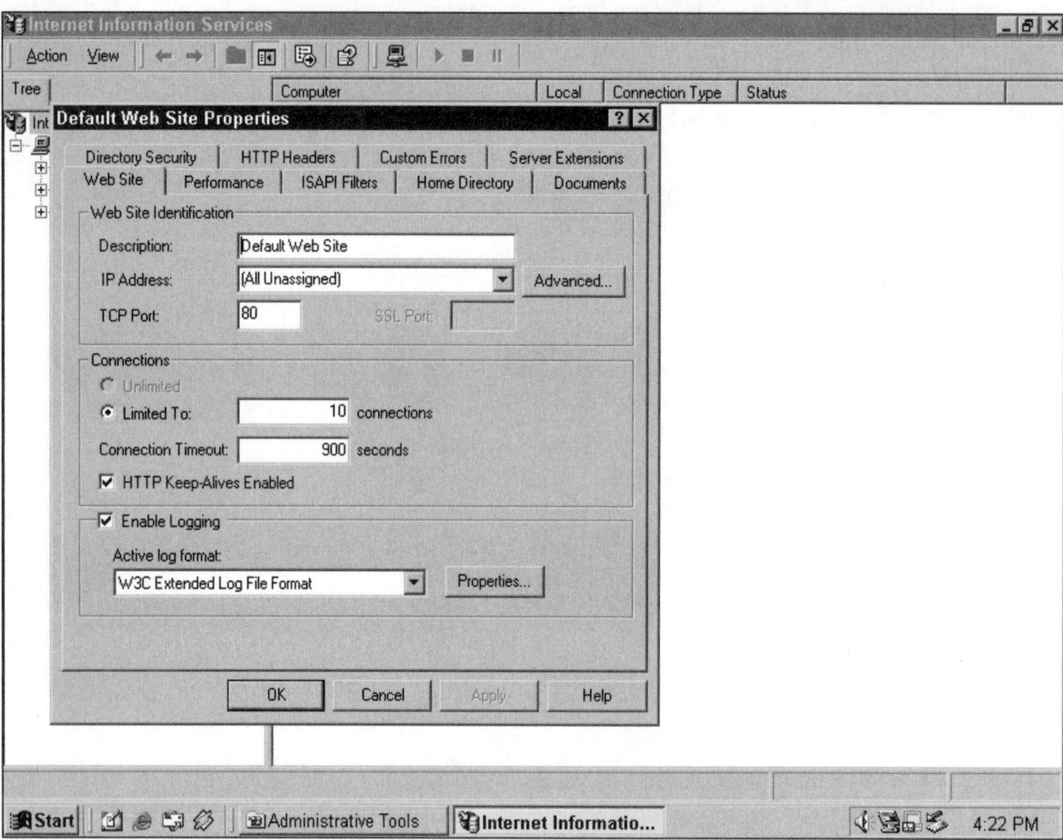

Figure 13-13: Tuning IIS with options for Keep-Alive and Connection Timeout.

Tuning the AJP Connector

Another optimization you can perform is configuring the number of request-processing threads in the Tomcat worker. The AJP13 Connector defined in the `server.xml` file enables you to set the minimum and maximum number of threads, as shown here:

```
<Connector className=" org.apache.ajp.tomcat4.Ajp13Connector"
           port=" 8009"
           minProcessors="5"
           maxProcessors="75"
           acceptCount="10"
           debug=" 0" />
```

The `<Connector>` tag has attributes such as `minProcessors`, `maxProcessors`, and `acceptCount`, which can be tuned for performance. A general rule of thumb is to set the number of `maxProcessors` to the maximum number of concurrent users expected per Tomcat worker. Set `minProcessors` to the average number of concurrent users expected per Tomcat worker. The `acceptCount` attribute controls the number of threads initialized at startup. If these values are too high, then the operating system suffers the overhead required for allocating memory and CPU for these threads. If these values are set too low, then user requests will be queued or not serviced at all.

Load-Balanced AJP Workers

In addition to the AJP worker, a load-balanced worker consisting of multiple `ajp13` workers can be defined. Chapter 12 describes the details for setting up a load-balanced environment. The concepts discussed in Chapter 12 are specified for Apache and Tomcat, but are applicable regardless of the Web server used. More advanced load balancing configurations are covered in Chapter 19.

Using SSL

Secure Socket Layers (SSL) provides a secure communication channel between the browser and the Web server. Chapter 10 discusses how SSL is set up for the HTTP Connector. When IIS is used with Tomcat, you can use SSL at either the IIS end or the Tomcat end. Using SSL with IIS is often preferred, as other Web pages and deployed applications (for example, ASP applications) on the same server can use it, too.

- *Configuring SSL in Tomcat*—This configuration is explained in detail in Chapter 15. In brief, it involves the following steps:
    1. Download and install an SSL implementation.
    2. Create a certificate keystore and add a self-signed certificate to it.
    3. Purchase a certificate from a certificate authority (such as VeriSign, Thawte, or Trustcenter). The self-signed certificate created the preceding step is used to generate a certificate-signing request.
    4. Configure Tomcat for SSL.
- *Configuring SSL in IIS*—Refer to the documentation provided with your IIS installation for details.

Summary

This chapter presented details about using IIS as a Web front end to Tomcat. To conclude this chapter, let's review some of the key points that have been discussed:

- Setup of the ISAPI filter for IIS, which enables it to communicate with Tomcat
- Some useful troubleshooting tips to help administrators deal with any configuration issues
- Performance-tuning tips

Chapter 14 covers JDBC connectivity in Tomcat.

14

JDBC Connectivity

Most Web applications process data, and that data is often stored in a database. The most popular database management systems are based on relational concepts, and are appropriately called **relational database management systems** (or **RDBMSs**).

All popular databases (including Oracle, MySQL, SQL Server, Sybase, Interbase, PostgreSQL, and DB2) are relational databases. Tomcat administrators must be well versed in RDBMSs. In addition, an understanding of the nature of interactions between an RDBMS and Tomcat is required in order to better anticipate the requirements that may arise.

This chapter addresses the following topics:

- Java Database Connectivity (JDBC), which is Java's database connectivity API
- JDBC version evolution
- JDBC driver types and advantages
- Importance of connection pooling
- Interactions between RDBMS and Tomcat
- JNDI-based JDBC configurations
- Standard configuration for a JDBC data source
- Alternative JDBC configurations that may be required
- Configuring alternative JDBC access

This chapter also covers a variety of situations that may arise when configuring Tomcat to work with relational databases. The examples within the discussion feature hands-on configuration. Special emphasis is placed on the recommended or preferred way of interacting with databases.

By the end of this chapter, you will be comfortable with the integration of RDBMSs with Tomcat, and will be able to handle the most common requests for configuring RDBMSs to work with the Tomcat server.

JDBC Basics

JDBC is a programming interface for accessing RDBMSs. Its operation is based on the transmission and execution of Structured Query Language (SQL) on the database server. SQL is a text-based query language for performing operations with data stored in a relational database. In fact, JDBC is based on a Call-Level Interface (CLI) to an engine that processes SQL statements. More specifically, JDBC uses the X/Open SQL CLI (X/Open is an international standards organization) conforming to the SQL92 language syntax standard. Figure 14-1 illustrates how SQL CLI, and, therefore, JDBC, operates underneath the hood.

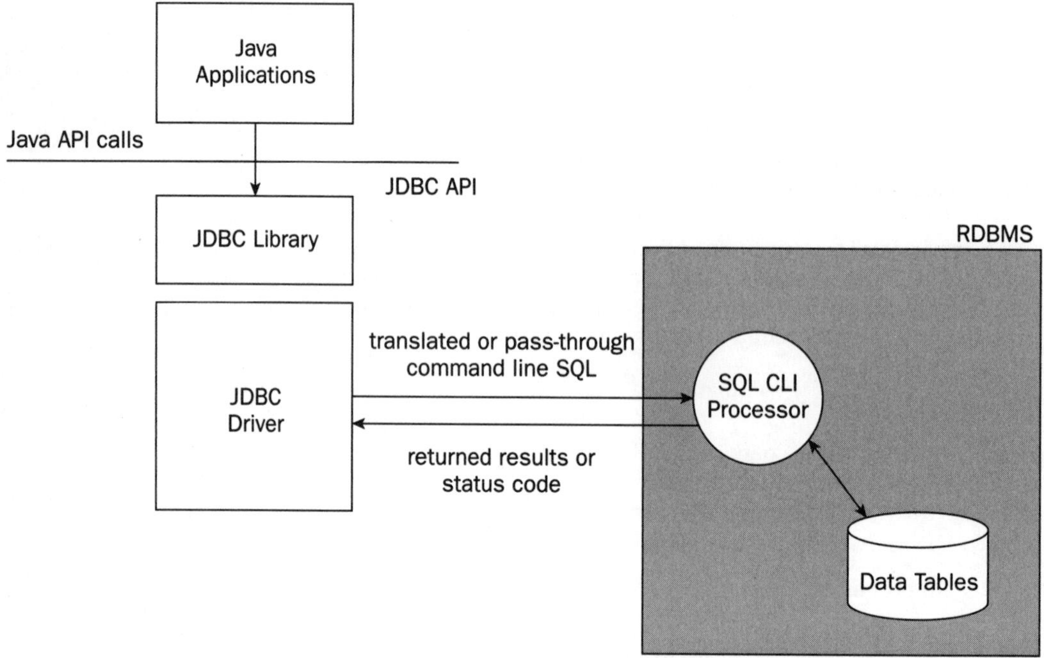

Figure 14-1: JDBC operation model.

In Figure 14-1, the JDBC engine submits SQL query statements to the remote SQL processing engine (part of the RDBMS, it typically handles multiple simultaneous connections via a connection manager), and the SQL processing engine returns the result of the query in a set of data called a **result set.** A result set is typically zero or more rows of data. Think of result sets as temporarily created tables.

Therefore, JDBC operations are designed to do the following:

- Take the JDBC API calls and transform them into an SQL query
- Submit that query to the SQL processing engine on the RDBMS

- Retrieve the result set that is returned from the query and transform it into a Java-accessible data structure

Not all statements return a result set. If a search is not successful, the returned result set will be empty (called a `NULL` result set). In addition, the SQL language includes statements that are used to create tables, update data, delete rows, and so on; these statements do not return any result sets either.

In JDBC programming, developers typically perform the following steps:

1. Obtain a connection to the remote database server (in JDBC 1.x, it is necessary to instantiate a database driver prior to obtaining a connection)
2. Create and prepare an SQL statement for execution (or call a stored procedure in the RDBMS)
3. Execute the SQL statement
4. Obtain the returned result set (if any) and work on it
5. Disconnect from the remote database

Administrators are most interested in facilitating the first step—obtaining a connection to the desired database.

Establishing and Terminating Connections to RDBMSs

Other than providing a unified way of accessing, modifying, and manipulating data in RDBMSs, JDBC also provides a unified way of connecting to RDBMSs from different vendors. While normal native connections to Oracle will be very different from connections to MySQL (which will be different from working with Microsoft's SQL server), connecting to any of these RDBMSs can be accomplished using the same JDBC API calls.

Evolving JDBC Versions

In the early days of JDBC, most Java developers were coding to the JDBC 1 standard. Under this standard, all of the code needed to establish a connection to an RDBMS (as well as the code to disconnect from the RDBMS) was written by the developers. In fact, even the code to select and activate a JDBC driver was coded by the developers.

While simple and straightforward to code, this approach created a problem; in some cases where the driver used was hard-coded by the developers, the code to obtain a connection only worked with RDBMSs from a specific vendor.

With the arrival of JDBC 2, this restriction was relaxed. JDBC 2 introduced the concept of a **data source.** This is an indirect way of specifying the JDBC driver to be used for making the connection. Developers can now obtain a connection from the data source in their code, enabling the same JDBC code to work with drivers from any vendor. Meanwhile, an administrator can switch database vendor support by simply configuring a different data source, and no code changes are needed. The selection and configuration of data sources shifted from the developer to the administrator.

As Web applications became more complex, the demand for high-performance concurrent access to database connections increased. The code that developers write to maintain and share database connections becomes highly complex and error-prone. Because this code is utilitarian, and can be used by all applications, it is another area that JDBC 2 attempts to improve on (see "Database Connection Pooling," covered in detail later in this chapter).

While JDBC 2's introduction of data source and connection pooling support opens up new possibilities for RDBMS developers, it falls short of specifying standard ways in which these features should (or must) be used. As a result, many of the architectural issues are left for the JDBC driver writers to solve, and code can quickly become vendor-specific again (this time, depending on the JDBC driver vendor).

Furthermore, the rapid maturation of J2EE has consolidated its overall architecture. There is growing momentum to adopt the same resource adapter model to the Enterprise Information System (EIS) throughout the J2EE stack. Architecturally, JDBC connections are connections to external/legacy systems, which are considered part of the EIS. In the J2EE architecture, these connections should be managed through a well-defined connector architecture. This is the subject matter of J2EE Connector Architecture (JCA). For more information, see the following URL:

```
http://java.sun.com/j2ee/connector/
```

In this architecture, J2EE software components access EIS resources via resource adapters with a common set of well-defined interfaces. These interfaces enforce well-defined contracts (between application server and resource adapter) in connection management, transaction management, and security. The evolution of the JDBC standard is migrating to this new JCA architecture as it becomes better defined.

The first step toward this migration is to detach any direct coupling between the application logic and the specific EIS resource that it needs. This can be accomplished by an intermediary indirect lookup mechanism. JNDI is a Java-based industry standard that can serve this purpose. JDBC 3 is the first version to be designed with this migration in mind.

In fact, JDBC 3 is the first specification that clearly spells out the different architectures that JDBC can operate in—including two-tier and three-tier models. The three-tier model corresponds to the application server model and the model of operation favored by J2EE applications.

The JDBC specification also attempts to accommodate JDBC 1 and 2 drivers and model of operations, while formalizing JNDI as the preferred way for applications to obtain a data source. It also formalizes connection pooling as a value-added service of the application server or Servlet container.

Regardless of the JDBC version, the JDBC driver still must translate the unified JDBC commands into native commands to connect to the different servers. JDBC drivers have evolved significantly over the past few years and most of them today are high-performance Type IV drivers (explained in the next section). However, some legacy systems still exist that support only the older Type I to Type III drivers. It is a good idea to gain some familiarity with different types of JDBC drivers that may be around.

JDBC Driver Types

There are four different types of JDBC drivers: Type I to Type IV. In general, the higher driver types represent an improvement on architecture and performance, as described in the following paragraphs:

- *Type I*—These drivers are the most primitive JDBC drivers, as they are essentially data access adapters. They adapt another data access mechanism (such as ODBC) to JDBC. These drivers completely rely on the other data access mechanism to work and as such create double the administrative and maintenance headaches. These drivers are also typically hardware/OS-specific (because of the data access mechanism that they depend on), making them completely nonportable.
- *Type II*—These drivers are partially written in Java and partially written in native data access languages (typically C or C++). The non-Java portion of these drivers limits the portability of the final code and platform-migration possibilities. The administrative and maintenance burden of Type I still exists.
- *Type III*—These drivers are pure Java drivers on the client side, which gives them the portability benefit of Java. However, they rely on a middleware engine running externally to operate. The client code communicates with the middleware engine, and the engine talks to the different types of databases. The administration and maintenance burden is somewhat reduced, but far from eliminated.
- *Type IV*—These drivers are 100 percent Java and talk directly to the network protocols supported by the RDBMSs. This results in the highest performance connection and the most portable application code. Administration and maintenance is greatly simplified (only the driver needs to be updated).

Fortunately, most modern day JDBC drivers are of the Type IV variety. All the major RDBMSs available today (MySQL, Oracle, DB2, and MS SQL Server) have Type IV JDBC drivers available, either through the database vendors themselves or via a third-party driver vendor.

Database Connection Pooling

When a Web application accesses a remote RDBMS, it may do so through a **JDBC connection.** Typically, a physical JDBC connection is established between the client application and the RDBMS server via a TCP/IP connection. Establishing such a connection is CPU-, memory,- and time-intensive. It involves multiple layers of software, and the transmission and receipt of network data. A typical physical database connection may take several seconds to establish. Contrast this with the "cost" of doing a simple database query, which typically takes milliseconds to complete. It is obvious why it would be wise to decrease the number of connects and disconnects between queries.

Modern Web applications consist of JSPs and Servlets that may need data from a database on every HTTP request (for example, a Servlet that prints the current employees from a specific department, or an electronic auction system that enables you to see all your current open bids). On a well-loaded server, the time it takes to establish, disconnect, and reestablish actual connections (physical connections) can substantially slow down Web-application performance.

To create high-performance and scalable Web applications, JDBC driver vendors and application servers are incorporating database connection pooling into their products.

Connection pooling reduces expensive session establishment times (connects, disconnects, and re-connects) by creating a pool of physical connections when the system starts up. When an application requires a connection, one of these physical connections is provided. Normally, when an application finishes using a connection, it is disconnected. However, in the case of a logical connection, the associated physical connection is merely returned to the pool and awaits the next application request. Figure 14-2 illustrates database connection pooling.

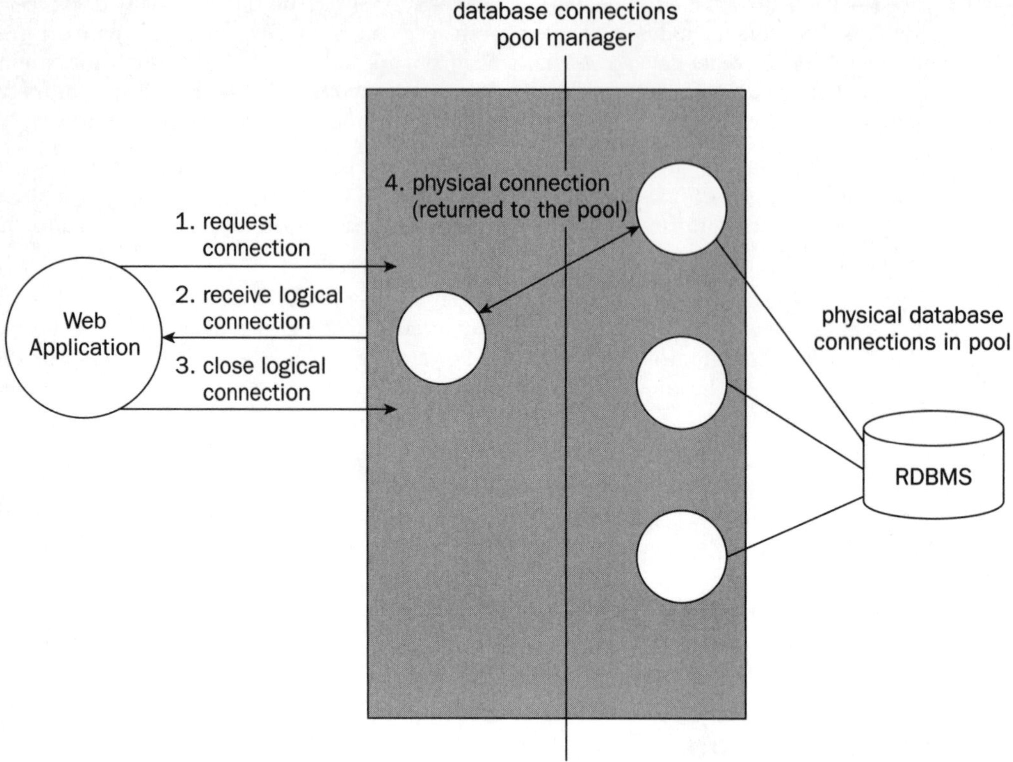

Figure 14-2: JDBC connection pooling.

A **pool manager** creates the initial physical connections, manages the distribution of the physical connections to the Web applications in the form of a logical connection, returns any closed logical connection to the pool, and handles any exception or error that may arise—potentially disconnecting the physical connection or recovering from error conditions. Note that closing a logical connection does not actually close any physical connection, but merely returns the connection back to the pool. This pool manager functionality may be provided by one of the following three sources:

- An application server such as Tomcat 5
- A third-party pool manager software vendor
- The JDBC driver vendor

When configuring Web applications to run on Tomcat 5, the preferred and recommended pool manager to use is one that is supplied with the Tomcat server.

Tomcat and the JDBC Evolution

Application developers and system designers using Tomcat 5 and 4 have a wide choice of JDBC support mechanisms from which to choose. Tomcat 5 and 4 servers provide JDBC 3 support while offering full backward compatibility to JDBC 2 (as well as JDBC 1). The remainder of this chapter examines the recommended mechanism to access JDBC resources while working with Tomcat, and explores one alternative access mechanism.

The major new JDBC features that are part of Tomcat 5 include the following:

- *Application server-managed database connection pools* — Tomcat 5 uses Jakarta Commons Database Connection Pooling (DBCP) to provide container-managed connection pooling. This also enables flexible configuration for the pooling mechanism (see the section "Resource and ResourceParams," later in this chapter). JDBC 3 is the first specification that defines standard configuration parameters for pooling (such as `maxStatements`, `initialPoolSize`, `minPoolSize`, `maxPoolSize`, `maxIdleTime`, and `propertyCycle`), making the mechanism more configurable in a standards-compliant manner.
- *Using the JNDI-API to look up data sources within an application server* — Tomcat 5 emulates JNDI for Web applications running under it. This is a portable and configurable way of obtaining data sources for JDBC operations without hard-coding the driver and associated properties. It makes the selection of the JDBC driver and RDBMS instance a deferred deployment-time decision. JDBC 3 specifies JNDI as the preferred method for applications to locate a data source.
- *Ease of migration to the connector architecture* — Tomcat 5's decoupled architecture for access to JDBC data sources (through JNDI lookup) is a first step in the migration toward the JCA connector-based architecture.

JNDI Emulation and Pooling in Tomcat 5

Tomcat provides valuable services for hosted Web applications that use JDBC connections. More specifically, Tomcat enables running Web applications to do the following:

- Access JDBC data sources using standard JNDI lookup
- Use connection pooling value-added service

The role of a Web-tier container as an intermediary between client Web applications and an RDBMS is defined by the set of J2EE specifications — most recently in the Servlet 2.4 specifications and the JDBC 3 specifications (both are can be located at `http://jcp.org/aboutJava/communityprocess/final/jsr154/` and `http://java.sun.com/products/jdbc/download.html#corespec30`, respectively). The value-added service that Tomcat provides is compliant with these specifications, and is documented as a three-tier architecture (see Figure 14-3).

Figure 14-3 shows how JDBC drivers are configured with Tomcat as JNDI resources. These resources are made available during Web application run-time via standard JNDI lookups. The following steps are depicted in the diagram:

1. A Web application obtains a JNDI `InitialContext` from Tomcat; it then performs a lookup on the resource (JDBC data source) by name.
2. Tomcat handles the JNDI lookup by consulting the configuration files (`server.xml` and `web.xml`) to determine which JDBC driver to use for obtaining a data source. Tomcat can also use Database Connection Pooling (DBCP) to pool the connections made; the connections obtained from Tomcat are logical connections.

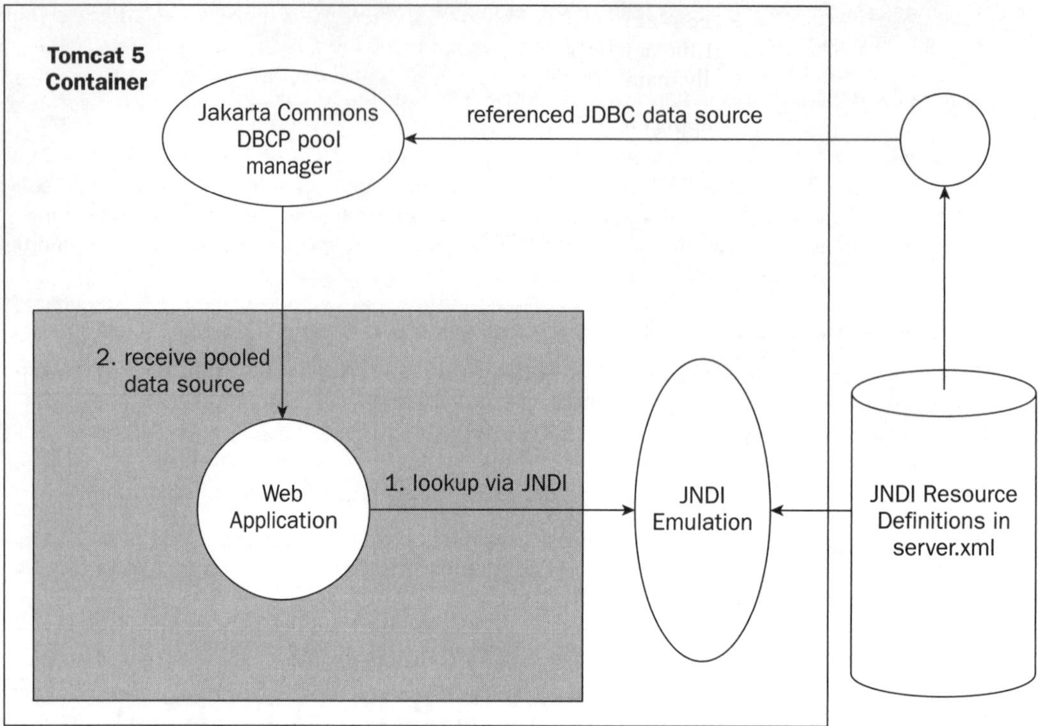

Figure 14-3: JNDI lookup of a JDBC data source in Tomcat 5.

Even though no true JNDI-compatible directory services are involved, the Tomcat container emulates the action of a JNDI provider. This enables code that is written with JNDI as the JDBC data source lookup mechanism to work within the Tomcat container (and other Servlet 2.4—compliant application servers).

As you can see in Figure 14-3, Tomcat 5 does more than merely provide JNDI emulation. It can also provide database connection pooling. Tomcat 5 uses another Apache Jakarta project, called the **Commons DBCP** (**Database Connection Pooling**), for its built-in pool manager functionality.

Preferred Configuration: JNDI Resources

Using JNDI resources in Tomcat to configure JDBC data sources is the recommended way to provide Web applications with access to JDBC connections. While other methods are possible (and at least one alternative is discussed later in this chapter), this approach will result in code that is portable to other Web containers over the long term.

Following are the steps that must be followed to configure JNDI resource for a JDBC data source:

1. Add `<Resource>` and `<ResourceParams>` tags in the `<Context>` element of the Web application, or in a `<DefaultContext>` sub-element of the `<Host>` element to configure the JNDI resource.

2. Ensure that a `<resource-ref>` element is defined, corresponding to the `<Resource>` from above, in the `web.xml` file of the Web application using the JDBC resource (note that the `web.xml` file is typically maintained by the application developer).
3. Use JNDI calls in the application code to look up the JDBC data source.

The following sections provide more detail on how to perform each of these steps.

Resource and ResourceParams tags

The `<Resource>` tag is used to specify the JNDI resource that represents a JDBC data source, and the `<ResourceParams>` tag is used to configure the associated data source factory. Here is a typical `<Resource>` element found in the `server.xml` configuration file:

```
<Resource name="jdbc/WroxTC5" auth="Container"
          type="javax.sql.DataSource"/>
```

This resource statement essentially says the following:

- Create a JNDI resource that is accessible from the context (logical name) `java:comp/env/jdbc/WroxTC5` by the Web application. The `java:comp/env/` portion of the context is added on for all Tomcat-managed contexts. The Web application can use this context to look up the data source. The type of resource that will be returned during this lookup is a `javax.sql.DataSource`. It also specifies that the container should authenticate against the RDBMS on behalf of the Web application.

You may want to check Chapter 8 for a detailed examination of the attributes allowed in the `<Resource>` element. A `<ResourceParams>` element is associated with the `<Resource>` element. The `<ResourceParams>` element (also covered in Chapter 8), is used to parameterize the associated resource. For example, you may have the following `<ResourceParams>` for the previously defined `<Resource>` element (note that this is where the example become database-specific):

```
<ResourceParams name="jdbc/WroxTC5">
  <parameter>
    <name>driverClassName</name>

    <value>com.mysql.jdbc.Driver</value>
  </parameter>
  <parameter>
    <name>url</name>
    <value>jdbc:mysql://localhost/wroxtomcat</value>
  </parameter>
  <parameter>
    <name>username</name>
    <value>empro</value>
  </parameter>
  <parameter>
    <name>password</name>
    <value>empass</value>
  </parameter>
  <parameter>
```

```
    <name>maxActive</name>
    <value>20</value>
  </parameter>
  <parameter>
    <name>maxIdle</name>
    <value>30000</value>
  </parameter>
  <parameter>
    <name>maxWait</name>
    <value>100</value>
  </parameter>
</ResourceParams>
```

Note that the name attribute of the <ResourceParams> element must match the <Resource> element that it is configuring. The actual name and value of the parameters depends on the data-source connection factory that is used. The settings here assume that you are configuring Tomcat's default DataSource factory (called the DBCP factory).

Data-Source Factory

A data-source factory is a Java class that assigns data sources. In some sense, this class manufactures data sources (hence the "factory" name). In actual operations, however, it may simply supply a customized data source class that will work with (as well as hand out) pooled data sources.

Working with Other RDBMS

Tomcat's default DBCP factory will work with JDBC drivers for any RDBMSs. For example, here is the setting for accessing an Oracle database:

```
<ResourceParams name="jdbc/WroxTC5">
  <parameter>
    <name>driverClassName</name>
    <value>oracle.jdbc.driver.OracleDriver</value>
  </parameter>
  <parameter>
    <name>url</name>
    <value>jdbc:oracle:thin:@xpserver:1521:ORCL</value>
  </parameter>
  <parameter>
    <name>username</name>
    <value>empro</value>
  </parameter>
  <parameter>
    <name>password</name>

    <value>empass</value>
  </parameter>
  <parameter>
    <name>maxActive</name>
    <value>20</value>
  </parameter>
```

```
    <parameter>
      <name>maxIdle</name>
      <value>30000</value>
    </parameter>
    <parameter>
      <name>maxWait</name>
      <value>100</value>
    </parameter>
  </ResourceParams>
```

DBCP—Jakarta Commons Pooling Support

To return a JDBC data source to the application, Tomcat 5 uses a data source factory to create the data source. Tomcat 5 and recent versions of Tomcat 4 use the Jakarta Commons DBCP (by default) to supply a data source factory and implement connection pooling.

Very old versions of Tomcat 4 (4.0.4 to 4.1.3), however, use the third-party licensed Tyrex data-source factory. Although it is relatively easy to override the default data-source factory, the procedure is not well-documented. For example, to make the older Tomcat 4 use the DBCP mechanism, you must add the following `<parameter>` element in the `<ResourceParams>`:

```
<parameter>
  <name>factory</name>
  <value>org.apache.commons.dbcp.BasicDataSourceFactory</value>
</parameter>
```

You might consider using DBCP pooling even if you must use very old Tomcat 4 versions, as it is the default (and pool manager of choice for the Tomcat distribution) for all new Tomcat 5 and 4 releases. It is very well supported and enhancements are added regularly.

Transactions and Distributed Transactions Support

RDBMSs offer varying levels of support for transactions. A transaction can be viewed as a unit of work that is composed of multiple operations, but can only be committed (all operations complete successfully) or rolled back (no operation completed). For example, MySQL 4 supports transactional access by default via the use of InnoDB tables.

When a transaction involves work that crosses multiple physical RDBMSs, it is called a **distributed transaction.** One standard that enables RDBMSs (and other products supporting transactions, such as Message Queue Servers) from different vendors to participate in the same distributed transaction is called **XA.**

In the XA operation model, an external **transaction manager** coordinates a two-phase-commit protocol between multiple **resource managers** (RDBMSs in this case). The two-phase-commit protocol ensures that the pieces of work, scattered across multiple physical RDBMSs, are either all completed or all rolled back.

JDBC 3 and 2 both accommodate data sources that support XA operations. Administrators who work with XA data sources and data-source factories should consult the vendor's documentation for proper parameterization and ensure that they work with Tomcat.

Hands-On JNDI Resource Configuration

Now it is time to put theory into practice. The actual example presented here configures a DBCP data source, through Tomcat 5's JNDI resources support, with a Type IV JDBC driver. A JSP will be created that accesses the data in an actual RDBMS and displays it within a table on a generated HTML page. This example uses a popular, widely available RDBMS: MySQL.

Installation and configuration of the MySQL database is beyond the scope of this chapter. The discussion in this chapter assumes that you have MySQL already configured and tested, and that you have an account with privileges to create tables and add records to create the test database. The latest version of MySQL is available for download from the following URL:

```
www.mysql.com
```

The Type IV JDBC driver that we will use is the `Connector/J`, supplied by the MySQL vendor, which can be downloaded from the following URL:

```
www.mysql.com/products/connector-j/index.html
```

The latest version available as of this writing is 3.0.9, and is the version on which this example is based.

Note that you must unzip the driver JAR file from the download and use the **`mysql-connctor-java-X.X.XX-stable-bin.jar`** *file within it. In our example, place this file under* **`$CATALINA_HOME/common/lib`**. *The example here is tested with MySQL Connector/J version 3.0.9, the latest stable version available as of this writing. However, any newer version should work identically.*

Creating the MySQL Test Database

To prepare for the example, you must create the MySQL database that will be used by the JSP. The employee database contains a number of employees from different branches of a company and details about those employees. Assuming you have a MySQL user account that can create table privileges on a database called `wroxtomcat`, you can create the three tables.

If you have database system administrator privileges on MySQL, access can be granted via the `mysql` command line:

```
mysql> GRANT ALL ON wroxtomcat.* TO
    -> 'mike'@'localhost' IDENTIFIED BY 'abc123';
```

Follow this with a flush of the MySQL cache. This ensures that the change is immediately valid:

```
mysqladmin --uXXXX --pYYYY  flush-privileges
```

Use your MySQL administrator credentials for XXXX and YYYY. This enables the user `mike` to connect from `localhost` and create tables in the `wroxtomcat` database. The user `mike` must log on using the password `abc123`.

To make things easy, here is a makedb.sql script to create all the required tables:

```
CREATE DATABASE IF NOT EXISTS wroxtomcat;

USE wroxtomcat;

CREATE TABLE employee (
   employeeid VARCHAR(10) NOT NULL,
   name VARCHAR(50) NOT NULL,
   phone VARCHAR(15) NOT NULL,
   department VARCHAR(15) NOT NULL,
   password VARCHAR(15) NOT NULL,
   PRIMARY KEY (employeeid)
);

CREATE TABLE vacation (
   employeeid VARCHAR(10) NOT NULL,
   fiscal INT(3) NOT NULL,
   approved CHAR(1) NOT NULL,
   PRIMARY KEY (employeeid, fiscal)
);

CREATE TABLE dept (
   department VARCHAR(15) NOT NULL,
   address VARCHAR(30) NOT NULL,
   zipcode VARCHAR(6) NOT NULL,
   PRIMARY KEY (department)
);
```

Use makedb.sql to create the database, as follows:

```
$ mysql < makedb.sql
```

Next, load the tables with the data that will be used. This is performed via the SQL script loaddb.sql, which contains the following:

```
USE wroxtomcat;

INSERT INTO dept (department, address, zipcode) VALUES ( 'Engineering', '33
Mexicali Road', '25763');
INSERT INTO dept (department, address, zipcode) VALUES ( 'Sales', '15 Navel
Circle', '98322');
INSERT INTO dept (department, address, zipcode) VALUES ( 'Administration', '1
Lawless Court', '66699');
INSERT INTO employee (employeeid, name, phone, department, password) VALUES ( '2901',
'Joe', '333-3331', 'Engineering', 'junior');
INSERT INTO employee (employeeid, name, phone, department, password) VALUES ( '2202',
'Matt', '434-3333', 'Engineering', 'perlguru');
INSERT INTO employee (employeeid, name, phone, department, password) VALUES ( '3021',
'Jane', '231-0001', 'Sales', 'milseller');
```

```
INSERT INTO employee (employeeid, name, phone, department, password) VALUES ( '0001',
'Bill', '343-0012', 'Administration', 'gatorshaq');

INSERT INTO employee (employeeid, name, phone, department, password) VALUES ( '0015',
'Steve', '342-2212', 'Administration', 'billion');
INSERT INTO vacation (employeeid, fiscal, approved) VALUES ( '0001', '1', 'Y');
INSERT INTO vacation (employeeid, fiscal, approved) VALUES ( '0001', '2', 'Y');
INSERT INTO vacation (employeeid, fiscal, approved) VALUES ( '0001', '3', 'Y');
INSERT INTO vacation (employeeid, fiscal, approved) VALUES ( '0001', '4', 'Y');
INSERT INTO vacation (employeeid, fiscal, approved) VALUES ( '2901', '12', 'N');
INSERT INTO vacation (employeeid, fiscal, approved) VALUES ( '2202', '51', 'N');
```

This script simply fills the table with the data. Run the script from the `mysql` console using the following command:

```
$ mysql < loaddb.sql
```

Now that the tables are created and you have populated them with data, you must create a user account that the developers will use to access the data within the database. Because the JSP functionality requires only read access to the data, creating a read-only user account for developer access is a good secure practice. This ensures that data cannot be accidentally or maliciously modified or altered.

Setting Up the Read-Only User

If you do not have database system administrator privileges, you will need to seek help. You need the user setup shown in the following table.

User Property	Value
Username	`empro`
Password	`empass`
Access	`SELECT` privilege only on the `wroxtomcat` database (that is, use the following command on the mysql console: `GRANT SELECT ON wroxtomcat.* TO 'empro'@'localhost' IDENTIFIED BY 'empass';`)

This creates a user who has read-only access to the `wroxtomcat` tables, which the developer will be using to access the data in the table.

Adding the JDBC JNDI Resource to the Default Context

Finally, to configure the JNDI resource for the data source, follow the three-step approach outlined earlier and described in the following sections.

Step 1 — <Resource> and <ResourceParam>

The first step is to make the JNDI data source accessible to all the Web applications running on this host. By adding the resource definition in the `<DefaultContext>` section, all the Web applications can gain access to this resource.

In the $CATALINA_HOME/conf/server.xml configuration file, within the scope of the localhost <Host> component, add the following <DefaultContext> element:

```
<DefaultContext>
  <Resource name="jdbc/WroxTC5" auth="Container"
            type="javax.sql.DataSource"/>
  <ResourceParams name="jdbc/WroxTC5">
    <parameter>
      <name>driverClassName</name>
      <value>com.mysql.jdbc.Driver</value>
    </parameter>
    <parameter>
      <name>url</name>
      <value>jdbc:mysql://localhost/wroxtomcat</value>
    </parameter>
    <parameter>
      <name>username</name>
      <value>empro</value>
    </parameter>
    <parameter>
      <name>password</name>
      <value>empass</value></parameter>
    <parameter>
      <name>maxActive</name>
      <value>20</value></parameter>
    <parameter>
      <name>maxIdle</name>
      <value>30000</value></parameter>
    <parameter>
      <name>maxWait</name>
      <value>100</value>
    </parameter>
  </ResourceParams>
</DefaultContext>
```

*The **url** parameter is often named **driverName** in old documentation for legacy reasons (older version name), and can still be specified using the old name. For all new work, use **url**.*

This configuration will work fine with Tomcat 5 or 4, as they both use DBCP connection pooling.

Two optional parameters (removeAbandoned and removeAbandonedTimout) help with the recycling of database connections, even for those that may not be released properly because of faulty developer coding. When the number of available connections in the pool runs low, the DBCP pool management code will recycle connections based on an elapsed idle timeout. For example, the following additional parameters will cause the DBCP pool management code to recycle all JDBC connections that are idled for more than 15 minutes:

```
<parameter>
  <name>removeAbandoned</name>
  <value>true</value>
</parameter>
<parameter>
  <name>removeAbandonedTimeout</name>
  <value>15</value>
</parameter>
```

If you are running an older Tomcat release that uses the Tyrex (licensed) data-source factory by default (Tomcat 4.0.4 or later up to 4.1.3), you will need to add the following parameter to the `<ResourceParams>` element:

```
<ResourceParams name="jdbc/WroxTC5">
  <parameter>
    <name>factory</name>
    <value>org.apache.commons.dbcp.BasicDataSourceFactory</value>
  </parameter>
  ...
```

In addition, because Tomcat 5 includes the required Jakarta Commons libraries by default, you will find the DBCP and dependent libraries in the `$CATALINA_HOME/common/lib` directory. These binaries include the following:

- `commons-dbcp-1.1.jar`
- `commons-collection.jar`
- `commons-pool-1.1.jar`

Tomcat 4 also already uses the DBCP library code by default since the release of Tomcat 4.1.3. If you are using versions prior to 4.1.3, you will need to download the aforementioned JAR files from the Jakarta Commons site at the following URL and copy them into the directory manually:

```
http://jakarta.apache.org/commons/index.html
```

Step 2—Add the <resource-ref/> entries to web.xml

Instead of creating a new Web application, an easy way to add a test JSP is by adding it to an existing example application from Tomcat. To do this, change directory to `$CATALINA_HOME/webapps/jsp-examples/WEB-INF` and edit the `web.xml` file (this is the deployment descriptor of the `jsp-examples` Web application). Add the following highlighted code to `web.xml` (note that it should be added immediately after the last `<env-entry>` element in the file):

```
...
<env-entry>
      <env-entry-name>foo/name4</env-entry-name>
      <env-entry-type>java.lang.Integer</env-entry-type>
      <env-entry-value>10</env-entry-value>
</env-entry>
<resource-ref>
  <res-ref-name>jdbc/WroxTC5</res-ref-name>
  <res-type>javax.sql.DataSource</res-type>
  <res-auth>Container</res-auth>
</resource-ref>
```

This `<resource-ref>` entry makes the `jdbc/WroxTC5` context, via JNDI APIs, available within the `jsp-examples` Web application.

Step 3 — Use JNDI to look up a data source

Finally, it is time to write the code that will look up the data source and start querying the database. The following JSP, `JDBCTest.jsp`, will do exactly this. Put it into a `$CATALINA_HOME/webapps/jsp-examples/wroxjdbc` directory (create this directory yourself). Pay special attention to the way JNDI is used to obtain the data source (code highlighted).

```
<html>
  <head>
    <%@ page errorPage="errorpg.jsp"
             import="java.sql.*,
                     javax.sql.*,
                     java.io.*,
                     javax.naming.InitialContext,
                     javax.naming.Context" %>
  </head>
  <body>
    <h1>JDBC JNDI Resource Test</h1>

    <%
    InitialContext initCtx = new InitialContext();
    DataSource ds = (DataSource)
                    initCtx.lookup("java:comp/env/jdbc/WroxTC5");

    Connection    conn = ds.getConnection();

    Statement stmt = conn.createStatement();
    ResultSet rset = stmt.executeQuery("select * from employee;");
    %>
    <table width='600' border='1'>
      <tr>
        <th align='left'>Employee ID</th>
        <th align='left'>Name</th>
        <th align='left'>Department</th>
      </tr>
      <%
      while (rset.next()) {
      %>
        <tr><td> <%= rset.getString(1)  %></td>
          <td> <%= rset.getString(2)  %></td>
          <td> <%= rset.getString(4)  %></td>
        </tr>
      <%  }
      rset.close();
      stmt.close();
      conn.close();
      initCtx.close();
      %>
    </table>
  </body>
</html>
```

The JNDI code highlighted here first obtains the `InitialContext` from Tomcat. It then uses this context to look up the JNDI resource that we have configured. Note that all Tomcat JNDI resources are found relative to `java:comp/env/`. Once the data source is obtained through JNDI, it is used to create a connection (actually pooled through DBCP). The JSP then performs a `SELECT *` on the `employee` table, and prints out all the rows that are retrieved. Finally, it creates an HTML table containing all the table rows.

Any exception caught during execution of this JSP is redirected to a very simple error-handling page called the `errorpg.jsp` file. This file is specified via the `errorPage` attribute of the `@page` directive. Here is the content of `errorpg.jsp`:

```
<html>
  <body>
    <%@ page isErrorPage="true" %>
    <h1> An error has occurred </h1>
    <%= exception.getMessage() %>
  </body>
</html>
```

This page will simply display a message indicating the exception caught.

Testing the JNDI Resource Configuration

At this point, the JNDI resources are prepared, the database tables are populated, the `<resource-ref>` to the deployment descriptor has been added, and a JSP that will use JNDI to obtain a JDBC data source has been created. It is time to give the new JSP code a test.

Start Tomcat 5 and then, from a browser, attempt to reach the following URL:

```
http://localhost:8080/jsp-examples/wroxjdbc/JDBCTest.jsp
```

This will compile and execute the JSP code. If everything is configured correctly and working, your browser display should be similar to what is shown in Figure 14-4.

The Web page shown in Figure 14-4 is the result of a JDBC query to the MySQL database data, via a connection obtained from the JNDI lookup.

You may face exceptions such as the server denying access to the data source, or some server connection failures, which are caused by the MySQL user account not having enough privileges.

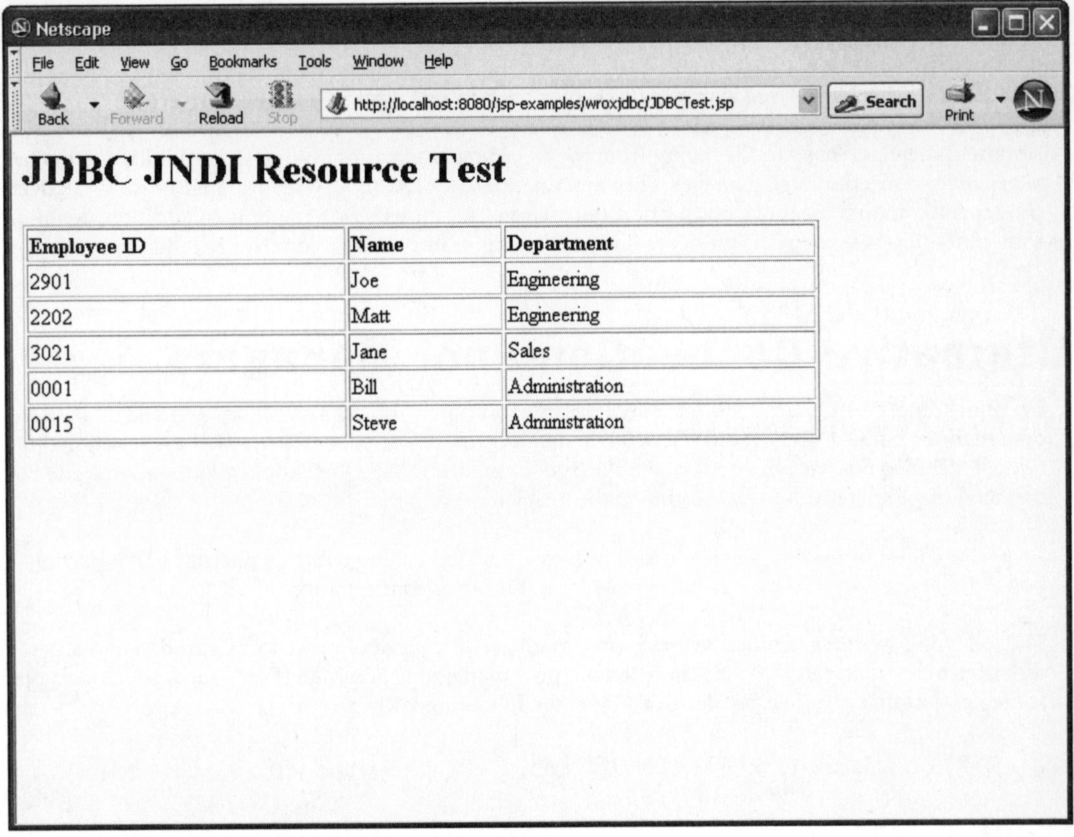

Figure 14-4: Display of MySQL RDBMS data in a JSP.

Alternative JDBC Configuration

In Tomcat 5, the JNDI API is the preferred and recommended way to pass a JDBC data source to your Web applications. It is currently the best-supported mechanism to access JDBC data sources.

However, in production, you might encounter situations in which you have to consider alternative means of JDBC data source or connection access.

Typically, there is no reason why newly developed database access code slated for Web application deployment should not use the preferred JNDI mechanism for data access. However, because JDBC 1 was a widely used and highly functional API long before the arrival of JDBC 2 and JDBC 3, a large legacy base of working JDBC code remains unaware of data sources and connection pooling.

There may be circumstances in which you must integrate legacy code, and the source code is either not available or cannot be changed. Typically, legacy JDBC 1 code has both the JDBC driver and the URL of the database hard-coded. Thankfully, JDBC 2 and JDBC 3 continue to maintain backward compatibility with JDBC 1. This means that legacy code can continue to run, even in Tomcat 5 servers.

Another potential reason for deviating from the recommended configuration is the deployment of an alternative connection pool manager. This could happen, for example, with a shared hosting ISP using a commercial product that does not support the Jakarta Commons DBCP pooling. In addition, developers sometimes disagree about the merits of one pool manager implementation over another.

Alternative Connection Pool Managers

Up until Tomcat 4.1.x, connection-pooling implementation on Tomcat servers has evolved in a roll-your-own manner. Because Tomcat did not provide default support, anyone who needed the functionality (which included anyone who deployed any large- or medium-scale Web application) had to write their own code, or find a third-party solution to the problem.

As a result, it is quite likely that some legacy projects on Tomcat are using an alternative connection-pooling manager, with its own requirements for data-source configuration.

The following section examines one such pool manager, and shows how its configuration and access differ from the preferred method. The alternate pool manager is PoolMan (Pool Manager). It is an open-source project that is hosted on Source Forge at the following URL:

```
http://sourceforge.net/projects/poolman/
```

About PoolMan

Since well before the introduction of DBCP, the open-source PoolMan has provided flexible object pooling for developers. PoolMan provides a generic pooling mechanism for Java language objects, with specialized focus on JDBC connections. PoolMan 2.0 (the latest version available as of this writing) provides the following features:

- Flexible pool configuration across server instance, Web application, or other boundaries
- Support for multiple pools operating concurrently
- Timeout-based automatic connection recovery (this feature has been recently implemented in DBCP)
- API-based programmatic access to all pools and pooled resources
- Managed cached SQL queries
- JMX-based run-time management
- Support for JDBC 2 and 3 style drivers, and provision of multiple ways to integrate with applications or servers

Some of the these features may be attractive to developers, and may indeed be the reason why PoolMan is deployed in specific production scenarios.

The choice of one pool management strategy over another is highly dependent on the application, the system configuration, the data-access pattern, and subjective designer/developer preferences.

Deploying PoolMan

The PoolMan binary is packaged as a single JAR file, called `poolman.jar`. The placement of this library will depend on your specific pool-management strategy. For example, if you were to pool JDBC connections on a per-Web-application basis, the `poolman.jar` file should be placed under the `WEB-INF/lib` directory of your Web application. The following example assumes that you will be using PoolMan to manage server-wide pool(s) of JDBC connections. In this case, `poolman.jar` must be copied into the `%CATALINA_HOME%/common/lib` directory.

When using JDK 1.4 with Tomcat 5, simply copying `poolman.jar` to `common/lib` is sufficient. This is because XML parser support and JDBC 2+ libraries are standard with JDK 1.4. If you are using JDK 1.3, however, you must add the dependent libraries manually. These libraries are included with the PoolMan code download and include the following:

- `xerces.jar`
- `jta.jar`
- `jdbc2_0-stdext.jar`

PoolMan supports its own XML-based configuration file. The configuration of the JDBC driver, `Connector/J` for MySQL in this case, must be performed within PoolMan's configuration file.

PoolMan's XML Configuration File

It is of utmost importance for PoolMan to find its configuration file (called `poolman.xml`). Otherwise, you may encounter strange run-time errors. To locate the `poolman.xml` configuration file, PoolMan looks at the system classpath (essentially, the `CLASSPATH` environment when the JVM is started). The best way to ensure that the `poolman.xml` file will be loaded is as follows:

1. Create a `c:\home\poolman` directory in which to place the `poolman.xml` file.
2. Include the path `c:\home\poolman` in the `%CATALINA_HOME%\bin\setclasspath.bat` (or `setclasspath.sh` for Linux/Unix) file.

In this case, the addition of the path into `setclasspath.bat` is used:

```
...
rem Set standard CLASSPATH
rem Note that there are no quotes as we do not want to introduce random
rem quotes into the CLASSPATH
set CLASSPATH=%JAVA_HOME%\lib\tools.jar;c:\home\poolman
rem Set standard command for invoking Java.
...
```

The content of the poolman.xml file provides instructions for PoolMan to access the MySQL database. The configuration parameters are similar to those of DBCP. The following is a listing of the poolman.xml configuration used:

```
<?xml version="1.0" encoding="UTF-8"?>
<poolman>
  <management-mode>local</management-mode>
  <datasource>
    <dbname>wroxtomcat</dbname>
    <jndiName>mysqlsrc</jndiName>
    <driver>com.mysql.jdbc.Driver</driver>
    <url>jdbc:mysql://localhost/wroxtomcat</url>
    <username>empro</username>
    <password>empass</password>
    <minimumSize>0</minimumSize>
    <maximumSize>10</maximumSize>
    <connectionTimeout>600</connectionTimeout>
    <userTimeout>12</userTimeout>
    </datasource>
</poolman>
```

The following table provides a brief description of the elements in this configuration file. For a more detailed description of the elements and allowed values, consult the PoolMan documentation.

Configuration Element	Description
poolman	Must be the outermost element (XML document element) of the XML configuration file
management-mode	Can be local or jmx. Local mode is started without JMX support.
datasource	Describes a pool of JDBC connections. Each <datsource> element describes one pool of JDBC connections.
dbname	The name for the pool of JDBC connections
jndiname	The name used in the JNDI lookup context to locate the pool of JDBC connections
driver	The Java language class name of the JDBC driver to use
url	The URL passed to the driver to access the RDBMS for connections in this pool
username	The login name for accessing the RDBMS
password	The password for accessing the RDBMS
minimumSize	The smallest number of connections in the pool
maximumSize	The maximum number of connections allowed in the pool
connectionTimeout	The number of seconds to hold a connection in the pool before closing it. A value of 600 is for 10 minutes.

Configuration Element	Description
userTimeout	The number of seconds before a JDBC connection claimed by a user is placed back into the pool. This is used to reclaim user connections in case user code forgets to give them back. Here, 12 seconds is more than adequate for the short queries that you perform.

Note that the `userTimeout` parameter in PoolMan is directly analogous to the new `removeAbandonTimeout` parameter in Tomcat 5's DBCP pool manager.

Obtaining JDBC Connections Without JNDI Lookup

PoolMan has a rich heritage that includes support of connection pooling back in the days of JDBC 1, before JDBC 2 became popular. In those times, it was necessary to hard-code the JDBC driver instantiation and connection establishment right into the JSP. To illustrate how different such an approach may look, this first example uses the JDBC 1 method to obtain the JDBC connection. The JSP that you create is placed in the `%CATALINA_HOME%/webapps/jsp-examples/wroxjdbc` directory. The file is called `JDBCTestPM.jsp`. The code is listed here, with the hard-coded JDBC portion highlighted:

```
<html>
  <head>
    <%@ page errorPage="errorpg.jsp"
             import="java.sql.*,
                     javax.sql.*,
                     java.io.*" %>
  </head>
  <body>
    <h1>JDBC JNDI Resource Test</h1>
    <%!
        public void jspInit() {
        try {
            Class.forName("com.codestudio.sql.PoolMan").newInstance();
            // Use the Connection to create Statements and do JDBC work
        } catch (Exception ex) {
        // JSP init() cannot throw any exception

       ex.printStackTrace();
     }
    }
    %>
```

By overriding `jspInit()`, the PoolMan driver class is loaded the first time `JDBCTestPM.jsp` is executed. The following highlighted code shows how to use the JDBC `DriverManager` class to get a JDBC connection from PoolMan. This is the way JDBC connections were obtained with JDBC 1, before the arrival of the JDBC 2 data source:

```
    <%
    Connection conn = DriverManager.getConnection("jdbc:poolman://wroxtomcat");
    Statement stmt = conn.createStatement();
    ResultSet rset = stmt.executeQuery("select * from employee;");
    %>
    <table width='600' border='1'>
      <tr>

        <th align='left'>Employee ID</th>
        <th align='left'>Name</th>
        <th align='left'>Department</th>
      </tr>

      <%
      while (rset.next()) {
      %>
        <tr><td> <%= rset.getString(1)    %></td>
          <td> <%= rset.getString(2)  %></td>
          <td> <%= rset.getString(4)  %></td>
        </tr>
      <%  }
      if (stmt != null)
        stmt.close();

      conn.close();
      %>
    </table>
  </body>
</html>
```

The highlighted explicit call to `conn.close()` ensures that the connection is returned to the pool. Note that once the connection to the database is obtained, the code is almost identical to that of `JDBCTest.jsp`. However, the necessity to hard-code the driver class loading makes the code specific to the PoolMan connection manager. While this is backwardly compatible with JDBC 1, and supported by Tomcat 5, it is not a recommended practice.

Testing PoolMan with a Legacy Hard-coded Driver

To test the JDBC 1 method of obtaining JDBC connections using PoolMan, start Tomcat 5 and try to access the JSP via the following URL:

```
http://localhost:8080/jsp-examples/wroxjdbc/JDBCTestPM.jsp
```

The screen that you see should display data from the `employee` table, similar to what is shown in Figure 14-5. This is identical to the result from `JDBCTest.jsp`, where the default DBCP pooling was used.

The first time the preceding URL is accessed, Tomcat 5 will compile the JSP and call `jspInit()`, loading the `PoolMan` class. The DriverManager URL lookup will then obtain the JDBC connection from PoolMan. Your browser should display the `employee` table, similar to what is shown in Figure 14-5.

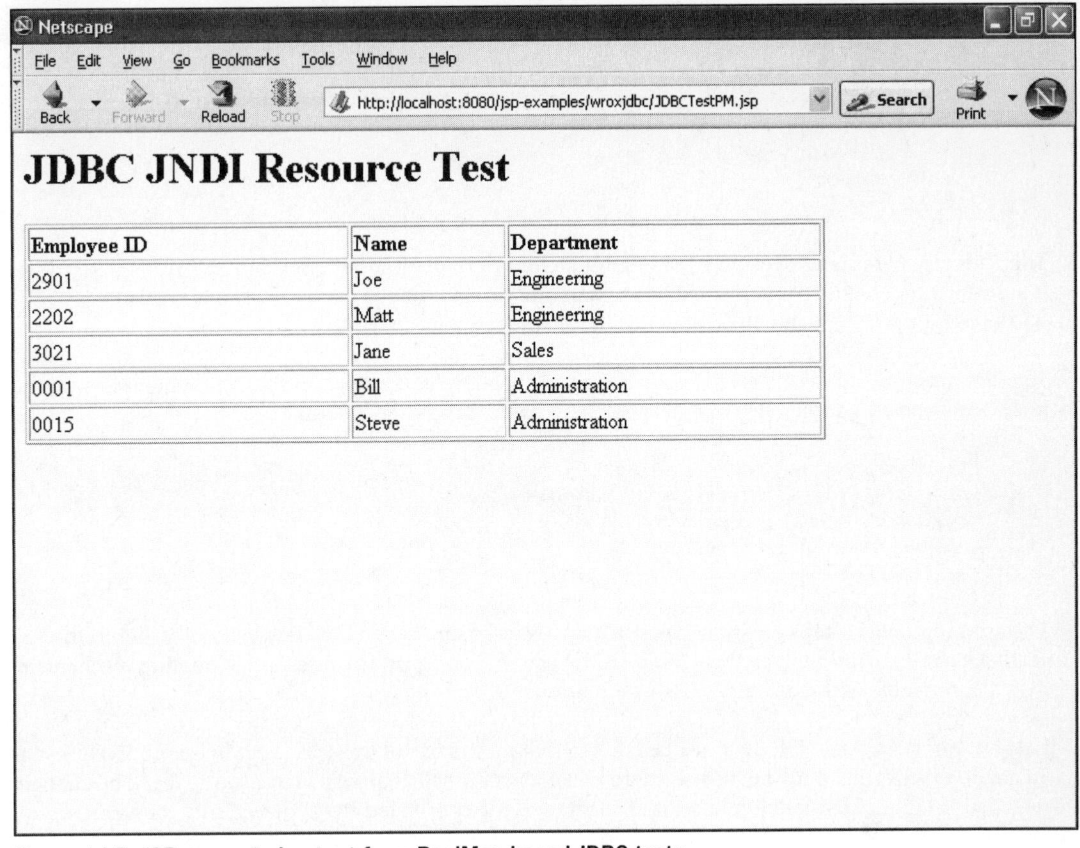

Employee ID	Name	Department
2901	Joe	Engineering
2202	Matt	Engineering
3021	Jane	Sales
0001	Bill	Administration
0015	Steve	Administration

Figure 14-5: JSP-generated output from PoolMan-based JDBC tests.

Obtaining a Connection with JNDI Mapping

The PoolMan 2.0 open-source project provides JNDI support when locating a JDBC data source. However, because of PoolMan's vintage (the last update was in 2001), Tomcat 5–styled JNDI emulation is not directly supported.

All that is needed for compatibility with Tomcat 5, however, is an object factory class to hand out the required data source. This class (called `com.wrox.protc5.pmfact.PoolManFactory`) is provided within the `poolfact.jar` file included with the code distribution (`code/ch14` directory). You can use this class to replace Tomcat's DBCP pool manager with PoolMan as an alternative. This will enable you to maintain JNDI-based access, keeping the application code highly portable. To use this class, copy it to the `%CATALINA_HOME%/common/lib` directory.

To enable the access of PoolMan through Tomcat 5's JNDI, it is necessary to edit the `conf/server.xml` file . Within the `<DefaultContext>` of the host named `localhost`, add the following resource and parameter declaration for the `jdbc/wroxtomcat` context:

```
<Resource name="jdbc/wroxtomcat" auth="Container"
            type="javax.sql.DataSource"/>
  <ResourceParams name="jdbc/wroxtomcat">
    <parameter>
       <name>factory</name>
       <value>com.wrox.protc5.pmfact.PoolManFactory</value>
    </parameter>
  </ResourceParams>
```

The `factory` parameter overrides the default factory of `org.apache.commons.dbcp.BasicDataSourceFactory`. Instead, it is using our version (in `com.wrox.protc5.pmfact.PoolManFactory`), which will create PoolMan-managed data sources.

To place a test JSP into the `jsp-examples` Web application, you must edit the deployment descriptor (`web.xml`) and add a reference `<resource-ref>` to the preceding resource:

```
<resource-ref>
  <res-ref-name>jdbc/wroxtomcat</res-ref-name>
  <res-type>javax.sql.DataSource</res-type>
  <res-auth>Container</res-auth>
</resource-ref>
```

These configuration steps are identical to what was necessary when DBCP was used earlier in the setup of `JDBCTest.jsp`. In general, this would be the way to configure any alternative pooling mechanism that is compatible with Tomcat 5's JNDI emulation.

Last but not least, a test JSP file must be created that makes use of the `jdbc/wroxtomcat` JNDI resource. To create this JSP file, it is only necessary to make a very small change to `JDBCTest.jsp`. The change required is highlighted in the following snippet, and the completed file is placed into the `wroxjdbc` subdirectory of the `jsp-examples` Web application. The new JSP is called `JDBCTestPJ.jsp`.

```
<html>
  <head>
    <%@ page errorPage="errorpg.jsp"
             import="java.sql.*,
                     javax.sql.*,
                     java.io.*,
                     javax.naming.InitialContext,
                     javax.naming.Context" %>
  </head>
  <body>
    <h1>JDBC JNDI Resource Test</h1>
    <%
    InitialContext initCtx = new InitialContext();
    DataSource ds = (DataSource)
                       initCtx.lookup("java:comp/env/jdbc/wroxtomcat");
    Connection    conn = ds.getConnection();
    Statement stmt = conn.createStatement();
    ResultSet rset = stmt.executeQuery("select * from employee;");
    ...
```

Note that the code of `JDBCTest.jsp` and `JDBCTestPJ.jsp` is essentially identical. This demonstrates the advantage of decoupling the application code from the RDBMS accessed via JNDI. The same code can be used with connection pooling mechanisms from different vendors without change; only the configuration must be modified.

The name of the JNDI resource is `jdbc/wroxtomcat`. Our custom `com.wrox.protc5.pmfact.PoolManFactory` code uses the part after `jdbc/` to find the pool to be used. In this case, `wroxtomcat` matches a configured `<dbname>` element (see `poolman.xml`).

Testing PoolMan with JNDI-Compatible Lookup

To test PoolMan's JNDI-compatible operation mode, shut down Tomcat 5 and restart it. This restart is not strictly necessary. However, restarting Tomcat will ensure that you begin with a clean slate, as the previous example loaded PoolMan. Next, try to access the JSP via the following URL:

```
http://localhost:8080/jsp-examples/wroxjdbc/JDBCTestPJ.jsp
```

The output from this example is again similar to what is shown in Figure 14-5.

Note that the output is indistinguishable from that of `JDBCTest.jsp` or `JDBCTestPM.jsp`, although they each use distinctively different means to access and manage the JDBC connection used.

As of this writing, the PoolMan 2.x project has been dormant on Source Forge for more than two years. In fact, some developers have started to fork the code base to add new functionality and fix bugs. While the coding and design is well ahead of its time with respect to application for Tomcat, it does bring up the issue of ongoing support for anyone who may decide to adopt this pool manager.

Deploying Third-Party Pools

Having explored the issues surrounding the integration of third-party pool managers, carefully consider the consequences of doing so before proceeding.

Following are two main points that must be considered:

- *Support* — How well is the third-party pool manager supported? If there is any future incompatibility with Tomcat, who will resolve it and how soon?
- *Code portability* — Must one sacrifice configuration flexibility when using the pool manager? Is it necessary to hard-code driver and data source information?

Because DBCP is an Apache Commons project, it is used by many Apache Jakarta projects. As such, it is likely to evolve and stabilize rapidly with contributions from the Jakarta community. Third-party connection pool managers are unlikely to enjoy the same level of contribution and support.

In addition, because it is an essential and integral part of Tomcat 5, DBCP technology will track Tomcat evolution and will always be tested for compatibility with every new Tomcat release.

Even if a production scenario forces the deployment of a non-standard pool manager, it is wise to consider a gradual migration to standard DBCP. This is especially true if Tomcat 5 deployment is important.

Summary

This chapter explored JDBC connectivity in the context of Tomcat 5. The most obvious interaction is the need for Web applications to connect to relational database sources.

To conclude this chapter, let's review some of the key points that have been discussed:

- Java supports the accessing of RDBMSs in the form of JDBC. The evolution of JDBC versions was examined, including coverage of each type of JDBC driver that is available.
- With the latest Servlet 2.4 and JDBC 3.0 standards, the recommended way of providing a JDBC data source to Web applications involves the configuration of JNDI resources in the Tomcat configuration file. In addition, Tomcat 5 provides a value-added database connection pooling service. This pooling service draws on the code from the Jakarta Commons DBCP project.
- Using the latest MySQL and its Connector/J driver, JNDI resources can be configured for a custom JSP that accesses RDBMS tables to generate a dynamic HTML page.
- Database connection pooling is required functionality for any serious Web application, but standard connection pooling on Tomcat is a relatively recent phenomenon. As a result, many current third-party solutions are not standards-compliant. As administrators, it is important to realize the existence of such alternatives. In fact, many legacy systems today still deploy them, and some shared hosting ISPs require the use of them.
- A third-party pool manager called PoolMan can be deployed with Tomcat 5. This pool manager replaces the built-in DBCP-based connection pool. PoolMan can use a legacy JDBC 1 mechanism for providing pooled JDBC connection access to a Web application. As a result, the Web application coding becomes specific to the pool manager, despite the fact that most of the application code can be reused. This raises serious questions about the actual value of such a third-party pool manager. However, it is possible to make this pool manager "Tomcat 5 JNDI-compatible" using a custom adapter/factory class. By using the custom factory, the Web application coding remains portable, and independent of the pool manager mechanism used. This example illustrates that the flexible JNDI-based data source distribution is not limited to Tomcat 5's built-in DBCP based pool manager, but can be leveraged by any third-party pool manager as well.

Chapter 15 examines Tomcat security.

15

Tomcat Security

Perhaps no topic in the computing industry receives more emphasis than security, and for good reason. As network computing enters the twenty-first century, it is more clear than ever that the Internet is not a safe place. Attacks can be simple pranks (such as defacing a Web site), or take much more serious forms, such as industrial espionage, sabotage, or the theft of consumer information. System administrators must take many steps to secure network-exposed systems and services (such as Tomcat) against such aggressions.

This chapter describes several steps you can take to secure Tomcat against intrusions:

- Securing Tomcat against common attacks
- Running Tomcat with an unprivileged user account
- Locking down the file system
- Limiting access to Web applications with authentication Realms
- Encrypting communications between Tomcat and application clients with SSL

The discussion of these security issues is not entirely platform-agnostic. However, this chapter does not attempt to provide platform-specific instructions for all operating systems. Where appropriate, specific instructions are provided for Windows 2000/XP and Linux operating systems. Despite some pockets of platform-specificity, the principles shared in this chapter are applicable to any secure operating system.

Securing the Tomcat Installation

By default, Tomcat ships with several Web applications installed and ready to run, including the following:

- *ROOT*—Contains the simple default welcome page
- *tomcat-docs*—Tomcat documentation

- `jsp-examples` *and* `servlets-examples`—Simple examples of JSPs and Servlets demonstrating Tomcat's standards compliance
- `admin` *and* `manager`—Two powerful Web applications to make administering Tomcat more convenient

Some of these applications present a security risk. The following sections examine the risks posed by each application and, where necessary, offer solutions to reduce or eliminate those risks.

ROOT and tomcat-docs

The `ROOT` and `tomcat-docs` applications present a very minimal risk. Many users will define a new root Web application; in these situations, `ROOT` will be effectively removed. Otherwise, `ROOT` should be deleted. It is implemented as a JSP so a potential exploit could exist. The risk is remote, but because the `ROOT` application provides no useful functionality, no benefit is obtained by keeping it around.

`tomcat-docs` contains no JSPs or Servlets, and its content is freely available in many other locations on the Web. It poses no known security risks.

Admin and Manager

Of the default applications, `admin` and `manager` present the greatest security risks by virtue of their powerful functionality. If Tomcat is installed by extracting files from an archive, these two applications are effectively disabled; no account has access to use them. For maximum security, system administrators can leave these applications disabled, or even delete them completely by removing their directories:

```
$CATALINA/server/webapps/admin
$CATALINA/server/webapps/manager
```

Note, however, that users who have installed Tomcat via the Windows installation program are prompted to create an account that has access to these applications. In this situation, the applications are not effectively disabled by default, and the steps listed below are especially important.

These applications are very useful, and they are not inherently insecure. Deleting them is certainly not a requirement for securing a Tomcat installation. Two simple steps can be taken to reduce the chances that these applications will be exploited.

First, **choose a non-obvious account name and a secure password.** Chapter 5 and Chapter 7 discuss how to configure these applications; be sure to use a user name other than "tomcat," "root," "admin," or the like. In addition, choose passwords with a combination of mixed case letters, numbers, and punctuation characters.

Second, **change the default context of these applications** (that is, the URL used to access these applications) by editing the following two files:

```
$CATALINA/conf/Catalina/localhost/admin.xml
$CATALINA/conf/Catalina/localhost/manager.xml
```

The context can be changed to any value. The following code listing shows two lines from `admin.xml` that reconfigure the `admin` application from its default context of `/admin` to the new value of `/mytomcatadminapp`:

```
<Context path="/mytomcatadminapp" docBase="../server/webapps/admin"
         debug="0" privileged="true">
```

After making this change, the `admin` application would be accessible at the following URL:

```
http://localhost:8080/mytomcatadminapp
```

A similar change to `manager.xml` can also be made. By changing the context path, it will be much more difficult for malicious hackers to mount brute force attacks against these applications.

Further Security

Changing the context and choosing a good user name and password are two effective, simple ways to increase the security of the management applications. However, you can take some additional steps to lock them down even further, including the following:

- Change the application's authentication mechanism from BASIC to a more secure type. See the section "Authentication and Realms," later in this chapter for more details on this approach.
- Only allow specific client addresses (hosts) to access these applications. This is covered in the section "Host Restriction," later in this chapter.

jsp-examples and servlets-examples

While neither of these applications presents any known security risks (other than providing obvious targets for Denial of Service attacks), it's a good idea to delete them. They provide no useful functionality, and the possibility exists that attackers can exploit them. They are located as follows:

```
$CATALINA/webapps/jsp-examples
$CATALINA/webapps/servlets-examples
```

Deleting these applications is as simple as erasing these directories recursively.

Changing the SHUTDOWN Command

By default, the Tomcat `SHUTDOWN` command works by connecting to a special Tomcat socket on port 8005 and sending the following character sequence:

```
SHUTDOWN
```

Tomcat provides no authentication mechanism to restrict clients from connecting to Tomcat, sending these characters, and shutting down Tomcat. You can try it yourself by using telnet.

The easiest way to prevent unauthorized use of this functionality is by blocking port 8005 with a firewall. If this is not possible for whatever reason, system administrators should change both the port and the SHUTDOWN character sequence. This can be done by editing the following line of the $CATALINA/conf/server.xml file:

```
<Server port="8006" shutdown="putdown" debug="0">
```

In this example, the port has been changed to 8006 and the character sequence to putdown.

Running Tomcat with a Special Account

Despite the best efforts of Tomcat's authors, application developers, and system administrators, there is a chance that Tomcat can be exploited. Thus, it is prudent to consider mechanisms that prevent the amount of damage that an attacker could incur by gaining control of Tomcat.

Perhaps the most effective damage-control mechanism is running Tomcat under its own account, an account with only those privileges necessary to run Tomcat and nothing more. If this strategy is used, hackers who gain control of Tomcat are presented with few ways to wreak havoc.

The following sections describe the process of running Tomcat with its own account.

Creating a Tomcat User

The first step in the process is to create an account for running Tomcat. For simplicity, this account will referred to as tomcat in the remainder of this section.

Be sure to configure the tomcat account with the environment variables required to run Tomcat—notably, the JAVA_HOME and CATALINA_HOME variables.

Windows Tip

To ensure that unintentional privileges are not extended to the account, the tomcat account should be removed from all groups. When creating a user from the Users and Passwords control panel (called User Accounts in Windows XP), Windows automatically adds tomcat to at least one group. The Computer Management utility must be used to remove the tomcat account from all groups. System administrators may want to consider creating a special "Restricted Services" group for the tomcat account (more on this strategy will follow in subsequent paragraphs). Note also that the tomcat account should be given a password that never expires, which can be accomplished with the same Computer Management utility.

Linux Tip

Create both a tomcat user and a tomcat group. This is the default behavior of the useradd command. By assigning tomcat to its own new group, system administrators ensure that privileges are not unintentionally granted to the account.

Running Tomcat with the Tomcat User

After creating the tomcat account, the operating system must be configured to use the account when launching Tomcat.

Configuring Windows

If Tomcat is configured to run as a service (see Chapter 3 for details), the Services utility can be used to select a user account for use when launching Tomcat. The Services utility can be found in the Administrative Tools folder, which in turn is located in the Control Panel folder.

To change the account, double-click on the Tomcat service and select the Log On tab. That tab provides the capability for the service to "log on as" a specific account. Enter the `tomcat` account and its password in the appropriate locations. The service should then be restarted for the new setting to take effect.

If Tomcat is *not* configured to run as a service, the Windows `runas` utility can be used to run Tomcat as the tomcat user. The syntax of this utility is shown here:

```
runas /user:tomcat c:\tomcat\bin\startup.bat
```

Configuring Linux

There's no one way to configure a Linux system to start up Tomcat with its own user account. The basic idea is to launch Tomcat using a syntax similar to the following in whatever startup scheme is used:

```
/bin/su tomcat $CATALINA_HOME/bin/startup.sh
```

A typical configuration might use a script such as the following in `/etc/init.d` (or wherever `init` scripts are stored):

```
#!/bin/bash
RETVAL=$?
export JAVA_HOME=/usr/java/jdk
export CATALINA_HOME=/usr/local/java/jakarta-tomcat

case "$1" in
 start)
        if [ -f $CATALINA_HOME/bin/startup.sh ];
          then
            echo $"Starting Tomcat"
            /bin/su tomcat $CATALINA_HOME/bin/startup.sh
        fi
        ;;
 stop)
        if [ -f $CATALINA_HOME/bin/shutdown.sh ];
          then
            echo $"Stopping Tomcat"
            /bin/su tomcat $CATALINA_HOME/bin/shutdown.sh
        fi
        ;;
 *)
        echo $"Usage: $0 {start|stop}"
        exit 1
        ;;
esac

exit $RETVAL
```

The script in `/etc/init.d` can then be configured to load on startup by creating links to it in the desired run-level directories or by using a graphical configuration client, depending on the distribution of Linux used.

Securing the File System

Configuring Tomcat to run with its own user account is only useful if the account is sufficiently impotent, to prevent havoc from being wreaked. Effectively, this means reducing the scope of the account's file system permissions to the minimum set required to perform the job.

Windows File System

Windows has two different types of file systems: FAT32 and NTFS. FAT32 is inherently insecure and not capable of being "locked down." It is, however, an excellent choice for system administrators if instability, limitations, and inefficiency are considered virtuous. NTFS, conversely, has all the necessary features for restricting the `tomcat` user's capabilities.

The type of file system being used can be determined by viewing the properties of the hard drive partition in question in the My Computer window. Windows supports upgrading FAT32 partitions to NTFS. Note, however, that once a partition has been changed to NTFS, it cannot revert back to FAT32.

Access Control Lists

NTFS security is built around the concept of **access control lists** (**ACLs**). Every resource in the file system (that is, files and directories) has an ACL that is associated with it. The ACL contains a list of users and groups and the operations that the users/groups are permitted to perform. The set of allowed operations for a user or group is that entity's **permissions.**

By default, Windows allows all users to access any resource in the file system, with the exception of sensitive areas, such as the Windows directory itself and the profile resources of other users. For the purposes of securing a Tomcat installation, these permissions are too liberal.

The instructions in this section are intentionally minimal, because this book is not intended for use as a Windows administration guide.

Restricting Permissions

To accomplish the stated goal of reducing `tomcat`'s permissions to the minimum required, all default permissions granted to the account must be revoked. To do this, the `tomcat` account must be explicitly denied access to every resource in the file system, and then selectively granted access to the necessary resources.

Use the following steps to revoke `tomcat`'s permissions:

1. Right-click on the first drive partition in the My Computer window.
2. Select the Properties context menu item.
3. Select the Security tab.

4. Click on the Add... button.
5. Select the `tomcat` account.
6. Click every Deny checkbox.
7. Click the Advanced... button.
8. Select the "Reset permissions on all child objects and enable propagation of inheritable permissions" checkbox.
9. Click OK.
10. Wait while Windows modifies every ACL in the partition's file system.
11. Repeat these steps with all partitions.

Granting Permissions

To do its job, the `tomcat` account must have permission to read and execute the JRE files. Thus, the next step in the process is to grant these permissions to the `tomcat` account. This is accomplished by a similar process to the one discussed previously. To start, select the directory containing the JRE used to run Tomcat, and view the Security properties of the directory. The `tomcat` account should be present in the list of groups and users. Removing the `tomcat` account with the Remove button is sufficient to grant access to run Tomcat. Propagating this change to all child objects is also necessary using the same process discussed previously.

For maximum security, the Everyone group should be removed from the JRE directory's ACL, and the `tomcat` user should be added to it, and given only the following permissions: "Read & Execute, List Folder Contents, and Read. However, this necessitates explicitly granting these permissions to *every* user who needs to use Java, which can become tedious. This illustrates the utility of creating a series of groups that has access to certain areas of the file system. For example, users who need access to Java can be given membership in the Java Users group. Users who need the capability to manipulate the contents of the Java directory can be given membership in a group called Java Developers. The extra time required to configure such a setup can be well worth the added security and scalability as more users are added.

The `tomcat` account also needs access to the `tomcat` directory. These permissions can be granted with the same procedure used to grant access to the `Java` directory. For maximum security, only grant read access to the following directories:

```
$CATALINA/bin
$CATALINA/common
$CATALINA/server
$CATALINA/shared
$CATALINA/webapps
```

Note that `$CATALINA/conf` must have write permissions to function if Tomcat's default UserDatabase implementation is used for user authentication. In addition, note that making the `$CATALINA/webapps` directory read-only can cause problems if Web applications modify files in their directories, or if the Tomcat `manager` application is used to deploy new Web applications.

Linux File System

Securing the Linux file system requires two steps: granting the `tomcat` account read and execute permissions on the JRE directory (recursively), and granting it read, write, and execute permissions on the Tomcat directory. There are numerous ways to effectively grant these permissions. Following is one strategy:

- Recursively set the "other" permissions on the JRE directory to read and execute with the `chmod` command:

```
chmod -R o=rx *
```

- Recursively set the owner of the Tomcat directory to the tomcat account:

```
chown -R tomcat:tomcat *
```

For additional security, the owner, group, and other permissions for the following Tomcat directories can be set to read-only:

```
$CATALINA/bin
$CATALINA/common
$CATALINA/server
$CATALINA/shared
$CATALINA/webapps
```

Note that `$CATALINA/conf` must have write permissions to function if Tomcat's default UserDatabase implementation is used for user authentication. In addition, note that making the `$CATALINA/webapps` directory read-only can cause problems if Web applications modify files in their directories, or if the Tomcat `manager` application is used to deploy new Web applications.

Securing the Java Virtual Machine

Configuring the file system for maximum security is an important part of securing a Tomcat installation. Java's Security Manager architecture exposes an entirely different level of configurability. With the Security Manager, Java applications can be restricted from accessing features of the Java language and platform in a remarkably fine-grained manner.

This security architecture is turned off by default, but it can be turned on at any time. In this section, the Security Manager architecture is reviewed in general terms, followed by a discussion of how this architecture specifically applies to Tomcat.

Overview of the Security Manager

As with the file system, the Security Manager architecture is based on the concept of permissions. Once the Security Manager is turned on (using a command-line switch that will be discussed shortly), applications must have **explicit permission** to perform certain security-sensitive tasks (such as creating a custom class loader or opening a network socket).

To make effective use of the Security Manager architecture, it is therefore necessary to know how to grant permissions to applications and to understand the set of possible permissions.

Granting Permissions to Applications

Policy files are the mechanism used by the Security Manager to grant permissions to applications. Policy files are simple text files composed of individual actions that applications are allowed to perform.

A policy file is composed of `grant` entries, which look like the following:

```
// first grant entry
grant {
  permission java.lang.RuntimePermission "stopThread";
}

// second grant entry
grant codeBase "file:${java.home}/lib/ext/*" {
  permission java.security.AllPermission;
};
```

The first `grant` entry in this example demonstrates the simplicity of the syntax. It grants all applications the capability to access the deprecated `Thread.stop()` method.

The second `grant` entry illustrates that code in specific locations can also be granted permissions. This is, of course, useful for extending permissions to certain trusted code while denying permissions to all other code. In this case, all code in the `$JAVA_HOME/lib/ext` directory is granted all permissions, which effectively disables the Security Manager architecture for that code.

Grant Entry Syntax

Each `grant` entry must be composed of the following syntax:

```
grant codeBase "URL" {
  // this is a comment
  permission permission_class_name "target_name", "action";
  ...
};
```

Note that comments in policy files must begin with `//` on each line. As shown in the first `grant` entry earlier, the `codeBase` attribute is optional. `codeBase` specifies a URL to which all the permissions should apply. The syntax is shown in the following table.

codeBase Example	Description
`file:/C:/myapp/`	Indicates that code in the directory `c:\myapp` will be assigned the permissions in the `grant` block. Note that the slash (`/`) indicates that only class files in the directory will receive the permissions, not any JAR files or subdirectories.
`http://java.sun.com/*`	All code from the specified URL will be granted the permissions. In this case, the "`/*`" at the end of the URL indicates that all class files and JAR files will be assigned the permissions, but not any subdirectories.
`file:/funstuff/-`	All code in the `/funstuff` directory will be granted the permissions. The slash (`/-`) indicates that all class files and JAR files in the directory and its subdirectories will be assigned the permissions.

Within the `grant` block, one or more permissions can be assigned. Each permission consists of a permission class name and, in some cases, an additional **target** that identifies a specific permission within the permission class. Some permission targets can additionally take parameters, called **actions.** Following are some examples of permissions:

```
grant {
  // allows applications to listen on all ports
  permission java.net.SocketPermission "localhost", "listen";

  // allows applications to read the "java.version" property
  permission java.util.PropertyPermission "java.version", "read";
}
```

Available Permissions

Permissions are defined by special classes that ultimately inherit from the abstract class `java.security.Permission`. Most permission classes define special targets that represent a security permission that can be turned on and off.

For example, the `java.lang.RuntimePermission` class defines the targets shown in the following table. (Note that this is not a complete list.)

Target Name	Description
`createClassLoader`	Allows an application to create a custom class loader
`exitVM`	Allows an application to exit the JVM via the `System.exit()` method

As of Java 1.4, there are 19 different permission classes offering control over various permissions. The following table shows a partial list of these classes to demonstrate the breadth of what is possible with permissions. This list is not an exhaustive listing of all possible permission targets. The complete list of permission classes and their targets can be viewed at the following URL:

```
http://java.sun.com/j2se/1.4/docs/guide/security/permissions.html
```

Permission Class	Description
`java.security.AllPermission`	By granting this permission, all other permissions are also granted. Granting this permission is the same as disabling the Security Manager for the affected code.
`java.security.SecurityPermission`	Allows programmatic access to various security features of the Java language

Permission Class	Description
`java.security.UnresolvedPermission`	This permission class is not defined in policy files. Rather, it is used as a placeholder when a policy file makes reference to a user-defined permission class that had not been loaded at the time of processing the policy file. This permission is only relevant to those interacting with the Security Manager system programmatically at run-time.
`java.awt.AWTPermission`	Controls various AWT permissions
`java.io.FilePermission`	Restricts read, write, execute, and delete access to files in specified paths
`java.io.SerializablePermission`	Allows serialization permissions
`java.lang.reflect.ReflectPermission`	Allows applications to circumvent the `public` and `private` mechanism's access checks and reflectively access any method
`java.lang.RuntimePermission`	Allows access to key run-time features, (such as creating class loaders, exiting the VM, and reassigning `STDIN`, `STDOUT`, and `STDERR`)
`java.net.NetPermission`	Allows various network permissions
`java.net.SocketPermission`	Allows incoming socket connections, outgoing connections, listening on ports, and resolving host names. These permissions can be defined for specific host names and port combinations.
`java.sql.SQLPermission`	While this may sound intriguing, it only controls a single permission: setting the JDBC log output writer. This file is considered sensitive because it may contain user names and passwords.
`java.util.PropertyPermission`	Controls whether properties can be read from or written to
`java.util.logging.LoggingPermission`	Allows the capability to configure the logging system
`javax.net.ssl.SSLPermission`	Allows the capability to access SSL-related network functionality
`javax.security.auth.AuthPermission`	Controls authentication permissions
`javax.security.auth.` and `PrivateCredentialPermission`	Controls various security permissions
`javax.security.auth.kerberos.` and `DelegationPermission`	Controls various security permissions related to the Kerberos protocol
`javax.security.auth.kerberos.` and `ServicePermission`	Controls various security permissions related to the Kerberos protocol
`javax.sound.sampled.AudioPermission`	Controls access to the sound system

Enabling the Security Manager System

The Security Manager system is enabled by passing the `-Djava.security.manager` parameter to the Java Virtual Machine at startup, in the following manner:

```
$ java -Djava.security.manager MyClass
```

By default, Java looks for the file `$JAVA_HOME/lib/security/java.policy` to determine what permissions to grant when the Security Manager is turned on.

For more information on enabling the Security Manager and using custom policy files, see the following URL:

```
http://java.sun.com/j2se/1.4/docs/guide/security/PolicyFiles.html
```

Advanced Security Manager Topics

There are additional Security Manager topics that are simply beyond the scope of this chapter. For example, it is possible to subclass the default Java Security Manager implementation to provide for custom permission classes. It is further possible to define `grant` blocks in policy files based on code signatures. For information on these and other advanced topics, check out the following URL:

```
http://java.sun.com/j2se/1.4/docs/guide/security/
```

Using the Security Manager with Tomcat

Now that the basics of the Security Manager system have been covered, their use with Tomcat will be explained.

Enabling Tomcat's Security Manager

The preferred way to start Tomcat with the Security Manager enabled on Linux systems is as follows:

```
$ $CATALINA_HOME/bin/catalina.sh start -security
```

On Windows systems, the command is quite similar:

```
> %CATALINA_HOME%\bin\catalina start -security
```

Tomcat's Policy File

Tomcat uses the `$CATALINA_HOME/conf/catalina.policy` file to determine its own permissions and those of its Web applications.

What follows is the file as of Tomcat 5. Note that it is divided into three sections: system code permissions, Catalina code permissions, and Web application code permissions.

System Code Permissions

Tomcat's policy file grants all permissions to the `javac` tool, which is used to compile JSPs into Servlets, and grants all permissions to any Java standard extensions. Four `grant` lines are used instead of two to deal with multiple path possibilities. Note that administrators may need to add additional `grants` to this section if the JRE used to run Tomcat uses different paths for its standard extensions (such as Mac OS X) and Tomcat Web applications are using JARs or classes in those paths.

```
// ========== SYSTEM CODE PERMISSIONS =========================================

// These permissions apply to javac
grant codeBase "file:${java.home}/lib/-" {
        permission java.security.AllPermission;
};

// These permissions apply to all shared system extensions
grant codeBase "file:${java.home}/jre/lib/ext/-" {
        permission java.security.AllPermission;
};

// These permissions apply to javac when ${java.home] points at $JAVA_HOME/jre
grant codeBase "file:${java.home}/../lib/-" {
        permission java.security.AllPermission;
};

// These permissions apply to all shared system extensions when
// ${java.home} points at $JAVA_HOME/jre
grant codeBase "file:${java.home}/lib/ext/-" {
        permission java.security.AllPermission;
};
```

Catalina Code Permissions

Note that Catalina grants all permissions to the following:

- Tomcat's startup classes (`$CATALINA/bin/bootstrap.jar` and `$CATALINA/bin/commons-launcher.jar`)
- The common class loader files (`$CATALINA/common/lib` and `$CATALINA/common/classes`)
- The server class loader files (`$CATALINA/server/lib` and `$CATALINA/server/classes`)

```
// ========== CATALINA CODE PERMISSIONS =======================================

// These permissions apply to the launcher code
grant codeBase "file:${catalina.home}/bin/commons-launcher.jar" {
        permission java.security.AllPermission;
};

// These permissions apply to the server startup code
grant codeBase "file:${catalina.home}/bin/bootstrap.jar" {
        permission java.security.AllPermission;
};

// These permissions apply to the servlet API classes
// and those that are shared across all class loaders
// located in the "common" directory
grant codeBase "file:${catalina.home}/common/-" {
        permission java.security.AllPermission;
```

```
};

// These permissions apply to the container's core code, plus any additional
// libraries installed in the "server" directory
grant codeBase "file:${catalina.home}/server/-" {
        permission java.security.AllPermission;
};
```

Web Application Permissions

Tomcat allows read access to various system properties and other miscellaneous permissions as commented here:

```
// ========== WEB APPLICATION PERMISSIONS =====================================

// These permissions are granted by default to all web applications
// In addition, a web application will be given a read FilePermission
// and JndiPermission for all files and directories in its document root.
grant {
    // Required for JNDI lookup of named JDBC DataSource's and
    // javamail named MimePart DataSource used to send mail
    permission java.util.PropertyPermission "java.home", "read";
    permission java.util.PropertyPermission "java.naming.*", "read";
    permission java.util.PropertyPermission "javax.sql.*", "read";

    // OS Specific properties to allow read access
    permission java.util.PropertyPermission "os.name", "read";
    permission java.util.PropertyPermission "os.version", "read";
    permission java.util.PropertyPermission "os.arch", "read";
    permission java.util.PropertyPermission "file.separator", "read";
    permission java.util.PropertyPermission "path.separator", "read";
    permission java.util.PropertyPermission "line.separator", "read";

    // JVM properties to allow read access
    permission java.util.PropertyPermission "java.version", "read";
    permission java.util.PropertyPermission "java.vendor", "read";
    permission java.util.PropertyPermission "java.vendor.url", "read";
    permission java.util.PropertyPermission "java.class.version", "read";
    permission java.util.PropertyPermission "java.specification.version", "read";
    permission java.util.PropertyPermission "java.specification.vendor", "read";
    permission java.util.PropertyPermission "java.specification.name", "read";

    permission java.util.PropertyPermission "java.vm.specification.version", "read";
    permission java.util.PropertyPermission "java.vm.specification.vendor", "read";
    permission java.util.PropertyPermission "java.vm.specification.name", "read";
    permission java.util.PropertyPermission "java.vm.version", "read";
    permission java.util.PropertyPermission "java.vm.vendor", "read";
    permission java.util.PropertyPermission "java.vm.name", "read";

    // Required for OpenJMX
    permission java.lang.RuntimePermission "getAttribute";

    // Allow read of JAXP compliant XML parser debug
```

```
        permission java.util.PropertyPermission "jaxp.debug", "read";

        // Precompiled JSPs need access to this package.
        permission java.lang.RuntimePermission
            "accessClassInPackage.org.apache.jasper.runtime";
        permission java.lang.RuntimePermission
            "accessClassInPackage.org.apache.jasper.runtime.*";
};
```

Note that system administrators are not only free to modify Tomcat's policy file, they are encouraged to do so. Once the Security Manager has been enabled, it's likely that changes to it will be required in order for certain aspects of deployed Web applications to function.

Recommended Security Manager Practices

Now that the process of enabling the Security Manager with Tomcat has been described, as well as the location of Tomcat's policy file, recommended practices for granting permissions to applications can be discussed.

Using the Security Manager

If the Security Manager is not used with Tomcat, any JSP or class file is free to perform any action it desires. This includes opening unauthorized connections to other network hosts, destroying the file system, or abnormally terminating Tomcat itself by issuing the `System.exit()` command.

Clearly, to maintain a secure Tomcat installation, the Security Manager should be enabled, and fine-grained permissions should be set.

Understanding Application Requirements

If Tomcat's default policy file is enabled, Web applications are likely to find themselves unable to perform certain required functions. Consider the following tasks that are unauthorized with Tomcat's default policy configuration:

- Creating a class loader
- Accessing a database via a socket (for example, the MySQL JDBC driver trying to establish a connection with a MySQL database)
- Sending an e-mail via the JavaMail API
- Reading or writing to files outside of the Web application's directory

There are a myriad of permissions that an application may require. System administrators must communicate with the application developers to understand which permissions the Web applications will require.

Examples for enabling some of the common permissions listed here are reviewed in the next section. To learn about other permissions, review the Java Security documentation links provided earlier in this chapter.

Enabling Creation of a Class Loader

The following example shows how to give a specific Web application, `yourWebApp`, the capability to create a class loader:

```
grant codeBase "file:${catalina.home}/webapps/yourWebApp/WEB-INF/-" {
  permission java.lang.RuntimePermission "createClassLoader";
};
```

Enabling JDBC Drivers to Open Socket Connections to Databases

The following example shows how to allow all Web applications access to a specific database running on the host `db.server.com` on port 54321:

```
grant codeBase "file:${catalina.home}/webapps/-" {
  permission java.net.SocketPermission "db.server.com:54321", "connect";
};
```

Note that the preceding example allows all code in all of your Web applications to connect to `db.server.com:54321`. If this is too much of a security risk, the JDBC driver can be explicitly granted permission individually:

```
grant codeBase "file:${catalina.home}/webapps/webAppName/WEB-INF/lib/JDBC.jar" {
  permission java.net.SocketPermission "db.server.com:54321", "connect";
};
```

Sending E-Mail with JavaMail

Sending e-mail requires that a Web application have access to port 25 on an SMTP server. The following example shows how to grant this permission to all classes in a Web application:

```
grant codeBase "file:${catalina.home}/webapps/myWebApp/WEB-INF/classes/-" {
  permission java.net.SocketPermission "mail.server.com:25", "connect";
};
```

Reading or Writing to Files Outside of the Web Application's Directory

Earlier in this chapter, the topic of securing the file system was discussed. If the file system has been properly secured, the following grant can be used to give Web applications full access to the file system (and thus rely on the operating system to enforce permissions):

```
grant {
  java.io.FilePermission "<<ALL FILES>>", "read,write,execute,delete";
};
```

While it may be tempting to use the Java Security Model in place of securing the file system via operating system permissions, such a tactic would be unwise. Relying on the operating system provides an important extra layer of security in the event that the Java Virtual Machine itself becomes compromised and exploited. Additionally, in many configurations, it is likely that Tomcat is not the only exploitable network service on the server — another good reason to utilize the operating system's security model, as Tomcat's security settings would not apply to the other services.

In addition, note that by default, all Java applications do have read access to the directory in which they are located, including its subdirectories.

Securing Web Applications

The previous sections have been concerned with securing the Tomcat installation and the Java Virtual Machine. In this section, techniques for securing individual Web applications are considered. These techniques fall under the following categories:

- Authentication and Realms
- Encryption
- Host Restriction

Note that these techniques can also be applied to Tomcat's built-in applications, as mentioned earlier in the section "Admin and Manager."

Authentication and Realms

Authentication is the process of determining and validating the identity of an application's client. The Servlet specification provides an integration with the Java Authentication and Authorization Service (JAAS) API. This enables Web applications to authenticate their users in a standard way that is portable across different Servlet containers.

Some Java developers have been known to eschew open standards in favor of their own. It is entirely possible (and indeed somewhat common) for Servlet developers to authenticate users via some home-grown mechanism, rather than via the JAAS/Servlet standard mechanism discussed subsequently in this section. System administrators should be aware that in such circumstances, this section will be of little utility.

Authentication Mechanisms

Serlvet-based applications have four standards-based authentication mechanisms from which to choose:

- BASIC
- DIGEST
- Form
- HTTPS Client Certificate

A brief description of these mechanisms follows. Later in this chapter, their use is demonstrated.

BASIC

As its name implies, the BASIC authentication mechanism is simplistic. The browser sends base64-encoded credentials to the server, which then decodes them and uses them to authenticate the user. This mechanism has two somewhat serious problems:

- Base64 encoding is not secure. Base64 is intended as a means of encoding binary data as ASCII data for transmission via protocols that lack support for binary data. It is not a type of secure encryption mechanism. In the case of the BASIC authentication mechanism, base64 is better than sending credentials in plaintext, but not much better.
- Browsers cache credentials after authentication. Once a user authenticates, there is no way for the user to log out other than exiting the browser. This disadvantage also applies to the other browser-managed authentication mechanisms, such as Digest and HTTPS Client Certificate.

Nevertheless, despite its insecurity, BASIC remains a good option for a simple level of security designed to keep out the "mindless hordes." When administrators really don't care if the protected resource is compromised, BASIC is not a bad mechanism to use.

DIGEST

DIGEST is a step up from BASIC. Another browser-based mechanism, DIGEST is very similar to BASIC with the exception that the password is transmitted in a secure fashion. The browser performs a **digest** on the password (a digest is a one-way hash, as explained shortly) and transmits the digest to the server. The server then digests the password to which the browser-provided password digest will be compared, and if the two match, the authentication is successful.

DIGEST is reasonably secure, but it too suffers from two flaws:

- In Tomcat, the original password must be stored somewhere in plaintext. This is especially unfortunate when the password is stored in a file, as it can then be easily viewed by anyone with access to the file. (A workaround is possible using file permissions to secure access to the file.)
- It has the same cached credential problem that BASIC has. (See the preceding section, "BASIC," for details.)

A digest, also called a **hash,** is used to provide proof that a set of data hasn't been nefariously (or unintentionally) altered.

A hashing algorithm takes some data as input and from it creates a unique fingerprint (which is usually 16 or 20 bytes long). This is a one-way process, meaning that the digest cannot be undigested to discover the original data. Because each fingerprint is unique, the digest of the original data can be compared with a digest of a second set of data. If the digests match, then the second set of data is proved to be identical to the original digest of data. If two sets of data are purported to be identical, they are confirmed as such.

This process can be applied to passwords by digesting the password and storing its digest in a file or database. Thus, even if the stored password digest is compromised, an attacker cannot "undigest" the password the hash represents, and it is thus unusable. To determine whether a user has entered the same password, the user's password is digested and compared with the digest value on file. If they match, it is the same password.

Java supports two digest algorithms:

- *MD5*—This algorithm is used in several password-storage mechanisms, including many Unix systems. MD5 produces a 16-byte message digest.
- *SHA*—This algorithm is more secure than MD5 as it uses a 20-byte message digest.

Form

In form-based authentication, the browser does not knowingly cooperate in the authentication process. Instead, the Web application creates an HTML form wherein the form name and user name and password fields all have special names. These fields can then be intercepted by the Servlet container, which uses the data to provide authentication.

Because an HTML form can be transmitted over an encrypted connection (HTTPS), form-based authentication can be made reasonably secure. It does suffer from at least one disadvantage, however:

- Reliance on user names/passwords as credentials. While the form-based mechanism can transmit credentials after they have been encrypted with HTTPS, the authentication mechanism is still reliant on passwords, which can be defeated either by brute force or by social engineering.

HTTPS Client Certificate

When a browser establishes a secure connection with a server, the browser is sent a public key certificate from the server. This certificate enables the browser to authenticate the server. That is, it enables the browser to know the true identity of the server as certified (signed) by a trusted third party (such as VeriSign). This authentication mechanism enables the browser to be certain of the identity of the server, so that sensitive transactions such as e-commerce can be conducted. Note, however, that this process is asymmetric; the server does not receive a certificate from the client.

The HTTPS client certificate mechanism upgrades this process to be symmetrical. With this mechanism, the Web browser transmits a public key certificate to the server, which can then use the certificate to authenticate the client. Both parties, therefore, are authenticated with each other. Note, however, that most server-based applications rely on simpler mechanisms to authenticate their clients (such as an HTML form-based mechanism).

The HTTPS client certificate mechanism is, of course, quite secure. If the public key architecture upon which HTTPS client authentication is based were defeated, the very basis of secure e-commerce would fall with it. Beyond this apocalyptic scenario, however, are some potential weaknesses:

- *Key length*—The most important factor in the security of public key encryption is the length of the key used to encrypt the messages. As computing evolves and computing power increases, ever larger keys will be needed to maintain security against brute force hack attempts. Administrators should stay informed about public key architecture issues and upgrade the keys used should this become necessary in the future.
- *Theft*—The fundamental assumption of public key authentication is that the corresponding private key is only available to the trusted party. Should the private key be stolen, the authentication would be compromised.

While quite secure, the HTTPS client certificate mechanism is rarely used outside of business-to-business applications because of the complexity of the process one must go through to obtain a certificate.

Configuring Authentication

In order for a Web application to use one of the authentication mechanisms just described, it must be configured to do so inside its deployment descriptor (`web.xml file`). This is accomplished by adding `<security-constraint>` and `<login-config>` elements to the `<web-app>` element. These elements are discussed in Chapter 6. An example of their use is shown here:

```
<web-app ...>
  <security-constraint>
    <web-resource-collection>
      <web-resource-name>Entire Application</web-resource-name>
      <url-pattern>/*</url-pattern>
    </web-resource-collection>
    <auth-constraint>
       <role-name>user</role-name>
    </auth-constraint>
  </security-constraint>

  <login-config>
    <auth-method>FORM</auth-method>
    <realm-name>My Application</realm-name>
    <form-login-config>
      <form-login-page>/login.jsp</form-login-page>
      <form-error-page>/notAuthenticated.jsp</form-error-page>
    </form-login-config>
  </login-config>

</web-app>
```

In this code excerpt, the `<security-constraint>` element is used to define a portion of the application that is restricted to users belonging to a specific role. The `<url-pattern>` element uses URL pattern matching to determine the protected portion of the application (in this case, the entire application), and the `<role-name>` element is used to restrict that portion of the application to authenticated users who belong to the "user" role. For more information on roles, see the section "Users and Roles," later in this chapter.

The `<login-config>` element is used to specify how users authenticate with the Web application. `<auth-method>` determines which of the authentication mechanisms described here is used. Possible values include `BASIC`, `DIGEST`, `FORM`, and `CLIENT-CERT`. Because we've chosen `FORM`, the `<form-login-config>` element must be nested in the `<login-config>` element. `<form-login-config>` identifies which page in the Web application is used to authenticate the user (`/login.jsp`) and which page is displayed when authentication fails (`/notAuthenticated.jsp`). No page is configured to be displayed when authentication succeeds. Instead, the user is presented with the URL that triggered the authentication in the first place.

Authentication Form

In the preceding example, the URL /login.jsp is used to specify the login form. While any valid HTML page containing an HTML form may be used, the HTML form used to send the credentials to the server must be configured in three specific ways:

- The value of its <form> element's action attribute must be "j_security_check".
- The user name must be sent in a field named "j_username".
- The password must be sent in a field named "j_password".

Following is an example of a conforming form:

```
<html>
  <head><title>Please Log In</title>
  <body>
    <form method="POST" action="j_security_check">
      <table>
        <tr>
          <th>Username:</th>
          <td><input type="text" name="j_username"></td>
        </tr>
        <tr>
          <th>Password:</th>
          <td><input type="password" name="j_password"></td>
        </tr>
        <tr>
          <td><input type="submit" value="Log In"></td>
          <td><input type="reset"></td>
        </tr>
      </table>
    </form>
  </body>
</html>
```

The error page can contain any HTML that conveys to the user the fact that the authentication attempt failed.

Security Realms

The authentication mechanism descriptions detailed how the credentials used for the authentication process (for example, user name and password) are obtained. However, for authentication to take place, Tomcat must also have access to the real credentials against which those sent from the browser must be compared. This section describes where Tomcat stores the actual credentials on the server and how it obtains them.

Realms are the standard mechanism used for storing the credentials used by Tomcat to authenticate the client. Tomcat's Realm mechanism is an implementation of the Realm support mandated in the Servlet specification.

A Realm is a standard programming interface defined in Tomcat for accessing a user's user name, password, and roles. Tomcat 5's built-in default authentication implementations (including the login mechanisms for the `admin` and `manager` utilities and the Single Sign-on Valve) depend on Realms to authenticate the user.

Users and Roles

The Web application security model is built around the concept of users and roles. Users are assigned to a role, which determines the resources that the user is allowed to access. For example, a Web application can declare that the resource "/admin" can only be accessed by users belonging to the "admin" role. Then, a Realm can be configured to consider the users "alice" and "bob" as belonging to the "admin" role. Thus, when "alice" and "bob" authenticate, they will be allowed access to "/admin."

The advantage of roles is that they enable the Web application to be configured independently of the permissions of the users who access the application. Using the preceding example, the deployment descriptor of the application only needs to specify that an "admin" role is required, and is not concerned with the identities of the users who are allowed access.

The actual mapping of users to roles can be specified at deployment time—and can be changed dynamically without having to change the application code. This clean separation of the authentication code from the actual method of authentication is the main advantage of Realms. This separation allows for many different ways of creating Realms. The following four built-in Realm implementations can be deployed with Tomcat 5:

- File-based, in-memory Realms
- JDBC Realms
- JNDI-based Realms
- JAAS-based Realms

In addition to these built-in Realms, it is also possible for developers to create custom Realms—supplying the authentication data via arbitrary custom means.

The following sections provide detailed coverage of each of the built-in Tomcat 5 Realm implementations. Where applicable, a basic deployment configuration is first described to familiarize you with the particular Realm implementation, followed by the presentation of a more secured method of deployment.

File-Based Realm: UserDatabase

A file-based Realm maintains its authentication data in flat files. These files can be edited using a normal text editor. The data is kept in human-readable format (such as XML). The primary built-in file-based Realm implementation for Tomcat 5 is called **UserDatabase.**

UserDatabase is Tomcat 5's greatly enhanced implementation of a MemoryRealm (note that UserDatabase has actually been available since Tomcat 4.1). A MemoryRealm reads authentication data from a specified XML file for use by Tomcat 5 during startup. A MemoryRealm is a read-only Realm; no update is possible. UserDatabase is a Realm implementation that still reads authentication data from an XML file, but is improved in many aspects:

- It is no longer a read-only Realm. The data in the Realm can be programmatically changed during the lifetime of the engine. This enables various possibilities for building administrative utilities.

- UserDatabase is persistent. That is, upon modification and shutdown, the UserDatabase can also persist any changes back to its associated XML (`tomcat-users.xml`) data file.
- The `admin` utility supports the graphical editing of authentication data within a UserDatabase Realm.

The intention of UserDatabase goes beyond simply serving as a refined version of a memory Realm. It is an integral part of Tomcat 5's authentication and programmatic security support.

Configuring UserDatabase

In the default `server.xml` (in the Tomcat 5 server distribution), the UserDatabase Realm is already configured. The UserDatabase is typically configured in the `<GlobalNamingResources>` element as a JNDI Resource. Here is a typical configuration:

```
<Resource name="UserDatabase" auth="Container"
          type="org.apache.catalina.UserDatabase"
          description="memory based user database"/>
<ResourceParams name="UserDatabase">
   <parameter>
      <name>factory</name>
      <value>org.apache.catalina.users.MemoryUserDatabaseFactory</value>
   </parameter>
   <parameter>
      <name>pathname</name>
      <value>conf/tomcat-users.xml</value>
   </parameter>
</ResourceParams>
```

This will make the UserDatabase accessible from application via JNDI lookup, relative to the `java:comp/env` naming context. Furthermore, it also provides an easy reference in a later scope. For example, you can use the UserDatabase as a Realm at the `<Engine>` container level by adding the following `<Realm>` definition:

```
<Realm className="org.apache.catalina.realm.UserDatabaseRealm"
                 debug="0" resourceName="UserDatabase"/>
```

In fact, this is precisely the content of the default Tomcat 5 `server.xml` file. This means that both the `manager` application and the `admin` application actually rely on UserDatabase as the Realm for authentication.

To see how UserDatabase is a modifiable, updateable Realm, use the `admin` application to add a user/password entry. Start up Tomcat, and then start the `admin` application via the following URL:

```
http://localhost:8080/admin/
```

Log on using the user ID and password that you have chosen for the admin role (as described in the section "Admin and Manager," earlier in this chapter).

Now, click the Users item in the tree view on the left. You should see a view similar to what is shown in Figure 15-1.

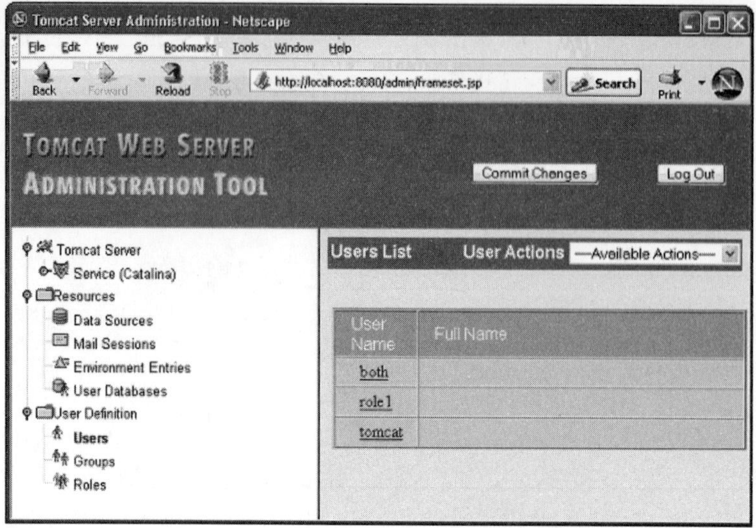

Figure 15-1: Using the admin application to test the UserDatabase Realm.

Next, select Create New User from the Available Actions list in the User Actions menu in the right pane. Fill it in as shown in Figure 15-2 (the password is `joe`):

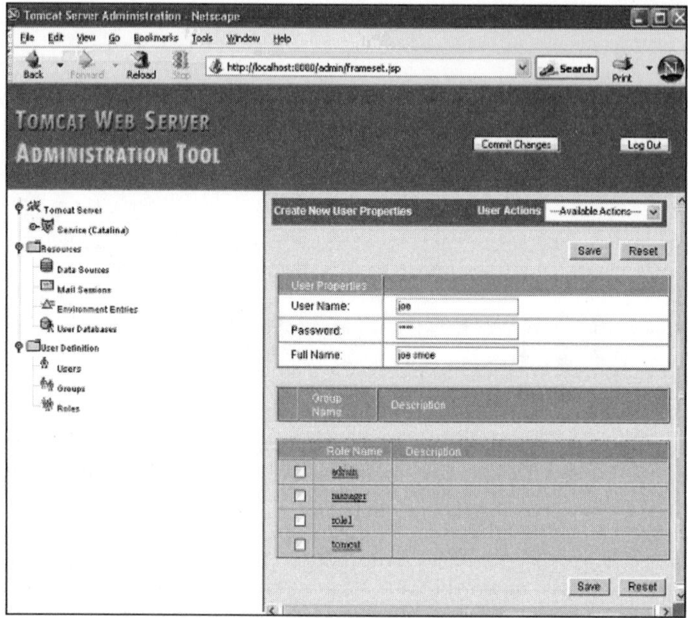

Figure 15-2: Adding a new user via the UserDatabase Realm.

Click the Save button. Note that all the user, password, and role information shown in `admin` are accessed through the configured UserDatabase. Now, after clicking Save, and without shutting down Tomcat, go to the `tomcat-users.xml` file and confirm that the following entry has been added:

```
<user username="joe" password="joe" fullName="Joe Smoe"
roles="admin,manager,role1"/>
```

The Save command caused the UserDatabase implementation to save the changes made to the database to the XML-persistent representation on disk.

In the approach detailed here, the user name and password used for authentication are stored on the server in plaintext. The next section describes how to secure a file-based Realm.

Securing a File-Based UserDatabase Realm

A UserDatabase Realm can be configured in a more secure manner than previously illustrated. While UserDatabase can be made reasonably secure, the ideal solution for secure authentication is to use an alternative Realm (JDBC, JNDI, or JAAS), which is discussed shortly.

The UserDatabase Realm stores passwords in cleartext in the `tomcat-users.xml` file. This is not very secure Therefore, a way must be found to store these passwords in a less readable format. There are four steps to configuring UserDatabase in a secure fashion:

1. Select the password digest algorithm.
2. Create a digested password.
3. Add the digested password to the Realm.
4. Test the digested password.

Selecting the digest algorithm

The choice of digest algorithm is limited to those supported by the `java.security.MessageDigest` class (SHA or MD5). To choose one, the `digest` attribute of the `<Realm>` element in the `$CATALINA/conf/server.xml` file must be set. In this example, SHA will be used:

```
<Realm className="org.apache.catalina.realm.UserDatabaseRealm"
       debug="0" resourceName="UserDatabase" digest="sha" />
```

When a user enters a password at the authentication stage, Tomcat will digest it with the algorithm specified here and then compare it with the value stored in the authentication file.

Creating a digested password

A digested version of the password must now be created. Tomcat comes with a script (`digest.sh` on Linux; `digest.bat` on Windows) located in `$CATALINA/bin` that calculates digests. The algorithm to use (SHA in this case) and the string to digest (`tomcat`, which is our password) must be specified as parameters:

```
$ $CATALINA_HOME/bin/digest -a sha tomcat
tomcat:536c0b339345616c1b33caf454454d8b8a190d6c
```

The output (highlighted in bold) is the string entered, followed by a colon and the SHA hash needed.

Note that as of this writing, Tomcat 4.1 and Tomcat 5 contain a bug that prevents the successful execution of the digest utility. The bug is caused by missing JMX class files in the `CLASSPATH` variable when the digest utility is executed. The following error message is symptomatic of this problem:

```
Tool: Exception creating instance of org.apache.catalina.realm.RealmBase
java.lang.NoClassDefFoundError: javax/management/MBeanRegistration
```

On Windows systems, the bug can be fixed by the following method:

- Change the following line in `$CATALINA/bin/tools-wrapper.bat`

```
set CLASSPATH=%CLASSPATH%;%CATALINA_HOME%\bin\bootstrap.jar
```

  to the following (all on one line):

```
set CLASSPATH=%CLASSPATH%;%CATALINA_HOME%\bin\bootstrap.jar;
%CATALINA_HOME%\common\lib\jmx.jar
```

- Tomcat 4.1 users should change the previous line to the following:

```
set CLASSPATH=%CLASSPATH%;%CATALINA_HOME%\bin\bootstrap.jar; %CATALINA_HOME%\
server\lib\mx4j-jmx.jar
```

On Linux systems, this can be accomplished by a similar process:

- Change the following line in `$CATALINA/bin/tools-wrapper.sh`

```
CLASSPATH="$CLASSPATH":"$CATALINA_HOME"/bin/bootstrap.jar
```

  to the following (all on one line):

```
CLASSPATH="$CLASSPATH":"$CATALINA_HOME"/bin/bootstrap.jar: "$CATALINA_HOME"/
common/lib/jmx.jar
```

- Tomcat 4.1 users should change the line to the following:

```
CLASSPATH="$CLASSPATH":"$CATALINA_HOME"/bin/bootstrap.jar: "$CATALINA_HOME"/
server/lib/mx4j-jmx.jar
```

Adding the digested password to the UserDatabase Realm

The final step is to add the digested password to the UserDatabase Realm for the Tomcat installation. This is accomplished by copying the digested output of the preceding step and adding it as the `password` attribute of a user in `tomcat-users.xml`:

```
<?xml version="1.0"?>
<tomcat-users>
  <role rolename="admin"/>
  <user username="maharaja"
        password="536c0b339345616c1b33caf454454d8b8a190d6c"
        roles="admin"/>
</tomcat-users>
```

Here, a user named `maharaja` with the role of `admin` has been added. This role allows the user to access the example application (as well as the `admin` application that ships with Tomcat).

Testing the digested password

The digested password can be tested by accessing the example Web application. Browse to the following URL:

```
http://localhost:8080/secure/
```

A login page should be presented. Enter **maharaja** as the User name and **tomcat** as the password and click the Log In button. If all goes well, access to the application will be granted.

File-based Realms (such as UserDatabase) are easy to configure and do not depend on external resources to operate. However, they are rather limited because all authentication and authorization data must reside in a file. When the size of the data is large, file-based Realms can become inefficient to manage. The security of file-based Realms is also rather limited. By using an external relational database for authentication data, JDBC-based Realms overcome these limitations. The next section explores the administration of JDBC Realms.

JDBC Realms

A JDBC Realm is a Realm implementation that uses tables maintained in a relational database (such as MySQL or Oracle). Authentication and authorization data reside in an external database, potentially an existing one containing user data. Unlike file-based Realms, JDBC Realms enable the flexible addition, updating, modification, and deletion of authentication data and user/role mappings. Because data in an RDBMS is maintained dynamically, any changes that are made to the content of the authentication data are immediately reflected in the Realm. In addition to the these advantages, sophisticated maintenance and administration tools can be readily created using JDBC to access and maintain the tables within the Realm.

Mapping columns to the required view

The JDBC Realm implementation in Tomcat 5 has a particular view of how the tables in the Realm must be maintained. Fortunately, the configurable parameters of Realms enable you to map to any existing schema containing the same data.

More specifically, the JDBC Realm implementation expects the following tables—in a standard normalized relation.

Table Name	Description
`users`	Contains user name and password information
`user_roles`	Contains user-to-roles mapping information

The `users` table is expected to contain the following two columns as a minimum. It has `user_name` as the primary key (indexed).

Column	Type	Length
`user_name`	`varchar` not `null`	15
`user_pass`	`varchar` not `null`	15

The `user_roles` table is expected to contain the following two columns as a minimum.

Column	Type	Length
`user_name`	`varchar` not `null`	15
`role_name`	`varchar` not `null`	15

Note that the datatype can be any type that results in a character string, and longer length fields will be accommodated.

The compound primary key in this table is `{user_name, role_name}`. This means that a single user can have multiple roles. The `user_name` column in both the `users` and `user_roles` tables can be relationally joined during regular queries.

For maximum flexibility, the mentioned table names and column names are not imposed on the underlying table. Instead, they are mapped during Tomcat run-time to the underlying table. The mapping is specified in the configuration of the `Realm` element.

The JDBC Realm implementation, contained in the `org.apache.catalina.realm.JDBCRealm` class, will assume this configuration while using a JDBC driver to access the data in the Realm.

Realm definitions must be configured in a Realm element within the scope of any container component. Specifically, the JDBC Realm implementation may be configured with the attributes shown in the following table.

Attribute	Description	Required?
`className`	The Java programming language class that implements the JDBC Realm. This should be the implementation provided by Tomcat — `org.apache.catalina.realm.JDBCRealm`.	Yes
`connectionName`	The JDBC connection user name to be used	Yes
`connectionPassword`	The JDBC connection password to be used	Yes
`connectionURL`	The JDBC connection URL used to access the database instance	Yes
`debug`	Controls the level of debugging information that is printed to the log file	No

Attribute	Description	Required?
digest	Specifies the digest algorithm used when the Container Managed Security uses the digest method of authentication. Takes a value that specifies the digest algorithm, such as SHA, MD2, MD5, and so on. (For a complete list of current values, consult the Javadoc java.security.MessageDigest class.)	No
driverName	Name of the JDBC driver, a Java programming language class name	Yes
userTable	The actual name of the table in the database that matches the Users table in the required view	Yes
userNameCol	The actual column name of the column in both the userTable and userRoleTable that matches the user column in the required view	Yes
userCredCol	The name of the column in the userTable that matches the password column in the required view	Yes
userRoleTable	The actual name of the table in the database that matches the user_roles table in the required view	Yes
roleNameCol	The name of the column in the userRoleTable that matches the role_name column in the required view	Yes

The combination of the attributes userTable, userNameCol, userCredCol, userRoleTable, and roleNameCol enables you to map the existing database table and columns containing authentication and role information to the view required by the Realm.

Configuring JDBC Realms with digested passwords

To gain some experience in configuring JDBC Realms, an external MySQL database server will act as the example relational database system. MySQL is free and is available on Linux and Windows; download a copy at www.mysql.com. The installation of MySQL is not covered in this chapter.

Setting up MySQL tables

For JDBC authentication, Tomcat requires a database with at least two tables: users and user_roles. The database is named authority. Here's the SQL to create the database:

```
CREATE DATABASE IF NOT EXISTS authority;

USE authority;

CREATE TABLE users (
   user_name VARCHAR(15) NOT NULL PRIMARY KEY,
   user_pass VARCHAR(32) NOT NULL
);
```

```
CREATE TABLE user_roles (
   user_name VARCHAR(15) PRIMARY KEY NOT NULL REFERENCES users(user_name),
   role_name VARCHAR(10) NOT NULL
);
```

This code can be entered into MySQL interactively through its console, or run as a script:

```
$ mysql < authority.sql
```

After creating the database and tables, users and roles must be added. To make the installation secure, the passwords of the users stored in the `authority` table will be digested. Most databases provide functions for digesting information, and MySQL is no exception. The `MD5()` function will be used in this case. Here's the SQL to add an `admin` user:

```
INSERT INTO users (user_name, user_pass) VALUES ('maharaja', MD5('tomcat'));
```

The JDBC Realm has an attribute called `digest` that is used to specify the digest algorithm to use on the password entered at the authentication stage.

Finally, the role database table must be populated. Here, the `admin` role is added, as it will grant access to the example application:

```
INSERT INTO user_roles (user_name, role_name) VALUES ('maharaja', 'admin');
```

Adding a Tomcat user to MySQL

Tomcat must be given a user name and password in `$CATALINA_HOME/conf/server.xml` that can be used to connect to the database in a JDBC Realm. Therefore, this user must be in the `mysql.user` table. The best way to create a new user is to use the `GRANT` command.

The `GRANT` command creates a user in the `mysql.user` table. MySQL uses this table to determine access privileges to its databases. It is important to restrict access to this table, because unlimited access would allow anyone to change the access rights to every database on the server.

The passwords should not be stored in cleartext, so it is fortunate that MySQL encrypts them automatically with `GRANT`. The following example creates a user called `tomcat` who will be accessing the database from the local machine with the password `tomcat`:

```
mysql> GRANT SELECT ON authority.*
    -> TO 'tomcat'@'localhost' IDENTIFIED BY 'tomcat';
mysql> FLUSH PRIVILEGES;
```

Here, `tomcat` is given `SELECT` privileges on all tables in the `authority` database. This access is sufficient for authentication, but real-world applications may well need more access. The `IDENTIFIED BY` clause specifies the user's password. MySQL automatically obfuscates this value and inserts it into the `user` table as shown here:

```
mysql> SELECT Host, User, Password, Select_priv FROM mysql.user;
+---------------+----------+------------------+-------------+
| Host          | User     | Password         | Select_priv |
+---------------+----------+------------------+-------------+
| localhost     | tomcat   | 22e3be3e311d37ea | N           |
+---------------+----------+------------------+-------------+
```

(Note that there will be a few other records besides the one shown. They don't concern us here.) Older versions of MySQL might not hide the password automatically. In these cases, the following command is needed in place of the earlier command:

```
mysql> GRANT SELECT ON authority.*
    -> TO 'tomcat'@'localhost' IDENTIFIED BY PASSWORD('tomcat');
mysql> FLUSH PRIVILEGES;
```

Remember the `FLUSH PRIVILEGES` line; MySQL won't update its privileges tables without being explicitly told to do so.

The `SET` command can be used to change the password of a user without having to create it afresh:

```
SET PASSWORD FOR 'tomcat'@'localhost' = PASSWORD('new_password');
```

To confirm that the `tomcat` user has indeed been given the appropriate privileges on `authority`, the following query can be used (note the `authority` database in the `Db` column):

```
mysql> SELECT Host, Db, User, Select_priv FROM mysql.db;
+---------------+-----------+--------+-------------+
| Host          | Db        | User   | Select_priv |
+---------------+-----------+--------+-------------+
| localhost     | authority | tomcat | Y           |
+---------------+-----------+--------+-------------+
```

Here, the `Y` in the `Select_priv` column indicates that the user in the `User` column (`tomcat`) has `SELECT` privileges on the table in the `Db` column (`authority`).

A user's privileges can be cancelled with the `REVOKE` command, as shown here:

```
mysql> REVOKE SELECT ON authority.* FROM 'tomcat'@'localhost';
mysql> FLUSH PRIVILEGES;
```

Now that a user for Tomcat has been created, the appropriate Tomcat Realm can be configured.

Defining the MySQL-based JDBC Realm

To define the JDBC Realm, the default `UserDatabase` Realm must be disabled. To do so, comment out the following lines in the `server.xml` file:

```
<!--
<Realm className="org.apache.catalina.realm.UserDatabaseRealm"
       debug="0" resourceName="UserDatabase"/>
-->
```

Next, define a JDBC Realm, mapping the tables and columns from the `authority` database:

```
<Realm className="org.apache.catalina.realm.JDBCRealm" debug="99"
       driverName="com.mysql.jdbc.Driver "
       connectionURL="jdbc:mysql://localhost/authority"
       connectionName="tomcat" connectionPassword="tomcat"
       userTable="users" userNameCol="user_name" userCredCol="user_pass"
       userRoleTable="user_roles" roleNameCol="role_name"
       digest="md5"/>
```

The `connectionURL` points to the database that contains the authentication details, which is accessed using the credentials supplied in the `connectionName` and `connectionPassword` attributes. The lines beginning with `userTable` and `userRoleTable` specify which tables in the database you should be using to look up the user and role for authentication purposes. The `digest` attribute is the algorithm that Tomcat uses to digest the password entered by the user (in this case, MD5). As mentioned earlier, this attribute can be one of the two digest algorithms supported by `java.security.MessageDigest` (SHA or MD5).

Tomcat may already have a MySQL JDBC Realm very similar to the one shown here in `server.xml` but commented out.

The `mm.mysql` JDBC driver must be installed in Tomcat for this Realm to function. This process is detailed in Chapter 14.

Testing the JDBC Realm

To see the Realm in action, start Tomcat and connect to the example Web application via the following URL:

```
http://localhost:8080/secure/
```

You should be presented with the login screen, as shown in Figure 15-3. Enter **maharaja** in the Username field and **tomcat** in the Password field.

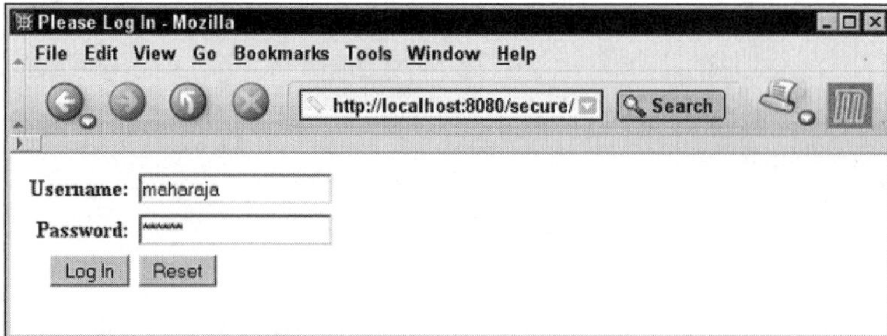

Figure 15-3: Login screen.

Using the JDBC Realm, authentication is now performed against MySQL instead of against the `tomcat-users.xml` file (that is, the UserDatabase file-based Realm). By replacing the JDBC driver and changing the table/column mappings in the Realm configuration, other databases (for example, Oracle) with completely different schemata can be used. As long as the user name, password, and role data are stored somewhere in the database, Tomcat can use this for authentication.

As demonstrated so far, changing the authentication method is easy and requires no code changes to the Web application. Custom login and authentication error forms have also been demonstrated. Some methods for making the authentication process a lot more secure have also been explained.

In some production scenarios, the user authentication and authorization information may not be available in a JDBC-accessible manner. The information may already be stored in directory services and/or external authentication and authorization systems. In some of these cases, configuring a JNDI Realm can enable Tomcat 5 to interoperate with the external systems. The next section describes JNDI Realms.

JNDI Realms

The Java Naming and Directory Interface (JNDI) is a standard Java API that provides applications with a unified interface to several different naming and directory services (such as SUN's NIS, Microsoft's ADS or NT Domains, and Novell's Netware Directory Service).

The JNDI architecture has two components: an API that is used by client-side applications to access the naming/directory services, and a Service Provider Interface (SPI), which allows vendors to develop custom Providers for their naming/directory servers. These Providers enable different directory servers to be "plugged in" in a manner transparent to the client application.

Lightweight Directory Access Protocol (LDAP) is one such directory protocol. OpenLDAP (`www.openldap.org`) and Netscape Directory Server (`http://enterprise.netscape.com/products/identsvcs/directory.html`) are two popular implementations of LDAP.

Further information on JNDI can be found at the following URL:

```
http://java.sun.com/products/jndi/docs.html
```

Similar to JDBC Realms, JNDI Realms enable you to use existing data in a directory service for a Realm. To use a JNDI Realm, you must be able to successfully map the various configuration attributes to an existing directory schema. This again is similar to the JDBC table and column name mapping. To better understand how this mapping works, the following table describes the configuration attributes that are available with a JNDI Realm.

Attribute	Description	Required?
`className`	Java programming class name of the JNDI Realm implementation. Must be set to `org.apache.catalina.realm.JNDIRealm`.	Yes
`connectionName`	The user name used to authenticate against the directory service via JNDI	Yes
`connectionPassword`	The password used to authenticate against the directory service via JNDI	Yes
`connectionURL`	The URL used to locate the directory service using JNDI	Yes
`contextFactory`	Configures the Java programming language class used to create a context for the JNDI connection. The default LDAP-based factory is sufficient in all noncustom cases.	No

Table continued on following page

Attribute	Description	Required?
`debug`	Controls the level of debugging messages that will be logged	No
`digest`	Specifies the digest algorithm used to store a password. By default, passwords are store as plaintext.	No
`userPassword`	Maps the name of the directory attribute from the user element that contains the password information	Yes
`userPattern`	Specifies an LDAP pattern for searching the directory for selecting user entry. Use the `{0}` as a placeholder for the distinguished name.	Yes
`roleName`	Maps the name of the directory attribute that contains the role name	Yes
`roleSearch`	Specifies an LDAP pattern for searching the directory for selecting roles entry. Use the `{0}` as a placeholder for the distinguished name, or `{1}` as a placeholder for the user name.	Yes
`roleBase`	Specifies the base element for role searches. The default is the top-level element.	No
`roleSubtree`	The default is `false`. If set to `true`, a subtree search will be conducted for the role.	No

The configurable attributes reveal that the user name must map to individual elements at the top-level directory context. Each group of users assigned to the same role must also map to the individual element at the top-level directory context.

Configuring the JNDI Realm

A JNDI Realm stores data in an LDAP directory server (such as Netscape Directory Server, OpenLDAP, and so on) and accesses it using a JNDI Provider.

This configuration example uses OpenLDAP as the directory server. OpenLDAP can be downloaded from `www.openldap.org/software/download/` and is available in open source under the OpenLDAP Public License (`www.openldap.org/software/release/license.html`).

Coverage of OpenLDAP is beyond the scope of this chapter. You can find information on LDAP at the following Web sites:

- *OpenLDAP: A quick start guide*

  `www.openldap.org/doc/admin/quickstart.html`

- *OpenLDAP 2.1 Administrator's Guide*

  `www.openldap.org/doc/admin/`

Configuring a JNDI Realm is more complex than configuring UserDatabase or JDBC Realms. The configuration involves a five-step process, as described in the following sections.

Installing the JNDI Driver

Place the JNDI driver JAR file in the `$CATALINA_HOME/server/lib` directory (if you do not need it visible to Web applications) or the `$CATALINA_HOME/common/lib` directory. The JNDI driver JAR file is typically named `ldap.jar` and can be downloaded from `http://java.sun.com/products/jndi/`.

Creating the LDAP Schema

After installing the JNDI driver, you create the LDAP schema for storing the user and role data. This step is different for each directory server: Refer to your LDAP server documentation for further information.

Before creating the schema, there are some design issues to be considered. Connections to the directory server can be made either anonymously or by using the user name and password specified in the Realm configuration by the `connectionName` and `connectionPassword` properties (see the section "Configuring the Realm," later in this discussion). An anonymous connection is sufficient in most cases.

Authentication of a user by a directory server can be done in two "modes": **bind mode** and **comparison mode:**

- *Bind mode* — In bind mode, user authentication is done by "binding" to the directory server using the **distinguished name** (**DN**) of the user and the password presented by the user. If the bind succeeds, the user is considered authenticated.

  Thus, in bind mode, the directory server does the actual authentication. The directory server saves a digested version of the user's password, and it converts the user's password to its digested version before comparing it. Therefore, the `digest` attribute in the Realm configuration in `server.xml` is ignored. However, this means that the password is transmitted as cleartext from Tomcat to the directory server. This is not the same as transmitting the password from the user's browser to the Tomcat end. Here, mechanisms such as HTTP Digest or even HTTPS may be used. Several LDAP servers support SSL connections, so this can be used to protect the transmission of passwords as cleartext.

- *Comparison mode* — In comparison mode, the Realm retrieves the password from the directory and does the comparison of the passwords itself. To enable comparison mode, you must specify the `userPassword` attribute of the Realm directive to the directory attribute that contains the user's password.

Bind mode is more secure, because in comparison mode the configuration enables the Realm to read the user's password.

Another disadvantage of comparison mode is that the Realm implementation must handle password digests (in case the directory server stored the digested version of the password) and all the variations of the digest algorithms.

There are two approaches to storing roles in the JNDI directory:

- *Explicit directory entries*—Roles can be represented as explicit directory entries. In this case, the `roleBase`, `roleSubtree`, `roleSearch`, and `roleName` attributes in the Realm directive are used. These are discussed in more detail in the section "Configuring the Realm," later in this chapter.
- *Attributes of the user entry*—Alternatively, roles can also be represented as attributes in the user's LDAP directory entry. In this case, the `userRoleName` attribute (discussed later) in the Realm configuration should be set appropriately.

Populating the Directory

Now you are ready to populate the LDAP directory with the users for the `admin` and `manager` roles. This is required to use the `admin` and `manager` Web applications.

The following shows sample entries for the `admin` and `manager` roles, and a user (user1) who is listed in both roles:

```
# Top-level entry
dn: dc=companyname,dc=com
objectClass: dcObject
dc:companyname

# Entry to contain people
# The searches for users are based on this entry.
dn: ou=people,dc=companyname,dc=com
objectClass: organizationalUnit
ou: people

# User entry for role 'admin' and 'manager'
dn: uid=user1,ou=people,dc=companyname,dc=com
objectClass: inetOrgPerson
uid: user1
sn: user1
cn: super user1
mail: root@companyname.com
userPassword: secret

# Entry to contain LDAP groups
# The searches for roles are based on this entry.
dn: ou=groups,dc=companyname,dc=com
objectClass: organizationalUnit
ou: groups

# Entry for the "manager" role
dn: cn=manager,ou=groups,dc=companyname,dc=com
objectClass: groupOfUniqueNames
cn: manager
uniqueMember: uid=user1,ou=people,dc=companyname,dc=com

# Entry for the "admin" role
dn: cn=admin,ou=groups,dc=companyname,dc=com
objectClass: groupOfUniqueNames
cn: admin
uniqueMember: uid=user1,ou=people,dc=companyname,dc=com
```

The previous data is in LDIF format, and it can be uploaded into OpenLDAP using the `ldapadd` tool:

```
$ ldapadd -f tomcat.ldif -x -D "cn=LDAPRootuser,dc=companyname,dc=com" -w password
```

In this example, `tomcat.ldif` is the file that contains the data about the roles and users in LDIF format. The value passed via the `-D` flag is that of the distinguished name used to bind to the directory server. This is the DN of a super-user who has the right to update the LDAP directory, and it authenticates itself via a password (the `-w` option). This super-user was configured in the `rootdn` directive in `slapd.conf`. The following is a sample entry:

```
database ldbm
suffix dc="companyname",dc="com"
rootdn "cn=LDAPRootUser,dc=companyname,dc=com"
rootpw password
```

Creating a user to access the directory

Next, create an OpenLDAP user who has read access to the data published in the LDAP directory. The default OpenLDAP configuration gives read access to all users (except the super-user, who has write access too). This is a security risk, especially if the passwords are being stored as cleartext. The following code is a sample from the OpenLDAP configuration file, which indicates restricted access to the `userPassword` attribute (the name of the attribute, in this configuration, that contains the Realm user password):

```
access to attr=userPassword
   by dn="cn=tomcatuser,dc=companyname,dc=com" read
   by * none
```

Configuring the Realm

The Realm directive varies depending on how users bind to the LDAP directory. The following sample configuration is for an LDAP server running on the same machine (hence the localhost in the `connectionURL`), and has users logging in using a user ID (see the `userPattern` attribute specifying this):

```
<Realm   className="org.apache.catalina.realm.JNDIRealm"
         connectionURL="ldap://localhost:389"
         userPattern="uid={0},ou=people,dc=companyname,dc=com"
         roleBase="ou=groups,dc=companyname,dc=com"
         roleName="cn"
         roleSearch="(uniqueMember={0})"
/>
```

Finally, restart Tomcat 5 in order to make it re-read the Realm configuration.

Adding Roles and Users

You can add a role or a user using the `ldapadd` command as discussed earlier in the section "Populating the Directory."

Other LDAP implementations (such as Netscape Directory Server) have GUI-based interfaces that make this simpler.

Removing a Role or a User

The `ldapremove` command is used to remove a user or role from the LDAP database:

```
$ ldapremove  "uid=user1,ou=people,dc=companyname,dc=com" -x -D
"cn=LDAPRootuser,dc= companyname,dc=com" -w password
```

Here `"uid=user1,ou=people,dc=companyname,dc=com"` is the distinguished name of the user being deleted. The same command works for removing a role. You just specify the DN of the role to be deleted.

As before, the value passed via the `-D` flag is that of the distinguished name used to bind to the directory server. This is the DN of a super-user who has rights to update the LDAP directory, and it authenticates itself via a password (the `-w` option).

The latest addition to Tomcat 5's built-in Realm support is the JAAS Realm. With the integration of JAAS into the JDK platform starting with JDK 1.4, this Realm implementation is likely to become more relevant and important in the near future. The next section shows how to work with a JAAS Realm.

JAAS Realm

The JAAS Realm uses the Java Authentication and Authorization Service (JAAS) to authenticate a user and provide access control.

JAAS enables the use of Pluggable Authentication Modules (PAM). With PAMs, the authentication technology is abstracted out, and thus the back-end authentication technology can be rendered transparent to the application making the request.

Following is some of the basic terminology relevant to JAAS Realms. This is not a tutorial on JAAS, and further information, including Javadocs and downloads, can be found at the following URL:

```
http://java.sun.com/products/jaas/
```

- *Subject* — The Subject (`javax.security.auth.Subject` class) is the identity that you wish to authenticate
- *Principal* — The Principal (`java.security.Principal`) represents the interaction of a Subject with an authenticating authority
- *LoginContext* — This is a Java class that acts as a session with the authentication Provider. It also loads the Provider class after reading its configuration file.
- *Provider* — This is a class that implements the `javax.security.auth.spi.LoginModule` interface, and contains the code for the actual authentication strategy.

JAAS is packaged along with JDK 1.4, although an optional download is available for JDK 1.3 from the following URL:

```
http://java.sun.com/products/jaas/
```

Configuration of a JAAS Realm

Configuring JAAS Realms is a five-step process:

1. Perform the setup required for the actual authentication technology.
2. Write or obtain a Provider for the authentication technology.
3. Configure the Provider.
4. Make changes to the Java security policy (if required).
5. Configure the Realm directive.

Performing the setup required for the actual authentication technology

JAAS provides an API interface to the authentication technology. You first need to perform setup steps, if required, for this. For example, if you were using JNDI at the back end, you would need to install and configure a JNDI directory server.

Writing or obtaining a Provider for the authentication technology

The Provider (discussed earlier) is a Java class that implements the `javax.security.auth.spi.LoginModule` interface. A Provider must implement the methods of this interface—namely, those shown in the following table.

Method	Description
`initialize`	Initializes the LoginModule
`abort`	Aborts the authentication process
`commit`	Commits the authentication process
`login`	Authenticates a Subject
`logout`	Logs out a Subject

The Provider would also make use of a `Principal` class (an implementation of the `java.security.Principal` interface) that represents users and roles in this particular implementation. For example, JAAS comes with implementations for Windows NT users and domains (`com.sun.security.auth.NTUserPrincipal` and `com.sun.security.auth.NTDomainPrincipal`).

JAAS also provides some Provider implementations as a part of the `jaasmod.jar` JAR file. These include a JNDI Provider (`com.sun.security.auth.module.JndiLoginModule`), an NT Login Provider (`com.sun.security.auth.module.NTLoginModule`), and a Solaris Login Provider (`com.sun.security.auth.module.SolarisLoginModule`).

In some cases, third-party vendors also provide Providers for their products.

Configuring the Provider

You must add configuration statements for the Provider in a configuration file. For some Providers (such as the Solaris and NT Login Providers), this is a very simple setup. The following code is a sample of the JAAS Provider configuration for Solaris' Login Provider:

```
SolarisLogin {
  com.sun.security.auth.module.SolarisLoginModule required;
};
```

Other Providers (such as the JNDI Provider) have a more complex setup (see following sample). In general, the configuration attributes are Provider-specific:

```
JNDILogin {
  com.sun.security.auth.module.JndiLoginModule required
  user.provider.url="ldap://localhost:389/ou=People,dc=companyname,dc=com"
  group.provider.url="ldap://localhost:389/ou=Group,dc=companyname,dc=com";
};
```

The configuration for the Provider is passed to the JRE through the `java.security.auth.login.config` environment parameter.

Making changes to the Java security policy (if required)

The JAAS authentication Provider class is a trusted part of the system, and hence requires special access permissions. The following code is a sample Java policy file that shows the kind of permissions required:

```
//trust the Provider
grant codeBase "file:./provider/" {
  permission java.security.AllPermission;
};

//trust JAAS
grant codeBase "file:/path/to/jaas.jar" {
  permission java.security.AllPermission;
};

//these permissions are needed by the client
grant codeBase "file:./client/" {
  permission javax.security.auth.AuthPermission
                              "createLoginContext";
  permission
         javax.security.auth.AuthPermission "doAs";
  permission java.util.PropertyPermission
                               "user.home", "read";
};
```

This policy file is passed to the JRE through the `java.security.policy` environment parameter.

In addition, JAAS has a format for specifying access rights for authenticated users. In the following example, the user `user1` has read permissions in the `user.home` directory:

```
grant Principal com.sun.security.auth.NTUserPrincipal "user1" {
   permission java.util.PropertyPermission
                              "user.home", "read";
};
```

This policy file is passed to the JRE through the `java.security.auth.policy` environment parameter. From JDK 1.4 onward, you don't need a separate policy file for this, and you can combine it with the previous security policy file.

Configuring the Realm directive

The following table describes the configuration attributes for the JAAS Realm element.

Attribute name	Description	Required
`className`	This is the classname of the java class that implements JAAS Realms. This must be `org.apache.Catalina.realm.JAASRealm`.	Mandatory
`debug`	The debug level. A missing or '`0`' (zero) valued debug level turns off debugging.	
	The log file to which log messages are sent is specified in a Logger directive.	Optional
`appName`	The application name passed to the JAAS `LoginContext`, which uses it to select the set of relevant LoginModules. This name should match the name of the enclosing block in the JAAS Provider configuration.	Mandatory
`roleClassNames`	Comma-delimited list of `javax.security.Principal` classes that represent security roles	Mandatory
`userClassNames`	Comma-delimited list of `javax.security.Principal` classes that represent individual users	Mandatory

A sample configuration directive from `server.xml` is shown here:

```
<Realm className="org.apache.catalina.realm.JAASRealm"
       appName="Tomcat"
       roleClassNames="com.wrox.APrincipalImpl"
       userClassNames="com.wrox.AnotherPrincipalImpl"/>
```

Tomcat must be restarted in order for the Realm configuration changes to take effect.

Adding or deleting users and roles

Adding or removing users and roles in a JAAS Realm is specific to the back-end technology being used for authentication. For example, if NT Realms are used, adding a user would be equivalent to creating a new NT login account.

Single Sign-on

If two or more Web applications deployed in Tomcat are configured to use authentication, the user will be prompted to authenticate, even if the same user uses the same credentials for both applications.

Fortunately, a special Tomcat mechanism enables users to only log in once in such scenarios: the Single Sign-on Valve. For detailed information on using this Valve, see Chapter 8.

In the next section, you will examine SSL, which adds another level of security to the sample application in this chapter by preventing prying eyes from looking at data in transit.

Encryption with SSL

Secure Sockets Layer (**SSL**) is a protocol that enables secure communication between clients and servers in a network environment. Originally developed by Netscape, it has since been adopted as an Internet standard. SSL enables the encryption of traffic between the client and the server, and also provides an authentication mechanism. (This was briefly described earlier in this chapter in the discussion about the HTTP client certificate).

The security protocols on which SSL is based are **public key encryption** and **symmetric key encryption.** In public key encryption, a pair of encryption keys are used to encode a message: one is a publicly available key, and the other is a private key that is not disclosed to anyone else. Clients who want to send a message to an application that has a known public key need to encrypt it with that key. Only the corresponding private key can then decrypt the message, and thus the transmission is secure. Symmetric key encryption, conversely, uses the same (secret) key for both encryption and decryption. This algorithm, however, needs a reliable way to exchange the secret key between the two end points in the transmission.

When a client opens an SSL connection with a server, an **SSL handshake** is performed. The procedure for an SSL handshake is as follows:

1. The server sends its digital certificate to the client. This contains the public key of the server, information about the server, the authority that issued the certificate to the server, and the validity of the certificate.
2. The client then authenticates the server based on the validity of the certificate and the trustworthiness of the authority that issued the certificate. Certificates issued by well-known and trusted **Certificate Authorities** (**CAs**), such as VeriSign and Thawte, are recognized by most Web browsers. If the certificate cannot be validated, the user is warned and can choose to either accept the certificate or deny it.
3. A session key is then generated and exchanged over the connection. At this point, the connection is secured by the public key encryption mechanism, and so the exchange is secure. The session key is a symmetric key and is used for the duration of the session to encrypt all subsequent data transmissions.

The server configuration may also require the client to present its own authentication. Later in this chapter, you will see how the `clientAuth` Tomcat attribute is used to enable this feature. In this situation, another step is introduced in the SSL handshake. Such a requirement is not common, and is used only in some business-to-business application environments.

The HTTPS (HTTP over SSL) protocol, as the name suggests, uses SSL as a layer on top of HTTP. Transport Layer Security (TLS) is the IETF (Internet Engineering Task Force) version of the SSL protocol. It is defined by RFC 2246 (`www.ietf.org/rfc/rfc2246.txt`), and is intended to eventually supersede SSL.

Adding support for SSL or TLS in Tomcat is a four-step process:

1. An SSL implementation must be downloaded and installed.
2. A certificate **keystore** must be created, to which a self-signed certificate is added.
3. A certificate must be obtained from a third-party CA such as VeriSign (`www.verisign.com/`), Thawte (`www.thawte.com/`), or Trustcenter.de (`www.trustcenter.de/`). The self-signed certificate created above is used to generate a certificate-signing request.

   If Tomcat is being used in a test/development environment, this step can be skipped. In production environments, a CA-signed certificate may be desirable so that users will be willing to accept the certificate.
4. Tomcat must be configured for SSL.

JSSE

Java Secure Socket Implementation (**JSSE**) is Sun's implementation of the SSL and TLS protocols. JSSE is available free, but is not open source. For more information on JSSE, please see the following URL:

```
http://java.sun.com/products/jsse/
```

Installing JSSE

JSSE is bundled with Java starting with JDK 1.4.0. Users of earlier JDK versions will need to install it manually (note that JDK 1.2 or newer is required).

JSSE can be downloaded from `http://java.sun.com/products/jsse/`. The three JSSE JAR files (`jsse.jar`, `jnet.jar`, and `jcert.jar`) can be either installed in the JDK for use by all applications, or placed in an application-specific location. To make JSSE available to all applications, copy all three JAR files to the JDK Standard Extensions directory, which is located at `$JAVA_HOME/jre/lib/ext`.

Preparing the Certificate Keystore

JSSE uses a keystore for the storage and retrieval of certificates. The keystore is simply a file. The commands for preparing a certificate keystore are as follows:

On Windows:

```
> %JAVA_HOME%\bin\keytool -genkey -alias tomcat -keyalg RSA
```

On Linux:

```
$ $JAVA_HOME/bin/keytool -genkey -alias tomcat -keyalg RSA
```

The `–genkey` option specifies that a key pair (private key and public key) must be created. This key pair is enclosed in a self-signed certificate. The `-keyalg` option specifies the algorithm (which in this case is RSA) to be used for the key pair. All keystore entries are accessed via unique aliases using the `-alias` option. Here, the alias is specified as `tomcat`.

The `keytool` command will ask for a password. The password can be set to the value Tomcat expects by default (`changeit`) or some other value. If the password is something other than the default, Tomcat's `keystorePass` attribute will need to be changed, as shown later.

The default name for the keystore file is `.keystore` and it is stored in the user's home directory. This directory will vary depending on the operating system. On Linux, the `keystore file` would need to be in `/home/[`*`username`*`]`. On Windows 2000/XP, the `keystore` file would be in `C:\Documents and Settings\[`*`username`*`]`. An alternative keystore filename can be specified using the `-keystore` option. The password can also be specified on the command line with the `-keypass` option. Both of these methods are shown here:

```
$ $JAVA_HOME/bin/keytool -genkey -alias tomcat -keyalg RSA -keypass somepass
-keystore /path/to/keystorefile
```

Figure 15-4 shows the `keytool` command being run.

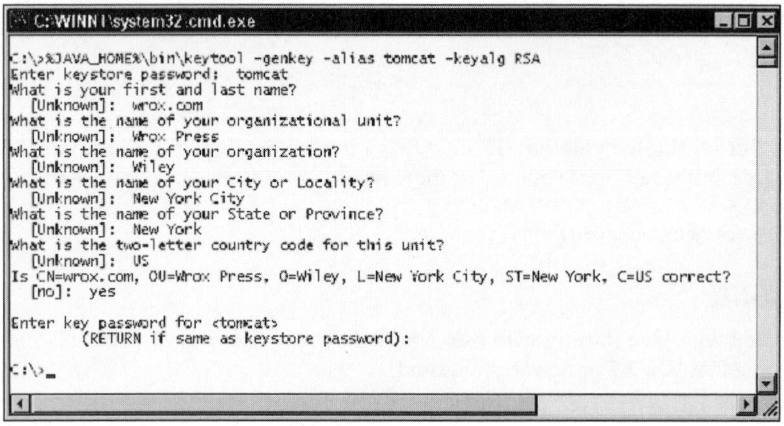

```
C:\WINNT\system32\cmd.exe

C:\>%JAVA_HOME%\bin\keytool -genkey -alias tomcat -keyalg RSA
Enter keystore password:  tomcat
What is your first and last name?
  [Unknown]:  wrox.com
What is the name of your organizational unit?
  [Unknown]:  Wrox Press
What is the name of your organization?
  [Unknown]:  Wiley
What is the name of your City or Locality?
  [Unknown]:  New York City
What is the name of your State or Province?
  [Unknown]:  New York
What is the two-letter country code for this unit?
  [Unknown]:  US
Is CN=wrox.com, OU=Wrox Press, O=Wiley, L=New York City, ST=New York, C=US correct?
  [no]:  yes

Enter key password for <tomcat>
        (RETURN if same as keystore password):

C:\>_
```

Figure 15-4: Creating the certificate keystore.

Notice the Common Name (CN) field that has been entered as "wrox.com." This must be of the format "www.domainname.com," "hostname.domainname.com," or just "domainname.com." This name is embedded in the certificate. The CN should be the fully qualified host name for the machine on which Tomcat is deployed. If not, users will get a warning message in their Web browser when they try to access a secure page from Tomcat.

If this is a test/development environment, or a CA-issued certificate is not desired, the SSL setup is completed and now Tomcat-related setup changes must be performed.

The steps for obtaining a CA-signed certificate are covered in the next section.

Installing a Certificate from a Certificate Authority

To obtain a certificate from a CA, first a local certificate must be created using the `keytool` command:

```
$ keytool -genkey -alias tomcat -keyalg RSA
```

Next, this certificate is used to create a Certificate Signing Request (CSR):

```
$ keytool -certreq -keyalg RSA -alias tomcat -file certreq.csr
```

The `keytool` option (`-certreq`) creates a CSR file called `certreq.csr` that can be submitted to the CA to get a certificate. Figure 15-5 shows an example of this process.

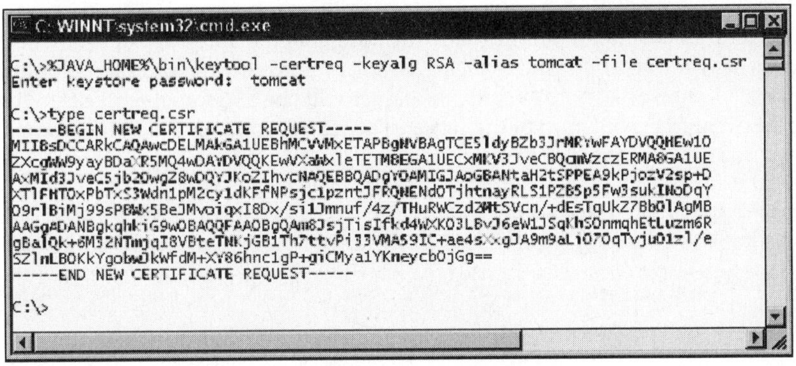

```
C:\WINNT\system32\cmd.exe

C:\>%JAVA_HOME%\bin\keytool -certreq -keyalg RSA -alias tomcat -file certreq.csr
Enter keystore password:  tomcat

C:\>type certreq.csr
-----BEGIN NEW CERTIFICATE REQUEST-----
MIIBsDCCARkCAQAwcDELMAkGA1UEBhMCVVMxETAPBgNVBAgTCESldyBZb3JrMRYwFAYDVQQHEw1O
ZXcgWW9yayBDaXR5MQ4wDAYDVQQKEwVXaWxleTETMBEGA1UECxMKV3JveCBQcmVzczERMA8GA1UE
AxMId3JveC5jb20wgZ8wDQYJKoZIhvcNAQEBBQADgYOAMIGJAoGBANtaH2tSPPEA9kPjozV2sp+D
XTlFHTOxPbTxS3Wdn1pM2cy1dKFfNPsjclpzntJFRQNENdOTjhtnayRLS1PZBSp5Fw3sukINoDqY
O9rlBiMj99sPBWx5BeJMvoiqxI8Dx/si1Jmnuf/4z/THuRWCzdZMtSVcn/+dEsTqUkZ7BbOlAgMB
AAGgADANBgkqhkiG9w0BAQQFAAOBgQAm8JsjTisIfkd4WXKO3LBvJ6eW1JSqKhSOnmqhEtLuzm6R
gBalQk+6M32NTmjqI8VBteTNKjGB1Th7ttvPi33VMA59IC+ae4sXxgJA9m9aLiO7OqTvjuO1zl/e
SZlnLBOKkYgobwJkWfdM+XY86hnc1gP+giCMya1YKneycbOjGg==
-----END NEW CERTIFICATE REQUEST-----

C:\>
```

Figure 15-5: Generating the Certificate Signing Request.

Obtaining a certificate requires payment to the CA for the authentication services. However, some CAs offer test certificates at no cost, although they are usually valid only for a limited time. To submit the CSR, visit VeriSign (`www.verisign.com`), Thawte (`www.thawte.com`), or Trustcenter.de (`www.trustcenter.de`).

After you have the certificate from the CA, you must get the Chain Certificate (also called the Root Certificate) from the CA. For VeriSign, this can be downloaded from the following site:

```
www.verisign.com/support/install/intermediate.html
```

The Chain Certificate is a self-signed certificate from the CA that contains its well-known public key. You can view the contents of a certificate using the `–printcert` option:

```
$ keytool -printcert -file /path/to/certificate
```

This is good practice before importing a third-party certificate into the keystore. You then import the Chain Certificate into the keystore:

```
$ keytool -import -alias root -trustcacerts -file
<filename_of_the_chain_certificate>
```

Here, the `<filename_of_the_chain_certificate>` contains the Chain Certificate that you got from the CA.

Finally, you import the new certificate:

```
$ keytool -import -alias tomcat -trustcacerts -file <your_certificate_filename>
```

In the next section, you will examine Tomcat-related setup changes.

Protecting Resources with SSL

Resources can be protected with SSL just as they can be protected with authentication constraints. The `<user-data-constraint>` sub-element of `<security-constraint>` in `web.xml` is used to specify the guaranteed integrity of the data flowing between the client and the server for this resource. There are three levels of integrity: `NONE`, `INTEGRAL`, and `CONFIDENTIAL`.

`NONE` means there is no guarantee that the data has not been intercepted and tampered with, while `INTEGRAL` guarantees the integrity of the data (meaning that the data has not been interfered with). The strongest guarantee is `CONFIDENTIAL`, which guarantees that a third-party has not intercepted the data. If you specify `INTEGRAL` or `CONFIDENTIAL`, the server will use SSL for all requests to this resource by redirecting the client to the SSL port of the server. The redirection port is configured in the `redirectPort` attribute of the HTTP Connector.

For the `secure` application introduced earlier, the `CONFIDENTIAL` level will be used. This is accomplished by adding the following element to the `<security-constraint>` in the example `web.xml` file:

```
<security-constraint>
  ...
  <user-data-constraint>
    <description>
     Constrain the user data transport for the whole application
    </description>
    <transport-guarantee>CONFIDENTIAL</transport-guarantee>
  </user-data-constraint>
</security-constraint>
```

This will force all requests for the `secure` Web application to use HTTPS, even if the original came in over HTTP. This is the only setup required in `web.xml`. The next section considers changes to `server.xml`.

Tomcat Setup

The setup procedure for Tomcat is straightforward, but different for Tomcat 4.1 and Tomcat 5. Both versions come with a handy HTTP Connector already set up for SSL, so it will only need to be modified.

Tomcat 4.1

Locate the following `<Connector>` element in `server.xml`:

```
<!--
<Connector className="org.apache.coyote.tomcat4.CoyoteConnector"
           port="8443" minProcessors="5" maxProcessors="75"
           enableLookups="true"
           acceptCount="10" debug="0" scheme="https" secure="true"
           useURIValidationHack="false">
  <Factory className="org.apache.coyote.tomcat4.CoyoteServerSocketFactory"
           clientAuth="false" protocol="TLS" />
</Connector>
-->
```

To use this Connector, the `<!--` and `-->` comment tags must be removed from around the `<Connector>` element. Next, the SSL-related settings are configured within the `<Factory>` element. If a nondefault password was used for the keystore (that is, any password but "changeit"), that password must be added here (shown in bold):

```
<Factory className="org.apache.coyote.tomcat4.CoyoteServerSocketFactory"
         clientAuth="false" protocol="TLS"
         keystorePass="tomcat" />
```

Tomcat 5

Locate the following `<Connector>` element in `server.xml`:

```
<!--
<Connector port="8443"
           maxThreads="150" minSpareThreads="25" maxSpareThreads="75"
           enableLookups="false" disableUploadTimeout="true"
           acceptCount="100" debug="0" scheme="https" secure="true"
           clientAuth="false" sslProtocol="TLS" />
-->
```

To use this Connector, the `<!–` and `–>` comment tags must be removed from around the `<Connector>` element. Next, if a nondefault password was used for the keystore (that is, any password but "changeit"), the `keystorePass` attribute must be added to the `<Connector>` element containing the keystore password, as shown in the following example (in bold):

```
<Connector port="8443"
           maxThreads="150" minSpareThreads="25" maxSpareThreads="75"
           enableLookups="false" disableUploadTimeout="true"
           acceptCount="100" debug="0" scheme="https" secure="true"
           clientAuth="false" sslProtocol="TLS" keystorePass="tomcat" />
```

To test this feature, start Tomcat and request the following URL:

```
http://localhost/secure/
```

If a CA-signed certificate was not used, the browser will display a warning about the certificate (note that this warning may vary depending on your browser), as shown in Figure 15-6.

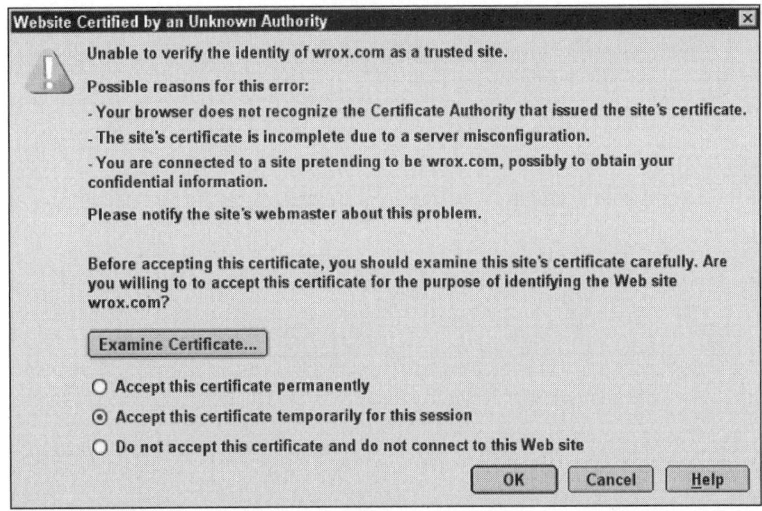

Figure 15-6: Warning about a certificate not signed by a Certificate Authority.

Host Restriction

The last security mechanism to be considered in this chapter is perhaps one of the most effective and least complex: host restriction.

Rather than allow any user from any location in the entire Internet to use a Web application, system administrations may configure Tomcat to only accept HTTP requests from either a specific IP address or a range of IP addresses. Requests from any other source will simply be ignored.

Tomcat restricts the hosts allowed to access an application through the use of the Request Filter Valve. For details, see Chapter 8.

Summary

This chapter has covered a broad range of techniques for securing Tomcat itself and Tomcat-hosted applications. To conclude this chapter, let's review some of its key points:

- Unnecessary default Tomcat applications that may pose potential security risks should be disabled.
- The default Tomcat security-related settings should be changed as these could be used to attack the Web site.
- Tomcat should be run under a Tomcat-specific account with limited permissions.
- The Java Security Manager can be used to limit the operations that Web applications may perform.
- Web applications can be secured by using standard mechanisms for authentication and access control.
- SSL can be used to secure important data communication between the Web server and the browser.
- Access to Web applications can be restricted to certain IP addresses or range of IP addresses.

Chapter 16 discusses shared hosting using Tomcat.

16

Shared Tomcat Hosting

With the introduction of the Tomcat JSP/Servlet container by the Apache Software Foundation, hosting providers around the world have started providing world-class Servlet/JSP support to their customers. Typically, these hosting services are based on shared hosting in which hundreds of sites can be running on a single computer. The hosting services allow for the sharing of resources such as the Web server, the database server, the mail server, and various other services. Thus, all the services that are typically used in this scenario must have built-in support for shared hosting.

The following shared hosting topics are covered in this chapter:

- An introduction to virtual hosting terminology
- Virtual hosting using Apache HTTPd and Tomcat
- Setting up Tomcat to work behind Apache HTTPd using `mod_jk2`
- Options for tuning Tomcat resource usage in a hosting situation

This chapter examines how Tomcat lends itself for use in a shared hosting scenario. The first concept to be covered is virtual hosting that helps Web servers (such as Apache) to work. This is fundamental because Tomcat interacts with Web servers quite intimately. The development cycles of Tomcat 4 and now Tomcat 5 has enabled the integration of Tomcat and Apache to progress to a mature stage of development.

During the evolution of Tomcat and Apache, many incompatible versions of the integration software were developed. This meant that upgrading Tomcat from version 3 to version 4 would require significant changes to the integration configuration. Fortunately for everyone using the well-integrated Apache HTTPd server and Tomcat, the configuration of Tomcat 4 and Tomcat 5 with Apache using `mod_jk2` are identical.

Apache 2.0.43, Tomcat 5, and `mod_jk2` are used for all of the examples in this chapter.

Virtual Hosting

In this chapter, a Web site refers to the contents of a distinct **Fully Qualified Domain Name (FQDN)**, which is served by a Web server. Strictly, a FQDN consists of two parts: a host name and a domain name. For example, the FQDN `www.wrox.com` consists of the host name `www` and the domain name `wrox.com`. The domain name `wrox.com` has other hosts such as `customer` and `xmail`, whose FQDNs would be `customer.wrox.com` and `xmail.wrox.com`. However, because the distinction between an FQDN and a domain name is not relevant in this discussion, the terms are used interchangeably.

As of November 2003, nearly 45 million Web sites were contacted by Netcraft (source: `http://news.netcraft.com/archives/web_server_survey.html`) as part of their monthly Web server survey. This shows the enormous number of Web servers that provide their services on the Internet. A standard Web server in a default configuration only allows one domain to be served from the machine. For a host provider to serve hundreds of domains from its location would mean setting up hundreds of computers for serving all the Web sites. Certainly, this is not a scalable solution.

In addition, IP addresses are an increasingly scarce resource. A Web-hosting provider gets a limited number of IP addresses from its connectivity providers for hosting. Using one IP address for every Web host would quickly eat up all the allocated IP addresses. To overcome these limitations, **virtual hosting** is used to make optimal use of all our available resources (be it services, IP addresses, or other computing resources).

The first topic to examine is the Apache Web server and how it implements Web virtual hosting in two ways:

- *IP-based virtual hosting*—Based on **multihoming hosts** (that is, machines with multiple network interface cards (NICs), each with distinct IP addresses), every domain to be served is allocated one IP address. The Web server listens to each of these network interfaces, and serves resources from the relevant domain based on the IP address from which the request arrived.
- *Name-based virtual hosting*—The Web server listens on the IP addresses configured on the host, and serves resources from the relevant Web site, based on the HTTP request headers from the Web client.

IP-Based Virtual Hosting

In **IP-based virtual hosting**, a machine is configured to have a number of IP addresses equal to the number of hosts it will serve. Therefore, a machine that is to host 10 Web sites would need 10 IP addresses configured. These additional IP addresses may be configured either by adding physical network interfaces (NICs) to the machine, or, as is more common, by adding aliased network interfaces to the computer.

Normally, when an NIC is added to a machine, it is configured with a single IP address, which is used by various services. However, it is possible to configure the same NIC with more than one IP address. Adding these additional IP addresses involves using operating-system-specific commands for first creating a virtual interface and then configuring it with a virtual IP address. This process normally involves using a physical NIC and adding virtual interfaces on top of it, a process also commonly known as **aliasing.**

For example, on Linux, using the `ifconfig` command adds a virtual interface and configures the NIC with an IP address at the same time. If an Ethernet interface named `eth0` has already been configured, it is simple to add an aliased interface called `eth0:1` (in Linux, virtual Ethernet interfaces are named with the syntax `<physical-interface-name>:<virtual-interface-index>`), using the following command:

```
$ ifconfig eth0:1 <virtual-IP> netmask <virtual-IP-netmask>
```

Implementing IP-Based Virtual Hosting in Apache

Adding IP-based virtual hosts in Apache is trivial. Merely add a `<VirtualHost>` block to Apache's `httpd.conf` file for each corresponding Web site, and a few associated parameters. Let's look at a sample configuration:

```
<VirtualHost 192.168.1.200>
    ServerName www.somedomain.com
    DocumentRoot /home/websites/www.somedomain.com/web
    ServerAdmin support@somedomain.com
    ErrorLog /home/sites/www.somedomain.com/log/error
    TransferLog /home/sites/www.somedomain.com/log/access
</VirtualHost>

<VirtualHost 192.168.1.201>
    ServerName www.otherdomain.com
    DocumentRoot /home/websites/www.otherdomain.com/web
    ServerAdmin support@otherdomain.com
    ErrorLog /home/websites/www.otherdomain.com/log/error
    TransferLog /home/websites/www.otherdomain.com/log/access
</VirtualHost>
```

Here, two IP-based virtual hosts, `www.somedomain.com` and `www.otherdomain.com`, were configured to run on the IP addresses `192.168.1.200` and `192.168.1.201`, respectively.

Each of the virtual hosts is defined in a `<VirtualHost>` section:

- The `ServerName` directive sets the domain name to be served by this virtual host.
- The `DocumentRoot` directive points to the base directory to be used for serving pages for this domain.
- The `ServerAdmin` directive lists the e-mail address of the Web server administration personnel.
- `TransferLog` and `ErrorLog` point to the log files to be used for Web site access and Web site error messages, respectively.

The two IP addresses used in the `<VirtualHost>` directives should belong to network interfaces for the machine on which Apache would be running. You may have noticed that each of the Web sites has its own document root and its own log files for access and error logging. Various other directives can be placed in these virtual host definitions to enable further customization. Omitting these other directives would cause the virtual host to inherit any values from the global settings in the configuration file.

Avoiding Common Mistakes

Some common mistakes to avoid include the following:

- Apache, in its default configuration, starts up and listens on all the configured network interfaces on the machine. If, for some reason, Apache is configured to listen on only a restricted number of IP addresses on the machine (using the `Listen` directive), it is important to ensure that Apache is listening on all the IP addresses of the various IP-based virtual hosts in order for all of them to work.
- Using any random combination of IP addresses and Web host names will not always work as expected. This is commonly done by configuring the client machine to use a Domain Name Service (DNS) server. The Web client would query this DNS server for the IP address of the given host name, and then use the IP address returned by the DNS server to connect to the Web server. Similarly, the Web server would expect requests for the host name at the IP address specified in the corresponding `NameVirtualHost` directive.

  Needless to say, if the IP address given in the `NameVirtualHost` directive doesn't match the one returned by the DNS server for the host name, the Web client and the server won't be able to talk to each other.
- The FQDN of the Web site can be used in place of the IP address in the `<VirtualHost>` directive. In this case, there should not be any problems in the DNS resolution of the host names in the machine. This is because when Apache starts up, it resolves each of the FQDNs in its `<VirtualHost>` directives to their IP addresses before offering the Web service. Problems in resolving these addresses (for example, when a DNS server cannot be reached in time) during startup can cause Apache to abort prematurely.

Name-Based Virtual Hosting

While IP-based virtual hosts help maximize the use of resources, they are still not feasible in places where hundreds of domains must be hosted on the same machine. Obtaining one IP address for each host or configuring many network interfaces on the same machine becomes a logistical nightmare. In these cases, **name-based virtual hosting** is used.

Name-based virtual hosting depends solely on an extension of the HTTP 1.0 protocol. In an HTTP 1.0 protocol, a Web client or a browser merely had to make a TCP connection to port 80 of a Web server and request a document using a relative location identifier in order for the Web resource to be fetched. For example, to access the document `http://www.somedomain.com/help.txt`, the browser could look up the IP address of `www.somedomain.com`, make a TCP connection to port 80 of the IP address, and get the complete resource just by using the HTTP `GET` command, as shown here:

```
$ telnet 192.168.1.200 80

Trying 192.168.1.200...
Connected to 192.168.1.200.
Escape character is '^]'.
GET /help.txt HTTP/1.0
```

Following is the response returned by the Apache HTTPd server:

```
HTTP/1.1 200 OK
Date: Fri, 21 Nov 2003 05:35:29 GMT
Server: Apache/1.3.26 (Unix) mod_watch/3.12 PHP/4.3.3
Last-Modified: Tue, 23 Jul 2002 02:37:16 GMT
ETag: '77e2ef-199-3d3cc15c'
Accept-Ranges: bytes
Content-Length: 409
Connection: close
Content-Type: text/plain

[... rest of the contents of help.txt]
```

However, this enables only one Web site to be accessed per IP address; otherwise, it would be impossible to discover the host for which the request was intended.

To tackle this problem, the `Host:` header, as introduced in HTTP 1.1, is used to determine the Web site from which the resource is requested. With this new header, the HTTP headers exchanged between an HTTP/1.1-compliant Web client and a server would look like the following from the client:

```
GET /help.txt HTTP/1.0
Host: www.somedomain.com
```

The response from the server would look as follows:

```
HTTP/1.1 200 OK
Date: Fri, 21 Nov 2003 05:36:45 GMT
Server: Apache/1.3.26 (Unix) mod_watch/3.12 PHP/4.3.3
Last-Modified: Tue, 23 Jul 2002 02:37:16 GMT
ETag: '77e2ef-199-3d3cc15c'
Accept-Ranges: bytes
Content-Length: 409
Connection: close
Content-Type: text/plain

[... rest of the contents of help.txt]
```

The additional `Host:` header in the client request helps the Web server distinguish between all the domains that share the same IP address.

Implementing Name-Based Virtual Hosting in Apache

Implementing name-based virtual hosting in Apache is not very different from implementing IP-based virtual hosting. It only requires the addition of the `NameVirtualHost` directive. This directive configures the IP address on which the Apache server will receive HTTP requests for the name-based virtual hosts. Documents should be subsequently fetched depending on the value of this parameter and the related virtual host definition specified later in the configuration.

A sample Apache name-based configuration would look like the following:

```
NameVirtualHost 192.168.1.200

<VirtualHost 192.168.1.200>
    ServerName www.somedomain.com
    DocumentRoot /home/websites/www.somedomain.com/web
    ServerAdmin support@somedomain.com
    ErrorLog /home/websites/www.somedomain.com/log/error
    TransferLog /home/websites/www.somedomain.com/log/access
</VirtualHost>

<VirtualHost 192.168.1.200>
    ServerName www.otherdomain.com

    DocumentRoot /home/websites/www.otherdomain.com/web
    ServerAdmin support@otherdomain.com
    ErrorLog /home/websites/www.otherdomain.com/log/error
    TransferLog /home/websites/www.otherdomain.com/log/access
</VirtualHost>
```

In this configuration, two Web sites, `www.somedomain.com` and `www.otherdomain.com`, are being hosted on the same IP address: `192.168.1.200`. After a request comes to the IP address, Apache uses the `Host:` parameter and the `ServerName` parameter of each of the virtual host definitions to determine the definition to which this request should be sent. The only configuration that must be specified in order to use name-based virtual hosting is to set up DNS settings for each of the FQDN to be hosted so that the client can resolve the IP addresses correctly. Compare this to IP-based virtual hosting, whereby each of the IP addresses also had to be configured on the network interfaces of the machine.

Avoiding Common Mistakes

Some common mistakes to avoid in name-based virtual hosting include the following:

- If a Web request has been made to an IP address listed in the `NameVirtualHost` and the applicable virtual host could not be determined, Apache sends the request to the *first* virtual host block in the Apache configuration for that IP address. The request is *not* sent to the default document root of the whole server. Therefore, the first `<VirtualHost>` section for every `NameVirtualHost` IP address should be a domain where unresolved Web requests could also be handled.
- Because SSL connections are not on HTTP, headers such as `Host:` cannot be extracted in advance. Therefore, it is not possible to have multiple SSL servers running on the same IP address. For this reason, each SSL-enabled Web site must be configured on a unique IP address.
- Older Web clients and many Web access software libraries still use the old HTTP 1.0 protocol. Because they don't send the `Host:` header to the Web server, name-based virtual hosting would not work properly with them. However, these incompatible clients are incredibly rare. It is unlikely that excluding them from a list of supported clients would cause a significant problem. Prominent browsers such as Netscape 2.0+, IE 3.0+, and Lynx 1995+ all support the `Host:` header.

Virtual Hosting with Tomcat

The preceding section explained how to configure Apache to support virtual hosts. This section contains the main focus of this chapter: virtual host support in Tomcat. Before reading further, it is important to consider what would be expected from Tomcat in a shared hosting environment.

Tomcat could work either in a standalone mode (in which it includes support for both an HTTP server and the JSP/Servlet container) or in a cooperative manner (with a Web server such as Apache). For more information about this topic, Chapter 12 provides details on setting up Tomcat with Apache in various ways.

Expecting Tomcat to provide virtual hosting support would mean the following: Given that two or more Web hosts are served from the same machine, when a request comes for a particular resource on one of these hosts, Tomcat should be able to successfully identify the host for which the request had been received, and fetch the required resource from the host document base.

For Tomcat working in a standalone mode, the request in question can target static pages, as well as JSP and Servlets. When working along with another Web server such as Apache, the Web server itself handles the virtual hosts and the processing of subsequent static pages. Therefore, the only thing that must be determined is whether Tomcat could handle the Servlets and JSPs while distinguishing the various hosts involved.

Of course, the Apache Web server can be used to perform additional tasks such as load balancing and clustering. These configuration options are not generally considered for virtual hosting, and are discussed separately in Chapter 12 and Chapter 19.

Because of the extreme similarity of the configuration between Tomcat 4.1 and Tomcat 5 using the JK2 Connectors, the version of Tomcat covered in this section is Tomcat version 5.0 — the upcoming version of Tomcat implementing Servlet 2.4 and JSP 2.0 specifications.

Example Configuration

For the purpose of assigning IP addresses to private networks, the Internet Assigned Numbers Authority (IANA) has assigned three blocks of IP addresses, as specified in the specification document RFC 1918 (`http://www.rfc-editor.org/rfc/rfc1918.txt`). Following are these IP address blocks:

- 10.0.0.0 – 10.255.255.255
- 172.16.0.0 –172.31.255.255
- 192.168.0.0 –192.168.255.255

The following discussion examines how to configure Tomcat to serve two virtual hosts: `europa.dom` and `callisto.dom`.

These virtual hosts will be running on the same machine with the common IP address `10.0.0.1` as an example of name-based virtual hosting. Our private network uses the IP range block `10.0.0.0-10.0.0.255` (that is, every IP address in our network is of the form `10.xxx.xxx.xxx`, with the exclusion of `10.0.0.0` and `10.0.0.255`, which have special meaning in networks). Every IP address in our network is also allocated a host name in the domain named `.dom`.

As is likely in a production scenario, both these domains would be hosted on a directory outside the Tomcat base directory. The hosting scheme that is to be used is as follows.

Each of the domains would have its own document area in `/home/websites/<domain-name>`. Web applications or WAR files would be deployed in a subdirectory named `webapps`. Static HTML pages and scripts, if required, can be kept separate from the Web applications, and would be deployed in a subdirectory named `web`.

As an example for the domain `europa.dom`, a Web application called `shop` would be deployed under `/home/websites/europa.dom/webapps/shop`. Alternatively, the `shop.war` Web application archive could be deployed under `/home/websites/europa.dom/webapps/`. If Apache is required to serve static pages and scripts, they must be deployed using `/home/websites/europa.dom/web/` as the document root. If Tomcat is to be used to serve static pages in a default context, an additional default Web application called `ROOT` is to be deployed as `/home/websites/europa.dom/webapps/ROOT/`, and all static content is to be served from this directory itself.

The Web applications should be kept separate from the static pages because in many cases of a shared hosting scenario, the hosting requirement of the clients would include Tomcat support as an additional feature to their regular Web needs. For most of the clients' static site content, the separate Web directory would suffice, and Apache would handle them without any problems. For clients who want to add Web applications, it is a simple matter to drop their WAR files in the `webapps/` directory without mixing them up with the static content.

For performance reasons, Tomcat is often configured to extract a WAR file to a directory with a similar name. For a Web administrator, the WAR directories would create confusion with those directories created for serving static content. Thus, keeping these two entities (static files and Web applications) separate aids in keeping the directory structure clean and more maintainable, as shown here:

```
/home/websites/
            europa.dom/
                       web/
                       webapps/

            callisto.dom/
                         web/
                         webapps/
```

For the purposes of providing a simple test example, create a sample JSP file, appropriately named `test.jsp`, in the document base of the default context Web application of each of these domains. For example, the file `/home/websites/europa.dom/webapps/ROOT/test.jsp` should contain the following simple code:

```
<html>
  <head>
    <title>Welcome to Europa!</title>
  </head>
  <body>
    <%
      out.println('You are currently viewing the contents of '
                 +'the Europa web server');
    %>
  </body>
</html>
```

Create a similar file as /home/websites/callisto.dom/webapps/ROOT/test.jsp. Remember to change the names for the callisto.dom domain.

Note that the more flexible request.getServerName() method has not been used. This is because if the virtual host setting is not configured correctly, Tomcat (which provides the server environment to the JSP file) would send incorrect host information to the internal JSP handler. The resulting server name displayed on our browsers could be confusing while debugging the configuration for virtual hosting.

Another alternative to this would be to just write the server name in HTML. The JSP as it stands is incredibly simple and unlikely to cause problems, but it is a JSP, and you want to ensure that the configuration is able to serve JSP (and hence Servlets) properly. Incorrectly setting up a virtual hosting scenario could, for example, cause the external Web server itself to serve the JSP file. Because it cannot interpret the JSP source, it would display the unparsed contents of the JSP file itself.

Feel free to change these setup details, such as modifying the contents of the JSP or including additional Web application contexts to suit the server hosting policy required.

Introduction to Virtual Hosting with Tomcat

The task of configuring virtual host support in Tomcat consists of two steps — adding virtual host supporting Web application definitions, which is sufficient if Tomcat is being run as a standalone server, and adding suitable directives in the Apache configuration file ($APACHE_HOME/conf/httpd.conf), if Tomcat is being run as an external Servlet engine. Let's look first at the scenario in which Tomcat is used as a standalone server, serving static pages as well as JSPs and Servlets.

Tomcat Components

Figure 16-1 illustrates the relationship between the various components of Tomcat when Tomcat is being used as a standalone server.

In this case, the Web client directly sends the HTTP request to the Tomcat process listening at port 8080. The HTTP Connector handles the Web client interaction. Tomcat then takes a look at the Host: header present in the HTTP request. If one is present, it tries to look up a virtual host with a name matching the one requested. If such a virtual host is found, the context parameter of the virtual host is taken and merged with the context parameters of the default configuration, and the file served accordingly. The resultant output is sent back to the Web client using the HTTP Connector again.

If no context with the given virtual host is found, Tomcat tries to match the context path to the contexts that do not belong to any virtual hosts. If one is found, that context is used to send back the results. If no such context is found, either the default (with the empty context path) context is used to send back the result (in which case, the context path is matched to a physical directory or filename) or an HTTP 404 error is generated and sent back to the client.

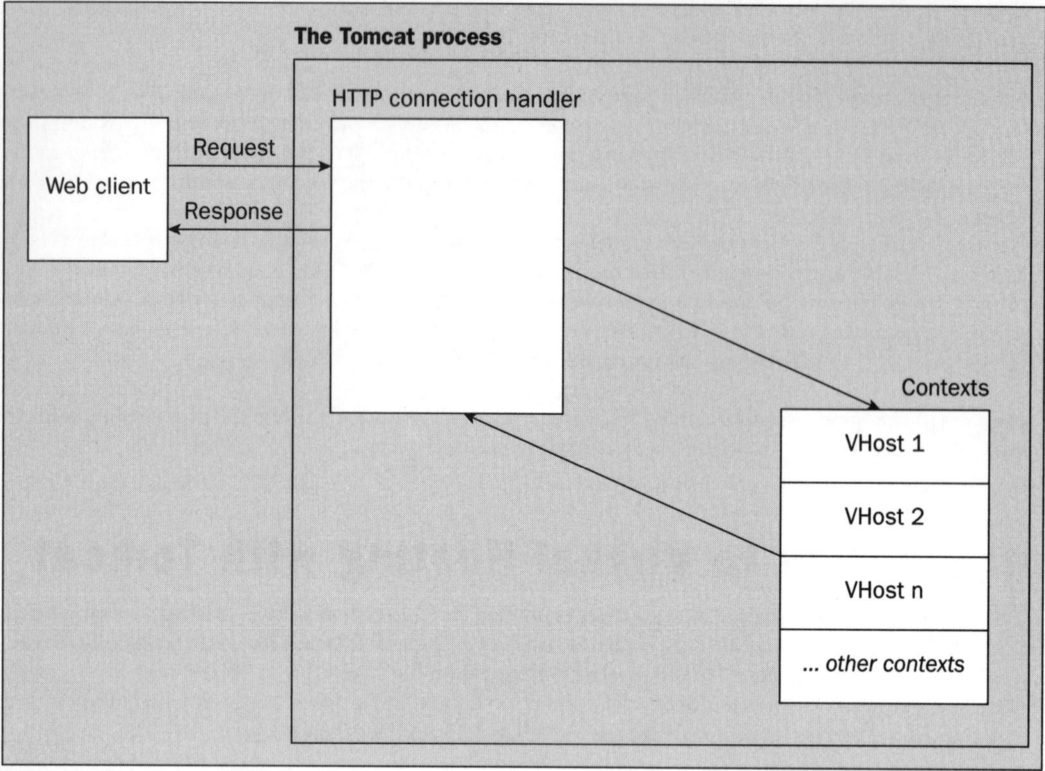

Figure 16-1: Tomcat handling request for a virtual host.

Tomcat 5 as a Standalone Server

Adding a virtual host is as simple as adding additional `<Engine>` entries in `server.xml`. Once these additions have been done, you simply restart Tomcat to use the virtual host definitions.

The default sample `server.xml` file of the Tomcat 5 build contains two services—one for the standalone server and one for the server that cooperates with an Apache Web server using the JK2 protocol. You can remove the definition for the second service and reuse that of the first service. Most of the following configuration already exists in the default `server.xml` file.

The top-level `<Service>` element for the standalone server would look like the following:

```
<Server port='8005' shutdown='SHUTDOWN' debug='0'>
  <Service name='Catalina'>

  </Service>
</Server>
```

The rest of the configuration would be placed inside this `<Service>` container element. The next step is to add the Connectors to be used for this service. Because this is a standalone server, the only Connector required to be configured is the HTTP/1.1 Connector, to enable communication with the outside world.

Add the following Connector definition inside the <Service> element:

```
<!-- Define a non-SSL Coyote HTTP/1.1 Connector on port 8080 -->
<Connector port='8080'
           maxThreads='150' minSpareThreads='25' maxSpareThreads='75'
           enableLookups='false' redirectPort='8443' acceptCount='100'
           debug='0' connectionTimeout='20000'
           disableUploadTimeout='true' />
```

This will configure Tomcat to listen to port 8080 for incoming Web requests.

Now add the <Engine> element to the <Service> element by adding the following lines just after the <Connector> element and inside the <Service> element:

```
<Engine name='Catalina' defaultHost='europa.dom' debug='0'>

</Engine>
```

This specifies an Engine for the service that processes incoming requests from the Connectors. After any request is received by the Connector and passed on to the Engine, the Engine examines the HTTP headers (especially the `Host:` tag) to determine which of the virtual host definitions that it handles should receive the request. If none of the virtual hosts seems to match the request headers, the Engine passes on the request to a default host. The name of the default virtual host is specified in the attribute `defaultHost`. The value of this attribute must match a <Host> definition in the Engine.

The configuration of the `defaultHost` property in the Engine element specifies that any Web requests that are not matched directly by the configured host elements should be served by the virtual host definition for `europa.dom`.

Adding the virtual host definition of `europa.dom` to the Engine is completed by including the following content inside the <Engine> element:

```
<Host name='europa.dom' debug='0'
      appBase='/home/websites/europa.dom/webapps'
      autoDeploy='true'
      unpackWARs='true'>
</Host>
```

This defines a virtual host entry for `europa.dom` in Tomcat. Logging functionality can be added to this virtual host by placing the following content within the <Host> element:

```
  <Valve className='org.apache.catalina.valves.AccessLogValve'
         directory='/home/websites/europa.dom/logs'
         prefix='europa_access.'
         suffix='.log'
         pattern='common'/>

   <Logger className='org.apache.catalina.logger.FileLogger'
           directory='/home/websites/europa.dom/logs'
           prefix='europa_catalina.'
           suffix='.log'
           timestamp='true'/>
```

This defines two logging services for this virtual host. Chapter 5 discusses the <Logger> element.

Finally, the configuration is completed by adding the contexts to serve for this virtual host, inside the <Host> element:

```
        <Context path='' docBase='ROOT' debug='0'/>
        <Context path='/shop' docBase='shop' debug='0' />
```

This has added two contexts here. The first one is the default context with an empty context path. This context has to be either defined explicitly or provided automatically by Tomcat (that is, without explicitly defining it in server.xml) if there is a Web application called ROOT in the appBase of the virtual host.

One important new convenience provided by Tomcat 4 and 5 is that it creates automatic contexts if they exist in the appBase, even if you haven't defined them in the host definition. To provide this functionality, Tomcat looks at directories inside the appBase directory. If these directories follow the Web application structure (specifically, if they contain a WEB-INF/web.xml file in them), Tomcat automatically provides contexts with context paths equal to the name of the directory under appBase.

Remember that the default parameters for these contexts are picked up from ***$CATALINA_HOME/conf/web.xml****.*

However, if there is a need to override some global parameters to these contexts, that configuration is required within the <Context></Context> elements. Examples would include logging for this context in a separate file, context parameters, resource definitions, and so on.

This completes the virtual host definition for europa.dom. For the virtual host callisto.dom, add another virtual host entry similar to that of europa.dom:

Save this file as $CATALINA_HOME/conf/server.xml and restart the Tomcat service.

Now, check the test JSP file in the europa.dom virtual host using the following URL, as shown in Figure 16-2.

```
http://europa.dom:8080/test.jsp
```

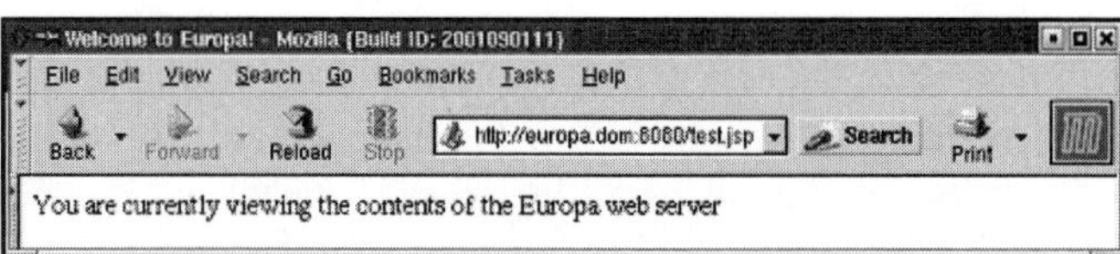

Figure 16-2: test.jsp executing in the Europa virtual host.

Do the same for callisto.dom by using the following URL, as shown in Figure 16-3.

```
http://callisto.dom:8080/test.jsp
```

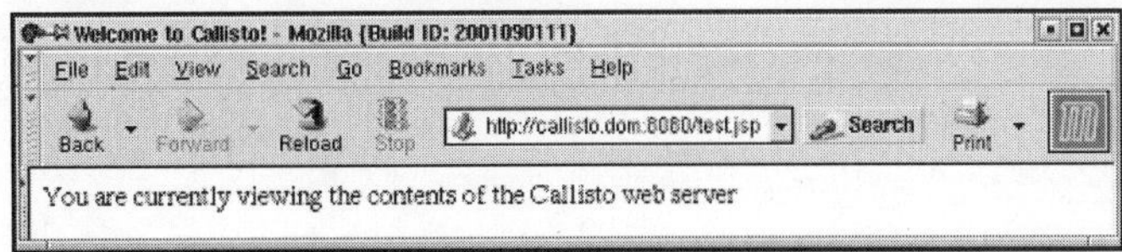

Figure 16-3: test.jsp executing in the Callisto virtual host.

Finally, perform a quick check to determine whether the default host setting of the `<Engine>` element is working properly. For this, use a host name other than the ones specified explicitly as `<Host>` definitions. The easiest way to do this is to try accessing the Tomcat server using the IP address `10.0.0.1` and view the results, as shown in Figure 16-4.

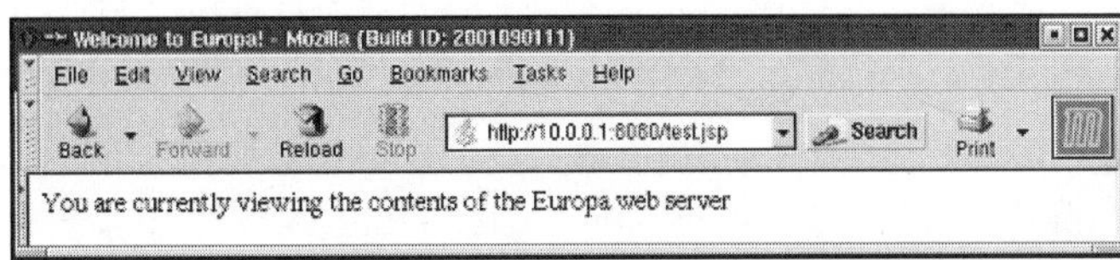

Figure 16-4: test.jsp executing in the Europa virtual host, using the IP address.

As shown in Figure 16-4, Tomcat serves the contents of the `europa.dom` virtual host, as defined in the default virtual host entry of the Engine. Now that Tomcat 5.0 is working as a standalone server for the virtual hosts, the next section provides instructions for creating the configuration to work with the Apache HTTPd.

Tomcat 5 with Apache

When Tomcat is used as an out-of-process Servlet container along with Apache, two sets of configuration must be done: one in Tomcat and the other in Apache.

For Tomcat, the configuration shown in the preceding section remains more or less the same. The only difference is that you can disable the HTTP Connector in the `server.xml` configuration file because it is not being used.

To disable the HTTP Connector, either comment out or remove the following section in `server.xml`:

```
<!-- Define a non-SSL Coyote HTTP/1.1 Connector on port 8080 -->
<Connector port='8080'
           maxThreads='150' minSpareThreads='25' maxSpareThreads='75'
           enableLookups='false' redirectPort='8443' acceptCount='100'
           debug='0' connectionTimeout='20000'
           disableUploadTimeout='true' />
```

At Apache's end, as shown in the previous chapters, an adapter for Tomcat must be used. Here, we will use the `mod_jk2` adapter using the AJP 1.3 protocol for communicating with Tomcat. The AJP protocol is covered in Chapter 11, and `mod_jk2` is covered in Chapter 12.

Figure 16-5 shows a diagrammatic representation of how the components are related. The differences between Figure 16-1 and Figure 16-5 reflect the different information pathways.

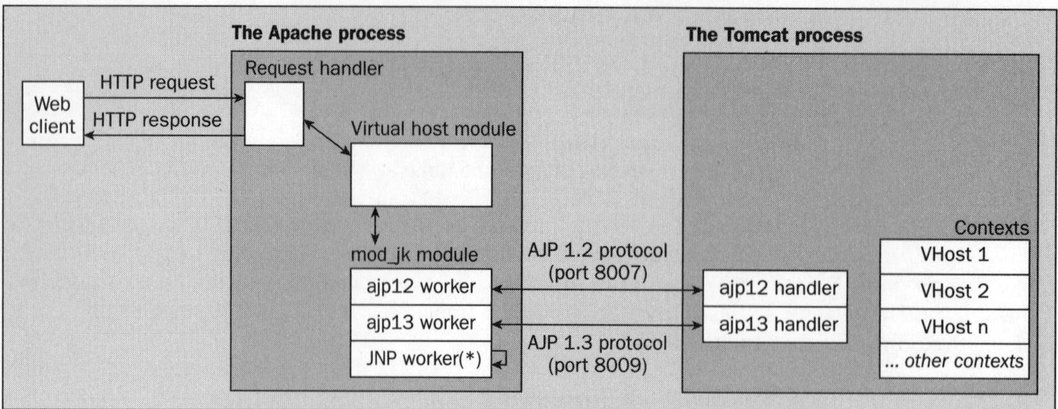

Figure 16-5: Apache and Tomcat serving HTTP requests.

Here, Apache receives the HTTP request from the client. It then looks up the appropriate virtual host entry using the `Host:` parameter in the request. In the virtual host entry, `mod_jk2` is configured to forward all appropriate Servlet and JSP requests to the appropriate worker. The worker would use the AJP 1.3 protocol, or a JNI interface could be used to communicate with a Tomcat process started within the Apache adapter.

While it is possible for all the types of workers to be simultaneously used, it is more common to use a single kind of worker throughout the installation. If the worker is an `ajp13`, it opens a TCP-based AJP 1.3 protocol connection to the Tomcat server, which receives the request via its AJP 1.3 Connector. Tomcat then examines the request to determine whether any of its virtual host definitions match the request. This is similar to the matching process in the standalone Tomcat server. The Servlet response is then sent back through the AJP 1.3 Connector to the `mod_jk2` module. This, in turn, instructs Apache to send the reply back to the Web client.

Configuring Apache

Assuming that `mod_jk2` has been appropriately set up in Apache to communicate with Tomcat as explained in Chapter 12, we now take a look at adding virtual host support to this configuration.

As explained in the section "Apache Name-Based Virtual Hosting," earlier in this chapter, for every virtual host definition you need to add a `<VirtualHost>` section in Apache (in fact, the Tomcat `<Host>` configuration definition is very similar to this concept). Now, along with the rest of the virtual host contents, we add some directives to connect certain resources to Tomcat.

You have two distinct ways available to configure the mapping of the requests within Apache. The first is to use the `<Location>` directive as shown next. This method doesn't require any changes to the `workers2.properties` file and will pass all requests ending in `jsp` to Tomcat.

Modify the `httpd.conf` `<VirtualHost>` elements as follows:

```
NameVirtualHost *
<VirtualHost *>
    ServerName europa.dom
    DocumentRoot /home/websites/europa.dom/web

    <Location '/*.jsp' >
        JkUriSet worker ajp13:localhost:8009
    </Location>

</VirtualHost>

<VirtualHost *>
    ServerName callisto.dom
    DocumentRoot /home/websites/callisto.dom/web

    <Location '/*.jsp' >
        JkUriSet worker ajp13:localhost:8009
    </Location>

</VirtualHost>
```

The `workers2.properties` file consists of the following:

```
[logger.file:0]
level=DEBUG
file=/usr/local/tomcat5/logs/apache_jk2.log
debug=1

[shm:]
info=Shared memory file. Required for multiprocess servers
file=/usr/local/tomcat5/work/jk2.shm
size=1000000

[channel.socket:localhost:8009]
info=Forwarding over socket connection to localhost tomcat instance
host=localhost
port=8009
tomcatId=TC5

[ajp13:localhost:8009]
info=AJP13 worker, connects to tomcat instance using AJP 1.3 protocol
channel=channel.socket: TC5
```

When compared to the Apache virtual host directives shown at the beginning of this chapter, the only major difference is the new `<Location>` and `JkUriSet` directives. These directives are an alternative to providing the `[uri:/*.jsp]` directives in the `workers2.properties` file.

Restart the Apache HTTPd server and access the following previously used test URL:

```
http://europa.dom/test.jsp
```

However, this time, instead of sending the request to port 8080 of the Tomcat Web server, use the standard HTTP port 80 on which Apache should be listening. Notice how the page is rendered correctly.

The second method is to use the `workers2.properties` to control the URI mapping. In this case, the configuration files look as follows:

```
NameVirtualHost *
<VirtualHost *>
    ServerName europa.dom
    DocumentRoot /home/websites/europa.dom/web
</VirtualHost>

<VirtualHost *>
    ServerName callisto.dom
    DocumentRoot /home/websites/callisto.dom/web
</VirtualHost>
```

and

```
[logger.file:0]
level=DEBUG
file=/usr/local/tomcat5/logs/apache_jk2.log
debug=1

[shm:]
info=Shared memory file. Required for multiprocess servers
file=/usr/local/tomcat5/work/jk2.shm
size=1000000

[channel.socket:localhost:8009]
info=Forwarding over socket connection to localhost tomcat instance
host=localhost
port=8009
tomcatId=TC5

[ajp13:localhost:8009]
info=AJP13 worker, connects to tomcat instance using AJP 1.3 protocol
channel=channel.socket: TC5

[uri:europa.dom/*.jsp]
worker=ajp13:localhost:8009

[uri:callisto.dom/*.jsp]
worker=ajp13:localhost:8009
```

The advantage of using the first configuration option is that the entire configuration is made in one place. Unfortunately, the disadvantage is that it does not offer sufficiently fine-grained control over the mapping to the Tomcat server. Because there is only one Tomcat and Apache server, all the requests are passed over the same AJP Connector; then a `<VirtualHost>` configuration with a `<Location>` element in the `httpd.conf` will be mapped and a different `<VirtualHost>` will be successfully displayed, even though this is not what is expected. This behavior is definitely to be avoided., and therefore, it is recommended that the second configuration method be used.

After adding these directives to the Apache `httpd.conf` file, restart Apache and access the following previously used test URL:

```
http://europa.dom/test.jsp
```

However, this time, instead of sending the request to port 8080 of the Tomcat Web server, use the standard HTTP port 80 on which Apache should be listening.

By now, you might be wondering about all the other files that are part of our Web applications. What if Servlets, or HTML pages and images, are part of the deployed Web applications? Trying to access any of those will result in an `Error 404: Not found`.

The easiest way to test this error behavior is to copy the `$CATALINA_HOME/webapps/servlets-examples` directory to `/home/websites/europa.dom/webapps`. This will result in the following directory structure:

```
/home/websites/
           europa.dom/
                     web/
                     webapps/
                       ROOT/
                       servlets-examples/
```

Browse to the following URL and notice how this results in an error:

```
http://europa.dom/servlets-examples/
```

Clearly, there must be a better way to map the requests to Tomcat that doesn't rely on matching the filename suffixes.

The next section describes the resolution to this dilemma.

Request Sharing Between Tomcat and Apache

The Apache server only sends requests to Tomcat when it matches the URI specified in the `workers2.properties` file. Therefore, while there is a defined mapping for the JSPs, there is not a mapping for any of the Web-application contexts.

What is happening is that `mod_jk2` is not listening for requests on the `servlets-examples` context, and those requests are being handled by Apache itself. Because the document root of Apache is different from that of the Tomcat contexts, Apache doesn't find the file and returns an error. Even if the document root of Apache and the `servlets-examples` context are the same, it still wouldn't solve the problem, because Apache doesn't understand JSP—Tomcat does. Therefore, Apache would end up displaying the contents of the JSP file instead of parsing and interpreting it as required.

What you need is a way to pass the requests made to the context to Tomcat. Fortunately, Tomcat enables you to do this with a small addition to `workers2.properties`. Modify the `uri` for the context so the configuration is as follows:

```
[uri:europa.dom/*]
worker=ajp13:localhost:8009

[uri:callisto.dom/*.jsp]
worker=ajp13:localhost:8009
```

Pay careful attention to the differences between the files, and note that the URI extension for europa.dom has been changed from *.jsp to *.

With this configuration in place, the expected contents of http://europa.dom/servlets-examples/ should be displayed.

However, is this current configuration what is desired? To see why this might not be the best configuration, put a sample HTML file in the <VirtualHost> document root (/home/websites/europa.dom/web) and try to access it through the browser. This will result in an HTTP 404 error, and careful scrutiny of the error message that appears indicates that Tomcat, not Apache, is generating the error this time.

What is happening now is that Tomcat has taken over all the references of the root URL, including static files, but this is not what is wanted. Tomcat is needed to handle only Servlets and JSPs.

Unfortunately there is no easy solution for this. With the JK2 configuration, there is no way to easily separate the Servlets and JSPs. The best solution is to map to non-ROOT contexts on the Tomcat server. An example using the servlets-examples context is to modify the workers2.properties file as follows:

```
[uri:europa.dom/servlets-examples/*]
worker=ajp13:localhost:8009

[uri:callisto.dom/*.jsp]
worker=ajp13:localhost:8009
```

Now, instead of blindly sending all root references to Tomcat, mod_jk2 is sending much more specific URLs.

Upon restarting the Apache server, try to access the test JSP file. The results should confirm that it works. Now try to access the file that you created earlier in the static HTML document root (for example, in /home/websites/europa.dom/web) and try to access it. This time it works.

However, it is important to note an important constraint while deploying Tomcat in this configuration. If Tomcat has a default context in the Web application, you *must* have the DocumentRoot of the <VirtualHost> directive point to the docbase of the default context. Otherwise, default context documents would simply not be accessible.

Fine-Tuning Shared Hosting

The previous sections have provided examples for standard configuration of shared hosting with Tomcat. However, every host provider has several other specific requirements for providing Tomcat-based services to multiple clients. This section provides two common configuration enhancements for Tomcat:

- Creating separate JVMs for each virtual host
- Setting memory resource limits for each Tomcat JVM

Creating Separate JVMs for Each Virtual Host

The entire preceding configuration focused on how multiple hosts could be served from the same Tomcat process. While this would suffice for many providers, others would rightly raise the issue of security between the virtual hosts.

Because all the virtual hosts lie in the same request-processing Engine, trusted contexts in these virtual hosts (which can access Tomcat internal objects, load/unload other `webapps`, and so on, such as the default `manager` Web application) would have access to the common Tomcat internal classes and can hence encroach on each other's territory.

This would be a logistical nightmare. One possible solution would be to set up one `<Engine>` per virtual host in the same `server.xml` file. Because each `<Service>` container element in the file could have only one child `<Engine>` element, this would mean adding one service per virtual host, with the accompanying Engine. However, because every Service has its own set of Connectors, this would also mean setting up different Connectors listening on different ports for each Engine. Therefore, each virtual host in the Apache configuration would have to forward to a different worker.

While this removes the problem of sharing information between the virtual hosts, it still causes a bit of discomfort when one considers how a relaxed security policy in Tomcat can give one domain enough privileges to bring down the whole Tomcat process.

The more secure (albeit more resource-intensive) solution to such possible security problems is to have one Tomcat process per virtual host. Luckily, Tomcat has support for running multiple Tomcat processes using the same Tomcat binary installation.

Tomcat depends on two environment variables to find its internal classes. These variables are used to find the configuration-specific files, and are named `$CATALINA_HOME` and `$CATALINA_BASE`:

- `$CATALINA_HOME` is needed for any Tomcat build to function properly. Tomcat uses this variable to find the location of internal classes and libraries.
- `$CATALINA_BASE` is used by Tomcat to find the location of the configuration-specific files and directories, such as configuration files, the scratch directory in which JSPs are compiled, log files, and the various Web applications. In case `$CATALINA_BASE` is not set, it defaults to the value of `$CATALINA_HOME`.

Therefore, to have separate Tomcat processes, all that is required is to set the value of `$CATALINA_BASE` to a different area of the disk for each virtual host, with its own `server.xml` file. This `server.xml` file would have only one virtual host definition, different Connector port numbers, and different directories for logs, scratch areas, and so on.

This setup requires the duplication of the directory trees that are specific to each implementation. While disk space is relatively cheap, this does introduce additional system administration overhead. Later in this chapter, some simple scripts are provided to illustrate how Tomcat server instances can be more easily managed.

As an example, for the two virtual domains that we would be serving, we can store their respective configurations in two different directories under `/home/websites/<domain-name>/catalina`. Therefore,

$CATALINA_HOME could be equal to /usr/local/tomcat/build. For europa.dom, $CATALINA_BASE could be /home/websites/europa.dom/catalina, and for callisto.dom, $CATALINA_BASE could be set to /home/websites/callisto.dom/catalina.

The server.xml file of europa.dom located at /home/websites/callisto.dom/catalina/conf/server.xml should then be modified as follows:

- Change the attribute port of the <Server> root element that is used to shut down the Tomcat process. We'll keep it at 8105.
- Change the AJP Connector port to 8109.
- Ensure that only the virtual host definition of europa.dom is present, and that the default host of the <Engine> is set to this domain.

The relevant sections of the europa.dom server.xml file should end up looking like the following:

```
<Server port='8105' shutdown='SHUTDOWN' debug='0'>
  <Service name='Catalina'>

    <Connector port='8109'
               enableLookups='false' redirectPort='8443' debug='0'
               protocol='AJP/1.3' />

    <Engine name='Catalina' defaultHost='europa.dom' debug='0'>

      <Host name='europa.dom' debug='0'
          appBase='/home/websites/europa.dom/webapps'
          autoDeploy='true'
          unpackWARs='true'>

          <Valve className='org.apache.catalina.valves.AccessLogValve'
              directory='/home/websites/europa.dom/logs'
              prefix='europa_access.'
              suffix='.log'
              pattern='common' />

          <Logger className='org.apache.catalina.logger.FileLogger'
              directory='/home/websites/europa.dom/logs'
              prefix='europa_catalina.'
              suffix='.log'
              timestamp='true'/>

          <Context path='' docBase='ROOT' debug='0' />
      </Host>

    </Engine>
  </Service>

</Server>
```

For the server.xml file of callisto.dom located at /home/websites/callisto.dom/catalina/conf/server.xml, the changes should be as follows:

- Change the <Server> port to 8205.
- Change the AJP Connector port to 8209.
- Ensure that only the virtual host definition of callisto.dom is present, and that the default host of the <Engine> element is set to this domain.

The relevant sections of the callisto.dom server.xml file should end up looking like the following:

```
<Server port='8205' shutdown='SHUTDOWN' debug='0'>
  <Service name='Catalina'>

    <Connector port='8209'
               enableLookups='false' redirectPort='8443' debug='0'
               protocol='AJP/1.3' />

    <Engine name='Catalina' defaultHost='callisto.dom' debug='0'>

      <Host name='callisto.dom' debug='0'
          appBase='/home/websites/callisto.dom/webapps'
          autoDeploy='true'
          unpackWARs='true'>

          <Valve className='org.apache.catalina.valves.AccessLogValve'
              directory='/home/websites/callisto.dom/logs'
              prefix='callisto_access.'
              suffix='.log'
              pattern='common' />

          <Logger className='org.apache.catalina.logger.FileLogger'
              directory='/home/websites/callisto.dom/logs'
              prefix='callisto_catalina.'
              suffix='.log'
              timestamp='true'/>

      </Host>

    </Engine>
  </Service>

</Server>
```

With the addition of the extra Tomcat instance, the Apache configuration needs updating. However, in this case, we are running two different Tomcat instances, each with an AJP 1.3 worker listening on a unique port. Therefore, we need to inform our Apache Connector, using the workers2.properties file, that we would be connecting to two different workers running on different ports.

The AJP worker properties file is changed to look like the following. This example simply reflects the addition of the new worker with the modified ports, and the configuration changes to send the requests to the appropriate worker. While making these changes, make sure that the ports specified for the workers match the ports specified in the `workers2.properties` file for the correct hosts:

```
[uri:europa.dom/*]
worker=ajp13:europa.dom:8109

[uri:callisto.dom/*]
worker=ajp13:callisto.dom:8209

[channel.socket:europa.dom:8109]
host=europa.dom
port=8109
tomcatId=europa.dom

[channel.socket:callisto.dom:8209]
host=callisto.dom
port=8209
tomcatId=callisto.dom

[ajp13:europa.dom:8109]
channel=channel.socket: europa.dom

[ajp13:callisto.dom:8209]
channel=channel.socket: callisto.dom
```

For example, the Tomcat instance serving the `europa.dom` domain has its AJP1.3 Connector listening on port 8109. Therefore, the `ajp13:europa.dom` port is set to `8109`.

The Apache `workers2.properties` file is now changed to reflect the new worker names. Notice how the names have changed from `localhost` to the domain name of the servers that are serviced by the Connectors.

All that is required now is to start the two instances of Tomcat with the `$CATALINA_BASE` set to the `catalina` subdirectory of the domains. To aid in the system administration task, write a shell script to start all the Tomcat instances as required. Create the following shell script with the name `start_sites.sh` in `$CATALINA_HOME` and make it executable:

```
#!/bin/bash

SITE_ROOT='/home/websites'
SITES=`ls ${SITE_ROOT}`

for x in ${SITES}
do
        CATALINA_BASE='${SITE_ROOT}/${x}/catalina'
        echo 'Starting server: ${x} . Using CATALINA_BASE=${CATALINA_BASE}'

        export CATALINA_BASE
        ${CATALINA_HOME}/bin/startup.sh
done
```

Similarly, create a shell script for shutting down all the servers. This shell script is created with the name `shut_sites.sh` in `$CATALINA_HOME` and should also be made executable:

```
#!/bin/bash

SITE_ROOT='/home/websites'
SITES=`ls ${SITE_ROOT}`

for x in ${SITES}
do
        CATALINA_BASE='${SITE_ROOT}/${x}/catalina'
        echo 'Shutting server: ${x} . Using CATALINA_BASE=${CATALINA_BASE}'

        export CATALINA_BASE
        ${CATALINA_HOME}/bin/shutdown.sh
done
```

Now, stop all the instances of Apache and Tomcat in the system. Start the Tomcat instances using the `start_sites.sh` script and follow it by starting the Apache daemon.

These startup and shutdown scripts could now be used in a system initialization script such as the `rc` init scripts kept in `/etc/init.d` on Linux systems.

This section has provided the necessary configuration to have independent Tomcat processes for each of the virtual sites.

Setting Memory Limits on the Tomcat JVM

Whether all the virtual hosts are running under the same Tomcat process or separate Tomcat processes are allocated for each of them, there is still the risk of a resource problem.

> *The problem is that a Java VM at startup allocates a fixed amount of memory for dynamic allocation. With several JVMs running, this number might be either too high (choking the virtual hosts that need more memory, or too low (causing sub-optimal performance for the various hosts).*

Depending on the number and the type of virtual hosts running on the one machine, it is likely that a hosting environment will want to optimize these settings. This setting of memory (more specifically, heap memory that is used while allocating all dynamic data structures) is done by setting a command-line parameter for the Java executable when the Tomcat process is started.

The options that can be set are as follows:

- Initial Java heap size — using parameter `-Xms`
- Maximum Java heap size — using parameter `-Xmx`
- Java thread stack size — using parameter `-Xss`

For example, to set an initial heap size of 20MB (or 20 × 1024 × 1024 = 20971520), the value to be passed to the JVM as a parameter is `-Xms20971520` (or the more succinct `-Xms20m`).

Factors Determining Memory Requirements

The nature of the applications being run on the JVM determines the optimum heap sizes. Heavy multi-threaded servers such as Tomcat that have a tendency to frequently allocate/de-allocate objects are quite sensitive to heap size because a lot of memory can be held up at times, waiting to be garbage-collected. Increasing the heap size in such scenarios can help a lot.

Conversely, very large heap sizes should be avoided by keeping `-Xmx` low. If other apps overload the machine, the heap could start using the swap space (that is, space allocated on the hard disk as an extension of RAM, when all the memory in RAM has been used up). This is also known as **virtual memory.** It reduces the performance of the system significantly. While a reasonable amount of swap usage is common for production servers, serious cases of continuous swapping, commonly known as **thrashing,** could slow the machine to a crawl.

The JVM normally starts with as little memory as possible, as specified in `-Xms`, and then slowly increases memory needs as required by the application, to the limit specified in `-Xmx`. If there is enough memory, it is possible to set `-Xms` to the same value as `-Xmx`. This could result in a faster startup time for the Java application. Always keep `-Xms` to a reasonable size to make applications more responsive.

The default value for `-Xms` and `-Xmx` (which differs from platform to platform) is normally too small for server applications. In addition, the heap resizing from `-Xms` to `-Xmx`, happening slowly over time, causes the server to slowly pick up performance. To reduce this startup latency, set both these limits to the same value. However, if memory needs are minimal, this configuration will lose the advantage of the JVM automatically choosing the optimum heap size (between `-Xms` and `-Xmx`) for the Tomcat server.

When adding processors to a Symmetric MultiProcessing (SMP) machine, be sure to increase memory, because unlike memory allocations, which can be parallelized over the SMP, garbage collection cannot be. Therefore, it could soon become the bottleneck in the application.

Heavy, database-oriented applications consume a lot of memory because of result sets, temporary tables resulting from `JOIN` statements, and so on.

Ultimately, optimum heap sizes can only be determined by examining specific parameters such as the following:

- How many Tomcat instances will be running?
- What kind of traffic is expected by the site?
- Does the Web application use a lot of data transactions involving heavily filled up databases?
- How much RAM is available to be installed in the machine?
- How many processors does the machine have?

Setting Memory Limits in Tomcat

The parameters for setting the memory that is passed to the JVM can be set in the environment variable `JAVA_OPTS`. For easy system administration, the simplest option is to modify the multiple-Tomcat-process starting script created earlier to send these options to the JVM, so that each of the virtual hosts is restricted to these limits.

The modified script would look like the following. Here, the configuration parameters set the minimum and maximum heap limits of each Tomcat instance to 20MB and 50MB, respectively:

```
#!/bin/bash

JVM_OPTIONS='-Xms20m -Xmx50m'
SITE_ROOT='/home/websites'
SITES=`ls ${SITE_ROOT}`

for x in ${SITES}
do
        CATALINA_BASE='${SITE_ROOT}/${x}/catalina'
        echo 'Starting server: ${x} . Using CATALINA_BASE=${CATALINA_BASE}'

        export CATALINA_BASE
        JAVA_OPTS='${JVM_OPTIONS}'
        export JAVA_OPTS
        ${CATALINA_HOME}/bin/startup.sh
done
```

It is important to modify the values in `JVM_OPTIONS` as appropriate for the specific hosting requirements.

Summary

This chapter covered various topics related to using Tomcat-based sites in a shared hosting scenario. Following are some of the key points discussed:

- Apache's HTTP server supports IP as well as name-based virtual hosting.
- Tomcat can be set up for virtual hosting both in its standalone configuration as well as with an Apache HTTP server front-end.
- Running separate JVMs for each virtual host is a recommended security practice, although it is resource intensive.
- Controlling resource usage is important in a shared environment, and hence parameters such as initial/maximum heap size and thread stack size can be configured for each virtual host.

This chapter specifically discussed the configuration of Tomcat for a shared hosting scenario. More information on configuration of Apache HTTPd and Tomcat for load balancing can be found in Chapter 12.

Chapter 17 discusses server load testing.

17

Server Load Testing

So far in this book, the topics of installing, configuring, and securing a distributed Tomcat environment have been examined. After expending the effort needed to install, configure, and tweak an installation, it is indeed a sad moment for a system administrator to see it all subverted because the application server buckles under a production load. Therefore, it is vital that administrators verify the performance characteristics of their Web applications *before* they are deployed for production use.

Server load testing is a commonly used technique for measuring the performance of a Web application. Server load testing is the process of simulating client requests so that a server can experience large amounts of activity in a controlled environment. If the performance of the application fails to live up to its requirements, steps can, and should, be taken to correct the situation.

This chapter illustrates the process of server load testing and describes some general optimization techniques. By the end of the chapter, you will

- Understand the importance of load testing
- Know how to load test with the Jakarta JMeter framework and interpret the results
- Learn some basic strategies for optimizing Tomcat's performance

The Importance of Load Testing

The goal of load testing is to determine both the *performance* and *scalability* of a Web application. **Scalability** is the ability of a system to handle an increased load without a severe degradation of performance. Thus, the notion of scalability is related to (but distinct from) that of **performance.**

To illustrate this point, consider two fictional Web sites: Widget World and Foo Bar. Suppose that when one or two Web clients request pages from Widget World or from Foo Bar simultaneously, they receive them in an average of 250 milliseconds (ms). Thus, the two sites can be said to perform fairly well. However, when 20 Web clients request pages from the two sites, Foo Bar's performance degrades to an average of 1,800 ms per request, while Widget World continues to serve up pages at an average rate of 250 ms per request. Widget World, therefore, is considered *scalable* (that is, it can handle scaled up loads gracefully), whereas Foo Bar is not.

The concept of scalability goes beyond designing a Web application to handle as many users as possible. Software, no matter how well written, cannot defy the laws of physics. There is a point at which even the best Web application will fail to scale up to ever-increasing demands because of the hardware limitations of the physical server upon which it runs. Therefore, scalability also reflects the capability of a Web application to maintain an acceptable level of performance when new hardware resources are added to it. Many Web applications fail to scale because they were never designed to function across multiple servers, or they fail to take advantage of all the hardware resources available to them.

Without load testing, administrators cannot know how scalable a Web application is, so they cannot accurately predict if a Web application will be able to perform adequately to service its anticipated load levels. Furthermore, load testing can tell an administrator at what point the application will fail, which is important information to know as the popularity of a Web application increases. Thus, it is very important to load test Web applications before placing them in production.

Load Testing with JMeter

Unless an administrator has a large number of people with Web browsers and a lot of spare time, special software is required to load test a Web application by simulating a heavy load.

There are numerous such load testing applications available, including open source software and commercial packages (some affordable, some extremely expensive), and some people even choose (usually erroneously) to write their own load tester. In this chapter, one of the sister projects of Tomcat, Apache Jakarta JMeter, is used as the load testing solution. JMeter is one of the finer solutions available. It is even capable of load testing FTP, JDBC data sources, and Java objects! This chapter's discussion focuses on load testing HTTP servers and applications.

The following sections describe how to install and use JMeter.

Installing and Running JMeter

As of this writing, JMeter's home page is located at `http://jakarta.apache.org/jmeter/`, from which the latest JMeter distribution can be downloaded as either a GZIP or ZIP archive. To install JMeter, simply extract the contents of the archive into its own directory. Launching JMeter is accomplished by entering the `bin` directory of JMeter and running either `jmeter.bat` (on Windows) or the `jmeter` shell script (on Linux or Unix).

The following sections demonstrate the use of JMeter. You may want to install JMeter at this point to try it out as specific features are explained. All of the examples and figures in this chapter are from JMeter 1.9.1.

Making and Understanding Test Plans with JMeter

Upon launching JMeter, you will see JMeter's Swing interface, as shown in Figure 17-1.

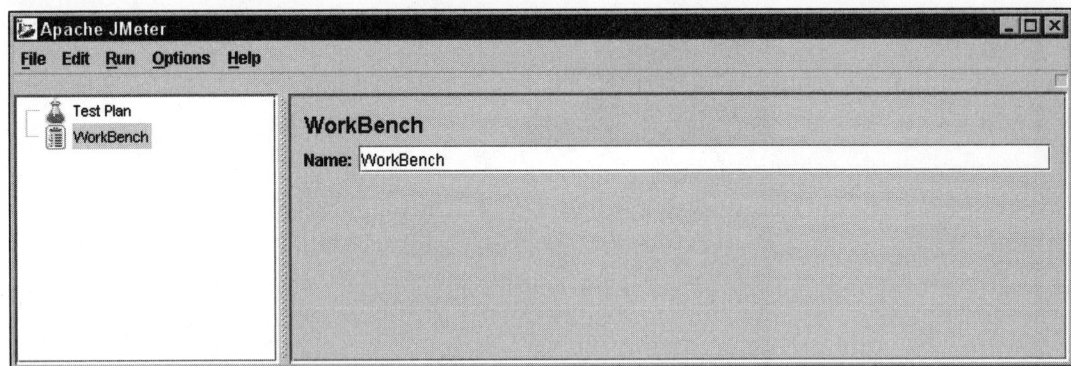

Figure 17-1: The JMeter interface.

JMeter's user interface consists of a tree in the left-hand pane, representing those items and actions that you have added, and a right-hand pane that provides configuration forms and output windows for items added to the left-hand pane.

At the heart of any JMeter session is the **test plan,** which is a list of actions that JMeter will perform. The test plan is a top-level node in the test tree. Elements are added to the test plan by right-clicking on its node and selecting `Add` from the pop-up menu.

The second icon on the first screen, the **workbench,** is a container for test elements that are not yet part of a test plan. The workbench is a great place for experimenting with configurations and moving them back and forth between test plans.

The simplest possible test plan for testing an HTTP server will be demonstrated before the discussion moves into more advanced options in the sections to come. The first element in every test plan is a **thread group.** A **thread group** is a collection of elements, and each thread group has its own set of Java threads and a separate configuration.

By right-clicking the Test Plan node in the left-hand pane and selecting Add, the thread group item can be selected. After adding the thread group, its icon can be selected in the left-hand pane to expose the thread group configuration pane (see Figure 17-2). For now, the configuration options will be left at their default values, but the available options will be explained.

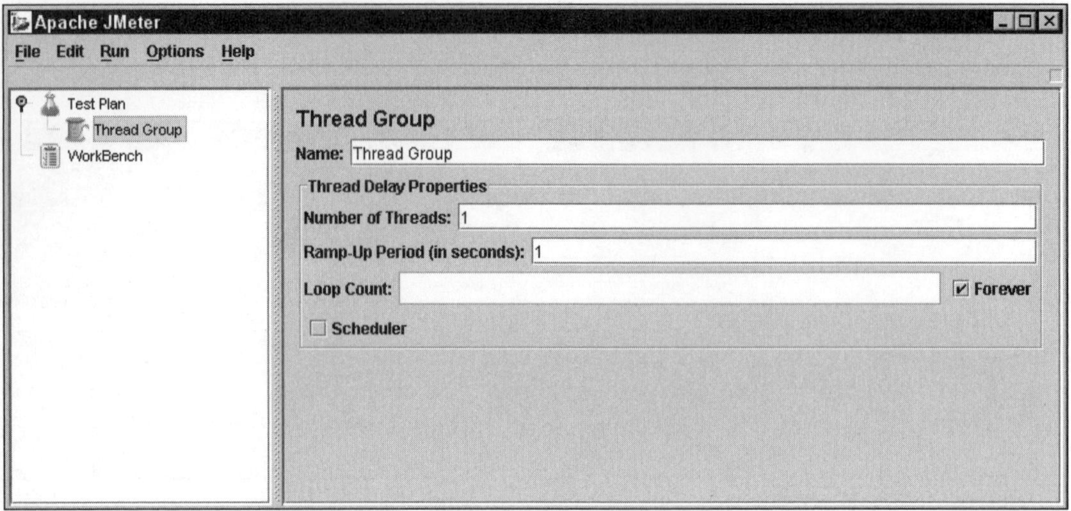

Figure 17-2: Adding a thread group.

The following configuration options are available:

- *Name* — The name doesn't need to be changed in a simple test plan, but when multiple thread groups are used, the name can come in handy to distinguish the groups.
- *Number of Threads* — This indicates the number of threads the group will spawn to carry out its assigned work. Each thread is basically equivalent to an additional simultaneous user performing the tasks assigned to the group.
- *Ramp-Up Period (in seconds)* — JMeter will start the group with one thread and add threads evenly over the course of the specified period until the value specified in Number of Threads has been reached.
- *Loop Count* — This specifies how many times the thread group will execute the elements of its assigned workload. The default is Forever, which means the elements of the test plan will be executed by the thread group until it is told to stop.
- *Scheduler* — This option enables the thread group to be configured to start and stop at a specific date/time.

Now that a thread group has been added, it's time to actually start doing something with it. Right-click the Thread Group icon to produces a pop-up menu, select Sampler, and then select HTTP Request, as shown in Figure 17-3.

Clicking on the freshly added HTTP Request icon exposes its configuration panel to the right. This is a much busier screen than the thread group configuration (see Figure 17-4).

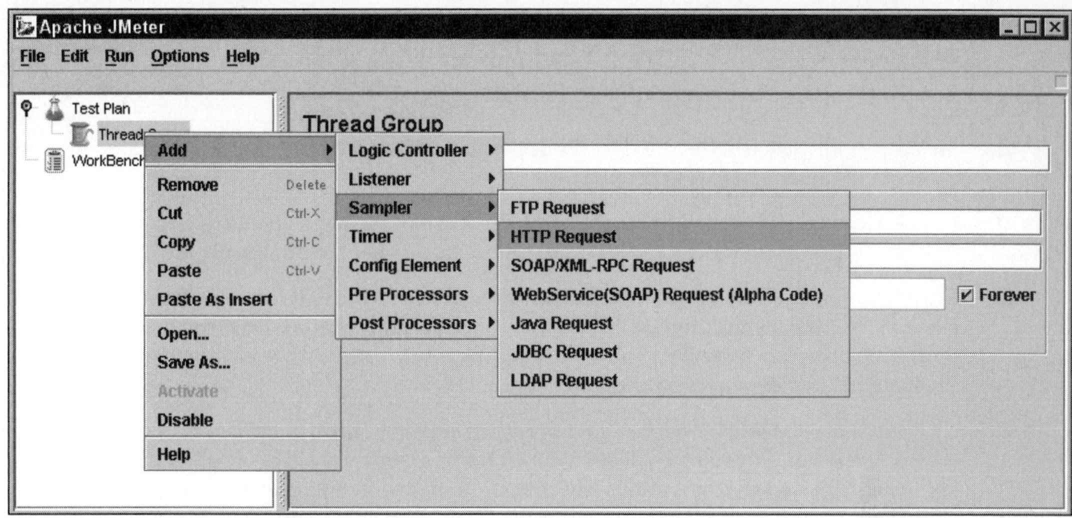

Figure 17-3: Adding an HTTP Request.

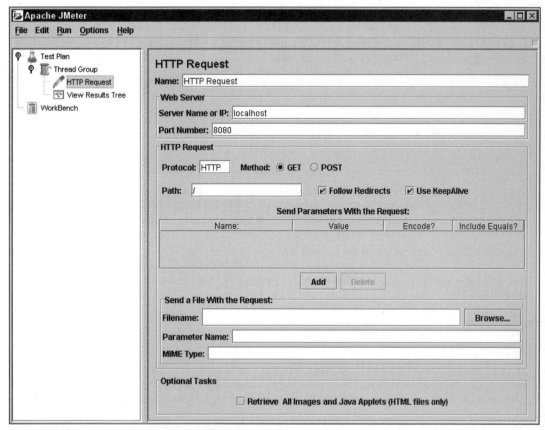

Figure 17-4: HTTP Request configuration panel.

Several options are available on this screen, many of which are quite obvious. Following are explanations of some of the less intuitive options:

- *Protocol*—HTTP or HTTPS should be entered here.
- *Method*—Indicates whether the test should send a `GET` or a `POST` request, which depends on what the requested page is expecting.
- *Path*—This is the Universal Resource Identifier (URI) of the page you are going to test. Note that `GET`-style parameters (for example, `index.html?name=ben`) should *not* be included on this line.
- *Follow Redirects*—Web servers can return a special redirect HTTP response that instructs Web clients to request an additional URL (as opposed to HTML or some other type of response content). Web browsers typically follow these redirects in a process that is transparent to the user. This option should usually be checked.
- *Use KeepAlive*—Most Web servers and browsers support "keep-alive" connections. This type of connection is not immediately closed when a browser receives a response from the server. It is kept open for a server-configurable, short amount of time in anticipation of an additional request from the same browser. Selecting this option eliminates socket-opening latency from the load testing process, which is almost always a good idea.
- *Parameters*—Here's the correct place to specify `GET/POST` parameters. The Encode? column indicates whether the name and value should have the HTTP encoding rules applied to them. For example, characters such as the ampersand (&) or spaces need to be encoded. The Include Equals? column is for those rare situations in which the application is not expecting an equals character (=) between the name and value.
- *Filename*—Some Web applications accept file uploads via HTTP `POST`. This field is for specifying which file should be uploaded with the request.
- *Parameter Name*—The file will be uploaded as a key-value pair. Use this field to specify the name of the key that the Web application will use to reference the file in the request.
- *MIME Type*—This is the type of the file you are uploading. For example, an HTML file would have a MIME type `text/html`, and an Adobe Acrobat file would be `application/pdf`.
- *Retrieve All Images and Java Applets*—Of course, Web browsers must request images and all other content referenced in an HTML page (such as CSS pages, etc.) separately from the initial HTML page request. This option specifies whether JMeter parses the HTML and requests such resources.

Assuming Tomcat is installed on the same machine from which you are running JMeter, the server name can be set to `localhost`, the port to `8080` (the default HTTP Connector port for Tomcat), and the path to `/`. If JMeter were to be run on a different physical machine from the server, the server name would simply need to be set to the appropriate host or IP of the server to be load tested. All other parameters can remain unchanged for now. The completed configuration for this section should look like what is shown in Figure 17-4.

With the preceding configuration steps taken, JMeter can now be instructed to start pounding a Web application with requests for its index page. The test can be started by selecting Start from JMeter's Run menu. However, the example isn't very practical so far, as there's no way to capture or view the results of the test. A few more options should be examined before running this first test.

JMeter was designed to internally separate the execution of a test plan from the collection and analysis of the test plan's results. For those who are interested, this is accomplished internally by use of the **Observer** or, as it is sometimes called, the **Event Listener design pattern.** This is reflected in the JMeter UI by its use of the listener terminology. **Controllers** are responsible for performing actions, and listeners are responsible for reacting to those actions. Thus, to access to the results of a test plan, one of the JMeter listeners must be used.

To complete this simple test plan, you need to add a listener. This is accomplished by right-clicking the Thread Group icon, selecting Add, and then Listener. From the several built-in listeners, select the View Results Tree option.

Selecting the View Results Tree icon in the left-hand pane will expose its output window on the right. There is no configuration required for this listener. When running a test with a View Results Tree listener, you can watch each response as it is received from the server. As items are selected in the tree component of the right-hand pane, the response from the server can be viewed in the Response Data section in the bottom part of that pane.

Before starting the test, the current JMeter configuration can be saved. Right-click the Test Plan icon in the left-hand pane and choose Save As from the pop-up menu.

This first test is now ready to be run. Tests are begun by selecting Start from the Run menu on the menu bar. Click the View Results Tree element before running the test. After the test is started, the Root node in the right pane's tree changes to a folder icon as test results start to trickle in. The node can be double-clicked to open it, revealing the individual test results contained within. Selecting any of the results will change the bottom pane to show the data received in the response, as well as the load time (in milliseconds), the HTTP response code, and the HTTP response message.

Figure 17-5 shows the completed test plan with the View Results Tree listener activated.

Since we didn't define a duration scope for the thread group, JMeter will continue making requests until either the JMeter application is closed or Stop is chosen from the Run menu on the menu bar.

JMeter Features

Manually clicking through each result in the View Results Tree window isn't an effective way to analyze the load testing data that JMeter provides. Moreover, the simplistic mechanism used in the preceding example to generate a load is somewhat limiting. Fortunately, JMeter provides many more features to aid in capturing and analyzing load data. Following are some of the other major feature types in JMeter that will help:

- Timer
- Listener
- Logic controller
- Sampler
- Config element

The following sections examine the HTTP-related highlights of these feature groups.

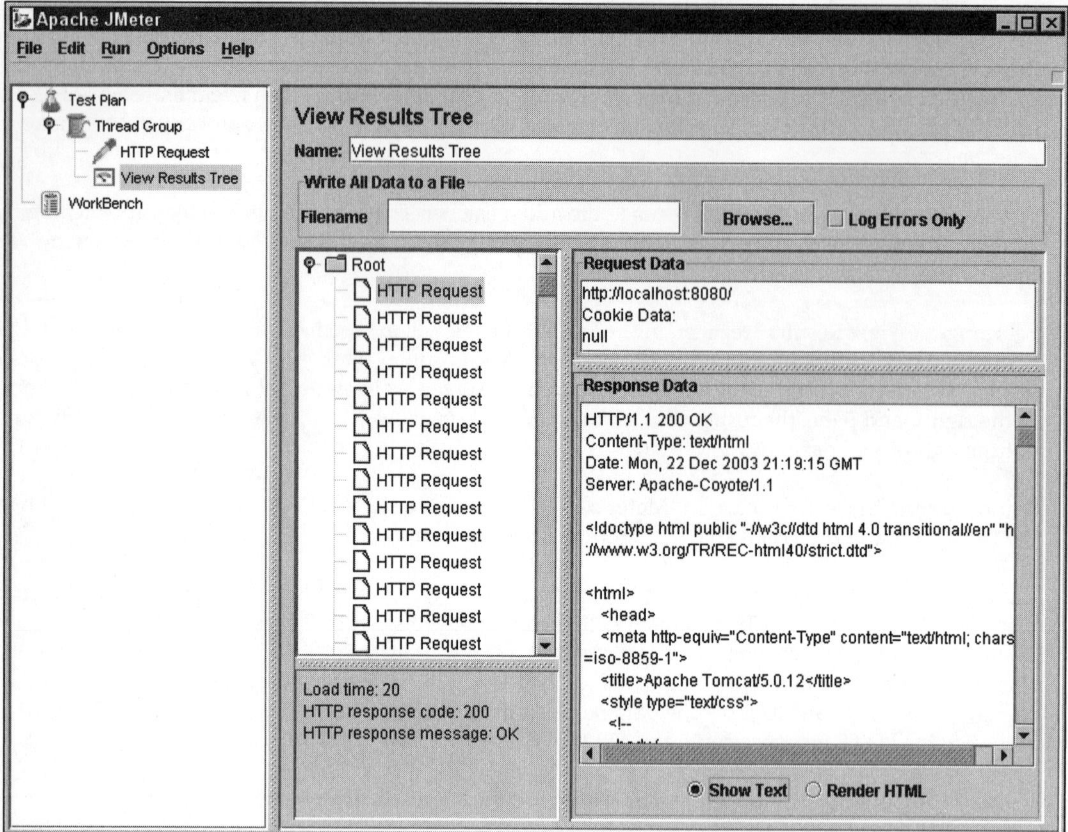

Figure 17-5: Viewing the results of a test.

Timer

In the sample test presented in the previous example, JMeter spawned one thread and started making requests as fast as it and the server being tested could keep up. In real-world cases, it might not make sense to so relentlessly pound a server with a constant onslaught of requests. Only in exceptional cases will a server be faced with a large number of simultaneous requests with no delay in between them.

To spare the server the full brunt of this load (and to make the load more representative of the real world), a timer can be added to the thread group. This will introduce some intelligent logic, which regulates the frequency and speed of each thread's requests. Four types of timers are currently included with JMeter: two random timers and two constant timers.

The constant timers are the **constant timer** and the **constant throughput timer.** The constant timer inserts a configurable and constant delay between each request issued by each thread in the group. The delay interval is specified in milliseconds; the default value is 300. The constant throughput timer, conversely, enables users to avoid the millisecond arithmetic and tell JMeter how many requests per minute each thread in the group should make. The default value is 60 requests (called **samples**) per minute.

The two random timers are the **uniform random timer** and the **Gaussian random timer.** These timers both simulate real-world traffic more accurately by inserting randomly calculated delays between the requests for each thread. The uniform random timer appends a truly random delay to a configurable constant delay, while the Gaussian random timer uses a statistical calculation to generate a pseudo-random delay. Each random timer takes a configurable constant time to which its random calculation will be appended.

To add a timer, right-click a thread group, select Timer from the Add menu, and choose the desired timer. Timers added to a thread group will affect the entire thread group to which they are added, but will not affect peer thread groups. Adding multiple timers to a thread group will have an additive effect on the delay between requests.

Listener

As discussed previously, listeners are JMeter's way of monitoring and reacting to the results of the requests it sends. The previous example used the View Results Tree listener to show the data returned from the server, as well as the response time, the HTTP response code, and the HTTP response message. As shown previously, a listener is added by right-clicking on a thread group and selecting the desired listener from the Listener submenu under the Add menu.

The listener only listens to activity from the thread group to which it is added. For example, given two thread groups in a test plan, thread group A and thread group B, a listener added to thread group B will be oblivious to anything that happens in the scope of thread group A. The following table shows the listeners currently provided by default with JMeter.

Listener	Description
Assertion Results	Views the output of the `Assertion` elements of a thread group
Graph Full Results	A cumulative graph of the response times of each request made
Graph Results	A simple graph view, plotting individual data points, mean response time, and standard deviation of response time for all requests in its parent thread group
Simple Data Writer	Writes the URLs sampled and their associated response times to a file for further analysis or posterity
View Results in Table	Provides a real-time view of test results organized into a table
View Results Tree	Provides a real-time view of test results organized into a tree
Aggregate Report	Displays aggregate information about each resource requested, such as the number of requests, the average response time, and so on
Spline Visualizer	A graph view of all data points made during a test plan run. The results are shown as an interpolated curve.

Each listener can be grouped into one of the following categories:

- Visualization listeners
- Data listeners
- Other listeners

Visualization Listeners

Graph Full Results, Graph Results, and Spline Visualizer all create graphical, real-time depictions of the test results. Graph Results (shown in Figure 17-6) is the simplest and most popular of these, plotting average response time in blue, standard deviation in red, median in purple, throughput in green, and each individual data point in black. In the graph shown, the median and throughput graphs are hidden; the other values are not shown in color in this book, but the standard deviation is the upper line, the average response time is the lower line, and the data points are the dots.

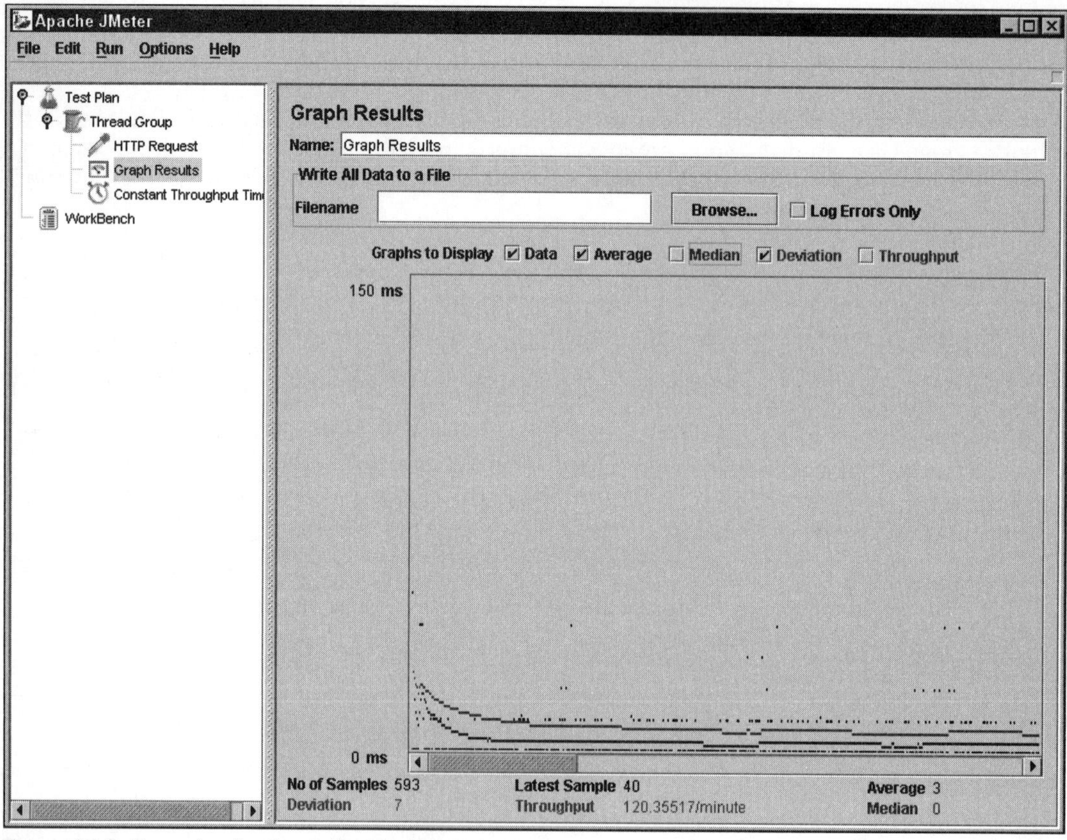

Figure 17-6: Example of a Graph Results listener.

More information about how to make sense of this data is explained in the section "Interpreting Test Results," later in this chapter.

Data Listeners

Simple Data Writer, View Results in Table, and View Results Tree capturing the raw data, response time, and return codes retrieved from the server. Simple Data Writer is somewhat redundant, as all of the other listener tools enable the raw data to be saved to a file. However, if no other listener is used, it can be useful to use Simple Data Writer by itself to record the data. Having the raw data is an important tool, because it enables users to keep their data for posterity, as well as to potentially import the data into other tools for more detailed analysis.

When data is written to a file, using Simple Data Writer or the Write All Data to a File option of any of the listeners, it is created in an XML format using a simple ad hoc XML grammar (that is, the names and organization of the elements and attributes in the XML file are undefined in any normative XML schema such as a DTD or W3C XML Schema document). A sample of the data is shown here:

```
<testResults>
    <sampleResult timeStamp="1072187462821" dataType="text"
                  threadName="Thread Group1-1" label="HTTP Request"
                  time="731" responseMessage="OK" responseCode="200"
                  success="true"/>
    <sampleResult timeStamp="1072187465264" dataType="text"
                  threadName="Thread Group1-1" label="HTTP Request"
                  time="10" responseMessage="OK" responseCode="200"
                  success="true"/>
</testResults>
```

The XML format is fairly intuitive. `timeStamp` is measured as the number of milliseconds since January 1, 1970, and `time` is the number of milliseconds before the response was received.

Aggregate Report, another data listener (see Figure 17-7), does more than display raw data. It organizes the raw data by requested URL, and provides a summary of all the data points involving that URL. It is a useful and concise way to track performance, striking a balance between the graphical visualizations and the other raw data listeners.

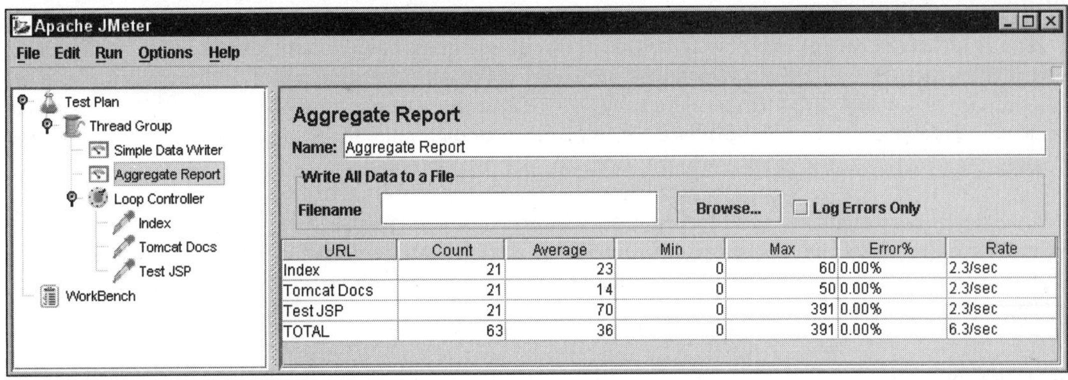

Figure 17-7: Aggregate Report makes the results of a test easy to interpret.

Assertion Results

Assertion Results enables users to view the results of `Assertion` elements that have been added to samplers. Both assertion and assertion results are discussed in the section "Sampler," later in this chapter.

Logic Controller

A Logic Controller's primary purpose is to manage the execution flow of a test plan. It is a container for other executable test plan elements. Logic Controllers that are added to a thread group (or even as a subnode of another Logic Controller) will be treated by their parent execution context as a single node to be executed. Elements added beneath logic controller nodes will be executed according to the rules of the specific Logic Controller to which they are added.

Like thread groups, Logic Controllers create a separate visibility space for listeners, timers, and other elements that are context-specific. Logic Controllers can be thought of as the closest approximation JMeter test plans have to the `while`, `for`, and `function` constructs of typical programming languages.

The following sections discuss the built-in Logic Controllers that currently ship with JMeter:

- Interleave Controller
- Simple Controller
- Loop Controller
- Module Controller
- Once Only Controller
- Random Controller
- Throughput Controller
- Recording Controller

Interleave Controller

The **Interleave Controller** will execute one of its sub-elements each time its parent container loops. It executes them in the order in which they are listed in the configuration tree. For example, if a user were to create an Interleave Controller with four elements under a thread group set to loop 14 times, JMeter would execute the entire set of Interleave Controller sub-elements three times, and would then execute only the first two sub-elements a fourth time (4 + 4 + 4 + 2 = 14).

Interleave Controllers are good for testing a sequential process in which each request depends on the successful completion of the previous request. An obvious example is an online shopping application, whereby a user searches for an item, adds it to a shopping cart, enters credit card details, and finalizes the order.

Simple Controller

With **Simple Controller,** each sub-element is executed each time the thread group loops. The Simple Controller can be used to logically organize test elements in much the same way as folders are used on a file system to logically separate their contents. If a site were to be load tested with a nontrivial amount of functionality, it would make sense to use Simple Controller elements to separate the tested functionality into related modules to keep the test plan more maintainable. This enhances the maintainability of the test plan in the same way that dividing large software projects into modules and functions enhances maintainability of the software.

Loop Controller

The **Loop Controller** will loop through all of its sub-elements as many times as specified in the Loop Controller's configuration panel. Therefore, any elements under the Loop Controller will execute the specified number of times, multiplied by the number of times the parent thread is set to loop. If a Loop Controller were configured to loop four times under a thread group that loops four times, each sub-element of the loop controller would be executed 16 times.

Module Controller

The **Module Controller** enables users to insert elements of the test plan *from entirely different locations* into the context of the module controller. In other words, the Module Controller can be thought of as a way to execute a method (or function or subroutine, depending on your preferred lexicon). Module Controllers can be particularly useful for applying to testing all of those reuse principles that programmers espouse. The Module Controller can also be used to radically design a test without physically moving testing elements around. Figure 17-8 shows the Module Controller.

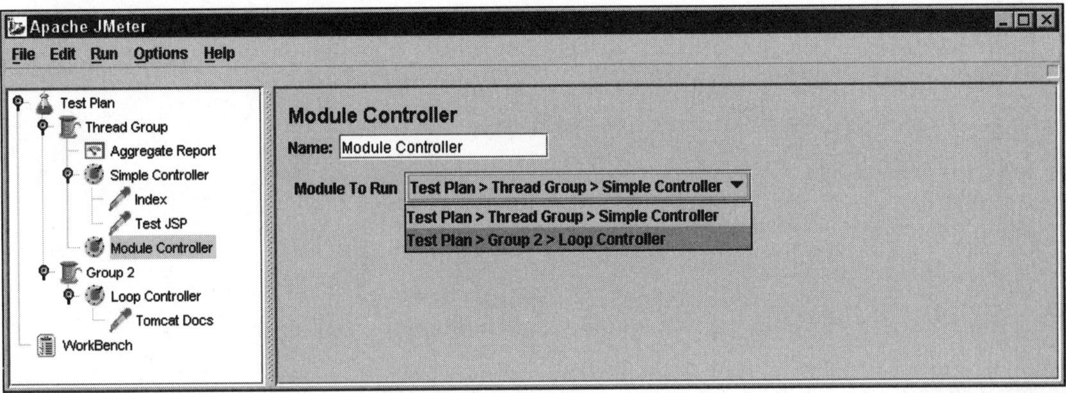

Figure 17-8: Configuring a Module Controller.

Once Only Controller

Not surprisingly, the **Once Only Controller** executes its child elements only once during the run of a load test. This controller can be used to execute an initial login, to create an application entity on which other tests depend (for example, creating an order in a sales application so you can manipulate it with other requests), or to perform any other operation that needs to happen only once.

Random Controller

The **Random Controller** works just like the Interleave Controller, with one exception. Whereas the Interleave Controller executes one item from its list in sequential order, the Random Controller picks an item in its collection of sub-elements at random each time it is executed.

Throughput Controller

The **Throughput Controller** provides another mechanism to testing creators for throttling the number of requests sent. The Throughput Controller will only send a subset of the requests sent to it on to its sub-elements. This subset can be defined in terms of **total executions** or **percent executions.** For example, the Throughput Controller can be configured to send only 50 percent of its requested executions on to its sub-elements, or it can be configured to only send the first ten requests on to its sub-elements. Thus, the Throughput Controller could be configured to emulate the Once Only Controller mentioned previously.

The Throughput Controller can be configured to limit *all* of the threads in a group collectively, or it can be set to limit them individually. This is controlled by selecting the Per User checkbox. When it is on, each thread in the group is individually subject to the throughput control. Otherwise, the controls apply to the group.

Recording Controller

The **Recording Controller** is used much differently from the other controllers. The Recording Controller is used by the **HTTP Proxy Server** feature of JMeter. The HTTP Proxy Server enables JMeter to record requests made by a Web browser and incorporate them as part of a test plan. The HTTP Proxy Server uses the Recording Controller to save the data it receives.

Sampler

As mentioned in our first JMeter example, samplers generate requests to be sent to a server. Following are the six types of built-in samplers:

- FTP Request
- HTTP Request
- SOAP/XML-RPC Request
- Java Request
- JDBC Request
- LDAP Request

As shown, JMeter can be used to load test more than just Web servers. A variety of test plans can be created by using some of these sampler types. While all of these sampler types are interesting, this chapter focuses on the HTTP Request sampler. The basic parameters of HTTP requests were previously discussed. This section addresses some of the advanced configuration options of the HTTP Request sampler.

Config Elements

Config Elements enable various configurable attributes to be applied globally to a series of samplers. In the case of HTTP requests, four different Config Elements can be used:

- HTTP Header Manager
- HTTP Authorization Manager
- HTTP Cookie Manager
- HTTP Request Defaults

While Config Elements are normally added to thread groups or other containers for samplers, they can also be added to individual samplers to override global values.

HTTP Header Manager

In some cases, application testing will require specific HTTP headers to be set in order to get a valid reflection of true application performance. For example, if an application performs different actions depending on the browser type making the request, it is necessary to set the `User-Agent` header when making test requests. The **HTTP Header Manager** is used to explicitly set header keys and values to be sent as part of each request. If added as a node under an `HTTP Request` element, the custom headers will only be sent for the request under which they are added. These headers will be sent with every request in the same branch if they are set at the thread group level.

Configuring the HTTP Header Manager is simple and very similar to configuring the `Name/Value` parameters in an `HTTP Request` element.

HTTP Authorization Manager

The **HTTP Authorization Manager** handles requests that require HTTP authentication. Like the HTTP Header Managers, they can be added either directly underneath an `HTTP Request` element or to an entire branch of a tree. Their configuration parameters are simple, accepting a base URL from which they will attempt to send authentication credentials, plus the obligatory user name and password.

HTTP Cookie Manager

Many modern Web applications use cookies in some manner. In these cases, an **HTTP Cookie Manager** element will need to be added to the test plan. Like HTTP authorization managers and HTTP Header Managers, HTTP Cookie Managers can accept a hard-coded list of cookies that should be sent for every request. In this way, a test sampler can emulate a browser that has previously visited a site. Additionally, HTTP Cookie Managers can mimic a browser's ability to receive, store, and resend cookies. Therefore, for example, if a cookie is dynamically assigned to each visitor, the HTTP Cookie Manager will receive it and resend it with every appropriate subsequent request.

HTTP Cookie Managers can be added either to a thread group or directly to an `HTTP Request` element, depending on the scope of their intended influence.

Note that the HTTP Cookie Manager stores cookies on a per-thread (also called **per-user** in JMeter) basis. That is, given a thread group of ten threads, if each thread receives a different cookie for the same base URL, each thread will continue to resend that unique cookie. *However,* when cookies are added manually to the Cookie Manager, *all* threads will resend that cookie. Future versions of JMeter may correct this limitation.

HTTP Request Defaults

HTTP Request Defaults provides a convenient mechanism for using common values among unique HTTP request samplers. The basic request parameters (such as `protocol`, `host`, `port`, `path`, and `name/value` parameters) can be specified in one location to be shared among the samplers.

Assertions

Even if an application is responding lightning fast, there is no cause for celebration if its output is invalid. An **assertion** provides a way to validate the actual data returned as a result of each request so that users can be sure that the server is both responsive *and* reliable. Assertions are created as sub-elements of samplers (such as the HTTP Request sampler). An assertion is a declaration of some truth that should be verified.

For example, you could create an assertion that posits that the response from a server should contain the word `Hello`. When this assertion exists, the response of the HTTP request to which it is added will be checked for the existence of `Hello`, and will throw an assertion failure if the string is not present.

Using the following simple HTML file, we'll see how an assertion is used to validate it:

```
<html>
  <body>
    Hello, World!
  </body>
</html>
```

Given that the preceding HTML has already deployed to an accessible HTTP server, the first step is to add an HTTP Request sampler into a test plan. After creating the HTTP Request sampler, it can be selected and right-clicked. From the context menu, choose Assertions ➪ Response Assertion from the Add menu. Clicking the new Response Assertion icon will display a panel like the one shown in Figure 17-9.

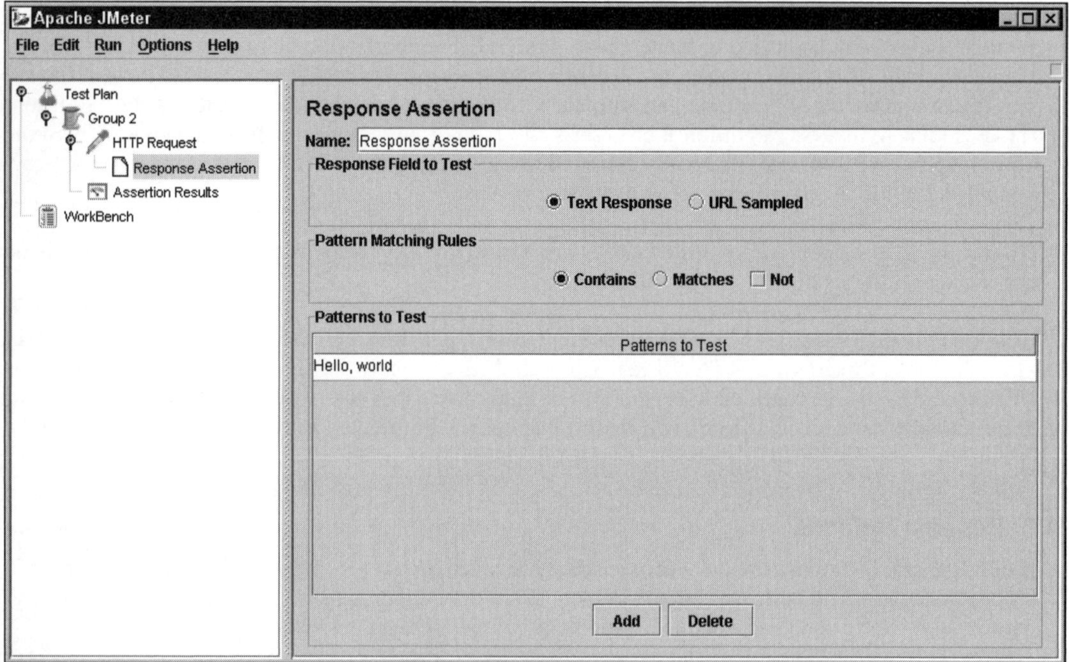

Figure 17-9: The Response Assertion configuration screen.

In Figure 17-9, the text "Hello, world" has already been added to the assertion. This is accomplished by clicking the Add button and writing the text into the entry area that appears. In this example, the Contains option has been selected. This indicates that the assertion will verify that the response from the HTTP request contains the pattern "Hello, world." When the Matches option is selected, the entire response must match the pattern.

Now that an assertion has been added, an **Assertion Results listener** (mentioned previously) will need to be added to view the successes and failures of the assertion. The Assertion Results listener should be added to the parent thread group of the HTTP Request sampler. Assertion Results listeners require no configuration. They will display all assertion results for any assertion in their thread group. If the assertion passes, it will print the string identifying the resource request (in this case, the URL). If there is a failure, it will print an indented failure message directly below the resource identifier, stating the pattern match that failed.

The Response Assertion can be used to verify that a response URL or body contains some pattern of text. Three other assertion types exist:

- *Duration Assertion*—Verifies that a response occurs within a specified time period
- *Size Assertion*—Checks the size of the response, in bytes, and verifies that it is equal to, not equal to, greater than, less than, greater than or equal to, or less than or equal to a specified value
- *XML Assertion*—Ensures that the response is well-formed XML. It does not check validity against a Document Type Definition (DTD) or other schema type.

These assertions can be added to a test plan and configured in the same manner as the Response Assertion.

HTTP Proxy Server

Creating HTTP Request elements can get tedious. JMeter provides an **HTTP Proxy Server** that enables it to monitor browser activity and auto-generate HTTP Request elements based on the requests made from the Web browser. As depicted in Figure 17-10, the proxy works by intercepting all requests that are made during the browsing session, converting them into JMeter HTTP Request elements, and passing the request on to the destination Web server.

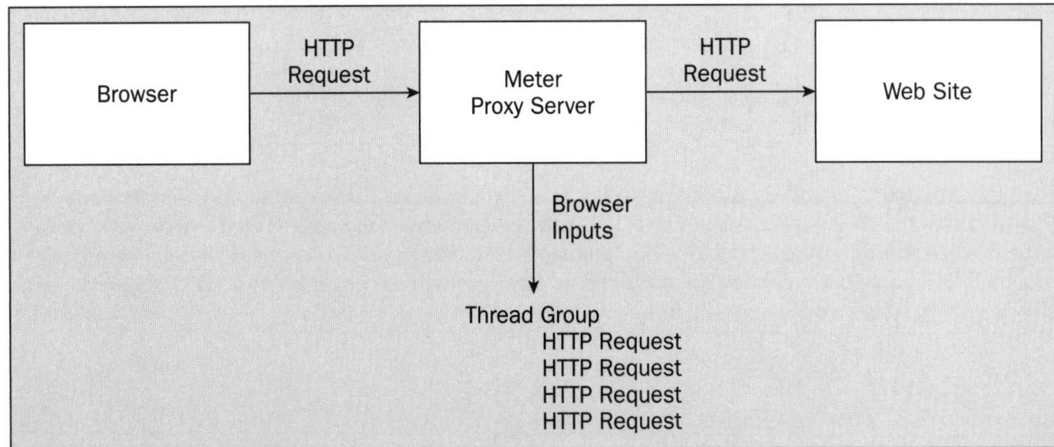

Figure 17-10: The JMeter Proxy Server sits in between a browser and a Web site.

Generating a large number of HTTP Request elements for a test plan is as simple as reconfiguring a browser's HTTP proxy setting and clicking through the features that should be load tested.

To start using the HTTP Proxy Server, it must be added to the JMeter WorkBench. This is done by right-clicking the WorkBench icon and selecting Add ➪ Non-Test Elements ➪ HTTP Proxy Server. The proxy's configuration screen is shown in Figure 17-11.

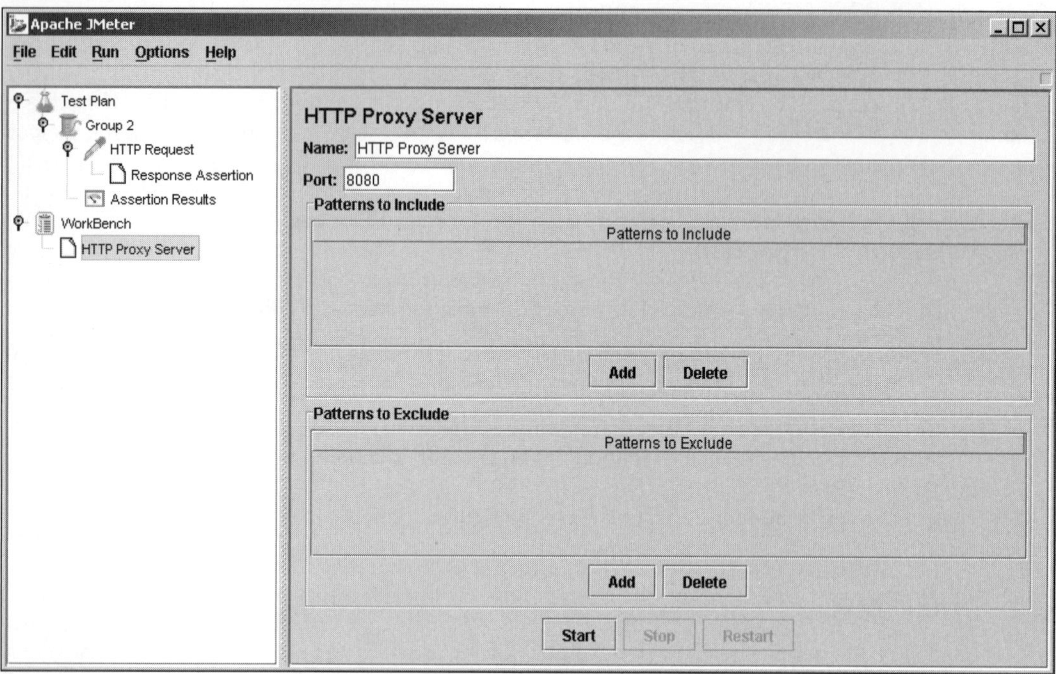

Figure 17-11: Configuration screen of the HTTP Proxy Server.

Note the default port number of 8080.

> **If Tomcat is running on the same machine as JMeter and is using its default port of 8080, the proxy's default port will conflict. On such machines, JMeter's proxy port will need to be changed to an unused port on the system.**

In the Patterns to Include and Patterns to Exclude text boxes, regular expressions can optionally be added that match the URLs for which HTTP Request elements will be generated. All browser traffic will be proxied through the HTTP Proxy element. However, if any patterns are listed here, only requests that match an include pattern or are not excluded by a pattern will be converted into HTTP Request elements.

The following instructions will aid in configuring browsers to use a proxy server:

- *Internet Explorer 5+* — Select the Tools ➪ Internet Options pull-down menu. Now select the Connections ➪ Settings button for the appropriate network connection (that is, dial-up versus LAN). Select Use a proxy server. In the Address field, type **localhost** (or the host name of the computer running the JMeter HTTP proxy — it need not be the local machine), and in the Port field, type the port chosen for the JMeter proxy.
- *Netscape 6/Mozilla* — Bring up the preferences dialog box by choosing Edit ➪ Preferences. Expand the Advanced tree element in the left-hand pane. Select Proxies ➪ Manual Proxy Configuration. Type **localhost** in the HTTP Proxy field, and the proxy port setup in JMeter in the `Port` field. Note that any HTTPS requests will need to be entered in the SSL Proxy field.

After configuring the proxy server, it must be started by clicking the Start button. From this point on, all requests made by the browser will be captured by JMeter and converted into HTTP Request items in WorkBench. These items can then be dragged into the test plan.

Distributed Load Testing

JMeter has the capability to coordinate multiple JMeter instances distributed across a network, instructing them to perform the same load test. To enable this functionality, one or more JMeter instances starts in **server mode.** Server mode enables a JMeter client (that is, the normal JMeter GUI interface) to attach to the JMeter instance in server mode and control it. The JMeter client's listeners receive the data generated by the JMeter server mode instances. There are two potential use cases for this capability:

- *Scalability* — For various reasons, a single JMeter instance might not be enough to generate a load heavy enough to bring a Web application to its knees. In these rare circumstances, JMeter's distributed capability can be used to generate a truly massive barrage of requests. This capability could also be used to coordinate a massive distributed denial of service (DDoS) attack, which highlights a good point: *Don't ever load test a Web site that you don't control!*
- *Server Proximity* — As an extreme example, imagine trying to load test a server in the Eastern United States while sitting in India. It would be difficult to have any acceptable degree of confidence in the tests, as network latency and packet loss would play such a critical role in the process. In a case such as this, it's possible to install a JMeter server somewhere physically close to the server being tested, and then use that server to perform the tests remotely.

Figure 17-12 illustrates the method by which JMeter interacts remotely between a JMeter client, a JMeter server, and a Web server:

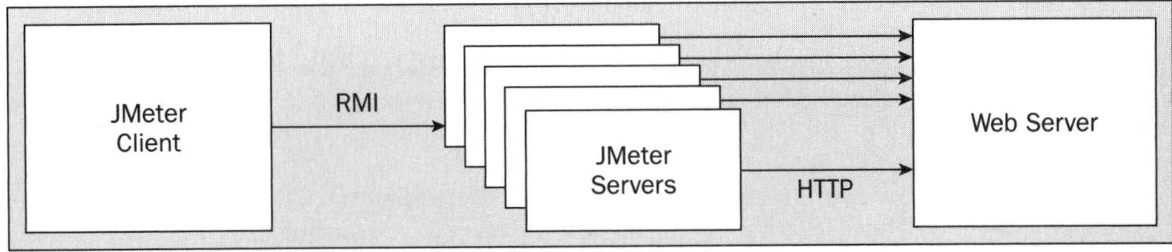

Figure 17-12: One JMeter client can control multiple JMeter servers.

The following is a step-by-step guide to setting up and running tests using the JMeter server:

1. Install the standard JMeter distribution on the intended JMeter server machine(s).
2. For each JMeter instance to be controlled, start the JMeter server process by entering JMeter's `bin/` directory and executing *either* `jmeter-server.bat` or the `jmeter-server` shell script, depending on your host operating system.
3. On the client machine, edit the `jmeter.properties` file (located in the `bin` directory of JMeter's installation directory).
4. Uncomment and change the `remote_hosts` property to include a comma-separated list of the JMeter server machines. These can be either DNS-resolvable host names or IP addresses.
5. Start the JMeter client by running `jmeter.bat` or the `jmeter` shell script.
6. Load or create a new test plan.
7. Two new options will be present in the Run menu: Remote Start and Remote Stop. In each of these options, any servers listed in the `remote_hosts` property will be available for stopping and starting.
8. Proceed with the JMeter GUI as usual.

Interpreting Test Results

Generating reams of raw data is one thing; knowing what the data means is quite another. There are two basic ways to analyze the resulting data:

- Set performance goals and test them.
- Establish the scalability limitations.

Setting Goals and Testing Them

A particularly effective way to create a Web application is to establish up front the performance goals for the system. These goals might include one or more of the following metrics:

- What's the average amount of time a user should wait for a request to be fulfilled?
- What's the longest amount of time a user should be made to wait?
- How many concurrent requests should be supported before errors occur?

Once such goals are established, it is a simple matter to determine if the tested Web application lives up to them. Both the Aggregate Report and the Graph Results listeners are perfectly adequate for such an analysis.

As an example, consider the following scenario: A simple Web site must support five concurrent users, where concurrent is defined as users making requests no more than a second apart. Each user should receive a response in an average of 250 milliseconds, although outlying delays up to 3 seconds are acceptable.

To continue the scenario, suppose a load test were created that measured the application using the criteria established in the goals. Figure 17-13 shows the Aggregate Report created by the test plan.

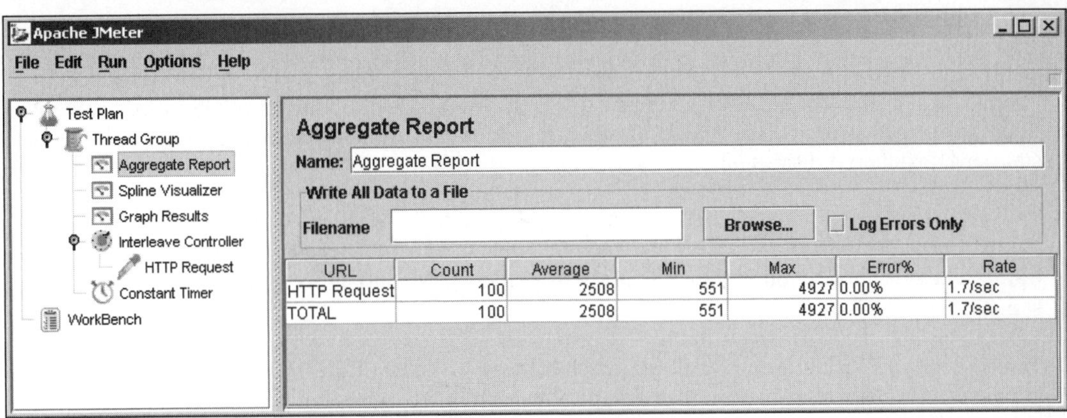

Figure 17-13: The example scenario's Aggregate Report screen.

Using the Aggregate Report's presentation of the data, it is clear that the Web application did not meet its goals. The average delay was 2,508 milliseconds (ms), roughly ten times the goal. The outlying delay was 4,927 ms, or almost 5 seconds! However, on a positive note, no requests resulted in an error from the Web application. Nonetheless, because the shortest response time was 551 ms, not one user ever received a single response within the desired parameters.

The Graph Results listener can provide additional valuable information (such as the true distribution of the responses), as shown in Figure 17-14.

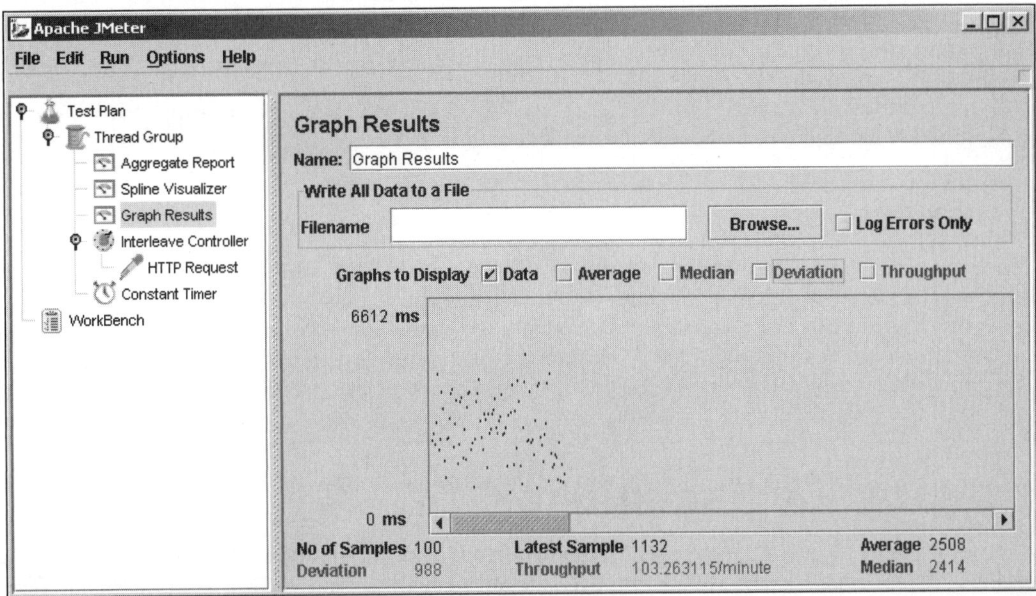

Figure 17-14: Graph Results output for the example scenario.

Note that all the graphs except Data have been disabled. This makes the graph easier to interpret in black and white. The dots on the graph indicate each individual sample, and how long the response took in milliseconds. Higher dots represent longer delays. Thus, the graph provides greater granularity regarding the application's performance. You can clearly see that the application's performance wasn't consistent at all!

A separate statistic, the **deviation,** confirms this observation. Deviation (commonly called the **standard deviation**) is a measure of how widely values in a sample are dispersed from the average value. A higher standard deviation indicates more variance in response time.

The graph also provides a new statistic: the **median.** If all the response times were placed in a sorted list, the median is the number in the middle. The median is similar to the **average,** which is the number produced when the total amount of time for each response is added together and divided by the number of samples.

The throughput number provided in the graph is the same value as the "rate" in the Aggregate Report. However, it is given at a different scale (minutes instead of seconds).

Establishing Scalability Limitations

Sometimes, goals aren't important, and the only real motivating factor is determining the point at which a Web application breaks. This methodology is also much more fun than simply verifying goals. Bringing a Web application to its knees is a hidden desire of many system administrators.

Here, JMeter comes in very handy, especially with its distributed testing capabilities. It is important to remember, however, that even these stress tests should be configured in such a way that they are representative of real-world scenarios. It is not very useful to know that if 10,000 users made concurrent requests for the same URL every 10 ms that the tested Web application fails. Such a scenario is unlikely to occur in the real world. It is more helpful to know that if 500 simultaneous users follow 1 of 10 realistic sequences of requests (averaging a 3-second delay between each request), the Web application will generate errors for 4 percent of the responses.

When performing such stress tests, the Aggregate Report can handily show the error rate, and it can be configured to log all errors that occur, for further analysis.

Further Analysis

JMeter can, of course, save all of its performance data for analysis by other tools. While at this time there are no (well-known) performance analysis tools designed specifically with JMeter in mind, popular programs such as Microsoft Excel can import JMeter data and generate all sorts of handy reports and graphs. By default, JMeter records output in XML, but it can be configured to use CSV (comma-separated values) by changing the `jmeter.save.saveservice.output_format` property in `jmeter.properties` to `CSV`.

Optimization Techniques

As the famous computer science guru Donald Knuth has said, "Premature optimization is the root of all evil." In other words, it's very difficult for even the most talented of individuals to know what a complex Web application's performance bottleneck will be in the real world. It's rather unwise to start twisting knobs and tweaking settings until the performance results have come in.

However, what should happen when the test is run and the performance is subpar? What can an administrator do to increase performance? While many performance problems can be solved by having the application developers optimize their code, there are some things an administrator can do to increase performance.

Some of the simplest optimizations are hardware-related: adding memory, increasing CPU power, faster hard drives, and so on. Some of the most complex optimizations involve operating system tweaks, all of which are very specific to the operating system involved. Obviously, these optimizations deserve their own references and are beyond the scope of this book.

Java and Tomcat-related optimizations, however, are right up our alley.

Java Optimizations

The JVM has received quite a few "dials and knobs" in recent years that enable administrators to tweak its settings. The techniques described here are specific to Sun Microsystem's own JVM implementations, and are subject to removal in future versions of their JVMs. Most, however, have been around since Java 1.3 and are probably here to stay for many years.

Considering the Server VM

Surprisingly few system administrators realize that the JVM actually contains two different virtual machines inside the binary that's executed to start up Java applications: the client VM and the server VM. Each of these two VMs is optimized according to the needs of client and server applications. The client VM's top priority is reducing startup time and minimizing the latency produced when the garbage collector reclaims memory. The server VM trades these priorities for an emphasis on greater scalability for server-type applications.

By default, Java uses the client VM. The server VM can be selected by passing the `-server` command-line option to the Java VM on startup. Administrators should experiment with this setting to increase their application's performance. Never assume that the server VM will be faster, however. Test the application with JMeter!

Optimizing Memory Allocation

The JVM will not take more memory from the operating system than it has been given permission to consume. This limit is configurable via command-line switches to the JVM. These two switches are shown in the following table.

Argument	Description
`-Xms<size>`	The initial heap size for the JVM
`-Xmx<size>`	The maximum heap size for the JVM

If these parameters are not explicitly set, the JVM will use its defaults. The defaults are dependent on the version of the JVM in use, but are generally inappropriately small for production use. The **heap** is the area of memory in which the JVM allocates new Java objects; the vast majority of the JVM's memory usage is its heap.

Initial heap size specifies the amount of operating system RAM to allocate to the Java heap at the time the JVM starts up. Generally, this setting is not important. However, in a memory-intensive application operating under a heavy load, initial heap size can be significant. If the JVM starts up with a very small heap size and is quickly pounded by many requests that require many object instantiations, the JVM must repeatedly increase its allocation until it reaches a sufficiently large size for the heap. For this reason, some administrators set the `-Xms` and `-Xmx` arguments to the same values. Others prefer to have the JVM scale up to its maximum heap size only when necessary.

The maximum heap size specifies the upper limit of RAM that the JVM will allocate to the heap. In a data-intensive application with long-lived objects, memory usage may quickly build up. If the memory required to run an application exceeds the maximum heap size configured, the JVM will fail with a `java.lang.OutOfMemory` error. It is a good idea to set the maximum heap size to the largest possible value.

Choosing a Different Vendor's JVM

Sun isn't the only company producing Java virtual machines. Several other vendors (such as IBM and BEA) also produce JVMs compatible with the Sun Java specification. The performance characteristics of these JVMs is rarely better or worse than their competitors. Rather, they are typically better at *some* tasks, but *worse* at others. The best course of action is to test an application with different JVMs.

Tomcat Optimizations

Tomcat has several settings that can affect its performance. Adjusting these settings is often the easiest way to achieve enhanced performance.

Combining Tomcat with Another Web Server

One of the best ways to increase an application's performance is to remove the burden of serving static resources from Tomcat by mating it with an HTTP server (such as Apache or IIS). This process is discussed in Chapter 12 and Chapter 13.

Connector Settings

Tomcat's `server.xml` file contains a `Connector` element for each port on which Tomcat listens. The performance-related attributes shown in the following table can be modified on the `Connector` element.

Parameter	Description
`maxThreads`	Tomcat uses a thread to handle each request that it receives. This value determines the maximum number of threads that Tomcat can create to service requests.
`acceptCount`	When all of its threads are being used, Tomcat can queue incoming connections until a thread is available. This setting controls the number of connections that can be queued. Note that when this queue fills up, errors will be sent to the clients.

Parameter	Description
connectionTimeout	Clients have a certain amount of time to send a request after a socket connection has been established with Tomcat. This value controls the number of milliseconds a client has to send a request before the connection is closed.
minSpareThreads	The number of threads Tomcat will initially create to service requests
maxSpareThreads	Tomcat will close socket threads when they are no longer necessary once the amount of open threads exceeds this number.

The preceding attributes are those that are likely to provide the largest performance return on investment when tweaking Tomcat settings. However, check the Tomcat documentation of the version being used to spot additional attributes that may have an impact.

Exploring Alternatives to JMeter

Though this chapter's discussion focused on JMeter for load testing, numerous other tools are available, both in the public domain and as commercial products. Two of the market leaders are Segue's **Silk Performer** and Mercury Interactive's **Load Runner.** Both offer very advanced scripting features, thus providing end users with great flexibility in specifying load test behaviors. With this flexibility comes the price of increased complexity, but both companies offer comprehensive documentation as well as training programs for their products.

The open source world also has more to offer in terms of load testing tools. From the up-and-coming OpenLoad (`http://openload.sourceforge.net`) to the more mature Grinder (`http://grinder.sourceforge.net`), numerous options are available. A great resource for finding the latest in open source load testing tools is the FreshMeat open source software archive site (`www.freshmeat.net`), which includes a category specifically for these kinds of tools under Topic :: Software Development :: Testing :: Traffic Generation.

Additionally, many other testing resources are available on the Web. A great place to look for an ever-evolving list of sites is the Open Directory Software Testing list (`www.dmoz.org/Computers/Programming/Software_Testing/`), which is a directory of sites that focus on testing topics.

Summary

Load testing is an important but often overlooked activity of the system administrator. It can help administrators make initial architectural decisions as well as validate decisions made previously. This chapter examined the following topics:

- Scalability (a system's capability to handle increased load without experiencing degraded performance or reliability) is driven by many factors. In a Tomcat installation, some of those factors are server hardware, software configuration, and deployment architecture.
- JMeter is a full-featured, open source load tester, which is part of the Jakarta project. Various JMeter load testing techniques were explored.

Chapter 18 explores Tomcat's support for JMX.

18

JMX Support

The updated architecture of Tomcat 5 improved the performance and modularity of the previous version. The refactoring of formerly mingled code into distinct components, and the subsequent pipelining of components for request processing, helped make Tomcat 5 one of the most flexible versions ever. Simultaneously, the J2EE 1.4 specification has evolved to include manageability as a requirement for compliance with the standard. Being the reference Web-tier server implementation, Tomcat 5 naturally must conform to the specification. To this end, Tomcat 5 has integrated support for Java Management Extensions (JMX), the management standard for Java services. This chapter discusses the following topics:

- JMX and manageability requirements
- Introduction to JMX
- JMX internals
- Configuring Tomcat 5 for JMX operations
- Utilizing the JMX support of Tomcat 5

A hands-on example shows you how JMX can be used to obtain live run-time information directly from the components that comprise the Tomcat 5 server.

Administrators should be familiar with JMX and its implications because all future administrative and management tools for the Tomcat servers will be based on JMX.

The Requirement to Be Manageable

The original intent of Tomcat was to provide a workable reference implementation of the Servlet and JSP specifications. Because of its reliability, however, Tomcat has been increasingly adopted for production purposes. Features formerly offered only as enhancements by commercial vendors are making their way into the Tomcat wish list. Near the top among the list of requirements is a well-defined means of configuring, administrating, monitoring, and managing a large group of servers or server clusters.

Because of the increasing demand from today's Web applications and Web services, many Tomcat deployments span multiple servers. To provide for the scalability, availability, and throughput demands, many production environments involve multiple physical servers.

Added to this trend is the increasing popularity of shared hosting for JSPs, Servlets, and Web applications. Shared hosting provides a cost-effective way to deploy Web applications for consumption over the Internet. In a typical hosting center, an individual physical server machine may have many independent JVMs concurrently running Tomcat. Often, a single instance of Tomcat may provide service for tens of virtual hosts. Until the arrival of JMX, managing these Tomcat and virtual host instances across a network of servers was an administrator's nightmare. Ad hoc solutions often require painstaking custom coding, are operating-system dependent, and are difficult to maintain. Figure 18-1 illustrates this management problem with Tomcat servers.

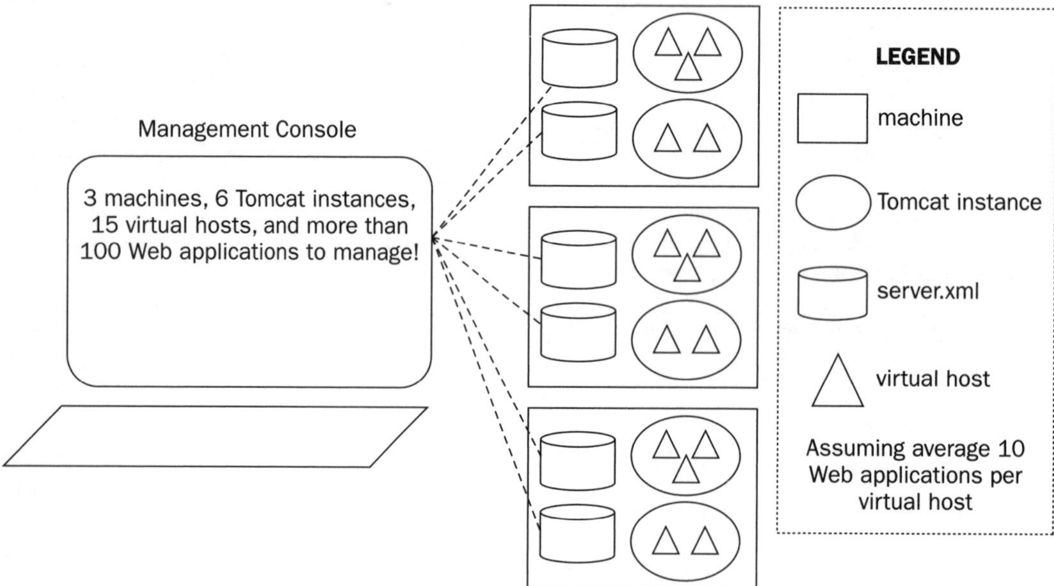

Figure 18-1: Management of a bank of Tomcat servers is problematic.

In Figure 18-1, management involves ad hoc maintenance and editing of individual configuration files at each of the physical servers. Operating system-specific scripts are used to automate certain frequently repeated operations. These scripts are difficult to maintain and must be changed for servers with different operating systems.

Tomcat 5's JMX support can eliminate this situation. Management, monitoring, and administrative tools created using Java can access and control Tomcat servers (and components within them, such as virtual hosts) across a network with ease. All the benefits of the Java language (including write-once run-anywhere behavior and easy code maintainability) can be leveraged in all these new management solutions. Figure 18-2 illustrates the JMX solution to Tomcat server management.

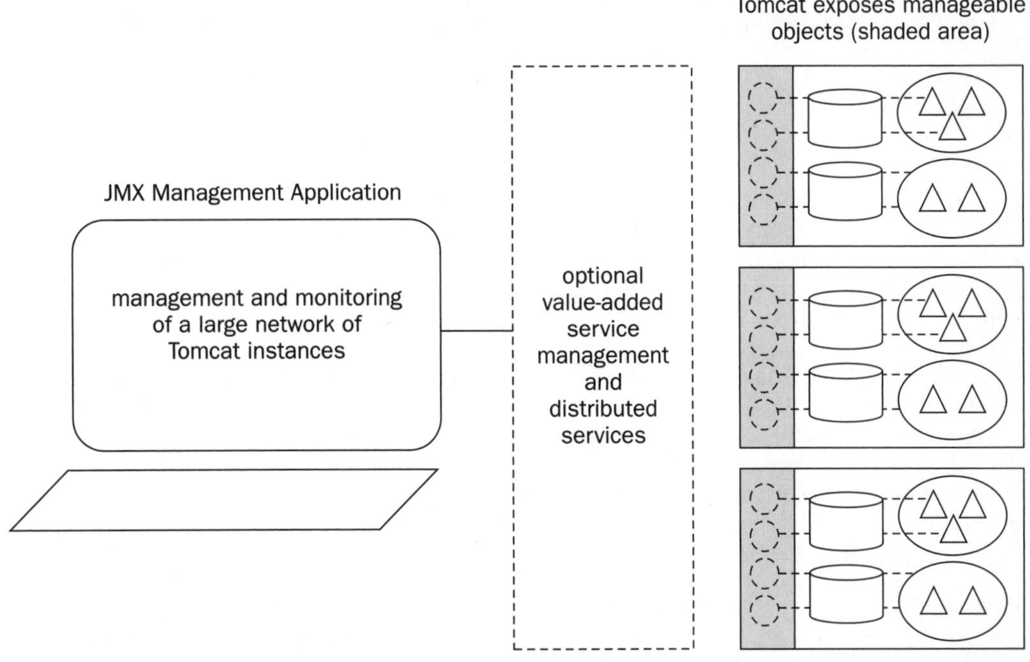

Figure 18-2: JMX solution to the Tomcat management problem.

In Figure 18-2, Tomcat 5 is JMX-ready. Tomcat exposes a set of Java-based objects for external management. This set of objects involves all configurable aspects of Tomcat, and provides run-time control for operational tuning/tweaking and run-time statistics for monitoring. JMX enables these objects to be accessed by local or remote management agents. Optional distributed services and value-added agent logic may further consolidate and intelligently aggregate the exposed information, providing users with a simplified view of the management application.

This is a definite improvement over the ad hoc management alternative. The following section examines exactly what JMX offers.

All About JMX

JMX is the subject matter of JSR-3, a specification developed over several years by an industry-wide network management experts group that is part of the Java Community Process (JCP). Major vendors of network management systems have active representation in this group and have ensured a balance of coverage. The main goal of this group was to develop a set of well-defined and related specifications that together describe an architecture for the management of manageable entities (devices, software services, and so on) over a network using the Java programming language. The deliverables from this exercise include the following:

- A set of specifications with a detailed architectural framework, including detailed descriptions of required components and their operations
- A functional reference implementation, with associated documentation
- A compatibility test suite to test compliance with the specification

While the subject of network management or enterprise management is certainly not new, a Java-specific standard is. Until JMX, most network management systems (sometimes called enterprise-management systems) are proprietary in nature. They are typically designed using specific operating system and programming language combinations. This leads to a proliferation of different versions of the same software base, maintained for different platforms.

The entities managed by a network management system have traditionally been hardware devices. Because of this origin, the de facto standard that makes devices generically manageable over a network is called **Simple Network Management Protocol** (**SNMP**). The protocol was originally defined for hardware devices, and is very restrictive when applied to modern software services that must be managed (such as Tomcat 5 servers). Because of the turbulent evolution of the network management industry, many proprietary extensions in addition to the SNMP protocol were introduced for vendor-specific device/management system combinations.

With the benefit of hindsight, JMX was designed to be flexible and adaptive from the start. Leveraging the benefits of the Java platform, the JMX specification is designed to facilitate the development of manageable entities and management systems without cornering vendors into restrictive implementations. At the same time, it must also be capable of co-existing and interoperating with the extensive body of already existing SNMP-based (or proprietary) managed systems in an evolutionary manner.

The JMX Architecture

Distilling decades of accumulated experience, the designers involved in JSR-3 made sure that the result is flexible and adaptable to both existing and future manageability needs. The architecture of JMX is layered as well as modular. The layers are well defined, yet loosely coupled. Existing networking and Java standards are used wherever applicable. As a result, the components of each layer can be built without prior intimate knowledge of the others. Being well defined and standards-based ensures that any specific implementation of one layer will directly work with an implementation of another.

Each layer within the JMX cake is called a **level.** The three levels in the JMX architecture are as follows:

- Instrumentation
- Agent
- Distributed Services

Figure 18-3 shows a high-level view of the levels and components involved in a JMX-based system. The next section explores these levels.

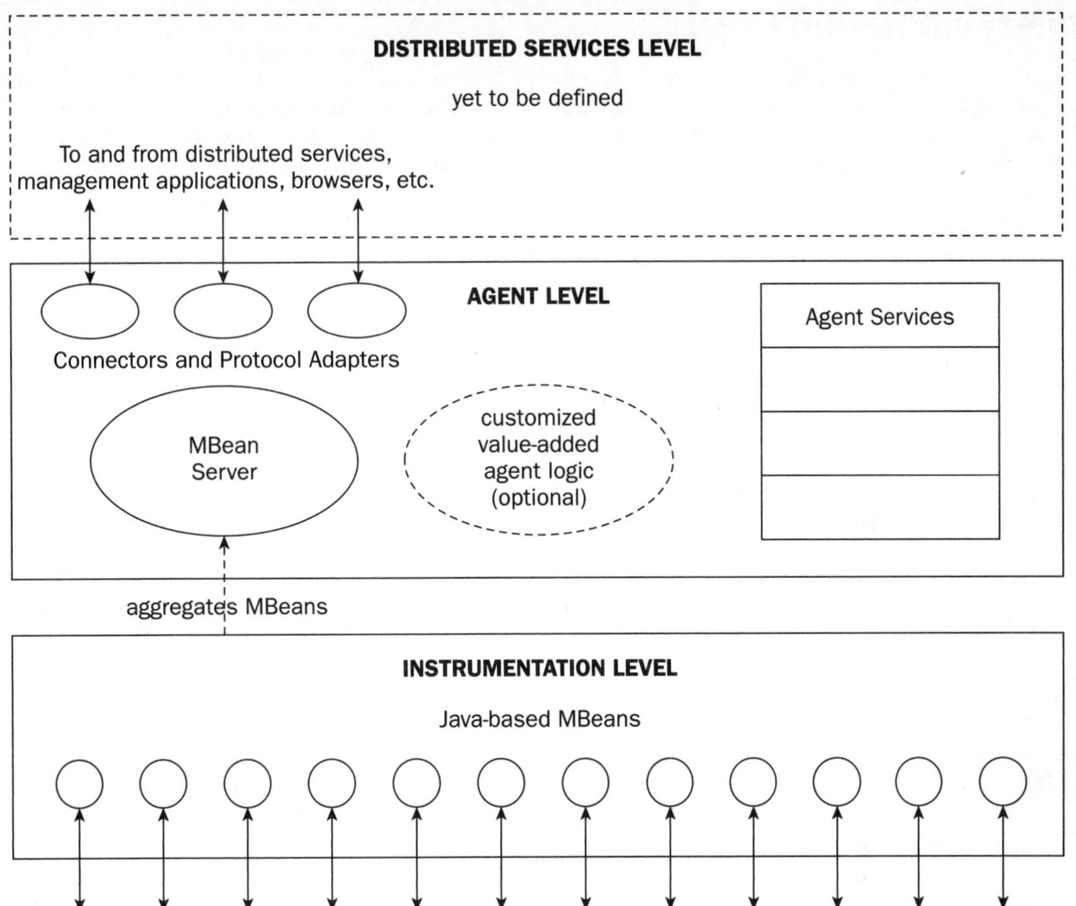

Figure 18-3: JMX architecture.

The complete JMX picture involves many different related standard specifications (JSRs). In fact, each JMX level is defined in its own specification, created by a different group of experts. Taken altogether, there are quite a few JMX-related JSR specifications, and this number can grow as the different levels become more fully defined. Currently, the two most important specifications to Tomcat administrators are the following:

- Java Management Extension Instrumentation and Agent Specification 1.2
- Java Remote API Specification 1.0

This chapter summarizes the important aspects of JMX that are relevant to Tomcat administration. You should consult the specifications for other details.

Now let's take a look at the components and interactions within each of the JMX levels.

Instrumentation Level

Within the **instrumentation level,** resources and objects that can be managed and/or monitored are enumerated. The act of defining what can be managed/monitored is called **instrumentation.** For example, the set of Web applications running in a Tomcat 5 server may be a candidate for JMX management, and thus can be instrumented at the instrumentation level. This entails the creation of **Managed Beans (MBeans).**

MBeans are Java components that live within the instrumentation level. They present a well-defined Java interface for the resources being managed. The resources, in this case, can be a hardware device, a software service, an application, or another entity (such as Web applications in a Tomcat 5 server). Instrumentation can be added to any existing resource simply by creating an MBean for the resource and hosting it on a network-connected Java VM. Typically, this is in the same physical box as the resource being managed. Figure 18-4 shows the high-level anatomy of an MBean.

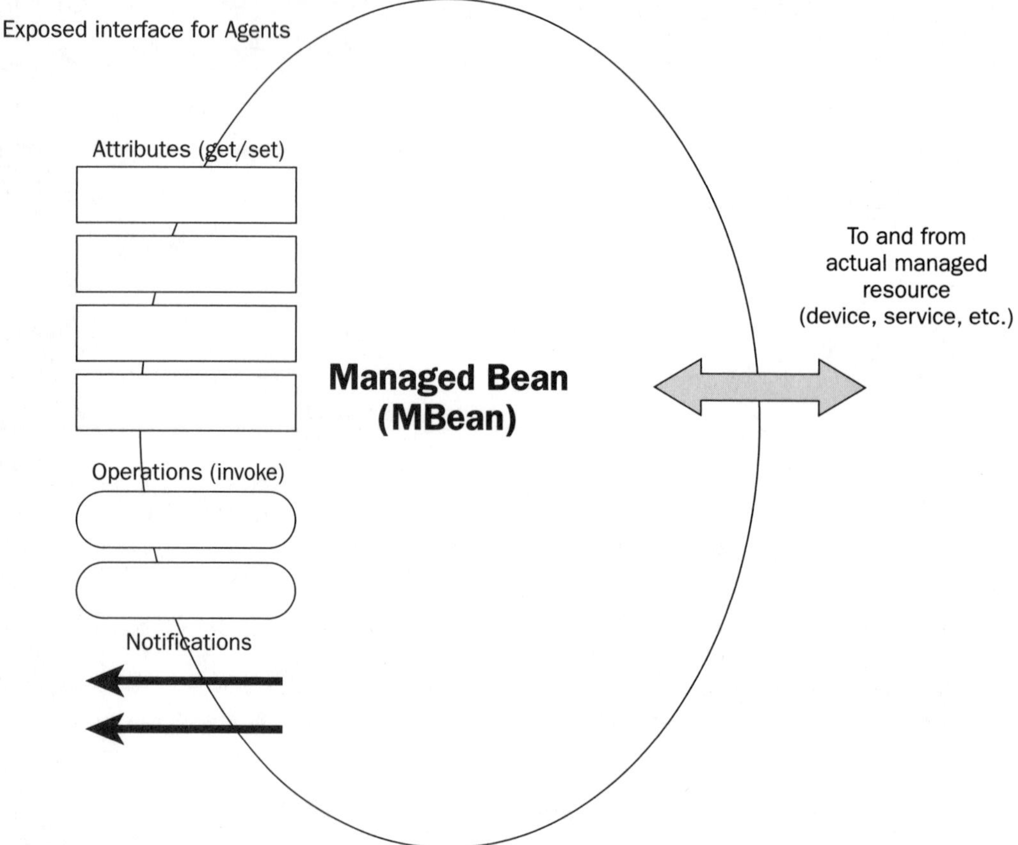

Figure 18-4: A Managed Bean (MBean).

Conceptually, MBeans are similar to JavaBeans, and expose attributes (such as properties that can be get and set), operations (such as methods that can be invoked), and notification events (distributed over the network, in this case) that can be caught by other levels. MBeans are oblivious to the agent that may be managing them, enabling instrumented resources to be managed by any JMX-compliant system.

Agent Level

At the agent level, the MBeans exposed by the instrumentation level are aggregated by the agent logic and present as manageable entities to higher-level distributed services and/or management applications. Most agents simply provide the same interface exposed by the MBeans for management. However, the interface exposed to higher levels need not be the same as those exposed by the individual aggregated MBeans. For example, an intelligent agent may expose a single attribute called `GlobalMaxThreads` that will update attributes of thread pool management MBeans across all the Tomcat 5 server instances that the agent is aggregating.

Another major purpose of the agent level is to decouple the interdependency between the management applications and the resources being managed. This decoupling enables instrumentation to be added independently (by coding MBeans), without being concerned about how the MBeans will be ultimately used. For example, hundreds of MBeans have been created and are available within any running Tomcat 5 server today. However, JMX management applications that make clever use of these MBeans are yet to be created.

The agent level can mediate and facilitate multiple concurrent accesses to the set of aggregated MBeans. It can also convert to and from different access protocols, enabling access from different management applications/services. Other value-added features at the agent level may include monitoring, data filtering, data reduction, intelligent consolidation, and so on.

Figure 18-3 shows the components that reside in the agent level, including the following:

- *MBean Server* — Aggregates MBeans; receives run-time registration of MBeans and makes them available for external management via connectors and protocol adapters.
- *Connectors and protocol adapters* — Provide external access to the MBeans and services aggregated by the MBean Server.
- *Agent Services* — A mandatory standard set of services that are available to a developer creating MBeans or agent logic.

The following sections describe each of these components in more detail.

The MBean Server

The MBean Server is a component in the agent level that aggregates the MBeans being exposed by the agent. A managed device or service needs to register the MBeans that it wants to expose with the MBean Server before it can be accessed by higher-level management applications. This registration happens at run-time (when a JMX-managed box is booted, at the startup of the Tomcat 5 server, and so on).

Management applications can only access MBean attributes, operations, or events through the management interface provided by the MBean Server. The access is not direct, as most higher-level management applications are external to the process/physical box of the server/device being managed. Instead, it is performed through the assistance of connectors and protocol adapters (described in the next section).

Note that many agent-level services are typically also implemented as MBeans. In these cases, they must also be registered with the MBean Server.

Connectors and Protocol Adapters

Management applications can access managed resources only through the MBeans Server component at the agent level. However, the MBean Server component has no direct means of communicating with external applications. Instead, the MBean Server relies on available connectors and protocol adapters to interface with external management applications, as shown in Figure 18-5.

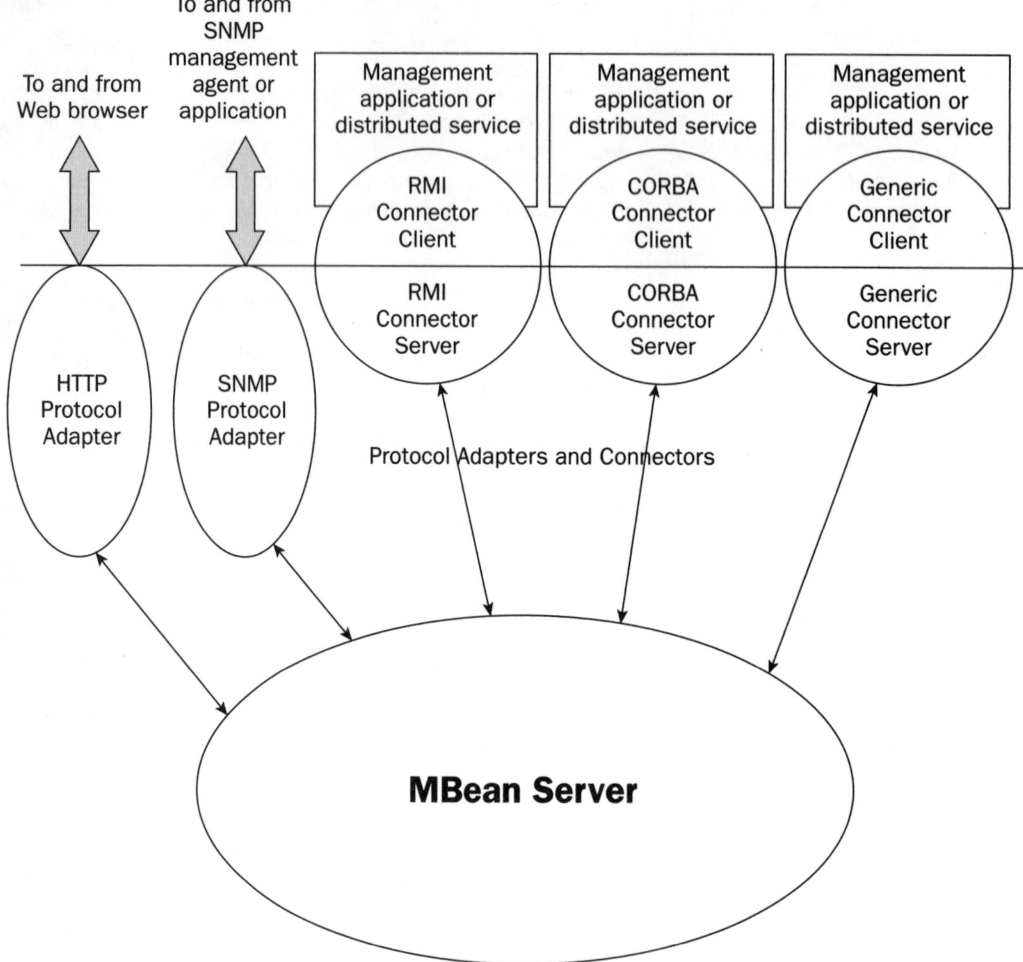

Figure 18-5: Connectors and protocol adapters.

Connectors typically utilize standard remote-access mechanisms (RMI, CORBA, Java Socket, and so on) to directly expose the interface of the agent remotely. Protocol adapters provide access to the agent by mapping JMX requests to and from specific protocols. For example, an HTTP protocol adapter may enable users to directly access the agent using a simple browser.

The JMX agent logic within Tomcat 5 supports both an HTTP protocol adapter in the form of the `manager` application's JMX proxy (more details about this later in this chapter), and an RMI Connector for remote JMX access. Figure 18-6 shows the connector and protocol adapter support within Tomcat 5.

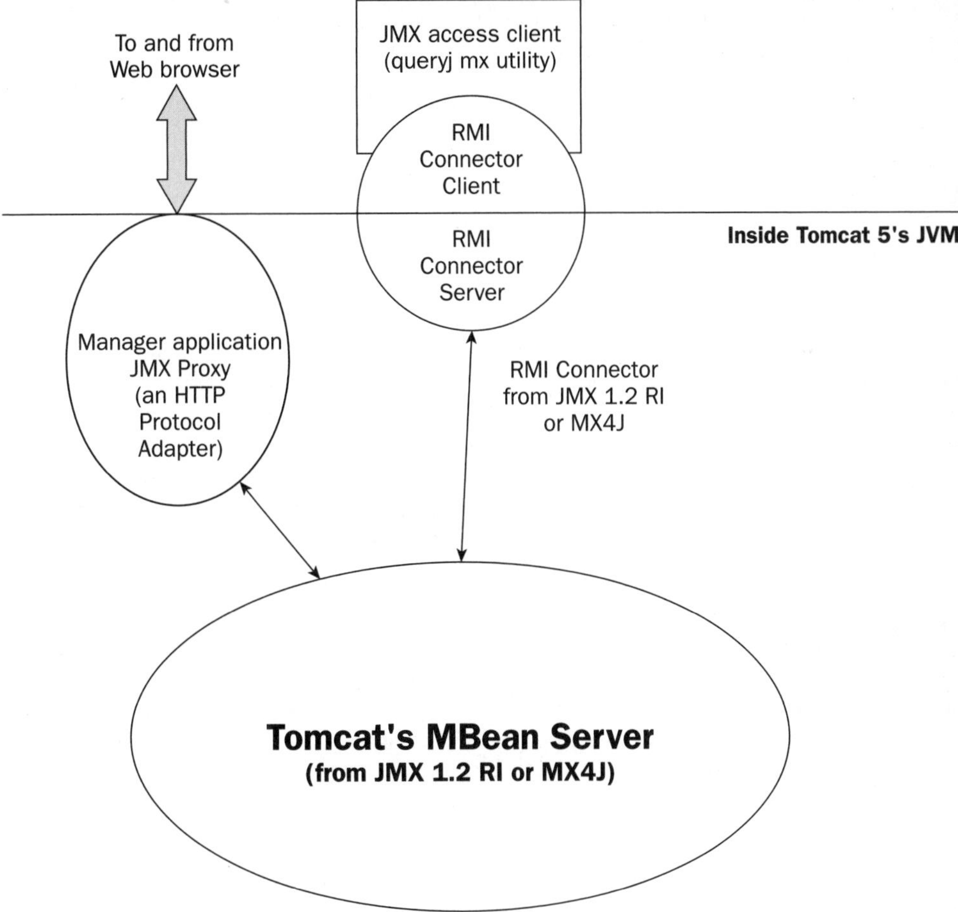

Figure 18-6: Tomcat 5 agent implementation.

Agent Services

JMX specifies a set of mandatory services that every compliant agent implementation must provide. These services include the following:

- A dynamic class loading service for loading management applets (mlets)
- A monitoring service to monitor changes in specified MBean attributes
- A timer service for periodic or one-shot timing
- A relation service for enforcing relationships between MBeans

Agent services are used mainly by developers to implement customized agent logic and/or management applications. Tomcat administrators need not be concerned with their programmatic features. However, an awareness of their existence may facilitate useful discussions with development and network management staff.

Distributed Services Level

The **distributed services level** is the topmost level in the JMX architectural diagram (see Figure 18-3). This level includes applications and services that access the functionality provided by the agent level.

This level specifies standard high-level management interfaces for the creation of management applications. These interfaces and their associated components enable management applications (or other services applications) to interact with the agent level. The specification for the distributed services level is still a work in progress and has not yet been finalized. No further public information is currently available.

JMX Remote API

While connectors and protocol adapters can be seen as agent level components, specifications for them are not part of JMX Instrumentation and Agent 1.2 specification. Instead, different connectors and adapters are covered under different specifications. Specifically, JSR-160 (the JMX Remote API specification) covers the details for a set of connectors that can be used to remotely access the agent level.

Originally, it was called JMX Remoting, and was destined to be included with a new release of the base JMX. However, the experts group decided to factor out elements that enable remote access to the agent layer and place them in its own specification. This enabled the earlier release of the base specification.

Before working with Tomcat 5's JMX agent, you should have an understanding of how developers typically create MBeans. This is necessary because the terminology introduced is a prerequisite for the Tomcat 5 MBeans examined later in this chapter.

An Anthology of MBeans

MBeans are software modules that expose the capabilities of a hardware device, a software service, or a software component. In JMX literature and technical discussions, you will see references to different types of MBeans, including the following:

- Standard MBean
- Dynamic MBean
- Model MBean
- Open MBean

It is not necessary for administrators to fully understand their differences. They all appear the same to management software that may work with them. Developers, however, will be very intimate with their differences. The following sections provide a brief explanation of each.

Standard MBeans

In standard MBeans, the features (attributes, operations, and notifications) that are exposed for management are fixed and cannot change (without a software or firmware change). Standard MBeans are typically the easiest to code for developers.

Dynamic MBeans

In dynamic MBeans, the features that are exposed for management are determined at run-time. Therefore, the exposed features can change over time.

Model MBeans

Because of the flexible nature of dynamic MBeans, they are quite difficult and tedious to code. Model MBeans are a type of dynamic MBean used by developers to expedite the creation of their own dynamic MBeans. For example, Tomcat 5 makes extensive use of the model MBean support provided by the Apache Jakarta Commons (modeler) project.

Open MBeans

Open MBeans are a type of dynamic MBean. The unique quality of open MBeans is their capability to be managed by any compliant management software. This is because the exposed features of an open MBean are guaranteed to be compliant with a universally manageable set of data types. Management software can then explore the set of exposed features at run-time to use the MBean. Open MBeans are a new feature of JMX 1.2, and are not required for compliance with previous JMX versions.

With all the basic technicalities out of the way, it's now time to take a look at the manageable elements exposed by Tomcat 5 through JMX MBeans.

JMX Manageable Elements in Tomcat 5

Almost all configurable elements of Tomcat 5 will become JMX-manageable in the near future. As developers build new attributes into the Tomcat 5 architectural components, they will create the corresponding MBean to expose these attributes for external management and monitoring.

In addition, the Tomcat 5 server creates some MBeans at run-time (see Chapter 8) to make dynamic run-time-only objects manageable. For example, elements in a UserDatabase (such as Users, Roles, and Groups) are created at run-time. When a Web application is deployed or re-deployed, Tomcat 5 will also create a manageable object for the context that supports the application.

Much of this support is still work in progress with Tomcat 5 (to be solidified in later releases). The following list describes MBean-exposed objects in Tomcat 5 and the attributes that are accessible via JMX:

- *Manageable Tomcat 5 Architectural Components* — These include Service, Server, Engine, Connector, and Host.
- *Manageable Nested Components* — These include Realm, Logger, Valve, and Manager

- *Manageable Run-Time Data Objects*—These include `UserDatabase`, `User`, and `Role`.
- *Manageable Resource Objects*—These include NamingResources, Environment, Resource, ResourceLink, application-related objects, WebModule, internal Tomcat objects, RequestProcessor, Cache, and ThreadPool.

Included with the following discussion of these items are step-by-step instructions for accessing these manageable components via either of the following means:

- The JMX proxy of the manager application (this is, architecturally, an HTTP protocol adapter)
- The RMI connector

The listing can be used as your reference guide to probe around the manageable components of Tomcat 5.

If you cannot wait to start probing around your own Tomcat 5 instance using JMX, skip right ahead to the section "Accessing Tomcat 5's JMX Support via the Manager Proxy," later in this chapter and consult the MBean list as necessary for reference.

Manageable Tomcat 5 Architectural Components

The first set of manageable objects are the components that we are familiar with when working with the `server.xml` file or the `admin` application. This section describes their accessible attributes, together with the data type expected for the attribute and whether the attribute is read-only (RO) or read/write (R/W).

If you need a refresher on any of the manageable components and/or their configurable attributes, you may want to revisit Chapter 5 and Chapter 8.

Service

Note that the `modelerType` attribute exists on every manageable component. This is because Tomcat 5 uses library code from The Apache Jakarta Project's Commons Modeler to simplify its own implementation of JMX. MBeans created using Apache's Commons Modeler typically expose this `modelerType` attribute.

In the following table, the column labeled Read/Write indicates whether an attribute can be changed (R/W) or cannot be changed (RO—Read-Only) via JMX control.

Attribute Name	Read/Write	Type
`modelerType`	R/W	`java.lang.String`
`debug`	R/W	`int`
`managedResource`	R/W	`java.lang.Object`
`name`	R/W	`java.lang.String`
`connectorNames`	RO (Read Only)	`javax.management.ObjectName[]`
`container`	RO	`javax.management.ObjectName`

Server

Because JMX MBeans expose both configuration and run-time attributes, many new attributes provide a run-time relationship between the components. For example, the `serviceNames` attribute provides an array of services that is associated with the Server component, as shown in the following table.

Attribute Name	Read/Write	Type
`modelerType`	R/W	`java.lang.String`
`debug`	R/W	`int`
`managedResource`	R/W	`java.lang.Object`
`port`	R/W	`int`
`shutdown`	R/W	`java.lang.String`
`serviceNames`	R/W	`javax.management.ObjectName[]`

Engine

In the following table, it is interesting to note that at run-time, the Engine maintains a list of configured Valve components. This list can be accessed via JMX using the `valveObjectNames` attribute.

Attribute Name	Read/Write	Type
`modelerType`	R/W	`java.lang.String`
`debug`	R/W	`int`
`defaultHost`	R/W	`java.lang.String`
`managedResource`	R/W	`java.lang.Object`
`name`	R/W	`java.lang.String`
`baseDir`	R/W	`java.lang.String`
`jvmRoute`	R/W	`java.lang.String`
`valveObjectNames`	RO	`javax.management.ObjectName[]`

Connector

As shown in the following table, each connector configured has its own run-time MBean. Some connectors (for example, JK Connectors) may have additional run-time MBeans that are accessible via JMX.

Attribute Name	Read/Write	Type
modelerType	R/W	java.lang.String
acceptCount	R/W	int
address	R/W	java.lang.String
algorithm	R/W	java.lang.String
bufferSize	R/W	int
className	RO	java.lang.String
clientAuth	R/W	boolean
ciphers	R/W	java.lang.String
compression	R/W	java.lang.String
connectionLinger	R/W	int
connectionTimeout	R/W	int
connectionUploadTimeout	R/W	int
debug	R/W	int
disableUploadTimeout	R/W	boolean
enableLookups	R/W	boolean
keystoreFile	R/W	java.lang.String
keystorePass	R/W	java.lang.String
keystoreType	R/W	java.lang.String
keyAlias	R/W	java.lang.String
maxKeepAliveRequests	R/W	int
maxProcessors	R/W	int
minProcessors	R/W	int
maxSpareThreads	R/W	int
maxThreads	R/W	int
minSpareThreads	R/W	int
minProcessors	R/W	int
port	R/W	int
protocol	R/W	java.lang.String
protocolHandlerClassName	RO	java.lang.String
proxyName	R/W	java.lang.String
proxyPort	R/W	int

Attribute Name	Read/Write	Type
redirectPort	R/W	int
scheme	R/W	java.lang.String
secret	WO	java.lang.String
secure	R/W	boolean
sslProtocol	R/W	java.lang.String
sslProtocols	R/W	java.lang.String
tcpNoDelay	R/W	boolean
tomcatAuthentication	R/W	boolean
URIEncoding	R/W	java.lang.String
xpoweredBy	R/W	boolean

Host

As shown in the following table, each configured virtual host in the Engine exposes its own JMX-accessible MBean.

Attribute Name	Read/Write	Type
modelerType	R/W	java.lang.String
appBase	R/W	java.lang.String
autoDeploy	R/W	boolean
debug	R/W	int
deployOnStartup	R/W	boolean
deployXML	R/W	boolean
managedResource	R/W	java.lang.Object
name	R/W	java.lang.String
unpackWARs	R/W	boolean
xmlNamespaceAware	R/W	boolean
xmlValidation	R/W	boolean
children	R/W	javax.management.ObjectName[]
aliases	R/W	java.lang.String[]
valveNames	R/W	java.lang.String[]
valveObjectNames	R/W	javax.management.ObjectName[]

Manageable Nested Components

Following is the set of noncontainer nested components that are exposed on Tomcat 5 via JMX. Chapter 8 provides a detailed description of most of their attributes. The existence and number of these elements depend on the current configuration (that is, `server.xml` settings).

Realm

The components in the following table correspond to a configured `<Realm>` element.

Attribute Name	Read/Write	Type
modelerType	R/W	java.lang.String
className	RO	java.lang.String
debug	R/W	int
resourceName	R/W	java.lang.String

Logger

The components in the following table correspond to a configured `<Logger>` element.

Attribute Name	Read/Write	Type
modelerType	R/W	java.lang.String
className	RO	java.lang.String
debug	R/W	int
directory	R/W	java.lang.String
prefix	R/W	java.lang.String
suffix	R/W	java.lang.String
timestamp	R/W	boolean
verbosity	R/W	int

Valve

The components in the following table correspond to a configured `<Valve>` element.

Attribute Name	Read/Write	Type
modelerType	R/W	java.lang.String
className	RO	java.lang.String
debug	R/W	int

Manager

The components in the following table correspond to a configured `<Manager>` element, representing a session manager implementation (that is, a Persistent Session Manager).

Attribute Name	Read/Write	Type
`modelerType`	R/W	`java.lang.String`
`algorithm`	R/W	`java.lang.String`
`randomFile`	R/W	`java.lang.String`
`className`	RO	`java.lang.String`
`debug`	R/W	`int`
`distributable`	R/W	`boolean`
`entropy`	R/W	`java.lang.String`
`managedResource`	R/W	`java.lang.Object`
`maxActiveSessions`	R/W	`int`
`maxInactiveInterval`	R/W	`int`
`name`	RO	`java.lang.String`
`pathname`	R/W	`java.lang.String`
`activeSessions`	RO	`int`
`sessionCounter`	R/W	`int`
`maxActive`	R/W	`int`
`rejectedSessions`	R/W	`int`
`expiredSessions`	R/W	`int`
`processingTime`	R/W	`long`
`duplicates`	R/W	`int`

Manageable Run-Time Data Objects

Chapter 8's overview of lifecycle listeners revealed that Tomcat 5 uses lifecycle listeners to create MBeans for run-time objects. For example, the UserDatabase that is used by Tomcat for authentication and authorization (if it is configured to use a UserDatabase Realm) can be accessed via these JMX MBeans. The listeners also create MBeans for each user, role, and group within the database.

The following tables list the attributes that are available with these run-time data objects.

UserDatabase

In the following table, note that UserDatabase contains attributes that contain users, groups, and roles information. This information is managed in memory by the UserDatabase Realm.

Attribute Name	Read/Write	Type
`modelerType`	R/W	`java.lang.String`
`encoding`	R/W	`java.lang.String`
`groups`	RO	`java.lang.String[]`
`pathname`	R/W	`java.lang.String`
`roles`	RO	`java.lang.String[]`
`users`	RO	`java.lang.String[]`

User

In the following table, note the wide-open availability of a password for the user via this MBean. This underscores the need for careful security considerations before enabling JMX access on production systems.

Attribute Name	Read/Write	Type
`modelerType`	R/W	`java.lang.String`
`fullName`	R/W	`java.lang.String`
`groups`	R/W	`java.lang.String[]`
`password`	R/W	`java.lang.String`
`roles`	RO	`java.lang.String[]`
`username`	R/W	`java.lang.String`

Role

The following table lists the attributes available with the Role object.

Attribute Name	Read/Write	Type
`modelerType`	R/W	`java.lang.String`
`description`	R/W	`java.lang.String`
`rolename`	R/W	`java.lang.String`

Manageable Resource Object

Any global resources, Web-application resources, or environments that are configured for JNDI access within the configuration files become manageable through an MBean instance.

NamingResources

As shown in the following table, this object maintains a live list of all the defined JNDI-accessible global naming resources.

Attribute Name	Read/Write	Type
`modelerType`	R/W	`java.lang.String`
`environments`	RO	`java.lang.String[]`
`resources`	RO	`java.lang.String[]`
`resourceLinks`	RO	`java.lang.String[]`

Environment

As shown in the following table, any global `<Environment>` definition has an associated Environment MBean.

Attribute Name	Read/Write	Type
`modelerType`	R/W	`java.lang.String`
`className`	RO	`java.lang.String`
`description`	R/W	`java.lang.String`
`name`	R/W	`java.lang.String`
`override`	R/W	`boolean`
`type`	R/W	`java.lang.String`
`value`	R/W	`java.lang.String`

Resource

As shown in the following table, any global `<Resource>` definition will cause the creation of an associated MBean instance with the following attributes.

Attribute Name	Read/Write	Type
modelerType	R/W	java.lang.String
auth	R/W	java.lang.String
description	R/W	java.lang.String
name	R/W	java.lang.String
scope	R/W	java.lang.String
type	R/W	java.lang.String

ResourceLink

A `<resource-link>` definition creates an associated ResourceLink MBean instance with the following attributes.

Attribute Name	Read/Write	Type
modelerType	R/W	java.lang.String
global	R/W	java.lang.String
name	R/W	java.lang.String
type	R/W	java.lang.String

Exposed Application-Related Objects

Several internal Tomcat 5 objects correspond to J2EE-defined run-time objects. They are accessible via JMX and are described in the following sections.

WebModule

A `WebModule` is a deployable unit. Tomcat 5 keeps track of currently deployed modules internally, and the information can be accessed via the MBeans shown in the following table. A WebModule MBean roughly corresponds to the combination of a single context descriptor and a deployment descriptor.

Attribute Name	Read/Write	Type
modelerType	R/W	java.lang.String
allowLinking	R/W	boolean
cacheMaxSize	R/W	int
cacheTTL	R/W	int
cachingAllowed	R/W	boolean
caseSensitive	R/W	boolean

Attribute Name	Read/Write	Type
children	R/W	javax.management.ObjectName[]
cookies	R/W	boolean
compilerClasspath	R/W	java.lang.String
crossContext	R/W	boolean
debug	R/W	int
defaultWebXml	R/W	java.lang.String
delegate	R/W	boolean
deploymentDescriptor	R/W	java.lang.String
docBase	R/W	java.lang.String
engineName	R/W	java.lang.String
environments	RO	java.lang.String[]
eventProvider	R/W	boolean
javaVMs	R/W	java.lang.String[]
loader	R/W	org.apache.catalina.Loader
logger	R/W	org.apache.catalina.Logger
managedResource	R/W	java.lang.Object
manager	R/W	org.apache.catalina.Manager
managerChecksFrequency	R/W	int
mappingObject	R/W	java.lang.Object
objectName	R/W	java.lang.String
override	R/W	boolean
parentClassLoader	R/W	java.lang.ClassLoader
path	R/W	java.lang.String
privileged	R/W	boolean
reloadable	R/W	boolean
resourceNames	RO	java.lang.String[]
server	R/W	java.lang.String
servlets	RO	java.lang.String[]
startupTime	R/W	long
state	R/W	int

Table continued on following page

Attribute Name	Read/Write	Type
stateManageable	R/W	boolean
statisticsProvider	R/W	boolean
staticResources	RO	javax.naming.directory.DirContext[]
swallowOutput	R/W	boolean
tldScanTime	R/W	long
useNaming	R/W	boolean
valveObjectNames	RO	javax.management.ObjectName[]
welcomeFiles	RO	java.lang.String[]
workDir	R/W	java.lang.String

Servlet

As shown in the following table, each activated Servlet also has its own MBean, which provides valuable information on the Web application and Servlet granularity.

Attribute Name	Read/Write	Type
modelerType	R/W	java.lang.String
engineName	RO	java.lang.String
eventProvider	R/W	boolean
objectName	R/W	java.lang.String
stateManageable	R/W	boolean
statisticsProvider	R/W	boolean
processingTime	RO	long
maxTime	RO	long
requestCount	RO	int
errorCount	RO	int
loadTime	RO	long
classLoadTime	RO	int

Exposed Internal Tomcat Objects

A few core internal Tomcat objects have MBeans exposed. The following sections describe several of the more interesting ones.

RequestProcessor

Each virtual host implements its own request processor. The following table shows how MBeans expose some interesting information. Information such as request count and error count may be relevant to administrators when troubleshooting.

Attribute Name	Read/Write	Type
modelerType	R/W	java.lang.String
virtualHost	RO	java.lang.String
bytesSent	R/W	long
method	RO	java.lang.String
remoteAddr	RO	java.lang.String
requestBytesSent	RO	long
contentLength	RO	int
bytesReceived	R/W	long
requestProcessingTime	RO	long
globalProcessor	R/W	org.apache.coyote.RequestGroupInfo
protocol	RO	java.lang.String
currentQueryString	RO	java.lang.String
maxRequestUri	R/W	java.lang.String
requestBytesReceived	RO	long
serverPort	RO	int
stage	R/W	int
requestCount	R/W	int
maxTime	R/W	long
processingTime	R/W	long
currentUri	RO	java.lang.String
errorCount	R/W	int

Cache

As shown in the following table, the object cache and thread pool objects exposed through JMX can provide administrators with valuable information for tuning the performance of a Tomcat system or cluster.

Attribute Name	Read/Write	Type
modelerType	R/W	java.lang.String
accessCount	RO	long
cacheMaxSize	R/W	int
hitsCount	RO	long
maxAllocateIterations	R/W	int
spareNotFoundEntries	R/W	int
cacheSize	RO	int
desiredEntryAccessRatio	R/W	long

ThreadPool

The following table shows attributes associated with the ThreadPool object.

Attribute Name	Read/Write	Type
modelerType	R/W	java.lang.String
name	R/W	java.lang.String
minSpareThreads	R/W	int
currentThreadsBusy	RO	int
daemon	R/W	boolean
threadStatus	RO	java.lang.String[]
sequence	RO	int
currentThreadCount	RO	int
maxSpareThreads	R/W	int
maxThreads	R/W	int
threadParam	RO	java.lang.String[]

Accessing Tomcat 5's JMX Support via the Manager Proxy

The `manager` application (featured in Chapter 7) has a JMX proxy that can be used to interact with Tomcat's agent level directly. The proxy enables the monitoring of Tomcat components through the exposed MBeans. It also enables you to read the value of an MBean attribute, or change/set the value of writeable MBean attributes. Figure 18-7 illustrates the operation of the JMX proxy.

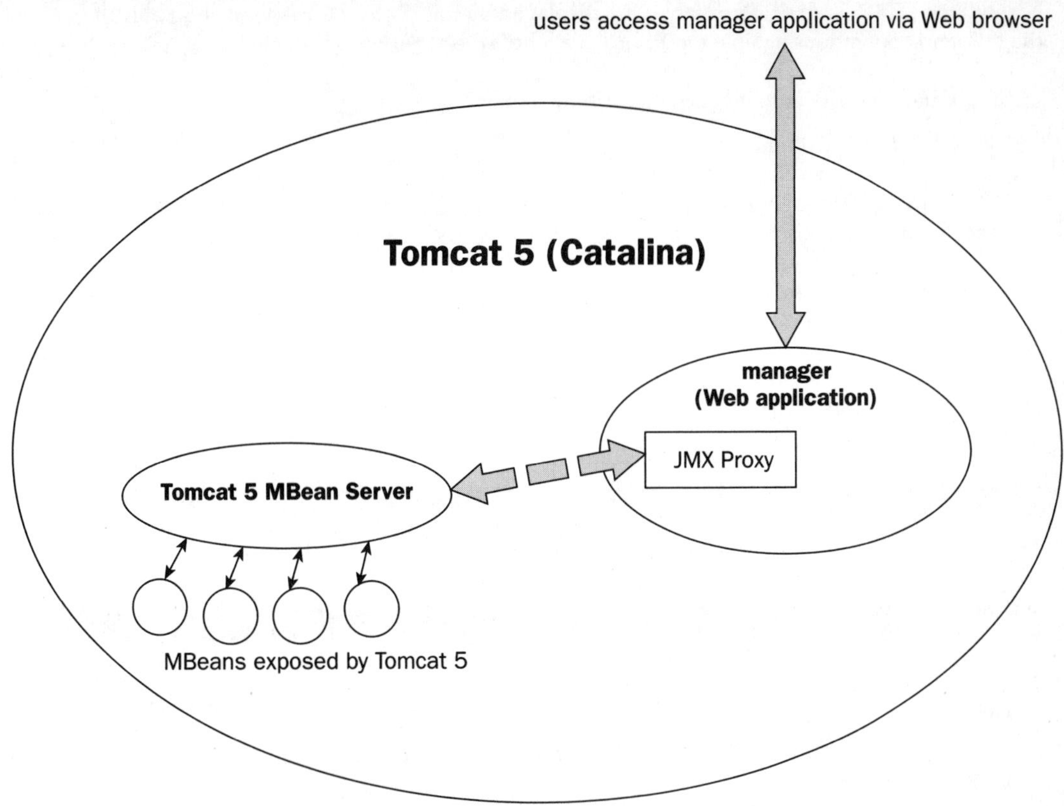

Figure 18-7: The manager application's JMX proxy.

In Figure 18-7, notice that the `manager` application provides an HTML-based interface to the JMX MBean server, acting as an HTTP protocol adapter for the agent. The `manager` application adds essential value in this scenario. It provides querying capabilities and will authenticate the user before granting access to the JMX proxy.

Architecturally, because the `manager` JMX proxy actually runs within the same JVM as the Tomcat server, it can be viewed as a part of Tomcat's agent level implementation. As mentioned previously, it acts as an HTTP protocol adapter.

Working with the JMX Proxy

The URL for accessing the JMX proxy using a browser is as follows:

```
http://<host>:<port>/manager/jmxproxy/<operation details>
```

If Tomcat is running locally with the default configuration, the URL is as follows:

```
http://localhost:8080/manager/jmxproxy/<operation details>
```

No stylized HTML Web pages or tables are displayed by this proxy. However, it is capable of performing the following operations against the Tomcat 5 agent (MBean Server) implementation:

- Query for MBeans and current attribute values
- Set MBean attribute values

WARNING: *Modifying the value of a Tomcat internal MBean during production operation can potentially cause problems that may result in an application and/or system crash. Use this feature at your own risk*

The general form for a query operation using the JMX proxy is as follows:

```
?qry=<query details>
```

For example, you can get a complete listing of all the available MBeans using the following wildcard query:

```
http://localhost:8080/manager/jmxproxy/?qry=*:*jmxproxy
```

The result will be similar to what is shown in Figure 18-8.

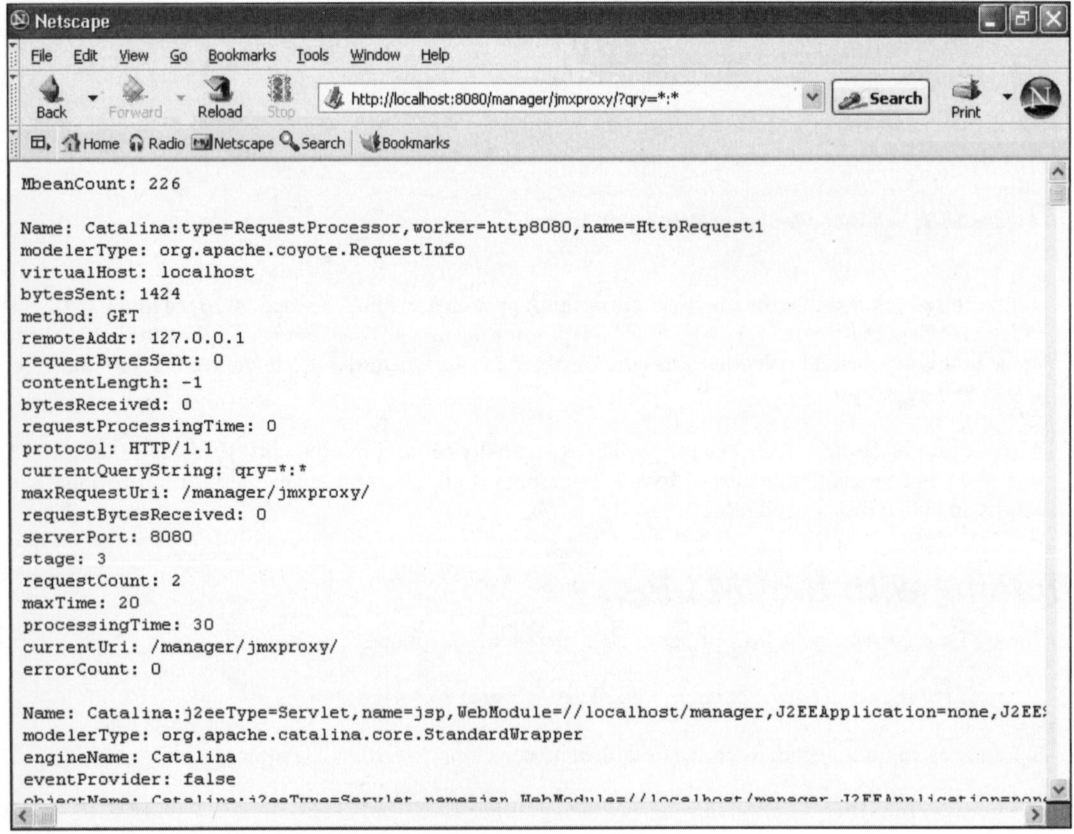

Figure 18-8: Listing of all the MBeans in Tomcat 5.

As another example, you can get a listing of all the connector MBeans using the following query:

```
http://<host>:<port>/manager/jmxproxy/?qry=*:type=Connector,*
```

The result will be similar to what is shown in Figure 18-9.

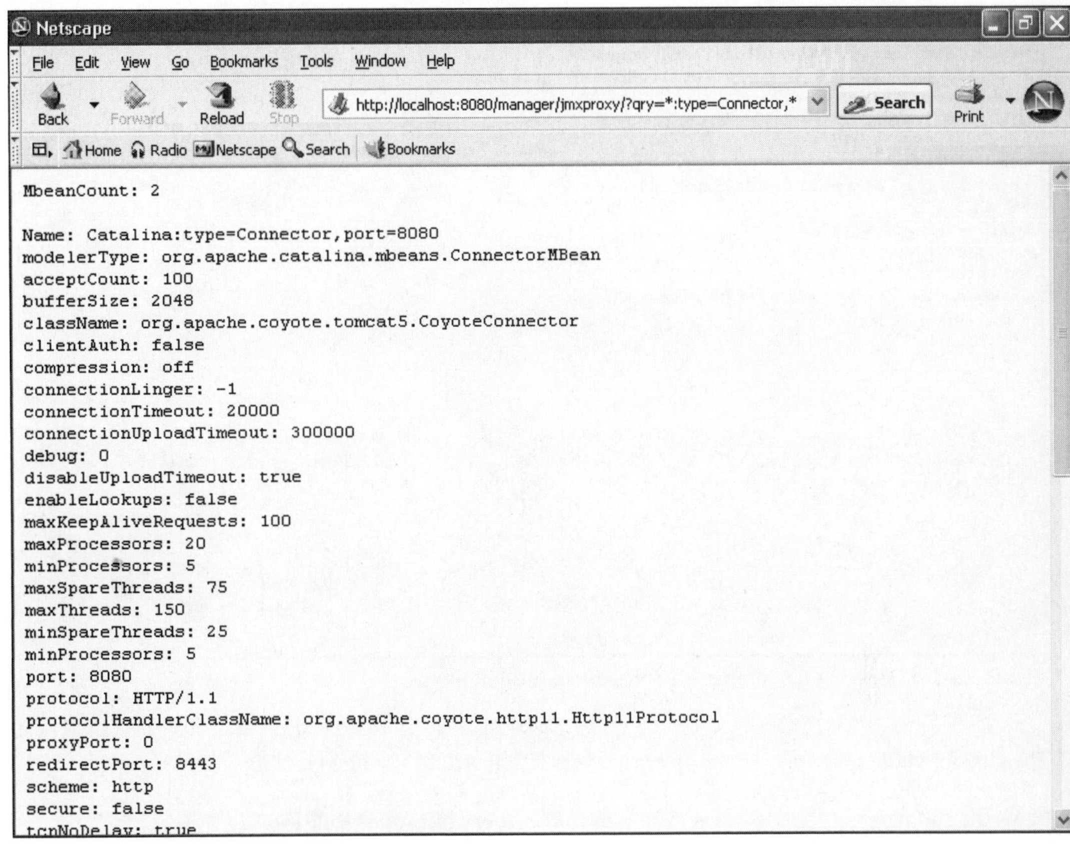

Figure 18-9: Listing of all Connector MBeans.

Modifying MBean Attributes

Another operation you can perform with the JMX proxy is to change the attribute of an MBean. The general syntax for this operation is as follows:

```
http://<host>:<port>/manager/jmxproxy/?set=<full MBean name>&att=<attribute
name>&val=<value to change to>
```

For example, the following procedure can be used during performance tuning to change the maximum number of threads managed by Tomcat 5's thread pool in real time. You first need to query for the full MBean name of the exposed thread pool, as shown in the following example:

```
http://<host>:<port>/manager/jmxproxy/?qry=*:type=ThreadPool,*
```

The output of the query will be similar to what is shown in Figure 18-10.

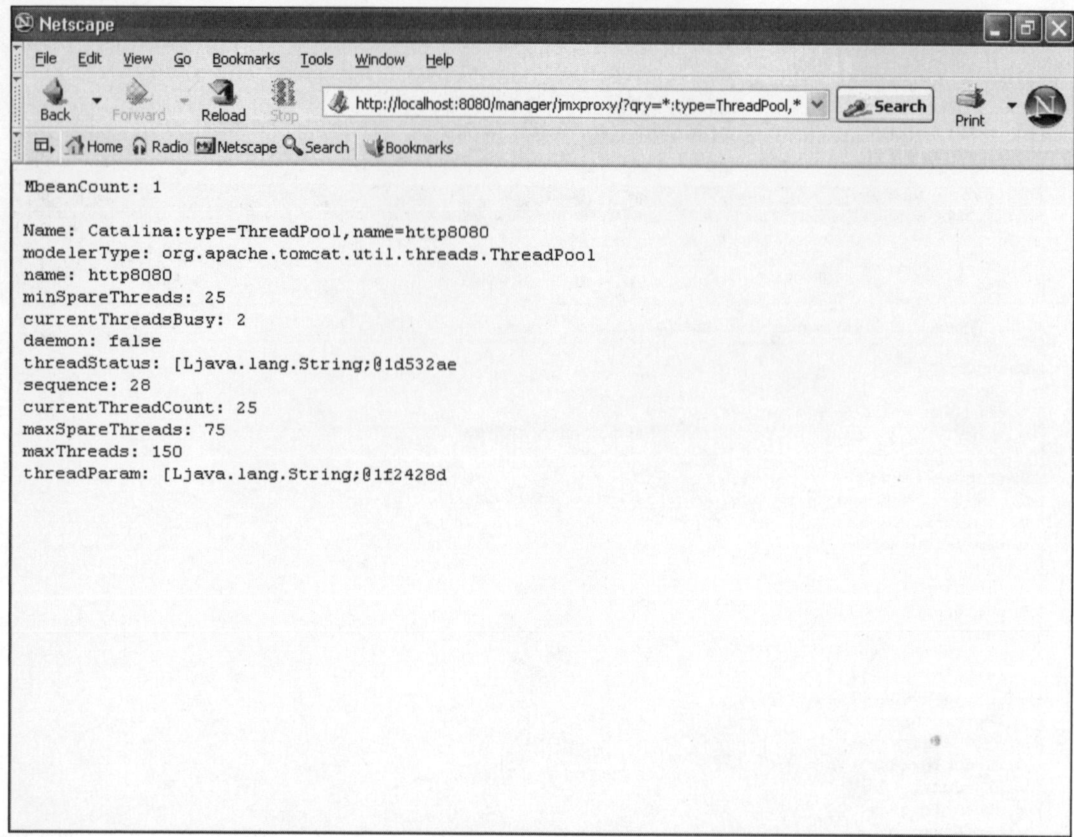

Figure 18-10: Querying for Tomcat 5's ThreadPool MBean name.

The current value of the `maxThreads` attribute is 150. It will be changed to 200.

Now, the full name of the MBean is visible from the query output as follows:

```
Catalina:type=ThreadPool,name=http8080
```

Next, by consulting the Tomcat 5 MBeans description listing in this chapter, you can determine that the `maxThreads` attribute is a writeable property.

Finally, the URL for the `set` operation is as follows (type the entire URL on one line):

```
http://<host>:<port>/manager/jmxproxy/?set= Catalina:type=ThreadPool,name=http8080
&att=maxThreads&val=200
```

Upon successful operation, the output is similar to what is shown in Figure 18-11. If you try to modify a read-only attribute, you will receive a message reporting an "attribute not found" exception.

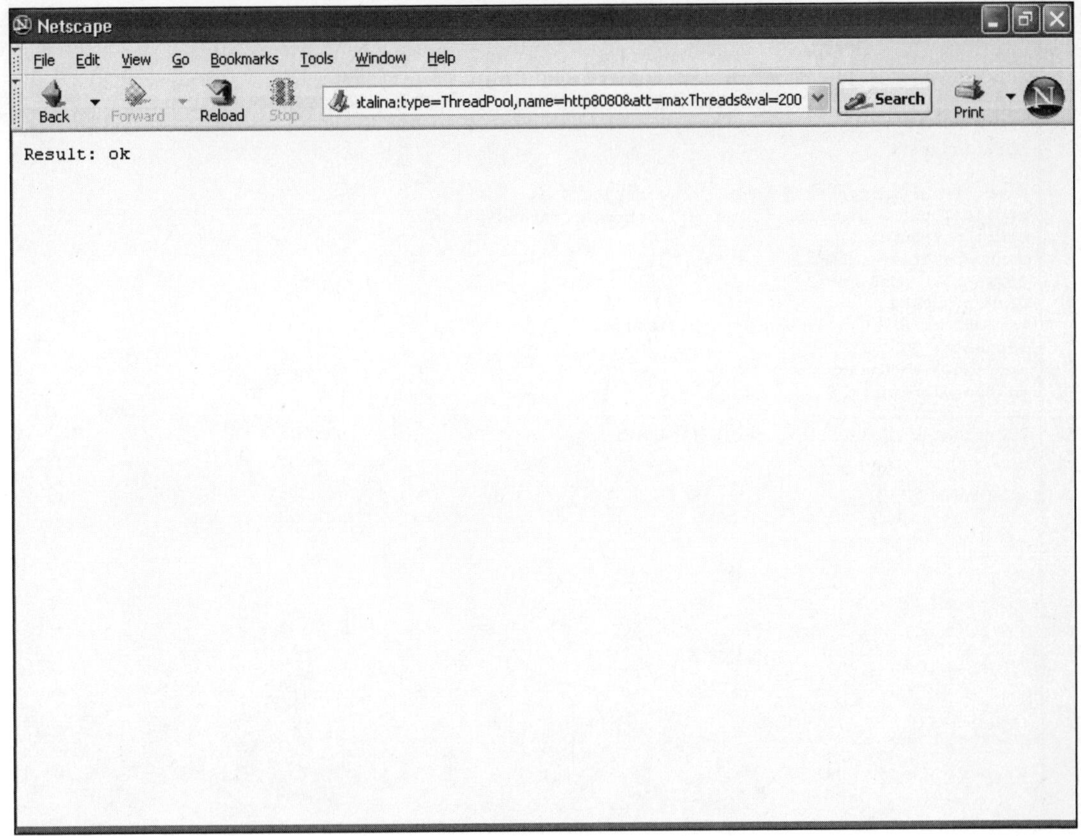

Figure 18-11: Increasing the maxThreads attribute of Tomcat 5's ThreadPool object.

If you perform another query for the ThreadPool information, you will see the change as shown in Figure 18-12.

The capability to peek into Tomcat internals during run-time and tweak the running server is an extremely attractive feature. Tomcat 5's support for JMX is essential in carrying out these tasks.

The JMX proxy accesses the MBean Server within the same JVM. Typical network-management scenarios call for the `management` application to run on an external JVM, and often on another machine over the network. Chapter 7 explains how to perform management tasks in an external JVM running Ant. The next section examines a method of accessing the Tomcat 5 agent remotely over a network.

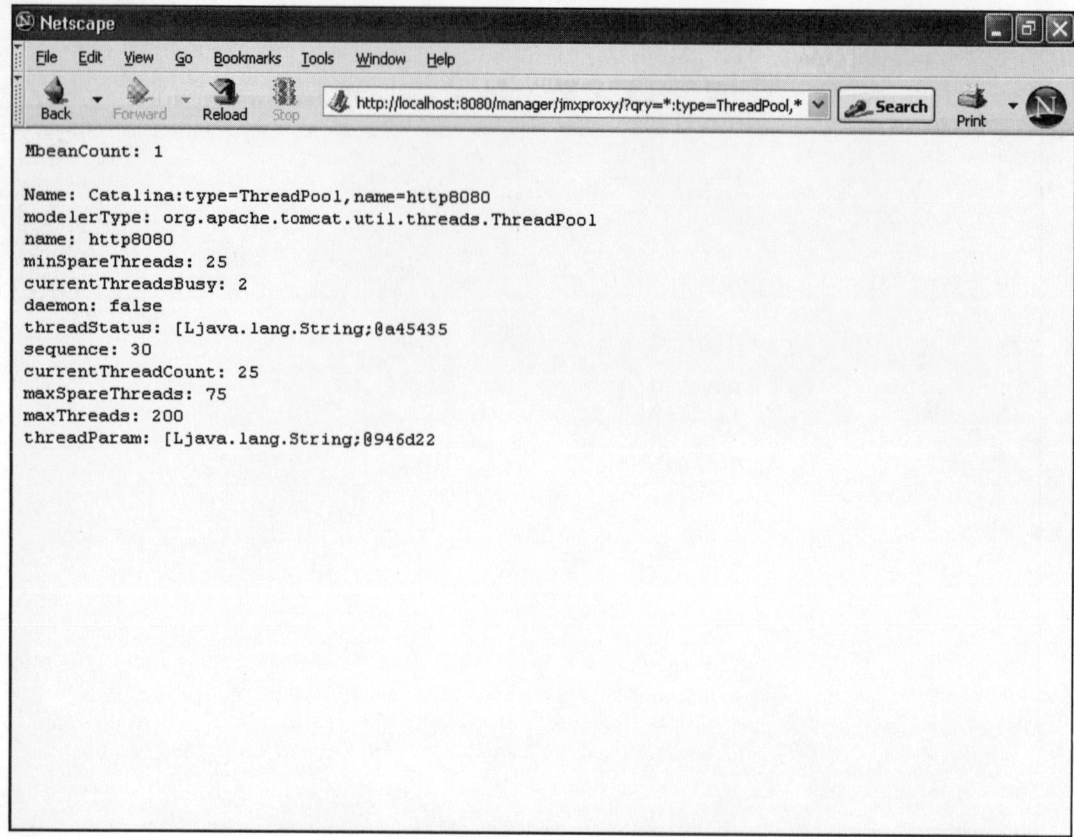

Figure 18-12: Verifying the new value of the maxThreads attribute.

Accessing Tomcat JMX Support Remotely via the RMI Connector

Most of Tomcat's JMX support has been implemented using an open source implementation of JMX called MX4J because the specification for the JMX Remote API was not finalized until October 2003, well into the final beta cycle of the initial Tomcat 5 release. You can download the latest release of MX4J at the following URL:

```
http://mx4j.sourceforge.net/
```

MX4J contains an implementation of an RMI connector that can be used to remotely access the MBeans exposed by Tomcat 5's agent level implementation. The following sections provide a step-by-step guide to configuring Tomcat 5 for remote JMX access, including the installation of the MX4J library.

Including JMX Support in server.xml

The first task is to check the `conf/server.xml` configuration file to ensure that both the `ServerLifecycleListener` and `GlobalResourcesLifecyleListener` are configured (that is, not commented out):

```
<Server port="8005" shutdown="SHUTDOWN" debug="0">
<Listener className="org.apache.catalina.mbeans.ServerLifecycleListener"
          debug="0" />
  <Listener className="org.apache.catalina.mbeans.GlobalResourcesLifecycleListener"
          debug="0"/>
```

Patching an Undocumented Attribute

Next, you must add an undocumented attribute (called `adaptor`) to the `ServerLifecycleListener` element. This tells Tomcat to start the MX4J RMI connector upon startup. The required modification is highlighted here:

```
<Server port="8005" shutdown="SHUTDOWN" debug="0">
<Listener className="org.apache.catalina.mbeans.ServerLifecycleListener"
          debug="0"  adaptor="jrmp" />
  <Listener className="org.apache.catalina.mbeans.GlobalResourcesLifecycleListener"
          debug="0"/>
```

This indicates to Tomcat the protocol to be used for the RMI Connector. In this case, it is the proprietary RMI-native `jrmp` protocol. The other allowed protocol is `iiop`, and it is compatible with distributed services or management applications based on the Common Object Request Broker Architecture (CORBA), which is a distributed network standard. A discussion of CORBA is beyond the scope of this book.

Replacing Reference Implementation JMX with MX4J

Because the RMI adapter is part of MX4J, you must replace the included reference JMX implementation with MX4J. Look into the `common/lib` directory and delete the following library files:

- `jmx.jar`
- `jmx-remote.jar`
- `jmx-remote-tools.jar`

Copy to the `common/lib` directory the following library files from the MX4J distribution:

- `mx4j-jmx.jar`
- `mx4j-tools.jar`

Starting Tomcat with JMX Remoting Enabled

The previous steps conclude the setup for the Tomcat 5 JMX agent. You can now start Tomcat 5 and attempt to access the JMX agent from another JVM, or even a remote machine. The next section demonstrates how to do this with a utility called `queryjmx`.

Peeking into Tomcat 5 with the queryjmx Utility

The code distribution of this book includes the `queryjmx` utility. This is a simple custom-coded utility program that can be used to access remote JMX agents using MX4J's RMI connector. The utility has been tested against MX4J version 1.1.1 (which is the latest available as of this writing).

The usage of `queryjmx` utility is straightforward. The command syntax is as follows:

```
queryjmx <JMX component type>
```

For example, if you want to view all the connectors, you would use the following:

```
queryjmx Connector
```

Alternatively, for all the roles defined in the UserDatabase, use the following:

```
queryjmx Role
```

You will find the `query.class` binary executable and a `queryjmx.bat` batch file that start the command. Edit the `queryjmx.bat` file to ensure that the classpaths are set to a location in which you can find the MX4J libraries. For example, the following edit of the `queryjmx.bat` file shows that the libraries are located under `c:\mx4j`:

```
java -classpath c:\mx4j\lib\mx4j-tools.jar;c:\mx4j\lib\mx4j-jmx.jar;. Queryjmx  %1
```

On a *nix system, you can edit and use the `queryjmx.sh` file, which contains the following:

```
java -classpath /usr/local/lib/mx4j-tools.jar:/usr/local/lib/mx4j-jmx.jar:.
Queryjmx $1
```

Setting Up the JNDI Initial Context

The `queryjmx` utility uses JNDI to locate the RMI registry in which the Tomcat's JMX connector server can be located. It is necessary to set up the JNDI run-time to use the RMI registry context factory. This involves setting up two Java system properties. The easiest way to accomplish this is to include a `jndi.properties` file within a directory in the classpath of the `queryjmx`. Because `.`, or current directory, is part of the classpath, the following `jndi.properties` file in the same directory as the executable will do the trick:

```
java.naming.factory.initial=com.sun.jndi.rmi.registry.RegistryContextFactory
java.naming.provider.url=rmi://localhost:1099
```

This assumes that you are running the `queryjmx` utility on the same host as Tomcat 5 (`localhost`). If the Tomcat 5 instance is located on a remote machine, simply change the `java.name.provider.url` system property to reflect the remote host's address.

Remote Tomcat Probing with queryjmx

Now you can try the `queryjmx` utility. The following is typical output from the utility. The query is for the Connector:

```
C:\Tomcat5>queryjmx Connector

MbeanCount: 2

Name: Catalina:type=Connector,port=8080
modelerType: org.apache.catalina.mbeans.ConnectorMBean
acceptCount: 100
bufferSize: 2048
className: org.apache.coyote.tomcat5.CoyoteConnector
clientAuth: false
compression: off
connectionLinger: -1
connectionTimeout: 20000
connectionUploadTimeout: 300000
debug: 0
disableUploadTimeout: true
enableLookups: false
maxKeepAliveRequests: 100
maxProcessors: 20
minProcessors: 5
maxSpareThreads: 75
maxThreads: 150
minSpareThreads: 25
minProcessors: 5
port: 8080
protocol: HTTP/1.1
protocolHandlerClassName: org.apache.coyote.http11.Http11Protocol
proxyPort: 0
redirectPort: 8443
scheme: http
secure: false
tcpNoDelay: true
tomcatAuthentication: true
xpoweredBy: false

Name: Catalina:type=Connector,port=8009
modelerType: org.apache.catalina.mbeans.ConnectorMBean
acceptCount: 10
bufferSize: 2048
className: org.apache.coyote.tomcat5.CoyoteConnector
clientAuth: false
compression: off
connectionLinger: -1
connectionTimeout: 60000
connectionUploadTimeout: 300000
debug: 0
disableUploadTimeout: false
enableLookups: false
maxKeepAliveRequests: 100
maxProcessors: 20
minProcessors: 5
minProcessors: 5
port: 8009
```

```
protocol: AJP/1.3
protocolHandlerClassName: org.apache.jk.server.JkCoyoteHandler
proxyPort: 0
redirectPort: 8443
scheme: http
secure: false
tcpNoDelay: true
tomcatAuthentication: true
xpoweredBy: false
```

Using this queryjmx utility, it is possible to monitor remote Tomcat servers in real time, as long as the remote JMX Connector support is configured.

Security Concerns

JMX access needs to be enabled explicitly in the Tomcat 5 distribution, and so administrators running default Tomcat installations do not have to worry about its security risks.

Enabling remote JMX access in the current Tomcat version leaves the running Tomcat server wide open to external elements. This is indeed one of the intentions of a JMX implementation. This is the primary reason why we had to use an undocumented attribute and external MX4J binaries to enable remote JMX access.

Developers or expert administrators familiar with MX4J can configure Secure Socket Layer (SSL) connections and user authentication if they need remote JMX capabilities in a production environment. It is also possible to configure mutually exclusive hardware-based subnetworks for server management.

In due time, with subsequent Tomcat releases, finer-grained access control and security measures will likely be implemented to enable safe and secure remote JMX access.

Summary

To conclude this chapter, let's review some of its key points:

- JMX is a standard for the management of hardware devices, software services, and other manageable entities. The JMX architecture has three levels and each level is componentized. Each level is decoupled from the others.
- The bottom level is instrumentation, and it requires that manageable devices and/or services expose their manageable attributes, operations, and events via a set of MBeans.
- The top level is distributed services. It involves management applications or higher-level agent functionality and is not well defined at this time.
- The middle level is called the agent level. This level aggregates the MBeans from devices and services, and provides a set of services, customized value-added logic, and external/remote access to managed elements.

- Tomcat 5 is fully JMX-compliant. It is also fully instrumented. This means that all of its configuration, internal, and run-time components have MBeans associated with them, enabling these components to be accessed through a JMX agent.
- The `manager` application in Tomcat provides a JMX proxy that can be used to access these Tomcat MBeans. The proxy provides a Web interface for querying the MBean Server, reading and writing MBean attribute values.
- Whereas the `manager` JMX proxy acted as an HTTP protocol adapter, replacing the JMX implementation with open source MX4J provides a fully functional RMI Connector for Tomcat 5. This RMI Connector enables external Tomcat 5 management across a network. Using a custom-coded `queryjmx` utility, it is possible to query the Tomcat 5 server remotely for its managed components. All attributes of the managed component can be accessed remotely using the `queryjmx` utility.
- One major benefit of Tomcat's JMX support is exemplified by the `queryjmx` utility, which enables the capability to consolidate the monitoring and management of Tomcat servers via remote JMX access. Ultimately, this occasions the management, administration, and monitoring of a large number of Tomcat servers — a requirement that has not been satisfied by Tomcat previously.

In Tomcat 5, one beneficial side effect of componentization and the exposure of internal components via JMX is the capability to configure, start, and operate Tomcat from within an external program or script file (external to the JVM running Tomcat). This is known as the **embedded mode** of operation for Tomcat. Chapter 20 has extensive coverage of this new mode of Tomcat server operation.

Before looking at this new mode of Tomcat server operation, however, let's take a look at Chapter 19, which explores clustering with Tomcat 5.

19

Tomcat 5 Clustering

The Tomcat server has grown up, from a reference implementation of a Servlet container for demonstrating and testing new APIs to a robust and high-performance Web-tier server. Increasingly, Tomcat is being used in production scenarios to handle real-world Web applications. It is a prime example of a prototype becoming the product. In a sense, the designers and architects realized that their mission changed direction, and redesigned the Tomcat product for high-stress production deployments.

Tomcat 5 is further along the evolutionary path of improved performance. Real-world deployments place many tough demands on the Tomcat server. Many of these requirements were not important to the Tomcat development team when it was a mere reference implementation. Two such areas are support for **horizontal scalability** (the ability to handle increasing user requests by utilizing a group of physical machines) and **high availability** (the ability to survive hardware or software failures and maintain a high percentage of application uptime). In other words, what happens when there are so many users that Tomcat servers start to crash, and how can you ensure that no user loses data? These are real-world problems, and Tomcat 5 attempts to solve them by providing built-in support for clustering. Clustering, in this context, refers to running multiple instances of the Tomcat server so that it appears to users as a single server.

This chapter covers the many facets of Tomcat 5 clustering, including the following:

- Basic principles of clustering
- How Tomcat implements clustering
- Internal software components that implement Tomcat clustering
- Technologies that underlie Tomcat clustering
- Various alternative configurations

Last but not least, the chapter will give you hands-on experience with configuring and experimenting with this new and exciting feature of Tomcat. You will be working with three different clustered configurations along the way. As an epilogue, the chapter offers some practical suggestions about clustering that may affect your decision to deploy the technology.

Clustering Benefits

Clustering in Tomcat 5 enables a set of Tomcat instances on a LAN (called a **cluster**) to appear to incoming users as a single server. This enables the distribution of work among the servers, called **load balancing.** Chapter 12 covers a load-balancing configuration with the Coyote AJP Connector and `mod_jk2`. Figure 19-1 illustrates the load-balancing concept.

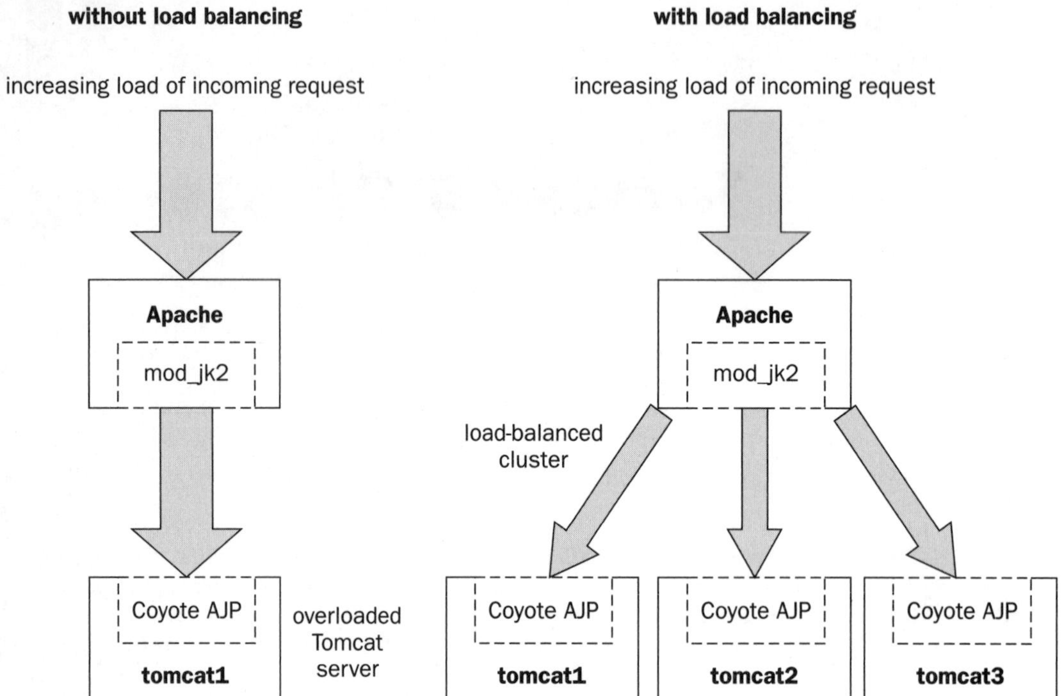

Figure 19-1: Load balancing with Tomcat 5.

In Figure 19-1, if an increasing stream of incoming requests were sent to the tomcat1 server, at some point the server will overload and crash by running out of resources. By deploying a load-balanced cluster, however, more requests can be handled.

Scalability and Clustering

Using the load-balanced configuration shown in Figure 19-1, incoming requests are distributed over the tomcat1, tomcat2, and tomcat3 servers. This means that each server is only handling a portion of the incoming requests. If the load-balancing distributor and algorithm are efficient, the system as a whole can handle significantly more requests before overloading.

Scalability refers to the capability to provide service for an increasing number of users. Formerly, scaling an application to more users required an upgrade to expensive, multiple CPU systems and corresponding memory expansion. This approach is often called **scaling up.** The way that clustering is handled in Tomcat 5 leverages inexpensive high-speed LAN interconnections to share the computing resources of multiple server machines. This approach is called **scaling out** or **horizontal scaling.** It provides an obvious cost advantage, as a server farm of low-cost commodity hardware is less expensive than a single multiple-CPU server.

Load balancing can solve the scalability problem by enabling the cluster to handle significantly more simultaneous requests than a single nonclustered server. Tomcat servers can support horizontal scaling through the use of the Coyote AJP Connector and the `mod_jk2` plug-in with the Apache Web server.

The Need for High Availability

Another difficult real-world problem that can be solved via horizontally scaled clustering is the **high availability** (HA) issue. The challenge here is avoiding situations in which server software/hardware crashes and becomes unavailable.

In a regular system, all requests being processed by the server are lost, and all users must wait until the server restarts properly before starting their work from the beginning. For example, if the users are online shoppers in a Web store, they will lose the contents of their shopping carts and any data that they may have entered during the checkout process when the server crashed.

This is clearly an unacceptable set of consequences for serious real-world applications. What is desired is a system capable of continuing to handle incoming requests, making a single server crash completely transparent to the end user. The crash and recovery of any individual hardware system should not affect the user experience with the hosted application. Systems with the capability to survive server crashes typically exhibit very high **uptime** or **availability.** These systems are called high-availability (HA) systems.

Tomcat 5 clusters can be used to implement an HA solution. In this scenario, the following occurs:

1. A request that is destined for the crashed server is redirected to another functioning server in the cluster.
2. The original incoming request is processed by the functioning server.
3. The Tomcat server that failed is logically removed from the cluster, so no further requests will be forwarded to it.
4. When and if the crashed Tomcat server recovers, it is logically added back into the cluster, and once again used to handle incoming requests.

The key to enabling this scenario is to realize that any state information maintained by the application in the crashed server (typically, carried in the session) must be somehow made available to the functioning server.

Tomcat 5 provides a workable solution to both the scalability and the HA problem. As such, Tomcat 5 has made major inroads in establishing itself as a serious and robust contender for enterprise-level production deployment.

To better understand how Tomcat 5 achieves scalability and HA, a few words on some basic clustering concepts are appropriate.

Clustering Basics

Several basic system design patterns are found in clustered systems (a specific applied instance of the general-distributed computing problem). This section briefly describes two. The preceding discussion in this chapter and Chapter 12 cover a third: the load-balancing front-end pattern.

Master-Backup Topological Pattern

Figure 19-2 illustrates the master-backup topological pattern. In this pattern, two (or more) machines are identically configured in hardware and OS, and they both host the same software. Interconnection exists between the machines (for example, over a LAN). One machine is designated as the **master server** and processes incoming requests. The rest of the machines are **backup servers.** The health of the master server is monitored constantly, either by the backup servers or by an independent hardware/software component. Whenever the master server crashes, one of the backup servers is made the master and request processing continues as if no crash has occurred. This is the basis of most HA implementations.

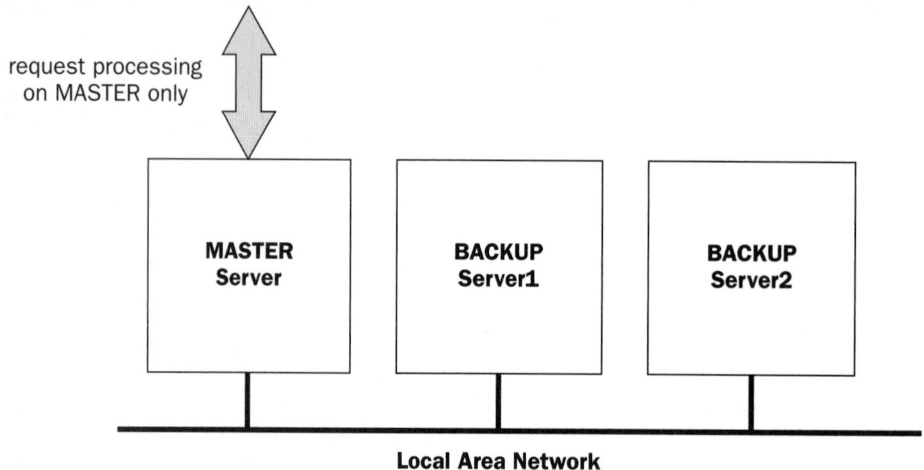

Figure 19-2: The master-backup topological pattern.

Fail-Over Behavioral Pattern

Figure 19-3 illustrates the fail-over behavioral pattern. Fail-over occurs when a server crashes in a master-backup system. It refers to the way and means by which the master server is taken over by the former backup server. While in a hardware implementation, this may involve sophisticated switching and communications link isolation; in a software scenario, a state transfer and synchronization mechanism must be in place.

In other words, simply having identically configured hardware, OS, and software applications (as in the master-backup pattern) is not enough to guarantee a logically transparent fail-over.

The backup server taking over the duties of the master server must know "what the master server is up to," and continue from where it left off. This requires the sharing of dynamic state information.

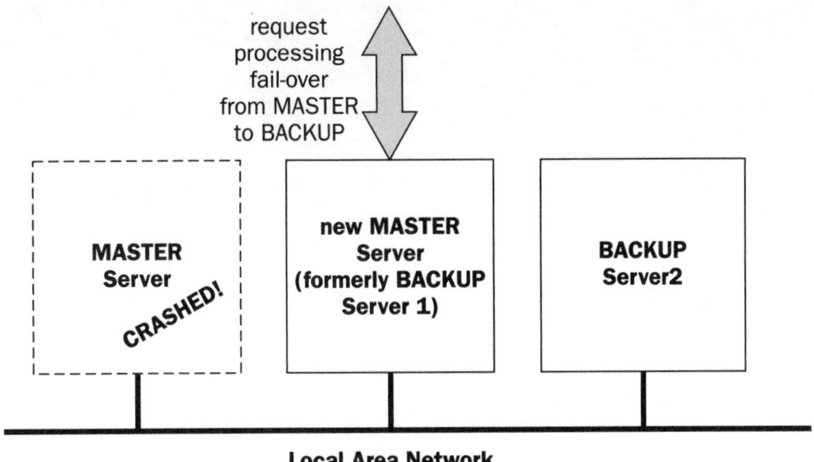

Figure 19-3: The fail-over behavioral pattern.

Of course, when the master server has crashed, it is too late to query it for information about what it was doing. In all likelihood, the crashed master server is not in any condition to respond.

Therefore, almost all fail-over solutions rely on maintaining and sharing state information between the master and backup servers *before* any crashes occur. Keeping this information current is the only way to ensure that the backup server can take over from where the master server left off during a fail-over.

This state sharing is much tougher to implement than it sounds. State information on a system refers to *any* changes to the system. On a hardware level, this could mean any memory or register write. Imagine having to let all servers in a cluster know about every register and memory write on the master system!

Thankfully, in a J2EE-compliant Servlet/JSP container, a well-accepted convention for tracking state information within Web applications is available. It involves the use of server-side sessions. Tomcat 5's cluster implementation takes advantage of this to provide fail-over capability.

Now it's time to see how Tomcat 5 incorporates the load-balancing, master-backup, and fail-over patterns in its clustering implementation to provide scalable, HA features for end users.

Tomcat 5 Clustering Model

This section explores the specific clustering implementation supported by Tomcat 5. Based on the discussion thus far, the implementation can be divided into two layers and various components. Figure 19-4 illustrates this.

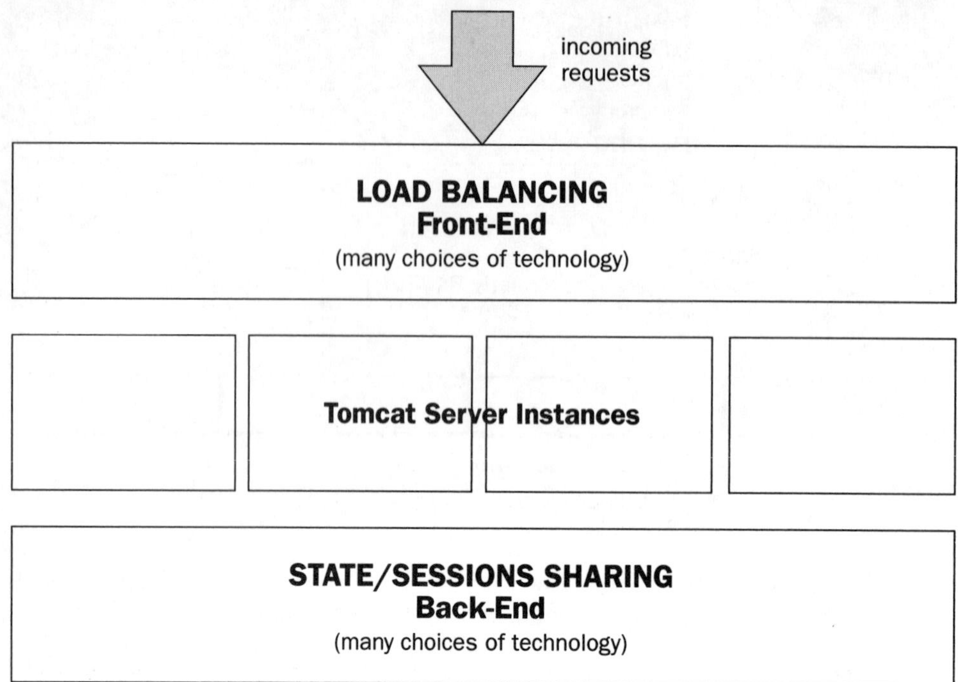

Figure 19-4: Tomcat 5 clustering-implementation architectural model.

The two layers that enable clustering are the load-balancing front-end and the state-sharing/synchronization back-end. In particular, Tomcat's load-balancing front-end distributes incoming requests to the Tomcat instances, while the back-end is concerned with ensuring that shared session data is available to the different instances.

Load Balancing

There are many options for implementing the load-balancing front-end. What you should choose depends on your specific application. These alternatives include (but are not restricted to) the following:

- Round-robin DNS, whereby a domain name resolution results in a set of IP addresses
- A hardware-based load balancer
- A software-based load balancer (including `balance`, a popular open-source TCP-based load balancer. See the following URL:

```
http://sourceforge.net/projects/balance/
```

- Apache `mod_jk` as load balancer
- Apache `mod_jk2` as load balancer
- The balancer Web application included with Tomcat 5 for rule-based, application-level load balancing

A discussion and detailed comparison of all of these options is beyond the scope of this book. However, the last two options are covered in this chapter because they are the most popular and least expensive options with Tomcat 5 deployments.

mod_jk2 Load Balancing and Sticky Sessions

The `mod_jk2` load balancer distributes incoming requests in a round-robin manner among the available Tomcat workers, but will also respect a **load factor** that you can specify. In addition, the `mod_jk2` load balancer supports sticky sessions.

Understanding Sticky Sessions

When sticky sessions (or **session affinity**) is enabled on `mod_jk2`, it ensures that all incoming requests with the same session are routed to the same Tomcat 5 worker. Figure 19-5 illustrates this concept.

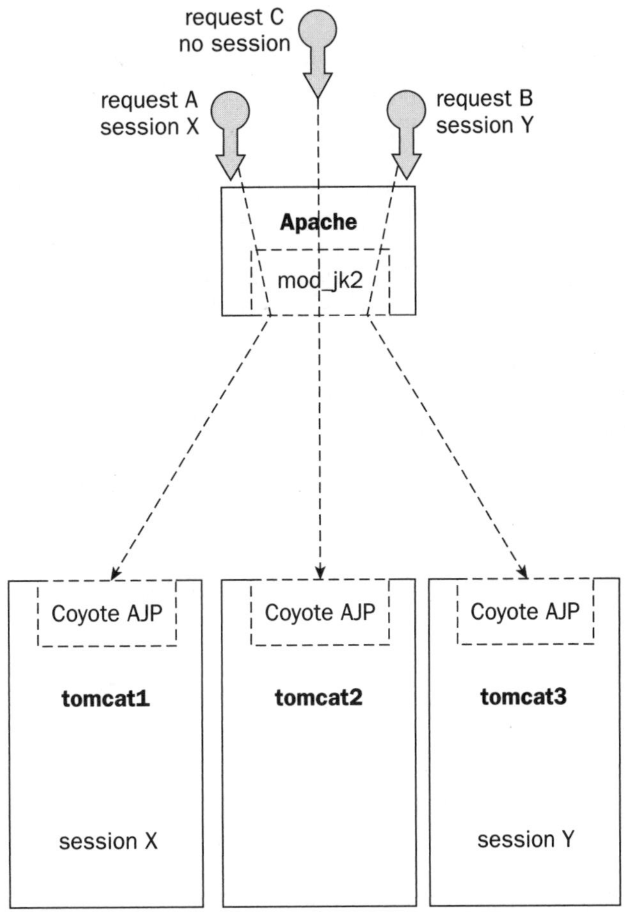

Figure 19-5: mod_jk2 load balancing with session affinity.

In Figure 19-5, incoming request A is routed to tomcat1 because session X is created and maintained on the tomcat1 instance. Meanwhile, request B is routed to tomcat3 because session Y is created and maintained on the tomcat3 instance. Request C has no session, so it is routed to the next server in the round-robin distribution, which is tomcat2.

This is a highly functional clustering configuration that is relatively easy to configure, and it can be used to scale a Web application across a cluster of Tomcat 5 servers.

The only disadvantage of this configuration is that sessions are Tomcat instance-specific. If a Tomcat instance is lost, all its sessions are lost.

For example, in Figure 19-5, if the tomcat1 instance crashes, session X is lost forever. Request A will not be handled by the system, and the user will lose the session (and whatever was being done at the time the failure occurred). However, if there is some way to help the clustered Tomcat instances to share session information, then one of the other Tomcat instances still up and running can take over and service incoming requests with sessions created by the crashed server.

Session Sharing

As with the load-balancing front-end, you have numerous session-sharing back-ends from which to choose. Each provides a different level of functionality, as well as implementation complexity.

Session sharing is the secret behind most implementations of an application server fail-over mechanism. It ensures transparent transfer of the sessions that were being handled by the crashed server.

In the following discussion, it is assumed that the `mod_jk2` load balancing front-end is used. This is the most popular production configuration for clustered Tomcat 5 instances. The available session-sharing configuration options include the following:

- Sticky sessions with no session sharing
- Sticky sessions with a Persistent Session Manager and a shared file store
- Sticky sessions with a Persistent Session Manager and a JDBC store to RDBMS
- In-memory session replication

Sticky Sessions with No Clustered Session Sharing

This is the scenario that was tested in Chapter 12, when `mod_jk2` and an AJP Connector were used to round-robin requests amongst a cluster of Tomcat 5 server instances. In this scenario, the `mod_jk2 lb` (load balance) worker ensures that requests destined for the same session are always handled by the same Tomcat worker instance. The session ID is encoded with the route name of the server instance that created it, assisting in the routing of the request.

While this setup may sound contrived, it is extremely practical and pragmatic in many production scenarios. The advantages of this simple clustering setup include the following:

- Application scalability through round-robin load balancing (new sessions are always created on the next worker in the round-robin queue)
- Simplicity in setup and maintenance (the `mod_jk2 lb` worker will detect crashed servers and reinstate recovered ones)
- No additional configuration or resource overhead (as no session sharing is occurring)

The major disadvantage is the lack of HA features. A crashed server means lost sessions.

In situations where server crashes are rare occurrences, and when session losses during these rare occasions are acceptable, this should be the clustering solution deployed.

Sticky Sessions with a Persistent Session Manager and a Shared File Store

Tomcat 5 is packaged with a Persistent Session Manager component that can be configured into any application context. Chapter 8 covers the configuration of this component. The main purpose of persistent session management is to provide continuity to sessions when a server shuts down and is restarted. Because the sessions are persisted to either the disk or an RDBMS, they can have a life cycle that is longer than the server's. In addition, because sessions can be configured to be "swapped out to the store" after a specified idle time, the Persistent Session Manager also provides a form of protection against system crashes (that is, any persistent session can be recovered when the system restarts after a crash).

Note that the Persistent Session Manager in Tomcat 5 is designed with no consideration for clustering. It deals only with the life cycle and session of one single Tomcat instance. However, by sharing the store between multiple Tomcat 5 server instances (via either a shared file system or an RDBMS), a certain level of session sharing can be accomplished.

Figure 19-6 illustrates the Persistent Session Manager with a shared file store. In this case, all the Tomcat server instances use the same directory to store their sessions. This directory is accessible from all the servers via the OS's shared file mechanism (NFS, SMB, and so on). Now, any sessions created by any Tomcat instance will **eventually** be visible to the other instances. Any modifications made by any instance will also be **eventually** visible to the other instances. It is important to reiterate the importance of the word **eventually** here, because the Persistent Session Manager does not guarantee exactly when a session will be persisted to the store (either after creation or modification). Until a session (or a change in the session) is persisted to the store, that information is not available to the other instances.

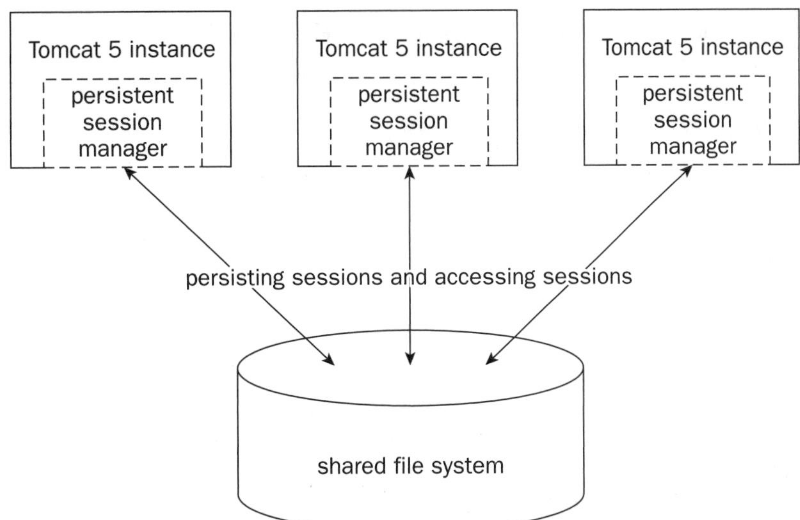

Figure 19-6: Tomcat 5's Persistent Session Manager with a shared file store.

At this point, you may be wondering what good is a clustering system that **eventually** shares its session information?

There is actually a very good and pragmatic answer. It is *slightly better* than the sticky session with *no* session sharing solution previously discussed.

In clustering situations where server crashes happen very infrequently, using this scheme can further minimize the loss of sessions during the moment of system crash and fail-over. This is because any persisted session at fail-over time can be immediately handled by any one of the remaining servers in the cluster.

Note that sticky sessions must still be configured in the `mod_jk2` Connector with this scheme. This means that most of the time, a session will be serviced throughout its lifetime by the same Tomcat instance. The only exception occurs when the original server crashed during the session's lifetime. Sticky sessions also increase the probability that the session will be persisted to the store, because the longer the session lingers around, the greater is the probability of it being persisted.

The advantages of this session-sharing scheme include the following:

- Application scalability through round-robin load balancing (new sessions are always created on the next worker in the round-robin queue)
- Relatively easy setup and maintenance. The `mod_jk2 lb` (load balance) worker will detect crashed servers and reinstate recovered ones.
- It provides a measure of HA in most situations because any persisted session is shared and can be handled by another server in the cluster.

The disadvantages of this session-sharing scheme include the following:

- Some sessions may still be lost during fail-over.
- Access traffic on the network supporting the shared file system can be heavy in a highly loaded server cluster.

Sticky Sessions with a Persistent Session Manager and a JDBC-Based Store

Note in Figure 19-6 that there is no conceptual difference between this session-sharing scheme and the previous one. In fact, they both use the same Persistent Session Manager component. In this case, JDBC is used to persist session information onto an RDBMS. The set of benefits and weaknesses remains identical to the previous scheme.

The only additional benefit of going to a JDBC-based scheme is the potential performance improvement on systems persisting a large number of sessions. If the applications running on the cluster are using the same RDBMS as the Persistent Session Manager, however, this slight performance edge may disappear (because of increased contention).

In-Memory Session Replication

Unlike the other two session-sharing schemes, this session-sharing mechanism is not built on top of a shared persistent storage. With in-memory session replication, session information is maintained in synchronization within the memory, across all the clustered server instances.

Because all server instances share the same session information, this mechanism has the potential to provide the full benefits associated with clustering. Figure 19-7 illustrates how this is accomplished.

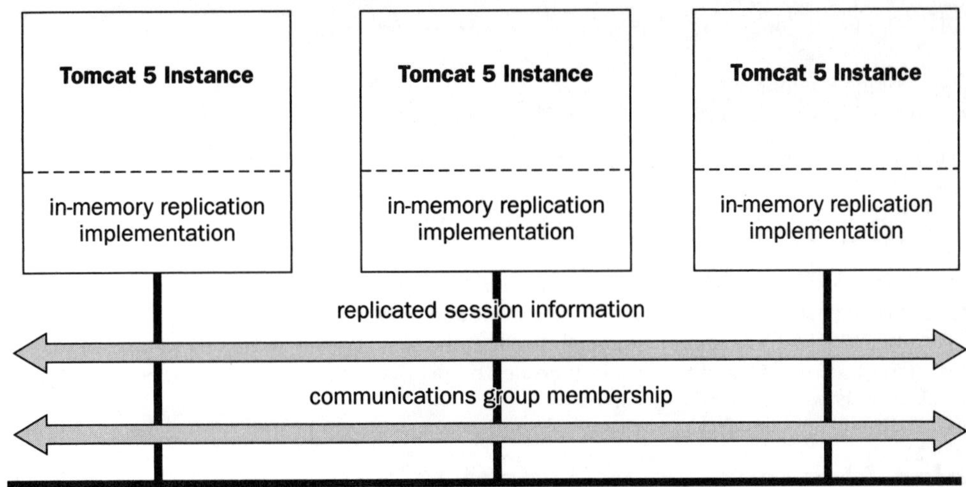

Figure 19-7: Tomcat 5 in-memory session replication.

In Figure 19-7, the Tomcat 5 server instances running in the cluster form a communications group (or peer group, as they are all equal in stature). Group membership is maintained by the clustering implementation. If a server crashes, it is automatically removed from the group. A recovered server is automatically made a member of the group again.

Any session-creation and modification activities on any of the Tomcat 5 instances are sent to all the instances within the communications group. The receiving members then update their own session image in memory to reflect the change. In this way, sessions and changes are replicated immediately—in memory, and within the group.

The main benefits of this approach are as follows:

- Full round-robin load balancing without sticky sessions enables an even distribution of requests (subject to prefigured `lb` factor on the `mod_jk` Connector). Any server can handle any request.
- With full HA support, any server can crash and fail-over with no session loss.

The second benefit is the major benefit delivered by the in-memory session replication scheme. The other schemes examined thus far cannot deliver this benefit.

However, with the benefit comes substantial cost. Here are the items of concern for this approach:

- The traffic on the interconnection (usually a LAN) can quickly become very heavy because all changes to all sessions are sent to all members of the group.

- Sessions are *not* persistent. This means that this model assumes that the overall system operates continuously (sometimes called **twenty-four-seven** or **nonstop operation**). All sessions are lost if the entire cluster is shut down. This is not the case with persistent session management
- Configuration, tuning, and maintenance can be quite complex.

The remaining sections in this chapter cover each of the clustering mechanisms in more depth, and provide hands-on configuration with working examples.

Working with Tomcat 5 Clustering

As discussed earlier, Tomcat 5 clustering implementation depends on a load-balancing front-end and a session-sharing back-end. The load balancing front-end may implement sticky sessions (using Apache `mod_jk` or `mod_jk2` Connectors), which ensure that the same clustered Tomcat 5 instance will always handle the same session. Taking a peek underneath the hood will reveal why this is very important in several of the clustering configurations.

Session Management in Tomcat 5

Sessions are created and managed by the Tomcat 5 container during application execution, and are made available to JSP and Servlets via the application context. In a single server instance, Tomcat 5 sessions are objects (which can contain and reference other objects) that are kept on behalf of a client.

Because the HTTP protocol is stateless, there is no simple way to maintain application state using the protocol alone. For example, consider a shopping cart application. Each product page accessed by a user comes into the server as a separate and distinct HTTP request. There is no way for the server to match up independent incoming requests that represent an application flow.

However, most Web applications need to maintain state information associated with a user (for example, the items in the user's shopping cart). A server-side session is the main mechanism used to maintain state. It works as follows:

1. The server writes a cookie to the user's browser instance. The cookie contains a token to retrieve the server-side session (data structure).
2. The cookie is supplied by the browser instance every time it accesses a page on the site.
3. The server reads the token in the cookie to extract the corresponding session.

An analogy to a session is the coat check tag that one may obtain prior to entering a theatre or concert. In this case, the cookie is the tag (smaller and simpler to carry) and the session is the coat (larger, but important data that is kept on the server side). You, the client, hold the tag and return the tag for the coat, which the establishment holds on your behalf. The browser client holds the cookie, and returns the cookie each time in a connection to the server. Using the cookie, the server is able to locate the session on which the browser client is working.

For browsers that do not support cookies, it is possible to use **URL rewrite** to achieve a similar effect. In URL rewrite, any URL that is being supplied by the application is decorated with the session ID being used. This enables the Web application to extract the session ID from the incoming URL during run-time.

The Role of Cookies and Modern Browsers

All popular modern-day browsers (Internet Explorer, Opera, Netscape, Mozilla, etc.) support the use of cookies. Cookies are managed on the browser's host PC, and indexed by the Web site's host name. In addition, all modern-day browsers support multiple concurrent connections to the same server. For example, you can start as many instances of Internet Explorer as you want (subject to machine resource constraints) and have them all connect to the following URL:

```
www.wrox.com/
```

Each instance you start manages its own client-side session. This is not to be confused with server-side sessions. In essence, when you start multiple instances of a browser pointing to the same server, it appears to the server as if different users are accessing it (each instance manages its own copy of a cookie from the server). In other words, each client-side browser instance will have its own independent, associated server-side session.

Note that if a load-balancing mechanism redirects an incoming request to a different host, the cookie supplied will be different (because cookies are indexed by host names) and the session information will not be maintained.

Configuring a Tomcat 5 Cluster

This section describes the configuration of an actual Tomcat 5 cluster. The cluster consists of three independent Tomcat 5 instances, and makes use of the following:

- `mod_jk2` load-balancing front-end (without sticky session)
- In-memory session replication back-end

This configuration is very similar to the one featured in the AJP Connector load-balancing example presented in Chapter 12. The main difference is in the use of multiple `%CATALINA_BASE%` settings (`$CATALINA_BASE` on Unix/Linux) for each Tomcat instance, and the cluster naming of the server instances.

Ideally, the following configuration experiments should be performed on an actual cluster of physical machines running Tomcat 5 on a network. However, not everyone has access to such extensive hardware. To provide all readers with a hands-on configuration experience, the example utilizes multiple instances of Tomcat 5 running on the same machine.

Setting Up Multiple Tomcat Instances on One Machine

To enable multiple instances of Tomcat 5 to run on the same physical machine, each instance must have at least the following:

- Its own configuration directory
- Its own `webapps` directory
- Its own `temp` directory
- TCP ports (for the Coyote AJP Connector) that do not conflict with other instances
- Optionally, other private TCP or JDBC resources, depending on the back-end session-sharing mechanism being deployed

Three batch files, called `start1.bat`, `start2.bat`, and `start3.bat`, respectively, are created and placed into the `%CATALINA_HOME%/bin` directory.

These batch files set the `CATALINA_BASE` environment variable and then call the `startup.bat` Tomcat startup script. Tomcat 5 will check for the existence of the `CATALINA_BASE` environment variable and use it to locate the base directory for startup. Each of the `start1.bat`, `start2.bat`, and `start3.bat` files sets the `CATALINA_BASE` variable to a different directory, allowing for variation in configuration. For example, `start1.bat` contains the following:

```
set CATALINA_BASE=c:\cluster\machine1
call startup
```

This tells Tomcat 5 to look for configuration information and Web application in the `c:\cluster\machine1` directory. Figure 19-8 shows the directory hierarchy that we will use in the subsequent cluster testing.

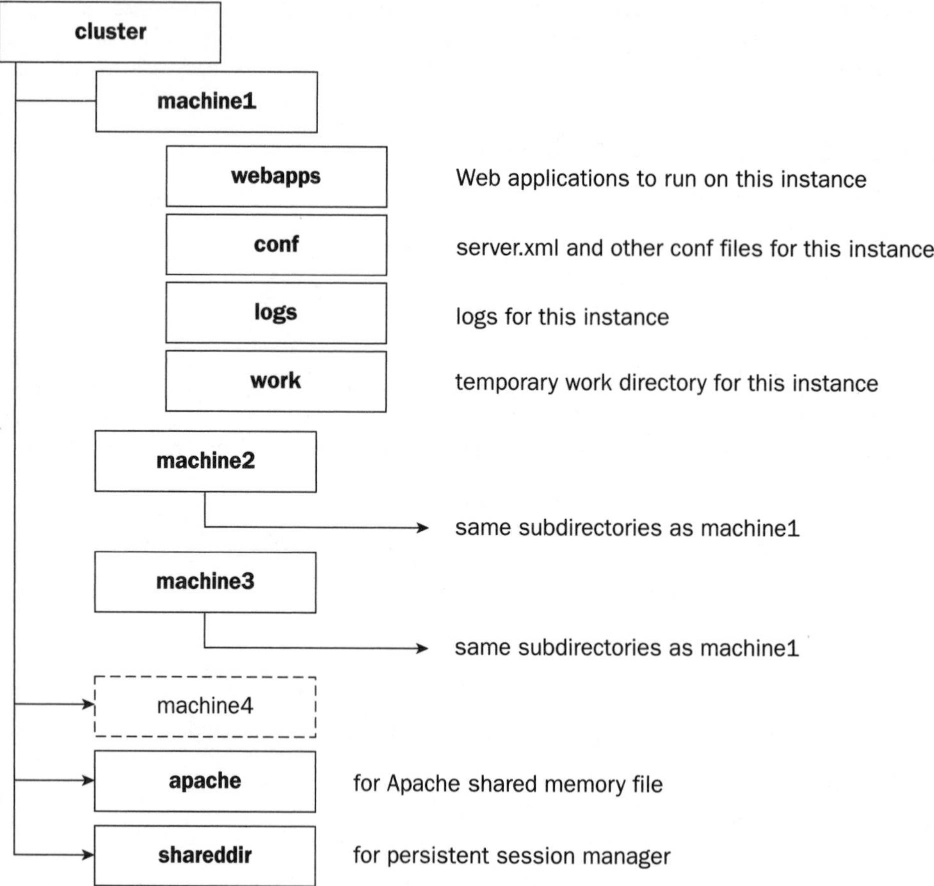

Figure 19-8: Directory tree of the in-memory replication example.

Note in Figure 19-8 that each machine1, machine2, and machine3 directory houses the configuration files for the respective Tomcat 5 instances to be started.

Shutting Down the Tomcat Cluster

Similar to the startn.bat files, there exists three stopn.bat files for shutting down the individual server instances. These batch files set the CATALINA_BASE environment variable and then call the shutdown script for the server. For example, following is the content of stop3.bat:

```
set CATALINA_BASE=c:\cluster\machine3
call shutdown
```

Configuring Minimal Web Applications

Only the jsp-examples application will be loaded for each of the three machine instances. In general, when setting up a cluster, you should try to minimize the number of applications loaded. This is because considerable overhead is associated with each clustered application (session management, network traffic, and so on). The webapps subdirectory on clustered machines should be thoroughly clean, except for the clustered Web applications.

Disabling the HTTP Connectors

The default server.xml file included with the Tomcat 5 distribution sets up two Connectors. One is an HTTP 1.1 Connector listening on port 8080, and the other one is an AJP 1.3 Connector listening on port 8009. You must first comment out the HTTP Connector if you are using the standard server.xml file. This ensures that the three instances will not fight for the 8080 port during startup:

```
<Server port="8005" shutdown="SHUTDOWN" debug="0">
...
<Service name="Catalina">
 <!--
   <Connector port="8080"
              maxThreads="150" minSpareThreads="25" maxSpareThreads="75"
              enableLookups="false" redirectPort="8443" acceptCount="100"
              debug="0" connectionTimeout="20000"
              disableUploadTimeout="true" />
  -->
    <Connector port="8009"
              enableLookups="false" redirectPort="8443" debug="0"
              protocol="AJP/1.3" />
...
```

Note that if you use the code distribution provided with this book, the HTTP Connectors are already removed from the server.xml files.

Configuring AJP TCP Ports for Clustered Tomcat Instances

In order for the three Tomcat 5 instances to coexist peacefully on a single physical machine, it is necessary to give the AJP Connectors different TCP ports on which to listen. By default, the server is listening on port 8005 for shutdown, and the AJP Coyote Connector listens on 8009. The relevant lines in server.xml that must be customized for each instance are highlighted here:

```
<Server port="8005" shutdown="SHUTDOWN" debug="0">
<GlobalNamingResources>
    <Resource name="UserDatabase" auth="Container"
              type="org.apache.catalina.UserDatabase"
       description="User database that can be updated and saved">
```

```
      </Resource>
      <ResourceParams name="UserDatabase">
        <parameter>
          <name>factory</name>
          <value>org.apache.catalina.users.MemoryUserDatabaseFactory</value>
        </parameter>
        <parameter>
          <name>pathname</name>
          <value>conf/tomcat-users.xml</value>
        </parameter>
      </ResourceParams>
    </GlobalNamingResources>

    <Service name="Catalina">
    <Connector  port="8009" protocol="AJP/1.3"/>
      ...
```

The following table shows what you need to configure in each instance.

Instance Name	File to Modify	TCP Ports (shutdown, AJP Connector)
machine1	\cluster\machine1\conf\server.xml	8005, 8009
machine2	\cluster\machine2\conf\server.xml	8105, 8109
machine3	\cluster\machine3\conf\server.xml	8205, 8209

The settings chosen here ensure that there will be no conflict starting the three Tomcat 5 instances simultaneously on the same physical machine. If you are actually setting up the test across three physical machines on the network, they can all use the setting of `machine1` in the table.

Servlet 2.4's Distributable Attribute for Web Applications

Instead of creating a Web application from scratch, this experiment will take advantage of the existing `jsp-examples` Web application. To indicate to the Servlet container (Tomcat 5) that this application can be clustered, a Servlet 2.4 standard `<distributable>` element is placed into the application's deployment descriptor: the `web.xml` file. The following code shows the placement of the `<distributable>` element. If you remove this element, the session maintained by this application across the three Tomcat 5 instances will not be shared:

```
<?xml version="1.0" encoding="ISO-8859-1"?>
<web-app xmlns="http://java.sun.com/xml/ns/j2ee"
    xmlns:xsi="http://www.w3.org/2001/XMLSchema-instance"
    xsi:schemaLocation="http://java.sun.com/xml/ns/j2ee web-app_2_4.xsd"
    version="2.4">
    <description>
      JSP 2.0 Examples.
    </description>
    <display-name>JSP 2.0 Examples</display-name>
    <distributable/>

    <!-- Define servlet-mapped and path-mapped example filters -->
```

```
<filter>
    <filter-name>Servlet Mapped Filter</filter-name>
    <filter-class>filters.ExampleFilter</filter-class>
...
```

This element must be manually added to the `web.xml` file in all three instances:

- `\cluster\machine1\webapps\jsp-examples\WEB-INF\web.xml`
- `\cluster\machine2\webapps\jsp-examples\WEB-INF\web.xml`
- `\cluster\machine3\webapps\jsp-examples\WEB-INF\web.xml`

If you are configuring three physical machines, make sure that the `web.xml` file on each machine has the `<distributable/>` element added.

Configuration Consistency

The three clustered instances of Tomcat 5 should be identically configured. This is a wise practice, in general, to reduce potential problems arising from dissimilar configuration. Typically, if the application or system requires machines with different hardware/software configurations, they are maintained in separate clusters (or in a nonclustered configuration).

Common Front End: Load Balancing via Apache mod_jk2

The load-balancing front end consists of an Apache server with `mod_jk2` installed. The following is only a brief recap of the configuration procedure. See Chapter 12 for a detailed step-by-step explanation of this configuration.

Apache Server Configuration

Make sure you are using matching versions of the Apache server and `mod_jk2.dll` (or `mod_jk2.so`). Many problems may arise from version mismatch. The examples in this chapter are tested with Apache 2.0.43 and `mod_jk.dll` for Apache 2.0.43.

On the Apache server side, you must make sure the `mod_jk.dll` is loaded at startup. This can be done by adding the following line to the `conf/http.conf` file.

```
LoadModule jk2_module modules/mod_jk2.dll
```

This line should immediately follow all the `LoadModule` directives in the file. Note that the downloaded `mod_jk2` library needs to be renamed to `mod_jk2.dll`. It should be placed in the `modules` directory of the Apache server.

mod_jk2 Configuration

When the `mod_jk2` plug-in starts up, it will look for a `workers2.properties` file. The following `workers2.properties` file should be placed into the `conf` subdirectory of the Apache server:

```
[logger.apache2]
file="c:\cluster\apache\error.log"
level=INFO
```

```
debug=1

[config]
file=conf/workers2.properties
debug=0

[channel.socket:localhost:8009]
host=localhost
port=8009
tomcatId=machine1
group=balanced
lb_factor=1

[ajp13:localhost:8009]
channel=channel.socket:machine1

[channel.socket:localhost:8109]
host=localhost
port=8109
tomcatId=machine2
group=balanced
lb_factor=1

[ajp13:localhost:8109]
channel=channel.socket:machine2


[channel.socket:localhost:8209]
host=localhost
port=8209
tomcatId=machine3
group=balanced
lb_factor=1

[ajp13:localhost:8209]
channel=channel.socket:machine3

[lb:balanced]
worker=ajp13:localhost:8009
worker=ajp13:localhost:8109
worker=ajp13:localhost:8209
timeout=90
attempts=3
recovery=30
StickySession=0
noWorkersMsg=Server Busy please retry later
noWorkerCodeMsg=503

[shm]
file=c:\cluster\apache\jk2.shm
size=1000000

[uri:/jsp-examples/*]
info=mapping the jsp-examples context of Tomcat
context=/jsp-examples
group=balanced
```

For a detailed explanation of the configuration directives, refer to Chapter 12. Note that unlike the Chapter 12 load-balancing example, the `StickySession` property for the load balancer is set to `0`, or disabled. You may need to adjust some of the file paths in this configuration, depending on where you have placed the cluster directory.

Preparation for Using Different Session-Sharing Back-Ends

This completes the basic common setup for the upcoming cluster examples. Each of the session-sharing back-ends that will be configured requires very specific configuration and customization, and each is covered individually. More specifically, the following example shows how to configure the following back-ends:

- In-memory replication
- The Persistent Session Manager, using a shared-file system
- The Persistent Session Manager, using JDBC-to-MySQL RDBMSs

The following section covers the configuration of the in-memory replication mechanism.

Back-End 1: In-Memory Replication Configuration

Two components need to be configured to enable in-memory configuration with Tomcat 5. Figure 19-9 depicts the position and function of the two components.

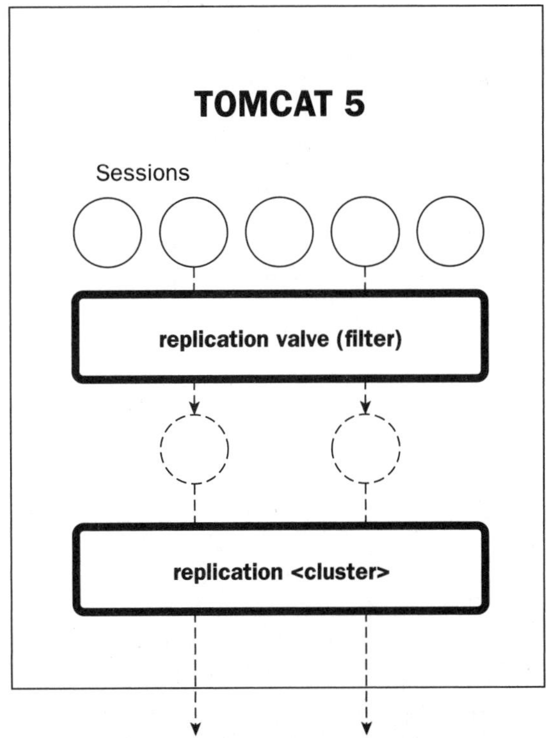

Figure 19-9: Tomcat components for In-memory session replication.

In Figure 19-9, a new `<Cluster>` component is responsible for the actual session replication. This includes the sending of new session information to the group, incorporating new incoming session information locally, and management of group membership. Another component, a replication Valve, is used to reduce the potential session replication traffic by ruling out (filtering) certain requests from session replication.

Operation of the Default Tomcat 5 SimpleTcpCluster

The default implementation of in-memory replication for Tomcat 5 is called `SimpleTcpCluster`. It is the only one available as of this writing.

This implementation uses a very simple multicast-based "ping" or heartbeat to determine membership. Any node that is up and running must multicast heartbeat ping messages at a minimum regular interval (see Figure 19-10). Nodes within the same cluster listen to and broadcast at the same multicast address and port. Nodes that do not send their heartbeat ping within the required interval are considered dead and are removed from the cluster (until they start multicasting the heartbeat again). The membership service simply listens at this port to determine the current set of nodes in the cluster.

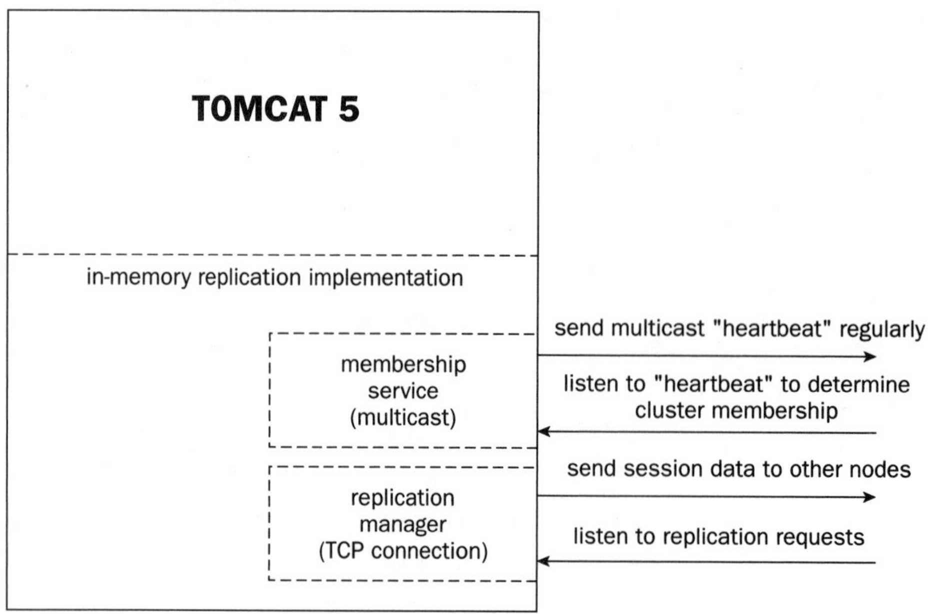

Figure 19-10: Operational model of Tomcat 5 SimpleTcpCluster implementation.

Session replication requests and session updates are sent between member nodes in the cluster using TCP connections directly, in an end-to-end connection. This means that a node sending replication data will make a direct TCP connection to each and every member node in the cluster when replicating a session.

Because of the amount of network traffic generated, this simple implementation is useful only for clusters with a small membership size. More efficient implementation is scheduled to follow in later Tomcat 5 releases.

Cluster Session Manager Configuration with the <Cluster> Element

The first component is a new <Cluster> component. This component should be nested inside an enclosing <Host> element. Including this component in a <Host> will essentially enable session replication for all applications in the host. The standard manager component used to manage sessions in Tomcat will be replaced with a session replication-enabled manager. Here is the configuration for our <Cluster> element:

```
<Cluster  className="org.apache.catalina.cluster.tcp.SimpleTcpCluster"
            name="wroxtomcat5"
            debug="10"
            serviceclass="org.apache.catalina.cluster.mcast.McastService"
            mcastAddr="228.0.0.4"
            mcastPort="45564"
            mcastFrequency="500"
            mcastDropTime="3000"
            tcpThreadCount="2"
            tcpListenAddress="auto"
            tcpListenPort="4001"
            tcpSelectorTimeout="100"
            printToScreen="false"
            expireSessionsOnShutdown="false"
            useDirtyFlag="true"
            replicationMode="synchronous"
  />
```

Note that the highlighted line is the TCP port on which the clustered session manager will listen for incoming session update information. Because all three of the Tomcat instances are running on the same physical machines, the port must be different for machine1, machine2, and machine3. The following table shows the port assignments that you need to use. Make sure you configure them properly in the corresponding `server.xml` file.

Instance Name	tcpListenPort
machine1	4001
machine2	4002
machine3	4003

The following table shows the attributes available for the <Cluster> element.

Attribute Name	Description	Default
className	The implementation Java class for the cluster manager. Currently, only `org.apache.catalina.cluster.tcp.SimpleTcpCluster` is available.	
name	A name for the cluster. The same name should be used on all instances.	

Table continued on following page

Attribute Name	Description	Default
serviceClass	The implementation Java class for the cluster's membership service. Currently, only org.apache.catalina.cluster.mcast.McastService is available.	
debug	Specifies the debug level	0
mcastAddr	The multicast address to use for the cluster. Should be the same on all instances. Can be used to form multiple clusters on the same LAN.	
mcastPort	The multicast port to use for the cluster. It should be the same on all instances, and it can be used to form multiple clusters on the same LAN.	
mcastFrequency	The interval (in milliseconds) between heartbeat multicast pings	
mcastDropTime	The maximum interval, in milliseconds, between heartbeats before a node is considered dead	
tcpThreadCount	The number of TCP threads used to handle incoming replication requests. This should be set to the number of nodes in the group.	2
tcpListenAddress	The address to listen to for incoming replication requests—either "auto" or an IP address. "Auto" means the local adapter address will be used. An IP address can be specified for nodes with multiple Ethernet cards.	
tcpListenPort	The port to listen to for incoming replication requests	1234
tcpSelectorTimeout	The maximum number of milliseconds to wait for a socket select() call. Used to bypass an NIO library bug. Setting to 100 is recommended.	
printToScreen	Set this to true if you want to see output from the manager on the console.	false
expireSessionsOnShutdown	Indicates if sessions should be expired upon shutdown of the node. Set to false except for debugging.	false
useDirtyFlag	This flag indicates if the session should be replicated with each incoming request. When the flag is false, the session will be replicated with every incoming request associated with a session. If true, session replication will occur only if setAttribute() or removeAttribute() has been called. Session replication is also affected by the replication Valve. See the next section in this chapter for more information.	false

Attribute Name	Description	Default
replicationMode	Either synchronous or asynchronous. In synchronous mode, the same thread is used for request processing and replication. In asynchronous mode, a thread is associated with each node in the cluster and the request processing thread queues the replication work for these threads to process. In most cases, synchronous replication mode is adequate.	

The configuration included with the Tomcat 5 default `server.xml` file is adequate for most in-memory replication scenarios. You can simply uncomment the configuration to use it.

A Replication <Valve> Element

The second component essential for in-memory replication is a replication `<Valve>` element. This element acts as a filter. The filter reduces the actual session replication network traffic by determining if the current session needs to be replicated at the end of the request processing cycle. A `useDirtyFlag` attribute can be set to `false` in the `<Cluster>` element, indicating the need to replicate session information with every request. Otherwise, when the flag is `true`, a session is only replicated when it is first created, or when `setAttribute()` or `removeAttribute()` is called. In any case, the filter attribute of the replication Valve may be used to override and stop session replication for specific matching requests. For example, the replication `<Valve>` element in our `server.xml` file is configured as follows:

```
<Valve className="org.apache.catalina.cluster.tcp.ReplicationValve"
       filter=".*\.gif;.*\.js;.*\.jpg;.*\.htm;.*\.html;.*\.txt;"/>
```

The filter setting here filters out any requests for static pages, graphic pages, or JavaScript pages. These pages do not modify the session values. Without this filtered set, session replication will occur for these static requests if the `useDirtyFlag` is set to `false`. The following table shows the attributes of the replication Valve.

Attribute	Description
className	The Valve's implementation class. It must be `org.apache.Catalina.cluster.tcp.ReplicationValve`.
filter	A semicolon-delimited list of URL patterns for requests that are to be filtered out (i.e., excluded for session replication)

Setting Up the Test JSP for Tomcat Session Replication

The JSP that will be used in the testing is named `sesstest.jsp`. The listing is as follows:

```
<%@page language="java" %>
<html>
<body>
<h1><font color="red">Session serviced by machine1</font></h1>
<table aligh="center" border="1">
```

```
<tr>
<td>
  Session ID</td>
<td><%= session.getId() %></td>
<% session.setAttribute("abc","abc"); %>
</tr>
<tr>
<td>
  Created on</td>
  <td><%= session.getCreationTime() %></td>
</tr>
</table>
</body>
</html>
```

Note that this is very similar to the JSP used in Chapter 12. It simply gets the session ID and date and displays them. The `setAttribute()` method is also called explicitly to cause a change in the session, triggering the replication mechanism to be tested. When accessing this JSP across server instances, a matching session ID indicates that a session has migrated/replicated from server to server in the cluster. In addition, each server has a JSP that will display the heading in a different color. The following code examples show the single-line difference for each copy of `sesstest.jsp`.

For machine1, the line would be

```
<h1><font color="red">Session serviced by machine1</font></h1>
```

For machine2, the line would be

```
<h1><font color="green">Session serviced by machine2</font></h1>
```

For machine3, the line would be

```
<h1><font color="blue">Session serviced by machine3</font></h1>
```

The `sesstest.jsp` is placed into the `%CATALINA_BASE%/webapps/jsp-examples` directory of each of the tomcat instances in the cluster. For example, the `sesstest.jsp` for machine1 is placed into the `\cluster\machine1\webapps\jsp-examples` directory. This enables simple access to the test JSP without the need to configure another Web application.

Testing Tomcat 5's In-Memory Session Replication Cluster

To test the in-memory session replication cluster, perform the following steps:

1. In the `server.xml` files of the three instances, ensure that the `<Cluster>` and the replication `<Valve>` elements are uncommented, and that the `<Manager>` element (for later examples) is commented out. In addition, ensure that the `<Context>` element is commented out, as this is only used for the Persistent Session Manager example later.
2. Start up the three configured Tomcat 5 instances, with the batch files in the `%CATALINA_HOME%/bin` directory (start1, start2, and start3); be sure to wait sufficient time until one fully starts up before starting another. (The replication manager takes a little longer than normal to start up.)

3. Start up the Apache server with the `mod_jk2` module.
4. Start an instance of a browser and point it to the following URL:

```
http://localhost/jsp-examples/
```

Initially, your display should be similar to what is shown in Figure 19-11. This indicates that machine1 is servicing your incoming request, and a session is created with the ID as displayed.

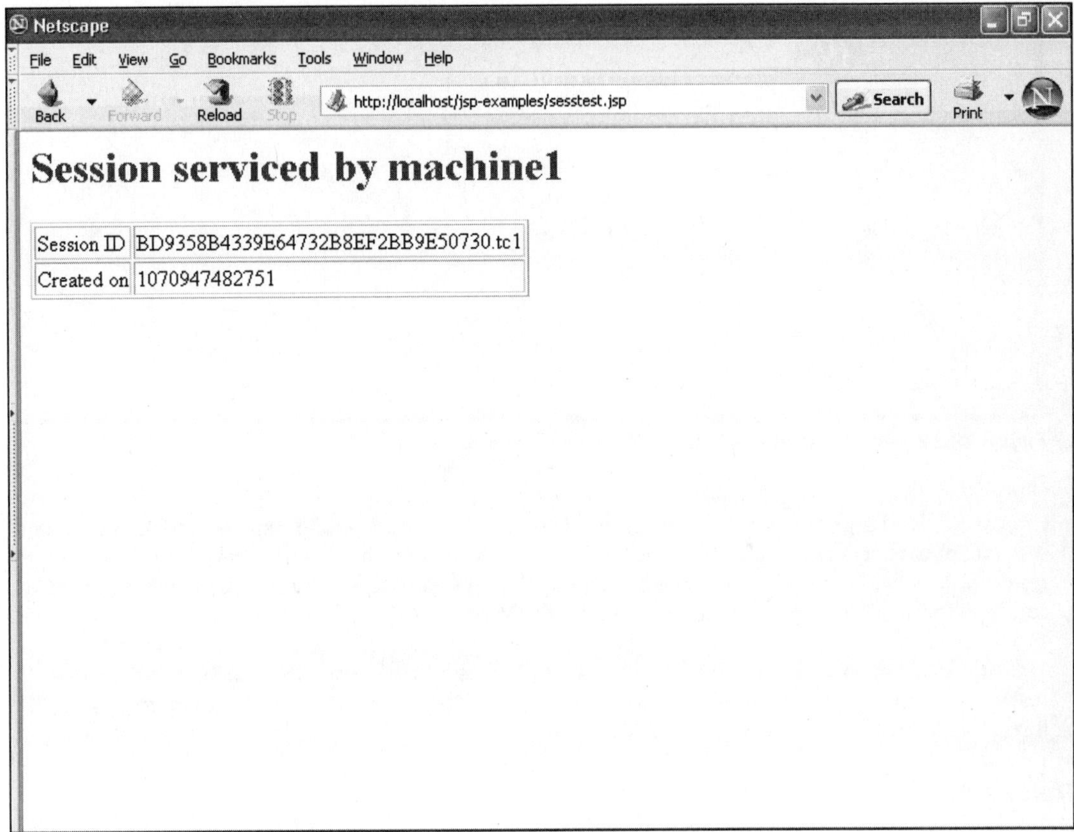

Figure 19-11: Establishing a session on machine1 in the cluster.

Observing Load Balancing for Requests with Same Session

Now, click the Reload button. Note that machine2 is servicing your request. Only round-robin request dispatch is observed because `mod_jk2` is configured with sticky sessions disabled. However, pay special attention to the session ID (see Figure 19-12). This is the same session ID as observed on machine1! The in-memory session replication mechanism has sent the session information to machine2.

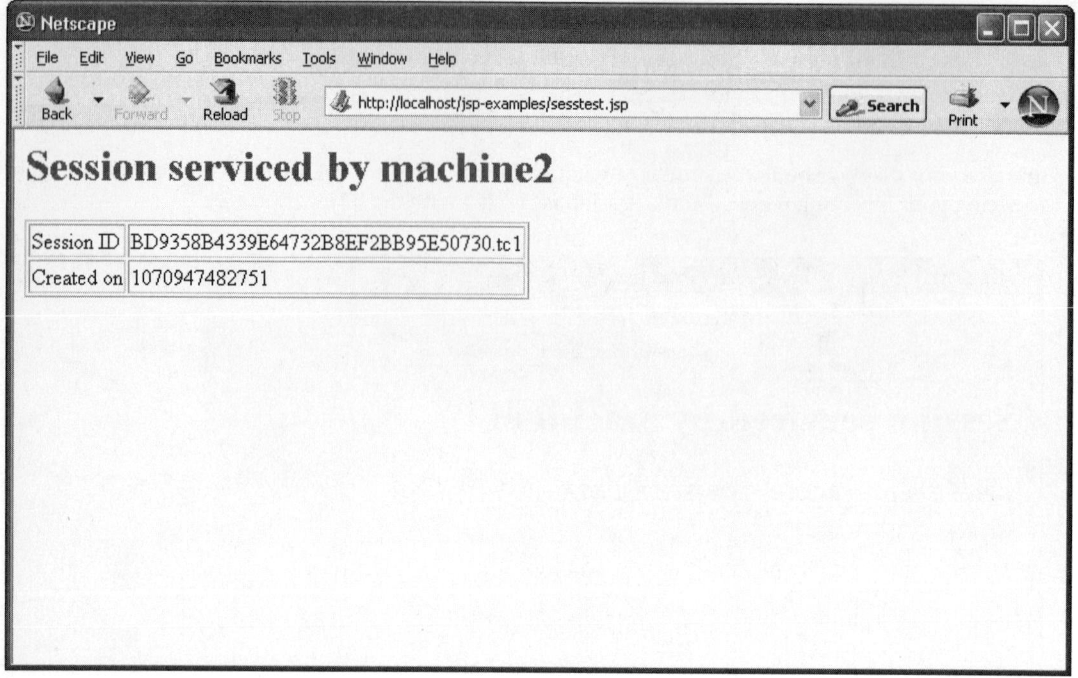

Figure 19-12: Load-balanced session serviced by machine2.

Click the Reload button again. Now, machine3 is servicing your incoming request, and again the same session appears. It is clear from this experiment that HA behavior has been achieved with in-memory replication. Any of the machines in the cluster has the capability to service any incoming request and continue the session(s) established. This enables transparent fail-over behavior.

You should try opening more browser instances and accessing the same URL. Each of the browser instances should have its own unique session ID, and will be serviced in a round-robin fashion by the three Tomcat instances in the cluster.

Observing HA Fail-Over

To see fail-over at work, note both the machine that is servicing your request and the session ID. Now, go to the console of that Tomcat instance and terminate it (press Ctrl+C or close the console window). This represents a sudden failure. Wait a little while (30 seconds or so) and then click Reload. Notice that your session is now handled by one of the remaining servers, with no change in the session ID.

If you have the means to observe network traffic over the LAN (that is, a hardware Ethernet monitor), you should see significant traffic even with this simple example. Devising a load test (as described in Chapter 17) will enable you to determine if the typical incoming request rate will be adequately served by this clustering back-end.

This completes the exploration of memory session replication. Next, an alternative back-end using a Persistent Session Manager will be covered.

Back-End 2: Persistent Session Manager with a File Store

This section describes the configuration for a Persistent Session Manager. This Persistent Session Manager will use a shared directory to store its persistent session.

To configure the cluster to work with a Persistent Session Manager, first comment out the <Cluster> and replication <Valve> elements in each of the server.xml files. This will disable the in-memory replication mechanism.

Configuring the <Manager> Element

Next, modify the server.xml file of each of the clustered nodes to add the following context and session manager definition at the end of the existing <Host> element. If you are using the code distribution, the following element is already in place:

```
...
<Context docBase="jsp-examples" path="/jsp-examples">
  <Manager  className="org.apache.catalina.session.PersistentManager" >
     <Store className="org.apache.catalina.session.FileStore"
      directory="c:\\cluster\\shareddir" />
</Manager>
</Context>
</Host>
```

You can change the c:\cluster\shareddir directory to any other directory that you are using to store shared session information. Just make sure that you change the directory attribute of the <Valve> element.

Unlike the previous example, note that the context for the jsp-examples Web application is explicitly specified here (instead of letting Tomcat 5 create a default one for us). This is because the Persistent Session Manager must be configured in the form of a nested <Manager> element. The <Manager> element can only reside within a <Context> element to persist the sessions created within that particular Web application. See Chapter 8 for more details on the specific allowed attributes for the <Manager> element.

The <Store> Nested Element

The only allowed sub-element of a <Manager> element is a <Store> element. Only two different stores are available with Tomcat 5: One uses a shared file directory to store the sessions, and the other one uses an RDBMS through JDBC to store the sessions. In this case, the Tomcat instance is configured with the shared file system store.

Note that the exact mechanism to share the specified directory is system- and installation-specific. In this case, the shared directory is actually the same physical directory because all the Tomcat instances executed reside on the same physical machine. In production systems, where each Tomcat instance runs on a different physical machine in the cluster, the directory may be shared by operating system–specific means (NFS on Solaris, SMB on Win32 servers, and so on).

Adding Sticky Session Support with the mod_jk2 Load Balancer

Recall from earlier discussions in this chapter that a Persistent Session Manager back-ended cluster should typically be deployed with sticky session support. In situations where server crashes are relatively rare, this configuration will minimize the number of sessions that may be lost during a fail-over.

Because the last configuration disabled sticky session support, it must be re-enabled. This involves an update to the `worker2.properties` file. Make sure you add or change the lines highlighted:

```
...
[channel.socket:localhost:8009]
host=localhost
port=8009
tomcatId=machine1
group=balanced
lb_factor=1
route=tc1

[ajp13:localhost:8009]
channel=channel.socket:machine1

[channel.socket:localhost:8109]
host=localhost
port=8109
tomcatId=machine2
group=balanced
lb_factor=1
route=tc2

[ajp13:localhost:8109]
channel=channel.socket:machine2


[channel.socket:localhost:8209]
host=localhost
port=8209
tomcatId=machine3
group=balanced
lb_factor=1
route=tc3

[ajp13:localhost:8209]
channel=channel.socket:machine3

[lb:balanced]
worker=ajp13:localhost:8009
worker=ajp13:localhost:8109
worker=ajp13:localhost:8209
timeout=90
attempts=3
recovery=30
StickySession=1
noWorkersMsg=Server Busy please retry later
noWorkerCodeMsg=503
...
```

Next, it is necessary to modify the `server.xml` files of the instances to label the `jvmRoute` attribute of the corresponding `<Engine>` element.

On machine1, add the following `jvmRoute`:

```
<Engine name="Catalina" defaultHost="localhost" debug="0"  jvmRoute="tc1">
```

On machine2, add the following `jvmRoute`:

```
<Engine name="Catalina" defaultHost="localhost" debug="0" jvmRoute="tc2" >
```

On machine3, add the following `jvmRoute`:

```
<Engine name="Catalina" defaultHost="localhost" debug="0" jvmRoute="tc3" >
```

This completes the configuration for the Persistent Session Manager with a file-based store. Of course, you should make sure that the shared directory specified in the `<Store>` element of the `server.xml` file indeed exists and is accessible.

Testing a Shared File System–Based Persistent Session Cluster

To test and see the level of HA provided by this solution, first start the three Tomcat instances using the start1, start2, and start3 batch files in the `%CATALINA_HOME%/bin` directory. Next, start the Apache server.

Start a browser instance and try accessing the following URL:

```
http://localhost/jsp-examples/sesstest.jsp
```

You should see machine1 servicing your request, and the session ID displayed. Write down this session ID. Click reload a few times, and notice that machine1 continues to service your request and that the session ID remains identical. This is sticky session working as desired.

Open another browser instance and access the same URL. This time, machine2 will service the request (thanks to round-robin load balancing). If you reload the page, machine2 will continue to service the request, again sticky session is working as configured.

Observing an Orderly Fail-Over

To observe HA at work, try to simulate a fault by machine1. Go to the `%CATALINA_HOME%/bin` directory and execute the following batch file:

```
C:\>  stop1
```

This will shut down the machine1 instance. Because the machine1 instance is no longer running, if you click reload on the browser serviced by machine1, it will be round-robin load-balanced to machine3 (machine2 serviced an earlier request from another browser instance). Note that even though machine3 is now handling the request, the session ID stays the same. In other words, the application has successfully failed over from machine1 to machine3, and in a manner transparent to the user.

The main reason why this works is because an orderly shutdown was performed. During the orderly shutdown, all of the sessions in the Persistent Session Manager were persisted to the store (shared directory). This may be useful in many situations. For example, a server can be taken out of service for maintenance and upgrades without affecting the ongoing cluster operation. In some cases, it may also be possible for a fault-detection mechanism to detect a problem and perform an orderly shutdown (hardware-uninterruptible power backup sources often offer this feature).

The picture is slightly different, however, when the server instance shutdown is not orderly.

Observing a Sudden Fail-Over

The key limitation to remember when working with a Persistent Session Manager shared-store back-end is that any sessions or changes not persisted at crash time are lost.

To observe this limitation, start a new browser instance and point it to the following URL:

```
http://localhost/jsp-examples/sesstest.jsp
```

Note the session ID. (Don't use any old browser instance, because an older session may already be persisted.)

Also note the Tomcat instance that is servicing this request/session. Now, go to the console running the Tomcat instance and press Ctrl+C or close the window.

This simulates a sudden system crash shortly after the session is created. Next, click your browser's Reload button. Note that a new instance is now servicing the request, but the session ID you observe may be either of the following:

- *The same session ID*—In this case, the fail-over was successful because the session was persisted before the crash.
- *A brand-new session ID*—In this case, the session was lost during fail-over because it was not persisted before the crash.

If you repeat this test a few times, you are likely to see both behaviors. It is possible to tweak the attributes of a Persistent Session Manager or the store to alter the time between session creation or modification and session persistence. However, the Persistent Session Manager is not designed with sharing sessions across clustered machines in mind, and it does not provide a hard guarantee for the time window between creation/update and persistence.

Despite the small potential of lost sessions, this level of HA support (which improved over the scenario with no session sharing at all) can be adequate for many real-world deployments. Its simplicity of configuration and inexpensive implementation are two advantages that should not be overlooked.

The next section takes a look at an alternative store mechanism for the Persistent Session Manager.

Back-End 3: Persistent Session Manager with a JDBC Store

Instead of sharing a directory between the Tomcat instances, it is also possible to write all shared session information into an RDBMS through JDBC. This is done through the same Persistent Session Manager, but using a JDBC <Store> element instead of a shared file system–based <Store> element.

A few scenarios in which you may want to use the JDBC store instead of a shared file-system store include the following:

- When a shared file system is not available to all the physical machines in the cluster, but a common JDBC connection is
- When the JDBC connection and RDBMS offer higher performance or provide the robustness guarantee that you may need
- When the JDBC connection to the shared RDBMS is made through a separate physical hardware connection (another LAN, firewire, proprietary communication link, and so on) that is less prone to failure (that is, it may be redundantly implemented through an RDBMS-level cluster)
- When the shared file system access traffic is over the same LAN that is handling the routed `mod_jk` requests, and the JDBC connection is made over a separate LAN or communications link
- When normal operations of the cluster involve a large number of sessions that may be swapped out at any moment in time

In this example, a MySQL RDBMS table will be used to store session information and enable a cluster of Tomcat servers to share session information via the Persistent Session Manager, through JDBC.

All the front-end configurations and `server.xml` modifications made in the previous example will continue to work. All that you need to do is replace the previous shared file system–based <Store> with the JDBC-based <Store> sub-element within each of the <Manager> elements:

```
    <Store className="org.apache.catalina.session.JDBCStore"
connectionURL="jdbc:mysql://localhost/wroxtomcat?user=empro&amp;password=empass"
      driverName="com.mysql.jdbc.Driver"
      sessionIdCol="session_id"
      sessionValidCol="valid_session"
      sessionMaxInactiveCol="max_inactive"
      sessionLastAccessedCol="last_access"
      sessionTable = "tomcat_sessions"
      sessionAppCol = "app_context"
      sessionDataCol = "session_data"
    />
```

Note that the JDBC <Store> element implementation is missing the usual user and password attributes required for a JDBC connection (this is an oversight that may be corrected in later versions). This forces you to add the user and password information as part of the `connectionURL`. Because the syntax of the URL requires the ampersand (`&`), it must be escaped within this XML-based configuration file as `&`.

The creation of the corresponding MySQL table called `tomcat_sessions` is shown later. The following table describes the attributes supported by the JDBC <Store> element.

Attribute Name	Description	Default
className	The JDBC Store implementation, which must be org.apache.catalina.session.JDBCStore	
connectionURL	The JDBC URL used to connect to the database instance. Note that user and password must also be part of the URL, as there are no corresponding user or password attributes.	
driverName	The Java language class name for the JDBC driver to use	
sessionTable	The name of the RDBMS table that is used to tomcat$sessions store session information	tomcat$sessions
sessionIdCol	The name of the database table column that contains the session ID information. This column should be the primary key of the table because it is the key used for lookup most frequently.	Id
sessionValidCol	The name of a database table column that contains a flag indicating if the associated session (row) is still valid	Valid
sessionMaxInactiveCol	The name of the database table column used to persist the value of the MaxInactiveInterval property for the session	Maxinactive
sessionLastAccessedCol	The name of the database table column used to persist the value of the lastAccessedTime property for the session	lastaccess
sessionAppCol	The name of the database table column used to persist the Engine, Host, and Context information for the session	app
sessionDataCol	The name of the database table column used to persist the actual session data (serialized session attributes)	data

*Make sure you have copied MySQL Connector/J into the common **lib** directory; otherwise, the Persistent Session Manager may fail silently. If you have the examples shown in Chapter 14 working, you are all set.*

To create the tomcat_sessions table, the following SQL script can be used. This script is found in the mksesstbl.sql file within the code distribution:

```
USE wroxtomcat;

drop table if exists tomcat_sessions;

create table tomcat_sessions (
  session_id     varchar(100) not null primary key,
  valid_session  char(1) not null,
  max_inactive   int not null,
  last_access    bigint not null,
  app_context       varchar(255),
  session_data   mediumblob,
  KEY kapp_context(app_context)
);
```

An additional complication can arise during configuration when multiple instances of Tomcat run on the same physical machine. This is because the combination of host name and user is not unique during RDBMS access. Therefore, it is necessary to create three different users for machine1, machine2, and machine3 access, respectively. The following MySQL commands will create these additional users (provided you have the necessary administrator privilege on the MySQL server):

```
GRANT SELECT,INSERT,UPDATE,DELETE ON wroxtomcat.tomcat_sessions TO
'empro'@'localhost' IDENTIFIED BY 'empass';
```

```
GRANT SELECT,INSERT,UPDATE,DELETE ON wroxtomcat.tomcat_sessions TO
'empro1'@'localhost' IDENTIFIED BY 'empass';
```

```
GRANT SELECT,INSERT,UPDATE,DELETE ON wroxtomcat.tomcat_sessions TO
'empro2'@'localhost' IDENTIFIED BY 'empass';
```

These commands will create the users and passwords shown in the following table for concurrent access of the `tomcat_sessions` table.

Tomcat Instance	User	Password
machine1	empro	empass
machine2	empro1	empass
machine3	empro2	empass

If you examine the actual `mksesstbl.sql` file in the code distribution, you will also see the SQL grant statements for creating the `empro`, `empro1`, and `empro2` JDBC access accounts. This will save you from entering the commands manually.

The following command line will execute the SQL script (assuming that you have a create table privilege on the database):

```
$ mysql < mksesstbl.sql
$ mysqladmin -u???? -p????? flush-privileges
```

The second statement is needed to flush the privileges cache and make the `grant` statements effective immediately.

After the table is created and the JDBC-based `<Store>` element has been added to the `server.xml` file of each clustered Tomcat instance, you are ready to test the JDBC-based Persistence Session Manager back-end.

Testing a Tomcat Cluster with JDBC Persistent Session Manager Back-End

The steps for testing the Tomcat cluster with a JDBC Persistent Session Manager back-end are exactly the same as those for the shared file system Persistent Session Manager. See the instructions for the preceding example for more details. There should be no observable difference between the behaviors of the two examples. A JDBC-based back-end provides a robust store mechanism, and is a potentially higher performance mechanism when numerous sessions need to be persisted/shared.

An Application-Level Load Balancing Alternative (Balancer)

One new load-balancing alternative, recently made available with the Tomcat 5 distribution, is an example Tomcat 5 Web application called `balancer`. It is located in the `%CATALINA_HOME%/webapps/balancer` directory.

Unlike the `mod_jk` solution, which uses an internal Tomcat server component (Manager), the `balancer` works on the application level. The `balancer` is actually a Tomcat filter (Servlets 2.3 specifications-compliant) that will perform load balancing by redirecting incoming requests using a **rules-based engine.** Figure 19-13 illustrates the action of the `balancer`.

The `balancer` uses a distinctly different means to balance the load: It redirects the incoming URL. The balancer performs the following steps:

1. Incoming URL requests are directed to the `balancer` Web application according to the URL pattern specified in the deployment descriptor's (`web.xml`) `<filter-mapping>` definition.
2. The `balancer` then examines the intercepted incoming URL and applies its chain of rules to it. The rules are configured in the `rules.xml` file.
3. When a rule is matched against a URL, the associated redirect URL is sent back to the browser.
4. The browser now attempts to access the new URL.

Note the following two main points:

- Each redirection requires an extra round-trip as the browser receives the redirection and connects to the new URL.
- This scheme is effective only for an initial request redirect, unless there exists a rule for dynamically generating the redirect URL (based on portion of the original incoming URL).

The second point is important because in the current version of the `balancer` application (Tomcat 5.0.16 as of this writing), the `balancer` cannot redirect to a dynamically created URL.

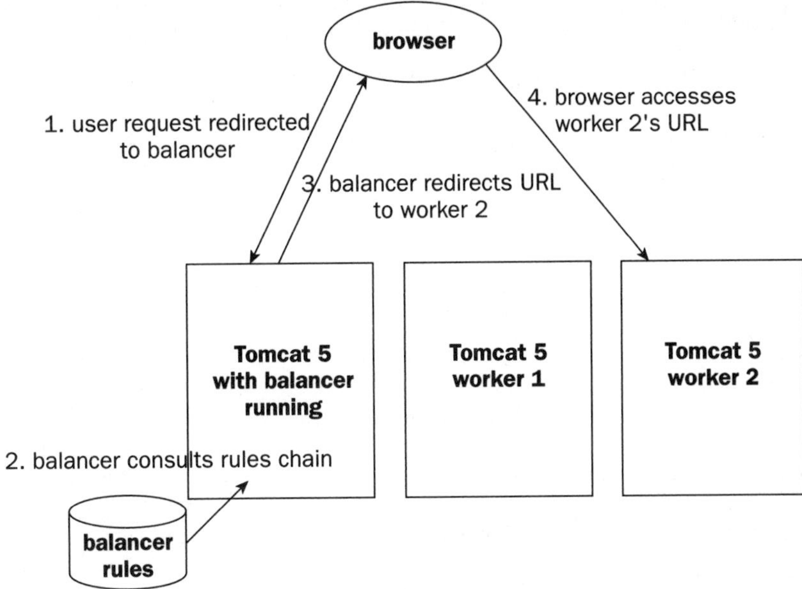

Figure 19-13: Operation of the balancer application.

Load Balancing with the balancer Filter

The typical use for `balancer` is to redirect initial incoming requests to a set of specialized servers that perform specific functionality. The rules-based engine adds additional value in that the exact server to which a request is directed can potentially change with dynamic system conditions. This can be achieved with custom Java rule coding.

For example, `balancer` can be used to forward any image processing request to a set of image processing servers, while sending accounting requests to accounting servers. You can use any arbitrary complex logic for load balancing too, such as a condition specifying that if it is outside of business hours and the accounting servers' average load is below 50 percent, then any overload of imaging processing requests should be sent to the accounting server.

Again, note that `balancer` is best used for the **initial request redirect.** This means that once the request is redirected, the client will continue to work with the same redirected server (e.g., continue to work with the same image processing server in the earlier example). Sessions are then created and maintained on the same server, with overall behavior similar to the `mod_jk` sticky sessions scenario.

Some benefits of performing balancing on the application level using `balancer` include the following:

- *Portability* — Filters are not container-specific and can be deployed in other Servlet 2.3-compliant (and later) containers in addition to (or instead of) Tomcat.

- *Easy configurability and testing*—Changes to the load-balancing logic can be made and redeployed without shutting down the host container.
- *Flexibility*—The rules-based load balancing and rule-chain handling provide unlimited algorithmic possibilities.

The main drawbacks to balancing on the application level are as follows:

- *Efficiency*—Redirection at the application level requires an additional round-trip for every incoming request because the browser receives a redirection response and has to send another request.
- *Loading*—It is necessary to quarantine the `balancer` application on its own physical server (or at least its own JVM/Tomcat instance) on a heavily loaded site, as its loading may affect the operation of other Web applications.

In any case, when running Tomcat 5 in standalone mode (without Apache or other Web servers), the `balancer` is a viable clustering front end that is easy to configure, maintain, and modify. The next section describes the configuration and deployment of `balancer` in detail.

> *IMPORTANT: The **`balancer`** makes use of Jakarta **`commons digester`** and **`beanutils`** libraries. These libraries are not included with the default Tomcat 5 distribution. Make sure you download them from **http://jakarta.apache.org/site/binindex.cgi**, and place them in **`%CATALINA_HOME%/common/lib`** before proceeding. This example has been tested with **`commons digester`** 1.5 and **`beanutils`** 1.6.1.*

Working with the balancer Filter

It is a good idea to configure the `balancer` to run on its own Tomcat instance. A new instance directory under the `\cluster` directory, called `machine4`, is created just for this purpose. It will simulate a fourth independent machine in our cluster.

Reconfiguring Tomcat Instances for Standalone Mode of Operations

Next, it is necessary to reconfigure the machine1, machine2, machine3, and machine4 `server.xml` file for standalone operation. This basically means that the Coyote HTTP Connector will be configured instead of the AJP Connector.

In each of the `server.xml` files, comment out the AJP Connector and add the following highlighted line:

```
...
<Service name="Catalina">
<!--  <Connector  port="8009" protocol="AJP/1.3"/>
-->
<Connector port="8080" />

    <Engine name="Catalina" defaultHost="localhost" debug="0" >
...
```

The port number used in this line must be changed for each instance. Because all the instances are running on the same physical machine, it is necessary to ensure that each instance uses a different TCP port. The example configuration uses the assignments shown in the following table.

Machine Name	Port Number
`machine1`	8080
`machine2`	8180
`machine3`	8280
`machine4`	8090

In addition, the new instance, machine4, needs a unique shutdown TCP port. This example uses port 8405. In machine4's `server.xml` file, make sure that the first configuration line is as follows:

```
<Server port="8405" shutdown="SHUTDOWN" debug="0">
```

Finally, configure the shared file–based Persistent Session Manager back-end for experimentation. Make sure that the machine1, machine2, and machine3 `server.xml` files have the following statements toward the end:

```
<Context docBase="jsp-examples" path="/jsp-examples">
  <Manager  className="org.apache.catalina.session.PersistentManager" >
     <Store className="org.apache.catalina.session.FileStore"
      directory="c:\\cluster\\shareddir" />
  </Manager>
</Context>
```

In addition, make sure that machine4's `server.xml` file has this segment removed. The `balancer` server instance does not need session sharing.

This completes the reconfiguration of the Tomcat instances for standalone mode of operation. The Tomcat instances will now serve both dynamic and static content.

Configuring the balancer Filter

The following configuration is related only to the `balancer` filter, and therefore should be performed only on the machine4 instance.

The `balancer` filter is a standard Servlet 2.3/2.4–compliant filter. As such, it is configured in the Web application through the deployment descriptor (`web.xml`). Make sure the `\cluster\machine4\webapps\balancer\WEB-INF\web.xml` file contains the following lines:

```
<filter>
    <filter-name>BalancerFilter</filter-name>
    <filter-class>org.apache.webapp.balancer.BalancerFilter</filter-class>
    <init-param>
      <param-name>configUrl</param-name>
      <param-value>/WEB-INF/config/rules.xml</param-value>
    </init-param>
  </filter>
  <filter-mapping>
    <filter-name>BalancerFilter</filter-name>
    <url-pattern>/*</url-pattern>
  </filter-mapping>
...
```

The /* url pattern ensures that all incoming URLs for the balancer application will pass through the filter. This means that any URL starting with http://localhost:8090/balancer/.... will be passed to this filter regardless of the exact URL.

Configuring the balancer Filter Rule Chain

In the web.xml configuration, the file WEB-INF/config/rules.xml is used to set balancer's filtering rules. The following is what the rules.xml file contains:

```
<?xml version="1.0" encoding="UTF-8"?>
<rules>
  <rule className="org.apache.webapp.balancer.rules.URLStringMatchRule"
    targetString="NewUser"
    redirectUrl="http://localhost:8080/jsp-examples/sesstest.jsp" />

  <rule className="org.apache.webapp.balancer.rules.RequestParameterRule"
    paramName="req"
    paramValue="3"
    redirectUrl="http://localhost:8180/jsp-examples/sesstest.jsp" />

  <rule className="org.apache.webapp.balancer.rules.AcceptEverythingRule"
    redirectUrl="http://localhost:8280/jsp-examples/sesstest.jsp" />
</rules>
```

All rules are specified inside the <rules> XML element. Each rule must have a className attribute that specifies the Java class containing the rule logic to use.

The preceding rules basically state the following:

- If the URL has the string NewUser in it, let machine1 service the request (at port 8080).
- If the URL has a parameter called req with a value of 3, then let machine2 service the request.
- Otherwise, let machine3 service the request.

Developers may create their own custom rules. However, the balancer application comes with several prefabricated rules. Note that all of the prefabricated rules shown in the following table reside in the org.apache.webapp.balancer.rules package. Additional custom rules by developers may reside in any Java package.

Rule className	Description
AcceptEverythingRule	Matches anything, and is used for the last entry in the rule chain
CharacterEncodingRule	Has an encoding attribute that specifies the character encoding of the incoming request to match
RemoteAddressRule	Has a remote address attribute that specifies the request's remote address to match
RequestAttributeRule	Has attributeName and attributeValue attributes that specify the request attribute and value to match

`RequestHeaderRule`	Has `headerName` and `headerValue` attributes that specify the request header and value to match
`RequestParameterRule`	Has `paramName` and `paramValue` attributes that specify the request parameter and value to match
`SessionAttributeRule`	Has `attributeName` and `attributeValue` attributes that specify the session attribute and value to match
`URLStringMatch`	Has a `targetString` attribute that specifies a substring to match against the incoming request's URL
`UserRoleRule`	Has a `role` attribute that indicates the role of the user needed for a match. This is verified against the user database.

You can specify as many rules as you want in the `<rules>` element of the `rule.xml` file. The rules form a chain, with the rules first appearing in the file at the top of the chain. The rules matching is attempted from the top of the chain to the bottom of the chain, and the first matching entry causes the redirection of the incoming request to the associated redirect URL.

Testing the balancer Filter

To test the `balancer` filter, start up the server instances and the `balancer`. This can be accomplished using the `start1`, `start2`, `start3`, and `start4` batch files in `%CATALINA_HOME%/bin` directory. Note that `start4.bat` and `stop4.bat` are similar in content to the other batch files and are used to start up the `balancer` instance.

Now, start a browser instance and then point it to the following URL:

```
http://localhost:8090/balancer/NewUser
```

You should observe that machine1 has serviced this request, as the `balancer` filter matches the first rule and redirected the request to machine1.

Wait about a minute, and then try the following URL in the same browser instance:

```
http://localhost:8090/balancer/abc?req=3
```

This time, machine2 services the instance because `balancer` has matched the second rule and redirects the request to machine2. If you are lucky, the back-end persistent session sharing would have kicked in, and you will see the same session ID as the one serviced by machine1.

Finally, try the following URL on the same browser instance:

```
http://localhost:8090/balancer/anything
```

Because the first two rules do not match, the final "catch all" rule is used and the request is redirected to machine3. Again, if the back-end has persisted the session, you will see the same session ID as the one serviced by machine1 and machine2 previously.

Note that in this example, the Reload button was not used. This is because the URL has been changed by the `balancer`, and reloading will access the same redirected URL and will not pass through the `balancer` filter again. This is the reason why the `balancer` filter is primarily good for one single initial redirection when the user first accesses the cluster.

Redirection and the Cookie Problem

You need to be careful when using the `balancer` filter for more than load balancing during the initial redirection. In production, the load-balanced Tomcat instances are typically running on independent machines, not on the same machine (using different ports). This means that the target-redirected URL will contain a different host name or IP address. Because cookies on a browser are indexed according to the host name or IP address, existing cookies will not follow the indirection. This means, unfortunately, that session information (which depends on cookies, as discussed earlier in this chapter) will also not be preserved if the request is redirected to a different host.

Hardware-Assisted Request Distribution with Common NAT

One solution to the preceding problem (if you need to solve it) is to use some inexpensive hardware assistance. Internet sharing devices, sometimes called Network Address Translation (NAT), are commonly available from manufacturers such as LinkSys, SMC, and Dlink, among others. These devices can be used to route incoming requests destined for one IP, but at different ports, to different IPs on an internal LAN. Figure 19-14 illustrates this configuration.

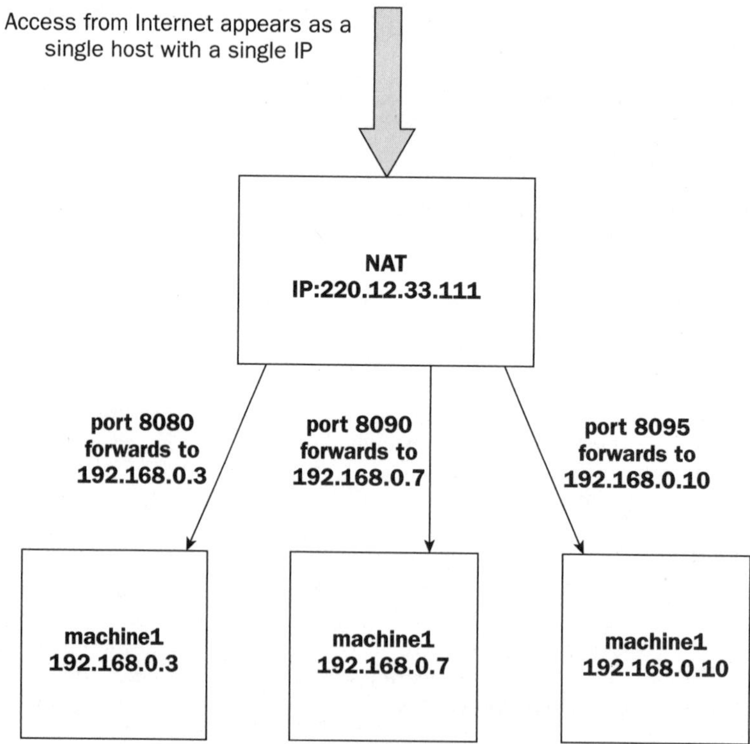

Figure 19-14: Using a NAT for request distribution.

Because all the incoming requests now contain the same host name or IP (only differ on ports), the cookies associated with the host will be preserved, and sessions will continue to work across the redirected hosts.

The Complexity of Clustering

While the setup and configuration of Tomcat 5 clustering can be a daunting task, the capability to obtain tangible benefits from a clustered configuration is the most complex. Several misconceptions (sometimes called urban legends) prevail:

- Performance of a Web application will increase with clusters.
- Response time to the user will improve (decrease) with clusters.
- Clustering is the most inexpensive way to solve performance and response-time problems observed with Web applications.

Clustering and Performance

The word "performance" means different things to different people. Often, it is not politically correct or survival savvy to correct marketing gurus or system architects on this point, but to state a general "performance improvement" objective without specific metrics is akin to saying that computers will solve all our problems.

Many aspects of what is perceived as performance improvement by the end user cannot be achieved by a clustering solution. The scenario that most naturally lends itself to a clustering solution, and the one that will clearly benefit from such a configuration, derives from the following:

- A Web application running on a single Tomcat instance on one physical machine handles all incoming requests with no problem during normal incoming load volume.
- The machine starts to slow down or fail under heavy incoming traffic volume.
- Most important, analysis of the failure/slowdown reveals that the bottleneck is in CPU saturation while processing Tomcat Servlets/JSPs.

It is of utmost importance to reiterate the last point.

> *Until an observed performance slowdown caused by incoming load on a single machine can be isolated to the single factor of CPU saturation due to Tomcat hosted application processing, the benefits of a Tomcat 5 clustering configuration cannot be ascertained.*

For example, no amount of expensive hardware or sophisticated configuration spent on Tomcat clustering will solve system bottleneck problems that pertain to faulty nonscalable application logic, network bandwidth saturation, RDBMS access, and so on.

Obviously, a million other variations of real-world situations that do not quite fit this scenario are possible, and your success with applying Tomcat clustering to the problem will vary accordingly.

Clustering and Response Time

In general, the addition of clustering may actually increase observed individual response time, rather than reduce it, especially when contrasted with a lightly loaded single-server solution. This is because of the overhead involved in front-end load balancing (which, in the `balancer` case illustrated earlier, involves an additional TCP round-trip per redirected request) and session replication. Therefore, one cannot guarantee a user that he or she will observe improved response time when using a clustered solution (versus a single-server solution).

The single-performance metric that should improve with a properly configured and applied Tomcat 5 cluster is **system throughput** (measured in requests processed per time unit) under maximum load. This means that the clustered system as a whole should handle more requests without failing. This is the basic premise of horizontal scalability (**scaling out**).

Solving Performance Problems with Clustering

It should be clear by this point that clustering should not be used as "magic dust" to solve performance problems. Throwing more hardware at the problem may not make it go away. Instead, a proper analysis of the system, including isolation of the bottleneck element, must be performed before applying clustering as a solution. In many cases, the analysis will reveal other factors that cannot benefit from a clustering solution.

When a system performance bottleneck can be isolated to the saturation of computing resources related to Tomcat 5 application processing, horizontal scaling can be achieved via a Tomcat 5 clustering configuration.

Of course, if you have other nonperformance-related system design goals that can benefit from distributed replicated logic (such as high availability for certain Web applications), clustering may still provide benefits.

Summary

This chapter on clustering contained the following key points:

- Widespread production deployments of Tomcat servers have motivated the Tomcat development team to refactor the server for performance and give serious consideration to real-world deployment issues, including scalability and high availability.
- Originally exclusive to proprietary hardware solutions, scalable and highly available clusters can now be achieved inexpensively using Tomcat 5 servers running on PCs, and commodity networking hardware.
- Tomcat 5 is the first version of the Tomcat server to support clustering right out of the box. As such, most of the supported mechanisms are work in progress, and are likely to gain in popularity with the improvement of features in future releases.
- A clustering Web-tier server solution consists of a load-balancing front end and a state/session sharing back-end, with the cluster of Tomcat 5 servers sandwiched in between.

- You have many options for a load balancing front-end solution, but the Apache server with the `mod_jk2` Connector is the technology of choice for production use because of the popularity and performance of Apache. This solution supports a round-robin distributor that respects the specified load factor, and also supports sticky sessions.
- For the session-sharing back-end technology, Tomcat 5 comes with support for group communications based on the memory-session replication mechanism. When enabled, multicast packets are used to maintain cluster membership, while TCP connections are made between servers to share session information. This configuration enables any server in the cluster to service any session, providing a highly available clustering solution. However, this solution should be deployed with care because of its escalating network bandwidth requirement as cluster size and session replication traffic increase.
- The Persistent Session Manager built into Tomcat can also be used for a form of session sharing. Either a file-based store or a JDBC store can be configured. Once a shared file system or RDBMS is configured, any persisted session will become available to all the server instances. When configured together with a front end that supports sticky sessions, this solution can be a very effective high-availability solution that minimizes lost sessions during a fail-over.
- Tomcat 5 also includes an application-level load-balancing front-end mechanism called the `balancer` Web application. The `balancer` uses rules-based URL rewriting to redirect incoming requests. This is best used in a standalone mode configuration (that is, without an Apache front end), and is very effective for initial incoming request redirection. Its routing decisions can be made with the help of custom-coded rules, optionally taking into account dynamic system information (server loads and time of day, and so on).

In summary, Tomcat 5 provides the administrator with a rich toolbox of components and mechanisms at various layers of the server architecture, to design and build functional server clusters. These cluster mechanisms can fulfill most scalability and/or high availability requirements in today's production environments.

Chapter 20 discusses embedded Tomcat.

20

Embedded Tomcat

Ever since the initial availability of the Tomcat server, some developers have wanted or needed to create applications that have full control over the server's life cycle and internal operation. When the entire Tomcat server is contained within a custom application, it is said to be operating in **embedded mode.** While provisions were made for embedding Tomcat into applications in past releases (as far back as Tomcat 3.x), these older provisions were rather ad hoc and problem-prone because the earliest versions of Tomcat did not account for the embedded mode of operation. Tomcat 5 changes this landscape completely. Embedded operation is an explicitly supported mode, and future Tomcat 5 designs will evolve to satisfy the emerging requirements from embedded users.

This chapter explores the embedded mode of Tomcat 5 in the following areas:

- Why embedding Tomcat may be important for many projects
- How JMX-based scripting enables Tomcat's embedded operation
- The architectural elements that make Tomcat embeddable
- The various JMX-based mechanisms used to access Tomcat components from an external program
- How to create and administer an embedded Tomcat server installation

Actual hands-on examples are provided for you to experiment with configuring embedded Tomcat instances.

By the end of this chapter, you should have a comprehensive understanding of why you might use embedded mode and how to operate Tomcat in embedded mode. You will be able to facilitate the creation of (or participate in the configuration/administration/management of) applications and systems that operate embedded Tomcat instances.

Importance of Embedded Tomcat in Modern System Design

Tomcat 5 is a container for JSPs and Servlets. JSPs and Servlets are componentized building blocks for Web applications or services. These components (along with custom Java classes and other Web resources) are managed and processed by the Tomcat container. The componentized nature of the applications makes them easy to construct, deploy, and maintain.

One specific scenario for such a use of Tomcat involves Web applications that are deployed and undeployed dynamically on one or more general-purpose Tomcat containers. In some situations, however, the application running within the Tomcat server may not need to change, or the need to change may be highly infrequent.

One example might be the use of Tomcat to create a Web interface for the configuration of a piece of hardware equipment. Because the hardware equipment will not change, the need to modify the configuration application logic will be infrequent. Another example might be the display and management of a standalone (non-networked) interactive catalog from a CD-ROM. The items and prices in the catalog are fixed once the CD-ROM is printed.

In these situations, the application that is running under Tomcat may be considered to be an embedded application. While it is certainly possible to start the generalized standalone Tomcat server for running such an application, it makes more design sense to minimize the memory footprint and CPU utilization by running "just enough" Tomcat to support the application. Embedded Tomcat 5 provides this flexibility to run "just enough" Tomcat.

Figure 20-1 illustrates a custom hardware scenario that may require embedded Tomcat.

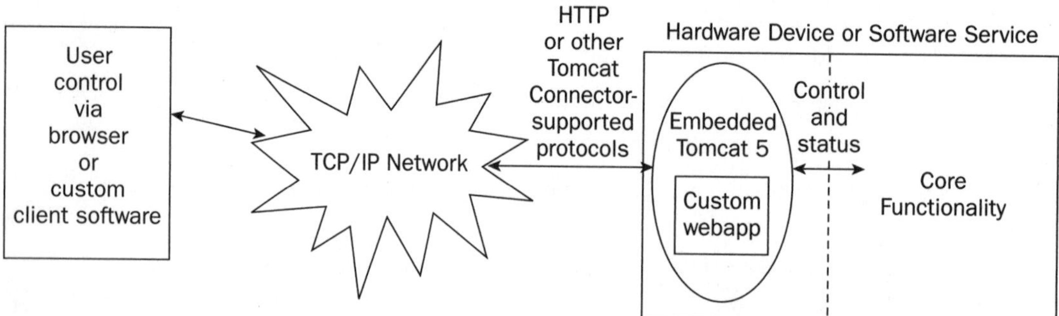

Figure 20-1: Embedded Tomcat 5 providing custom network facade for device/service.

In Figure 20-1, notice that a componentized Web application actually resides within the Tomcat container. This Web application provides the user with control over the device/service, as well as live status information. The Servlets and JSPs communicate directly with the internal logic. The Tomcat container, in turn, is embedded as part of the device or service.

Typical Embedded Application Scenarios

Traditionally, most embedded applications are created from scratch as a monolithic code module, potentially utilizing some proprietary or third-party software libraries. Applications that require Web-based networking are especially difficult to create because of the complexity of HTTP protocol handling and HTML generation. By embedding the Tomcat server, application creation is simplified, as all of this complexity is handled by Tomcat.

To device/service designers and developers, the appealing benefits of embedding a Tomcat server within an application include the following:

- Rapid development time and a shorter project cycle
- Large developer pool with training on Java, Servlets, and JSP
- Wide availability of supporting tools for Servlet and JSP coding and testing
- Ease of coding, testing, and maintaining application logic
- Getting an HTTP server and Web interface for "free"

Some typical scenarios in which embedding Tomcat in an application may make sense include the following:

- Providing a Web interface front end for a complex hardware and/or software system
- Creating a standalone "turnkey network appliance" box that hosts a Web-based application (sometimes called **network black-boxes** or **network appliances**)
- Creating a complex customized server in which serving HTML pages and/or Servlets and/or JSP is a part of the required application logic
- Creating a standalone, fat-client version of an existing Web application, whereby the application code is already available and tested
- Providing common operation/management code that can be scripted across multiple operating systems and hardware platforms

Note that you must abide by the Apache Software License (see the **`LICENSE`** *file in the top-level directory of the Tomcat Embedded Distribution) if your software product is being delivered with Tomcat 5 inside. This license is quite liberal, but must be followed carefully. In a production or vendor shop, this will typically be the responsibility of the marketing, productization, and legal staff.*

The Role of the Administrator with Embedded Tomcat

Most embedded Tomcat applications originally start life as standalone Web applications. In fact, applications that are ultimately targeted for embedded operations may be initially developed, tested, and tuned in a standalone Tomcat server. Because of this, the service of a competent Tomcat server administrator is indispensable during this prototyping stage.

With the ultimate goal of embedding the server, a Tomcat administrator can experiment with server loading and application tuning to determine the best configuration for the server and application. The role of the administrator may be to recommend a configuration that optimizes the use of resources in the final delivery system. The configuration details from this exercise can then be used by the developers to operate the embedded server. Figure 20-2 illustrates this workflow.

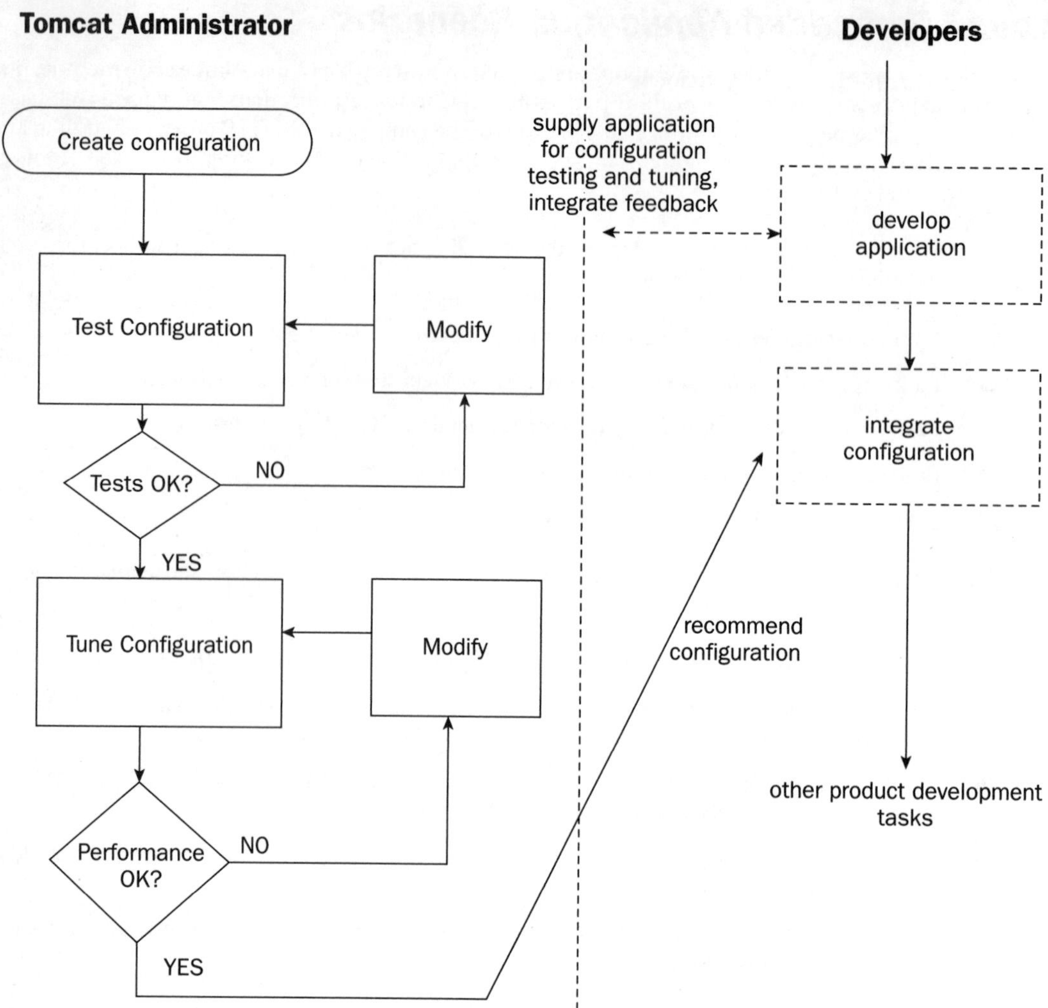

Figure 20-2: Possible role of Tomcat administrator in embedded development.

Note that it is possible to deploy administrative Tomcat applications such as the `manager` application (see Chapter 7) within an embedded server instance. By configuring the `manager` application with embedded Tomcat, administrators may use the familiar tool for the operation, troubleshooting, and maintenance of the embedded application/system. It may be necessary to create multiple configuration profiles, for instance one for normal operation that is optimized for resource utilization, another one for troubleshooting, and yet another one for JMX support, and so on. The troubleshooting instance would be the one that would start the `manager` application. A hands-on section later in this chapter will reveal how to provide multiple configuration profiles for embedded Tomcat systems.

Overview of Embedded Mode in Tomcat

Following are the two most common ways to work with embedded Tomcat:

1. Using explicit Java coding to call the helper methods of the `org.apache.catalina.startup.Embedded` class to configure and start the server
2. Using Ant scripts to start up and configure the server via JMX

The focus in this chapter is on the second method of working with embedded Tomcat. This scripting method is more relevant to Tomcat administrators because it involves only the creation of script files, and does not require custom coding in Java. The main enabler for this method is JMX. Tomcat 5's integrated JMX support provides a way for external scripts and applications to access the internals of Tomcat. This access includes the capability to configure, start, and stop internal Tomcat components.

Chapter 18 revealed that all configurable Tomcat architectural components have associated MBeans. The MBeans expose attributes that can be read and/or modified. They also expose operations that can be invoked. This corresponds to the instrumentation level in the JMX architecture. Putting it another way, Tomcat 5 is fully JMX-enabled for remote control.

According to the JMX specification, management applications do not communicate directly with MBeans. Instead, communications are facilitated through the agent layer in JMX. The most notable component in the agent layer is the component that loads and starts MBeans. This component is called the **MBean Server.**

The MBean Server and Object Bus

The main function of the MBean Server is to load and start MBeans. The loading of MBeans is not restricted to the local file system, but generalized to an arbitrary URL. This enables the possibility for remotely loading MBeans.

The way that the individual MBeans (software components) plug into the MBean server is similar to the way that hardware cards plug into the hardware bus of a PC machine. Often, a software module of this nature is called an **object bus.**

The specification for MBean Server functionality is rather generic, and not restricted only to beans that represent JMX instrumentation. Because of this, the MBean Server is often used as a flexible object bus for loading agent-layer logic. In fact, the reference JMX implementation uses the MBean Server to load several agent services. By coding agent-layer logic (such as agent services) in the form of MBeans, it is possible to use the MBean Server to manage the life cycle and operation of the individual agent services. This technique is not restricted to agent-layer services only; custom embedded application logic can also benefit from being loaded by the MBean Server. Figure 20-3 illustrates the use of the MBean Server to load custom application logic.

The dotted-line modules in Figure 20-3 are modular custom application logic (or services) that are coded to the MBean standard and can be loaded and controlled via the standard JMX MBean management protocol.

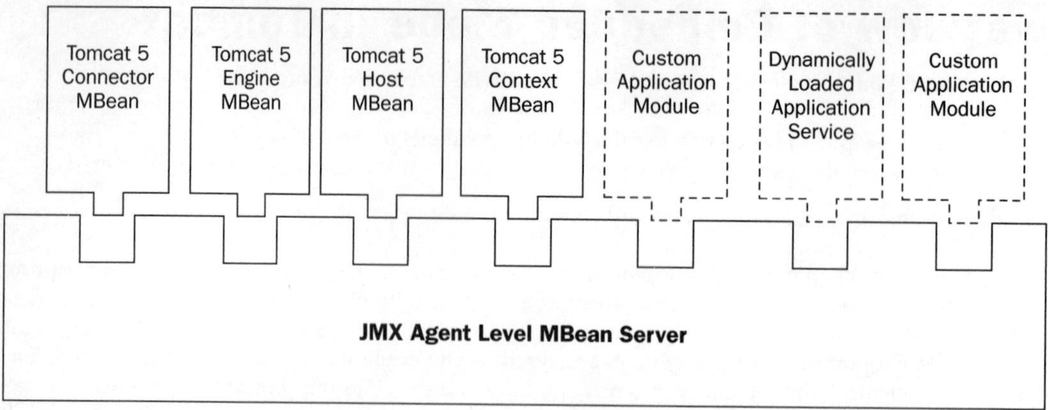

Figure 20-3: JMX agent-level MBean Server as a generic minimal object bus.

The JMX 1.2 specification explicitly states that the MBean Server is not designed to be a general-purpose object bus. This is largely because certain standard services (such as naming and directory services) must exist for a generalized object bus implementation. However, the basic features that an MBean Server provides are adequate to implement a minimal object bus for many application scenarios.

Internal Versus External Control

When the Tomcat 5 server is launched (either by the launcher application or the startup batch file), the following happens internally:

1. Catalina startup code reads the `server.xml` file using an XML parser.
2. The nested nature of Tomcat configuration syntax causes the XML parser to process the subelements most deeply nested before those in the outer nesting levels (inside-out parsing).
3. A Tomcat 5 internal component is created for every component encountered in the XML configuration file during the inside-out parsing. Configuration is also performed on the component by setting its attributes (for example, setting a port number attribute for a service component).
4. A container component is started after all of its nested elements are created and configured.

All of the preceding steps are preformed by Java code internal to Tomcat. However, it is entirely possible to use either a customized Java application or a Java-based scripting engine to perform the exact same sequence of operations.

Apache Ant as a Scripting Engine

Apache Ant (see Appendix C) is a tool that can be used as a scripting engine. In this case, an Ant build file can be created to customize the instance(s) of Tomcat being started.

As a scripting engine, the following features of Ant are utilized:

- Dependency checking
- Custom task definitions

Other features of Ant (such as built-in tasks to compile and process Java programs) are less important here.

Tomcat 5's integral JMX support enables the external script-driven configuration and operation of internal components. Earlier versions of Tomcat cannot support such scripting access because of the lack of JMX support, as well as the lack of internal componentization. Tomcat 5 eases both of these limitations, and future releases will further improve on such support.

Even though it is possible to use Ant as the scripting engine, Ant knows nothing about Tomcat. There still must be some "glue" code that can plug into Ant and work with the JMX elements in Tomcat 5. Thankfully, another Jakarta project called **Jakarta Commons** provides just such a solution.

> *In Chapter 7, Ant scripts are used to access the* **`manager`** *application functionality, including querying and setting JMX attributes via the* **`jmxproxy`**. *However, these Ant tasks require an already running Tomcat 5 instance, and cannot be used for configuring and starting embedded Tomcat.*

The Apache Jakarta Commons Modeler

In the interest of code reuse, the bulk of the repetitious code that is used in Tomcat 5 to support JMX is packaged as an external library. In fact, this library is kept separate from the main Tomcat development project. It is part of the Apache Jakarta Commons Open Source project tree. Specifically, this reusable portion of code is called the **Jakarta Commons Modeler,** or **Modeler** for short. The Jakarta Commons Modeler provides Tomcat 5, or any other Java application, with model MBean JMX support. This model MBean support substantially simplifies the coding of MBeans by eliminating the need for often tedious coding (see Chapter 18). The Modeler project and associated information can be located at the following URL:

```
http://jakarta.apache.org/commons/modeler.html
```

There is no need to download any Modeler binaries, as Tomcat 5 already includes them.

The Modeler makes the coding of MBeans simple because it can access metadata describing the MBeans and then assist in generating code that handles the attributes and operations of the MBeans. All of this can happen during run-time, without requiring the generation and compilation of static code. This certainly is a capability that can benefit many other applications that need to support JMX, and it is the core reason why the Modeler is stored as a separate reusable library.

The metadata describing an MBean is called an MBean descriptor. This is basically an XML file that describes the attributes and operations available for an MBean. These MBean descriptors must be registered with the Modeler's registry before the MBean's information can be accessed programmatically. Another very important component of the Modeler is a set of custom JMX Ant tasks. These custom tasks enable an Ant script to gain control of a Tomcat 5 component through the JMX agent.

Custom JMX Ant Tasks in the Commons Modeler

The set of custom Ant tasks in the Modeler can be used to load MBean descriptors into the Modeler's registry, to load MBeans into Tomcat's MBean Server, to set the attributes of an MBean, and to invoke an operation of an MBean.

The code for these custom Ant tasks are located in the `org.apache.commons.modeler.ant` package. The following table provides a description of the custom tasks relevant to Tomcat 5 embedded operations. Many of these tasks have aliased (multiple) names. The preferred name is shown in italics in this case.

Task Alias(es)	Task Class	Description
MLET mbean	MLETTask	Loads a specified MBean into the MBean Server. It can also be used to load a specified MLET, a piece of logic or service inside a loadable MBean.
jmx-attribute attribute	JmxSet	Sets an MBean attribute value
Jmx-operation	JmxInvoke	Invokes an MBean operation
mbeans-descriptors	RegistryTask	Loads an MBean descriptor into the registry of the MBean Server
jmx-service service	ServiceTask	Runs a service consisting of MBeans

The definitions of these tasks are kept in a properties file. This file is located at `org/apache/commons/modeler/ant/ant.properties` if you examine the Modeler's source code. The properties file for Modeler version 1.1, the latest available as of this writing, is reproduced here:

```
modeler=org.apache.commons.modeler.ant.ModelerTask
MLET=org.apache.commons.modeler.ant.MLETTask
mbean=org.apache.commons.modeler.ant.MLETTask
jmx-attribute=org.apache.commons.modeler.ant.JmxSet
jmx-operation=org.apache.commons.modeler.ant.JmxInvoke
mbeans-descriptors=org.apache.commons.modeler.ant.RegistryTask

jmx-service=org.apache.commons.modeler.ant.ServiceTask
service=org.apache.commons.modeler.ant.ServiceTask

# old names, to be removed
jmxSet=org.apache.commons.modeler.ant.JmxSet
jmx=org.apache.commons.modeler.ant.JmxInvoke
modelerRegistry=org.apache.commons.modeler.ant.RegistryTask
```

The next section examines each of the frequently used Ant tasks and the subelements that they can contain.

<jmx-service> Task

This custom Ant task processes its body elements to create a service. Typically, the body consists of a set of code modules that are loaded as MBeans. The `init` and `start` operations of the body elements are invoked to start the service. This element has a single attribute (shown in the following table) that is sometimes necessary to set.

Attribute Name	Description
`action`	If the name of the operation to start the body elements running is not `init` followed by `start`, then specify the operation name here.

A `<jmx-service>` task can contain any number of `<mbean>` subelements. Each `<mbean>` element specifies an MBean (code module) that must be loaded to create the service.

<mbean> Subelement

This subelement loads an MBean, or custom code module, into the MBean Server. The following table shows the available attributes.

Attribute Name	Description
`name`	Run-time name given to the MBean. It may be used to locate the MBean via the MBean Server.
`code`	Java code binary class of the MBean
`codebase`	Specifies a URL to load the MBean and/or support libraries
`modeler`	A Boolean value indicating whether this is a model bean.

An `<mbean>` element can have any number of `<attribute>` subelements. These subelements are used to set the values of attributes for the MBean during run-time.

<attribute> Subelement

The `<attribute>` subelement is used to set the value of an MBean attribute. The MBean whose attribute is being set must be previously loaded into the MBean Server via the `<mbean>` task. Currently, only MBean attribute values of string data type can be set via this element. The following table shows the attributes of this subelement.

Attribute Name	Description
`name`	Name of the MBean attribute to set
`value`	The string value to set

<modelerRegistry> or <mbean-descriptor> Task

This custom Ant task loads the metadata describing an MBean into the Modeler's registry. This is an internal function of Tomcat utilizing the Jakarta Commons Modeler. Using this metadata information, the Modeler is capable of creating model MBeans at run-time to support JMX operations for Tomcat's internal components. The following table shows the attribute for these tasks.

Attribute Name	Description
resource	Specifies an XML in the current classpath that contains MBean descriptor information to load into the Modeler's registry

<jmx-operation> Task

This custom Ant task is used when invoking an operation on an MBean. The following table shows the attributes for this task.

Attribute Name	Description
objectName	The name of the MBean instance to perform the operation
operation	The operation to execute

Ant Script Operational Flow

Ant scripts for an embedded Tomcat server typically contain Ant targets that are `<jmx-service>` task(s). Each `<jmx-service>` element will have one or more `<mbean>` elements within it. Each `<mbean>` element may in turn have zero or more `<attribute>` elements.

What actually happens when an Ant script is executed is governed by two external factors:

- The way that Ant works with nested XML elements and custom tasks
- The logic inside the Ant custom tasks provided by the Jakarta Commons Modeler

The details of these factors are outside the scope of this chapter. However, the combined result can be readily comprehended. The following procedure describes the JMX objects that are created and manipulated when the script is executed.

First, the script cycles through each `<mbean>` element within the `<jmx-service>` element in order, and performs the following actions:

1. Locates the MBean server
2. Creates the MBean and registers it with the MBean Server, using the attributes of the `<mbean>` XML element
3. Sets each of the MBean's attributes (nested `<attribute>` XML elements) in the order specified

Second, the script goes through the entire list of recently created MBeans again, but this time it performs the following single action:

- Invokes the MBean's `init` and `start` operations (unless the `action` attribute is specified in the `<jmx-service>` XML element, in which case the operation corresponding to the action is executed)

Embedded Tomcat 5 is designed to be started from JMX when this sequence event is executed. Note the following two important aspects about the aforementioned two-pass flow:

- The first pass instantiates the MBean (and associated Tomcat 5 component), and then sets the attributes.
- The second pass starts up the hierarchy of Tomcat 5 components.

This procedure is essentially what happens when Tomcat bootstrap code processes the `server.xml` configuration file. From a conceptual perspective, Figure 20-4 reveals that the Ant script essentially represents a flexible replacement for Tomcat 5 startup code.

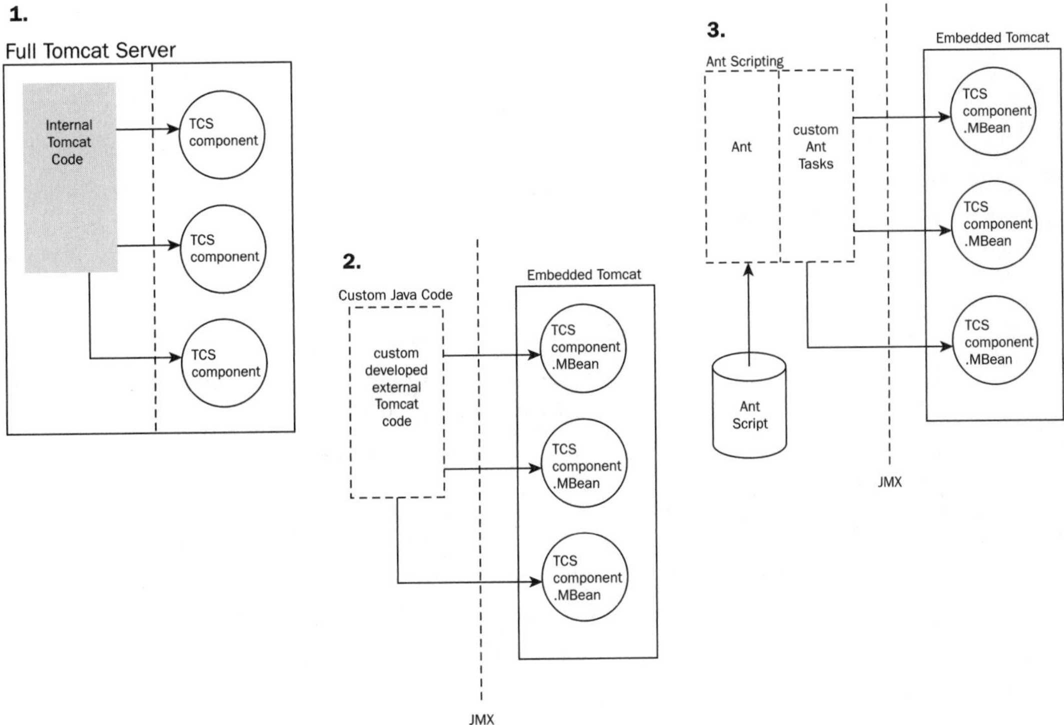

Figure 20-4: Replacing Tomcat control logic with custom code or Ant scripts.

In Figure 20-4, Scenario 1 depicts the normal start-up sequence of the non-embedded version of Tomcat. In this case, internal bootstrap Tomcat code reads the `server.xml` file, creates the configured Tomcat components, and starts up the server. In Scenario 2, custom Java code created by embedded developers replaces the internal Tomcat control code, and uses the `org.apache.catalina.startup.Embedded` helper class to access the embedded Tomcat server. In Scenario 3, instead of writing custom Java code, Ant is used to process a script that can replace the custom code to start up and control the embedded Tomcat server through JMX. Administrators will most likely deal with Scenario 3, and may be called upon to create these Ant scripts. The next section examines such an Ant script.

Using an Ant Script to Start Up a Minimal Embedded Server

It's now time to reveal how to create Ant scripts that can be used to start up embedded Tomcat. `min.xml` is a script that will start up a single Engine with a single Connector and Host.

Downloading and Installing Embedded Tomcat

To try out any of the following scripts, you must download the embedded distribution of Tomcat 5. Do not use the regular Tomcat 5 distribution. The embedded Tomcat 5 distribution can be downloaded from the following URL:

```
http://jakarta.apache.org/site/binindex.cgi
```

Select the `5.x.x_Embed.zip` download. To install, unzip this archive into your installation directory. You should see the familiar Tomcat directory hierarchy.

Figure 20-5 illustrates the default directory hierarchy of the embedded Tomcat 5 distribution, which is quite similar to that of the non-embedded version of Tomcat 5.

Note the following differences in this hierarchy:

- Under the `conf` directory, there is no `server.xml` file.
- A single `lib` directory holds all JAR libraries. Library code used in an embedded environment typically does not change within the lifetime of the product.
- The Ant script file to start the server is in the top-level directory, not in a `bin` subdirectory.

In fact, many of the directories used by the Tomcat 5 components are configurable via the component's attributes (see Chapter 8 for configuration details). The location of these directories can be further customized by developers creating their own embedded Tomcat applications.

If you look into the `webapps` subdirectory, you will see that only the `manager` application is included with this distribution. You can start up the embedded Tomcat instance with only `manager` running, and then use it to deploy any new application. If you need any other application (for example, the `admin` utility or the `servlet-examples` Web application) running at startup, you will need to copy them into the `webapps` directory from a regular non-embedded Tomcat 5 distribution.

For this example, the `servlets-examples` Web application will be started by the Ant script. This means that the application must be pre-installed. You need to copy the `servlet-examples` subdirectory from a regular installation of Tomcat 5 to the `webapps\servlet-examples` subdirectory of the embedded Tomcat installation.

The min.xml Minimal Embedded Startup Script

You can find the following `min.xml` script (an Ant project build file) in the book's code distribution under the `ch20/code` subdirectory (download the code samples for this book from `www.wrox.com`). Note its similarity to a `server.xml` file. Important sections in the script have been annotated with boldface numbers so that they can be referred to later.

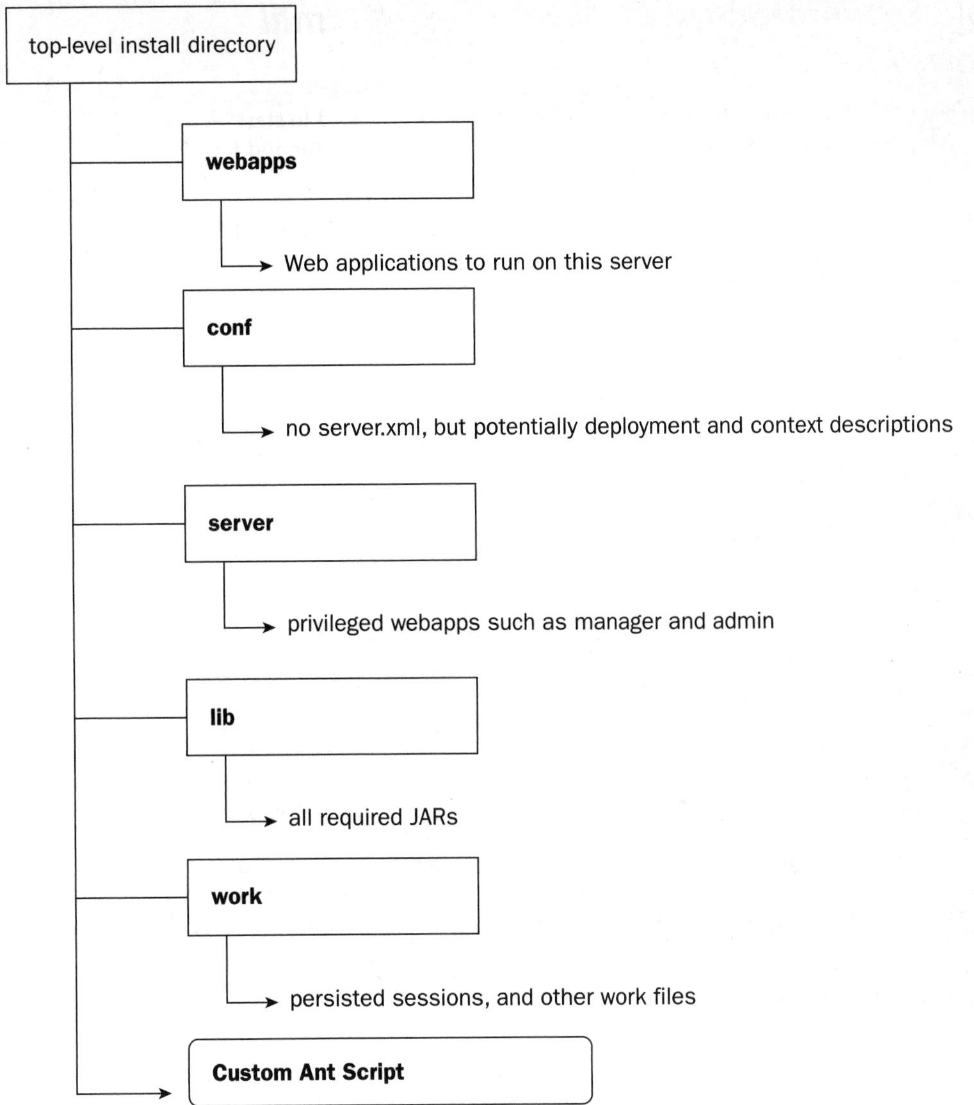

Figure 20-5: Default Directory Hierarchy of Embedded Tomcat 5 Distribution.

```
<project name="min-tc5" default="start" basedir=".">
  <property file="${user.home}/build.properties"/>
  <property file="build.properties"/>
     <property name="tomcat.home" location="." />
    <property name="tomcat.webapps" location="${tomcat.home}/webapps" />

  <path id="tomcatCP-extra" />

  <target name="init" unless="init.done">
    <path id="tomcatCP" >
      <path refid="tomcatCP-extra"/>
```

```
        <fileset dir="${tomcat.home}/lib" includes="*.jar"/>
        <pathelement  path="${tomcat.home}/conf"/>
      </path>
      <taskdef resource="org/apache/commons/modeler/ant/ant.properties"
               classpathref="tomcatCP" />
      <property name="init.done" value="true"/>
     </target>
   <property name="domain" value="Tomcat-Min-Standalone" />
   <property name="jsr77Domain" value=" Tomcat-Min-Standalone" />

     <target name="run" depends="init">
      <modelerRegistry resource="org/apache/catalina/mbeans/mbeans-descriptors.xml"
/>
      <modelerRegistry resource="org/apache/catalina/loader/mbeans-descriptors.xml"
/>
      <mkdir dir="${tomcat.home}/work/${domain}/" />

      <jmx-service>
      (1) <mbean name="${domain}:type=Server"
            code="org.apache.catalina.core.StandardServer"
               modeler="true">
          <attribute name="port" value="9005"/>
         </mbean>

       (2) <mbean name="${domain}:type=Service"
           code="org.apache.catalina.core.StandardService"
                modeler="true">
           <attribute name="name" value="Tomcat-Min-Standalone"/>
         </mbean>
       (3),(4) <mbean name="${domain}:type=Engine"
                code="org.apache.catalina.core.StandardEngine"
                modeler="true">
           <attribute name="name" value="Tomcat-Min-Standalone"/>
           <attribute name="defaultHost" value="localhost"/>
           <attribute name="baseDir" value="${tomcat.home}"/>
         </mbean>

       (5) <mbean name="${domain}:type=Realm"
                code="org.apache.catalina.realm.MemoryRealm" modeler="true">
           <attribute name="pathname"
                      value="${tomcat.home}/conf/tomcat-users.xml" />
         </mbean>

        (6) <mbean name="${domain}:type=Connector,port=9080"
                code="org.apache.coyote.tomcat5.CoyoteConnector"
                modeler="true">
                <attribute name="port" value="9080" />
          </mbean>
  (7)    <mbean
name="${jsr77Domain}:j2eeType=WebModule,name=//localhost/,J2EEApplication=none,J2EE
Server=none"
                code="org.apache.catalina.core.StandardContext"  modeler="true">
             <attribute name="docBase" value="${tomcat.webapps}/ROOT" />
             <attribute name="privileged" value="true" />
             <attribute name="engineName" value="${domain}" />
```

```
        </mbean>
    (7)  <mbean name="${jsr77Domain}:j2eeType=WebModule,name=//localhost/servlets-
examples,J2EEApplication=none,J2EEServer=none"
              code="org.apache.catalina.core.StandardContext"  modeler="true">
         <attribute name="docBase" value="${tomcat.webapps}/servlets-examples" />
         <attribute name="privileged" value="true" />
         <attribute name="engineName" value="${domain}" />
        </mbean>
      </jmx-service>
      <echo message="Tomcat5 running"/>
    </target>

    <target name="await" depends="init"
          description="Wait for tomcat stop. Call this target after run">
       <jmx objectName="${domain}:type=Server"
          operation="await" />
      <sleep hours="1"/>
    </target>

    <target name="start"
         depends="init,run,await"
         description="Start tomcat, wait for stop message"/>
</project>
```

To better understand how the script works, compare it against an equivalent `server.xml` file. You can find the source to such a `server.xml` file in the code distribution, also under the `ch20/code` subdirectory. The file is listed here. For ease of comparison, the equivalent sections that are compared are clearly numbered within the two listings.

```
(1) <Server port="9005">

(2)  <Service name="Tomcat-Min-Standalone">
(6)      <Connector port="9080"/>

(3)  <Engine name="Tomcat-Min-Standalone" defaultHost="localhost" debug="0">
(4)   <Host name="localhost" appBase="webapps"
       unpackWARs="true" autoDeploy="true">

(5)       <Realm className="org.apache.catalina.realm.MemoryRealm" />

(7)          <Context path="" docBase="ROOT" debug="0"/>
      </Host>

    </Engine>

  </Service>

</Server>
```

The following table provides a section-by-section comparison of the `min.xml` Ant script and the equivalent `server.xml` file.

Section	Description
1	A service component is created here. The only attribute specified for this component is a port number. Note that in the JMX script, we set the attribute of the component using an `<attribute>` nested element. The attributes of the `<mbean>` XML element (such as `code` and `modeler`) are used to create the MBean that represents the underlying component.
2	A server component is created with the name "Tomcat-Min-Standalone."
3, 4	An Engine component is created here. Note that when using JMX, it is necessary to create the Engine before any Connector. In the `server.xml` case, the Connector can be created before the Engine. In addition, in JMX, a Host is automatically created by default. The JMX attributes `defaultHost` and `baseDir` are used to specify the name of the Host created and to set its base directory. In `server.xml`, the Host and its attributes are specified explicitly.
5	A Realm nested component is created here. There is no difference between the JMX version and the `server.xml` version.
6	An HTTP Connector at port 9080 is created here. In the JMX case, it is necessary to create the Engine instance before the Connector instance.
7	The root context is created here. Note that in the JMX case, every application context must be created explicitly and manually. This provides finer-grained control over what needs to be started in the embedded application. If Tomcat had been started using the `server.xml` file, the creation of context descriptors and deployment of web applications in the `webapps` directory would have happened automatically.

It is worthwhile to review the main differences between the standard Tomcat 5 `server.xml` file and the Ant script using embedded Tomcat 5:

- The Connector is created after the Engine in the script.
- With the script, there is no need to create the default Host because it is created by the Engine by default.
- Each application context must be created explicitly in the script.
- With the script, an `await` target is used to ensure that the Ant script thread does not terminate upon completion (otherwise, it will also take down the Tomcat server).

It is evident from this comparison that any tested `server.xml` configuration may be translated to a corresponding Ant script. This provides a way to test embedded Tomcat 5 configurations first on the non-embedded server, and then migrate them to the embedded one.

Some embedded applications may only need to start up the Tomcat 5 server and a single Web application. Others may use the extended capabilities of Ant to start up other custom code modules. It is also possible for software developers to write their own application logic as MBeans and use the JMX capabilities to load these modules into the MBean Server. Finally, some applications may bypass Ant altogether and directly control the server (via either JMX or the **`org.apache.catalina.startup.Embedded`** *class, as mentioned previously). In all these cases, Ant-based scripting can still be used to test and experiment with configuration alternatives. Therefore, a basic understanding of its operation is vital to any Tomcat 5 administrator or developer.*

Now that you have some familiarity with the Ant script, it is an opportune time to test the embedded Tomcat 5 server.

Testing the Embedded Tomcat Server

The following section's hands-on experimentation will start up a minimal embedded server using JMX through an Ant script.

Starting Up a Minimal Server

Copy the `min.xml` file from the code distribution to the top-level directory of the embedded server installation. You can find this file under the `ch20/code` directory of the distribution. This file will be used in place of the default `build.xml` file that is supplied with the Tomcat 5 embedded distribution.

To start up the minimal server, issue the following command:

```
ant -f min.xml
```

It is assumed, of course, that you have Ant 1.5.2 or later installed and working.

At this point, Ant uses the Jakarta Commons Modeler's JMX Ant tasks to access the JMX support of Tomcat 5 and start up the server. The output on your console should be similar to what is shown in Figure 20-6.

Accessing Embedded Tomcat 5

You can now try the embedded server by starting a browser and pointing it to the following URL:

```
http://localhost:9080/
```

The browser should display the Tomcat introduction (static HTML) page at the root context (shown in Figure 20-7), just as a non-embedded server would.

Figure 20-6: Starting a minimal embedded Tomcat 5 distribution with an Ant JMX script.

To access the other Web application that has been started via JMX, connect to the following URL:

```
http://localhost:9080/servlets-examples/
```

The browser should display the `servlets-examples` main page, as shown in Figure 20-8.

Verify that this embedded server instance is indeed full-featured by trying some of the Servlet examples. In general, you will find that the embedded server instance performs identically to the non-embedded version. In fact, the exact same Tomcat 5 code is executing.

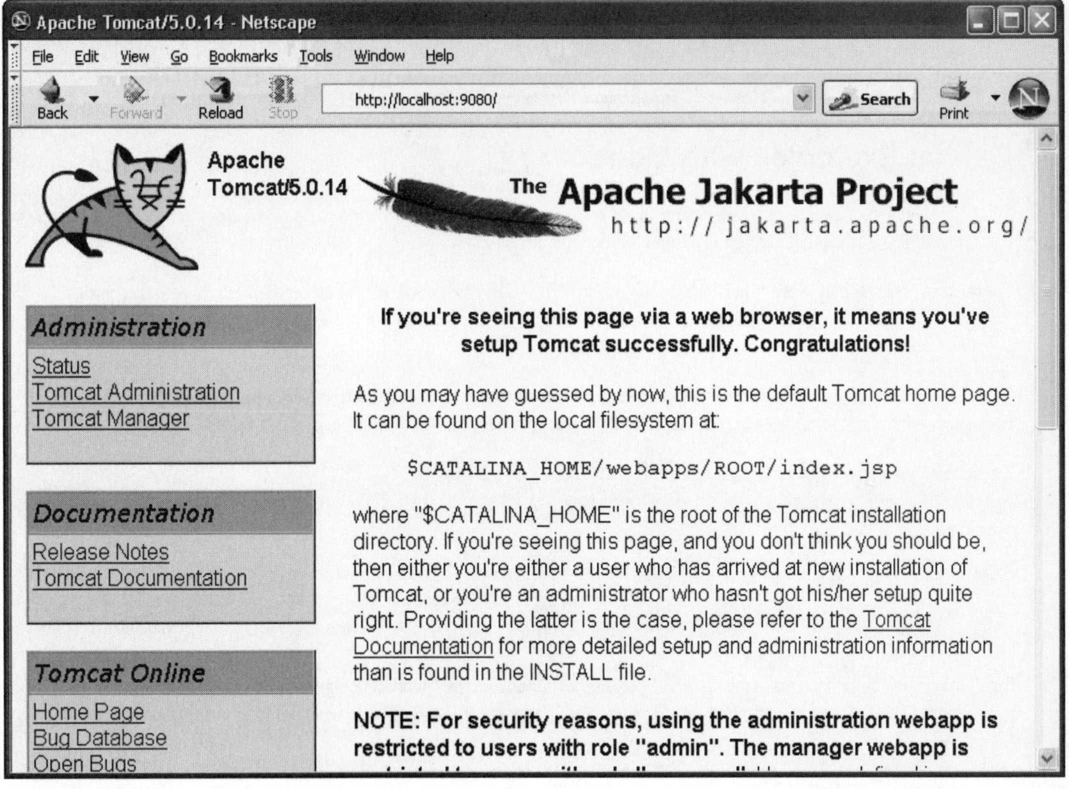

Figure 20-7: Tomcat 5's home page, displayed at the root context and loaded via the Ant script.

Shutting Down the Embedded Server

No readily available custom Ant task can be used to shut down the embedded server instance. In production-embedded scenarios, shutdown can be custom programmed.

It is possible, in this case, to do it manually. Press Ctrl+C in the command console where the Ant script is running. This will terminate the thread running the Ant `await` target, resulting in the shutdown of the server.

Adding the manager Web Application

To facilitate testing, deployment, and/or management, you may consider enabling the `manager` Web application for the embedded server. This section shows you how this can be done quite simply, building on the Ant scripting technique (and the `min.xml` file) demonstrated thus far.

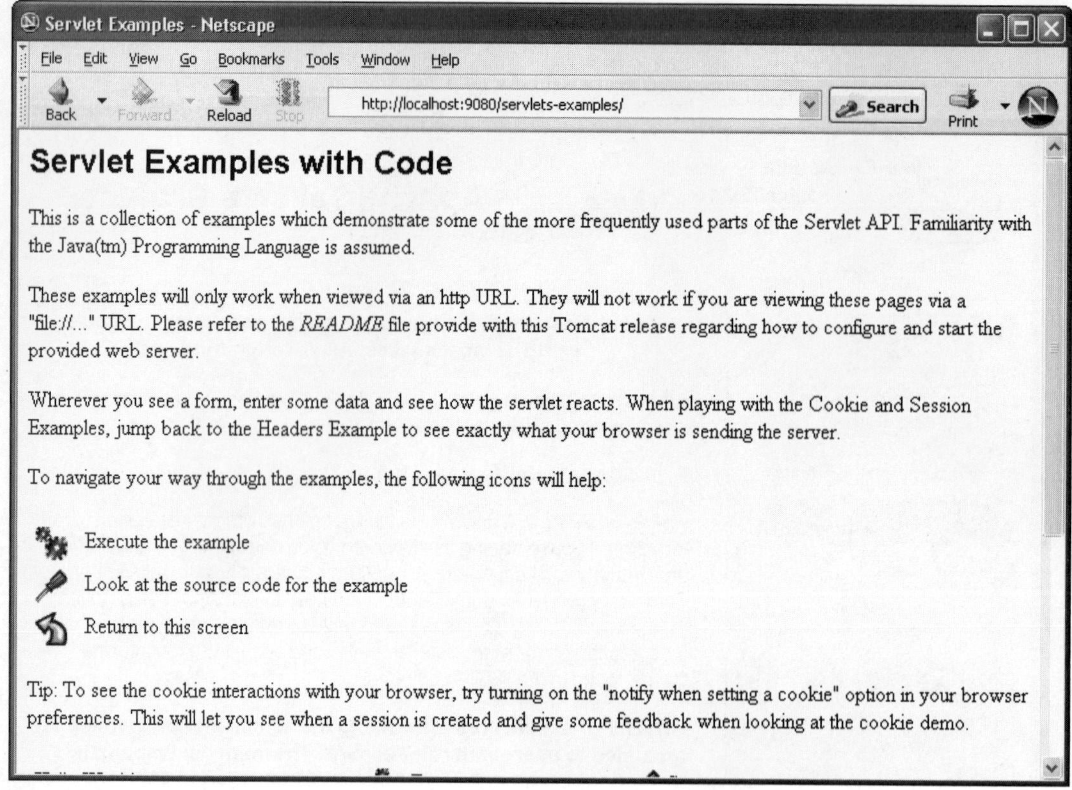

Figure 20-8: The servlets-examples Web application loaded via a JMX context MBean.

The necessary steps are as follows:

1. Modify the `tomcat-users.xml` file to enable the manager role for authentication.
2. Add the `<mbean>` element to create a context for the `manager` application.

The following sections describe both of these steps.

Adding the Manager Role for Authentication

In the `conf` directory of the embedded server, modify the `tomcat-users.xml` file as shown in the following code. This will add the manager role to the `tomcat` user, with the password `tomcat`. In production, you may want to use another user and password.

```
<tomcat-users>
<user name="tomcat" password="tomcat" roles="manager,tomcat" />
...
</tomcat-users>
```

Adding an <mbean> Element to the manager Context

To modify the minimal server startup Ant script to also start the `manager` application, the following highlighted modification must be made to the `min.xml` file:

```
<jmx-service>
...
       <mbean name="${jsr77Domain}:j2eeType=WebModule,name=//localhost/servlets-
examples,J2EEApplication=none,J2EEServer=none"
              code="org.apache.catalina.core.StandardContext"  modeler="true">
         <attribute name="docBase" value="${tomcat.webapps}/servlets-examples" />
         <attribute name="privileged" value="true" />
         <attribute name="engineName" value="${domain}" />
       </mbean>

  <mbean name="${jsr77Domain}:j2eeType=WebModule,name=//localhost/
manager,J2EEApplication=none,J2EEServer=none"
        code="org.apache.catalina.core.StandardContext"  modeler="true">
         <attribute name="docBase"
value="${tomcat.webapps}/../server/webapps/manager" />
         <attribute name="engineName" value="${domain}" />
         <attribute name="privileged" value="true" />
       </mbean>
  </jmx-service>
```

A modified Ant script called `minmgr.xml`. is included in the source distribution, under the `ch20/code` directory Copy this to your top-level directory of the embedded Tomcat server.

Using the manager Application on the Embedded Server

Now you can start the embedded server again, with the following command line:

```
ant -f minmgr.xml
```

Start a browser and point it to the following URL:

```
http://localhost:9080/manager/html
```

After authentication (use user `tomcat` and password `tomcat`), this will show the HTML interface of the `manager` application, as shown in Figure 20-9. You can now use the `manager` application to manage and monitor the server, deploy new Web applications, and so on.

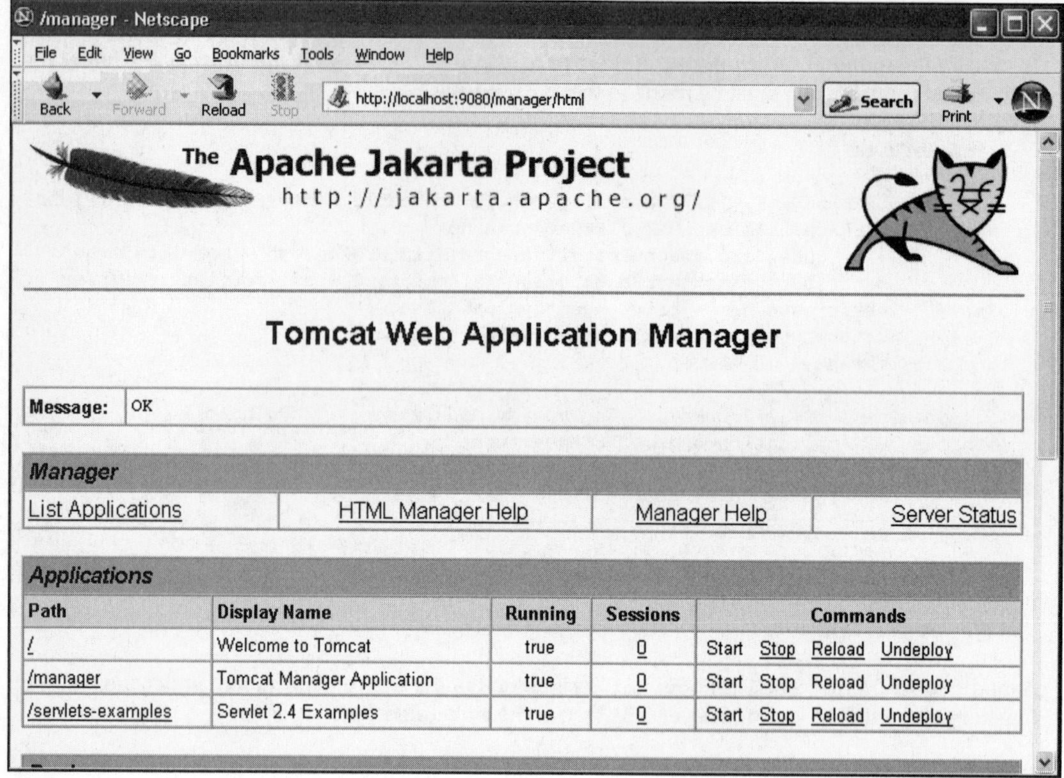

Figure 20-9: Tomcat's `manager` application, operating on the embedded server.

Summary

This chapter on embedded Tomcat included the following key points:

- Tomcat 5 formally supports embedded mode of operation. Using Tomcat in embedded mode, application developers can embed the functionality of a simple Web server, a Servlet, and a JSP container within their own applications or products. Servlet and JSP support provides developers with a modular and reusable way of constructing their application logic. Tomcat 5's inherent support for the HTTP protocol also makes it an attractive candidate for any application that requires a Web-based user interface.

- Tomcat 5's componentization and support for JMX are to enable the use of embedded mode operation. The coding of Tomcat 5 takes advantage of the Jakarta Commons Modeler library. This library contains a set of custom Ant tasks that can be used by Ant to access JMX elements. By scripting these custom Ant tasks, it is possible to gain control over Tomcat 5's internal components.

- During embedded mode operations, Tomcat 5 is not started up by internal coding that parses a `server.xml` configuration file. Instead, customized code can access Tomcat 5 to configure components and start the server. One way to do this easily is to use Ant scripts that start Tomcat via JMX.
- The examples in this chapter illustrate how to create Ant scripts to start and operate Tomcat 5. A section-by-section comparison associated `server.xml` configuration elements to Ant elements that do the same thing. This provides a straightforward way to translate any `server.xml` file into its equivalent Tomcat startup Ant script.
- Using a minimal Ant script, a minimal Tomcat 5 instance was started up to serve the `servlets-examples` application. Testing revealed that full functionality of the server was indeed available. The script was then modified to also start up the `manager` Web application. Enabling this application provided a familiar means to monitor and manage the embedded server instance.

The capability to embed Tomcat in a custom application opens up a whole new world of possibilities for networked solutions developers, and brand-new opportunities for seasoned Tomcat administrators.

Log4J

It is common to track data changes at various stages during the software development life cycle of an application. In a large application, it is sometimes difficult for developers and administrators to detect where a problem has occurred. Developers often get this information by adding statements using `System.out.println()` inside application code. This way, they can analyze the data and trace the root of the problem. This mechanism of outputting data values at run-time is called **logging**.

In addition to the data values, also needed is information about application state changes, and an execution context. Hard-coding trace messages using `System.out.println()` in the application code is not a good practice because it affects application performance and code readability.

Adding log statements is the only viable option for analyzing the execution of a long-running Web application. This approach, however, often affects efficiency, flexibility, and performance overhead. **Log4J** is a powerful logging API that addresses all these issues. It enables the logging of information in a more efficient and elegant way, and in a variety of formats.

This appendix discusses Log4J and its functionality. It also explains how to use Log4J effectively in your applications. Following are the main topics covered:

- Introduction to Log4J
- Components of Log4J
- Setting up and working with Log4J
- Logging in various formats

Introduction to Log4J

Log4J is an open-source Java framework for logging that you can download from the following URL:

```
http://logging.apache.org/log4j
```

This framework (developed by Ceki Gulcu, N. Asokan, and Michael Steiner) is currently a part of the logging services project of the Apache Software Foundation (ASF).

Log4J is designed as a pluggable component that can be used inside applications. It can be configured easily to log messages at run-time without greatly affecting the performance of the application. It also provides control over the kind of information that is to be logged, without changing the application code. It makes use of a simple configuration file. Changing this file controls the logging behavior of Log4J.

Java ships with its own Logging API since JDK 1.4. HoweverLog4J is a more mature and proven logging mechanism, and the more widely used one. More information on the Java Logging API can be found at ***http://java.sun.com/j2se/1.4.2/docs/guide/util/logging/index.html.***

Components of Log4J

Log4J uses a modular design that enables you to change the behavior of the application by modifying the Log4J configuration file. It contains the following components, which are used to log information about application state:

- Loggers
- Appenders
- Levels
- Layouts

The following sections briefly describe each of these components.

Loggers

Loggers are the main component of Log4J, and they control the scope of logging. Log4J components can be configured to log one or more messages associated with an application, as well as log messages for a specific scope (for example, the package or class).

An **Appender** must be assigned to a Logger (Appenders are discussed in the next section). The Appender controls the defined logging target (for example, a log file). Different kinds of Appenders can be assigned to the same Logger or to different Loggers. This means that different parts of an application can have different log destinations.

The following example shows what a Logger entry looks like in the Log4j configuration file:

```
# Define a Logger named 'WroxLogger'. Assign the Level DEBUG to it. Assign an
# Appender 'WroxAppender' to this Logger
log4j.WroxLogger = DEBUG, WroxAppender
```

Appenders

This Log4J component manages the logging of information to an actual location (for example, the console, a log file, etc.). The various kinds of log destinations are discussed later in this appendix. Every logging environment should have an Appender assigned. It is also possible to set different logging destinations for different parts of the application code. A Layout is assigned to each Appender. This Layout determines the actual formatting of the logged messages. Each Appender logs the message at the specified destination using the assigned Layout.

Log4J provides different kinds of Appenders. Every Appender is implemented by a class in the Log4J API. For example, `ConsoleAppender` logs information to the console, `FileAppender` logs information to a file, and `SMTPAppender` logs information to an SMTP server.

In the following example, the information is logged to the console:

```
# Set the type for 'WroxAppender' as ConsoleAppender (writes to system console).
log4j.appender.WroxAppender = org.apache.log4j.ConsoleAppender
```

Log4J is also capable of sending log messages to multiple destinations simultaneously (such as logging the same information to a file and the console).

Levels

Log4J uses various levels of logging. These are predefined priority values that can be used during logging. A log level refers to a particular priority of logging. Log4j can be configured to log messages at the following five different levels:

- `DEBUG` — This level logs debugging messages. These messages are not logged in a production scenario.
- `INFO` — This level is used to track the progress of a running application.
- `WARN` — This level is used to log potentially harmful messages. The application, however, continues to run.
- `ERROR` — This level is used to log application error messages. These are logged when there are serious errors in applications.
- `FATAL` — This level is used to log messages that lead to an application crash.

Each level is represented by a constant defined in the `Priority` class provided by the Log4J API. Log4J also provides the flexibility to extend these levels.

*An earlier implementation of Log4J used the **`Priority`** class instead of the **`Level`** class. Both of these are used in a similar manner, but the class **`Level`** extends the class **`Priority`**.*

Following are the priority levels in ascending order:

`DEBUG < INFO < WARN < ERROR < FATAL`

In addition to these levels, there are two special levels:

- `OFF` — This is the highest priority, where all logging is disabled.
- `ALL` — This is the lowest priority, where messages at all levels are logged.

Layouts

Layouts control the formatting of information. Log4J can be configured to arrange the logged information in a concise and comprehensive manner. This way, the information that is logged is easy to read, thus making it usable and easier to interpret. Log4J provides various classes that manage this, and these are discussed later in this appendix. The `SimpleLayout` Layout logs messages in the simplest possible form.

Every Layout component is associated with an Appender. Once the Appender sends the information to be logged to the specified destination, the Layout takes care of formatting these log messages in the required format. The Layout provides details such as date and time, name of the Java class, thread status, level, and so on.

Following is a sample entry of Layout from the Log4J configuration file:

```
# A Log4J Appender 'WroxAppender' is defined as shown in the Appenders section.
# SimpleLayout is assigned to WroxAppender.
log4j.appender.WroxAppender.layout = org.apache.log4j.SimpleLayout
```

A Sample Log4J Configuration File

Following is a sample Log4J configuration file. In this case, the `wroxAppender` (an Appender) is assigned to the `WroxLogger` (a Logger) with logging Level `DEBUG`. The `wroxAppender` is then set to `ConsoleAppender` to use the console as the destination. The Layout used for logging information is `SimpleLayout`:

```
# Define a Logger component 'WroxLogger'
# Set Level as DEBUG and assign the Appender 'WroxAppender' to the 'WroxLogger'
log4j.WroxLogger = DEBUG, WroxAppender

# Set the type for 'WroxAppender' as ConsoleAppender (writes to system console)
log4j.appender.WroxAppender = org.apache.log4j.ConsoleAppender

# Set the Layout as SimpleLayout for 'WroxAppender'
log4j.appender.WroxAppender.layout = org.apache.log4j.SimpleLayout
```

Setting Up Log4J

This section describes how to set up Log4J for the actual development environment. First, download a stable release of Log4J from the following URL:

```
http://logging.apache.org/log4j/docs/download.html
```

All examples discussed in this chapter are tested with Log4J version 1.2.8, J2SDK 1.4.1, Apache Jakarta Tomcat 5.0.16 on a MS Windows 2000 server. These examples will work on other operating systems (such as Linux) with appropriate path changes.

Extract the downloaded file into a convenient directory on your local machine (for example, `D:\Apps\Log4J`). This directory is denoted by `<Log4J_HOME>` in the remainder of this discussion.

Setting CLASSPATH

It is assumed that the environment variables `PATH` and `CLASSPATH` for Java are properly set. The classes of Log4J can be made available to the application by simply including the `log4j.jar` file in the `CLASSPATH`. This file is located under the distribution directory at `<Log4J_HOME>\dist\lib`.

To include the JAR file in the Tomcat Web application classpath, copy the file to the `<CATALINA_HOME>\common\lib` directory. The server will automatically include any classes from this location (usually in the form of a JAR) into the `CLASSPATH` at run-time. For other applications, you can put the `log4j.jar` file in the `CLASSPATH` or `<JAVA_HOME>\jre\lib\ext` directory. The configuration discussed in this chapter uses the following locations:

- `Log4J_HOME` — `D:\Apps\Log4J`
- `CATALINA_HOME` — `D:\Apps\Tomcat5`

Working with Log4J

Log4J can be configured in the following ways:

- Using a simple properties file
- Programmatically
- Using an XML configuration file

Using a Simple Properties File

The simplest way to configure a Logger is by using a Java properties file typically referred to as a **Log Configuration File** (**LCF**). It specifies all the configuration details. The entries are simple name-value pairs, and the pound symbol (#) is used to comment out a line.

The usual name for the configuration file is `log4j.properties`. The location of this file is important for the initialization of the application. By default, Log4J will look for the configuration file in the same directory as that of the application.

The following discussion shows how to build a sample log configuration file (`WroxSampleLog.properties`). You should first set up a Logger named `WroxSimpleLogger`. Assign an Appender named `wroxSimpleAppender` to this Logger. In addition, the logging level should be `DEBUG`:

```
log4j.logger.WroxSimpleLogger= DEBUG, wroxSimpleAppender
```

Once the Logger is in place, configure the Appender. Use the `FileAppender` to log all messages to a file. It is also needed to provide the name of the log file in this configuration:

```
log4j.appender.wroxSimpleAppender=org.apache.log4j.FileAppender
log4j.appender.wroxSimpleAppender.File= wroxSimpleLog.log
```

Finally, set the desired Layout for the logging. This example uses `SimpleLayout`:

```
log4j.appender.wroxSimpleAppender.layout=org.apache.log4j.SimpleLayout
```

Following is the complete sample log configuration file:

```
log4j.logger.WroxSimpleLogger = DEBUG, wroxSimpleAppender
log4j.appender.wroxSimpleAppender = org.apache.log4j.FileAppender
log4j.appender.wroxSimpleAppender.File = c:\wroxSimpleLog.log
log4j.appender.wroxSimpleAppender.layout = org.apache.log4j.SimpleLayout
```

The configuration file must be specified to the `PropertyConfigurator`, which enables it to read the configuration. In the application code, a simple statement such as the following does this:

```
PropertyConfigurator.configure("WroxSampleLog.properties");
```

Once the configuration is loaded, each class that requires logging capability within the application must have a reference to the Logger object. Because the Logger uses a package naming convention, it is common among developers to use the class name as the Logger, although this is not mandatory. In any case, a package style of Logger naming serves well. To use Log4J in the application, the property file is loaded by using a `PropertyConfigurator`. This is shown in the following line:

```
import org.apache.log4j.PropertyConfigurator;
PropertyConfigurator.configure("path_to_file/WroxSampleLog.properties");
```

Using Log4J Programmatically

Log4J can also be configured programmatically. In the application code, a new `Logger` object is created, and is configured in much the same way as the configuration file. The main steps for using Log4J programmatically are as follows:

1. Create a Logger object. Typically, the package hierarchy — including the class name — is used:

```
Logger WroxTestLogger = Logger.getLogger("wroxLogging.WroxLoggingTest");
```

2. Once the Logger is in place, set the logging level to the Logger object:

```
WroxTestLogger.setLevel(Level.DEBUG);
```

3. Create an instance of the Layout to be used:

```
SimpleLayout WroxSimpleLayout = new SimpleLayout();
```

4. Create an instance of the Appender to be used and use the Layout object:

```
FileAppender WroxFileAppender =
            new FileAppender(WroxSimpleLayout,"WroxSampleLog.log");
```

5. Finally, add this Appender object to the Logger object:

```
WroxTestLogger.addAppender(WroxFileAppender);
```

The following completed sample Java class shows a Logger being created and configured to log messages:

```
package wroxLogging;

import org.apache.log4j.Logger;
import org.apache.log4j.Level;
import org.apache.log4j.SimpleLayout;
import org.apache.log4j.FileAppender;
import java.io.IOException;

public class WroxLoggingTest {
public static void main(String[] args) {
     //Create an instance of Logger
     Logger WroxTestLogger = Logger.getLogger("wroxLogging.WroxLoggingTest");

    //Set the Logging Level
    WroxTestLogger.setLevel(Level.DEBUG);

    try {
      SimpleLayout WroxSimpleLayout = new SimpleLayout();

      //Assign a SimpleLayout to the FileAppender
     FileAppender WroxFileAppender=
            new FileAppender(WroxSimpleLayout,"WroxSampleLog.log");

      //Finally Assign the fileAppender to the Logger
      WroxTestLogger.addAppender(WroxFileAppender);

     //Now try to Log few messages at different 'Levels'
      WroxTestLogger.debug("Sample Message : DEBUG");
      WroxTestLogger.info("Sample Message : INFO");
      WroxTestLogger.warn("Sample Message : WARN");
      WroxTestLogger.error("Sample Message : ERROR");
      WroxTestLogger.fatal("Sample Message : FATAL");
    } catch(IOException e) {
      WroxTestLogger.warn("An IOException was thrown", e);
    }
  }
}
```

Note that each of the logging methods (such as `debug()`, `warn()`, and so on) shown here have an overloaded version available that accepts the `Throwable` object. Typically, such methods add the trace log to the same log file.

Using an XML Configuration File

The Log4J configuration file can also be in XML format. The way it works is very similar to the properties file. The only difference is that the Log4J class loading the configuration file — the XML file — is loaded using `DOMConfigurator`, instead of `PropertyConfigurator`.

The file begins with a standard XML declaration and the DTD declaration. This ensures that the XML configuration file conforms to the syntax of Log4J:

```
<?xml version="1.0" encoding="UTF-8" ?>
<!DOCTYPE log4j:configuration SYSTEM "log4j.dtd">
```

The root element in the XML file is `<log4j:configuration>`. The `log4j` portion is the namespace used for the configuration file. The root element `<log4j:configuration>` wraps the entire configuration. It has two main sub-elements, `appender` and `logger`.

```
<log4j:configuration>
```

The main attributes of the `appender` element are `name` and `class`. It also takes parameters such as the `Layout` as sub-elements. Here is how a sample entry looks:

```
  <appender name="wroxFileAppender" class="org.apache.log4j.FileAppender">
    <param name="File" value="log4j.log"/>
    <layout class="org.apache.log4j.SimpleLayout"/>
  </appender>
```

The next important element is `<logger>`. It also has attributes and a few sub-elements. The main attribute is `name`. The parameter it takes is the associated `appender` element. A typical entry looks like the following:

```
  <logger name="wroxLogging.WroxSimpleLogger">
    <level value="debug"/>
    <appender-ref ref="wroxFileAppender" />
  </logger>
```

Here is the complete sample configuration file `WroxSampleConfig.xml` for Log4J in XML format:

```
<?xml version="1.0" encoding="UTF-8" ?>
<!DOCTYPE log4j:configuration SYSTEM "log4j.dtd">
<log4j:configuration>
  <appender name="wroxFileAppender" class="org.apache.log4j.FileAppender">
    <param name="File" value="log4j.log"/>
    <layout class="org.apache.log4j.SimpleLayout"/>
  </appender>
  <logger name="wroxLogging.WroxSimpleLogger">
    <level value="debug"/>
    <appender-ref ref=" wroxFileAppender" />
  </logger>
</log4j:configuration>
```

Once the configuration is provided in the XML file, the `DOMConfigurator` can be used to load these settings. The `DOMConfigurator` looks for the XML configuration file in the same directory as that of the application. `DOMConfigurator` can also use a specific system path or URL:

```
public static void main(String[] args) {
  // Load the configuration through the DOMConfigurator and provide in the XML file
  DOMConfigurator.configure("WroxSampleConfig.xml");
  Logger WroxLogger = Logger.getLogger("wroxLogging.WroxSimpleLogger");

  // Now try to log few messages at different Levels
  WroxLogger.debug("Sample Message : DEBUG");
  WroxLogger.info("Sample Message : INFO");
  WroxLogger.warn("Sample Message : WARN");
  WroxLogger.error("Sample Message : ERROR");
  WroxLogger.fatal("Sample Message : FATAL");
}
```

Behavior of Loggers and Appenders

Loggers in Log4J follow a hierarchical model. This enables you to maintain a parent-child relationship between Loggers. Therefore, a well-defined hierarchy of such Loggers can be set up. It will provide fine-grained control during actual logging, and thus exploit the feature of inheritance. A simple implementation of a Logger hierarchy can contain a child Logger that can inherit the features provided by its ancestor. Therefore, if a Logger doesn't have any of its configuration parameters specified explicitly, it will inherit these values from its parent. As in the case of inheritance, the properties of a parent Logger can be overridden by its child.

The logging level can also be set at the application-code level. The logging level can be set using a Log4J API method from the class Category as shown here. This method accepts the logging level constant as a parameter.

```
myLogger.setLevel((Level) Level.DEBUG);
```

Log4J also provides the option to check whether a particular logging level is active or not, as shown here:

```
if(myLogger.isDebugEnabled()) {
  myLogger.debug("This is debug value for temp : " + temp);
}
```

Appenders are additive by nature. Therefore, by default, a Logger inherits all the Appenders from its ancestors. If an Appender is added to a Logger and it writes to the same underlying stream (console, file, and so on) as some other Appender, the same log message will appear twice. In addition, if two Loggers in a hierarchy are configured to use the same Appender name, Log4J will write twice to that Appender. Using the method `Logger.setAdditivity(false)` on a Logger, this behavior can be disabled. This way, log messages will only be sent to the Appenders specifically configured for that Logger.

Log4J Examples

This section presents various code samples to demonstrate Log4J capabilities. Note that each sample contains some specific settings that provide details about the exact locations of files referred to in the discussion. Modify the file paths as per your local settings.

Logging from a Java Class

This sample code presents a simple Java class that uses the Log4J API for logging. It also uses a properties file for configuring Log4J. The actual code for the class and the contents of the properties file are provided. After placing the files as specified in the settings, just compile the Java code. Invoking the class from the command prompt will log the sample messages. This can be verified by looking at the contents of the log file.

Ensure that the Log4J JAR file has been either included in the CLASSPATH or put under the **`<JAVA_HOME>\jre\lib\ext`** *directory.*

Settings

The following table shows the required settings for this example.

File	Location
Java class location	`D:\Apps\Test\wroxLogging\WroxTestLog4J.java`
Properties file location	`D:\Apps\Test\SampleLog.properties`
Log file location	`D:\Apps\Test\WroxSampleLog.log`

SampleLog.properties — Log Configuration File

The following code represents the log configuration file:

```
# Define a Logger named SampleLogTest
log4j.logger.wroxLogging.SampleLogTest = WARN, WroxTestFile, WroxTestConsole

# Define a second logger that is a child to wroxLogging.SampleLogTest
log4j.logger.wroxLogging.SampleLogTest.SampleSubLogTest

# Define an Appender named WroxTestFile, which is set to be a FileAppender
log4j.appender.WroxTestFile = org.apache.log4j.FileAppender
log4j.appender.WroxTestFile.file = D:/Apps/Tomcat5/logs/WroxSampleLog.log

# Define an Appender named WroxTestConsole, which is set to be a ConsoleAppender
log4j.appender.WroxTestConsole = org.apache.log4j.ConsoleAppender

# Assign a Layout to both Appenders
log4j.appender.WroxTestConsole.layout = org.apache.log4j.SimpleLayout
log4j.appender.WroxTestFile.layout = org.apache.log4j.SimpleLayout
```

WroxTestLog4J Java Class

The following code is the complete source of the Java class used for this example:

```
package wroxLogging;

import org.apache.log4j.Logger;
import org.apache.log4j.Level;
import org.apache.log4j.PropertyConfigurator;

public class WroxTestLog4J {
// Create an instance of Logger "wroxLogging.SampleLogTest" and it's subtype
static Logger WroxLogger = Logger.getLogger("wroxLogging.SampleLogTest");
static Logger WroxSubLogger =
          Logger.getLogger("wroxLogging.SampleLogTest.SampleSubLogTest");

public static void main(String[] args) {

   // Load the properties using the PropertyConfigurator
   PropertyConfigurator.configure("SampleLog.properties");

   // Logging using different Log Levels - WroxLogger in Action
   WroxLogger.debug("Wrox Logging in progress by : " + WroxLogger.getName());
   WroxLogger.info("Wrox Logging in progress by : " + WroxLogger.getName());
   WroxLogger.warn("Wrox Logging in progress by : " + WroxLogger.getName());
   WroxLogger.error("Wrox Logging in progress by : " +  WroxLogger.getName());
   WroxLogger.fatal("Wrox Logging in progress by : " +  WroxLogger.getName());

   // Logging using different Log Levels - wroxSubLogger in Action
   WroxSubLogger.debug("Wrox Logging in progress by : " + WroxSubLogger.getName());
   WroxSubLogger.info("Wrox Logging in progress by : " + WroxSubLogger.getName());
   WroxSubLogger.warn("Wrox Logging in progress by : " + WroxSubLogger.getName());
   WroxSubLogger.error("Wrox Logging in progress by : " + WroxSubLogger.getName());
   WroxSubLogger.fatal("Wrox Logging in progress by : " + WroxSubLogger.getName());
 }
}
```

Log Output

All the logged messages will appear on the console as well as in the log file. The contents of the file will look like the following:

```
WARN -- Wrox Logging in progress by : wroxLogging.SampleLogTest
ERROR -- Wrox Logging in progress by : wroxLogging.SampleLogTest
FATAL -- Wrox Logging in progress by : wroxLogging.SampleLogTest
WARN -- Wrox Logging in progress by : wroxLogging.SampleLogTest.SampleSubLogTest
ERROR -- Wrox Logging in progress by : wroxLogging.SampleLogTest.SampleSubLogTest
FATAL -- Wrox Logging in progress by : wroxLogging.SampleLogTest.SampleSubLogTest
```

Logging from a Web Application

Typically, in Web applications, the Log4J configuration is done in an initialization Servlet. This way, the properties are read at the time the application is started. The `<load-on-startup>` tag in the `web.xml` file should be set to 1. This ensures that the initialization Servlet is invoked at the time of Web application startup. You also need to copy the log4j.jar file to the WEB-INF\lib directory of the Web application.

Once the Log4J is configured, any JSP or Servlet within that Web application can use Log4J features, as demonstrated next. The example provided here shows a JSP using Log4J for logging. Set up the environment as stated in the settings and compile the initialization Servlet, and then restart the Tomcat Web container for the Servlet to be reloaded.

Settings

The following table shows the required settings for this example.

File	Location
Servlet location	D:\Apps\Tomcat5\webapps\jsp-examples\WEB-INF\classes\wroxLogging\WroxLogServlet.java
Properties file location	D:\Apps\Tomcat5\webapps\jsp-examples\WEB-INF\WroxLogging.properties
Log4J JAR	D:\Apps\Tomcat5\webapps\jsp-examples\WEB-INF\lib\log4j.jar
JSP location	D:\Apps\Tomcat5\webapps\jsp-examples\WroxLogPage.jsp
Log file location	D:\Apps\Tomcat5\logs\WroxLog.log

WroxLogServlet — Initialization Servlet

Here is the complete source code of the initialization Servlet:

```
package wroxLogging;

import javax.servlet.*;
import javax.servlet.http.*;
import java.io.*;
import java.util.*;
import org.apache.log4j.PropertyConfigurator;

public class WroxLogServlet extends HttpServlet {
  public void init()
  throws ServletException {
    // Get Fully Qualified Path to Properties File
    String config = getServletContext().getRealPath("/") +
                    getInitParameter("setup");
    System.out.println("LoggingServlet Initialized using file :" + config);
    // Initialize Properties for All Servlets
    PropertyConfigurator.configure(config);
}

  public void doGet(HttpServletRequest request, HttpServletResponse response)
  throws ServletException, IOException {
    PrintWriter out = response.getWriter();
    response.setContentType("text/html");
```

```
        out.println("<html>");
        out.println("<head>");
        out.println("<title>LoggingServlet</title>");
        out.println("</head>");
        out.println("<body>");
        out.println("<p>Called GET method of the Servlet.</p>");
        out.println("</body>");
        out.println("</html>");
        out.close();
    }

    public void destroy() {
    }
}
```

Deployment Descriptor Settings

Following are the `web.xml` settings:

```
<servlet>
    <servlet-name>WroxLogServlet</servlet-name>
    <servlet-class>wroxLogging.WroxLogServlet</servlet-class>
    <init-param>
        <param-name>setup</param-name>
        <param-value>WEB-INF\WroxLogging.properties</param-value>
    </init-param>
    <load-on-startup>1</load-on-startup>
 </servlet>
```

WroxLogging.properties — Log Configuration File

The Log4J configuration log file is as follows:

```
# Define a Logger "wroxLoggoing.WroxLogTest"
log4j.logger.wroxLogging.WroxLogTest=INFO,WroxTestFile

# Define a file Appender of type RollingFileAppender
log4j.appender.WroxTestFile = org.apache.log4j.FileAppender
log4j.appender.WroxTestFile.file = D:/Apps/Tomcat5/logs/WroxLog.log

# Assign a Layout to the Appender
log4j.appender.WroxTestFile.layout = org.apache.log4j.SimpleLayout
```

WroxLogPage.jsp — Sample JSP for Testing

The JSP uses the Logger (`wroxLogging.WroxLogTest`) initialized in the initialization Servlet. The following code demonstrates how the Logger can be used for logging in any Web component:

```
<%@ page language="java" import="org.apache.log4j.Logger" %>
<%
    out.println("Testing Log4J");
    Logger logger = Logger.getLogger("wroxLogging.WroxLogTest");
    logger.info("Testing Logging!");
%>
```

Log File Output

When the JSP is invoked, it logs messages to the log file (`WroxLog.log`) as shown in the following example:

```
INFO -- Testing Logging!
```

A Closer Look at Logging Options

The log configuration file stores all the Log4J options that control what information should be logged, and how it should be logged. The following sections provide details about various logging options.

Meta Level Options

The meta level offers full control over the logging behavior of the application. The logging can be disabled for all declared Loggers for a specific level. For the sample case shown, any log message that has a level equal to or lower than the one specified will not be logged:

```
log4j.disable=INFO
```

In the most basic and simplest format, the Application Root Logger can be used. In this case, all messages with the default level (`DEBUG`) or higher will be logged:

```
log4j.appRootLogger= LogDestination1
```

Logging to the Console

There may be an application requirement to log all the messages to the console. In addition, the messages may need to mention the output stream explicitly and control the flushing behavior. The `ConsoleAppender` supports all these features. The following sample shows a `ConsoleAppender` with all these options:

```
# Declare a Logger 'WroxLogger' and assign the Appender 'wroxAppender' to it.
log4j.logger.wroxLogging.WroxLogger = DEBUG, wroxAppender

# Set the type for wroxAppender as ConsoleAppender
log4j.appender.wroxAppender = org.apache.log4j.ConsoleAppender

# Mention the Level, where each message with equal or above Level gets logged
log4j.appender.WroxDest1.Threshold=WARN

# The behavior for the rendering on the console can be controlled, by deciding
# when to flush the contents on the console as shown below
log4j.appender.WroxDest1.ImmediateFlush=true

# Specify that which stream to be used, standard or error
log4j.appender.WroxDest1.Target=System.out
```

Logging to a File

The most familiar log destination is a file. Various options are available, which are supported by the `FileAppender`. The name and location of the log file can be configured. The following sample shows a `FileAppender` with these options:

```
# Declare a Logger 'WroxLogger' and assign the Appender 'wroxAppender' to it.
log4j.logger.wroxLogging.WroxLogger = DEBUG, wroxAppender

# Use a FileAppender
log4j.appender.wroxAppender = org.apache.log4j.FileAppender

# Provide the name and location of the log file
log4j.appender.wroxAppender.File = MyLogs.log

# Rendering option and flush attribute can be provided
log4j.appender.wroxAppender.ImmediateFlush=true
# Mention the Level, where each message with equal or above Level gets logged
log4j.appender.wroxAppender.Threshold=INFO

# Whether to append to existing contents or overwrite
log4j.appender.wroxAppender.Append=false
```

Log File Rolling

This important option prevents large amounts of log messages from collecting in the log files over time. The `RollingFileAppender` provides various options to control the rolling of log files. Here is a sample configuration for `RollingFileAppender`:

```
# Declare a Logger 'WroxLogger' and assign the Appender 'wroxAppender' to it.
log4j.logger.wroxLogging.WroxLogger = DEBUG, wroxAppender

# Set the Appender
log4j.appender.wroxAppender = org.apache.log4j.RollingFileAppender

# Provide the Level of Level.
log4j.appender.wroxAppender.Threshold=INFO

# Provide the log file name.
log4j.appender.wroxAppender.File= MyLogs.log

# An attribute which decides whether to append or overwrite
log4j.appender.wroxAppender.Append=false

# Set the Maximum log file size
log4j.appender.wroxAppender.MaxFileSize=100KB

# Mention the number of backup files.
# backup files = MaxBackupIndex * MaxFileSize.
log4j.appender.wroxAppender.MaxBackupIndex=4
```

Logging in Different Formats

This section explains how to configure Log4J to log information in a variety of formats. This includes options such as logging in HTML format, logging to an SMTP server, logging to the Windows System log, and so on.

Using HTML Format

Log4J provides an option to log all messages in HTML format. This is the most popular format when the logs are generated for Web applications. This format improves the overall presentation and readability of log files. A sample of logging output is shown in Figure A-1.

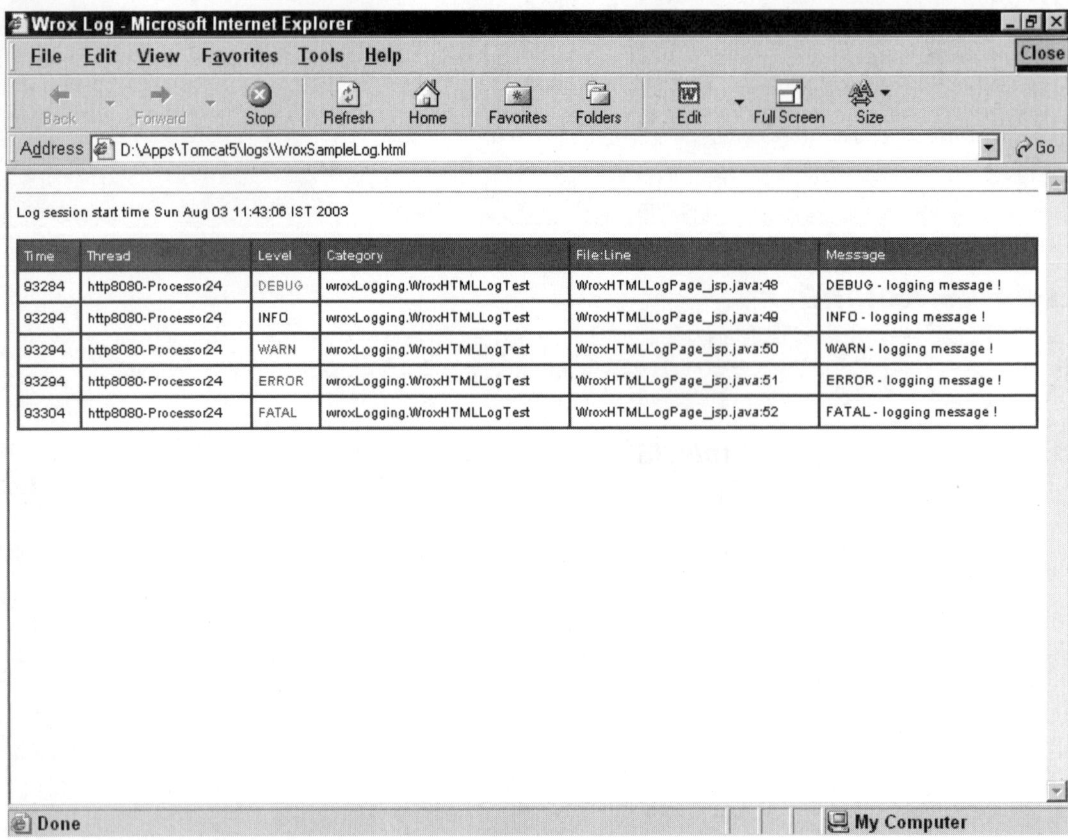

Figure A-1: Sample logging output.

Settings

The following table shows the required settings for this example.

File	Location
Properties file location	D:\Apps\Tomcat5\webapps\jsp-examples\WEB-INF\HTMLLog.properties
JSP location	D:\Apps\Tomcat5\webapps\jsp-examples\HTMLLayout.jsp
Log4J JAR	D:\Apps\Tomcat5\webapps\jsp-examples\WEB-INF\lib\log4j.jar
Log file location	D:\Apps\Tomcat5\logs\WroxSampleLog.html

HTMLLog.properties File — Log Configuration File

The following is the log configuration file:

```
# Declare a Logger 'WroxLogger'
log4j.logger.wroxLogging.WroxLogger = DEBUG , wroxAppender

# Set the type of 'wroxAppender' as FileAppender
log4j.appender.wroxAppender = org.apache.log4j.FileAppender
log4j.appender.wroxAppender.File = D:/Apps/Tomcat5/logs/WroxSampleLog.html
log4j.appender.wroxAppender.Append = false

# Set HTMLLayout to the 'wroxAppender'
log4j.appender.wroxAppender.layout = org.apache.log4j.HTMLLayout
log4j.appender.wroxAppender.layout.LocationInfo = true
log4j.appender.wroxAppender.layout.Title = WroxLog
```

HTMLLayout.jsp — Sample JSP for Testing

The following is the sample JSP for testing:

```
<%@ page language="java" import="org.apache.log4j.*" %>
<h2>HTML Logging Using Log4J</h2>
<%
    Logger logger = Logger.getLogger("wroxLogging.WroxLogger");
    PropertyConfigurator.configure(getServletContext().getRealPath("/") +
                                            "WEB-INF\\HTMLLog.properties");

    logger.debug("DEBUG -- logging message !");
    logger.info("INFO -- logging message !");
    logger.warn("WARN -- logging message !");
    logger.error("ERROR -- logging message !");
    logger.fatal("FATAL -- logging message !");
    out.println("Logging Tested !");
%>
```

Log Output

The output generated is shown in Figure A-2.

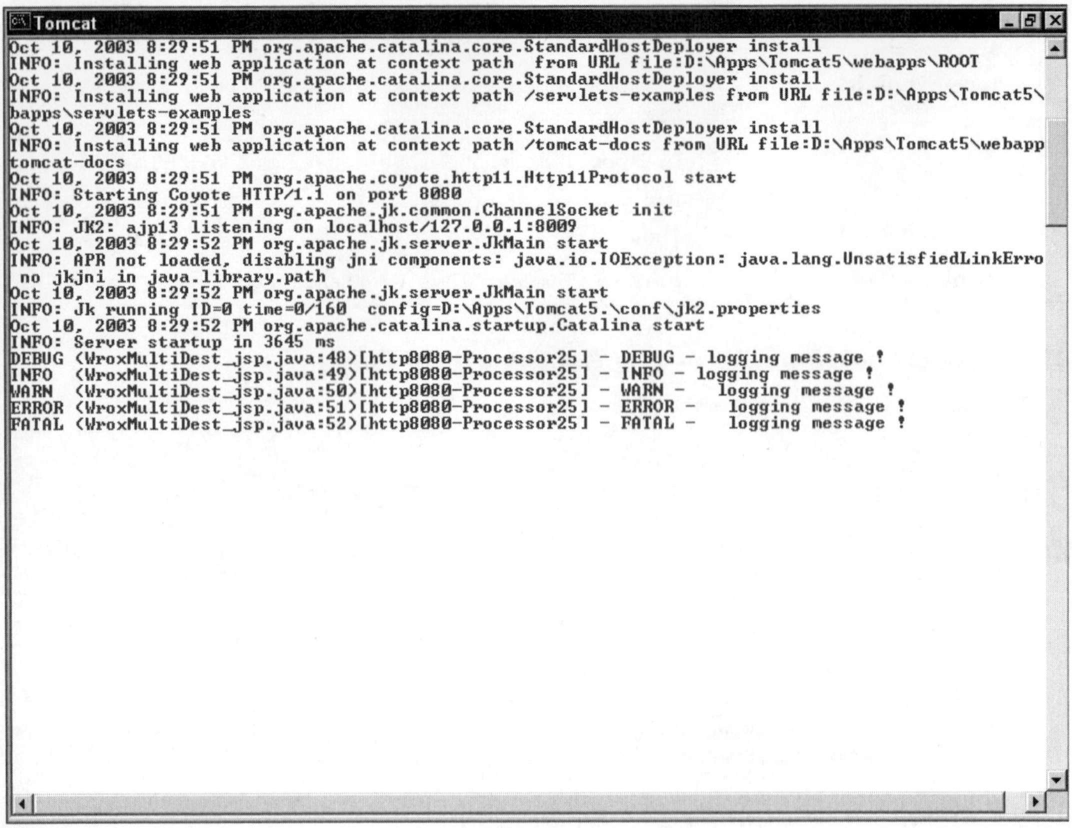

```
Tomcat
Oct 10, 2003 8:29:51 PM org.apache.catalina.core.StandardHostDeployer install
INFO: Installing web application at context path  from URL file:D:\Apps\Tomcat5\webapps\ROOT
Oct 10, 2003 8:29:51 PM org.apache.catalina.core.StandardHostDeployer install
INFO: Installing web application at context path /servlets-examples from URL file:D:\Apps\Tomcat5\
bapps\servlets-examples
Oct 10, 2003 8:29:51 PM org.apache.catalina.core.StandardHostDeployer install
INFO: Installing web application at context path /tomcat-docs from URL file:D:\Apps\Tomcat5\webapp
tomcat-docs
Oct 10, 2003 8:29:51 PM org.apache.coyote.http11.Http11Protocol start
INFO: Starting Coyote HTTP/1.1 on port 8080
Oct 10, 2003 8:29:51 PM org.apache.jk.common.ChannelSocket init
INFO: JK2: ajp13 listening on localhost/127.0.0.1:8009
Oct 10, 2003 8:29:52 PM org.apache.jk.server.JkMain start
INFO: APR not loaded, disabling jni components: java.io.IOException: java.lang.UnsatisfiedLinkErro
 no jkjni in java.library.path
Oct 10, 2003 8:29:52 PM org.apache.jk.server.JkMain start
INFO: Jk running ID=0 time=0/160  config=D:\Apps\Tomcat5.\conf\jk2.properties
Oct 10, 2003 8:29:52 PM org.apache.catalina.startup.Catalina start
INFO: Server startup in 3645 ms
DEBUG (WroxMultiDest_jsp.java:48)[http8080-Processor25] - DEBUG - logging message !
INFO  (WroxMultiDest_jsp.java:49)[http8080-Processor25] - INFO - logging message !
WARN  (WroxMultiDest_jsp.java:50)[http8080-Processor25] - WARN -   logging message !
ERROR (WroxMultiDest_jsp.java:51)[http8080-Processor25] - ERROR -   logging message !
FATAL (WroxMultiDest_jsp.java:52)[http8080-Processor25] - FATAL -   logging message !
```

Figure A-2: Log output.

Logging to Multiple Destinations

This section explains how to log messages to multiple destinations. In this example, messages are logged at two separate targets: the system console and a daily rolling log file.

Settings

The following table shows the required settings for this example.

File	Location
Properties file location	`D:\Apps\Tomcat5\webapps\jsp-examples\WEB-INF\MultiDest.properties`
JSP location	`D:\Apps\Tomcat5\webapps\jsp-examples\MultiDestLog.jsp`
Log4J JAR	`D:\Apps\Tomcat5\webapps\jsp-examples\WEB-INF\lib\log4j.jar`
Log file location	`D:\Apps\Tomcat5\logs\DailyRollingFile.log`

MultiDest.properties — Log Configuration File

The following is the log configuration file:

```
# WroxMultipleDest.properties
log4j.logger.wroxLogging.WroxLogger = DEBUG, WroxDest1, WroxDest2

# WroxDest1 is a ConsoleAppender
log4j.appender.WroxDest1 = org.apache.log4j.ConsoleAppender
log4j.appender.WroxDest1.layout = org.apache.log4j.PatternLayout
log4j.appender.WroxDest1.layout.ConversionPattern = %-5p (%F:%L)[%t] -- %m%n

# WroxDest2 is a DailyRollingFileAppender
log4j.appender.WroxDest2=org.apache.log4j.DailyRollingFileAppender
log4j.appender.WroxDest2.file=D:/Apps/Tomcat5/logs/DailyRollingFile.log
log4j.appender.WroxDest2.datePattern='.'yyyy-MM-dd
log4j.appender.WroxDest2.append=true
log4j.appender.WroxDest2.layout=org.apache.log4j.PatternLayout
log4j.appender.WroxDest2.layout.ConversionPattern=%-5p %d{ISO8601} [%t] -- %m%n
```

MultiDestLog.jsp — Sample JSP for Testing

The following code represents the sample JSP for testing:

```
<%@ page language="java" import="org.apache.log4j.*" %>
<h2>Logging At Multiple Destinations Using Log4J</h2>
<%
    Logger logger = Logger.getLogger("wroxLogging.WroxLogger");
    PropertyConfigurator.configure(getServletContext().getRealPath("/") +
                                    "WEB-INF\\MultiDest.properties");

    logger.debug("DEBUG -- logging message !");
    logger.info("INFO -- logging message !");
    logger.warn("WARN --   logging message !");
    logger.error("ERROR --   logging message !");
    logger.fatal("FATAL --   logging message !");

    out.println("Logging Tested !");
%>
```

Log File Contents

The following output is generated in the file `DailyRollingFile.log`:

```
DEBUG 2003-10-10 20:29:54,831 [http8080-Processor25] -- DEBUG -- logging message !
INFO  2003-10-10 20:29:54,841 [http8080-Processor25] -- INFO -- logging message !
WARN  2003-10-10 20:29:54,841 [http8080-Processor25] -- WARN --   logging message !
ERROR 2003-10-10 20:29:54,841 [http8080-Processor25] -- ERROR --   logging message !
FATAL 2003-10-10 20:29:54,841 [http8080-Processor25] -- FATAL --   logging message !
```

The output is displayed on the console.

Logging to SMTP Server — E-mail Log Messages

A very powerful feature of Log4J is its capability to send critical messages as e-mail. This makes it possible for administrators to get critical messages as alerts. For example, `FATAL` level messages can be sent to an SMTP server, which can get the immediate attention of the server administrator. Although it might look complicated, the Log4J implementation hides the complexities from the developer. This makes it easy to deploy this solution, as demonstrated in the following configuration files and sample JSP. Use the settings as stated in the following table and deploy the JSP in the Web container. On invoking the JSP, messages will be logged and sent as e-mail.

Settings

The following table shows the required settings for this example.

File	Location
Properties file location	`D:\Apps\Tomcat5\webapps\jsp-examples\WEB-INF\SMTPLog.properties`
JSP location	`D:\Apps\Tomcat5\webapps\jsp-examples\SMTPLog.jsp`
Log4J JAR	`D:\Apps\Tomcat5\webapps\jsp-examples\WEB-INF\lib\log4j.jar`
JavaMail JAR	`D:\Apps\Tomcat5\webapps\jsp-examples\WEB-INF\lib\mail.jar`
Java Activation JAR	`D:\Apps\Tomcat5\webapps\jsp-examples\WEB-INF\lib\activation.jar`
SMTP server address	`smtp.xyz.com`

In addition to the Log4J distribution, you will also need the JavaMail API and Java Activation Framework JAR files. Copy the `mail.jar` file from the Java Mail 1.2 distribution and `activation.jar` from the Java Activation Framework 1.0.2 to the `D:\Apps\Tomcat5\webapps\jsp-examples\WEB-INF\lib\` directory. This is needed in order for the JavaMail functionality to work. These JAR files are used by Log4J internally to send e-mail.

SMTPLog.properties — Log Configuration File

The following code shows the log configuration file:

```
# WroxSMTPLog.properties
log4j.logger.wroxLogging.WroxLogger = DEBUG, SMTPDest

# APPENDERS
log4j.appender.SMTPDest = org.apache.log4j.net.SMTPAppender
log4j.appender.SMTPDest.To = abc@xyz.com
log4j.appender.SMTPDest.SMTPHost = smtp.xyz.com
log4j.appender.SMTPDest.Subject = There is an Application ERROR !!!
log4j.appender.SMTPDest.From = abc@xyz.com
```

```
log4j.appender.SMTPDest.BufferSize = 1

# Set the Layout
log4j.appender.SMTPDest.layout=org.apache.log4j.PatternLayout
log4j.appender.SMTPDest.layout.ConversionPattern=%d %-5p [%t] %c{2} -- %m%n
```

SMTPLog.jsp — Sample JSP for Testing

Following is the sample JSP code for testing:

```
<%@ page language="java" import="org.apache.log4j.*" %>
<h2>SMTP Logging Using Log4J</h2>
<%
    Logger logger = Logger.getLogger("wroxLogging.WroxLogger");
    PropertyConfigurator.configure(getServletContext().getRealPath("/") +
                                            "WEB-INF\\SMTPLog.properties");

    logger.debug("DEBUG -- logging message !");
    logger.info("INFO -- logging message !");
    logger.warn("WARN -- logging message !");
    logger.error("ERROR -- logging message !");
    logger.fatal("FATAL -- logging message !");
    out.println("SMTP Logging Tested !");
%>
```

SMTP Message Contents

The log messages are sent as e-mail. The following lines show typical contents of the generated e-mail:

```
2003-08-03 12:35:27,569 ERROR [http8080-Processor25] wroxLogging.WroxLogger --
ERROR --   logging message !
2003-08-03 12:35:29,912 FATAL [http8080-Processor25] wroxLogging.WroxLogger -
FATAL -- logging message !
```

Logging to Native System Logs — NT Event Log

Some administrators prefer to integrate the application log and system log for convenience and maintenance. Log4J can use the native system log (such as the syslog on Linux/Unix and the Windows Application log on Windows).

Logging to the Linux/Unix syslog, though not shown here, can be done by using the SyslogAppender (`org.apache.log4j.net.SyslogAppender`) instead of the NTEventLogAppender in the Log4J configuration.

A communication channel with the native operating system is required for this. For Windows, the Log4J distribution provides a Dynamic Link Library (DLL), `NTEventLogAppender.dll`, to enable logging to the Event log.

Using the NTEventLogAppender DLL

The first step is registering this DLL. The `NTEventLogAppender` DLL is located under the `<LOG4J_HOME>\src\java\org\apache\log4j\nt` directory.

Copy the `NTEventLogAppender.dll` file into the `system32` directory under the Windows installation directory. For the discussion presented here, it is assumed that the `system32` folder is located at `c:\winnt\system32`. After copying the DLL file, execute the following command to register the DLL (the command can be executed by selecting Run from the Start menu):

```
regsvr32 c:\winnt\system32\NTEventLogAppender.dll
```

The DLL registration step is shown in Figure A-3.

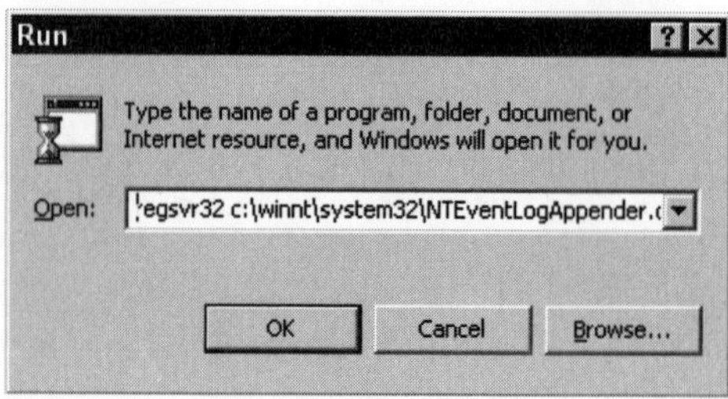

Figure A-3: Registering the DLL.

Settings

The following table shows the required settings for this example.

File	Location
Properties file location	`D:\Apps\Tomcat5\webapps\jsp-examples\WEB-INF\NTLog.properties`
JSP location	`D:\Apps\Tomcat5\webapps\jsp-examples\NTLog.jsp`
DLL Location	`C:\WINNT\system32\NTEventLogAppender.dll`

NTLog.properties — Log Configuration File

The following code shows the log configuration file:

```
# NT System Event Logger
log4j.logger.wroxLogging.WroxNTLogger=debug , WroxNTLogTester

# appender
log4j.appender.WroxNTLogTester.Threshold=FATAL
log4j.appender.WroxNTLogTester=org.apache.log4j.nt.NTEventLogAppender

# Layout
log4j.appender.WroxNTLogTester.layout=org.apache.log4j.HTMLLayout
log4j.appender.WroxNTLogTester.layout=org.apache.log4j.PatternLayout
log4j.appender.WroxNTLogTester.layout.ConversionPattern=%d %5p [%c] %x -- %m%n
```

NTLog.jsp — Sample JSP for Testing

Following is the sample JSP code for testing:

```
<%@ page language="java" import="org.apache.log4j.*" %>
<h2>NT System Logging Using Log4J</h2>
<%
  Logger logger = Logger.getLogger("wroxLogging.WroxNTLogger");
  PropertyConfigurator.configure(getServletContext().getRealPath("/") +
                                                   "WEB-INF\\NTLog.properties");

  logger.debug("DEBUG -- logging message !");
  logger.info("INFO -- logging message !");
  logger.warn("WARN --   logging message !");
  logger.error("ERROR --   logging message !");
  logger.fatal("FATAL --   logging message !");

  out.println("NT System Logging Tested !");
%>
```

After registering the DLL, the sample JSP can be invoked through the browser. This will log the messages to the Windows native Application log. Once this is done, the entries generated in the Windows system Application log can be reviewed through the Event Viewer. You can use it by selecting Start ➪ Control Panel ➪ Administrative Tools ➪ Event Viewer. All the messages logged through the sample JSP can be found under the Application log, as shown in Figure A-4.

Event Viewer

Action View

Tree

Event Viewer (Local)
Application Log
Security Log
System Log

Application Log 1,850 event(s)

Type	Date	Time	Source	Category	Event	User
Error	10/10/2003	8:39:31 PM	Log4J	(50001)	4096	N/A
Information	10/10/2003	7:37:35 PM	Norton AntiVirus	None	16	N/A
Information	10/10/2003	3:43:27 PM	Norton AntiVirus	None	16	N/A
Information	10/10/2003	3:30:15 PM	Norton AntiVirus	None	16	N/A
Information	10/10/2003	11:37:30 AM	Norton AntiVirus	None	16	N/A
Information	10/10/2003	10:30:18 AM	Norton AntiVirus	None	7	N/A
Information	10/10/2003	10:28:34 AM	Norton AntiVirus	None	16	N/A
Information	10/10/2003	10:04:48 AM	SceCli	None	1704	N/A
Information	10/9/2003	5:35:57 PM	Norton AntiVirus	None	16	N/A
Information	10/9/2003	1:51:39 PM	Norton AntiVirus	None	16	N/A
Information	10/9/2003	12:22:46 PM	MsiInstaller	None	11707	N/A
Information	10/9/2003	11:33:14 AM	Norton AntiVirus	None	16	N/A
Information	10/9/2003	9:05:14 AM	SceCli	None	1704	N/A
Information	10/8/2003	2:39:24 PM	Norton AntiVirus	None	16	N/A
Information	10/8/2003	2:04:58 PM	Norton AntiVirus	None	16	N/A
Information	10/8/2003	12:19:11 PM	Norton AntiVirus	None	16	N/A
Information	10/8/2003	11:25:38 AM	SceCli	None	1704	N/A
Information	10/7/2003	6:41:27 PM	Norton AntiVirus	None	16	N/A
Information	10/7/2003	6:02:06 PM	Norton AntiVirus	None	16	N/A
Information	10/7/2003	5:58:56 PM	Norton AntiVirus	None	23	N/A
Information	10/7/2003	5:58:01 PM	Norton AntiVirus	None	14	N/A
Information	10/7/2003	5:57:55 PM	WMDM PMSP Service	None	105	N/A
Information	10/7/2003	5:57:39 PM	Dazel Delivery Agent	None	105	N/A
Information	10/7/2003	5:38:55 PM	SceCli	None	1704	N/A
Information	10/7/2003	12:00:32 PM	Norton AntiVirus	None	16	N/A
Information	10/7/2003	12:28:14 AM	SceCli	None	1704	N/A
Information	10/6/2003	5:53:51 PM	Norton AntiVirus	None	16	N/A
Information	10/6/2003	3:13:02 PM	Norton AntiVirus	None	16	N/A

Figure A-4: The Windows Event Viewer.

When you click any one entry from the Application log, all the details for that entry are displayed. This includes the application name and the actual log message, with a date and time stamp, as shown in Figure A-5.

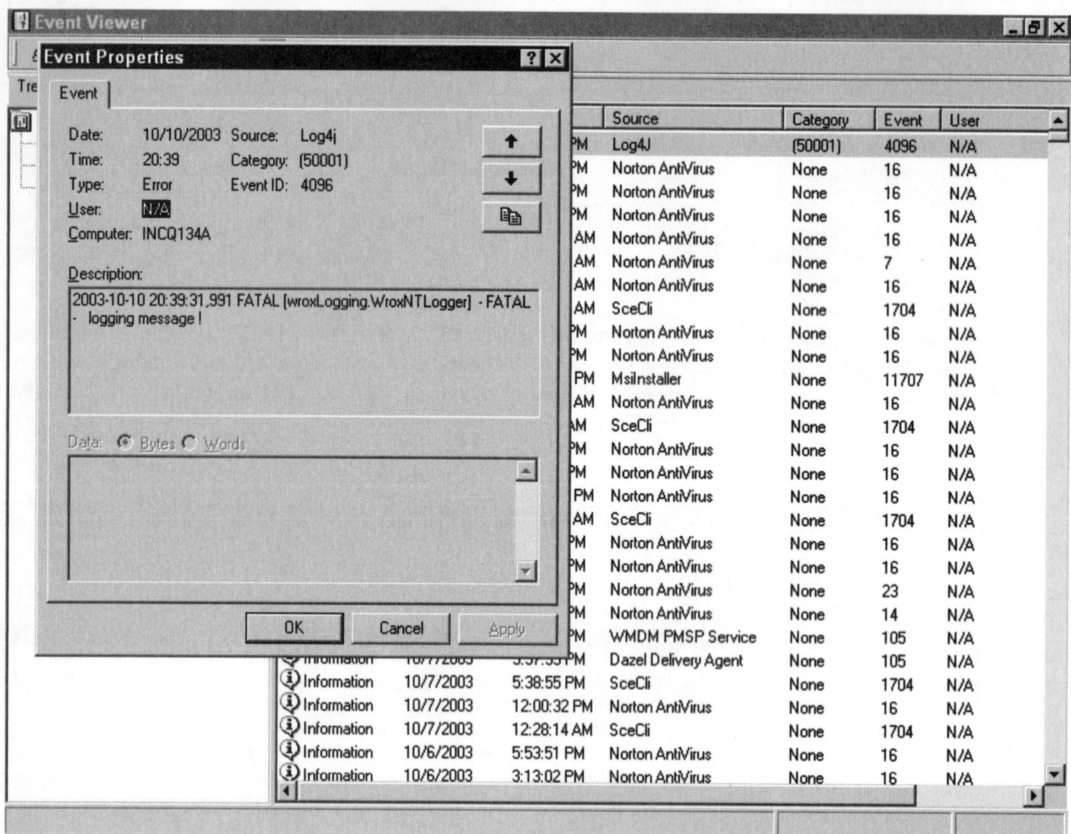

Figure A-5: Log message details.

Using PatternLayout

Log4J enables the customized formatting of log messages using the `PatternLayout`. This provides an option to log messages with detailed information. It is a preferred option used with the rolling file Appender. The following code snippet shows how to use the `PatternLayout` in the configuration file:

```
# Use the 'PatternLayout' as the layout
log4j.appender.wroxAppender.layout = org.apache.log4j.PatternLayout
```

Format Modifiers

Specifying the format of log messages is done via **format modifiers.** Following are some of the most commonly used format modifiers:

- `%m` — The actual log message
- `%n` — New line
- `%c` — Logger name
- `%t` — Current thread
- `%p` — Log level for the message (`DEBUG/INFO/WARN/ERROR/FATAL`)
- `%r` — Time (in milliseconds) since the code was executed

The default format modifier is `%m%n`. If the data item requires fewer characters, it is padded with space(s) on either the left or the right until the minimum width is reached. If the data item is larger than the minimum field width, the field is expanded to accommodate the data. In addition, a period followed by a positive integer to specify the maximum field width is also valid. The following lines show some samples of the commonly used combinations with `PatternLayout`:

```
log4j.appender.wroxAppender.layout.ConversionPattern = %-5p: %m%n
log4j.appender.WroxDest7.layout.ConversionPattern=[%d{yyyy-mm-dd hh:mm},%6.6r]%-
5p[%t]%x(%F:%L) -- %m%n
```

Format modifiers can be used between the percentage symbol and the conversion character to change the minimum field width, the maximum field width, and text justification within a field. Use the minus sign (–) to left-justify within a field. By default, it is right-justified (pad on left). Use a positive integer to specify the minimum field width.

Performance Tips

Adding Log4J statements to your code does impact performance. However, the performance can be improved by first determining whether a particular logging level is enabled or not. This saves the overhead of constructing the parameters of a logging method:

```
if (WroxLogger.isDebugEnabled()) {
    WroxLogger.debug("Logged the process ID : " + id);
}
```

When configured with the `SimpleLayout` (or a pattern using only `%p`, `%m`, or `%n`), tests have shown that logging via Log4J has the same performance characteristics as the equivalent `System.out.println()` statement.

The Apache Log4J developer teams provide performance figures for Log4J on its Web site. For example, on an AMD Duron clocked at 800 MHz and running the JDK 1.3.1, it took about 5 nanoseconds to determine if a logging statement should be logged or not. Actual logging was quite fast too, ranging from 21 microseconds using `SimpleLayout` to 37 microseconds using `TTCCLayout`.

Summary

This appendix explained how to log messages in applications by using Log4J. To conclude this appendix, let's review some of the key points that have been discussed:

- The major Log4J components are Logger, Appender, Level, and Layout.
- Configuring Log4J can be done using Log4J configuration files, programmatically and also via XML configuration files.
- Log4J can log to various destinations, such as the console, log files as well as to system loggers (for example, Unix/Linux syslog, NT Event Logger).
- Logging can be done in various formats and with custom log message patterns.
- When a simple output format is used, and a log message is sent to the console, Log4J's performance overhead is comparable to that of equivalent `System.out.println()` statements.

The appendix also discussed various examples, including code samples and configuration files. These illustrative examples showed the capability of Log4J to log messages to a file, the system console, the native system log, and in various formats, including HTML.

Appendix B outlines support for Tomcat in popular Java IDEs.

B

Tomcat and IDEs

As a general rule, programmers hate tedium. If a process can be automated, it should be. Web application deployment certainly fits into that category. While the popular Apache Ant tool excels at automating tasks such as Web application deployment, many Integrated Development Environments (IDEs) can top that: integration with Tomcat itself.

This appendix outlines the Tomcat support built into the following Java development tools:

- Intellij IDEA (`www.intellij.com`)
- Eclipse (`www.eclipse.org`)
- NetBeans/Sun Java Studio (`www.netbeans.org`)
- JBuilder (`www.borland.com/jbuilder`)

Remote Debugging

Starting with the JDK 1.3, the Java Virtual Machine (JVM) gained the capability to pass debugging information to external applications and receive debugging commands from them. The data can be transferred via either a network socket or shared memory on a local machine. Tomcat fully supports remote debugging (when used on a capable JVM). IDEs that support remote debugging can thus attach to a Tomcat instance remotely to step through Java code.

All the IDEs in this appendix support remote debugging, and thus all of the IDEs support step-through debugging of class files in a Tomcat Web application. While the instructions for attaching an IDE to a remote JVM are specific to each IDE, the instructions for configuring Tomcat to support remote debugging are generic. These configuration instructions are provided here; you can find each of the IDE-specific instructions later in the appendix.

To launch Tomcat in debug mode, use one of the following commands.

For Windows, use this command:

```
%CATALINA_HOME%\bin\catalina jpda start
```

For Linux, use this command:

```
$CATALINA_HOME/bin/catalina jpda start
```

Tomcat defaults to using the shared memory transport and a shared memory address of `jdbconn`. These settings are optimal for attaching to a Tomcat process on a local machine. If Tomcat resides on a separate server from the machine hosting the IDE, the transport should be changed to a socket and the port value set to 5050 (which is the remote debugging default, but not the Tomcat default). To change these values, set the following environment variables:

```
JPDA_TRANSPORT=dt_socket
JPDA_ADDRESS=5050
```

Notice that all of the IDE instructions in this appendix assume that Tomcat's default remote debugging settings are used.

IntelliJ IDEA 4.0

As of this writing, IntelliJ IDEA 4.0 has not been released, and its Tomcat integration was not finalized or functioning. As a result, this appendix cannot provide instructions for integrating Tomcat 5.0 with IntelliJ IDEA 4.0, but it does provide instructions for remote debugging with IDEA, which was quite stable in the pre-release version of IDEA 4.0 we used.

Remote Debugging with IDEA

With remote debugging, Tomcat is launched with remote debugging support turned on. Then, IDEA attaches to Tomcat and allows for stepping through class files.

See the section "Remote Debugging" at the beginning of this appendix for instructions on launching Tomcat in remote debug mode. Once Tomcat has been launched in debug mode, IDEA can be attached to it with the following steps:

1. Select Run from the Run pull-down menu.
2. Select the Remote tab.
3. Click the Plus button (Add New Configuration button).
4. Select the shared memory transport.
5. Enter **jdbconn** as the shared memory address.

After following these steps, clicking on Debug will attach IDEA to Tomcat. Breakpoints set in class files used by the Web application will now function.

Eclipse 3.0

Eclipse doesn't include Tomcat support out of the box. Instead, it relies on third parties to fill the void with plug-ins—and fill the void they have! Numerous Tomcat plug-ins are available for Eclipse. The most popular, the open-source Sysdeo plug-in, is discussed in the following section.

Sysdeo Tomcat Plug-in

The Sysdeo plug-in can be downloaded from `sysdeo.com`; as of this writing, the following URL worked:

```
www.sysdeo.com/eclipse/tomcatPlugin.html
```

Sysdeo supports Tomcat versions 3.3 through 5.x. Installing Sysdeo is straightforward:

1. Unzip the package to `ECLIPSE_HOME\plugins`.
2. Launch Eclipse.
3. Select Window from the pull-down menu, followed by Preferences.
4. Select the Tomcat node.
5. Select the desired version of Tomcat from the Tomcat Version box.
6. Enter the Tomcat home and base directories in the appropriate text fields (these values should be the same). The configuration file text field will auto-fill itself.
7. Press OK.

Upon completion of these steps, a new type of project can be created: a Tomcat Project. Use the following steps to create a Tomcat Project:

1. Select the File pull-down menu, followed by Project.
2. Select the Java node on the left and the Tomcat Project item on the right. Select Next.
3. Give the project a name and select Next.
4. Select Finish.

For simplicity, you can add to the project a special Tomcat menu containing links for starting, restarting, and stopping Tomcat. Usually, this menu will appear after installing the Sysdeo plug-in. If it does not, follow these steps to add this menu:

1. Select the Window pull-down menu, followed by Customize Perspective.
2. Click the Commands tab.
3. Check the Tomcat checkbox on the left, and select OK.

A new Tomcat pull-down menu with the aforementioned functions will appear while in this view.

Running and Debugging

After installing the Sysdeo plug-in via the steps outlined earlier, Eclipse will fully support running Tomcat, and debugging will be enabled when breakpoints are set in the Eclipse project.

Remote Debugging

Eclipse does not support the remote debugging shared-memory transport. Consequently, the first step in configuring Eclipse to attach to a Tomcat JVM is setting the environment variables to use the socket transport, as described in the "Remote Debugging" section at the beginning of this appendix.

Following that exercise, a remote debugging profile must be configured in Eclipse. This is accomplished by the following steps:

1. Select the Run pull-down menu, followed by Debug.
2. Double-click on the Remote Java Application node.
3. Select the appropriate project in the Project field.
4. Change the Port field to 5050.
5. Press the Debug button.

Eclipse will attach to the remote instance of Tomcat.

NetBeans 3.6

NetBeans 3.6 was in beta as of this writing; consequently, some of the details in this section may differ from the version you use. NetBeans 3.6 provides full support for Tomcat 5.0.

Embedded Tomcat

NetBeans includes an embedded version of Tomcat as part of its standard installation. This embedded version has been tightly integrated with NetBeans, and makes Web development a snap! Users of NetBeans simply click the Execute button when developing a Web Module (NetBeans term for a Web application) and the embedded version of Tomcat launches. Debugging of JSPs is enabled by default; just set breakpoints and run the application in the NetBeans debugger.

NetBeans also has an integrated HTTP monitor for viewing the requests and responses flying across the wire, as well as all kinds of other information derived from the HTTP requests/responses. Very cool!

External Tomcat

NetBeans also supports integration with external instances of Tomcat. To configure an external instance of Tomcat 5.0, first create a new Web Module project. Next, follow these steps:

1. View the Runtime edit pane, either by selecting the Editing tab followed by the Runtime tab, or by selecting Runtime from the View pull-down menu.
2. Expand the Server Registry tree node.
3. Right-click on the Tomcat 5 Servers tree node and select `Add New Server...` from the context menu.
4. Enter the Tomcat home directory (the `CATALINA_HOME` directory) in the Install Directory text field.
5. Leave the Base dir text field blank.
6. Enter a user name and password that has access to the manager role (see Chapter 7 for details on enabling access to the manager role).

After completion of these steps, a new node will appear in the Runtime tree under the Tomcat 5 Servers node. The title of this node will be the host name and port number on which the Tomcat installation is configured to listen. In order to use this new server, it should be set as the default Tomcat instance. This is accomplished by right-clicking on the new Tomcat node and selecting Set as DefaultContext from the context menu.

The integration is finished! Now, Tomcat can be controlled by right-clicking on the child node of the newly created Tomcat node.

Remote Debugging

When all else fails, NetBeans can remotely attach to the Tomcat VM to support debugging classes. After starting Tomcat in debug mode using the instructions at the beginning of this appendix, follow these steps to attach to Tomcat with NetBeans:

1. Select the `Debug` pull-down menu, the `Start Session` menu item, and the `Attach` menu item.
2. Choose `JPDA` as the Debugger, `SharedMemoryAttach` as the Connector, and enter **jdbconn** as the Name.
3. Click OK.

After completing these steps, NetBeans will be attached to the Tomcat JVM; breakpoints and other debug features will be active.

JBuilder X

JBuilder improves on NetBeans by including not one, but three versions of Tomcat embedded in their product: Tomcat 3.3.1, Tomcat 4.0.6, and Tomcat 4.1.27. JBuilder X supports class and JSP debugging with all three versions, although some file copying is necessary to enable JSP debugging in Tomcat 4.1. JBuilder X does not support Tomcat 5, nor is there currently a timeline for when Tomcat 5 support will be available. (Attempts to successfully coax JBuilder into working with Tomcat 5 by the authors failed.)

Embedded Tomcat

To enable use of the embedded Tomcat versions, a Web Module project must be created. This is accomplished by following these steps:

1. Create a new Project in JBuilder X (select `File` ➪ `New Project...` from the pull-down menu and accept the default settings).
2. Select the `File` pull-down menu, followed by `New`.
3. Select the Web node on the left, the Web Module icon on the right, and click OK.
4. Select `Create Empty Web Module` and click `Next`.
5. Enter **webapp** (or any desired value without spaces) in the Name and Directory fields, and click Next.
6. Click Finish.

After completing these steps, the project must be configured to use the appropriate Tomcat server. This can be achieved by the following steps:

1. Right-click the project icon in the Project window and select `Properties` from the context menu.
2. Select the Server node from the list on the left.
3. Select the desired Tomcat server from the `Single server for all services in project` combo box.

To launch Tomcat, right-click on either a Servlet/JSP in the project and select Web Run or Web Debug.

HTTP Monitor

Also like NetBeans, JBuilder X includes a handy HTTP monitoring tool called TCP Monitor that is accessible at any time from the Tools pull-down menu. The tool itself is an embedded version of the HTTP monitoring tool included with the Apache Axis project. In fact, JBuilder X didn't make this tool any easier to use than the original, which didn't win any "intuitive user interface" awards.

JSP Debugging with Tomcat 4.1

JSP debugging is not available by default for Tomcat 4.1. However, it can be enabled by copying the files `jasper-compiler.jar` and `jasper-runtime.jar` from the `CATALINA_HOME\lib` directory of a Tomcat 4.0.x installation into the `CATALINA_HOME\common\lib` directory of a Tomcat 4.1.x installation.

Remote Debugging

Just as with NetBeans, remote debugging can be used in JBuilder X to debug classes in any Tomcat version, including Tomcat 5. To configure JBuilder X for remote debugging, follow these steps:

1. Select the Run pull-down menu, followed by Configurations.
2. Select the New... button.
3. Select the Remote node, which is a child of the Debug node.

4. Check the Enable Remote Debugging checkbox.
5. Select the Attach radio button.
6. Select `dt_shmem` as the transport type and enter **jdbconn** as the transport address.
7. Give the configuration a name in the Name text field, and select OK to save the configuration.
8. Press the down arrow on the Debug Project button, and select the name entered in step 7.

You must launch Tomcat in debug mode (see the section "Remote Debugging," at the beginning of this appendix) in order to attach to it from JBuilder X or any other IDE.

Summary

This appendix covered the following items:

- Remote debugging overview
- Remote debugging with IntelliJ IDEA 4.0
- Tomcat integration and remote debugging with Eclipse 3.0, NetBeans 3.6, and JBuilder X

Appendix C provides a tutorial introduction to Apache Ant.

C

Apache Ant

Ant is quickly becoming the de facto standard for creating cross-platform build files for Java applications. One important feature that has led to its popularity is the capability it offers developers to extend Ant via custom tasks. In Chapter 7, "Web Application Administration," you learned how Tomcat's custom Ant tasks can be used to deploy and undeploy Web applications without the need to restart Tomcat. This means that not only can you build the Web application using the Ant build script, you can also go a step further by installing, removing, or reloading the application while running Tomcat.

This appendix provides a brief introduction to the features of Ant. It covers the following:

- A short tutorial introduction to Ant
- A sample Web application and its associated Ant build script, which is used to compile the application and get it ready for deployment to a Tomcat instance
- How the results of the build processes can be e-mailed back to developers
- References to additional information about Ant

Installing Ant

Ant started off as a subproject under the Jakarta project. Since then, its increasing popularity earned it a promotion—it's now a top-level project under Apache, and can be downloaded from `http://ant.apache.org`. This appendix uses the stable release currently available (Ant 1.5.4). This is the last release from the 1.5 code base, and the next new release (Ant 1.6) is currently in beta.

Installing Ant is simple:

1. Download Ant from www.apache.org/dist/ant/ and unzip it in a directory of choice. For the remainder of the appendix, $ANT_HOME is used as the environment variable that points to the installation directory of Ant.
2. Add $ANT_HOME/bin to your system PATH.

Ant is often used to perform additional tasks, other than building Java code. Typically, this requires copying JAR files for these custom tasks into $ANT_HOME/lib.

For example, when Ant is to be used to manage Web applications, you would need to copy the catalina-ant.jar file that contains Tomcat's Ant tasks from the $CATALINA_HOME/server/lib directory to $ANT_HOME/lib.

Introduction to Ant

As a system administrator, you have likely been exposed to a lot of build tools (make, jam, and so on), so why is another build tool required?

Ant is built around the following central ideas:

- Implement the tool using Java, and use XML to store the build information. This results in a platform-independent build tool.
- Enable extensibility of the tool. Developers can extend Ant by writing Java classes, and thus develop custom tasks. One example of this is Tomcat's management tasks, mentioned earlier. Another example of this kind of integration is the capability to run jUnit test cases from Ant build scripts, using the optional <junit> task.

The first thing most people miss when moving from make to Ant is the expressiveness of make. Make-like tools are based on the underlying shell, and while that enables a lot of expressiveness and compact build scripts, such tools are nonportable. However, if you absolutely need to execute a shell command, Ant does offer a way out. Ant's <exec> task allows for this for the cost of the portability of build scripts.

As mentioned earlier, Ant uses an XML file to store build information. This file contains the list of tasks to be performed. The general structure of an Ant build file is as follows:

```
Project
|_
+--Property
|
+--Path
|
+--Task Definition
|
+--Target
     |
     +--Property
```

```
       |
       +--Path
       |
       +--Task
```

A project consists of a number of properties, targets, paths, and task definitions. Properties at the project level are name-value pairs that are available throughout the project and to each target.

A target consists of a series of tasks. A target can define its own set of properties, which override the global project properties. A target can depend on other targets, which means that all targets that it depends upon will execute first, before running the tasks associated with it. Ant comes with several built-in tasks that can be called. Some of the built-in tasks include creating directories, copying files, compiling Java source files, and so on.

You can also define path elements at both the Project level and Target level. A path is used to include or exclude certain files and directories. For example, you can construct a path element to contain the directories and/or JAR files that comprise the classpath.

Let's take a look at a simple Ant file (`mybuild.xml`). This build file creates a directory and then copies a file to that directory.

First, the `<project>` element must be specified:

```
<project name="MyAntProject" basedir="." default="copyfile">
```

The `name` attribute in the `<project>` element is set to the name of the project (`MyAntProject`, in this case). The `basedir` attribute indicates the root directory, which will be used as a reference for all the tasks present in this project. The `default` attribute indicates the target that will be executed by default if none are specified while running Ant.

Next, the properties for the project are defined:

```
<property name="dir.name" value="${basedir}/mydir"/>
<property name="file.name" value="file1.txt"/>
```

Here, two global properties are defined: `dir.name` and `file.name`. The `dir.name` property specifies the name of the directory to be created, and `file.name` is the file to be copied.

After this, the targets to be performed are specified. In this project, these include creating a directory (`mydir`) and copying the file (`file1.txt`) into the newly created directory:

```
  <target name="makedirectory" description="Create directory mydir">
    <mkdir dir="${dir.name}"/>
  </target>

  <target name="copyfile" depends="makedirectory" description="Copy files">
    <copy file="${file.name}" todir="${dir.name}"/>
  </target>

</project>
```

In these two targets, makedirectory and copyfile, note that the target copyfile is dependent on makedirectory. Therefore, even if you specify the copyfile target, Ant will make sure that all the dependencies are run first, and makedirectory will be executed irrespective of the situation.

The target makediretory creates the directory. Note how the directory name is referenced via the ${dir.name} property. The built-in tasks <mkdir> and <copy> are used to perform the functions of making a directory and copying the file. The syntax of the Ant command is as follows:

```
ant -buildfile <filename> <target-name>
```

If the buildfile option is not used, Ant will look for a file named build.xml in the directory from which the Ant command was issued. If the target name is not specified, Ant will look for the default target to execute as specified by the default attribute of the root <project> element.

The following example shows the Ant command being run with the mybuild.xml build file:

```
$ ant -buildfile mybuild.xml

Buildfile: mybuild.xml

makedirectory:
    [mkdir] Created dir: /home/tomcat/AppendixC/mydir

copyfile:
     [copy] Copying 1 file to /home/tomcat/AppendixC/mydir

BUILD SUCCESSFUL
Total time: 1 second
```

Ant Tasks

A summary of Ant's core tasks is listed in the following table.

Task Name	Description
ant	Run Ant on a build file. This task can be used to build subprojects.
antcall	Call another target within the same build file.
antstructure	Generate a Document Type Definition (DTD) for Ant build files.
apply	Execute a system command. This task has an optional os parameter that specifies the operating system on which the command should be run.
available	Set a property if a resource (for example, file, directory, class, JVM system resource) is available at run-time.
basename	Determine the basename of a specified file. Also see dirname.

Task Name	Description
`buildnumber`	This is used to track build numbers.
`bunzip2`	Unzip a file using the BZip2 algorithm.
`bzip2`	Compress a file using the BZip2 algorithm.
`checksum`	Generate checksum for a file.
`chmod`	Change permissions of file(s).
`concat`	Concatenate a file or series of files to a file or console.
`condition`	Set a property if a condition is `true`.
`copy`	Copy a file or set of files to a new location.
`cvs`	Handle CVS modules.
`cvschangelog`	Generate a CVS Changelog in XML format.
`cvspass`	Add entries to the CVS .cvspass file (same effect as doing a cvs login).
`cvstagdiff`	Generate a diff between two CVS tags (or dates).
`delete`	Delete a file, a set of files, or a directory.
`dependset`	Manage arbitrary dependencies between files.
`dirname`	Determine the directory path of a specified file.
`ear`	An extension of the `jar` task for handling Enterprise ARchive (EAR) files.
`echo`	Echo a message to a logger or a listener (the default is to echo to the console).
`exec`	Execute an OS-specific system command.
`fail`	Exit the current Ant build.
`filter`	Set up a token filter. These filters are used by file copying tasks.
`fixcrlf`	Adjust a text file for local OS conventions.
`genkey`	Generate a key in a keystore.
`get`	Get a file from a URL.
`gunzip`	Uncompress a file using the Gzip protocol.
`gzip`	Compress a file using the Gzip protocol.
`input`	Prompt for input from the user.
`jar`	Create a JAR file.
`java`	Execute a Java class within the same virtual machine.

Table continued on following page

Task Name	Description
`javac`	Compile a Java source tree.
`javadoc`	Run `javadoc` to create project documentation.
`loadfile`	Load a text file into a property.
`loadproperties`	Load Ant properties from a file.
`mail`	Send e-mail.
`manifest`	Create a manifest file (used in JAR files).
`mkdir`	Create a directory.
`move`	Move a file, a set of files, or a directory to a new location.
`parallel`	Execute a set of tasks in parallel. Each task executes in its own thread.
`patch`	Apply a "diff" file patch to the original file.
`pathconvert`	Used for converting representations of a path from one form to another.
`property`	Set a property.
`record`	Listener to the current build process that records the output to a file.
`replace`	Replace a string with another string in a text file.
`rmic`	Run the `rmic` compiler.
`sequential`	Specify a set of tasks to be run in sequence. Typically used for grouping inside a nested parallel task.
`signjar`	Sign a JAR or ZIP file using the `signjar` command.
`sleep`	"Sleep" for a specified amount of time.
`sql`	Execute an SQL statement via JDBC.
`style`	Process a set of documents using XSLT.
`tar`	Create a tar archive.
`taskdef`	Add a task definition for new (optional) tasks.
`tempfile`	Set a property to the name of a temporary file.
`touch`	Change the modification time of a file.
`tstamp`	Set the timestamp-related properties in the build file.
`typedef`	Specify a new type definition for the project.
`unjar/untar/unwar/unzip`	Extract a JAR/TAR/WAR or ZIP file.
`uptodate`	Set a property if a target file (or set of files) is more current than a source file (or set of files).

Task Name	Description
`waitfor`	Block until a certain condition is `true`. Often used in conjunction with the Parallel task.
`war`	An extension of the JAR task for handling WAR files.
`xmlproperty`	Load properties from an XML file.
`xslt`	Process a set of documents using XML Stylesheet Language Transformations (XSLT).
`zip`	Create a ZIP file.

Other than these core tasks, Ant can perform a number of optional tasks. More details on these core and optional tasks can be obtained from the Ant manual at `http://ant.apache.org/manual/index.html`.

Having only built-in tasks would have severely limited the applicability of Ant to diverse project requirements. Therefore, Ant also enables you to create your own user-defined tasks. These tasks can be used like any other ordinary task in your target, but with one difference: You need to add a task definition (`<taskdef>`) for the user-defined task, specifying the mapping from the task name to the Java class that implements this optional task. Once you have referenced a task definition element, you can use it as you would any other ordinary task in your target. Using custom tasks also requires that you copy the JAR files containing the implementation for these custom tasks into `$ANT_HOME/lib`.

You saw examples of this earlier in the book when Tomcat's Ant tasks were used in Chapter 7. A part of this Ant script example is reproduced as follows:

```
<!-- Specify the mapping between the task name and the java class
     implementing the task -->
<taskdef name="deploy"
        classname="org.apache.catalina.ant.DeployTask"/>
 ...
<!-- Use the task just as a core Ant task is used -->
<target name="deploy" description="Deploy web application"
       depends="build">
  <deploy url="${url}" username="${username}" password="${password}"
         path="${path}" war="file:${build}/hello.war"/>
</target>
```

If you have a large number of such tasks, you can also put the task name and class mapping in a properties file and specify the file in the `resource` attribute of the `<taskdef>` task. An example of this was shown in Chapter 20 (reproduced here):

```
<taskdef resource="org/apache/commons/modeler/ant/ant.properties"
        classpathref="tomcatCP" />
```

The properties file should follow the Java property file syntax, with each mapping specified on a separate line (`taskname=fully.qualified.java.classname`, and so on).

The Ant Build Process

This section demonstrates how to build a sample Web application with Ant. The steps include compiling the files and creating the appropriate directory structure for the WAR file to get the application ready for deployment.

A sample development-time directory structure for a Web application project may look like the following example:

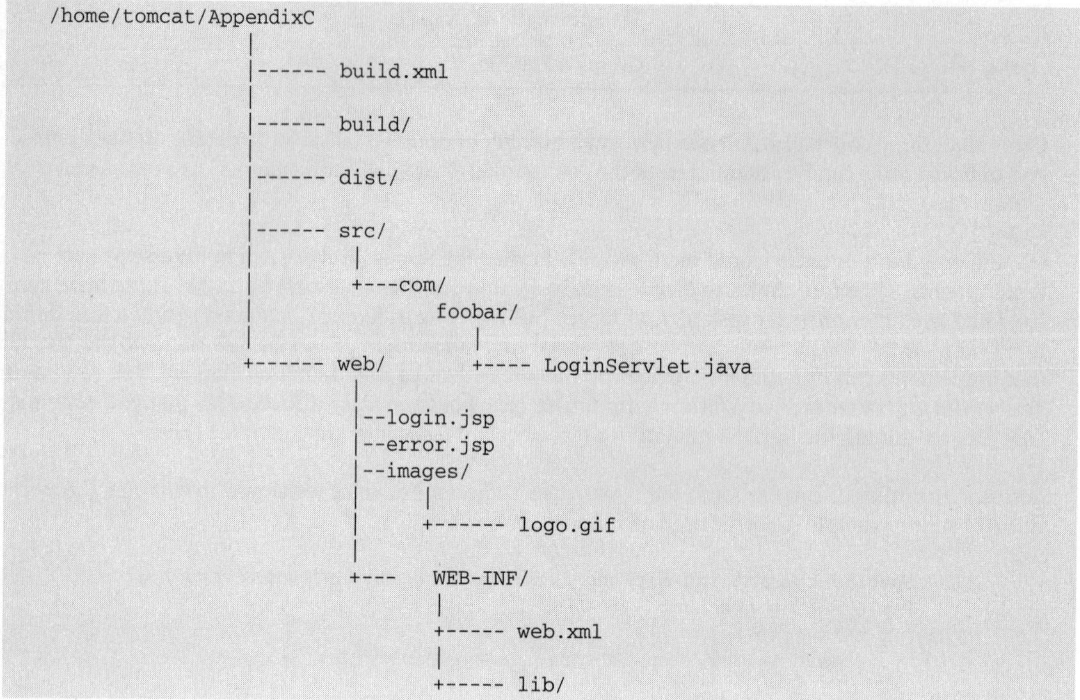

```
/home/tomcat/AppendixC
                      |
                      |------ build.xml
                      |
                      |------ build/
                      |
                      |------ dist/
                      |
                      |------ src/
                      |        |
                      |        +---com/
                      |              foobar/
                      |                 |
                      +------ web/      +---- LoginServlet.java
                               |
                               |--login.jsp
                               |--error.jsp
                               |--images/
                               |      |
                               |      +------ logo.gif
                               |
                               +---   WEB-INF/
                                       |
                                       +----- web.xml
                                       |
                                       +----- lib/
```

This directory structure consists of the following:

- The main build file (`build.xml`)
- A directory (`src`) containing all the Java source files of the Web application (for example, all the Servlet classes)
- A directory (`web`) containing the HTML and JSP files. It also contains any other resource directories — for example, images. Finally, it contains the `WEB-INF` directory with the deployment descriptor (`web.xml`). Chapter 6 discusses the deployment descriptor for the Web application in detail. The `WEB-INF` directory also has a `lib` directory that contains any third-party JAR files.
- A directory (`build`) in which the compiled Java classes would be built, and the expanded WAR structure created
- Finally, a directory (`dist`) in which the WAR file is generated from the build directory

The `build.xml` build file is shown here (the default target is the `compile` target):

```
<!-- Ant build file for Sample Web Application -->
<project name="myWebapp" default="compile" basedir=".">
```

The following section initializes the global properties that are used throughout the build file. Note that you might have to change some of these properties to suit your environment. For example, the `catalina.home` property should point to the root directory of your Tomcat installation:

```
    <property name="catalina.home"
                                  value="/usr/tomcat/jakarta-tomcat-5.0.15"/>
    <property name="app.name"     value="myWebapp"/>
    <property name="app.path"     value="/${app.name}"/>
    <property name="src.home"     value="${basedir}/src"/>
    <property name="web.home"     value="${basedir}/web"/>
    <property name="docs.home"    value="${basedir}/docs"/>
    <property name="build.home"   value="${basedir}/build"/>
    <property name="dist.home"    value="${basedir}/dist"/>
    <property name="war.file"     value="${dist.home}/${app.name}.war"/>
```

In this build file, the properties are included in the file itself for the sake of simplicity. A good programming practice is to move them to a separate properties file that contains the name-value property pairs. This enables you to use the same build script for different deployment environments. The property file can then be specified via a command-line option:

```
ant -buildfile <filename> <target-name> -propertyfile <propertyfilename>
```

The `clean` target deletes the `build` and `dist` directories and all subdirectories within them. This target is useful if you want to clean all the files generated by a build:

```
<!-- ====== Clean Target ====== -->
  <target name="clean"
        description="Deletes the build and dist directories">
    <delete dir="${build.home}"/>
    <delete dir="${dist.home}"/>
  </target>
```

The `prepare` target creates the expanded WAR directory structure and copies the static Web files from `web` and its subdirectories:

```
<!-- ====== Prepare Target ====== -->

  <target name="prepare">
    <mkdir  dir="${build.home}"/>
    <mkdir  dir="${build.home}/images"/>
    <mkdir  dir="${build.home}/WEB-INF"/>
    <mkdir  dir="${build.home}/WEB-INF/classes"/>

    <!-- Copy static content of this web application -->
    <copy todir="${build.home}">
      <fileset dir="${web.home}"/>
    </copy>

  </target>
```

The `compile` target compiles all the Java source files present in the `src` directory. The destination directory for the class files is `./build/WEB-INF/classes`:

```
<!-- ====== Compilation  ====== -->
    <target name="compile" depends="prepare">

        <javac srcdir="${src.home}"
               destdir="${build.home}/WEB-INF/classes"
               debug="true"
               deprecation="true">
            <classpath>
                <fileset dir="${web.home}/WEB-INF/lib">
                   <include name="*.jar"/>
                </fileset>

              <pathelement location="${catalina.home}/common/classes"/>
                <fileset dir="${catalina.home}/common/endorsed">
                     <include name="*.jar"/>
                </fileset>

                <fileset dir="${catalina.home}/common/lib">
                     <include name="*.jar"/>
                </fileset>

                <pathelement location="${catalina.home}/shared/classes"/>

                <fileset dir="${catalina.home}/shared/lib">
                     <include name="*.jar"/>
                </fileset>

            </classpath>
        </javac>

        <!-- Copy application resources -->
        <copy  todir="${build.home}/WEB-INF/classes">
              <fileset dir="${src.home}" excludes="**/*.java"/>
        </copy>
        <copy  todir="${build.home}/WEB-INF/lib">
             <fileset dir="${web.home}/WEB-INF/lib"/>
        </copy>
    </target>
```

The `dist` target creates a WAR file from the expanded WAR directory structure present in the `build` directory:

```
<!-- ====== Dist Target ====== -->

    <target name="dist" depends="compile"
          description="Create WAR file">

      <!-- Create WAR file -->
      <mkdir dir="${dist.home}"/>
      <jar jarfile="${war.file}"  basedir="${build.home}"/>
   </target>
```

The `all` target runs all the targets. Ant will run each target once in the order specified in the `depends` attribute for this target:

```
<!-- ====== All Target ====== -->

    <target name="all"
            depends="clean, prepare, compile, dist"
            description="Builds the web application and war file"/>

</project>
```

Let's run the different targets now to ensure that our environment is set up to run Ant correctly.

- *`clean`*—Open the console window and go to the `/home/tomcat/AppendixC` directory and run the `clean` target as shown here. Note that if you run the `clean` target after running the `compile` or `dist` targets, the `build` and `dist` directories will be cleared in the `clean` target:

```
$ant clean
Buildfile: build.xml

clean:
   [delete] Deleting directory /home/tomcat/AppendixC/build
   [delete] Deleting directory /home/tomcat/AppendixC/dist

BUILD SUCCESSFUL
Total time: 2 seconds
```

- *`dist`*—The `dist` target is responsible for generating the WAR file. Because this target depends on the `compile` target, by running it you ensure that not only will the files be compiled and copied into an expanded WAR directory structure, but that the WAR file is also generated:

```
$ ant dist
Buildfile: build.xml

prepare:
    [mkdir] Created dir: /home/tomcat/AppendixC/build
    [mkdir] Created dir: /home/tomcat/AppendixC/build/images
    [mkdir] Created dir: /home/tomcat/AppendixC/build/WEB-INF
    [mkdir] Created dir: /home/tomcat/AppendixC/build/WEB-INF/classes
    [mkdir] Created dir: /home/tomcat/AppendixC/build/WEB-INF/lib
     [copy] Copying 4 files to /usr/tomcat/AppendixC/build
     [copy] Copied 1 empty directory to /usr/tomcat/AppendixC/build

compile:
    [javac] Compiling 1 source file to /home/tomcat/AppendixC/build/WEB-INF/classes

dist:
    [mkdir] Created dir: /home/tomcat/AppendixC/dist
      [jar] Building jar: /home/tomcat/AppendixC/dist/myWebapp.war

BUILD SUCCESSFUL
Total time: 5 seconds
```

Now that you have the expanded WAR directory structure for the Web application as well as the .war file, you are ready to deploy it. This Web application can be deployed in a number of ways:

- Copy the WAR file to the $CATALINA_HOME/webapps directory.
- Create a context for the Web application by making a directory within $CATALINA_HOME/webapps — for example, $CATALINA_HOME/webapps/myWebapp — and copy the expanded WAR directory structure in the build directory to $CATALINA_HOME/webapps/myWebapp.
- Use the manager Web application GUI to deploy the application.
- Use the Ant interface to the manager application.

The last two methods are covered in detail in Chapter 7.

Ant Build Status (E-mail Notifications)

Developers often need to know the status of a build. If the Ant build script is run manually, the results can be e-mailed by the person running the build process. In big projects, or those with distributed development, it is common to have builds fired off automatically. This section describes how e-mail notifications of build status can be generated and automatically e-mailed.

Ant enables you to monitor the status of a build using listeners and loggers. The listeners are components that enable the monitoring of Ant events, such as the start and end of a task, a target, or a build. The loggers extend the functionality of listeners and are responsible for logging information about a build.

A logger class can be associated with a build process using Ant's -logger command-line option:

```
ant -logger <loggername>
```

Here <loggername> is the fully qualified class name of the logger class.

Similarly, a listener classes can be associated with the build process using the -listener command-line option:

```
ant -listener <listenername>
```

Ant 1.5 provides a built-in class called MailLogger (org.apache.tools.ant.listener.MailLogger) that can be used to e-mail results of the build process. This logger can be associated with a build process using the following command:

```
ant -logger org.apache.tools.ant.listener.MailLogger
```

When the build file finishes executing, the logger class sends an e-mail about the build's status. The behavior of the logger can be controlled via several properties, as described in the following table.

Property Name	Description
`MailLogger.mailhost`	The outgoing SMTP mail server that is used to send the e-mail. This property is mandatory.
`MailLogger.from`	The e-mail address of the account from which the e-mail is sent. This property is mandatory.
`MailLogger.failure.notify`	This Boolean property indicates whether an e-mail notification must be sent in case the build fails. This property is optional and is enabled by default.
`MailLogger.success.notify`	This Boolean property indicates whether an e-mail notification must be sent in case the build succeeds. If you are interested in sending an e-mail message only when there is a failure, you can set this property value to `false`. This property is optional and has a default value of `true`.
`MailLogger.failure.subject`	The subject of the e-mail in case the build fails. This property is optional and its default value is `Build Failure`.
`MailLogger.failure.to`	The e-mail address to which the build results must be sent in case of a failure. You can send the results to multiple e-mail addresses by separating them with commas. This property is only needed if you need to send an e-mail in case of a failure.
`MailLogger.success.subject`	The subject of the e-mail in case the build succeeds. This property is optional and its default value is `Build Success`.
`MailLogger.success.to`	The e-mail address to which the build results must be sent in case of success. You can send the results to multiple e-mail addresses by separating them with commas. This property is mandatory only if you need to send an e-mail if the build is successful.

Following is a sample properties file (`MailLogger.properties`):

```
MailLogger.mailhost=<your-smtp-servername>
MailLogger.from=<youraccount@someserver.com>

MailLogger.failure.subject=BUILD FAILURE : My Intranet Application
MailLogger.failure.to=<youraccount@someserver.com>

MailLogger.success.subject=BUILD SUCCESSFUL : My Intranet Application
MailLogger.success.to=<youraccount@someserver.com>
```

The property file is specified on the command line via the `-propertyfile` attribute:

```
> ant dist -logger org.apache.tools.ant.listener.MailLogger -propertyfile
MailLogger.properties
```

In addition to the MailLogger, the other Loggers and Listeners available are as follows:

- DefaultLogger (`org.apache.tools.ant.DefaultLogger`)

  This is the default Ant logger, and prints build-related messages to the console.

- NoBannerLogger (`org.apache.tools.ant.NoBannerLogger`)

  This logger functions similarly to the DefaultLogger, only it doesn't output messages for targets that don't perform any action.

- AnsiColorLogger (`org.apache.tools.ant.listener.AnsiColorLogger`)

  This logs the same messages that the DefaultLogger does, but in color.

- Log4jListener (`org.apache.tools.ant.listener.Log4jListener`)

  This is a listener that passes events to Log4J.

- XMLLogger (`org.apache.tools.ant.XmlLogger`).

  This logs messages in an XML format to a log file specified by the `-logfile` command-line option.

Developers can also write their own loggers/listeners by implementing the `org.apache.tools.antBuildListener` Java interface.

Summary

This appendix provided a tutorial introduction to Apache Ant. In addition to the simple examples covered here, Ant can be used to construct very elaborate build environments, and to perform tasks that include the following:

- Compiling source code
- Running test cases (when coupled with jUnit and Ant's jUnit-specific tasks)
- Building installable packages
- Deploying applications (for example, using Tomcat's Ant tasks to deploy a Web application)
- E-mailing the status of the test cases or the build to developers

Further information on Apache Ant (including a list of Ant tasks) is available at: `http://ant.apache.org/manual/index.html`

Index

B

C

E

I

M

N

O

Q

R

S

X

Z